Lecture Notes in Computer Science 3502

Commenced Publication in 1973
Founding and Former Series Editors:
Gerhard Goos, Juris Hartmanis, and Jan van Leeuwen

T0223709

Ferhat Khendek   Rachida Dssouli (Eds.)

Testing
of Communicating
Systems

17th IFIP TC6/WG 6.1 International Conference
TestCom 2005
Montreal, Canada, May 31 – June 2, 2005
Proceedings

 Springer

Volume Editors

Ferhat Khendek
Concordia University, Department of Electrical and Computer Engineering
1455, de Maisonneuve W., Montréal, Canada H3G 1M8
E-mail: khendek@ece.concordia.ca

Rachida Dssouli
Concordia University, Concordia Institute for Information Systems Engineering
1455, de Maisonneuve W., Montréal, Canada H3G 1M8
E-mail: dssouli@ciise.concordia.ca

Library of Congress Control Number: 2005925777

CR Subject Classification (1998): D.2.5, D.2, C.2

ISSN   0302-9743
ISBN-10   3-540-26054-4 Springer Berlin Heidelberg New York
ISBN-13   978-3-540-26054-7 Springer Berlin Heidelberg New York

Springer is a part of Springer Science+Business Media

springeronline.com

© 2005 IFIP International Federation for Information Processing, Hofstrasse 3, 2361 Laxenburg, Austria
Printed in Germany

Typesetting: Camera-ready by author, data conversion by Scientific Publishing Services, Chennai, India
Printed on acid-free paper   SPIN: 11430230   06/3142   5 4 3 2 1 0

Preface

This volume contains the proceedings of the 17th IFIP TC6/WG6.1 International Conference on Testing of Communicating Systems (TestCom 2005). The conference was held at Concordia University, Montréal, Canada, from May 31 to June 2, 2005. TestCom 2005 was organized by Concordia University and was sponsored by IFIP.

Following the trends initiated at the 16th edition of the conference held in Oxford, UK, the first call for papers issued in summer 2004 called for contributions from the general software testing community. The goal of the conference this year was to continue the broadening of the subject. The theme of the conference this year is "Meeting Software Testing." In response to the call for papers, we received 62 abstracts. Out of these abstracts, 53 turned into paper submissions. Each of these submissions was evaluated by at least 3 reviewers from the Technical Programme Committee, with the help of additional co-reviewers when needed. The Programme Committee meeting was held online from January 18 to January 30, 2005. Out of the 53 submitted papers, the Programme Committee selected 24 papers covering the traditional topics of TestCom, such as EFSM/FSM model-based testing, and also papers on general software testing reflecting the new trends in the conference.

We are very grateful to the keynote speaker, Prof. Tom Maibaum, from McMaster University, Hamilton, Canada. Prof. Maibaum addressed TestCom 2005 on this year's theme. He kindly provided an extended abstract, which is also included in this volume.

We are very grateful to the people who contributed to TestCom 2005 in one way or another. We would like to thank the authors of all submitted papers and the members of the Technical Programme Committee for their hard work during the evaluation of the papers and during the selection process. We are thankful to all the co-reviewers who are indispensable for any peer-reviewed volume. We are grateful to the members of the Steering Committee for their advice. Special thanks go to Prof. Guy Leduc, Université de Liège, Belgium, chairman of the Steering Committee, for his support since day one of the organization of TestCom 2005. We would like to thank also the members of the Organizing Committee for their devotion to the conference, and Dean Nabil Esmail from the Faculty of Engineering and Computer Science at Concordia University for his support. All the individuals who contributed to TestCom 2005 are listed in the following pages.

March 2005

Ferhat Khendek
Rachida Dssouli

Preface

Conferences Committees

Conference Chairs

R. Dssouli, CIISE, Concordia University, Canada
F. Khendek, ECE, Concordia University, Canada

Steering Committee

A.R. Cavalli, INT, France
R. Groz, LSR-IMAG, France
G. Leduc, Chairman, Université de Liège, Belgium
A. Petrenko, CRIM, Canada

Technical Programme Committee

G. von Bochmann, University of Ottawa, Canada
S. Dibuz, Ericsson, Sweden
P.G. Frankl, Polytechnic University, NY, USA
J. Grabowski, University of Göttingen, Germany
R.M. Hierons, Brunel University, UK
T. Higashino, Osaka University, Japan
D. Hogrefe, University of Göttingen, Germany
T. Jeron, IRISA, France
M. Kim, ICU University, Korea
D. Lee, Ohio State University, USA
G. Maggiore, TIM, Italy
M. Núñez, Universidad Complutense de Madrid, Spain
I. Schieferdecker, Fraunhofer FOKUS, Germany
K. Suzuki, Kennisbron Ltd., Japan
M. Toeroe, Ericsson, Canada
A. Ulrich, Siemens, Germany
H. Ural, University of Ottawa, Canada
M.U. Uyar, City University of New York, USA
J. Wu, Tsinghua University, China
N. Yevtushenko, Tomsk State University, Russia
H. Zhu, Oxford Brookes, UK

Additional Reviewers

Baptiste Alcalde
Gábor Bátori
Sergiy Boroday
Jiapeng Cai
Dongluo Chen
Ning Chen
John Clark
Michael Ebner
David de Frutos-Escrig
Xiaoming Fu
Mohammed Ghriga
Arnaud Gotlieb
Hesham Hallal
Toru Hasegawa
Hyoung Seok Hong
Cihui Huang

Jiale Huo
Akira Idoue
Lifa Jin
Sungwon Kang
Davy Khuu
Keqin Li
Tian Li
Luis Llana
Yan Liu
Natalia López
Stephane Maag
Helmut Neukirchen
Tomohiko Ogishi
Svetlana Prokopenko
Ismael Rodrguez
Fernando Rubio

Soonuk Seol
Xingang Shi
Guoqiang Shu
Tibor Szabo
Beihang Tian
Vadim Trennkaev
Dario Vieira
Elisangela R. Vieira
Dong Wang
Zhiliang Wang
Constantin Werner
Edith Werner
Xia Yin
Xing Yu
Gábor Ziegler

Local Organization Committee

S. Anderson, CIISE, Concordia University
R. Karunamurthy, ECE, Concordia University
S. Tablan, CIISE, Concordia University

Sponsors

Concordia University, Canada
IFIP
Springer, Germany

Table of Contents

The Epistemology of Validation and Verification Testing

T.S.E. Maibaum

Department of Computing and Software
McMaster University
tom@maibaum.org

Abstract. We wish to be able to give formal definitions (in the sense of science or engineering) for concepts like requirements validation and for the relationship between a requirements specification and an abstract design of the intended system. Ditto validation of designs and the final executable application with respect to the original "application concept", on the one hand, and the requirement specification, on the other. We have been developing a framework based on the work of the logical empiricists and other analytic philosophers over the last 80 years to support our understanding of software engineering concepts. Recent developments (dating from the 80s) in the area of "confirmation" (of a hypothesis concerning a theory by some (experimental) evidence) promises to illuminate some of these problematic concepts. In this talk we address the problem of establishing the very relation between requirement specifications and scenarios, as used, for example, in UML. The same framework can also be applied to the problem of testing implementations against designs, so called verification testing.

1 Introduction

Requirements engineering (RE) is a black art! We are forever confronted by the assertion that, whilst requirements specifications may be a formal entity, analysable even in a mathematical sense, it is informally related to an informal "entity", the so-called *application concept*. If we cannot define precisely (and meaningfully) the statement "this scenario confirms (or discomfirms) this behaviour specification", then how can we pretend we know what a behaviour specification (and therefore a requirements specification) specifies? Suppose further that we are interested in questions such as the following: Is requirements language X better than Language Y for defining the requirements of applications of class W? On what basis can we justify the fact that we like the work reported in [21,32,,22,23] and that it says something important about requirements engineering?

On what basis can we answer these questions so that the answers can be justified on a "scientific" or "engineering" basis? If we cannot answer the first question, how can we begin to address the others? If some entities and relationships are informal, what is there left aside from anecdote to support requirements "meta-analysis"? The

---

Original version co-authored with the late AM Haeberer and with the assistance of MV Cengarle, then of Institut für Informatik, Ludwig-Maximilians-Universität München.

F. Khendek and R. Dssouli (Eds.): TestCom 2005, LNCS 3502, pp. 1–8, 2005.

purpose of this talk is to demonstrate that a *framework* can be defined, turning the "informal" entities and relationships of the above discussion into well defined concepts that are amenable to formal analysis.

2 Gedanken Experiments, Requirement Specifications and Confirmation

In former papers [16,17, 6,7, 8] we have endeavoured to lay the basis for the epistemological analysis of software engineering. In [17], we analyse superficially the relationships among the various objects in a metamodel of the software process we posited (called W) and which is reproduced in Figure 1.

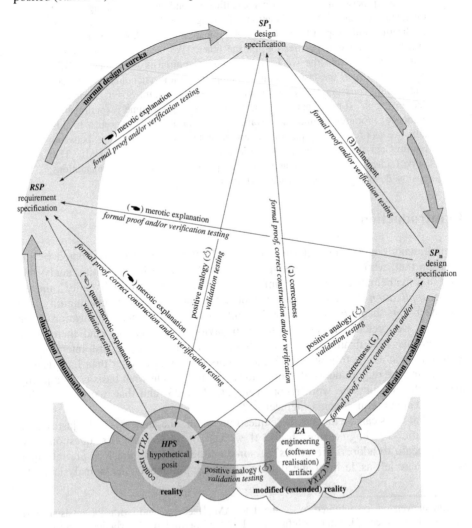

Fig. 1.

At the leftmost lower corner of this figure we see the factual[1] relation *HPS+CTXP* ☞ *RSP*, where *HPS* is what we called the hypothetical posit of the intended software artifact *EA* in [17], *CTXP* its context, and *RSP* the requirements specification for *EA*. In [17] we claim that the relation ☞, whose analysis is the purpose of this talk, is what we called there a *quasi merotic explanation*.

To be able to study formally the leftmost lower hollow arrow in Figure 1, which is nothing but the notorious process of *ab initio* requirements elicitation, we need a framework in which we can reason about the nature of this process, about the objects *HPS*, *CTXP*, and *RSP*, and about the relation ☞. It is the purpose oft his talk to analyse the nature of this relation and, in order to do that, to establish an adequate framework for reasoning about it and the objects involved. It is very important to bear in mind that, in its present state, the Ω meta-model is idealised in various ways; one of them is that we are considering *ab initio* development, meaning that we are not considering legacy artifacts. This means that we consider requirement specifications as being elicited from (hypothetical) scenarios in which there are no legacy software artifacts or systems, and therefore, this eliciation process does not involve design recovery. Moreover, we will assume that there is no existing software artifact or system from which we can glean a single clue about decomposition; thus, merotic explanations[2] are inhabitants of our post-requirements world.

The process we have in mind for devising a new engineering artifact is as follows. See the figure at the end of this extended abstract. We have a somewhat vague requirement (called *protoRSP*) for a new artifact to be, *EA*, which at this point is merely a hypothetical posit *HPS*. This vague requirement *protoRSP* is actually a set of properties we know (or we desire) the artifact to be (represented here by the hypothetical posit) should exhibit. These properties are of two kinds, i.e., abstract (theoretical) ones, such as, for instance, behaviours, and their observable counterparts, i.e., sets of observable instances of them, which we will call evidence *E* (e.g., scenarios). In our engineering setting, evidence is produced both by the operation of an engineering artifact *EA* (after its construction!), or by the operation of an hypothetical posit *HPS*, as in a gedanken experiment. The sets of such evidence are part of what we are calling here the context *CTXA* of the engineering artifact *EA*, or the context *CTXP* of the hypothetical posit, respectively. Then, we construct an extension of the language belonging to our underlying science/technology and to the already existing engineering discipline with the necessary symbols, etc., to enable us to state precisely the requirements specification *RSP*, and to show how evidence produced by the operation of the hypothetical posit *HPS confirms RSP*, and that (if the status of our current technology makes its construction viable) the resulting engineering artifact *EA* will be in a certain relation with *HPS* that enables us to expect that

---

[1] We classify the relationships among the objects in the Ω meta-model into factual and logical, as we have done in [H&M00]. We give an exact definition of these clasificatory terms below.

[2] An exact definition of what a merotic explanation is can be found in [17]. Informally speaking, we can consider that the structure of the resulting software artifact *EA* in a software process satisfying the Ω meta-model (or any of the series of increasingly reified design specifications SP_i) provides an explanation of why the requirements specification predicts (and retrodicts) correctly its operation. Since this explanation is composed from parts following *EA*'s (or SP_i's) structure, it was called "merotic".

EA will also produce evidence that *confirms RSP*. (As we argue in [17], this relation is a positive analogy, i.e., *HPS* ⚭ *EA*. See the figure.) Then, we construct *EA*, through a process of design and reification, which adds design and realisation detail to the above extension.

If, on the one hand, *protoRSP* is a description in everyday language, or in a previous stage in the development of our scientific/technological language, of the evidence produced by *HPS* and, on the other hand, *RSP* is the exact description of the behaviour confirmed by evidence produced by *HPS* or *EA*, then we may be tempted to characterise *protoRSP* as what Carnap [4] calls an *explicandum* and the corresponding requirement specification *RSP* as its *explicatum*, both related by an *explication*[3]. As Carnap stated [4] *"the task of explication consists in transforming a given more or less inexact concept into an exact one or, rather, in replacing the first by the second. We call the given concept (or the term used for it) the <u>explicandum</u>, and the exact concept proposed to take the place of the first (or the term proposed for it) the <u>explicatum</u>."*

The analysis of the reason why we said that this is a simplistic viewpoint will introduce the core points of this talk. Notice that we had distinguished between, on the one hand, evidence, which is observable (perhaps with the aid of certain apparata), such as scenarios, and, on the other hand, certain abstract (mathematical) objects, such as behaviours. These abstract properties are of a very dangerous kind, because if we become overenthusiastic in their introduction, we can obtain a complete zoo of scientifically useless abstractions, such as, for instance, phlogiston, vital force, or entelechy. (Software engineering, as all the novel disciplines whose corpus is not well defined, is especially prone to accept such useless abstractions.) However, *mass* in physics is one of these concepts (as is *force*); *mass* is needed to state Newton's principle for relating force with acceleration. Otherwise, Newtonian mechanics cannot be developed, or even stated. If we look to current scientific language, even that familiar to laymen, we find many abstract terms denoting abstract objects or properties, such as, for instance, *gene, electron, magnetic field, preservation of the angular momentum,* or *esprit de corps*. For instance, some of Kepler's laws can be stated in a language the designata of whose nouns would be accepted by everyone as observables. However, this is not the case with Newtoninan Dynamics; terms such as *angular momentum, gravitational field,* and *universal gravitational constant* have non observable designata. Notwithstanding, nobody will say that these terms are useless; without them Newtonian Mechanics is unthinkable. <u>The difference between Kepler's laws and Newtonian mechanics is the difference between empirical generalisations and scientific theories.</u> This difference resides in their respective predictive powers; from Kepler's laws we can infer the movements and positions of the planets, whilst from Newtonian Mechanics we can infer the same <u>but also particular laws</u>, such as Kepler's laws. Unfortunately, it seems that the existence of such terms (nouns) with non-observable designata, is a must if we want an expressive scientific theory, or a statement belonging to a scientific theory, and not an empirical generalisation.

---

[3] Notice that in this context (i.e., that of the Philosophy of Science) *explication* and *explanation* are not synonymous; we are using *explication* in the particular sense we are discussing, and *explanation* in the sense of *scientific explanation*.

However, an exaggerated use of theoretical terms leads us down the path to metaphysics, so Occam's razor comes into play. In our case, we have evidence, as for instance the collection of behavioural data *hypothetically* generated by an *hypothetical posit*, which can be stated in a language the designata of whose nouns are observable, and we have abstract objects, such as behaviours, which do not designate observable things, but from which we can infer hypotheses potentially confirmable by evidence (e.g., scenarios in UML). Thus, the vocabulary of the language whose nouns designate observable things and properties is smaller than the vocabulary of the language whose nouns designate representatives of these observable things plus abstract things and properties. Furthermore, the restriction of *observability*[4] of the former language makes wider the difference between the two languages, for it is obvious that universal quantifiers in the former must be finite, i.e., equivalent to generalised finite conjunctions (neither our senses nor any physical instrument enables us to observe a whole from infinitely many parts), whilst those of the latter language can be, and are usually, infinite. Moreover, we can have in the latter language modalities, such as *permission* and *obligation*, and *temporal quantifiers*, such as *forever, once*, and *sometime in the future*.

The principal problem is, in Clark Glymour's words [12], "How can evidence stated in one language confirm hypotheses stated in a language that outstrips the first? How can one make an inference from statements in the narrower language to statements in the broader language? The hypotheses of the broader language cannot be confirmed by their instances, for the evidence, if framed in the narrower tongue, provides none. Consistency with the evidence is insufficient, for an infinity of incompatible hypotheses may obviously be consistent with the evidence, and the same is true if it is required that the hypotheses logically entail the evidence. The structure of the problem is: what relations between [...] observation statements, on the one hand, and statements [...] about unobservable things or unobservable properties, on the other hand, permit statements of the former kind to confirm statements of the latter kind?".

From what we have said above, it seems plausible to say that the relation ☞ is one of confirmation between the evidence produced by *HPS*, on the one hand, and *RSP*, on the other. As a first approximation we can state the following:

Definition. *Evidence E confirms RSP iff we can use some hypotheses deduced from RSP to deduce from E other hypotheses deducible from RSP.*

This idea about the mechanism by which we can decide if a theory agrees or disagrees with a piece of evidence (observable) was first conceived by Carnap [5] and later explored and developed by Clark Glymour [12]. Let us call the former hypotheses in the above definition, *bootstrap hypotheses*; thus, our definition can be re-stated as: *evidence E confirms RSP iff we can deduce from RSP a set of <u>bootstrap</u>*

---

[4] We are using *observable, observability*, and *abstract*, without giving a precise definition of what we are referring to. We will give precise definitions for them, actually for their exact counterparts, which will have the same spelling but which will actually be different terms with exact meanings, i.e., *designata*.

subtheories of RSP which enable the deduction from E of other hypotheses deducible *from RSP*. It is exactly in the conditions established for the deduction of bootstrap *subtheories* where, for instance, the necessary application of Occam's razor we had talked about above must be embedded. Such requirements are the source of the complexity of the confirmation procedure (the so-called bootstrap strategy of confirmation) we introduce below in the talk.

In discussing confirmation, we must here make something very clear. We need to separate carefully two different issues. The frst is the mechanism by means of which we can decide that a certain piece of evidence "agrees" or "disagrees" with a given theory. We will talk below of two of them: one is that succinctly presented in the discussion that led to the definition above and the other is the notorious and flawed *hypothetico-deductive method* (of Newton and others). The second is the criterion of confirmation. We can informally explain this issue by contrasting some of the proposed criteria. One, which we will call Popperian falsifiability (also used in the hypothetico-deductive method), is: if the evidence disagrees with the theory (we need some mechanism for deciding this, i.e., the first issue), then the theory should be discarded; conversely, if the evidence agrees with the theory, then we do not have any new information about the appropriateness of the theory for describing the phenom-enon producing the evidence. Another criterion, advanced by Lakatos, says that a theory is something resulting from a difficult and expensive process and, therefore, nobody is willing to discard it because of a mere disagreement with a piece of evidence; so an auxilliary hypothesis is created to explain the disagreement. Finally, the Carnapian logical measure function [4] presents a criterion of confirmation based on degrees of confirmation: if the evidence disagrees with the theory, one can blame the theory or certain auxilliary hypotheses about the experimental method producing the evidence, the measurement instruments, etc. But actually, as in the Popperian case, we blame something, often the theory itself. The main difference between the Carnapian criterion of confirmation and Popperian falsifiability is about what we do when the theory agrees with the evidence. Here, instead of saying that we do not have more information about the appropriateness of the theory, we will say that the degree of confirmation of this theory is greater than the degree of confirmation of a theory not agreeing with this piece of evidence. Carnap associates with this degree of confirmation a logical function (which he calls Logical Probability [4]). This logical function is strongly related with Carnap's inductive logic (and today with theories about belief revision).

In this talk we will deal only with the first issue, i.e., how we can decide that a requirements specification *RSP* agrees or disagrees with a piece of evidence hypothetically produced by the hypothetical posit *HPS*. The second issue will be treated in a forthcoming paper, since if we adopt the Carnapian logical measure function, we should inspect also Carnap's inductive logic and his "continuum of inductive methods", which will bring us closer to the issue of requirements elicitation, and, therefore, to the leftmost lower hollow arrow in Figure 1. However, to be able to produce an effective setting for this talk, we need to append to the so-called bootstrap mechanism, which deals with the first issue above, some kind of confirmation crite-rion. We will use a not very complicated one, which is a modification of one put forward by Hempel.

References

1. Rudolf Carnap, *On Inductive Logic*. Philosophy of Science, Vol. 12, 72-97. 1945.
2. Rudolf Carnap, *Continuum of Inductive Methods*. Univ. of Chicago Press. 1952
3. Rudolf Carnap, *Meaning and Necessity*. Supplement A, *Empiricism, Semantics, and Ontology*. Midway Reprint Edition. 1988.
4. Rudolf Carnap, Logical Foundations of Probability. The University of Chicago Press. Second Edition. 1962.
5. Rudolf Carnap, *An Introduction to the Philosophy of Science* (re-edited from Philosophical Foundations of Physics, Basic Books, 1966). Ed. Martin Gardner, Dover Publications, Inc. 1995.
6. Maria V. Cengarle and Armando Haeberer, *Towards an epistemology-based methodology for verification and validation testing*. See http://www. informatik.uni-muenchen.de under M.V. Cengarle. 1999.
7. María V. Cengarle and Armando M. Haeberer, *Specifications, programs, and confirmation*. Proceedings of the Workshop on Requirements, Design, Correct Construction, And Verification: Mind The Gaps! F.A.S.T. Gesellschaft für angewandte Softwaretechnologie mbH- Munich April 2000. http://www.fast.de
8. Cengarle, M V., Haeberer, A. M.. *A formal approach to specification-based black-box testing*. Proceedings of the Workshop on Modelling Software System Structures in a fastly moving scenario. June 13-16, 2000. Santa Margherita Ligure, Italia. www.disi.unige.it/person/FerrandoE/MSSSworkshop.
9. David Christensen, *Glymour on evidential relevance*, Philosophy of Science. Vol 50. 471-481, 1983.
10. John Earman and Clark Glymour, What Revisions does Bootstrap Testing Need? A Reply. Philosophy of Science. Vol. 55. 261-264, 1988.
11. Clark Glymour, *Hypothetico-deductivism is Hopeless*. Philosophy of Science. Vol. 47. 322-325, 1980.
12. Clark Glymour, *Theory and Evidence*. Princeton Univ. Press. 1980.
13. Clark Glymour, *On testing and evidence*. *In John Earman ed. Testing Scientific Theories*, Minnesota Studies in the Philosophy of Science, Vol. X. Univesity of Minnesota Press. 1983.
14. Clark Glymour, *Revisions of bootstrap testing*, Philosophy of Science. Vol 50. 626-629, 1983.
15. Carl G. Hempel, International Encyclopedia of Unified Science, Vol. 2, No. 7: *Fundamentals of Concept Formation in Empirical Science*. University of Chicago Press. 23-38, 1952.
16. Armando M. Haeberer and Tom S. E. Maibaum, *The very idea of software development environments: a conceptual architecture for the arts environment*. In B. Nuseibeh and D. Redmiles, eds. Proc. of 13th IEEE Int. Conf. on Automated Software Engineering (ASE-98), IEEE CS Press, 260–269. 1998.
17. Armando M. Haeberer and Tom S. E. Maibaum, *Scientific rigour, an answer to a pragmatic question: a linguistic framework for software engineering*, to appear in Proc. of ICSE2001, 23rd Int. Conf. on Software Engineering. Toronto 2001.
18. Mary Hesse. *The Structure of Scientific Inference*. University of California Press. 1974.
19. Jako Hintikka, *Towards a Theory of Inductive Generalization*. In Y. Bar-Hillel, Proc. of the 1964 Congress for Logic, Methodology, and the Philosophy of Science. 274-288. Stanford University Press. 1962.

20. Michael Jackson, *Formal Methods and Traditional Engineering*. Journal of Systems and Software special issue on Formal Methods Technology Transfer. Vol. 40. 191-194. 1998.
21. Michael A. Jackson and Pamela Zave, *Deriving Specifications from requirements: an Example*. Proc. ICSE'95 - 17th International Conference on SE. IEEE Computer Society Press, 15-24. 1995.
22. Axel van Lamsweerde and Emmanuel Letier, *Handling Obstacles in Goal-driven Requirements Engineering*. IEEE Transactions on SE, Vol. 26, September 2000.
23. Axel van Lamsweerde and L. Willemet, *Inferring Declarative Requirements Specifications from Operational Scenarios*. IEEE Transactions on SE, Vol. 24, No. 12, 1089-1114. December 1998.
24. Tom S.E. Maibaum, *Mathematical Foundations of Software Engineering: a roadmap*. In Eds. A. Finkelstein and J. Kramer, Future of Software Engineering, ICSE 2000. IEEE C.S. Press. 2000.
25. 25.E. Nagel, *The Structure of Science*. Harcourt, Brace. 1961.
26. Bryan G. Norton, *Linguistic Frameworks and Ontology*: A Re-Examination of Carnap's Metaphilosophy. Mouton Publishers. 1977.
27. Karl R Popper, *The Logic of Scientific Discovery*. Hutchinson, London 1968.
28. Herbert Simon, *The axiomatization of physical theories*. Philosophy of Science. Vol 37. 16-26, 1970.
29. Wlad M. Turski, *An Essay on Software Engineering at the Turn of Century*. In Ed. Tom Maibaum, Proc.of Fundamental Approaches to Software Engineering 2000, LNCS 1783, Springer. 2000.
30. Wlad M. Turski and Tom S.E. Maibaum, *The Specification of Computer Programs*. Addison-Wesley, 1987.
31. Walter G. Vincenti, What Engineers Know and How They Know It : *Analytical Studies from Aeronautical History*. Johns Hopkins U. Press. 1993.
32. Pamela Zave and Michael A. Jackson, *Four Dark Corners of Requirements Engineering*. ACM Tansactions on SE and Methodology, Vol. 6, No. 1. 1-30. 1997.
33. Jan M. Zytkow, *What revisions does bootstrap testing need?*. Philosophy of Science. Vol 53. 101-109, 1986.

Passive Testing - A Constrained Invariant Checking Approach

Behrouz Tork Ladani[1], Baptiste Alcalde[2], and Ana Cavalli[2]

[1] Department of Computer Engineering, University of Isfahan, Isfahan, Iran
ladani@eng.ui.ac.ir
[2] Institute National des Telecommunications GET-INT, Evry, France
{ana.cavalli, baptiste.alcalde}@int-evry.fr

Abstract. Passive testing of a network protocol is the process of detecting faults in the protocol implementation by passively observing its input/output behaviors (execution trace) without interrupting the normal network operations. In observing the trace, we can focus on the most expected relevant properties of the protocol specification by defining some invariants on the specification and checking them on the trace. While intuitive extraction of the invariants from the protocol requirements with respect to the control portion of the protocol system is relatively simple, taking the data portion into account is difficult. In this paper we propose algorithms for checking the correctness of given invariants on the specification and extracting the required constraints on the variables (data portion). Once we generate the constraints for a given invariant, we can check if the execution trace is confirmed by the specification with respect to the invariant and its constraints. We show the applicability of the algorithm on a case study: the simple connection protocol (SCP).

Keywords: passive testing, invariants, invariant checking, constraint solving, SCP.

1 Introduction

Testing network protocol implementations, to assure that they work as their specification, is of high importance. Instead of conventional active testing, there are propositions to use passive testing for network protocol systems, which means observing the input/output behavior of the implementation (i.e. execution trace) without interfering its normal behavior ([1], [2]). The naive approach to passive testing is to record the execution trace and try to find its faults by comparing it with the specification ([3], [4], [5]). Other approaches try to extract the critical properties of the specification in the form of some invariants and then try to observe them on the implementation ([6], [7]).

Most of passive testing methods are focused on the control parts of the system under test without considering the data parts, so it is sufficient for them to use finite state machines (FSMs) as the specification method. To take the data part of the protocols into account, extended finite state machines (EFSMs) are used to specify the system. EFSM uses parameterized input/output signals including variable parameters to encode data as

F. Khendek and R. Dssouli (Eds.): TestCom 2005, LNCS 3502, pp. 9–22, 2005.

well as predicates and actions to control the firing of the transitions by manipulating the relevant data. There are some methods proposed to perform passive testing using EFSM ([5], [8], [9]). These methods are based on exploring constraints of the variables and comparing the whole specification with the implementation regarding the constraints in a backward or forward manner (i.e. the naive approach).

In this paper we represent a method to perform passive testing based on the invariants on the EFSM. In our approach, first we have to extract the invariants intuitively from the protocol specification requirements regarding only the control portion of the protocols. After that, to take the data portion into account, we consider the invariant parameters as some variables. We present two algorithms for finding the corresponding constraints over the variables of the invariants automatically. The algorithms use the unification method [10] for checking the correctness of the given invariants over the EFSM and finding the constraints over its variables. Having the invariants and their corresponding constraints in hand, we can check the execution trace with the invariants using pattern matching methods.

It should be noted that finding suitable control-driven invariants, especially with the help of an expert is relatively simple; also there are some methods to extract a limited set of invariants from an EFSM automatically [7]. We use the notion of invariant introduced in [11] with little changes in the definitions to extract the control driven invariants intuitively.

The rest of the paper is organized as follows: in section 2 some preliminary concepts needed in the rest of the paper are described. In section 3 the notions of forward and backward invariants are described. In section 4, our algorithms for checking invariants on a given EFSM and extracting corresponding constraints are presented. Section 5 reports some experiments of the algorithms on the Simple Connection Protocol (SCP) to show the applicability of the method in detecting subtle errors in some given traces of the protocol. In section 6 we conclude the paper.

2 Preliminaries

2.1 Extended Finite State Machine

We use Extended Finite State Machines (EFSMs) to specify the network protocols.

Definition 1. An *Extended Finite State Machine (EFSM)* M is a 6-tuple $M=(S, I, O, x, T, s_0)$ where S is a finite set of states, I and O are the finite sets of input and output parametric symbols respectively, x is a vector denoting a finite set of variables, T is the finite set of transitions, and s_0 is the initial state.

Each transition $t \in T$ is a tuple (s, s', i, o, P, A) where s, s' $\in$ S are the initial and final states of the transition respectively, i $\in$ I, o $\in$ O are the input and output symbols (possibly with parameters) respectively, P is the predicate (a Boolean expression), and A is the sequence of actions.

Definition 2. Let $M=(S, I, O, x, T, s_0)$ be an EFSM, the sequence $i_1/o_1, \ldots i_n/o_n$ is a *path* in M if for any $1 \leq j \leq n$, $i_j \in I$, $o_j \in O$, and there exist n transitions $t_1 \ldots t_n \in T$ and n+1 states $s, s_1, \ldots, s_{n-1}, s' \in S$ such that $t_1 = (s, s_1, i_1, o_1)$, $t_n = (s_{n-1}, s', i_n, o_n)$ and for any $1 < j < n$ we have $t_j = (s_{j-1}, s_j, i_j, o_j)$.

2.2 Substitution and Unification

Our algorithms use the unification method, so we borrow some definitions from the context of logic programming.

Definition 3. A *substitution* θ is a set of bindings, each of the form V/T, such that V is a distinct variable and T is a term. θ is called a *renaming* if it maps each variable to a new fresh variable.

Applying a binding V/T to an expression E, replaces each free occurrence of V in E by T. Applying a substitution θ on an expression E denoted by Eθ applies all the bindings in θ to E simultaneously and independently.

Definition 4. Let $\theta = \{V_1/T_1,...., V_m/T_m\}$ and $\alpha = \{U_1/S_1,....,U_n/S_n\}$ be substitutions. The *composition* of θ and α, denoted by $\theta o \alpha$ is defined as:

$$\theta o \alpha = \{V_1 / T_1 \alpha,....., V_m / T_m \alpha\} \cup \{U_k / S_k \mid U_k \notin \{V_1, ... , V_m\}\}$$

Definition 5. A *unifier* of two simple expressions E and F is a substitution θ such that Eθ = Fθ. If two simple expressions have a unifier, they are said to be *unifiable*; we also say that E is unified with F by the unifier θ. A *most general unifier*, abbreviated as *mgu*, of two simple expressions E and F is a unifier θ that is more general than any unifier of E and F. As an example two expressions P(X,f(X)) and P(b,f(a)) are not unifiable, while the most general unifier of the expressions P(X,f(a)) and P(b, f(Y)) is $\{X/b, Y/a\}$.

2.3 Normalizing Action Sequences

We need in our algorithms to track the changes in the variable values made by the action sequences in each transition, so we define a special normal action sequence and present an algorithm to normalize a given action sequence. In normalizing an action sequence of a transition, a special renaming substitution is produced which we name the *normalizer substitution* of that action. The normalizer substitution is then used to propagate the changes of the variable values in a transition to predicates and actions of the successive transitions.

Definition 6. Let x be the set of variables in an EFSM, also let $A=(l_1:=r_1, ... l_n:=r_n)$ be an action sequence of size n in a transition in the EFSM, in which $l_i \in x$ and r_i is an expression for $1 \leq i \leq n$. Also suppose that $R_k = \{V \in x \mid V$ is used in expressions $r_1, r_2, ... , r_k\}$ for $1 \leq k \leq n$. A is a *normal action sequence* if $l_j \notin R_j$ for $1 \leq j \leq n$.

The algorithm depicted in figure 1 change a given action sequence to a normalized one and returns its corresponding normalizer substitution. The algorithm renames the new appearances of the variables whose values are changed in an action sequence. The normalizer substitution of the action is in fact the set of variable renaming substitutions performed in the above process.

3 The Notion of Invariants

In this section we represent the notion of invariants on EFSM as introduced in [11] with little changes in the definitions. An invariant represents a specific property (which should be always true) on an EFSM which is in fact a statement about causal relationships between input/output pairs in the EFSM.

INPUT: An action sequence $A=(l_1 := r_1, \ldots l_n := r_n)$ in the EFSM
$M = M=(S, I, O, x, Tr, s_{in})$
OUTPUT: A normalizer substitution θ
SIDE EFFECT: Action sequence A is changed to a normal one
Begin
   $\theta := \varnothing;$
   for $i:=1$ *to* n **do begin**
      $R := \{ V \in x \mid V$ *is used in expressions* $r_1, \ldots, r_i \}$
      if $l_i \in R$ **then begin**
         $l'_i := new\ V;$ /* a new variable name */
         $\theta := \theta \cup \{ l_i / l'_i \};$
         $l_i := l'_i;$
         for $j := i+1$ *to* n **do begin**
            $l_j := l_j\ \theta;\ r_j := r_j\ \theta;$
         end;
      end;
   end;
End;

Fig. 1. Normalizing an action sequence

Regarding the way of expressing the temporal relationships of the input/outputs in an EFSM, two types of invariants are introduced. We call them forward and backward invariants. Note that to define the invariants we only consider the control parts of the protocol so we do not speak about the values of the variables in input or output parameters. In the next section we represent algorithms to find corresponding constraints on the variables of a given invariant that makes it correct on the EFSM.

3.1 Forward Invariants

A *forward invariant* is used to express properties in the EFSM such as "*each time the implementation performs a specific execution trace like* $i_1/o_1, \ldots, i_{n-1}/o_{n-1}, i_n,$ *the next observed output belongs to a specific set of output symbols*". Based on this definition, we can assume that a forward invariant contains three elements: A preamble I/O sequence, a preamble input and a test output set. Intuitively a forward invariant is correct if for all paths in the EFSM matching with the preamble I/O sequence, and followed by an I/O pair containing an input equal to the preamble input, then the corresponding output essentially belongs to the test output set.

Definition 7. Let $M=(S, I, O, x, Tr, s_{in})$ be an EFSM. We say that the F(PIO, PI, TOS) is a forward invariant for M if the following conditions are respected :

1. PIO is the preamble I/O sequence which is defined according to the following EBNF:
$$PIO ::= a/z, PIO \mid *,PIO \mid \varepsilon$$
   In which $a \in I \cup \{?\}, z \in O \cup \{?\}$ and ε is the null sequence.
2. $PI \in I$ is the preamble input and $TOS \subseteq O$ is the test output set.
3. Each time that the sequence PIO is matched with any path in the EFSM, and it is followed by any transition with input PI, then we get essentially an output belonging to TOS.

Note that we deal with the wildcard ? as the standard one in pattern matching, while modify the usual meaning of the symbol *. The symbol * replaces any sequence of input/outputs not containing any pair with input equal to PI.

3.2 Backward Invariants

Using a *backward invariant* we can express more subtle properties such as "*each time a specific output is produced by the implementation, then we must have that a specific trace had been produced before*". So a backward invariant contains three elements: A preamble output set, a test input and a test I/O sequence. Intuitively a backward invariant is correct if any transition in the EFSM in which its output symbol belongs to the preamble output set, have an input equal to test input and essentially preceded by a path matching with the test I/O sequence.

Definition 8. Let $M=(S, I, O, x, Tr, s_{in})$ be an EFSM. We say that the B(TIO, TI, POS) is a backward invariant for M if the following conditions are respected :

1. TIO is the test I/O sequence which is defined according to the following EBNF:
$$TIO ::= a/z, TIO \mid *,TIO \mid \varepsilon$$
in which $a \in I \cup \{?\}$, $z \in O \cup \{?\}$ and ε is the null sequence.
2. $TI \in I \cup \{?\}$ is the test input and $POS \subseteq O$ is the test output set.
3. All transitions of M with an output symbol belonging to POS must essentially have an input symbol equal to TI and proceed by a path matching with TIO.

Let us remark that, in contrast with forward invariants (for the case of preamble input symbol), we do not force the test input symbol here to be an input action (it can be also the wildcard character "?"). Furthermore, our matching method is modified such that the symbol * replaces any sequence of input/outputs not containing any pair with input equal to TI.

4   Extracting Invariant Constraints

To use an invariant for passive testing, it is needed to assure at first about the correctness of the invariant on the specification. While checking invariants on a FSM simply returns a Boolean value showing the correctness or fail of the invariant, checking an invariant on an EFSM either returns simply a false Boolean value showing that the invariant is incorrect on the EFSM or returns a set of constraints on the variables of the invariant showing that the correctness of the invariant depends on the set of constraints. For passively testing the implementation, it is sufficient to match the execution trace with the invariant while its constraints regarding the value of the variables in the trace don't conflict. In this section we represent algorithms for checking forward and backward invariants on an EFSM and extracting their corresponding constraint set. The constraint extraction process is done once and off-line.

4.1   Forward Invariant Constraints

To check a given forward invariant on an EFSM, first we have to find the paths in the EFSM which are unifiable with the preamble part of the invariant. After that we should check if the invariant test set is reachable using all the unified paths or not, and if it is reachable, then what is the constraint set to make it true. The constraint set is in fact constructed during the unification of the preamble part with the paths in the EFSM.

Definition 9. Let $\rho = i_1/o_1,\ldots,i_n/o_n$ be an input sequence of size n and $M=(S, I, O, x, Tr, s_{in})$ be an EFSM, we define U_n as the set of *forward matchers* of ρ containing quadruples (s,θ,C,δ) in which s is a state belongs to S, θ and δ are substitutions and C is a set of constraints (conjoined predicates) which is constructed inductively as follows:

- The initial forward matcher set is equal to $U_0=S\times\{\emptyset\}\times\{\emptyset\}\times\{\emptyset\}$
- If $t=(s,s',a,z,P,A)\in Tr$ is a transition in M, and U_{j-1} contains a forward matcher quadruple (s,θ,C,δ) such that $(a/z)\delta$ is unifiable with (i/o), then U_j contains quadruples (s',θ',C',δ') in which $\theta'= \theta_o mgu((a/z)\delta, (i/o))$, $C'=C\cup(P\wedge normalized (A))\delta$, and δ' is the normalizer of A.

Using the above definition we can describe our algorithm for checking the correctness of a given forward invariant on an EFSM and extracting its necessary constraints.

Let F(PIO, PI, TOS) be a forward invariant in which PIO is of size n. Suppose that U_n is the forward matcher set of PIO. If U_n is empty then the invariant is incorrect, else we check that for any transition labeled by the input PI , we receive an output unifiable with one of the items in the TOS. If there is no possible transitions, then the invariant is incorrect, else for each forward matcher quadruple (s,θ,C,δ) in U_n , if C is empty then the invariant is true, else the invariant is true constraint to $C\theta$. The set of constraints $C\theta$ can be simplified using the existing constraint simplification algorithms. The algorithm is depicted more formally and detailed in figure 2.

The algorithm deals with invariants containing the wildcard character *. Also we consider that both i=? and o=? hold. We have used some auxiliary functions: *head(I)* returns the first i/o couple of the sequence I and *tail(I)* removes the first i/o couple from I.

The Boolean function *path(s, s', i)* returns true if there exist a path $a_1/z_1, \ldots a_r/z_r$ from s to s' and for any $1 \leq j \leq r$ we have $a_j \neq i$. Also the function *simplified(C)* returns the simplified version of the constraint set C. In fact this function solves the constraints such that the most constraining predicates on a single variable are remained. We don't enter in the details of this function. There are some well known methods to do this in the literature [12].

4.2 Backward Invariant Constraints

To check a given backward invariant on an EFSM, first we have to find the set of transitions in the EFSM which have outputs unifiable with elements of the preamble output set in the invariant. After that, we should check whether the paths in the EFSM which are ended by the discussed outputs are unifiable with the test input and test I/O sequence in the invariant or not. And, if they are unifiable, what are the constraints on the variables of the invariant. The constraint set is in fact constructed during the unification of the test I/O sequence with the paths in the EFSM. We traverse the paths in the EFSM in a backward fashion to do the unification and extract the constraints.

Definition 10. Let $\rho = i_1/o_1,\ldots,i_n/o_n$ be an input sequence of size n and $M=(S, I, O, x, Tr, s_{in})$ be an EFSM, we define V_0 as the set of *backward matchers* of ρ containing quadruples (s,θ,C,δ) in which s is a state belongs to S, θ and δ are substitutions and C is a set of constraints (conjoined predicates) which is constructed inductively as follows:

Input: M=(S, I, O, x, Tr, s_{in}), I=F(PIO,PI,OTS)

Output: true/false or a set of constraints. Satisfaction of each constraint is sufficient to satisfy the invariant.

Begin

/* PIO Matching: Finding the paths in the EFSM which are unifiable with the PIO */
I' :=PIO; U :=$S \times \{\emptyset\} \times \{\emptyset\} \times \{\emptyset\}$;
while $I' \neq \varepsilon$ **and** $U \neq \emptyset$ **do begin**

$first = head(I'); I'=tail(I');$
if $first \neq *$ **then begin** /* first = i/o */
$T:=Tr; U':= \emptyset;$
while $T \neq \emptyset$ **do begin**
choose $t \in T;$ /* t=(s,s',a,z,P,A) */
$T:=T-\{t\};$
if $(s,\theta,C,\delta) \in U$ *and unifiable*$((a/z)\delta, i/o)$ **then begin**
$\theta':= \theta_o mgu((a/z)\delta, i/o); C':=C \cup (P \wedge normalized(A)) \&$
$\delta':=normalizer(A); U' := U' \cup \{(s',\theta', C',\delta')\};$
end
end
$U=U';$
end
else begin   /* first= * */
while $head(I')=*$ **do** $I':=tail(I');$
$first:= head(I');$ /* first=i/o */
$U := \{ (s,\theta,C,\delta)) \mid s \in S, \exists (s,\theta,C,\delta) \in U, p=path(s',s,i) \};$
end
end

/* TOS checking: Checking if TOS is reachable using the unified path or not and if so what is its constraints*/
if $U=\emptyset$ **then return**(false);
else begin
$tf := $ false; $T:= Tr; CS:= \emptyset;$
while $T \neq \emptyset$ **do begin**
choose $t \in T; T := T-\{t\};$ /* t=(s,s',a,z) */
if $(s,\theta,C,\delta) \in U$ *and unifiable*$(a\delta, i_n)$ **then begin**
$\theta' := \theta_o mgu(a\delta, i_n);$
if $\exists o \in O \bullet (z\delta)\theta' = o\theta'$ **then return**(false);
$tf:=$ true; $CS :=CS \cup simplified(C \cup (P \wedge normalized(A))\delta);$
end
end
end
if not tf **then return** false;
if $CS = \emptyset$ **then return** true **else return** (CS);
End

Fig. 2. Algorithm for checking forward invariants and finding its corresponding constraints

- The initial backward matcher set is equal to $V_n=S \times \{\emptyset\} \times \{\emptyset\} \times \{\emptyset\}$
- If t=(s, s', a, z, P, A)$\in$ Tr is a transition in M, and V_{j+1} contains a backward matcher quadruple q=(s',θ,C,δ) such that $(a/z)\delta$ is unifiable with (i_j/o_j), then V_j contains quadruples q'=(s,θ',C',δ') in which $\theta'= \theta_o mgu((a/z)\delta, (i_j/o_j))$, δ' is the normalizer of A and $C' = C\delta' \cup (P \wedge normalized (A))$. Delete the quadruple q from V_{j+1}.

```
Input: M=(S, I, O, x, Tr, s_in), I=B(TIO,TI,POS)
Output: true/false or a set of constraints. Satisfaction of each constraint is sufficient to
        satisfy the invariant.
Begin
    /* POS Matching: Finding states in the EFSM which are unifiable with elements of the POS */
    T:=Tr;  V:=S ×{Ø}×{Ø}×{Ø};  error:=false;
    while T≠Ø and not error do begin
            choose t∈ T;  /* t=(s,s',a,z,P,A) */
            T:=T-{t};
            if ∃o∈POS • unifiable((a/z)δ, (TI/o)) then begin
                    θ:=mgu(a/z, PI/o);        δ:=normalizer(A);
                    C:=P∧ normalized(A);    V := V∪{(s, θ, C, δ)};
            end else error :=true;
    end;
    if V=Ø then error :=true;

    /* TIO matching: Checking if the TIO is matched with all paths ending to the states found in
       previous step or not and if so what is the constraint set   */
    I' := reverse(TIO);
    while not empty(I') and not error do begin
            V' := Ø;    first :=head(I');    I':=tail(I');
            if first ≠ * then begin   /* first = i/o */
                    T:=Tr;
                    while T ≠Ø do begin
                            choose t∈ T;    /* t=(s,s',a,z,P,A) */
                            T:=T-{t};
                            if (s',θ,C,δ) ∈ V and unifiable((a/z)δ, i/o) then begin
                                    θ':= θ,mgu((a/z)δ (i/o));     δ':=normalizer(A);
                                    C':=Cδ ∪(P∧ normalized(A));   V' := V'∪{(s,θ', C',δ')};
                                    V=V-{(s',θ,C,δ)};
                            end  else error := True;
                    end
            end else begin    /* first =* */
                            while head(I') = *  do  I' := tail'(I');   /* skip a seq. of *'s */
                            first := head(I');    /* first = i/o */
                            V':={ (s,θ,C,δ) | s∈S,  ∀(s',θ,C,δ)∈ V • path(s, s', o)};
                    end
            if V'≠Ø then error:= true else V:= V';
    end;
    if error then return (false);
    CS:= Ø;
    while V ≠Ø do begin
            choose v∈ V;    /* v= (s,θ,C,δ) */
            V:=V-{v};    CS:= CS ∪ simplify(C);
    end;
    if CS=Ø then return(true) else return(CS);
End;
```

Fig. 3. Algorithm for checking backward invariants and finding its corresponding constraints

Using the above definition we can describe our algorithm for checking the correct-ness of a given backward invariant on an EFSM and extracting its necessary constraints.

Let B(TIO, TI, POS) be a backward invariant. For all elements $o_m \in$ POS ($1 \leq m \leq$ |POS| in which |POS| is the cardinality of POS) we concatenate the pair TI/o_m to the TIO to generate a set of input/output sequences like ρ_m = "TIO, TI/o_m". Let the size of ρ_m be n. For each ρ_m ($1 \leq m \leq$ |POS|) we try to find its backward matcher set. If after constructing V_j ($0 < j \leq$ n) in each iteration, V_j is empty or V_{j+1} is not empty, then the invariant is incorrect, else for each quadruple of the V_0, if C is empty, then the invariant is true without any condition, else the invariant is true constraint to simplified Cθ. The algorithm is depicted more formally and detailed in figure 3. Auxiliary functions used are the same as described for the forward invariant checking algorithm.

5 An Example: SCP Protocol

In this section we present the processing of the method we discussed in this paper for passively testing an implementation of the Simple Connection Protocol (SCP) to show the applicability of the method. SCP has the advantage of including most difficulties of passive testing in a protocol specification, and then is able to figure out the applicability of the algorithm on bigger protocols.

5.1 The Simple Connection Protocol

SCP allows us to connect an entity called upper layer to an entity called lower layer. The upper layer performs a dialogue with SCP to fix the quality of service desirable for the future connection. Once the negotiation is finished, SCP dialogues with the lower layer to ask for the establishment of a connection satisfying the previously negotiated quality of service. The lower layer accepts or refuses this connection request. If it accepts the connection, SCP informs the upper layer that connection was established and the upper layer can start to transit data towards the lower layer via SCP.

Once the transmission of the data finished, the upper layer sends a message to close the connection. On the other hand, if the lower layer refuses the connection, the system allows SCP to make three requests before informing the upper layer that the connection attempts all failed. If the upper layer wishes again to be connected to the lower layer, it is necessary to restart the QoS negotiation with SCP from beginning. Figure 4 shows the interactions of the SCP with its upper and lower layers.

5.2 Defining Invariants

Let consider the EFSM specification of the Simple Connection Protocol depicted in figure 5. We suppose that the values of TryCount, ReqQos, FinQos, CONreq.qos, and accept.qos are defined in the interval [0;3]. Suppose that we want to passively test an implementation of the SCP regarding the following properties of the specification which are described using the invariants:

- I_1 = B (< refuse/connect(x) > , (refuse) , { CONcnf(-) }), means that SCP fail to connect the two layers (CONcnf(-)) only if the lower layer refused the connection twice before (refuse/connect(x), refuse/).
- I_2 = F (< CONreq(x)/connect(y) > , (accept(w)) , { CONcnf(+,z) }) , means that if SCP accepts to connect with the upper layer at his requested QoS (CON-

req(x)/connect(y)) and the lower layer accept it at a given QoS, then a connection must be realized between the two layers.

- $I_3 = F (<> , (accept(x)) , \{ CONcnf(+,y) \})$, means that if the lower layer accept the connection (accept(x)), this connection must be realized (CONcnf(+,y)).
- $I_4 = B (<> , (accept(x)) , \{ CONcnf(+,y) \})$, means that a connection is realized (CONcnf(+,x)), only if the lower layer accepted it before (accept(y)).

Note that I_1 and I_4 are forward invariants while I_2 and I_3 are backward invariants. In definition of the above invariants we have used a control driven approach i.e. in this stage, parameters of the signals are not important so we have used some variables instead of them.

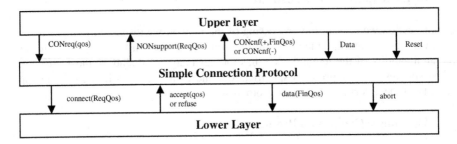

Fig. 4. Interactions of the SCP with its upper and lower layers

5.3 Finding Invariant Constraints

Now, we apply our method on the invariants to find their corresponding constraints. Table 1 shows the trace of the algorithms. For each forward (backward) invariant, the value of the intermediate forward (backward) matcher set i.e. U (i.e. V) and the ultimate constraint sets CS over the variables of the invariants have been shown. (See the algorithms in figures 2 and 3).

Applying the algorithms reveal that all the invariants are correct regarding the control part of the specification, but regarding the data part of the specification the invariants are true condition to some constraints which have been produced by the algorithms. For invariant I_1, there is no constraint over the variable of the invariant, so it should be matched by execution traces with any value for the variable x. For the other invariants, only such execution traces are matched with the invariants that the value of their input/output parameters does not cause any conflict with the corresponding constraints of the intended invariant.

5.4 Passive Testing Using the Constrained Invariants

Now suppose that the following execution traces are generated by a faulty implementation of the SCP:

- $Trace_1 = CONreq(1) / connect(1) , refuse / CONcnf(-)$
- $Trace_2 = CONreq(1) / connect(0) , accept(1) / CONcnf(+, 0)$.

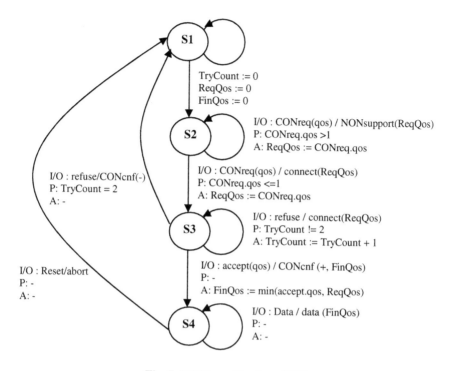

Fig. 5. EFSM specification of SCP

We know that a transition error has occurred in the first trace because the specification forces two loops on state s_3 before eventual transition to s_1, corresponding to the three requests SCP must do before failing the connection. In this trace, the connection is said to be failed on first try. For the second trace, there is an output error because the first I/O couple should be CONreq(1)/connect(1). We can imagine that the trace comes from an implementation in which the action on the transition from s_2 to s_3 is ReqQos:=CONreq.qos −1 and then such a trace is produced. This error has for consequence to connect the upper and lower layers with a QoS equals to 0 when it could be (normally) equal to 1.

Tables 2 and 3 show the invariants used in the checking of the first and the second trace respectively. We try to identify the constraints with the values of the variables extracted from the traces:

- **Trace₁:** Since the analysis found CONcnf(-) in the trace and failed looking for the couple refuse/connect(x), then the trace is erroneous regarding the invariant I_1. Note that the found error is control driven, so it is not needed to look at the constraints at all.
- **Trace₂:** There are three invariants which are candidate for this trace. Matching the trace with the invariants shows that there is not any control driven error, so we use constraints and the value of the variables in the trace to decide about the possibility of data driven errors:

Table 1. Using algorithms to extract required constraints for the example invariants

Invariant	U_1(or V_1)	U_2 (or V_2)	Constraint set (CS)
I_1 (Backward)	$V_1 = \{ (s_3, \theta_1, C_1, \delta_1) \}$ $\theta_1 = \varnothing$ $C_1 = \{ \text{TryCount} = 2 \}$ $\delta_1 = \varnothing$	$V_2 = \{ (s_3, \theta_2, C_2, \delta_2) \}$ $\theta_2 = \{ \text{ReqQos}/x \}$ $\delta_2 = \{ \text{TryCount}/y \}$ $C_2 = C_1 \delta_2 \cup$ $\{\text{TryCount}!=2, y=\text{TryCount}+1\} =$ $\{y=2, \text{TryCount}!=2, y=\text{TryCount}+1\}$ $= \{ \text{TryCount} = 1 \}$	$CS\_I_1 = C_2\theta_2 =$ $\{\text{TryCount}=2\}$
I_2 (Forward)	$U_1 = \{ (s_3, \theta_1, C_1, \delta_1) \}$ $\theta_1 = \{ \text{CONreq.qos}/x, \text{ReqQos}/y \}$ $C_1 = \{ \text{CONreq.qos} <=1, \text{ReqQos} = \text{CONreq.qos} \}$ $\delta_1 = \varnothing$	$U_2 = \{ (s_4, \theta_2, C_2, \delta_2) \}$ $\theta_2 = \theta_1 \circ \{ \text{accept.qos}/w, \text{FinQos}/z \}$ $= \{\text{CONreq.qos}/x, \text{ReqQos}/y,$ $\text{accept.qos}/w, \text{FinQos}/z \}$ $C_2 = C_1 \cup \{\text{CONreq.qos}=$ $\min(\text{accept.qos}, \text{ReqQos}) \} \delta_1$ $= \{\text{CONreq.qos} <=1,$ $\text{ReqQos}=\text{CONreq.qos},$ $\text{FinQos}=\min(\text{accept.qos},$ $\text{ReqQos})\}$ $\delta_2 = \varnothing$	$CS\_I_2 = C_2\theta_2 =$ $\{x<=1, y=x,$ $z=\min(w, y)\}$
I_3 (Forward)	$U_1 = \{ (s_3, \theta_1, C_1, \delta_1) \}$ $\theta_1 = \{ \text{accept.qos}/x, \text{FinQos}/y \}$ $C_1 = \{ y=\min(x, \text{ReqQos}) \}$ $\delta_1 = \varnothing$		$CS\_I_3 = C_1\theta_1 =$ $\{y=\min(x,$ $\text{ReqQos})\}$
I_4 (Backward)	$V_1 = \{ (s_4, \theta_1, C_1, \delta_1) \}$ $\theta_1 = \{ \text{accept.qos}/x, \text{FinQos}/y \}$ $C_1 = \{ y=\min(x, \text{ReqQos}) \}$ $\delta_1 = \varnothing$		$CS\_I_4 = C_1\theta_1 =$ $\{y=\min(x,$ $\text{ReqQos})\}$

$CS\text{-}I_2 \cup \{x=1, y=0, w=1, z=0\} = \{x<=1, y=x, z=\min(w, y)\} \cup \{ x=1, y=0, w=1, z=0 \}$
$\qquad = \{ 1=<1, 0=1, 0=\min(1, 0) \}$

$1=<1$ is true, $0=1$ is false and $0=\min(1, 0)$ is true, so the invariant I_2 is false on Trace_2.

$CS\text{-}I_3 \cup \{x=1, y=0\} = \{y=\min(x, \text{ReqQos})\} \cup \{x=1, y=0\} = \{ 0=\min(1, \text{ReqQos}) \}$

0 is the minimum of 1 and ReqQos only if ReqQos is equal to 0, so the invariant I_3 is true on the trace Trace_2 if ReqQos=0.

$CS\text{-}I_4 \cup \{x=1, y=0\} = \{y=\min(x, \text{ReqQos})\} \cup \{ x=1, y=0 \} = \{ 0=\min(1, \text{ReqQos}) \}$

0 is the minimum of 1 and ReqQos only if ReqQos is equal to 0 so the invariant I_4 is true on the trace Trace_2 if ReqQos=0.

As we found an inconsistency in the checking of the invariant I_2 with the trace Trace_2 we conclude that the trace T_2 is false. Checking the other invariants on the trace is not necessary but figure here as an example of variable simplification.

Table 2. Using invariant I_1 to check the execution trace Trace_1

Trace_1	CONreq(1)	connect(1)	Refuse	CONcnf(-)
I_1	Refuse	connect(x)	Refuse	CONcnf(-)

Table 3. Using invariants I_2, I_3 and I_4 to check the execution trace $Trace_2$

$Trace_2$	CONreq(1)	connect(0)	Accept(1)	CONcnf(+,0)
I_2	CONreq(x)	connect(y)	Accept(w)	CONcnf(+,z)
I_3			Accept(x)	CONcnf(+,y)
I_4			Accept(x)	CONcnf(+,y)

6 Conclusion

Passive testing methods for network protocols can be classified into naïve and invariant based approaches. In the naïve approach the implementation trace which is recorded during the execution of the protocol under test is compared with total of the specification in a forward or backward manner. This is where, in the invariant based approach only critical properties of the specification (i.e. invariants) which are extracted by an expert are compared with the implementation trace. By using invariant based approach, not only a lot of extra processing is reduced, but also we can focus on the critical properties of the program under test.

Passive testing methods can be compared from another aspect. Some methods are limited to testing only control driven aspects of the implementation, i.e. the order of occurrences of the input/output signals, while other methods are capable of testing both control driven and data driven aspects of the implementation i.e. the values of the signal's parameters. For testing control driven aspects it is sufficient to use FSM for specification, while for data driven aspects it is needed to use EFSM.

In this paper we presented a new method for passive testing of both control driven and data driven aspects of the network protocols using an invariant based approach. The intended properties of the specification are expressed using some control driven invariants given by an expert. After that, using the given algorithms, the invariants are checked on the specification off-line. Also to take the data driven aspects into account, for the correct invariants, some constraints over the variables of the invariants are extracted. For passively testing the implementation traces, it is sufficient to compare, on-line, the trace with the invariants regarding the constraints using pattern matching. A trace is correct while it is matched with the invariant and the invariant's constraints are not conflicting regarding the values of the signal's parameters.

To show the applicability of the presented method, passive testing of the Simple Connection Protocol (SCP) using the presented method was illustrated.

References

1. R. Lai, "A survey of communication protocol testing", Journal of Systems and Software 62(1): 21-46 (2002).
2. D. Lee, and M. Yannakakis, "Principles and methods of testing finite state machines--- A survey", Proc. IEEE 84, 8, (1996), 1089--1123.
3. D. Lee, A. N. Netravali, K. Sabnani, B. Sugla, A. John, "Passive testing and applications to network management", IEEE International Conference on Network protocols, ICNP'97, pages 113-122. IEEE Computer Society Press, 1997

4. R. E. Miller and K. A. Arisha, "On Fault Location in Networks by Passive Testing", IPCCC 2000, Pheonix, AZ, Feb. 2000.
5. M. Tabourier and A. Cavalli, "Passive Testing and application to the GSM-MAP Protocol", in Journal of Information and Software Technology 41(11) (15 Sept. 1999), Pages 813-821, Elsevier, 1999.
6. J. A. Arnedo, A. Cavalli and M. Nunez, "Fast Testing of Critical Properties through Passive Testing", LNCS, vol. 2644/2003, Pages 295-310, Springer, 2003.
7. A. Cavalli, C. Gervy and S. Prokopenko, "New Approaches for Passive Testing Using an Extended Finite State Machine Specification", in Journal of Information and Software Technology, 45:837-852, Elsevier, 2003.
8. D. Lee, D. Chen, R. Hao, R. E. Miller, J. Wu, and X. Yin, "A Formal Approach for Passive Testing of Protocol Data Portions", Proc. ICNP'2002.
9. B. Alcalde, A. Cavalli, D. Khuu, D. Chen, D. Lee, "Network Protocol System Passive Testing for Fault Management - a Backward Checking Approach", in the Proceedings of the 24th IFIP WG 6.1, International Conference on Formal Techniques for Networked and Distributed Systems, FORTE 2004, 27-30 September, 2004, Madrid, Spain.
10. F. Baader, W. Snyder, "Unification Theory, Handbook of Automated Reasoning", Alan Robinson, Andrei Voronkov, eds., Vol. 1, Chapter 8, 446–533.
11. E.Bayse, A. Cavalli, M. Nunez and F. Zaidi, "A Passive Testing Approach based on Invariants: Application to the WAP", To be published in journal of Computer Network, 2004.
12. K. Marriott and P. J. Stuckey, "Programming with Constraints: An Introduction", Book, The MIT Press, 1998.

Dependence Testing: Extending Data Flow Testing with Control Dependence

Hyoung Seok Hong[1] and Hasan Ural[2]

[1] Concordia Institute for Information Systems Engineering,
Concordia University
hshong@ciise.concordia.ca
[2] School of Information Technology and Engineering,
University of Ottawa
ural@site.uottawa.ca

Abstract. This paper presents a new approach to structural testing, called dependence testing. First we propose dependence oriented coverage criteria that extend conventional data flow oriented coverage criteria with control dependence. This allows one to capture the full dependence information of a program or specification systematically. We then describe a model checking-based approach to test generation for dependence testing. It is shown that dependence oriented coverage criteria can be characterized in the temporal logics LTL and CTL. This enables one to use any LTL and CTL model checkers as test generators. Finally, we show that the temporal logic-based characterization can also be used for reducing the cost of dependence testing.

1 Introduction

In structural testing, we are given a coverage criterion defining a set of entities in the structure of a program or specification and we generate a test suite satisfying the coverage criterion. A test suite is a set of test sequences and is said to satisfy a coverage criterion if for every entity defined by the coverage criterion, there is a test sequence in the test suite exercising the entity. There are two main types of structural testing. Control flow testing calls for exercising single entities such as statements, branches, decisions, and conditions. Data flow testing calls for exercising associations between definitions and uses of variables such as definition-use pairs and definition-use chains. These associations capture the dependence information of a program or specification mainly in terms of data dependence. Data flow testing has been widely used for program testing[34] and protocol conformance testing with formal specifications written in SDL and Estelle whose underlying model is extended finite state machine[11].

This paper presents a new approach to structural testing, called *dependence testing*. The main contributions of the paper are three-fold. First, we propose dependence oriented coverage criteria that extend conventional data flow oriented coverage criteria with control dependence. Our new coverage criteria are

F. Khendek and R. Dssouli (Eds.): TestCom 2005, LNCS 3502, pp. 23–39, 2005.
© IFIP 2005

motivated by the work of Podgurski and Clarke[30] which evaluates data flow oriented coverage criteria in terms of program dependence. In [30], it is shown that both data dependence and control dependence are necessary to detect the propagation of erroneous values caused by faults. It is also shown that although data flow oriented coverage criteria incorporate limited forms of control dependence, they are not powerful enough to detect the propagation of all of erroneous values. However, the question of how to extend data flow oriented coverage criteria has remained unanswered. In this paper, we show that the data flow oriented coverage criteria in [17, 28, 27, 32] can be naturally extended with control dependence. This allows one to capture the dependence information of a program or specification systematically based on both data dependence and control dependence.

Second, we discuss test generation for dependence testing. Recently there have been several proposals of model checking-based approaches to test generation for control flow testing[3, 7, 12, 14, 16, 29] and data flow testing[20, 21]. Model checking[9] is a formal verification technique for determining whether a system model satisfies a property written in temporal logic and model checkers such as SMV[26] and SPIN[18] are already used on a regular basis for the verification of real-world applications. In addition to being automatic, an important feature of model checking is the ability of explaining the success or failure of a temporal logic formula in terms of witnesses or counterexamples, respectively. The main idea of model checking-based test generation[3, 7, 12, 14, 16, 20, 21, 29] is to characterize test coverage in temporal logic in such a way that the problem of test generation is reduced to the problem of finding a set of witnesses or counterexamples for a set of temporal logic formulas. The capability of model checkers to construct witnesses and counterexamples enables efficient and scalable test generation. In this paper, we extend the model checking-based approach in [20, 21] for dependence testing. We show that dependence oriented coverage criteria can be characterized in the temporal logics LTL and CTL so that any LTL and CTL model checkers can be used as test generators for dependence testing.

Finally, we show that the temporal logic-based characterization of dependence oriented coverage criteria can also be used for reducing the cost of dependence testing. There have been several proposals of approaches to reducing the cost of control flow testing[1, 4, 5, 6, 8] and data flow testing[15, 24, 25]. The main idea of these approaches is to construct a subset of entities for a given coverage criterion such that exercising every entity in the subset guarantees exercising every entity defined by the coverage criterion. That is, if a test suite covers every entity in the subset, the test suite satisfies the coverage criterion. Following the terminology of [24, 25], we call such a subset a spanning set for the coverage criteria. Recently in [22], the authors show that the problem of finding a minimum spanning set for a family of data flow oriented coverage criteria can be reduced to the model checking problem of LTL. In this paper, we extend the results of [22] and show how LTL model checking can be used for reducing the cost of dependence testing.

The remainder of the paper is organized as follows. After introducing preliminary definitions in Section 2, we investigate test coverage, generation, and reduction for dependence testing in Section 3, 4, 5, respectively. We conclude the paper with a discussion of future work in Section 6.

2 Preliminaries

This section recalls the basics of LTL and flow graph, which are the logic and model employed in our approach, respectively.

2.1 Logics: LTL and CTL

In this paper we will make use of both LTL and CTL. We give a brief introduction to LTL here and refer the interested readers to [9] for the syntax and semantics of CTL. A formula f in LTL is built from a set AP of atomic propositions, the standard boolean operators, and the temporal operators $\mathbf{X}$ (next time) and $\mathbf{U}$ (until) according to the following grammar: $f := p \mid \neg f \mid f \wedge f \mid \mathbf{X}f \mid f\mathbf{U}f$ where $p \in AP$. We also use the temporal operators $\mathbf{F}$ (eventually) and $\mathbf{G}$ (always) defined by $\mathbf{F}f \equiv true\mathbf{U}f$ and $\mathbf{G}f \equiv \neg\mathbf{F}\neg f$.

The semantics of LTL is defined with respect to an infinite path $\pi = \sigma_0\sigma_1...$ where for every $i \geq 0$, σ_i is a subset of AP. For a position i, $\pi(i)$ is the i-th element of π and π^i is the suffix $\sigma_i\sigma_{i+1}...$ of π. We write $\pi \models f$ to indicate that π satisfies f.

- $\pi \models p$ iff $p \in \sigma_0$;
- $\pi \models \neg f$ iff $\pi \not\models f$;
- $\pi \models f_1 \wedge f_2$ iff $\pi \models f_1$ and $\pi \models f_2$;
- $\pi \models \mathbf{X}f$ iff $\pi^1 \models f$;
- $\pi \models f_1\mathbf{U}f_2$ iff there exists $i \geq 0$ such that $\pi^i \models f_2$ and $\pi^j \models f_1$ for every $0 \leq j < i$.

We also interpret LTL over a Kripke structure (Q, q_{init}, L, R) where Q is a set of states, $q_{init} \in Q$ is the initial state, $L : Q \to 2^{AP}$ labels each state with atomic propositions, and $R \subseteq Q \times Q$ is the total transition relation. We write $M \models f$ to indicate that for every infinite path π of M such that $\pi(0) = q_{init}$, $\pi \models f$. The model checking problem of LTL is to decide if for given M and f, it holds that $M \models f$.

2.2 Model: Flow Graph

Flow graphs are the standard model of programs in conventional program analysis and testing[2]. Flow graphs have also been used in analyzing and testing specification languages whose underlying model is extended finite state machine such as Estelle[32], SDL[33], and statecharts[19] as well as process algebra such as LOTOS[31].

A *flow graph* is a directed graph $G = (V, v_s, v_f, A)$ where V is a set of nodes, $v_s \in V$ is the start node, $v_f \in V$ is the final node, and $A \subseteq V \times V$ is a set of arcs. The start node v_s and final node v_f represent the single entry and single exit point, respectively. A node represents a simple statement (such as assignment, input, and output) or the predicate of a conditional or repetitive statement (such as if and while). An arc represents possible flow of control between statements. Each variable occurrence is classified as a definition or use. For a variable x and a node v, x is *defined* at v, denoted by $d(x, v)$, if x is assigned a value at v. x is *used* at v, denoted by $u(x, v)$, if v is referenced at v. A use $u(x, v)$ is a *computation-use* (c-use) if v represents a statement and is a *predicate-use* (p-use) if v represents a predicate. A path $v_1...v_n$ is *complete* if $v_1 = v_s$ and $v_n = v_f$. A *test sequence* is a complete path and a *test suite* is a finite set of test sequences. Figure 1 shows a simple program and its flow graph where v_1 is the start node and v_9 is the final node.

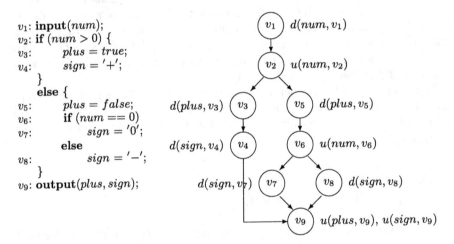

Fig. 1. A program and its flow graph

There are two types of program dependence. For two nodes v and v', we say that v *directly data-affects* v' *through variable* x (or equivalently, v' *is directly data-dependent on* v *through variable* x), denoted by $v \xrightarrow{x} v'$, if x is defined at v, x is used at v', and there is a path $vv_1...v_nv'$ such that x is not defined v_i for every $1 \leq i \leq n$. In this case, $v_1...v_n$ is a *definition-clear path* with respect to x. A test sequence *exercises* $v \xrightarrow{x} v'$ if $vv_1...v_nv'$ is a subpath of the test sequence where $v_1...v_n$ is a definition-clear path with respect to x. We say that v' *postdominates* v if every path from v to v_f contains v' and that v *directly control-affects* v' (or equivalently, v' *is directly control-dependent on* v), denoted by $v \xrightarrow{c} v'$, if v has two successors v_1 and v_2 such that v' postdominates v_1 but v' does not postdominate v_2. A test sequence *exercises* $v \xrightarrow{c} v'$ if $vv_1...v_nv'$ is a subpath of the test sequence.

3   Test Coverage

Let $v_1, v_2, ..., v_n$ be nodes. We say that $v_1 \to v_2 \to ... \to v_n$ is a *dependence-chain* if for every $1 \le i < n$, $v_i \to v_{i+1}$ is either a direct data dependence $v_i \overset{x}{\to} v_{i+1}$ or direct control dependence $v_i \overset{c}{\to} v_{i+1}$. Obviously the strongest coverage criterion based on the dependence information, which we call *all-dependence-chains coverage criterion*, is to require that every dependence-chain be exercised. However, this is in general impossible to achieve since the number of dependence-chains in a program may be large or even infinite in the presence of loops. In this section we investigate the data flow oriented coverage criteria in [17, 28, 27, 32], which capture the dependence information mainly in terms of data dependence, and extend them with control dependence. This allows one to generate test suites consisting of a finite and reasonable number of test sequences based on both data dependence and control dependence.

3.1   Direct Dependences

All-Dependence-Pairs Coverage Criterion. A pair $(d(x, v), u(x, v'))$ is a *definition-use pair* (du-pair) if there is a path $vv_1...v_nv'$ such that $v_1...v_n$ is a definition-clear path with respect to x. A test suite Π satisfies *reach coverage criterion*[17] if every du-pair $(d(x, v), u(x, v'))$ is exercised by some test sequence in Π.

It is straightforward to rephrase reach coverage criterion in terms of program dependence: A test suite Π satisfies *reach coverage criterion* if every direct data dependence $v \overset{x}{\to} v'$ is exercised by some test sequence in Π.

We extend reach coverage criterion with direct control dependence as follows: A test suite Π satisfies *all-dependence-pairs coverage criterion* if Π satisfies reach coverage criterion and every direct control dependence $v \overset{c}{\to} v'$ is exercised by some test sequence in Π. In Figure 1, all-dependence-pairs coverage criterion requires that the following direct data and control dependences be exercised.

- direct data dependences: $v_1 \overset{num}{\longrightarrow} v_2$, $v_1 \overset{num}{\longrightarrow} v_6$, $v_3 \overset{plus}{\longrightarrow} v_9$, $v_5 \overset{plus}{\longrightarrow} v_9$, $v_4 \overset{sign}{\longrightarrow} v_9$, $v_7 \overset{sign}{\longrightarrow} v_9$, $v_8 \overset{sign}{\longrightarrow} v_9$
- direct control dependences: $v_2 \overset{c}{\longrightarrow} v_3$, $v_2 \overset{c}{\longrightarrow} v_4$, $v_2 \overset{c}{\longrightarrow} v_5$, $v_2 \overset{c}{\longrightarrow} v_6$, $v_6 \overset{c}{\longrightarrow} v_7$, $v_6 \overset{c}{\longrightarrow} v_8$

All-Dependence-Pairs-with-Puses Coverage Criterion. Rapps and Weyuker's criteria[28] extend reach coverage criterion by distinguishing between c-uses and p-uses. A du-pair $(d(x, v), u(x, v'))$ is a *definition-cuse pair* (dcu-pair) if $u(x, v')$ is a c-use. Otherwise, it is a *definition-puse pair* (dpu-pair). Let $(d(x, v), u(x, v'))$ be a dpu-pair and v'' be a successor of v'. A test sequence *exercises* $(d(x, v), u(x, v'), v'')$ if $vv_1...v_nv'v''$ is a subpath of the test sequence where $v_1...v_n$ is a definition-clear path with respect to x. A test suite Π satisfies *all-uses coverage criterion*[28] if for every dcu-pair $(d(x, v), u(x, v'))$, the dcu-pair is exercised by some test sequence in Π and for every dpu-pair $(d(x, v), u(x, v'))$ and every successor v'' of v', $(d(x, v), u(x, v'), v'')$ is exercised by some test sequence in Π.

In all-uses coverage criterion, a test sequence exercising $(d(x, v), u(x, v'))$ reflects the direct data dependence $v \xrightarrow{x} v'$, whereas a test sequence exercising $(d(x, v), u(x, v'), v'')$ reflects the dependence-chain $v \xrightarrow{x} v' \xrightarrow{c} v''$, that is, the direct data dependence $v \xrightarrow{x} v'$ and direct control dependence $v' \xrightarrow{c} v''$ at the same time.

We extend all-uses coverage criterion with direct control dependence as follows: A test suite Π satisfies *all-dependence-pairs-with-puses coverage criterion* if Π satisfies all-uses coverage criterion and every direct control dependence $v \xrightarrow{c} v'$ is exercised by some test sequence in Π. In Figure 1, all-dependence-pairs-with-puses coverage criterion requires that the following dependences be exercised.

- dcu-pairs: $v_3 \xrightarrow{plus} v_9, v_5 \xrightarrow{plus} v_9, v_4 \xrightarrow{sign} v_9, v_7 \xrightarrow{sign} v_9, v_8 \xrightarrow{sign} v_9$
- dpu-pairs: $v_1 \xrightarrow{num} v_2 \xrightarrow{c} v_3, v_1 \xrightarrow{num} v_2 \xrightarrow{c} v_5, v_1 \xrightarrow{num} v_6 \xrightarrow{c} v_7, v_1 \xrightarrow{num} v_6 \xrightarrow{c} v_8$
- direct control dependences: $v_2 \xrightarrow{c} v_3, v_2 \xrightarrow{c} v_4, v_2 \xrightarrow{c} v_5, v_2 \xrightarrow{c} v_6, v_6 \xrightarrow{c} v_7,$ $v_6 \xrightarrow{c} v_8$

3.2   Indirect Dependences

All-k-Dependence-Chains Coverage Criterion. While reach coverage criterion and all-uses coverage criterion focus on definitions and uses of the same variable, Ntafos' criteria[27] emphasize interactions among different variables. These interactions are captured in terms of sequences of du-pairs. A sequence $[(d(x_1, v_1), u(x_1, v_1')) \ldots (d(x_n, v_n), u(x_n, v_n'))]$ of du-pairs is a *data flow chain* (df-chain)[32] if for every $1 \le i < n$, $v_i' = v_{i+1}$, that is, $u(x_i, v_i')$ and $d(x_{i+1}, v_{i+1})$ occur at the same node and hence x_{i+1} is defined in terms of x_i. A path $v_1\pi_1v_2...v_n\pi_nv_n'$ is an *interaction path* of a df-chain if for every $1 \le i \le n$, π_i is a definition-clear path with respect to x_i. A test sequence *exercises* a df-chain if an interaction path of the df-chain is a subpath of the test sequence. A test suite Π satisfies *required k-tuples coverage criterion* if every df-chain consisting of k' du-pairs, $1 \le k' < k$, is exercised by some test sequence in Π.

We rephrase required k-tuples coverage criterion in terms of program dependence: A test suite Π satisfies required k-tuples coverage criterion if every dependence-chain consisting of k' direct data dependences, $1 \le k' < k$, is exercised by some test sequence in Π. Since required k-tuples coverage criterion is based on data dependence, it can only partially capture the dependence information. For example, consider the nodes v_1 and v_3 in Figure 1. Although there is a dependence-chain $v_1 \xrightarrow{num} v_2 \xrightarrow{c} v_3$ from v_1 to v_3, required k-tuples coverage criterion fails to capture this dependence-chain since it contains control dependence.

We extend required k-tuples coverage criterion with control dependence as follows: A test suite Π satisfies *all-k-dependence-chains coverage criterion* if every dependence-chain consisting of k' direct dependences, $1 \le k' < k$, is exercised by some test sequence in Π. We note that required 2-tuples coverage criterion (resp. all-2-dependence-chains coverage criterion) is equivalent to reach coverage criterion (resp. all-dependence-pairs coverage criterion). In Figure 1, all-

3-dependence-chains coverage criterion requires that the following dependence-chains be exercised[1].

$$v_1 \xrightarrow{num} v_2 \xrightarrow{c} v_3, \; v_1 \xrightarrow{num} v_2 \xrightarrow{c} v_4, \; v_1 \xrightarrow{num} v_2 \xrightarrow{c} v_5, \; v_1 \xrightarrow{num} v_2 \xrightarrow{c} v_6,$$
$$v_1 \xrightarrow{num} v_6 \xrightarrow{c} v_7, \; v_1 \xrightarrow{num} v_6 \xrightarrow{c} v_8,$$
$$v_2 \xrightarrow{c} v_3 \xrightarrow{plus} v_9, \; v_2 \xrightarrow{c} v_4 \xrightarrow{sign} v_9, \; v_2 \xrightarrow{c} v_5 \xrightarrow{plus} v_9, \; v_2 \xrightarrow{c} v_6 \xrightarrow{c} v_7,$$
$$v_2 \xrightarrow{c} v_6 \xrightarrow{c} v_8,$$
$$v_6 \xrightarrow{c} v_7 \xrightarrow{sign} v_9, \; v_6 \xrightarrow{c} v_8 \xrightarrow{sign} v_9$$

Let $[(d(x_1, v_1), u(x_1, v_1')) \; ... \; (d(x_n, v_n), u(x_n, v_n'))]$ be a df-chain. We have that $u(x_i, v_i')$ is a c-use for every $1 \le i < n$ and the last use $u(x_n, v_n')$ may be either a c-use or p-use. By distinguishing between c-uses and p-uses, all-k-dependence-chains-with-puses coverage criterion may be defined. Due to space limit this coverage criterion will not be pursued in this paper.

All-IO-Dependence-Chains Coverage Criterion. Ural *et al.*'s coverage criteria[32, 33] also emphasize interactions among different variables. While required k-tuples coverage criterion considers df-chains consisting of a fixed number of du-pairs, all-IO-df-chains coverage criterion in [32, 33] considers df-chains consisting of an arbitrary (but finite) number of du-pairs which start with inputs and end with outputs. In this paper, we define an *input* as a definition occurring at an input statement and *output* as a use occurring at an output statement. For example, in Figure 1, there are one input $d(num, v_1)$ and two outputs $u(plus, v_9)$ and $u(sign, v_9)$. The rationale here is to capture the functionality of a module in terms of the interactions with its environment by identifying the effects of inputs accepted from the environment on outputs offered to the environment. Since the number of df-chains from an input to an output may be infinite, we consider only *simple* df-chains that are allowed to have at most one occurrence of each du-pair. A test suite Π satisfies *all-IO-df-chains coverage criterion* if for every input i, every output o, and every simple df-chain from i to o, the df-chain is exercised by some test sequence in Π.

As is done by required k-tuples coverage criterion, all-IO-df-chains coverage criterion also partially captures the dependence information in terms of only data dependence. For example, consider the input $d(v_1, num)$ and output $u(v_9, plus)$ in Figure 1. There are several dependence chains from v_1 to v_9, say $v_1 \xrightarrow{num} v_2 \xrightarrow{c} v_3 \xrightarrow{plus} v_9$, but all-IO-df-chains coverage criterion fails to capture those dependence-chains since they contain control dependence.

We extend all-IO-df-chains coverage criterion with control dependence as follows: A test suite Π satisfies *all-IO-dependence-chains coverage criterion* if for every input i, every output o, and every simple dependence-chain from i to o, the dependence-chain is exercised by some test sequence in Π. In Figure 1, all-IO-dependence-chains coverage criterion requires that the following dependence-chains be exercised.

$$v_1 \xrightarrow{num} v_2 \xrightarrow{c} v_3 \xrightarrow{plus} v_9, \; v_1 \xrightarrow{num} v_2 \xrightarrow{c} v_4 \xrightarrow{sign} v_9, \; v_1 \xrightarrow{num} v_2 \xrightarrow{c} v_5 \xrightarrow{plus} v_9,$$

---

[1] Dependence-chains consisting of one direct dependence are not shown.

$$v_1 \xrightarrow{num} v_2 \xrightarrow{c} v_6 \xrightarrow{c} v_7 \xrightarrow{sign} v_9, \; v_1 \xrightarrow{num} v_2 \xrightarrow{c} v_6 \xrightarrow{c} v_8 \xrightarrow{sign} v_9,$$
$$v_1 \xrightarrow{num} v_6 \xrightarrow{c} v_7 \xrightarrow{sign} v_9, \; v_1 \xrightarrow{num} v_6 \xrightarrow{c} v_8 \xrightarrow{sign} v_9$$

3.3 The Relationships Among Coverage Criteria

For two coverage criteria C_1 and C_2, C_1 *subsumes* C_2 if every test suite satisfying C_1 also satisfies C_2[28]. By definition, the four data flow oriented coverage criteria considered in this section are subsumed by their dependence oriented counterparts. For the other direction, the data flow oriented coverage criteria except all-uses coverage criterion do not subsume their counterparts.

It is interesting to investigate the relationship between all-uses coverage criterion and all-dependence-pairs-with-puses coverage criterion. Let A_P be the set of arcs starting from a node representing a predicate and A_C be the set of arcs (v, v') such that v directly control-affects v'. For example, in Figure 1,

$$A_P = \{(v_2, v_3), (v_2, v_5), (v_6, v_7), (v_6, v_8)\} \text{ and}$$
$$A_C = \{(v_2, v_3), (v_2, v_4), (v_2, v_5), (v_2, v_6), (v_6, v_7), (v_6, v_8)\}.$$

It is not hard to see that a test suite exercises every arc in A_P if and only if the test suite exercises every arc in A_C. Hence it follows that all-uses coverage criterion and all-dependence-pairs-with-puses coverage criterion subsume each other and hence they are equivalent with respect to the subsume relation.

One of the limitations of the subsume relation is that it does not always guarantee a better fault-detecting ability, that is, C_1 subsumes C_2 but there are test suites that satisfy C_2 that expose faults while test suites that satisfy C_1 do not expose any faults. The cover and properly cover relations in [13] address this limitation. For a coverage criterion C, let $SD(C)$ be the multiset of subdomains such that C requires the selection of one or more input values from each subdomain in $SD(C)$. C_1 *covers* C_2 if for every subdomain $D \in SD(C_2)$, there is a collection $\{D_1, ..., D_n\}$ in $SD(C_1)$ such that $D_1 \cup ... \cup D_n = D$. Roughly speaking, C_1 *properly covers* C_2 if C_1 covers C_2 and, in addition, the number of times a subdomain D_1 in $SD(C_1)$ is used to characterize the subdomains in $SD(C_2)$ is at most the number of times D_1 appears in $SD(C_1)$. It is not hard to see that if $SD(C_1)$ is a superset of $SD(C_2)$, then C_1 covers C_2 and C_1 properly covers C_2. We have that the multisets of subdomains for the dependence oriented coverage criteria defined in this section are supersets of those for their data flow oriented counterparts. Hence the dependence oriented coverage criteria cover and properly cover their data flow oriented counterparts but not vice versa.

4   Test Generation

This section shows how test generation for dependence testing can be formulated in the temporal logics LTL and CTL. We restrict ourselves to a fragment of LTL consisting of guarantee formulas. An LTL formula is a *guarantee formula* if there is a finite path π such that for every infinite path π', $\pi \cdot \pi'$ satisfies the formula.

The finite prefix π is called a *witness* of the formula. Intuitively, it is sufficient to use a finite path to explain the success of a guarantee formula while we need an infinite path for a general LTL formula. For a set F of guarantee formulas and a set Π of finite paths, we say that Π is a *witness-set* of F if for every formula f in F, there is a finite path in Π that is a witness of f. In the following sections, we show that test generation for dependence oriented coverage criteria can be reduced to the problem of finding a witness-set of guarantee formulas.

4.1 Direct Dependences

All-Dependence-Pairs Coverage Criterion. Let $def(x)$ be the disjunction of nodes at which x is defined. For example, in Figure 1, $def(num) ::= v_1$, $def(plus) ::= v_3 \vee v_5$, and $def(sign) ::= v_4 \vee v_7 \vee v_8$. For a direct data dependence $v \xrightarrow{x} v'$, we associate an LTL formula defined by

$$\text{ltl}(v \xrightarrow{x} v') = \mathbf{F}(v \wedge \mathbf{X}[\neg def(x)\mathbf{U}(v' \wedge \mathbf{F}v_f)])$$

with the property that a finite path π is a test sequence exercising $v \xrightarrow{x} v'$ if and only if there are $0 \leq i < j \leq k$ such that $\pi(i) \models v$, $\pi(l) \models \neg def(x)$ for $i < l < j$, $\pi(j) \models v'$, and $\pi(k) \models v_f$ if and only if π is a witness of $\text{ltl}(v \xrightarrow{x} v')$. For example, consider the direct data dependence $v_1 \xrightarrow{num} v_6$ in Figure 1. A test sequence exercising $v_1 \xrightarrow{num} v_6$ is shown in Figure 2, which is also a witness of $\mathbf{F}(v_1 \wedge \mathbf{X}[\neg def(num)\mathbf{U}(v_6 \wedge \mathbf{F}v_9)])$.

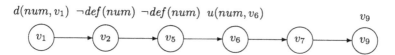

$d(num, v_1) \quad \neg def(num) \quad \neg def(num) \quad u(num, v_6) \qquad\qquad v_9$

Fig. 2. A test sequence exercising $v_1 \xrightarrow{num} v_6$

For a direct control dependence $v \xrightarrow{c} v'$, we associate an LTL formula defined by

$$\text{ltl}(v \xrightarrow{c} v') = \mathbf{F}(v \wedge \mathbf{XF}(v' \wedge \mathbf{F}v_f))$$

with the property that a finite path π is a test sequence exercising $v \xrightarrow{c} v'$ if and only if there are $0 \leq i < j \leq k$ such that $\pi(i) \models v$, $\pi(j) \models v'$, and $\pi(k) \models v_f$ if and only if π is a witness of the LTL formula $\text{ltl}(v \xrightarrow{c} v')$. For example, consider the direct control dependence $v_2 \xrightarrow{c} v_6$ in Figure 1. A test sequence exercising $v_2 \xrightarrow{c} v_6$ is shown in Figure 3, which is also a witness of $\mathbf{F}(v_2 \wedge \mathbf{XF}(v_6 \wedge \mathbf{F}v_9))$.

We characterize all-dependence-pairs coverage criterion in terms of witness-sets. A test suite Π satisfies all-dependence-pairs coverage criterion if and only if Π is a witness-set of

$$\bigcup_{v \xrightarrow{x} v'} \text{ltl}(v \xrightarrow{x} v') \cup \bigcup_{v \xrightarrow{c} v'} \text{ltl}(v \xrightarrow{c} v').$$

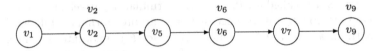

Fig. 3. A test sequence exercising $v_2 \xrightarrow{c} v_6$

CTL can also be used in the characterization of dependence oriented coverage criteria. A finite path is a witness of $\mathbf{ltl}(v \xrightarrow{x} v')$ if and only if the finite path is a witness of the CTL formula defined by

$$\mathbf{ctl}(v \xrightarrow{x} v') = \mathbf{EF}(v \wedge \mathbf{EX}[\neg def(x)\mathbf{U}(v' \wedge \mathbf{EF}v_f)]).$$

A finite path is a witness of $\mathbf{ltl}(v \xrightarrow{c} v')$ if and only if the finite path is a witness of the CTL formula defined by

$$\mathbf{ctl}(v \xrightarrow{c} v') = \mathbf{EF}(v \wedge \mathbf{EXEF}(v' \wedge \mathbf{EF}v_f)).$$

All-Dependence-Pairs-with-Puses Coverage Criterion. For a dependence chain $v \xrightarrow{x} v' \xrightarrow{c} v''$, we associate an LTL formula defined by

$$\mathbf{ltl}(v \xrightarrow{x} v' \xrightarrow{c} v'') = \mathbf{F}(v \wedge \mathbf{X}[\neg def(x)\mathbf{U}(v' \wedge \mathbf{XF}(v'' \wedge \mathbf{F}v_f))])$$

and a CTL formula defined by

$$\mathbf{ctl}(v \xrightarrow{x} v' \xrightarrow{c} v'') = \mathbf{EF}(v \wedge \mathbf{EX}[\neg def(x)\mathbf{U}(v' \wedge \mathbf{EXEF}(v'' \wedge \mathbf{EF}v_f))]).$$

A test suite Π satisfies all-dependence-pairs-with-puses coverage criterion if and only if Π is a witness-set of

$$\bigcup_{v \xrightarrow{x} v'} \mathbf{ltl}(v \xrightarrow{x} v') \cup \bigcup_{v \xrightarrow{x} v' \xrightarrow{c} v''} \mathbf{ltl}(v \xrightarrow{x} v' \xrightarrow{c} v'') \cup \bigcup_{v \xrightarrow{c} v'} \mathbf{ltl}(v \xrightarrow{c} v').$$

4.2   Indirect Dependences

All-k-Dependence-Chains Coverage Criterion. For a dependence-chain κ, we associate an LTL formula defined by

- $\mathbf{ltl}(\kappa) = \mathbf{F}ltl(\kappa)$,
- if κ is $v \xrightarrow{x} v'$, then $ltl(\kappa) = (v \wedge \mathbf{X}[\neg def(x)\mathbf{U}(v' \wedge \mathbf{F}v_f)])$,
- if κ is $v \xrightarrow{c} v'$, then $ltl(\kappa) = (v \wedge \mathbf{XF}(v' \wedge \mathbf{F}v_f))$,
- if κ is $v \xrightarrow{x} v' \cdot \kappa'$, then $ltl(\kappa) = (v \wedge \mathbf{X}[\neg def(x)\mathbf{U}ltl(\kappa')])$,
- if κ is $v \xrightarrow{c} v' \cdot \kappa'$, then $ltl(\kappa) = (v \wedge \mathbf{XF}(v' \wedge \mathbf{F}ltl(\kappa')))$.

The CTL formula $\mathbf{ctl}(\kappa)$ is defined in a similar way.

- $\mathbf{ctl}(\kappa) = \mathbf{EF}ctl(\kappa)$,
- if κ is $v \xrightarrow{x} v'$, then $ctl(\kappa) = (v \wedge \mathbf{EX}[\neg def(x)\mathbf{U}(v' \wedge \mathbf{EF}v_f)])$,
- if κ is $v \xrightarrow{c} v'$, then $ctl(\kappa) = (v \wedge \mathbf{EXEF}(v' \wedge \mathbf{EF}v_f))$,

- if κ is $v \xrightarrow{x} v' \cdot \kappa'$, then $ctl(\kappa) = (v \wedge \mathbf{EX}[\neg def(x) \mathbf{U} ctl(\kappa')])$,
- if κ is $v \xrightarrow{c} v' \cdot \kappa'$, then $ctl(\kappa) = (v \wedge \mathbf{EXEF}(v' \wedge \mathbf{EF} ctl(\kappa')))$.

By induction on the number of du-pairs in κ, it can be shown that a finite path is a test sequence exercising a df-chain κ if and only if the finite path is a witness of $\mathbf{ltl}(\kappa)$ if and only if the finite path is a witness of $\mathbf{ctl}(\kappa)$.

A test suite Π satisfies all-k-dependence-chains coverage criterion if and only if Π is a witness-set of

$$\bigcup_{\kappa \in DC(1) \cup \dots \cup DC(k-1)} \mathbf{ltl}(\kappa)$$

where $DC(n)$ is a set of dependence-chains consisting of n direct dependences.

All-IO-Dependence-Chains Coverage Criterion. A test suite Π satisfies all-IO-dependence-chains coverage criterion if Π is a witness-set of

$$\bigcup_i \bigcup_o \bigcup_{\kappa \in SDC(i,o)} \mathbf{ltl}(\kappa)$$

where $SDC(i, o)$ is a set of simple dependence-chains from input i to output o.

5 Test Reduction

This section shows how the problem of test reduction for dependence testing can be formulated as the LTL model checking problem.

5.1 Subsumption Graph

For a flow graph G and a coverage criterion C, $E(G, C)$ is the set of entities of G required to be exercised by C. A subset of $E(G, C)$ is a *spanning set* if exercising every entity in the subset guarantees exercising every entity in $E(G, C)$. Hence a test suite exercises every entity in a spanning set if and only if the test suite satisfies the coverage criterion. A *minimum spanning set* is a spanning set S such that $|S| \leq |S'|$ for every spanning set S'. The central notion used in constructing a minimum spanning set is *subsumption relation*. An entity subsumes another entity if a test sequence exercising the former also exercises the latter. Once we have a test sequence exercising an entity, we do not need to generate test sequences exercising the entities subsumed by the entity. In addition, if an entity is not subsumed by any other entities, a test sequence exercising the entity should be generated.

We construct a minimum spanning set using *subsumption graph* and *reduced subsumption graph*. For a flow graph G and a coverage criterion C, the subsumption graph is $(E(G, C), SR)$ where SR is the subsumption relation between the entities in $E(G, C)$. Note that the subsumption relation SR is not a partial order and hence subsumption graphs may have strongly connected components. A reduced subsumption graph is a directed acyclic graph obtained by collapsing each strongly connected component of a subsumption graph into one node. Let $v_1, ..., v_n$ be the nodes of the reduced subsumption graph that have no incoming arcs, that is, the nodes that are not subsumed by any other nodes. Let $V_1, ..., V_n$ be the strongly connected components corresponding to $v_1, ..., v_n$, respectively. A minimum spanning set is $\{v_1', ..., v_n'\}$ such that $v_i' \in V_i$ for every $1 \leq i \leq n$.

Figure 4 shows an algorithm for finding a subsumption graph in a generic fashion without being specific about any coverage criteria. For every pair (e, e') of entities, we determine whether e subsumes e' by model-checking the LTL formula $\mathbf{ltl}(e) \rightarrow \mathbf{ltl}(e')$ against the flow graph G, where $\mathbf{ltl}(e)$ and $\mathbf{ltl}(e')$ are the LTL formulas associated with e and e', respectively. The correctness of the algorithm can be understood as follows. Let $e, e' \in E(G, C)$. e subsumes e' if and only if for every finite path π, π is a test sequence exercising e implies π is a test sequence exercising e' if and only if for every finite path π, π is a witness of $\mathbf{ltl}(e)$ implies π is a witness of $\mathbf{ltl}(e')$ if and only if for every finite path π, π is a witness of $\mathbf{ltl}(e) \rightarrow \mathbf{ltl}(e')$ if and only if for every infinite path π, $\pi \models \mathbf{ltl}(e) \rightarrow \mathbf{ltl}(e')$ if and only if $G \models \mathbf{ltl}(e) \rightarrow \mathbf{ltl}(e')$.

INPUT: a flow graph G and a coverage criterion C
OUTPUT: the subsumption graph $(E(G, C), SR)$

1: construct the set $E(G, C)$ of entities of G required by C;
2: $SR := \emptyset$;
3: **for** every pair (e, e'), $e, e' \in E(G, C)$, $e \neq e$ **do**
4:     model check $\mathbf{ltl}(e) \rightarrow \mathbf{ltl}(e')$ against G;
5:     **if** $G \models \mathbf{ltl}(e) \rightarrow \mathbf{ltl}(e')$ **then** /* e subsumes e' */
6:         $SR := SR \cup \{(e, e')\}$;
7: **return** $(E(G, C), SR)$;

Fig. 4. An algorithm for constructing a subsumption graph

For example, consider all-dependence-pairs coverage criterion in Figure 1. The set of entities required to be covered are shown in Figure 5.(a). By model-checking the formula $\mathbf{ltl}(e) \rightarrow \mathbf{ltl}(e')$ for every pair (e, e') of entities, we construct the subsumption graph. We then construct the reduced subsumption graph by collapsing each strongly connected component in the subsumption graph into one node. Figure 5.(b) shows the reduced subsumption graph. Finally we construct a minimum spanning set by selecting one entity from each of the strongly connected components $\{v_3 \xrightarrow{plus} v_9, v_4 \xrightarrow{sign} v_9, v_2 \xrightarrow{c} v_3, v_2 \xrightarrow{c} v_4\}$, $\{v_7 \xrightarrow{sign} v_9, v_6 \xrightarrow{c} v_7\}$, and $\{v_8 \xrightarrow{sign} v_9, v_6 \xrightarrow{c} v_8\}$ that have no incoming arcs.

5.2   Subsumption Forest

In the above algorithm, the total number of model checking performed is $O(|E(G, C)|^2)$ both in the best case and worst case. Note that the subsumption graph is used to identify all possible minimum spanning sets. If we are only

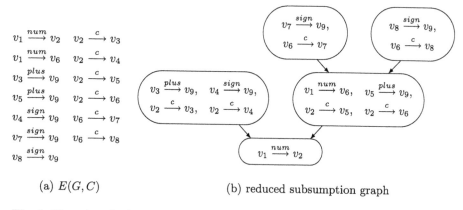

$$v_1 \xrightarrow{num} v_2 \qquad v_2 \xrightarrow{c} v_3$$
$$v_1 \xrightarrow{num} v_6 \qquad v_2 \xrightarrow{c} v_4$$
$$v_3 \xrightarrow{plus} v_9 \qquad v_2 \xrightarrow{c} v_5$$
$$v_5 \xrightarrow{plus} v_9 \qquad v_2 \xrightarrow{c} v_6$$
$$v_4 \xrightarrow{sign} v_9 \qquad v_6 \xrightarrow{c} v_7$$
$$v_7 \xrightarrow{sign} v_9 \qquad v_6 \xrightarrow{c} v_8$$
$$v_8 \xrightarrow{sign} v_9$$

(a) $E(G, C)$ (b) reduced subsumption graph

Fig. 5. The reduced subsumption graph for Figure 1 and all-dependence-pairs coverage criterion

interested in one minimum spanning set rather than all possible ones, we can significantly reduce the total number of model checking to $O(|E(G,C)|)$ in the best case using the new algorithm shown in Figure 6. The intuition behind the algorithm is that if e_i subsumes e_j (Line 10) then we do not consider e_j any more between Lines 5 and 12, which reduces the number of model checking that needs to be performed. It is not hard to see that the result of the new algorithm is a spanning forest of the subsumption graph $(E(G,C), SR)$. Moreover, the root nodes of the spanning forest comprise a minimum spanning set.

Figure 7 shows a subsumption forest for Figure 1 and all-dependence-pairs coverage criterion. We construct a minimum spanning set by finding the root nodes of the subsumption forest: $\{v_3 \xrightarrow{plus} v_9, v_7 \xrightarrow{sign} v_9, v_8 \xrightarrow{sign} v_9\}$.

INPUT: a flow graph G and a coverage criterion C
OUTPUT: a spanning forest $(E(G,C), SF)$

1: let $E(G,C)$ be $\{e_1, ..., e_n\}$;
2: $SF := \emptyset$;
3: **for** $i := 1$ to n **do**
4:     $marked[i] := false$;
5: **for** $i := 1$ to n **do**
6:     **if** $marked[i] = false$ **then**
7:         **for** $j := 1$ to n, $j \neq i$ **do**
8:             **if** $marked[j] = false$ **then**
9:                 model check $ltl(e_i) \rightarrow ltl(e_j)$ against G;
10:                 **if** $G \models ltl(e_i) \rightarrow ltl(e_j)$ **then** /* e_i subsumes e_j */
11:                     $SF := SF \cup \{(e_i, e_j)\}$;
12:                     $marked[j] := true$;
13: **return** $(E(G,C), SF)$;

Fig. 6. An algorithm for constructing a spanning forest

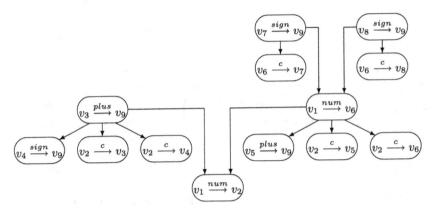

Fig. 7. The subsumption forest for Figure 1 and all-dependence-pairs coverage criterion

6   Conclusions and Future Work

We have presented an approach to structural testing, called dependence testing. For test coverage, we have extended data flow oriented coverage criteria with control dependence in order to capture the dependence information of a program or specification in terms of both data dependence and control dependence. For test generation, we have showed that dependence oriented coverage criteria can be characterized in temporal logic in such a way that test generation can be reduced to the problem of finding witnesses for LTL or CTL formulas. For test reduction, we have showed that the LTL-based characterization can also be used for reducing the cost of dependence testing. It will be interesting to empirically study the extent to which dependence testing actually provides tests which are more effective at identifying errors, provides better reliability for programs under test, or exhibits a better cost ratio for test development.

Our approach can be applied to more accurate models of programs. Traditionally, test generation has been performed upon flow graphs. Since a flow graph preserves only the control flow and ignores the values of data variables, it is often the case that the size of state space is not a concern. However, test generation is increasingly performed upon more accurate models that respect the values of data variables such as reachability graphs and abstract state graphs obtained by abstract interpretation. In this case, the size of state space is the primary concern and model checking has been proven to be effective for controlling the state explosion problem. We plan to conduct case studies to see how large and complex programs can be handled by our approach when reachability graphs or abstract state graphs are used.

Our approach can also be applied to requirements specifications written in state-based specification languages such as extended finite state machines, statecharts, and SDL. Test generation for such specifications is very different from that for programs since the specification languages typically provide a rich set of language constructs for modeling hierarchy, concurrency, and communications. Our approach is language-independent in the sense that the temporal logic formulas employed in the approach can be immediately used for various specification languages. In fact, the differences among specification languages (for example, synchronous computational model in statecharts versus asynchronous computational model in SDL and communications through event broadcasting in statecharts versus communications through message queues in SDL) only affect the rules for translating specifications into input to model checkers.

Acknowledgments

This research is supported in part by Natural Sciences and Engineering Research Council (NSERC) of Canada under grant RGPIN 976.

References

1. H. Agrawal, "Dominators, Super Blocks, and Program Coverage," *Proceedings of the 21st ACM Symposium on Principles of Programming Languages*, pp. 25-34, 1994.
2. A.V. Aho, R. Sethi, and J.D. Ullman, *Compilers, Principles, Techniques, and Tools*, Addison-Wesley, 1986.
3. P. Ammann, P. Black, and W. Majurski, "Using Model Checking to Generate Tests from Specifications," in *Proceedings of the 2nd IEEE International Conference on Formal Engineering Methods*, pp. 46-54, 1998.
4. A. Bertolino, "Unconstrained Edges and Their Application to Branch Analysis and Testing of Programs," *The Journal of Systems and Software*, 20(2):125-133, Feb. 1993.
5. A. Bertolino and M. Marré, "Automatic Generation of Path Covers Based on the Control Flow Analysis of Computer Programs," *IEEE Transactions on Software Engineering*, 20(12):885-899, Dec. 1994.
6. A. Bertolino and M. Marré, "How Many Paths are Needed for Branch Testing?" *The Journal of Systems and Software*, 35(2):95-106, Nov. 1996.
7. D. Beyer, A.J. Chlipala, T.A. Henzinger, R. Jhala, and R. Majumdar, "Generating Tests from Counterexamples," *Proceedings of the 26th International Conference on Software Engineering*, pp. 326-335, 2004.
8. T. Chusho, "Test Data Selection and Quality Estimation Based on the Concept of Essential Branches for Path Testing," *IEEE Transactions on Software Engineering*, 13(5):509-517, May 1987.
9. E.M. Clarke, O. Grumberg, and D.A. Peled, *Model Checking*, The MIT Press, 1999.
10. L.A. Clarke, A. Podgurski, D.J. Richardson, and S.J. Zeil, "A Formal Evaluation of Data Flow Path Selection Criteria," *IEEE Transactions on Software Engineering*, 15(11):1318-1332, Nov. 1989.
11. R. Dssouli, K. Saleh, E. Aboulhamid, A. En-Nouaary, and C. Bourhfir, "Test Development for Communication Protocols: towards Automation," *Computer Networks*, 31(7):1835-1872, June 1999.

12. A. Engels, L. Feijs, and S. Mauw, "Test Generation for Intelligent Networks Using Model Checking," in *TACAS '97*, Vol. 1217 of LNCS, pp. 384-398, Springer-Verlag, 1997.

13. P.G. Frankl and E.J. Weyuker, "A Formal Analysis of the Fault-Detecting Ability of Testing Methods," *IEEE Transactions on Software Engineering*, 19(3):202-213, Mar. 1993.

14. A. Gargantini and C. Heitmeyer, "Using Model Checking to Generate Tests from Requirements Specifications," in *Proceedings of ESEC/FSE '99* pp. 146-162, 1999.

15. R. Gupta and M.L. Soffa, "Employing Static Information in the Generation of Test Cases," *Software Testing, Verification and Reliability*, 3(1):29-48, 1993.

16. M.P. Heimdahl, S. Rayadurgam, W. Visser, G. Devaraj, and J. Gao, "Auto-Generating Test Sequences Using Model Checkers: A Case Study," *Proceedings of the 3th International Workshop on Formal Approaches to Testing of Software*, Vol. 2931 of LNCS, pp. 44-62, Springer, 2003.

17. P.M. Herman, "A Data Flow Approach to Program Testing," *Australian Computer Journal*, 8(3):92-96, Nov. 1976.

18. G.J. Holzmann, "The Model Checker SPIN," *IEEE Transactions on Software Engineering*, Vol. 23, No. 5, pp. 279-295, May 1997.

19. H.S. Hong, Y.G. Kim, S.D. Cha, D.H. Bae, and H. Ural, "A Test Sequence Selection Method for Statecharts," *Journal of Software Testing, Verification, and Reliability*, 10(4):203-227, Dec. 2000.

20. H.S. Hong, I. Lee, O. Sokolsky, and H. Ural, "A Temporal Logic Based Theory of Test Coverage and Generation," *TACAS '02*, Vol. 2280 of LNCS, pp. 327-341, Springer, 2002.

21. H.S. Hong, S.D. Cha, I. Lee, O. Sokolsky, and H. Ural, "Data Flow Testing as Model Checking," *Proceedings of the 25th International Conference on Software Engineering*, pp. 232-242, 2003.

22. H.S. Hong and H. Ural, "Using Model Checking for Reducing the Cost of Test Generation," *Proceedings of the 4th International Workshop on Formal Approaches to Testing of Software*, LNCS, Springer, 2004.

23. J.W. Laski and B. Korel, "A Data Flow Oriented Program Testing Strategy," *IEEE Transactions on Software Engineering*, 9(5):347-354, May 1983.

24. M. Marré and A. Bertolino, "Unconstrained Duas and Their Use in Achieving All-uses Coverage," *Proceedings of the International Symposium on Software Testing and Analysis*, pp. 147-157, 1996.

25. M. Marré and A. Bertolino, "Reducing and Estimating the Cost of Test Coverage Criteria," *Proceedings of the 18th International Conference on Software Engineering*, pp. 486-494, 1996.

26. K.L. McMillan, *Symbolic Model Checking — an Approach to the State Explosion Problem*, Kluwer Academic Publishers, 1993.

27. S.C. Ntafos, "On Required Element Testing," *IEEE Transactions on Software Engineering*, 10(11):795-803, Nov. 1984.

28. S. Rapps and E.J. Weyuker, "Selecting Software Test Data Using Data Flow Information," *IEEE Transactions on Software Engineering*, 11(4):367-375, Apr. 1985.

29. S. Rayadurgam and M.P. Heimdahl, "Coverage Based Test Generation Using Model Checkers," *Proceedings of the 8th Annual IEEE International Conference on the Engineering of Computer Based Systems*, pp. 83-91, 2001.

30. A. Podgurski and L.A. Clarke, "A Formal Model of Program Dependences and Its Implications for Software Testing, Debugging, and Maintenance," *IEEE Transactions on Software Engineering*, 16(9):965-979, Sept. 1990.

31. H. van der Schoot and H. Ural, "Data Flow Oriented Test selection for LOTOS," *Computer Networks*, 27(7):1111-1136, 1995.
32. H. Ural and B. Yang, "A Test Sequence Generation Method for Protocol Testing," *IEEE Transactions on Communications*, 39(4):514-523, Apr. 1991.
33. H. Ural, K. Saleh, and A. Williams, "Test Generation Based on Control and Data Dependencies within System Specifications in SDL," *Computer Communications*, 23(7):609-627, Mar. 2000.
34. H. Zhu, P.A. Hall, and J.H.R. May, "Software Unit Test Coverage and Adequacy," *ACM Computing Surveys*, 29(4):366-427, Dec. 1997.

Comparing Bug Finding Tools with Reviews and Tests*

Stefan Wagner[1], Jan Jürjens[1], Claudia Koller[1], and Peter Trischberger[2]

[1] Institut für Informatik,
Technische Universität München,
Boltzmannstr. 3, D-85748 Garching, Germany
[2] O2 Germany, Georg-Brauchle-Ring 23-25,
D-80992 Munich, Germany

Abstract. Bug finding tools can find defects in software source code using an automated static analysis. This automation may be able to reduce the time spent for other testing and review activities. For this we need to have a clear understanding of how the defects found by bug finding tools relate to the defects found by other techniques. This paper describes a case study using several projects mainly from an industrial environment that were used to analyse the interrelationships. The main finding is that the bug finding tools predominantly find different defects than testing but a subset of defects found by reviews. However, the types that can be detected are analysed more thoroughly. Therefore, a combination is most advisable if the high number of false positives of the tools can be tolerated.

1 Introduction

Software failures can have enormous consequences in terms of threatening peoples lives as well as economic loss because various critical systems rely on software. Furthermore, software becomes increasingly complex, which makes the prevention of failures even more difficult. However, software quality assurance accounts already for around 50% of the development time [13]. Therefore it is important to improve defect-detection techniques as well as reduce their costs. Automation can be an option in that direction. For example, automated test-case generation based on executable models is also under investigation as a possibility to make testing more efficient [16].

Extensive research has been done on finding defects in code by automated static analysis using tools called *bug finding tools*, e.g. [1, 7, 8]. Although the topic is subject of ongoing investigations, there are only few studies about how these tools relate among themselves and to other established defect-detection techniques such as testing or reviews.

---

* This research was supported in part by the *Deutsche Forschungsgemeinschaft (DFG)* within the project *InTime*.

F. Khendek and R. Dssouli (Eds.): TestCom 2005, LNCS 3502, pp. 40–55, 2005.

We will now discuss the problem situation in more detail. We briefly define the terms we use in the following: *Failures* are a perceived deviation of the output values from the expected values whereas *faults* are the cause of failures in code or other documents. Both are also referred to as *defects*. We mainly use *defect* in our analyses also if there are no failures involved as with defects related to maintenance only.

Problem. We address the question of how automated static analysis using bug finding tools relates to other types of defect-detection techniques and if it is thereby possible to reduce the effort for defect-detection using such tools. In detail, this amounts to three questions.

1. Which types and classes of defects are found by different techniques?
2. Is there any overlap of the found defects?
3. How large is the ratio of false positives from the tools?

Results. The main findings are summarised in the following.

1. Bug finding tools detect a subset of the defect types that can be found by a review.
2. The types of defects that can be found by the tools can be analysed more thoroughly, that is, the tools are better regarding the bug patterns they are programmed for.
3. Dynamic tests find completely different defects than bug finding tools.
4. Bug finding tools have a significant ratio of false positives.
5. The bug finding tools show very different results in different projects.

Consequences. The results have four major implications.

1. Dynamic tests or reviews cannot be substituted by bug finding tools because they find significantly more and different defect types.
2. Bug finding tools can be a good pre-stage to a review because some of the defects do not have to be manually detected. A possibility would be to mark problematic code so that it cannot be overlooked in the review.
3. Bug finding tools can only provide a significant reduction in the effort necessary for defect-detection if their false positives ratios can be reduced. From our case studies, we find the current ratios to be not yet completely acceptable.
4. The tools have to be more tolerant regarding the programming style and design to provide more uniform results in different projects.

Experimental Setup. Five industrial projects and one development project from a university environment were selected which are either already in use or in the final testing phase. We evaluated several bug finding tools and chose three representatives that were usable for the distributed web systems under consideration. The bug finding tools and dynamic tests were used on all projects. A review was only possible for a single project. The warnings issued from the tools were analysed with experienced developers to classify them as true and false positives. All defects that were found were classified regarding their severity and defect types. The comparison was done based on this classification.

Contribution. We are not aware of studies that compare the defects found by bug finding tools with the defects found by other techniques, in particular not of any based on several, mainly industrial, projects. A main contribution is also a thorough analysis of the ratio of false positives of the bug finding tools as this is a significant factor in the usability of these tools.

Organisation. Sec. 2 gives an overview of bug finding tools in general (Sec. 2.1) and the three tools that were used in the projects (Sec. 2.2). The projects are described in Sec. 3 with general characteristics in Sec. 3.1 and specific descriptions in Sec. 3.2. The approach for the comparison of the techniques can be found in Sec. 4 with a general discussion in Sec. 4.1, the defect classification in Sec. 4.2, and the introduction of the defect types in Sec. 4.3. The analysis of the study is described in Sec. 5 with the comparison among the bug finding tools in Sec. 5.1, bug finding tools versus reviews in Sec. 5.2, bug finding tools versus testing in Sec. 5.3, and the defect removal efficiensies in Sec. 5.4. We discuss our findings in Sec. 6 and describe related work in Sec. 7. Finally, we conclude in Sec. 8 and sketch intended future work in Sec. 9.

2   Bug Finding Tools

This section provides an introduction to bug finding tools in general and describes briefly the three tools that were used in the case study.

2.1   Basics

Bug finding tools are a class of programs that aim to find defects in code by static analysis similarly to a compiler. The results of such a tool are, however, not always real defects but can be seen as a warning that a piece of code is critical in some way. There are various techniques to identify such critical code pieces. The most common one is to define typical bug patterns that are derived from experience and published common pitfalls in a certain programming language. Furthermore, coding guidelines and standards can be checked to allow a better readability. Also, more sophisticated analysis techniques based on the dataflow and controlflow are used. Finally, additional annotations in the code are introduced by some tools [7] to allow an extended static checking and a combination with model checking.

2.2   Analysed Tools

The three bug finding tools that we used for the comparison are described in the following. We only take tools into account that analyse Java programs because the projects we investigated, as described below, are all written in that language. All three tools are published under an open source license. We used these three tools as representatives for tools that mainly use bug patterns, coding standards, and dataflow analysis, respectively. We deliberately ignored tools that need annotations in the code because they have quite different characteristics.

FindBugs. The tool *FindBugs* was developed at the University of Maryland and can detect potentially problematic code fragments by using a list of bug patterns. It can find faults such as dereferencing null-pointers or unused variables. To some extent, it also uses dataflow analysis for this. It analyses the software using the bytecode in contrast to the tools described in the following. The tool is described in detail in [8]. We used the Version 0.8.1 in our study.

PMD. This tool [15] concentrates on the source code and is therefore especially suitable to enforce coding standards. It finds, for example, empty try/catch blocks, overly complex expressions, and classes with high cyclomatic complexity. It can be customised by using XPath expressions on the parser tree. The version 1.8 was used.

QJ Pro. The third tool used is described in [17] and analyses also the source code. It supports over 200 rules including ignored return values, too long variable names, or a disproportion between code and commentary lines. It is also possible to define additional rules. Furthermore, checks based on code metrics can be used. The possibility to use various filters is especially helpful in this tool. We evaluated version 2.1 in this study.

3   Projects

We want to give a quick overview of the five projects we analysed to evaluate and compare bug finding tools with other defect-detection techniques.

3.1   General

All but one of the projects chosen are development projects from the telecommunications company O_2 Germany for backend systems with various development efforts and sizes. One project was done by students at the Technische Universität München. All these projects have in common that they were developed using the Java programming language and have an interface to a relational database system. The O_2 projects furthermore can be classified as web information systems as they all use HTML and web browsers as their user interface.

3.2   Analysed Projects

The projects are described in more detail in [12]. For confidentiality reasons, we use the symbolic names A through D for the industrial projects.

Project A. This is an online shop that can be used by customers to buy products and also make mobile phone contracts. It includes complex workflows depending on the various options in such contracts. The software has been in use for six months. It consists of 1066 Java classes that consist of over 58 KLOC (kilo lines of code).

Project B. The software allows the user to pay goods bought over the Internet using a mobile phone. The payment is added to the mobile bill. For this, the client sends the mobile number to the shop and receives a transaction number (TAN) via short message service (SMS). This TAN is used to authenticate the user and authorises the shop to bill the user. The software has not been put into operation at the time of the study. Software B has 215 Java classes with over 24 KLOC in total.

Project C. This is a web-based frontend for managing a system that is used to convert protocol files between different formats. The tool analysed only interacts with a database that holds administration information for that system. The software was three months in use at the time it was analysed. It consists of over 3 KLOC Java and JSP code.

Project D. The client data of O_2 is managed in the system we call *D*. It is a J2EE application with 572 classes, over 34 KLOC and interfaces to various other systems of O_2.

EstA. The only non-industrial software that we used in this case study is *EstA*. It is an editor for structuring textual requirements developed during a practical course at the Technische Universität München. It is a Java-based software using a relational database management system. The tool has not been extensively used so far. It has 28 Java classes with over 4 KLOC.

4   Approach

In this section, the approach of the case study is described. We start with the general description and explain the defect classification and defect types that are used in the analysis.

4.1   General

We use the software of the five projects introduced in Sec. 3 to analyse the interrelations between the defects found by bug finding tools, reviews, and tests. For this, we applied each of these techniques to each software as far as possible. While a review was only made on project C, black-box as well as white-box tests were done on all projects. We ran the bug finding tools with special care to be able to compare the tools as well. To have a better possibility for comparison with the other techniques, we also checked each warning from the bug finding tools if it is a real defect in the code or not. This was done by an inspection of the corresponding code parts together with experienced developers. The usage of the techniques was completely independent, that is, the testing and the review was not guided by results from the bug finding tools.

The external validity is limited in this case study. Although we mostly considered commercially developed software that is in actual use, we only analysed five systems. For better results more experiments are necessary. Furthermore, the tests on the more mature systems, i.e. the ones that are already in use, did not reveal many faults. This can also limit the validity. Moreover, the data from only one review is not representative but can only give a first indication. Finally, we only analysed three bug finding tools, and these are still under development. The results might be different if other tools would have been used.

In the following we call all the warnings that are generated by the bug finding tools *positives*. *True positives* are warnings that are actually confirmed as defects in the code, *false positives* are wrong identifications of problems.

4.2   Defect Categorisation

For the comparison, we use a five step categorisation of the defects using their severity. Hence, the categorisation is based on the effects of the defects rather than their cause or type of occurrence in the code. We use a standard categorisation for severity that is slightly adapted to the defects found in the projects. Defects in category 1 are the severest, the ones in category 5 have the lowest severity. The categories are:

1. *Defects that lead to a crash of the application.* These are the most severe defects that stop the whole application from reacting to any user input.
2. *Defects that cause a logical failure.* This category consists of all defects that cause a logical failure of the application but do not crash it, for example a wrong result value.
3. *Defects with insufficient error handling.* Defects in this category are only minor and do not crash the application or result in logical failures, but are not handled properly.
4. *Defects that violate the principles of structured programming.* These are defects that normally do not impact the software but could result in performance bottlenecks etc.
5. *Defects that reduce the maintainability of the code.* This category contains all defects that only affect the readability or changeability of the software.

This classification helps us (1) to compare the various defect-detection techniques based on the severity of the defects they find and (2) analyse the types of defects that they find.

4.3   Defect Types

Additionally to the defect classification we use defect types. That means that the same or very similar defects are grouped together for an easier analysis. This is not based on any standard types such as [2, 4, 9] but was defined specifically for the applications.

The defect types that we use for the bug finding tools can be seen as a unification of the warning types that the tools are able to generate. Examples for defect types are "Stream is not closed" or "Input is not checked for special characters".

5   Analysis

This section presents the results of the case study and possible interpretations. At first, the bug finding tools are compared among each other, then the tools are compared with reviews, and finally with dynamic tests.

5.1   Bug Finding Tools

We want to start with comparing the three bug finding tools described in Sec. 2 among themselves. The tools were used with each system described above.

Data. Tab. 1 shows the defect types with their categories and the corresponding positives found by each tool over all systems analysed. The number before the slash denotes the number of true positives, the number after the slash the number of all positives.

Observations and Interpretations. Most of the true positives can be assigned to the category *Maintainability of the code*. It is noticeable that the different tools predominantly find different positives. Only a single defect type was found from all tools, four types from two tools each.

Considering the categories, FindBugs finds in the different systems positives from all categories and PMD only from the categories *Failure of the application*,

Table 1. Summary of the defect types found by the bug finding tools

Defect Type	Category	FindBugs	PMD	QJ Pro
Database connection is not closed	1	8/54	8/8	0/0
Return value of function ignored	2	4/4	0/0	4/693
Exception caught but not handled	3	4/45	29/217	30/212
Null-pointer exception not handled	3	8/108	0/0	0/0
Returning null instead of array	3	2/2	0/0	0/0
Stream is not closed	4	12/13	0/0	0/0
Concatenating string with + in loop	4	20/20	0/0	0/0
Used "==" instead of "equals"	4	0/1	0/0	0/29
Variable initialised but not read	5	103/103	0/0	0/0
Variable initialised but not used	5	7/7	152/152	0/0
Needless if-clause	5	0/0	16/16	0/0
Multiple functions with same name	5	22/22	0/0	0/0
Needless semicolon	5	0/0	10/10	0/0
Local variable not used	5	0/0	144/144	0/0
Parameter not used	5	0/0	32/32	0/0
Private method not used	5	17/17	17/17	0/0
Empty finally block	5	0/0	1/1	0/0
Needless comparison with null	5	1/1	0/0	0/0
Uninitialised variable in constructor	5	1/1	0/0	0/0
For- instead of simple while loop	5	0/0	2/2	0/0

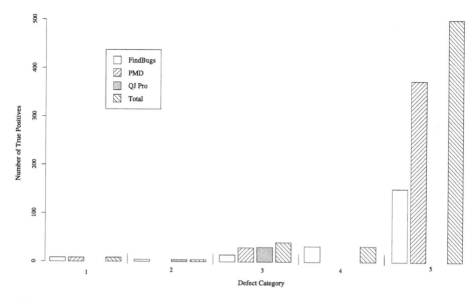

Fig. 1. A graphical comparison of the number of true positives found by each tool and in total

Insufficient error handling, and *Maintainability of the code.* QJ Pro only reveals positives from the categories *Logical failure of the application, Insufficient error handling,* and *Violation of structured programming.* The number of faults found in each category from each tool is graphically illustrated in Fig. 1. Also the number of types of defects varies from tool to tool. FindBugs detects defects of 13 different types, PMD of 10 types, and QJ Pro only of 4 types.

The accuracy of the tools is also diverse. We use the defect type "Exception is caught but not handled" that can be found by all three tools as an example. While FindBugs only finds 4 true positives, PMD reveals 29 and QJ Pro even 30. For this, the result from QJ Pro contains the true positives from PMD which in turn contain the ones from FindBugs. A reason for this is that QJ Pro is also able to recognize a single semicolon as an non-existent error handling, whereas the other two interpret that as a proper handling. This defect type is also representative in the way that FindBugs finds the least true positives. This may be the case because it uses the compiled class-files while PMD and QJ Pro analyse the source code.

A further difference between the tools is the ratio of true positives to all positives. PMD and FindBugs have a higher accuracy in indicating real defects than QJ Pro. Tab. 2 lists the average ratios of false positives for each tool and in total. It shows that on average, half of the positives from FindBugs are false and still nearly a third from PMD. QJ Pro has the worst result with only 4% of the positives being true positives. This leads to an overall average ratio of 0.66, which means that two thirds of the positives lead to unnecessary work. However, we have to notice that FindBugs and PMD are significantly better than that average.

Table 2. Average ratios of false positives for each tool and in total

FindBugs	PMD	QJ Pro	Total
0.47	0.31	0.96	0.66

An illustrative example is the defect type "Return value of function is ignored". FindBugs only shows 4 warnings that all are true positives, whereas QJ Pro provides 689 further warnings that actually are not relevant. Because all the warnings have to be looked at, FindBugs is in this case much more efficient than the other two tools.

The efficiency of the tools varied over the projects. For the projects B and D, the detection of the defect type "Database connection not closed" shows only warnings for true positives with FindBugs. For project A, it issued 46 warnings for which the database connection is actually closed. Similarly, the detection rate of true positives decreases for the projects D and A for the other two tools, with the exception of the well recognised positives from the maintainability category by PMD. This suggests that the efficiency of the defect detection depends on the design and the individual programming style, i.e. the implicit assumptions of the tool developers about how "good" code has to look like.

A recommendation of usage of the tools is difficult because of the issues described above. However, it suggests that QJ Pro, although it finds sometimes more defects than the other tools, has the highest noise ratio and therefore is the least efficient. FindBugs and PMD should be used in combination because the former finds many different defect types and the latter provides very accurate results in the maintainability category. Finally, PMD as well as QJ Pro can be used to enforce internal coding standards, which was ignored in our analysis above.

5.2 Bug Finding Tools Versus Review

An informal review was performed only on project C. The review team consisted of three developers, including the author of the code. The reviewers did not prepare specifically for the review but inspected the code at the review meeting.

Data. The review revealed 19 different types of defects which are summarised in Tab. 3 with their categories and number of occurrences.

Observations and Interpretations. All defects found by bug finding tools were also found by the review. However, the tools found 7 defects of type "Variable initialised but not used" in contrast to one defect revealed by the review. On the other hand, the review detected 8 defects of type "Unnecessary if-clause", whereas the tools only found one. The cause is that only in the one defect that was found by both there was no further computation after the if-clause. The redundancy of the others could only be found out by investigating the logics of the program.

Table 3. Summary of the defect types and defects found by the review

Defect Type	Category	Occurrences
Database connection is not closed	1	1
Error message as return value	1	12
Further logical case ignored	2	1
Wrong result	2	3
Incomplete data on error	2	3
Wrong error handling	2	6
ResultSet is not closed	4	1
Statement is not closed	4	1
Difficult error handling	4	10
Database connection inside loop opened and closed	4	1
String concatenated inside loop with "+"	4	1
Unnecessary parameter on call	5	51
Unnecessary parameter on return	5	21
Complex for loop	5	2
Array initialised from 1	5	21
Unnecessary if clauses	5	8
Variable initialised but not used	5	1
Complex variable increment	5	1
Complex type conversion	5	7

Apart from the two above, 17 additional types of defects were found, some of which could have been found by tools. For example, the concatenation of a string with "+" inside a loop is sometimes not shown by FindBugs although it is generally able to detect this defect type. Also, the defect that a database connection is not closed was not found, because this was done in different functions. Furthermore it was not discovered by the tools that the ResultSet and the corresponding Statement was never closed.

Other defect types such as logical faults or a wrong result from a function cannot be detected by bug finding tools. These defects, however, can be found during a review by following test cases through the code.

In summary, the review is more successful than bug finding tools, because it is able to detect far more defect types. However, it seems to be beneficial to first use a bug finding tool before inspecting the code, so that the defects that are found by both are already removed. This is because the automation makes it cheaper and more thorough than a manual review. However, we also notice a high number of false positives from all tools. This results in significant non-productive work for the developers that could in some cases exceed the improvement achieved by the automation.

5.3   Bug Finding Tools Versus Testing

We used black box as well as white box tests for system testing the software but also some unit tests were done. The black box tests were based on the textual specifications and the experience of the testers. Standard techniques

Table 4. Summary of the defect types and defects found by the tests

Defect Type	Category	Occurrences
Data range not checked	1	9
Input not checked for special characters	1	6
Logical error on deletion	1	1
Consistency of input not checked	2	3
Leading zeros are not ignored	2	1
Incomplete deletion	2	2
Incomprehensible error message	3	7
Other logical errors	2	3

such as equivalence and boundary testing were used. The white box tests were developed using the source code and path testing. Overall several hundred test cases were developed and executed. A coverage tool has also been used to check the quality of the test suites. However, there were no stress tests which might have changed the results significantly. Only for the projects *EStA* and *C*, defects could be found. The other projects are probably too mature to be able to find further defects by normal system testing.

Data. The detected defect types together with their categories and the number of occurrences are summarised in Tab. 4. We also give some information on the coverage data that was reached by the tests. We measured class, method, and line coverage. The coverage was high apart from project *C*. In all the other projects, class coverage was nearly 100%, method coverage was also in that area and line coverage lay between 60 and 93%. The low coverage values for project *C* might be explained by the fact that we invested the least amount of effort in testing this project.

Observations and Interpretations. The defects found by testing are in the categories *Failure of the application, Logical failure,* and *Insufficient error handling.* The analysis above of the defects showed that the bug finding tools predominantly find defects from the category *Maintainability of the code.* Therefore the dynamic test techniques find completely different defects.

For the software systems for which defects were revealed, there were no identical defects found with testing as well as the bug finding tools. Furthermore, the tools revealed several defects also in the systems for which the tests were not able to find one. These are defects that can only be found by extensive stress tests, such as database connections that are not closed. This can only result in performance problems or even a failure of the application, if the system is under a high usage rate and there is a huge amount of database connections that are not closed. The most defects, however, are really concerning maintainability and are therefore not detectable by dynamic testing.

In summary, the dynamic tests and the bug finding tools detect different defects. Dynamic testing is good at finding logical defects that are best visible

Table 5. The defect removal efficiencies per defect-detection technique

Technique	Number of Defects	Efficiency
Bug Finding Tools	585	76%
Review	152	20%
Tests	32	4%
Total	769	100%

Table 6. The defect removal efficiencies for each category

Category	Bug Finding Tools	Reviews	Tests	Total
1	22% (8)	35% (13)	43% (16)	100% (37)
2	15% (4)	50% (13)	35% (9)	100% (26)
3	85% (40)	0% (0)	15% (7)	100% (47)
4	70% (32)	30% (14)	0% (0)	100% (46)
5	82% (501)	18% (112)	0% (0)	100% (613)

when executing the software, bug finding tools have their strength at finding defects related to maintainability. Therefore, we again recommend using both techniques in a project.

5.4 Defect Removal Efficiency

The defect removal efficiency is as proposed by Jones in [11] the fraction of all defects that were detected by a specific defect-detection technique. The main problem with this metric is that the total number of defects cannot be known. In our case study we use the sum of all different defects detected by all techniques under consideration as an estimate for this number. The results are shown in Tab. 5. The metric suggests that the tools are the most efficient techniques whereas the tests where the least efficient.

However, we also have to take the defect categorisation into account because this changes the picture significantly. The Tab. 6 shows the efficiencies for each techniques and category with the number of defects in brackets. It makes obvious that tests and reviews are far more efficient in finding defects of the categories 1 and 2 than the bug finding tools which are the most severe defects.

6 Discussion

The result that bug finding tools mainly detect defects that are related to the maintainability of the code complies with the expectation an experienced developer would have. Static analysis only allows to look for certain patterns in the code and simple dataflow and controlflow properties. Therefore only reviews or tests are able to verify the logic of the software (as long as the static analysis is not linked with model checking techniques). The tools do not "understand" the code in that sense. The prime example for this is the varying efficiency over the projects. In many cases, the tools were not capable to realise that certain database connections are not closed in the same Java method but a different one. They only search for a certain pattern. Therefore, the limitation of static analysis tools lies in what is expressible by bug patterns, or in how good and generic the patterns can be.

However, it still is surprising that there is not a single overlapping defect detected by bug finding tools and dynamic tests. On the positive side, this implies that the two techniques are perfectly complementary and can be used together with great benefit. The negative side is that by using the automated static analysis techniques we considered, it may not be possible to reduce costly testing efforts. That there is only little overlapping follows from the observation above that the tools mainly find maintenance-related defects. However, one would expect to see at least some defects that the tests found also detected by the tools, especially concerning dataflow and controlflow. The negative results in this study can be explained with the fact that most of the projects analysed are quite mature, and some of them are already in operation. This resulted in only a small number of defects that were found during testing which in turn could be a reason for the lack of overlapping.

A rather disillusioning result is the high ratio of false positives that are issued by the tools. The expected benefit of the automation using such tools lies in the hope that less human intervention is necessary to detect defects. However, as on average two thirds of the warnings are false positives, the human effort could be even higher when using bug finding tools because each warning has to be checked to decide on the relevance of the warning. Nevertheless, there are significant differences between the tools so that choosing the best combination of tools could still pay off.

Bug finding tools that use additional annotations in the code for defect-detection could be beneficial considering the overlap of defects with other techniques as well as the false positives ratio. The annotations allow the tool to understand the code to a certain extent and therefore permits some checks of the logic. This deeper knowledge of the code might reduce the false positives ratio. However, to make the annotations requires additional effort by the developers. It needs to be analysed if this effort is lucrative.

The effort and corresponding costs of the determination of defects using the tools (including checking the false positives) was not determined in this study. This is however necessary to find out if the use of bug finding tools is beneficial at all.

7   Related Work

There are only few studies about how bug finding tools relate among themselves and to other established defect-detection techniques such as testing or reviews.

In [18] among others PMD and FindBugs are compared based on their warnings which were not all checked for false positives. The findings are that although there is some overlap the warnings generated by the tools are mostly distinct. We can support this result with our data.

Engler and Musuvathi discuss in [6] the comparison of their bug finding tool with model checking techniques. They argument that static analysis is able to check larger amounts of code and find more defects but model checking can check the implications of the code not just properties that are on the surface.

In [10] a static analysis tools for C code is discussed. The authors state that sophisticated analysis of, for example, pointers leads to far less false positives than simple syntactical checks.

An interesting combination of static analysis tools and testing in described in [5]. It is proposed to use static analysis to find potential problems and automatically generate test cases to verify if there is a real defect. However, the approach obviously does not work with maintenance-related defects.

Bush et al. report in [3] on a static analyser for C and C++ code which is able to find several more dynamic programming errors. However, a comparison with tests was not done. Nevertheless, our observation that the defect-finding capabilities depend strongly on the coding styles of different programmers is supported in this paper.

In [22] an evaluation of static analysis tools for C code regarding buffer overflows is described. The defects were injected and the fraction of buffer overflows found by each technique was measured. It is also noted that the rates of false positives or false alarms are unacceptably high.

Palsberg describes in [14] some bug finding tools that use type-based analysis. He shows that they are able to detect race conditions or memory leaks in programs.

8   Conclusion

The work presented is not a comprehensive empirical study but a case study using a series of projects mainly from an industrial environment giving first indications of how the defects found by bug finding tools relate to other defect-detection techniques.

The main findings are that the bug finding tools revealed completely different defects than the dynamic tests but a subset of the types of the review. The defect types that are detected by the tools are analysed more thoroughly than with reviews. The effectiveness of the tools seems to strongly depend on the personal programming style and the design of the software as the results differed strongly from project to project. Finally, a combination of the usage of bug finding tools together with reviews and tests would be most advisable if the number of false positives were lower. It probably costs more time to resolve the false positives than is saved by the automation using the tools.

Therefore, the main conclusion is that bug finding tools can save costs when used together with other defect-detection techniques, if the tool developers are able to improve the tools in terms of the false positives ratio and tolerance of different programming styles.

9   Future Work

This study is only a first indication and needs further empirical validation to be able to derive solid conclusions. For this, we plan to repeat this study on different subjects and also taking other tools into account, e.g. commercial tools or tools that use additional annotations in the source code. Also, the investigation of other types of software is important, since we only considered web applications in this study.

How the proper combination of the different techniques can be found is also subject to further research. As a first step more reliability-oriented measures, such as the failure intensity efficiency [19, 20] can be used to compare the bug finding tools with other techniques. This can give more clues in terms of the effect on the reliability of the usage of bug finding tools. However, a comprehensive treatment of the subject needs to incorporate the false positives ratio into a cost model based on [21] to be able to determine the economically best alternatives.

Acknowledgments

We want to thank the authors of the tools FindBugs, PMD, QJ Pro for investing such an amount of work in the tools and making them available to the public.

References

1. T. Ball and S.K. Rajamani. The SLAM Project: Debugging System Software via Static Analysis. In *Proc. 29th Annual ACM SIGPLAN-SIGACT Symposium on Principles of Programming Languages*, 2002.
2. B. Beizer. *Software Testing Techniques*. Thomson Learning, 2nd edition, 1990.
3. W.R. Bush, J.D. Pincus, and D.J. Sielaff. A static analyzer for finding dynamic programming errors. *Softw. Pract. Exper.*, 30:775–802, 2000.
4. R. Chillarege. Orthogonal Defect Classification. In Michael R. Lyu, editor, *Handbook of Software Reliability Engineering*, chapter 9. IEEE Computer Society Press and McGraw-Hill, 1996.
5. C. Csallner and Y. Smaragdakis. CnC: Combining Static Checking and Testing. In *Proc. 27th International Conference on Software Engineering (ICSE'05)*, 2005. To appear.
6. D. Engler and M. Musuvathi. Static Analysis versus Model Checking for Bug Finding. In *Proc. Verification, Model Checking and Abstract Interpretation (VMCAI'04)*, volume 2937 of *LNCS*, pages 191–210. Springer, 2002.
7. C. Flanagan, K.R.M. Leino, M. Lillibridge, G. Nelson, J.B. Saxe, and R. Stata. Extended Static Checking for Java. In *Proc. 2002 ACM SIGPLAN Conference on Programming Language Design and Implementation*, 2002.
8. D. Hovemeyer and W. Pugh. Finding Bugs is Easy. *SIGPLAN Notices*, 39(12), 2004. To appear.
9. IEEE. *IEEE Standard Classification for Software Anomalies*, 1993. IEEE Std 1044-1993.
10. R. Johnson and D. Wagner. Finding User/Kernel Pointer Bugs With Type Inference. In *Proc. 13th USENIX Security Symposium*, 2004.

11. C. Jones. *Applied Software Measurement: Assuring Productivity and Quality.* McGraw-Hill, 1991.
12. C. Koller. *Vergleich verschiedener Methoden zur analytischen Qualitätssicherung.* Diploma Thesis, Technische Universität München, 2004. In German.
13. G.J. Myers. *The Art of Software Testing.* John Wiley & Sons, 1979.
14. J. Palsberg. Type-Based Analysis and Applications. In *Proc. 2001 ACM SIGPLAN-SIGSOFT Workshop on Program Analysis for Software Tools and Engineering (PASTE'01)*, pages 20–27. ACM Press, 2001.
15. PMD. http://pmd.sourceforge.net (February 2005).
16. A. Pretschner, W. Prenninger, S. Wagner, C. Kühnel, M. Baumgartner, B. Sostawa, R. Zölch, and T. Stauner. One Evaluation of Model-Based Testing and its Automation. In *Proc. 27th International Conference on Software Engineering (ICSE'05)*, 2005. To appear.
17. QJ Pro. http://qjpro.sourceforge.net (February 2005).
18. N. Rutar, C.B. Almazan, and J.S. Foster. A Comparison of Bug Finding Tools for Java. In *Proc. 15th IEEE International Symposium on Software Reliability Engineering (ISSRE'04)*, pages 245–256, 2004.
19. S. Wagner. Efficiency Analysis of Defect-Detection Techniques. Technical Report TUMI-0413, Institut für Informatik, Technische Universität München, 2004.
20. S. Wagner. Reliability Efficiency of Defect-Detection Techniques: A Field Study. In *Suppl. Proc. 15th IEEE International Symposium on Software Reliability Engineering (ISSRE'04)*, pages 294–301, 2004.
21. S. Wagner. Towards Software Quality Economics for Defect-Detection Techniques. In *Proc. 29th Annual IEEE/NASA Software Engineering Workshop*, 2005. To appear.
22. M. Zitser, R. Lippmann, and T .Leek. Testing Static Analysis Tools using Exploitable Buffer Overflows from Open Source Code. In *Proc. 12th ACM SIGSOFT International Symposium on Foundations of Software Engineering (SIGSOFT'04/FSE-12)*, pages 97–106. ACM Press, 2004.

Cross-Language Functional Testing for Middleware

A. Puder[1] and L. Wang[2]

[1] San Francisco State University, Computer Science Department,
1600 Holloway Avenue, San Francisco, CA 94132
arno@sfsu.edu
[2] Computer Science Department, University of Southern California,
941 W. 37th Place, Los Angeles, CA 90089-0781
limeiwan@usc.edu

Abstract. Middleware is at the heart of any distributed application and its correctness therefore requires rigorous testing. Since middleware technologies typically support heterogeneous environments, its API is available for different programming languages. Functional tests written to test the functionality of a middleware platform therefore have to be re-written for all those programming languages. The framework introduced in this paper shows how functional tests written in Java can automatically be translated to other programming languages such as C++. This is achieved by using the XML-based programming language XMLVM. XMLVM can automatically be created from Java class files. The cross-language translations are accomplished by using XSL-transformations of XMLVM programs.

1 Motivation

Middleware allows the development of cross-platform, language-independent, distributed applications. Middleware is used in different contexts such as eCommerce applications or system-to-system integration, which places high demand on the correctness of middleware platforms. Several activities have created tens of thousands of test cases to ensure the correct behavior of a middleware technology. Among those efforts are CORVAL, COST, and WS-I (see [2], [15], and [4] respectively). One of the challenges of middleware functional testing is that by definition a middleware platform supports multiple programming languages. The implication of this heterogeneity is that functional tests have to be written in every language that is supported by a middleware technology, which leads to redundant and error-prone work.

Of the 100,000 lines of functional tests that were contributed as part of the COST (CORBA Open Source Testing, see [15]) effort, roughly half of the code tests C++ API whereas the other half tests the Java API of CORBA implementations. Every test therefore exists in two different implementations: C++ and Java. While these tests are functionally identical, they have to be re-written

F. Khendek and R. Dssouli (Eds.): TestCom 2005, LNCS 3502, pp. 56–68, 2005.

because of different language mappings for C++ and Java. The framework introduced in this paper allows a functional test to be written in Java and then to automatically derive the same test for other programming languages. This reduces manual work as well as potential for errors. We achieve this goal by making use of some advanced XML technologies. At the core of our framework is an XML-based programming language that allows cross-language translation of functional tests written in Java.

The paper is structured as follows: Section 2 introduces the problems related to writing functional tests for two different middleware technologies: CORBA and Web Services. Section 3 describes our framework. We present our XML-based programming language XMLVM and show how functional tests written in Java can automatically be translated to C++. Section 4 provides a conclusion and outlook.

2   Functional Testing of Middleware

This section highlights two real-life examples of functional testing for two different middleware technologies: CORBA and Web Services. In both cases it will become evident that a lot of testing code has to be virtually replicated in every programming language that is supported by the respective middleware technology.

2.1   Use Case 1: CORBA Functional Testing

CORBA (Common Object Request Broker Architecture) defines an architecture for a platform independent middleware for object-oriented applications (see [1]). The core specification of CORBA, as standardized by the OMG, consists of over 1000 pages with hundreds of API functions. A functional test written for any of those functions would need to be translated into all languages that are being supported by CORBA. The following example illustrates this problem. The Java code excerpt demonstrates a functional test for a *Dynamic Any* using JUnit (see [9]):

```
J1:  // Java
J2:  public class DynAnyBaseTest extends junit.framework.TestCase {
J3:
J4:      private org.omg.CORBA.ORB orb = null;
J5:      private org.omg.DynamicAny.DynAnyFactory dynany_factory = null;
J6:
J7:      // ...
J8:
J9:      public void testAccessBasicValue ()
J10:     {
J11:         int                    longVal1;
J12:         int                    longVal2;
J13:         org.omg.CORBA.TypeCode tc = null;
J14:         org.omg.DynamicAny.DynAny dynAny = null;
J15:
```

```
J16:              longVal1 = 700;
J17:              longVal2 = 0;
J18:              tc = orb.get_primitive_tc (org.omg.CORBA.TCKind.tk_long);
J19:              dynAny = dynany_factory.create_dyn_any_from_type_code (tc);
J20:              dynAny.insert_long (longVal1);
J21:              longVal2 = dynAny.get_long ();
J22:              assertEquals ("DynamicAny error", longVal1, longVal2);
J23:      }
J24:  }
```

The code above was taken from an actual functional test from the COST project. A Dynamic Any is a generic container for one data item. The type of the data item that can be contained in the Dynamic Any is determined when the Dynamic Any is created (lines J18 and J19). The Dynamic Any supports all types of the CORBA-IDL. The example above shows a simple functional test that first writes a long with value 700 into a Dynamic Any (line J20), extracts the value contained in the Dynamic Any (line J21) and then compares the two values to make sure that they are identical (line J22). Below is the same functional test, but now written in C++ using CPPUnit (see [8]):

```
C1:  // C++
C2:  class DynAnyBaseTest : public CppUnit::TestCase {
C3:    private:
C4:      CORBA::ORB_ptr                  orb;
C5:      DynamicAny::DynAnyFactory_ptr dynany_factory;
C6:
C7:      // ...
C8:
C9:    public:
C10:       void testAccessBasicValue()
C11:       {
C12:         CORBA::Long              longVal1;
C13:         CORBA::Long              longVal2;
C14:         CORBA::TypeCode_var     tc;
C15:         DynamicAny::DynAny_var dynAny;
C16:
C17:         longVal1 = 700;
C18:         longVal2 = 0;
C19:         tc = CORBA::TypeCode::_duplicate (CORBA::_tc_long);
C20:         dynAny = dynany_factory->create_dyn_any_from_type_code (tc);
C21:         dynAny->insert_long (longVal1);
C22:         longVal2 = dynAny->get_long ();
C23:         CPPUNIT_ASSERT_EQUAL_MESSAGE ("DynamicAny error",
C24:                                       longVal1, longVal2);
C25:       }
C26:  };
```

Conceptually the functional test above is doing exactly the same as the Java version, except that the CORBA's C++ API and CPPUnit are used in this case.

Despite the similarities there are some differences. E.g., the way the `TypeCode` is created (J18 vs. C19) or how to use the assert-API in JUnit and CPPUnit (J22 vs. C23).

2.2 Use Case 2: Web Services

Web Services are an emerging technology that have made a lot of head-waves over the past few years. Conceptually identical to CORBA, it has gained certain prominence because of Microsoft's commitment to support Web Services. XML is used extensively as the underlying foundation of many of the Web Services standards. The WS-I (Web Services Interoperability) organization issues the set of standards (called basic profile) that define the scope of Web Services (see [4]). It is interesting to note that Web Services do not support the concept of portability. I.e., the API for a certain programming language might differ significantly between different Web Services products.

The following code excerpt illustrates this problem:

```
// Java using Sun's WS Developer Kit
import java.rmi.Remote;
import java.rmi.RemoteException;

public interface AccountIF extends Remote {
    public void deposit (int amount) throws RemoteException;
    public void withdraw (int amount) throws RemoteException;
    public int balance () throws RemoteException;
}
```

The code excerpt above shows the server-side mapping of a simple bank account interface using Sun's Web Services SDK. In Sun's implementation of the Web Services standards, the server-side implementation must implement a Java interface that extends the `Remote` interface. Furthermore, every method that belongs to the interface must throw the exception `RemoteException`. Below is a code excerpt that shows the same bank account interface using BEA's WebLogic Server:

```
// Java using BEA's Web Logic Server
public class Account implements com.bea.jws.WebService
{
    static final long serialVersionUID = 1L;

    /**
     * @common:operation
     */
    public void deposit (int amount);
    {
        ...
```

As can be seen, BEA implements the bank account interface through a Java class that is derived from `com.bea.jws.WebService`. All remote methods are marked through a special JavaDoc comment `@common:operation`. It is apparent that functional testing for Web Services pose even greater challenges than for CORBA. Due to lack of portability, the functional tests have to be re-written for each Web Service product, even though Java is used in all instances.

3   Framework

This section introduces our framework. The goal is to write a functional test only once, and create the functional test for different languages automatically. In Section 3.1 we briefly discuss a non-solution. Section 3.2 gives an overview of Java's virtual machine. Based on those explanations, we introduce our XML-based programming language called XMLVM in Section 3.3. Section 3.4 finally describes how we use XMLVM to solve the problem of cross-language functional testing.

3.1   Non-solution

Before we present our solution to cross-language functional testing, we want to briefly discuss a non-solution. Initially we took the approach of defining a new programming language based on XML. Flow control statements (such as if and while) and other elements of an object-oriented programming language are represented by appropriate XML-tags. There are numerous projects that have created such XML-based programming languages (see [5, 12, 13, 7, 11]). Once a test case has been written in this language, it is relatively easy to translate it to another high-level programming language such as Java or C++. This can easily be accomplished by using XSL-transformations (see Figure 1).

However once we started to pursue this idea, we quickly realized that there were several disadvantages over using an XML-based programming language in this way. First and foremost programmers have to learn a new programming language. Someone using this approach would need to master a new programming language for which no tools (such as smart editors or syntax checkers) exist. Another problem resulted in the fact that XML tends to be very "verbose". By this we mean that it takes on the average more lines of code to express an

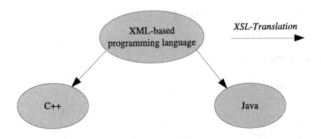

Fig. 1. Non-solution: Mapping XML to C++ and Java

algorithm in XML compared to other high-level languages. This is because of the rigid syntax that XML imposes on the structure of a document. For these reasons we took a different approach.

3.2   Java's Virtual Machine

As outlined in the previous section, it is not practical to expose a programmer to an XML-based programming language. Yet XML has much to offer due to the availability of rich tool sets. In order to exploit the benefits of XML, but make it transparent to programmers, we created a low-level XML-based programming language that is not intended for human readers. In order to use standards as much as possible, we decided to use the byte code executed by a Java virtual machine as a model for our XML-based programming language.

Before we explain our approach, we provide a few details on the Java Virtual Machine concept (for more details see [10]). A Java compiler translates the Java source code to hardware independent byte code that is stored in a class file. The byte code resembles the machine code of other hardware architectures. The Java virtual machine implements a simple stack based machine (see Figure 2).

The Java VM maintains an instruction pointer to the class file that points to the next instruction to be executed. Upon entering a method, a new frame consisting of a stack and local variables is created. This frame will be deleted upon exiting the method. The Java VM maintains a pointer to the current frame (which represents the most nested method call). A method has only access to its own stack and local variables. The actual parameters of a method are automatically stored in the local variables. Besides the stack frames, the Java VM maintains a garbage collected heap where a program can allocate new objects.

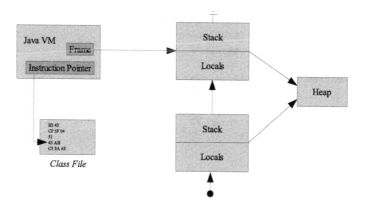

Fig. 2. Java VM

The Java byte code features a mix of low-level and high-level virtual machine instructions. On the one hand side one finds simple instructions such as iadd that pops two integers off the stack and pushes the sum back onto the stack. On the other side there exist high-level instructions such as new (for instantiating new objects) and invokevirtual (invoke a virtual method). These instructions go beyond the capabilities of normal machine languages and explain the difficulties in creating a real CPU that can execute Java byte code natively.

3.3   XMLVM

The Java byte code resembles the machine code of other hardware architectures. It is interesting to note that Sun Microsystems as the inventor of Java never standardized an assembly language of their own byte code. Several assemblers were developed, but they had to invent their own syntax. The most commonly used assembly syntax stems from the Jasmin project (see [14]).

The first step in creating a cross-language functional testing framework consist in defining an XML-based programming language that is based on the Java byte code. This effectively defines an assembly language for the Java virtual machine whose syntax is based on XML. Since we mimic the syntax very closely to the Java byte code instructions, there is a direct bi-directional mapping between Java class files and our XML-based programming language. Since the XML-based programming language is closely related to the byte code of the Java virtual machine, we call our language XMLVM.

In practice, programs are not directly written in XMLVM, but rather created automatically from class files. The programmer is thus not exposed to the details of XMLVM, but can implement his or her programs in Java. The following XML follows the XMLVM schema and demonstrates the translation of the Java functional test for Dynamic Any presented in Section 2.1:

```
X1:    <?xml version="1.0" encoding="UTF-8"?>
X2:    <xmlvm>
X3:      <class name="DynAnyBaseTest" isPublic="true"
X4:             isSynchronized="true" extends="junit.framework.TestCase">
X5:        <field isPrivate="true" name="orb"
X6:               type="org.omg.CORBA.ORB" />
X7:        <!-- ... -->
X8:        <method name="testAccessBasicValue"
X9:                isPublic="true" stack="3" locals="5">
X10:         <signature>
X11:           <return type="void" />
X12:         </signature>
X13:         <code>
X14:           <!-- ... -->
X15:           <getfield class-type="DynAnyBaseTest"
X16:                     type="org.omg.CORBA.ORB" field="orb" />
X17:           <getstatic class-type="org.omg.CORBA.TCKind"
X18:                      type="org.omg.CORBA.TCKind" field="tk_long" />
X19:           <invokevirtual class-type="org.omg.CORBA.ORB"
```

```
X20:                              method="get_primitive_tc">
X21:            <signature>
X22:              <return type="org.omg.CORBA.TypeCode" />
X23:              <parameter type="org.omg.CORBA.TCKind" />
X24:            </signature>
X25:          </invokevirtual>
X26:          <astore type="java.lang.Object" index="3" />
X27:          <!-- ... -->
X28:        </code>
X29:      </method>
X30:    </class>
X31:  </xmlvm>
```

The above XML was automatically created using our tool. The complete XML is much longer and cannot be reproduced here. A few details are worth mentioning. We will relate the XMLVM output with the original Java functional test from Section 2.1. Line X3 contains the class declaration (line J2). Line X5 contains the instance member orb (line J4). Line X8 contains the declaration of method testAccessBasicValue() (line J9). The stack and locals attributes in line X9 state how big the stack and how many local variables are needed for this method. Note that the Java compiler computes this information by doing a flow analysis. Lines X10 to X12 show the signature, and lines X13 to X28 the implementation of method testAccessBasicValue().

Lines X15 through X26 show an excerpt of the byte code generated by the Java compiler. Those lines represent the compiled version of Java source code at line J18. There are basically four byte code instructions: <getfield> (line X15) pushes the value of instance member orb onto the stack and <getstatic> (line X17) pushes the value of static variable org.omg.CORBA.TCKind.tk_long onto the stack. <invokevirtual> (line X19) calls the virtual method get_primitive_tc(). This instruction assumes that the object reference to the target object as well as the actual parameters are on the top of the stack (which was done by the previous two instructions). Once the call to get_primitive_tc() returns, the result is on the top of the stack. <astore> (line X26) pops this result off the stack and saves it in a local variable.

3.4   Mapping XMLVM to Other Languages

The XML presented in the previous section was automatically generated and it represents an intermediate artifact not intended to be inspected by programmers. The principal idea of our framework is to translate XMLVM to other high-level programming languages. The translation is done using XSL-translations (see [3]). Figure 3 shows the overall translation process.

API Transformation: As shown in the figure, the source program is first translated to XMLVM by a tool. The resulting XMLVM then undergoes an API transformation. The purpose of the API transformation is to adapt the API from the source to the target language. The original test case was written using specific

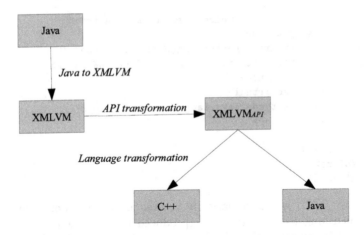

Fig. 3. XMLVM transformation process

APIs such as Java-CORBA and JUnit. If the test case is to be translated to C++, this API has to be adapted to the appropriate API available for the target language. For each API exist a XSL-stylesheet that adapts the API. The following list gives some examples of API transformations if the target language is C++:

- JUnit to CPPUnit:
    - Base class `junit.framework.TestCase` (J2) changes to `CppUnit.TestCase` (C2)
    - `assertEquals()` (J22) changes to `CPPUNIT_ASSERT_EQUAL_MESSAGE()` (C23)
- CORBA for Java to C++:
    - Namespace prefix `omg.org.CORBA` (J4) changes to `CORBA` (C4)
    - Method `get_primitive_tc()` (J18) changes to `_duplicate()` (C19)

Note that the output of API transformation is still an XMLVM program (referred to as XMLVM$_{API}$ in Figure 3) and consequently uses XMLVM notation, such as "." for the scope operator. The examples given above are mostly simple renaming operations that can easily be achieved by appropriate XSL-stylesheets. The more complex example is the creation of a `TypeCode` (J18). This situation can be handled by a more complex XSL-stylesheet. This XSL-template basically looks for a call to `get_primitive_tc()` and then transforms the API to a semantically equivalent version to be used for C++.

Each API transformation is handled by its own XSL-stylesheet and depending on how many different libraries (e.g., JUnit, CORBA, etc) are used, multiple stylesheets may be applied. The result of the API transformation is again an XMLVM program. The excerpt below demonstrates the resulting XMLVM after the applying the XSL-stylesheets for API transformation:

```
A1:   <getstatic class-type="CORBA"
A2:              type="CORBA.TypeCode" field="_tc_long" />
A3:   <invokestatic class-type="CORBA.TypeCode"
A4:                 method="_duplicate">
A5:     <signature>
A6:       <return type="CORBA.TypeCode" />
A7:       <parameter type="CORBA.TypeCode" />
A8:     </signature>
A9:   </invokestatic>
A10:  <astore type="CORBA.Object" index="3" />
```

The excerpt above shows the result of translating the original XMLVM code for creating a `TypeCode` (lines X15 to X26 in Section 3.3). Instead of using the ORB-singleton to create a `TypeCode` via get_primitive_tc(), the `TypeCode` is now created by duplicating the constant _tc_long that all CORBA conformant C++ ORBs are required to have.

Language Transformation: The result of the API transformation is another XMLVM program. The final step in this translation process consists in generating code for the target language. This translation is done by yet another XSL-stylesheet. The idea for this last step of our framework is to map XMLVM-instructions one-to-one to the target language, without attempting to reverse engineer (or de-compile) the original Java program. Since the Java VM is based on a simple stack-based machine, we simply mimic a stack-machine in the target language. An example helps to illustrate this approach. The XMLVM instruction <astore> pops an object reference off the stack and saves it to a local variable. Here is the XSL-template that creates C++ code for this instruction:

```
<xsl:template match="astore">
    <xsl:text>
    locals[</xsl:text>
    <xsl:value-of select="@index"/>
    <xsl:text>] = stack.pop();</xsl:text>
</xsl:template>
```

As an example, the <astore> instruction in line A10 would translate to the following C++ code:

```
locals[3] = stack.pop();
```

This C++ code makes reference to variables `locals` and `stack`. Those variables are declared for every method and it is with the help of those variables that we mimic the VM's stack-machine. The code below represents the C++ version of the XMLVM program shown in lines A1 to A10 of the previous section:

```
T1:   // C++
T2:   class DynAnyBaseTest
T3:           : public virtual CppUnit::TestCase
T4:   {
```

```
T5:        CORBA::ORB_ptr orb;
T6:        DynamicAny::DynAnyFactory_ptr dynany_factory;
T7:
T8:        // ...
T9:
T10:       void testAccessBasicValue()
T11:       {
T12:           XMLVM::Locals locals(5);
T13:           XMLVM::Stack stack(3);
T14:           XMLVM::Object op1;
T15:           XMLVM::Object op2;
T16:           locals[0] = this;
T17:
T18:           // ...
T19:           stack.push(CORBA::_tc_long);
T20:           op1 = CORBA::TypeCode::_duplicate((CORBA::TypeCode_ptr)
T21:                                             stack.top(0));
T22:           stack.remove(1);
T23:           stack.push(op1);
T24:           locals[3] = stack.pop();
T25:           // ...
T26:       }
T27:   }
```

As can be seen from the code excerpt, there is a natural mapping from XM-LVM to C++. The intention is not to generate readable code, but correct code that uses the API of the target language. The above code is automatically created by the XSL-language transformation and is not meant to be inspected by programmers. We mimic Java's VM via the two classes XMLVM::Locals and XMLVM::Stack (lines T12 and T13). Those two C++ classes are part of the XMLVM library for C++. Class XMLVM::Stack features common stack-operations such as push and pop. Both of these classes implement the garbage collection that is normally done by Java's VM. Variables op1 and op2 (lines T14 and T15) are used as temporary variables needed by some XMLVM-instructions.

4   Conclusions and Outlook

Functional testing for middleware requires individual tests to be re-written in all programming languages that are supported by that middleware. The framework introduced in this paper proposes a novel way to automate this manual and error prone task. In our framework functional tests are written once in Java. The class file that contains the compiled version of the functional test is then translated to XMLVM; an XML-based programming language. Then various XSL-transformations can be applied to first transform the API and then to translate the functional test to another high level language.

It is important to emphasize the fact that we effectively translate functional tests written in Java to other programming languages. This works well for APIs (such as Dynamic Any) that exists in all different languages, but there are limitations for language specific APIs. E.g., the CORBA C++ language mapping defines various helper types for C++ pointers that can be recognized by the suffix _ptr and _var. These helper types do not exist in Java, simply because C++ pointers are much more complex than Java object references. Functional tests that specifically test the correctness of these helper types would need to be written manually in C++.

XMLVM is at the core of our framework. We have implemented it based on the Byte Code Engineering Library (BCEL) which is part of Apache's Jakarta project (see [6]). We are currently investigating other uses of XMLVM in different contexts. One possible use could be in a code migration framework for web-based applications based on previous work (see [16]). Another potential use of XMLVM could be byte code instrumentation using XSL-transformation.

References

1. Common object request broker architecture (corba/iiop). Object Management Group. http://www.omg.org/technology/documents.
2. Vsorb test suite specification, release 1.0.0. Open Group, 1997. http://www.opengroup.org/corval/vsorbts.pdf.
3. Xsl transformations. World Wide Web Consortium (W3C), 1999. http://www.w3.org/TR/1999/REC-xslt-19991116.
4. Web Services Interoperability Organization, 2004. http://www.ws-i.org.
5. G.J. Badros. A markup language for java source code. May 2000. http://www.cs.washington.edu/research/constraints/web/badros-javaml-www9.pdf.
6. Markus Dahm. Byte code engineering. Java Informations Tage, pages 267–277, 1999.
7. W. Emmerich, C. Mascolo, and A. Finkelstein. Implementing incremental code migration with xml. pages 397–406. In M. Jazayeri and A. Wolf, editors, Proc. 22nd Int. Conf. on Software Engineering (ICSE2000) Limerick, Ireland, ACM Press., June 2000. http://www.cs.ucl.ac.uk/staff/W.Emmerich/publications/ICSE2000/MobXML/mobxml.pdf.
8. Paul Hamill. *Unit Test Frameworks*. O'Reilly; 1 edition, October 2004.
9. Andy Hunt and Dave Tomas. *Pragmatic Unit Testing in Java With JUnit*. The Pragmatic Programmers; 1 edition, September 2003.
10. Tim Lindholm and Frank Yellin. *The Java Virtual Machine Specification*. Addison-Wesley Pub Co, second edition, April 1999.
11. Jonathan I. Maletic, Michael L. Collard, and Andrian Marcus. Source code files as structured documents. pages 289–292, June 2002. http://www.sdml.info/papers/iwpc02.pdf.
12. E. Mamas and K. Kontogiannis. Towards portable source code representation using xml. pages 172–182. Proceedings of the Seventh Working Conference on Reverse Engineering, IEEE Computer Society Press, Brisbane Australia, November 2000.
13. G. McArthur, J. Mylopoulos, and S.K.K. Ng. An extensible tool for source code representation using xml. pages 199–208. Proceedings of the Ninth Working Conference on Reverse Engineering, IEEE Computer Society, Richmond, Virginia, USA, October 2002.

14. Jonathan Meyer. An assembler for the java virtual machine. 1996. http://jasmin.sourceforge.net/.

15. Arno Puder. Corba open source testing. OMG in Motion, Needham, 2001.

16. Arno Puder. Extending desktop applications to the web. Second Workshop on Distributed Objects Research, Experiences and Applications (DOREA 2004), pages 8–11, Dublin, July 2004. Computer Science Press.

Using Anti-Ant-like Agents to Generate Test Threads from the UML Diagrams

Huaizhong Li and C. Peng Lam

School of Computer and Information Science, Edith Cowan University,
Mt. Lawley, WA 6050, Australia
{h.li,c.lam}@ecu.edu.au

Abstract. The problem of generating the test cases is one of the most important issues in the software testing research and practice. Test threads, especially the thin-threads which are the usage scenarios in a software system, are frequently used to generate test cases for the scenario-based software testing. However, the derivation of the test threads is usually a manual and labor-intensive task. In this paper, we propose an automated approach using anti-ant-like agents to directly generate test threads from the UML artifacts. The generated test threads can then be used to generate and to prioritize the test cases for scenario-based software testing.

1 Introduction

Recently, great amount of attentions have been given to effectively using UML, which is the industrial de-facto standard for modeling object-oriented software systems, in software testing (see, for example, [9] and the references therein). One of the focused research topics is using UML artifacts for scenario based testing. Scenarios represent the sequences of executions in a software system. There are two important problems which are generally associated with the scenario-based testing techniques, namely the generation of the test scenarios [1, 3], and the prioritization of the testing scenarios [1, 4].

Properly generated test scenarios are essential for the scenario-based software testing to achieve the test adequacy and to guarantee the software quality. Test thread derivation, especially thin-thread derivation is a frequently used approach for the generation of the test scenarios [1, 3, 5, 15]. Thin-threads, in the forms of thin-thread trees and associated condition trees, can be derived from the scenarios-based business model [1, 5] or directly from the UML artifacts [3], and then test scenarios can be generated from the thin-threads. The generated test threads can also be used to prioritize the test cases for scenario-based software testing [4]. Additional data object tree can be generated to assist in analyzing the content-dependencies which may lead to couplings between the test scenarios [3]. One main problem with the generation of thin-threads is that the generation procedures are either manual/labor-intensive [1, 5], or can not be fully automated [3].

It is well-known that the development of techniques which support the automation of software testing will result in significant cost savings. Recently, the application of Artificial Intelligence (AI) techniques in Software Engineering (SE) emerges as an

F. Khendek and R. Dssouli (Eds.): TestCom 2005, LNCS 3502, pp. 69–80, 2005.

area of research that brings about the cross-fertilization of ideas across two domains [8]. It has been identified that one of the SE areas with a more prolific use of AI techniques is software testing [18]. The focus of these techniques involves the applications of genetic algorithms (GAs), for examples [19] and [21]. Recently, efforts have been made to apply Ant Colony Optimization (ACO) algorithms to software testing [11, 20, 21]. However, none of the reported investigations using ACO approaches addresses the generation of test threads from the UML artifacts for scenario-based software testing.

ACO simulates the behavior of real ants. The first ACO technique is known as Ant System [12] and it was applied to the traveling salesman problem. Since then, many variants of this technique have been produced. ACO can be applied to generate solutions for combinatorial optimization problems. The artificial ants in the algorithm represent the stochastic solution construction procedures which make use of (1) the dynamic evolution of the pheromone trails that reflect the ants' acquired search experience; and (2) the heuristic information related to the problem in hand, in order to construct solutions.

Using AI techniques, especially using ant-like agents, provides a potential avenue to automate the generation of test threads for scenario-based software testing. However, the original ACO algorithms as presented in [12] and [13] can not be directly used to tackle the problem of generating test threads from the UML artifacts, as the standard ACO ants are not designed to tackle the graphs which can be converted from the UML diagrams.

In this paper, we propose to use anti-ant-like agents to automatically generate test threads directly from the existing UML activity diagrams. The details of our approach are presented in the next section.

2   Generating Test Threads from the UML Activity Diagrams

Before presenting the details of our approach, we briefly review the principles underlying the representation of the thin-thread tree, the condition tree, and the data-object tree, as well their relationship with the UML activity diagrams.

2.1   The Three Trees

The UML use cases are the good sources for the derivation of the software testing requirements, because they represent high level functionalities provided by the system to the end-users. The use cases are usually not independent. They may have the Extend and the Include dependencies, and the sequential dependencies [7, 10] which stem from the logic of the supported business workflows. The sequential dependencies between use cases can be represented by activity diagrams for all the actors in the system. As the activity diagrams are relatively easy to be interpreted, such a representation facilitates the identification and visualization of these dependencies viewed by the application domain experts. Thin threads can be extracted from the system level activity diagrams.

A thin thread and a use case serve similar functionality, i.e., they both describe system scenarios. However, a thin thread contains more information than a use case, and thin threads for an application are organized into a tree style which is suitable for various analyses such as dependency analysis, risk analysis, traceability analysis, coverage analysis, completeness and consistency checking, and test scenario/test case generation [1]. Thin-threads that share certain commonalities can be grouped together to form a thin-thread group. Such grouping can be recursive, i.e., a collection of lower level thin-thread groups that share some commonalities can be further grouped to form a higher level thin-thread group. All thin-threads and thin-thread groups can be arranged hierarchically to form a thin-thread tree. Furthermore, conditions are generally associated with each thin thread or each thin thread group to identify their activation constraints [1]. A thin-thread can only be activated if its affiliated conditions are satisfied. The conditions can also be grouped and organized into a tree style.

On the other hand, the UML activity diagrams can contain data storage objects which can be read and/or updated by sub-scenarios. These data objects can affect or be affected by the associated conditions. For example, a multi-processing system or an interactive system may experience the racing problem in which the execution result is affected by the execution sequencing of the sub-scenarios, if two or more sub-scenarios update the same data objects in certain situations. Similar to the conditions, the data storage objects can also be classified and organized into a tree style. However, there is a difference between the classification of the data objects and that of the conditions, namely the hierarchy of the data objects closely resembles a normal data storage structure in a relational database. The top level of a data object hierarchy contains the data objects, and a leaf node only contains part of a data object since different sub-scenarios may operate on the different parts of the same data object. The operation attributes, namely reading or updating, are assigned to the leaf nodes to help identifying the data dependencies between the thin-threads. The data object tree was not part of the standard thin-thread based approaches reported in literature [1, 5, 22]. It was proposed in [3] to extend the thin-threads to capture the important content-dependent coupling relationships between the thin-threads.

Consequently, thin-threads, conditions and data objects can all be arranged hierarchically to form the thin-thread tree, the condition tree and the data-object tree, respectively. There are complex relationships amongst the three trees. A thin thread is composed of a group of sequential sub-scenarios, with each sub-scenario associated with one or more conditions in the condition-tree and one or more data object in the data-object tree. The thin-threads may share common sub-scenarios, conditions and data-objects.

Next we present the details of the proposed approach which aims at automating the generation of the trees.

2.2 Using Anti-Ant-like Agents to Build the Three Trees

A directed graph is defined as G = (V, E) where V is a set of vertices of the graph and E a set of edges of the graph. A UML activity diagram can be viewed as a directed graph where the vertices are the activity nodes, the object nodes, the branch nodes, the fork nodes, the join nodes, and the initial node, while the edges are the activity edges in the activity diagram. An extended activity diagram, namely an ATM machine, is shown in Figure 1. This activity diagram contains a data object *Account* which can be accessed by various activity nodes.

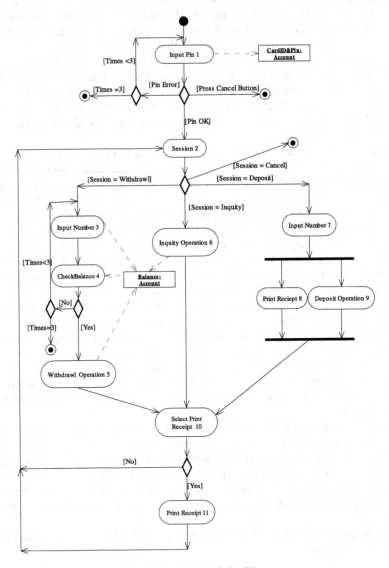

Fig. 1. An ATM Activity Diagram

An activity graph is a directed, dynamic graph in which the activity edges may only become accessible after the evaluation of their guards. It is difficult to apply the original ACO algorithms directly to this type of dynamic graphs to generate test threads.

Inspired by ACO algorithms, we consider the problem of sending a group of ant-like agents to cooperatively search a directed graph G. The objective of the ant exploration is to build the three trees as discussed in the previous sub-section.

The behavior of an artificial ant in our approach is governed by a state machine diagram illustrated in Figure 2. An artificial ant at a node in our paradigm can sense the pheromone trails on the edges emanating from the current vertex, and leave pheromone trails over the edges when it moves between the nodes.

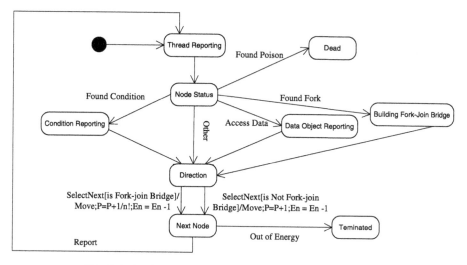

Fig. 2. Behavior of an Artificial Ant - The State Machine Diagram

Unlike the approach in [3], it is not necessary for the current framework to convert a UML activity diagram into an activity hypergraph first and then process the convert hypergraph which were two steps that could not be fully automated in [3]. The UML activity diagrams, in the form of XMI files exported from common UML tools can be directly used to generate the trees in the proposed approach. Graph conversion from the activity diagram, if necessary, is done on the fly instead.

There are two special sets of nodes in the activity diagram which need to pay special attention:

- *The final nodes in an activity diagram are considered as the poisoned food sources for the artificial ants.* An artificial ant is killed if it finds the poisoned food.

- *A fork node and its associated join node are considered as the two banks of a river, every path between the fork-join nodes is considered as a pontoon.* An artificial ant can not cross the river without building a pontoon bridge[1] over the river first. Every pair of fork/join nodes and all the nodes between the pair will be converted on the fly to execution sequences, called Fork-Join

---

[1] A type of temporary bridge which is quickly built using floating pontoons for the passage of troops.

Bridges, by the artificial ants. The details of Fork-Join Bridges will be discussed late.

In our framework, an artificial ant is powered by limited energy. An ant is terminated if it runs out of energy. The main purpose for the introduction of power consumption for the artificial ants is to avoid the situations in which an artificial ant runs into a cyclic loop, or in which an ant is stalled in a part of the activity diagram.

We now present the algorithm for the proposed ant exploration approach:

Algorithm

The pseudo codes of the proposed algorithm are illustrated as following:

```
/* Initialization */
for every edge (i,j) do
    P_ij = 0; /*Set 0 pheromone level to every edge*/
endfor;

/* Exploration of a group of m ants */
for k = 1 to m do
  EN_k = Energy; /*Charge every ant with default energy*/

  i = 0; /*Every ant starts from the initial node*/

  while ( EN_k > 0 ) do

    /*Thread reporting*/
    Report threads to the thread tree;

    Evaluate status at node i;

    if (Found Poison) do
       Kill ant;
       Break;
    endif;

    /*Condition reporting*/
    if (Found Condition) do
       Report conditions to the condition tree;
    endif;

    /*Data Reporting*/
    if (Access Data) do
       Report data access to the data object tree;
    endif;

    /*If arrives at a fork node*/
    if (Found Fork) do
       Building Fork-Join Bridge;
    endif;

    /*Not every edge is freely accessible*/
    Get access conditions for emanating edges from vertex i;

    Evaluate pheromone levels on all emanating edges;
```

```
    /*Find the destine node d which has the minimum pheromone
level, random selection if multiple*/
    Find min P_id;

    Take access conditions on edge (i,d);

    /*Move to the destine node*/
    i = d;

    /*Each move consumes energy*/
    EN_k = EN_k - 1;

    /*Update pheromone over the traversed edge*/
    if (is Fork-join Bridge) do
        P_id = P_id +1/n!; /*n pontoons*/
    else
        P_id = P_id + 1;
    endif;

  endwhile;

  if P_ij >= 1 for every edge (i,j) do
    Stop; /*Every edge has been traversed*/
  endif;

endfor;
```

The above pseudo codes are derived from the state machine diagram in Figure 2 to reflect an artificial ant's behavior in exploring the activity graphs. Similar to ACO, pheromone trails on edges are used to guide an artificial ant in selecting its direction for next move. However, unlike ACO and the real ants, our artificial ants exhibit repulsive behavior as pheromone trails in our approach are used in such a way that an ant will favor the unexplored or less-explored edges. This results in effective exploration of the activity diagrams, as the addressed problem here is the generation of various test threads which requires effective coverage of all activity edges instead of an optimal path achieved by original ACO algorithms.

Since the artificial ants in our framework exhibit repulsive behavior which is contrary to that of the real ants, we may better name our artificial ants as anti-ants. However, for simplicity, we will still use the name "ants" to call our artificial agents which actually exhibit anti-ant behavior.

The pseudo codes are straightforward to be followed. However, two segments of the pseudo codes, namely Building Fork-Join Bridge and Reporting need to be further explained.

Building Fork-Join Bridge

When an artificial ant arrives at a fork river bank, it has to utilize the pontoons between the two river banks to build a pontoon bridge over the river in order to cross the river. Assume that there are n pontoons, and then the procedure to build a fork-join bridge for an ant is:

1. Set $k = 1$;
2. From the remaining pontoons, find the k-th pontoon which has the minimum pheromone level on the first edge; randomly select a pontoon if there are multiple candidates with same minimum pheromone level;
3. Deposit pheromone level $1/k$ to the first edge of the k-th pontoon;
4. If $k = n$, sequentially connect all pontoons in the respective order to form a pontoon bridge; otherwise set $k = k + 1$ and go to step 2;
5. Temporarily replace all the inclusive nodes between the fork node and the join node in the activity diagram with the fork-join bridge constructed by the current ant.

For example, for the fork-join river in the ATM example shown in Figure 1, two consecutive ant explorations build two fork-join bridges as illustrated in Figure 3. Note that an ant deposits $1/n!$ pheromone level over each edge which it traverses on the fork-join bridge.

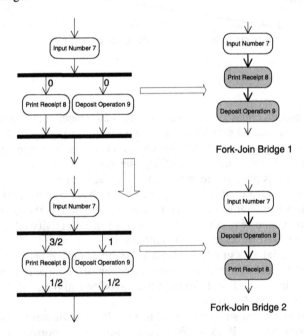

Fig. 3. Building a Fork-Join Bridge

The bridge building procedure ensures that every possible execution sequence combination of the paths between the fork node and the join node will be exercised by the proposed algorithm, and all corresponding traces will be recorded in the three trees. However, the bridge building procedure alone can not guarantee that every activity edge in a path between the fork and the join nodes will be visited by at least one ant. Therefore, the $1/n!$ pheromone level deposition is introduced which ensures that if there is an unexplored activity edge between the fork and the join nodes, the proposed ant exploration algorithm will not stop. Further exploration of other ants over the paths between the fork and join nodes will favor those edges which have not been fully explored. The number of ants m in the proposed algorithm can be increased to allow more exhaustive exploration. Eventually all activity edges between the fork and the join nodes will be visited at least once which serves as one of the necessary conditions for the termination of the ant exploration algorithm.

Reporting

For simplicity, we only discuss thread reporting here. Condition reporting and data reporting can be tackled in similar ways.

In the exploration of a UML activity diagram, an ant frequently reports its trace to a thin-thread tree. The completed trace of an ant, which is an execution thread, is represented as a branch in the thin-thread tree, as illustrated in Figure 4. When next ant enters and explores the activity diagram, its trace is also reported to the same thin-thread tree. However, for compactness, the part of the new ant's trace which overlaps an existing trace is merged with the existing trace to form the trunk, while the different part is allowed to branch away from the trunk, as shown in the right hand side of Figure 4.

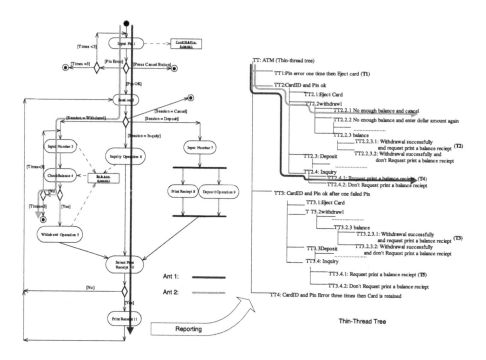

Fig. 4. Thread Reporting

Exploration a UML activity diagram using multiple ant-like agents will result in the automatic generation of three tree type structures, namely the thin-thread tree, the associated condition tree, and the associated data object tree. For the ATM example in Figure 1, application of the proposed approach results in the three trees which are partly shown in Figure 5. The three trees are accordant with the ones reported in [3].

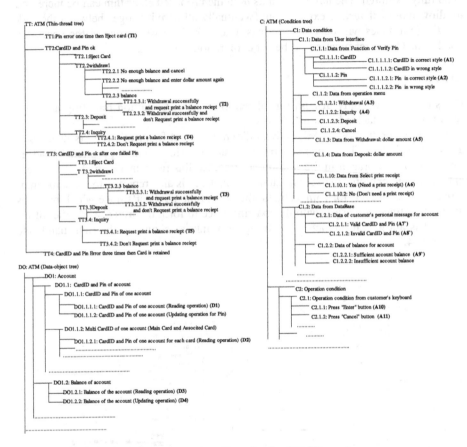

Fig. 5. The Three Trees for the ATM Example

It is possible that some variations may be adopted for the proposed algorithm:

- Use more sophisticated and complicated pheromone updating rules, or use evaporating pheromone deposit.

However, unlike the original ACO algorithms where convergence to an optimal path is desired, the proposed algorithm doesn't encourage cyclic exploration for the artificial ants. In contrary to the original ACO algorithms, the pheromone trails in our approach is used to discourage an artificial ants from exploring an edge which has already been well explored. We believe that the simple pheromone updating rules should serve our purpose well. Adoption of more sophisticated pheromone updating rules, or using evaporating pheromone deposit may complicate the algorithm without significant improvement. However, further research is required and is being carried out to verify this claim.

- Use goal-oriented approach to guide the ants to effectively explore these unexplored edges.

A goal-oriented evolutionary approach has been proposed in [18] for optimization of state-based test suites for software systems. In the current framework, the artificial ants used to explore the activity diagrams are simple memoryless creatures, they can not pre-fetch the future pheromone trails, and are unable to back-trace. Further research will be demanded to exploit the possibility of using ant-like simple agents in goal-oriented approach for the generation of test threads.

- Deploy ants to randomly assigned initial nodes to start exploration.

While ants can be deployed to random locations to start their exploration, the traces they create may not be meaningful in the sense of test threads. Thus the details of this variation will not be discussed further in this paper.

While the proposed algorithm works well for the exploration of UML activity diagrams of the ATM example scale, further experiments will be performed to verify the efficiency of the proposed algorithm for large scale activity diagrams. Results will be reported in sequential reports.

3   Conclusion

This paper extends the previous work in generation of test threads for software testing. In this paper, we propose to use anti-ant-like agents to automatically generate the thin-threads from the UML artifacts. Our approach has the following advantages: 1) the process to generate the thin-threads is simplified because the UML artifacts are directly used; 2) the generation process is *fully* automated; 3) redundant exploration for the test threads is avoided due to the use of the anti-ant-like ants.

References

1. Assistant Secretary of Defense for Command, Control, Communications, and Intelligence (ASD C3I), *End-to-End Integration Test Guidebook*, 2000.
2. F. Basanieri, A. Bertolino, and E. Marchetti, "CoWTeSt: A Cost Weighed Test Strategy", *Proc. Escom-Scope 2001*, London, 2001.
3. X. Bai, C. P. Lam, and H. Li, "An Approach to generate the Thin-threads from the UML Diagrams", *Proc. COMPSAC 2004*, Hong Kong, 2004.
4. X. Bai, H. Li, and C. P. Lam, "A Risk Analysis Approach to Prioritize UML-Based Software Testing", *Proc. SNPD 2004*, Beijing, 2004.
5. X. Bai, W. T. Tsai, R. Paul, K. Feng, and L. Yu, "Scenario-Based Business Modeling", *IEEE Proc. of APAQS*, 2001.
6. S. Bennett, S. McRobb and R. Farmer, *Object-Oriented Systems Analysis and Design Using UML (Second Edition)*, McGraw-Hill Education, 2002.

7. R. V. Binder, *Testing Object-Oriented Systems - Models, Patterns, and Tools*, Addison-Wesley, 1999.
8. L. Briand, "On the many ways Software Engineering can benefit from Knowledge Engineering", *Proc. 14th SEKE*, Italy, 2002.
9. L. Briand and Y. Labiche, "A UML-Based Approach to System Testing", *Software and Systems Modeling*, 1(1), 2002.
10. A. Cockburn, "Structuring use cases with goals", http://alistair.cockburn.us/.
11. K. Doerner and W. J. Gutjahr, "Extracting Test Sequences from a Markov Software Usage Model by ACO", LNCS, Vol. 2724, pp. 2465-2476, Springer Verlag, 2003.
12. M. Dorigo, V. Maniezzo, and A. Colorni, "Positive Feedback as a Search Strategy", Technical Report No. 91-016, Politecnico di Milano, Italy, 1991.
13. M. Dorigo, V. Maniezzo, and A. Colorni, "The Ant System: Optimization by a Colony of Cooperating Agents", *IEEE Transactions on Systems, Man, and Cybernetics-Part B*, 26(1), 1996.
14. J. Heumann, "Introduction to Business Modeling Using the Unified Modeling Language (UML)", http://www.therationaledge.com/content/mar_01/m_uml_jh.html.
15. J. Horgan, S. London, and M. Lyu, "Achieving Software Quality with Testing Coverage Measures", *IEEE Computer*, 27(9), 1994.
16. C. Kaner, J. Falk, and H. Q. Nguyen, *Testing computer software*, 2nd Edition, John Wiley & Sons, 1999.
17. Y. Kim and C. R. Carlson, "Scenario Based Integration Testing for Object-Oriented Software Development", *Proceedings of the Eighth Asian Test Symposium*, Shanghai, 1999.
18. C. P. Lam, M. C. Robey and H. Li, "Application of AI for Automation of Software Testing", *Proc. SNPD03*, Germany, 2003.
19. H. Li and C. P. Lam, "Optimization of State-based Test Suites for Software Systems: An Evolutionary Approach", *International Journal of Computer and Information Science*, 5(3), 2004.
20. H. Li and C. P. Lam, "Software Test Data Generation using Ant Colony Optimization", to appear in *Proc. ICCI 2004*, 2004.
21. P. McMinn and M. Holcombe, "The State Problem for Evolutionary Testing", *Proc. GECCO 2003*, 2003.
22. W. T. Tsai, X. Bai, R. Paul, W. Shao, and V. Agarwal, "End-To-End Integration Testing Design", *Proc. COMPSAC'01*, Chicago, 2001.
23. E. J. Weyuker, "Testing Component-Based Software: A cautionary Tale", *IEEE Software*, 15(5), 1998.

Action Refinement in Conformance Testing

Machiel van der Bijl[1,*], Arend Rensink[1], and Jan Tretmans[2]

[1] Software Engineering, Department of Computer Science, University of Twente,
P.O. Box 217, 7500 AE Enschede, The Netherlands,
{vdbijl, rensink}@cs.utwente.nl
[2] Informatics for Technical Applications,
Nijmegen Institute for Computing and Information Sciences (NIII),
Radboud University, P.O. Box 9010, 6500 GL Nijmegen, The Netherlands,
tretmans@cs.ru.nl

Abstract. In *model based testing* test cases are derived from a model (the specification) of the system we want to test. In general the model is more abstract than the implementation. This may result in test cases that are not executable, because their actions are too abstract; the implementation does not understand them. The standard approach is to rewrite the model by hand to the required level of detail and regenerate the test cases. This is error-prone and time consuming.

In this paper we present an approach to automatically obtain test cases at the required level of detail by means of action refinement. Action refinement is a way to add information to the abstract model. It relates actions from the abstract model to concrete actions of the system under test. We apply this approach to a simple case of action refinement, so-called atomic linear input-inputs refinement. In order to reason about correctness between an abstract model and a concrete implementation we introduce a new implementation relation. We show that this relation is equivalent with the **uioco** implementation relation on the refined model. Furthermore we show under which conditions the refinement of a complete abstract test suite is again complete.

1 Introduction

A problem in model based testing is that the generated test cases may not have the required level of detail, and hence are not executable against the implementation under test. The test cases are generated from the model (the specification) and in general, the model is more abstract than the implementation. The usual solution is to add the required level of detail to the model by hand. This has some obvious drawbacks; it is time consuming and error-prone.

In this paper we use *action refinement* to automatically obtain test cases at the required level of detail. Action refinement has been studied extensively; see Gorrieri and Rensink for an overview [2]. Action refinement adds extra information to the model by relating an action of the model to more detailed behavior.

---

* This research was supported by the dutch research program PROGRESS under project: TES5417: Atomyste – ATOm splitting in eMbedded sYStems TEsting.

F. Khendek and R. Dssouli (Eds.): TestCom 2005, LNCS 3502, pp.81–96, 2005.

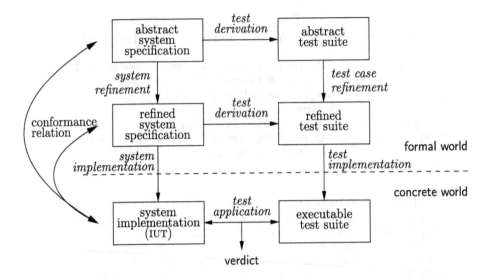

Fig. 1. Action refinement approach

Wherever we read the action in the model we replace it with the more detailed behavior. For example, suppose that the model specifies to input two euros and the implementation also allows the insertion of two one euro pieces. With action refinement we can define that wherever we read two euros we can also read the more detailed behavior one euro followed by one euro. Action refinement in model based testing has not been studied at all. This is surprising, because it is a well known problem in practice and occurs often.

Figure 1 shows our general approach for action refinement in testing. We see six objects in the figure. The objects on the left hand side denote models and the objects on the right hand side denote test suites. **System implementation** is the system that we want to test, also known as IUT (Implementation Under Test); a real system in the physical world. **Abstract system specification** is a (formal) model of the system implementation. It is called *abstract* because it does not have the required level of detail with respect to the system implementation. **Refined system specification** is the refined model of the system implementation with the required level of abstraction with respect to the system implementation. **Abstract test suite** is the test suite that is derived from the abstract system specification. As with the abstract system specification, it is too abstract with respect to the system implementation. **Refined test suite** is a test suite with the required level of abstraction with respect to the system implementation. There are two ways to derive such a test suite. One way is to refine the abstract test suite, another way is to derive test cases from the refined system specification. We do both and proof both approaches to be equivalent under certain restrictions. **Executable test suite** is a test suite in the physical world that we can execute against the system implementation. This results in a verdict whether or not the implementation is correct with respect to the refined (or abstract) system specification. This notion of correctness is defined in a so-called *implementation relation* between the system specification (abstract or refined) and the system implementation. The conformance relation is depicted on the left side of the Figure.

This paper is a first step in our effort towards action refinement in model based testing and we use a simple, though non-trivial case of action refinement: *atomic linear input-inputs refinement*.

In this paper we show how to refine traces, transition systems and test cases. In order to reason about correctness between an abstract specification and a concrete implementation we introduce the implementation relation **uioco**$_r$ and we show that it is equivalent with **uioco** between the refined specification and the same implementation (**uioco** is a further evolution of **ioco**; see [4] and [6]). We show under which conditions the refinement of a complete abstract test suite results in a complete refined test suite.

The main contribution of this paper is that refinement of a complete test suite results in a complete refined test suite (under certain restrictions). Furthermore we argue that our approach for atomic linear input-inputs refinement can be extended to more general types of action refinement. This extension is the next step in our research. One of the surprising (theoretic) consequences of this paper is that specification equivalence is not preserved by action refinement.

We start with summarizing some results and notations that we will use throughout the paper in Section 2. In Section 3 we introduce atomic linear input-inputs refinement. We present trace refinement in Section 4 and the refinement of labeled transition systems in Section 5. In Section 6 we present the implementation relation **uioco**$_r$, followed by the refinement of test cases in Section 7. Conclusions can be found in Section 8.

2   Formal Preliminaries

This section recalls some aspects of the theory behind **uioco** that are used in this paper; see [6] and [4] for a more detailed exposition.

Labeled Transition Systems. A labeled transition system (LTS) description is defined in terms of states and labeled transitions between states, where the labels indicate what happens during the transition. Labels are taken from a global set $\mathbf{L}$. We use a special label $\tau \notin \mathbf{L}$ to denote an internal action. For arbitrary $L \subseteq \mathbf{L}$, we use L_τ as a shorthand for $L \cup \{\tau\}$. We partition the label set of an LTS in an input and output set; a deviation from the standard definition of labeled transition systems.

Definition 1. *A labeled transition system is a 5-tuple $\langle Q, I, U, T, q_0 \rangle$ where Q is a non-empty countable set of states; $I \subseteq \mathbf{L}$ is the countable set of input labels; $U \subseteq \mathbf{L}$ is the countable set of output labels, $I \cap U = \emptyset$; $T \subseteq Q \times (I \cup U \cup \{\tau\}) \times Q$ is a set of triples, the transition relation; $q_0 \in Q$ is the initial state.*

We use L as shorthand for the entire label set $(L = I \cup U)$; furthermore, we use Q_p, I_p etc. to denote the components of an LTS p. We commonly write $q \xrightarrow{\mu} q'$ for $(q, \mu, q') \in T$. We use a question mark before a label to denote that it is input and an exclamation mark to denote that it is output. We denote the class of all labeled transition systems over I and U by $\mathcal{LTS}(I, U)$. We represent a labeled transition system in the standard way, by a directed, edge-labeled graph where nodes represent states and edges represent transitions.

A state that cannot do an internal action is called *stable*. A stable state from which no output action is possible is called *quiescent*. We use the symbol δ $(\notin \mathbf{L}_\tau)$ to represent quiescence: $p \xrightarrow{\delta} p$ stands for the absence of any transition $p \xrightarrow{\mu} p'$ with $\mu \in U_\tau$. For an arbitrary $L \subseteq \mathbf{L}$, we use L_δ as a shorthand for $L \cup \{\delta\}$. We use the label μ, respectively λ to range over $\mathbf{L}_\tau$, respectively $\mathbf{L}_{\tau\delta}$.

An LTS is *strongly responsive* if it always eventually enters a quiescent state; in other words, if it does not have any infinite U_τ-labeled paths. The **ioco** theory is restricted to strongly responsive systems, hence we also use this restriction.

A *trace* is a sequence of observable actions. The set of all traces over L $(\subseteq \mathbf{L})$ is denoted by L^*, ranged over by σ, with ϵ denoting the empty sequence. If $\sigma_1, \sigma_2 \in L^*$, then $\sigma_1 \cdot \sigma_2$ is the concatenation of σ_1 and σ_2. Concatenation is extended in the standard way to sets of traces and also to $\Sigma \cdot a$ where Σ is a set of traces and a an action. We use the standard notation with single and double arrows for traces: $q \xrightarrow{\lambda_1 \cdots \lambda_n} q$ denotes $q \xrightarrow{\lambda_1} \cdots \xrightarrow{\lambda_n} q'$, $q \xRightarrow{\epsilon} q'$ denotes $q \xrightarrow{\tau \cdots \tau} q'$ and $q \xRightarrow{\lambda_1 \cdots \lambda_n} q$ denotes $q \xRightarrow{\epsilon} \xrightarrow{\lambda_1} \xRightarrow{\epsilon} \cdots \xrightarrow{\lambda_n} \xRightarrow{\epsilon} q'$. We will use Σ to denote a set of traces. If $\sigma = \lambda_1 \cdots \lambda_n$ then $\sigma|i = \lambda_i$ where $1 \leq i \leq |\sigma| = n$, and $L(\sigma) = \{\lambda_1, \cdots, \lambda_n\}$. We use the symbol $\sqsubseteq$ to denote trace prefix and the symbol $\downarrow$ to denote prefix closure, as follows: $\sigma_1 \sqsubseteq \sigma \Leftrightarrow \exists \sigma_2 : \sigma_1 \cdot \sigma_2 = \sigma$, $\downarrow \sigma = \{\sigma' \mid \sigma' \sqsubseteq \sigma\}$, $\downarrow \Sigma = \bigcup \{\downarrow \sigma \mid \sigma \in \Sigma\}$

We will not always distinguish between a labeled transition system and its initial state. We will identify the process $p = \langle Q, I, U, T, q_0 \rangle$ with its initial state q_0, and we write, for example, $p \xRightarrow{\sigma} q_1$ instead of $q_0 \xRightarrow{\sigma} q_1$.

Input-output transition systems. We call a labeled transition system that is completely specified for input actions an *input-output transition system* (IOTS). This means that all states can do all input actions from the label set, if necessary by first doing one or more internal actions. The class of input-output transition systems with input actions in I and output actions in U is denoted by $\mathcal{IOTS}(I, U)$ $(\subseteq \mathcal{LTS}(I, U))$.

Definition 2. *An input-output transition system $p = \langle Q, I, U, T, q_0 \rangle$ is a labeled transition system for which all inputs are enabled in all states:* $\forall q \in Q, a \in I :$ $q \xRightarrow{a}$ *(weak input enabledness).*

Conformance. The testing scenario on which **uioco** is based wants to establish a notion of conformance between a specification and an implementation [4]. The specification is an LTS, specifying the required behavior. Since the testing approach is black box testing, we do not know anything about the implementation;

however, we *assume* that it is possible to model it as an IOTS. This assumption is referred to as the test hypothesis [1].

Given a specification s and an (assumed) model of the implementation i, the relation i **ioco**$_\mathcal{F}$ s expresses that i conforms to s based on a set of traces $\mathcal{F}$. This is formalized as follows: Let $s \in \mathcal{LTS}(I, U)$, $i \in \mathcal{IOTS}(I, U)$, $S \subseteq Q_s$ be a set of states in s, $\sigma \in \mathbf{L}_\delta^*$ and $\mathcal{F} \subseteq \mathbf{L}_\delta^*$.

$$s \text{ after } \sigma =_{\text{def}} \{s' \mid s \stackrel{\sigma}{\Longrightarrow} s'\} \tag{1}$$

$$out(s) =_{\text{def}} \{x \in U \mid s \stackrel{x}{\longrightarrow}\} \cup \{\delta \mid s \stackrel{\delta}{\longrightarrow}\} \tag{2}$$

$$out(S) =_{\text{def}} \bigcup \{out(s) \mid s \in S\} \tag{3}$$

$$Straces(s) =_{\text{def}} \{\sigma \in \mathbf{L}_\delta^* \mid s \stackrel{\sigma}{\Longrightarrow}\} \tag{4}$$

$$Utraces(s) =_{\text{def}} \{\sigma \in Straces(s) \mid \forall q, (\sigma_1 \cdot a) \sqsubseteq \sigma :$$
$$(a \in I \wedge s \stackrel{\sigma_1}{\Longrightarrow} q) \text{ implies } q \stackrel{a}{\Longrightarrow}\} \tag{5}$$

$$i \text{ ioco}_\mathcal{F} s =_{\text{def}} \forall \sigma \in \mathcal{F} : out(i \text{ after } \sigma) \subseteq out(s \text{ after } \sigma) \tag{6}$$

For $\mathcal{F} = Straces(s)$ we abbreviate **ioco**$_\mathcal{F}$ to **ioco** and for $\mathcal{F} = Utraces(s)$ to **uioco**. In other words **ioco** is based on suspension traces (*Straces*: traces in L_δ^*) whereas **uioco** is based on a subset of suspension traces: universal traces. All states that a universal trace leads to can do the same set of input actions. This is a necessary prerequisite to make **uioco** a pre-congruence for parallel composition and hiding.

Test cases. A test case is the specification of a tester in an experiment with the system under test. It is modeled as a special labeled transition system with **pass** and **fail** predicates on states to decide about the success of a test. It is a special LTS because it has the following restrictions:

Definition 3. *A test case* $t = \langle Q, S, R, T, t_0, \mathbf{pass}, \mathbf{fail} \rangle$ *over a set of stimuli* S *and a set of responses* R *is an acyclic labeled transition system such that:*
∘ t *is deterministic and has finite behavior.*
∘ **pass** $\subseteq Q$, **fail** $\subseteq Q$. **pass** *and* **fail** *states do not have outgoing transitions.*
∘ *A state in* Q *that is no* **pass** *or* **fail** *state has either* one *outgoing transition with a stimulus label, or has outgoing transitions for all labels in* R.

The class of test cases over S and R is denoted as $\mathcal{TEST}(S, R)$. A *test suite* T is a set of test cases: $T \subseteq \mathcal{TEST}(S, R)$. An implementation $i \in \mathcal{IOTS}(I, U)$ **passes** a test case $t \in \mathcal{TEST}(I, U_\delta)$ if there is no suspension trace of i that leads to a **fail** state in t. Note that a stimulus of the test case is an input of the implementation and vice versa for the responses.

Definition 4. *Let* $s \in \mathcal{LTS}(I, U)$ *be a specification and* $T \subseteq \mathcal{TEST}(I, U_\delta)$ *a test suite; then for the implementation relation* **uioco**:
T *is* **complete** $=_{\text{def}} \forall i \in \mathcal{IOTS}(I, U) : i$ **uioco** $s \Leftrightarrow i$ **passes** T
T *is* **sound** $=_{\text{def}} \forall i \in \mathcal{IOTS}(I, U) : i$ **uioco** $s \Rightarrow i$ **passes** T
T *is* **exhaustive** $=_{\text{def}} \forall i \in \mathcal{IOTS}(I, U) : i$ **uioco** $s \Leftarrow i$ **passes** T

3   Atomic Input-Inputs Action Refinement

As stated in the introduction we treat the problem that test cases derived from a specification may not be executable on the system under test. Example 1 illustrates this problem (we use this as our running example).

Example 1. In Figure 2 we see a specification (left) and a refined specification (right) of a simple data entry application (forget the state labels for now). The specification tells us that we can enter address data, push the store button after which the system either stores the address data (ok) or returns nok. Suppose that our specification is too abstract, because an address is entered in three steps: street, city and postal code, like the refined specification on the right.

The left hand side of Figure 3 shows a test case generated from the abstract specification. On the right we see two test cases with the required level of detail to test the actual system. We can read the abstract test case as follows: enter the address data, press the store button and then observe the response of the IUT. The IUT passes the test if we observe ok or nok, but fails when we observe quiescence. Note that the direction of inputs and outputs in the test case are reversed with respect to the specification.

Of course the data entry example is very simple, because of its educational purposes. This may give the illusion that refinement of transition systems and test cases is straightforward. The more extended technical report of this paper shows that simple refinements may quickly result in a complex system [7].

There are several types of action refinement [5]. In this paper we treat *atomic linear input-inputs refinement*. Atomic means that no actions are allowed to interfere with the refinement; we treat the behavior of the refinement as atomic. Linear means that we allow no branching behavior in the refinement and input-inputs means that we only refine an input action with one or more other input actions. The refinement in Figure 2 is an example of such a refinement. It is

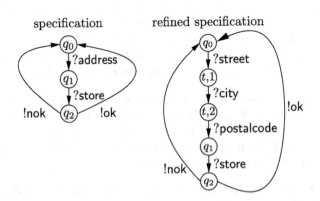

Fig. 2. Abstract and refined specification of data entry system

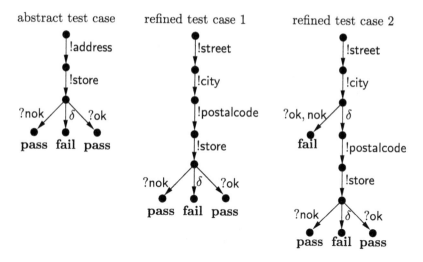

Fig. 3. Abstract and refined test cases for data entry example

our goal to extend this action refinement approach in the future to more general cases of action refinement. We believe that this can be done in a similar way as the atomic linear input-inputs refinement case that we treat in this paper, as we discuss in the concluding section.

In this paper we show what correctness means in terms of a conformance relation between the abstract system specification and the system implementation. Furthermore we show two ways to obtain a refined test suite as shown in Figure 1. One is to refine the abstract system specification and derive a refined test suite and the other is to refine the abstract test suite directly. We show that both approaches are equivalent under some restrictions.

Sometimes we use the terms abstract and concrete as synonyms for unrefined and refined, respectively .

4   Trace Refinement

We define refinement as a pair $r = (a_r, \sigma_r)$ with respect to an input label set I and an output label set U. a_r is the *refinement label*, i.e., the abstract label that we want to refine and σ_r is the *refinement trace*, i.e., the trace that we want to replace the refinement label with. There are the following restrictions: $a_r \in I$, $L(\sigma_r) \cap L_\delta = \emptyset$ (the labels in σ_r are fresh) and $\sigma_r \neq \epsilon$.

In cases where there may be confusion about label sets we use the subscript r to tag the label set after refinement, for example: $I_r = (I \backslash \{a_r\}) \cup L(\sigma_r)$.

The goal of trace refinement is to refine a trace from an abstract specification such that it becomes a trace of the refined system. In a refined trace all occurrences of the refinement label have been replaced with its refinement.

Input-inputs refinement allows quiescence within a refinement. To get all possible suspension traces within the refinement trace, we saturate the refinement trace with δ's (this technicality is explained in Example 2).

Definition 5 (δ-saturation). *Let* $\sigma = a_1 \cdots a_n$ *then* $\lceil \sigma \rceil = a_1 \cdot \delta^* \cdot a_2 \cdots \delta^* \cdot a_n$

The refinement of a trace results in a set of traces. All labels except the refinement label a_r are unchanged. The refinement label is substituted with every trace in $\lceil \sigma_r \rceil$. Formally this is expressed as follows.

Definition 6 (Trace refinement). *Let* $\sigma \in L_\delta^*$ *then* $\sigma[r]$ *denotes the refinement of a trace in the following way.*

$$\sigma[r] = \begin{cases} 1) \ \{\epsilon\} & \text{if } \sigma = \epsilon \\ 2) \ \{\sigma_2 \cdot \lambda \mid \sigma_2 \in \sigma_1[r]\} & \text{if } \sigma = \sigma_1 \cdot \lambda \wedge \lambda \in L_\delta \backslash \{a_r\} \\ 3) \ \{\sigma_2 \cdot \sigma' \mid \sigma_2 \in \sigma_1[r] \wedge \sigma' \in \lceil \sigma_r \rceil\} & \text{if } \sigma = \sigma_1 \cdot a_r \end{cases}$$

Likewise we define refinement on sets of traces by refining all traces in the set.

An important concept in this paper is the concept of an *r-complete* trace. This is a trace that does not end in the middle of a refinement; or in other words, a trace σ is r-complete when $\sigma \in L_\delta^*[r]$.

Trace *contraction* is the opposite of trace refinement. The goal of trace contraction is to transform a concrete trace to a trace of the abstract system.

Definition 7 (Trace contraction). *Let* $r = (a_r, \sigma_r), \sigma \in \downarrow(L_\delta^*[r])$.

$$\sigma\langle r \rangle = \begin{cases} 1) \ \epsilon & \text{if } \sigma = \epsilon \\ 2) \ \sigma_1\langle r \rangle \cdot a_r & \text{if } \sigma = \sigma_1 \cdot \sigma_2 \wedge \sigma_2 \in \lceil \sigma_r \rceil \\ 3) \ \sigma_1\langle r \rangle & \text{if } \sigma = \sigma_1 \cdot \sigma_2 \wedge \sigma_2 \in \downarrow \lceil \sigma_r \rceil \backslash (\lceil \sigma_r \rceil \cup \{\epsilon\}) \\ 4) \ \sigma_1\langle r \rangle \cdot \lambda & \text{if } \sigma = \sigma_1 \cdot \lambda \text{ and none of the above holds} \end{cases}$$

Likewise we define contraction on sets of traces by contracting traces in the set.

Example 2. Let us illustrate trace refinement and trace contraction with our running example in Figure 2. We refine the action address into street followed by city followed by postalcode: the refinement pair is $r = $ (address, street·city·postalcode). Suppose we want to refine the trace address·store·ok. This results in the following set of traces of the refined specification.

$$\begin{aligned} \text{(address·store·ok)}[r] &= \text{(address·store)}[r]\text{·ok} & \text{(rule 2)} \\ &= \text{address}[r]\text{·store·ok} & \text{(rule 2)} \\ &= \text{street·}\delta^*\text{·city·}\delta^*\text{·postalcode·store·ok} & \text{(rule 3)} \end{aligned}$$

To contract street·δ·city·postalcode·store·ok·street·δ, we obtain the following:

$$\begin{aligned} \text{(street·}\delta\text{·city·postalcode·store·ok·street·}\delta)\langle r \rangle & \\ &= \text{(street·}\delta\text{·city·postalcode·store·ok)}\langle r \rangle & \text{(rule 3)} \\ &= \text{(street·}\delta\text{·city·postalcode·store)}\langle r \rangle\text{·ok} & \text{(rule 4)} \\ &= \text{(street·}\delta\text{·city·postalcode)}\langle r \rangle\text{·store·ok} & \text{(rule 4)} \\ &= \text{address·store·ok} & \text{(rule 2)} \end{aligned}$$

5   Atomic Refinement of Transition Systems

In this section we present a way to refine transition systems. The crux of this refinement is that we make a transition system from our refinement trace and insert this into the abstract transition system at the place where there is a transition with the abstract refinement label. A formal definition is given in Definition 8, it is illustrated in Example 3.

Definition 8 (Atomic transition system refinement). *Let* $r = (a_r, \sigma_r)$ *be the refinement pair and let* $p = \langle Q, I, U, T, q_0 \rangle$ *be an LTS. We define the refinement of* p *as* $p[r] = \langle Q_r, I_r, U_r, T_r, q_0 \rangle$. *For a transition* $t = (q, a_r, q')$, *we use* $(t, 0) = q$ *and* $(t, n) = q'$ *for* $n = |\sigma_r|$.

$Q_r = Q \cup \{(t, i) \mid \exists q, q' \in Q : t = (q, a_r, q') \in T, 1 \leq i < n = |\sigma_r|\}$

$I_r = I \backslash \{a_r\} \cup I(\sigma_r)$

$T' = \{((t, i), \sigma_r|_{i+1}, (t, i+1)) \mid \exists q, q' \in Q : t = (q, a_r, q') \in T, 0 \leq i \leq |\sigma_r| - 1\}$

$T_r = \{(q, a, q') \in T \mid a \neq a_r\} \cup T'$

To prevent confusion between transitions in the abstract and refined transition system we add the subscript 'r' to the transition arrow for refined systems: $q \overset{\sigma}{\Longrightarrow}_r q'$. Likewise we use the subscript for the set of states, transitions, etc., as shown in the definition.

Example 3. We use our running example in Figure 2 to explain Definition 8 (the states are numbered according to this definition). For the abstract transition $t = (q_0, \mathsf{address}, q_1)$ we add the states $(t, 1)$ and $(t, 2)$ to Q_r ($(t, 0)$ and $(t, 3)$ correspond to states q_0 and q_1 respectively). T' consists of the transitions: $((t, 0), \mathsf{street}, (t, 1)), ((t, 1), \mathsf{city}, (t, 2))$ and $((t, 2), \mathsf{postalcode}, (t, 3))$. In T_r we delete the $\mathsf{address}$ transition from the set of abstract transitions and we add T'. We add all labels from the refinement trace: $\{\mathsf{street}, \mathsf{city}, \mathsf{postalcode}\}$ to I_r and delete the refinement label "$\mathsf{address}$" (the output label set stays the same).

Lemma 1 states that the prefix closure of the refined *Utraces* of the abstract specification equals the set of *Utraces* of the refined specification. This result holds because we defined trace refinement in such a way that the refinement of a trace results in a trace from the refined system. To include traces that end in the middle of the refinement, we apply the prefix closure.

Lemma 1. $\downarrow(Utraces(s)[r]) = Utraces(s[r])$

Lemma 2 states that for completely refined *Utraces* the set of outputs after such a trace in the refined system equals the set of outputs in the abstract system after the contracted trace. This holds because r-complete traces end in states that come from the abstract system (old states). Because atomic linear input-inputs refinement does not add outputs to the refined system, the output behavior of the old states is not altered by the refinement.

Lemma 2. $\forall \sigma \in Utraces(s)[r] : out(s[r] \ \mathbf{after} \ \sigma) = out(s \ \mathbf{after} \ \sigma \langle r \rangle)$

For not completely refined *Utraces* (traces in $\downarrow(Utraces(s)[r]) \backslash Utraces(s)[r]))$ Lemma 3 states that the only output of the refined specification after such a trace is quiescence. This holds because not r-complete utraces end inside the refinement (in new states). Because our refinement does not add outputs, the only allowed output inside the refinement is quiescence.

Lemma 3. $\forall \sigma \in \downarrow(Utraces(s)[r]) \backslash Utraces(s)[r] : out(s[r] \text{ after } \sigma) = \{\delta\}$

6   Uioco$_r$ for Testing Refined Systems

We introduce the implementation relation **uioco**$_r$ that express correctness of the concrete implementation in terms of the abstract specification and the refinement pair. We show that **uioco**$_r$ is equivalent to **uioco** for refined specifications.

Definition 9 (uioco$_r$). *Let* $s \in \mathcal{LTS}(I_1, U)$, $i \in \mathcal{IOTS}(I_2, U)$, $r = (a_r, \sigma_r)$, $I_2 = I_1 \backslash \{a_r\} \cup I(\sigma_r)$.
i **uioco**$_r$ $s =_{\text{def}} \forall \sigma \in \downarrow(Utraces(s)[r]) :$
$\qquad\qquad$ *if* $\sigma \in Utraces(s)[r]$ *then* $out(i \text{ after } \sigma) \subseteq out(s \text{ after } \sigma\langle r\rangle)$
$\qquad\qquad$ *else* $out(i \text{ after } \sigma) \subseteq \{\delta\}$

For completely refined *Utraces* the allowed output behavior of the implementation is restricted to the output behavior of the abstract specification after the contracted trace (see Lemma 2). For not completely refined *Utraces* the allowed output behavior of the implementation is restricted to quiescence (see Lemma 3). Because of Lemma 1 we know that we have covered all possible traces of the refined specification. Theorem 1 states the equality between **uioco**$_r$ and **uioco**.

Theorem 1. *Let* $s \in \mathcal{LTS}(I_1, U), i \in \mathcal{IOTS}(I_2, U)$, $r = (a_r, \sigma_r)$, *and* $I_2 = I_1 \backslash \{a_r\} \cup I(\sigma_r)$

$$i \text{ \textbf{uioco}}_r \ s \Leftrightarrow i \text{ \textbf{uioco} } s[r]$$

Example 4. We look again at the abstract and refined specification in Figure 2, to illustrate Definition 9 and Theorem 1. We use the following two traces: street·city·postalcode·store is a complete refinement of address·store and street·city a not complete refinement. Both traces are in the set of *Utraces* of the refined specification, as stated in Lemma 1. The trace address·store leads to state q_2 in the abstract specification and the trace street·city·postalcode·store leads to state q_2 in the refined specification; the set of outputs is in both states the same, conform to Lemma 2. The not r-complete trace street·city leads to state $(t, 2)$ in the refined specification. This state is quiescent, as stated in Lemma 3. When we put these results together, it illustrates that the **uioco**$_r$ definition for the abstract specification is equal to the **uioco** definition for the refined specification.

7   Test Case Refinement

In the previous sections we have shown how to obtain a refined test suite by refining the specification; from this refined specification we can generate a complete test suite. In this section we show how to refine existing abstract test cases, like the test cases shown in Figure 3. Furthermore, we show under what conditions the refinement of a complete abstract test suite results in a complete refined test suite with respect to **uioco**$_r$.

To test inside the refinement we need several test cases (we can make several observations). Therefore we generate a set of mini test cases that test the entire behavior of the refined action. We replace transitions with the refinement label in the abstract test case with these mini test cases.

7.1   Generation of Mini Test Cases

We present an algorithm to generate mini test cases that test the entire behavior inside the refinement. The algorithm is closely related to the test generation algorithm of Tretmans [4]. There are some minor differences:

1. The only pass state is at the end of a mini test case. A possible error can be anywhere within the refinement, so it is no use to stop testing before the end of the refinement.
2. There are no observations at the start and the end state of the mini test. Because atomic linear input-inputs refinement does not add or change output actions we use the observations of the abstract system in these states.

Definition 10 (Generation of mini tests). $MT \subseteq TEST(I(\sigma_r), U_\delta)$, a set of mini tests, is obtained from σ_r (with respect to an input label set I and and output label set U) in the following way. The stimulus and response step are executed in a non-deterministic manner. Let $n = |\sigma_r|$ and $1 \leq i < n$.

Stimulus step $t_i := \sigma_r|_i; t_{i+1}$
Response step $t_i := \sigma_r|_i; (\Sigma\{x; \textbf{fail} \mid x \in U\} \Box \delta; t_{i+1})$
Pass step $t_n \quad := \sigma_r|_n; \textbf{pass}$

The set of mini test is built with the process algebraic operators action prefix (;) and choice ($\Box$ and Σ) in the same style as Tretman's algorithm. For readers that are unfamiliar with this notation, formally we write this as follows:

Let t_i be test cases for $i = 1, 2$ and $\mu \in L_\delta$
; $(\mu; t_1) \xrightarrow{\mu} t_1$
$\Box$ if $t_1 \xrightarrow{\mu} t'_1$ then $t_1 \Box t_2 \xrightarrow{\mu} t'_1$ and $t_2 \Box t_1 \xrightarrow{\mu} t'_1$
Σ if $t_i \xrightarrow{\mu} t'_i$ for $i \in I$ then $\Sigma\{t_i \mid i \in I\} \xrightarrow{\mu} t'_i$

7.2   Test Case Refinement

Test case refinement is similar to LTS refinement. The main difference is that test case refinement results in a *set* of refined test cases, where LTS refinement results in one transition system. The definition is explained in Example 5.

Definition 11. *Given a test case* $t = \langle Q_t, I_t, U_t, T_t, t_0, \textbf{pass}_t, \textbf{fail}_t \rangle$ *and a refinement pair* (a_r, σ_r) *we define test case refinement as follows. Let* MT *be the set of mini tests generated with the algorithm from Definition 10. Let* f *be a*

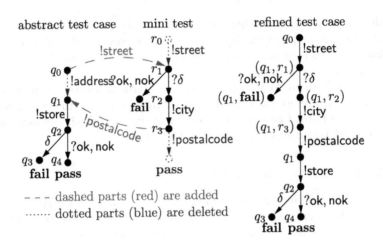

Fig. 4. Example of test case refinement

function from Q_t to MT. For better readability we denote a mini test obtained from f for a state q as $f(q) = \langle Q_q, I_q, U_q, T_q, start_q, \mathbf{pass}_q, \mathbf{fail}_q \rangle$. We assume all states to be unique.

$t[r] = \{t[f] \mid f : Q_t \to MT\}$ *where* $t[f] = \langle Q_f, I_f, U_t, T_f, t_0, \mathbf{pass}_t, \mathbf{fail}_f \rangle$ *is defined as follows.*

$Q_f = Q_t \cup \{(q_2, q) \mid \exists q_1 \in Q_t : (q_1, a_r, q_2) \in T_t \land q \in Q_{q_2} \backslash (\mathbf{pass}_{q_2} \cup \{start_{q_2}\}))\}$

$T_f = \{(q_1, \lambda, (q_2, q)) \mid (q_1, a_r, q_2) \in T_t \land (start_{q_2}, \lambda, q) \in T_{q_2}\}$
$\quad \cup \{((q_2, q), \lambda, q_2) \mid \exists q_1 \in Q_t : (q_1, a_r, q_2) \in T_t \land \exists q_3 \in \mathbf{pass}_{q_2} : (q, \lambda, q_3) \in T_{q_2}\}$
$\quad \cup T_t \backslash \{(q_1, a_r, q_2) \in T_t \mid q_1, q_2 \in Q_t\}$

$I_f = I_t \backslash \{a_r\} \cup I(\sigma_r)$

$\mathbf{pass}_f = \mathbf{pass}_t$

$\mathbf{fail}_f = \mathbf{fail}_t \cup \{(q_1, q_2) \in Q_f \mid q_1 \in Q_t \land q_2 \in \mathbf{fail}_{q_1}\}$

We apply a little mathematical trick with our function f. The function maps the states of the abstract test case to the set of mini tests. For every refinement label transition (q_1, a_r, q_2) we get a mini test $f(q_2)$. We replace the refinement label transition with this mini test. $t[f]$ results in one refined test case and when we combine all possible refinements with f we get a set of refined test cases in which a_r transitions are replaced with all possible mini tests. We illustrate test case refinement in the following example.

Example 5. In Figure 4 we show an abstract test case on the left, a mini test in the middle and the resulting refined test case on the right. We use different types of lines: dashed parts are added, dotted parts are deleted and solid parts remain unchanged.

We delete the refinement label transition, $(q_0, \mathbf{address}, q_1)$ from the abstract test case (dotted transition) and all other transitions are added to T_f. All states are copied to Q_f.

From the mini test we delete the start and pass states. All other states are added to Q_f as a pair with q_1. We delete the transitions from the start state and transitions leading to pass states and add all other transitions to T_f.

To finalize the test case refinement we let the first transition in the mini test start in q_0, the start state of the refinement transition: the striped transition labeled with **street** between q_0 and r_1. In a similar way we redirect the **postalcode** transition to the pass state to q_1. When we reorganize the dashed parts and the black solid parts we obtain the refined test case on the right.

7.3   Completeness of Test Case Refinement

The test suite derived from the refined specification is complete with respect to **uioco** and $s[r]$ and thus with respect to **uioco**$_r$ and s. If we can show that the refinement of a complete test suite results in a complete refined test suite with respect to **uioco**$_r$ and s, we know that both test suites are equivalent under completeness.

As usual we divide completeness in *soundness* and *exhaustiveness* [4]. A test case is sound when it does not end in a fail state when executed against a correct implementation. If every incorrect implementation is detected by the test suite, we call a test suite exhaustive.

Test case refinement is defined in such a way that the refinement of a sound test case with respect to **uioco** and s leads to a sound refined test case with respect to **uioco**$_r$ and s.

Theorem 2 (Soundness of the refined test suite).
   (t is **sound** *w.r.t.* **uioco** *and* s) $\Rightarrow$ ($t[r]$ is **sound** *w.r.t.* **uioco**$_r$ *and* s)

Intuitively this theorem can be explained as follows. Like with LTS refinement we have the property that completely refined *Utraces* of s end in states of the abstract test case, where the output behavior is completely determined by the abstract system (see Lemma 2). Soundness is guaranteed by the soundness of the abstract test case. Not completely refined *Utraces* test the behavior of the refinement, where the output behavior is limited to quiescence (see Lemma 3). Not completely refined traces lead to states from the mini tests. It can be easily seen that mini tests generated with the algorithm in Definition 10 only lead to fail if the observed output is not quiescent.

It turns out that exhaustiveness of the refined test suite does not necessarily follow from exhaustiveness of the abstract test suite. When the abstract test suite fulfills the following property, exhaustiveness of the refined test suite holds.

Definition 12. *Let* $s \in \mathcal{LTS}(I, U)$ *and* $r = (a_r, \sigma_r)$
   $r\text{-}cov(T, s) =_{\text{def}} \forall (\sigma \cdot a_r) \in Utraces(s) : (\exists t \in T : t \xrightarrow{\sigma \cdot a_r})$

The property states that a test suite T covers a specification s with respect to r if for every utrace of s ending in a_r, there is a test case in T that can perform this trace.

Theorem 3 (Exhaustiveness of the refined test suite). *Let $s \in \mathcal{LTS}(I, U)$ and $r = (a_r, \sigma_r)$ and let r-cov(T, s) then*
*(T is **exhaustive** w.r.t. **uioco** and s) $\Rightarrow$ ($T[r]$ is **exhaustive** w.r.t. **uioco**$_r$ and s)*

For exhaustiveness we follow the same line of thought as in the explanation of soundness. If the implementation is not **uioco**$_r$ correct there can be an error in the abstract behavior (from the abstract specification) or in the behavior of the refinement. In case of an error in the abstract behavior, we know that there is a test case that reveals the failure because the abstract test suite is exhaustive.

In case of incorrectness in the refined part of the specification, we run into a problem. It may be that there is an error inside the refinement, but no abstract test case that leads to the refinement. The reason for this is that a complete test suite remains complete when deleting test cases that always lead to pass. The deleted test case may just be the test case that we need to obtain exhaustiveness. We can illustrate this as follows. Suppose that we have a specification that allows all behavior. A test suite with one test case that only consists of a **pass** state is complete. Refinement of this test suite results in the same test suite. Suppose that we have an implementation that can only perform the first refinement action and after that is not quiescent. This implementation is not **uioco**$_r$ correct, but the refined test suite does not have a test case to detect this.

For r-cov test suites exhaustiveness holds, because there always is an abstract test case that leads us to the refinement. Within the refinement only quiescence is allowed as output and because the implementation is not **uioco**$_r$ correct, we know that it is not quiescent. In the mini test generation algorithm we can easily see that such behavior leads to a fail verdict. We illustrate the soundness and exhaustiveness results with an example.

Example 6. **Figure 5** shows an abstract test case (left), a refined test case and two implementations (right) for our data entry system. Both implementations have an error. Implementation 1 is quiescent in state i_3 and implementation 2 allows the output ok in state j_2.

For soundness we want to know if an error detected by a refined test case is indeed an error in the implementation. For implementation 1 we observe quiescence after street, city and postalcode. Our test case leads to fail because it expects ok or nok as observation. Because the fail state is a state from the abstract test case and because we know that the abstract test case is sound, we also know that our refined test case is sound.

For implementation 2, the execution of the refined test case leads to a fail verdict after observing ok after street followed by city. This is a failure within the refinement ($(q_2, \textbf{fail})$ is a new state). Our observation within the refinement is ok and we know that the only allowed output within a refinement is δ. This means that the **fail** verdict is correct and that the test case is sound.

For exhaustiveness we can follow the same line of thought. Suppose the implementation is not **uioco** correct, like implementations 1 and 2, do we have a

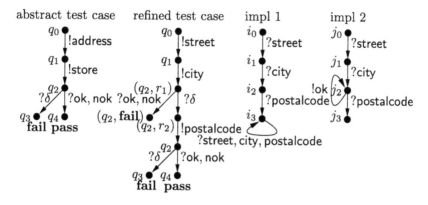

Fig. 5. Figure to illustrate soundness and completeness properties

test case that detects the error? For implementation 1 this is clear: the error is in the abstract part of the system and because the abstract test suite is complete, there is a test case that tests the specific abstract state of the specification. Because this abstract test case is present, we know that the refined test case will detect the error. For an error inside a refinement, like in implementation 2 we have a problem, because it requires that there is an abstract test case that starts with address. As explained earlier, the existence of such a test case is not guaranteed by completeness.

It may be unclear if the r-cov requirement for exhaustiveness can be met. The test case generation algorithm of Tretmans [4] fulfills this requirement (as it does not optimize test suites by deleting test cases).

Corollary 1. *The refinement of a complete test suite generated with Tretmans algorithm for test case generation, is complete with respect to* **uioco**$_r$ *and the abstract specification.*

8   Conclusion

In this paper we have filled in the parts of our action refinement approach in Figure 1 for atomic linear input-inputs refinement. For this special case of action refinement we showed how to refine traces, transition systems and test cases. This enables us to obtain test cases with the required level of detail in an automated way. Furthermore we introduced the implementation relation **uioco**$_r$ that relates the abstract specification to the concrete implementation by using the refinement information in the form of the refinement pair. We showed that a complete test suite can be derived from the refined specification and under which conditions this test suite is equivalent to the refinement of a complete abstract test suite.

Related work. In the light of conformance testing, the problem addressed by this paper is well known in practice. However, no research has been carried out in the field of conformance testing nor in the field of action refinement.

In the context of action refinement, the results of Section 7 have an unexpected consequence. The vast majority of research in action refinement has concentrated on the so-called *coarsest congruence* question (given two equivalent specifications, are they still equivalent after refinement?). In this paper we are not primarily interested in equivalences at all: the core issue is the conformance relation, embodied in **uioco**. Still, an obvious derived equivalence is that of *specification strength* — two specifications are equivalent if they are satisfied by the same set of systems. Surprisingly, this equivalence is *not* preserved even under atomic action refinement, as a side-effect of the fact that test case refinement does not always preserve completeness. This is in contrast to previously studied equivalences; see [2].

Future work. This paper is only a first step; it treats a non-trivial though rather simple form of atomic action refinement. Future research focuses on arbitrary atomic refinement. This means that no actions are allowed to interfere with the refinement, but we drop the linearity and input-inputs constraints. As a result we allow branching (including looping) behavior with a mix of input and output actions. Arbitrary atomic refinement is the next research step.

Some research has been done in comparing Finite State Machine (FSM) testing with LTS based testing [3]. With atomic action refinement we can refine the atomic input output pair from an FSM into two sequential actions. This might give an interesting basis for comparison.

References

1. G. Bernot, M. G. Gaudel, and B. Marre. Software testing based on formal specifications: a theory and a tool. *Software Engineering Journal*, (November), 1991.
2. R. Gorrieri and A. Rensink. Action refinement. In *Handbook of Process Algebra*, chapter 16, pages 1047–1147. Elsevier, 2001.
3. A. Petrenko, G. v. Bochmann, and R. Dssouli. Conformance relations and test derivation. In *IWPTSVI*, pages 157–178. North-Holland, 1994.
4. J. Tretmans. Test generation with inputs, outputs and repetitive quiescence. *Software—Concepts and Tools*, 17(3):103–120, 1996.
5. M. van der Bijl, A. Rensink, and J. Tretmans. Action refinement roadmap. Technical report, University of Twente, 2004. URL: http://www.cs.utwente.nl/~vdbijl/papers.
6. M. van der Bijl, A. Rensink, and J. Tretmans. Compositional testing with ioco. In *FATES 2003*, volume 2931 of *LNCS*, pages 86–100. Springer, 2004.
7. M. van der Bijl, A. Rensink, and J. Tretmans. Action refinement in conformance testing. Technical report, University of Twente, 2005. URL: http://www.cs.utwente.nl/~vdbijl/papers.

Multiplexing of Partially Ordered Events

Colin Campbell[1], Margus Veanes[1], Jiale Huo[2,*], and Alexandre Petrenko[3]

[1] Microsoft Research, Redmond, WA, USA
{colin, margus}@microsoft.com
[2] McGill University, Montreal, Quebec, Canada
jiale.huo@mail.mcgill.ca
[3] Centre de Recherche Informatique de Montreal, Quebec, Canada
petrenko@crim.ca

Abstract. This paper introduces a method to correctly order events in model-based testing for concurrent systems, in particular multi-threaded programs, whose events are only partially ordered. For a sequential, centralized tester, we need to merge (local) traces of each component into a (global) trace of a system in such a way that the ordering constraints are observed. To this end, we instrument a multi-threaded program under test so that the order of lock events is visible. This additional information helps a so-called multiplexer to reconstruct a fully serial trace consistent with the partial order. We describe programs and the multiplexer as labeled transition systems and give pseudo-code of the algorithm implementing the latter. The implementation of the algorithm presented is used in an industrial context.

1 Introduction

Model-based conformance testing checks whether an implementation is behaviorally consistent with its specification. Formally, this check is performed with respect to a correctness criterion called conformance relation. Such testing is carried out by a tester or a testing tool. An industrial software test engineer usually writes a test harness to provide an interface (API) between the tester and the implementation under test (IUT), so that the two entities can interact with each other. The interface is symmetric in the sense that it specifies the methods that the tester can use to influence the IUT and the methods that the IUT can use to pass information back to the tester.

The tester uses a model or specification as a reference of the IUT's behavior. The verdict of a particular test run depends on whether the observed behavior conforms to the specified behavior or not. For sequential systems, such as single-threaded programs, events can be observed in the order they occur. In concurrent systems, such as multi-threaded programs and distributed systems, events of individual agents (an agent being a thread or, in distributed systems, a process) can still be observed in the order they occur, but there are typically many possible ways in which events of different agents can be

---

* Part of the work was carried out during the author's internship at Microsoft Research, Redmond.

F. Khendek and R. Dssouli (Eds.): TestCom 2005, LNCS 3502, pp. 97–110, 2005.

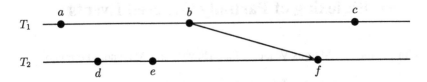

Fig. 1. Example of partially ordered events of a concurrent system

interleaved. In this paper, we consider the problem that a sequential, centralizaed tester is used to test concurrent systems. Due to its sequential nature, the tester requires a linearized view of all the events of all agents. Other approaches consider using several distributed testers to test concurrent systems, see e.g. [5].

A problem with the single tester scenario is that, even if all the events of all agents are totally ordered according to a timeline with sufficiently fine precision, the order in which the events are observed by the tester may still differ from the actual one due to buffering and communication delays. If the agents in the IUT interact and this interaction is important to the conformance relation, observing the events out of order may result in false positives (a correct IUT failing a test) or false negatives (a wrong IUT passing a test), rendering the conformance checking unsound. (On the other hand, if the agents do not interact, they can be tested independently or concurrently by independent testers, and the need to observe the events in the corret order does not arise in the first place.) Inter-agent communication usually imposes a partial order of events defined by constraints on message communication, e.g. send-events happen before corresponding receive-events. In multi-threaded programs, a partial order of events is defined by the access of shared resources. For example, a lock has to be released by a thread before it can be acquired by another thread. In general, an event of one agent may depend on an event of another agent and therefore cannot occur before the latter. The sequence of events observed by the tester must not violate the dependency among the events.

Figure 1 illustrates events of a concurrent system with two agents using a space-time diagram [15]. The events of each agent are depicted as dots located on a per-agent timeline, on which an event x of the agent is drawn to the left of an event y of the agent if and only if x occurs before y, i.e. y depends locally on x. Inter-agent dependencies are indicated by arrows. In this system, event f of agent T_2 depends on event b of agent T_1, and therefore b must precede f. In this case the trace *daebfc* is consistent with the dependencies whereas the trace *daefbc* is not. In general, a trace is consistent with the partial order if and only if the trace represents an outcome of topological sorting, called a linearization, of the partial order.

In a system where all agents and all events are observed, it is straightforward to produce a linearization of the partial order of the events. For example, this is the case in a distributed system where each process is instrumented to produce unique send-events and receive-events of messages exchanged between the processes [11]. By using time stamps [14] all processes need not be observed but all communication relations must be augmented with a vector time stamps. When dealing with multi-threaded programs such instrumentations are often either impossible or undesirable. Threads do not directly communicate with each other, but synchronize through shared resourses, such as locks. Lock events are not normally observable to the tester because they are internal to the implementation. The abstraction level at which they occur is lower than that of the model; as a consequence, lock events are not even mentioned in the model.

A naive attempt to reorder events in multi-threaded programs could be achieved by assigning a time stamp to each observable event with respect to a global clock and then sorting the events using the time stamps. However, modern computer hardware architectures may render the time stamping approach infeasible. For example, consider a program written for a multi-processor hardware architecture in which memory writes are local to each processor until an explicit memory-serialization operation occurs. Between two memory-serialization operations, the system never arrives in a single global state that can be seen uniformly by all processors. Hence, it seems impossible to use time stamps of a global clock to serialize the events occurring between two memory-serialization operations. Moreover, using a global clock may substantially alter the behavior being tested by introducing unwanted synchronization when the clock itself is a shared resource.

Another attempt to reconstruct a linearization from the observations would be to keep a centralized log of events [16]. In this scheme, each agent reports its events to a central, serialized log. Unfortunately, such a log introduces additional synchronization in multi-threaded programs because the very operation of writing into the log by each thread requires locking and unlocking the log. This additional synchronization could affect the possible behavior of the system and could eliminate certain errors. In other words, the instrumentation of the system would itself prevent some invalid behaviors from occurring. Undetected errors would occur once the system is no longer in "testing mode".

Our solution relies on additional assumptions about the implementation and instruments the implementation in such a way that the order in which locks are used becomes observable. We use a program called multiplexer that takes as its input sequences of events (with lock events included) of each agent and merges the event sequences into a single sequence that preserves the order of lock events. We show that if all the shared resources in the implementation are protected by locks then the merged event sequence is a valid linearization.

In 1978, Lamport described the inadequacy of using fully sequential time as a way to understand the runs of distributed systems [15]. His formulation of partially ordered distributed runs is consistent with the view presented in this paper, and like Lamport we use incrementing counters as a way to encode ordering constraints. However, the algorithm he presented focuses more on runtime synchronization (for example, as a way to solve the mutual exclusion problem), whereas our algorithm assumes proper synchronization in the concurrent system under test and validates its behavior with respect to a serial model of evolving system state.

The rest of the paper is organized as follows. Preliminaries are provided in Section 2. In Section 3, we formalize threads, shared resources and locks. Then, we describe the multiplexer formally in Section 4. The instrumentation of lock events is realized by extending the events with *usage counts* that indicate the order in which a lock is used by agents. We show that by using the multiplexer, the behavior of a multi-threaded program can be given a consistent serial interpretation. In Section 5, we outline the algorithm underlying the multiplexer and mention its application in Section 6. Conclusions and discussions of future work are provided in Section 7.

2   Preliminaries

We use labeled transition systems (LTS) to describe the behavior of multi-threaded programs. A labeled transition system L has the following components: a nonempty set S of *states*; a nonempty subset S^{init} of S called *initial states*; a set Σ of *external actions*; a set Σ^{H} of *internal actions*, $\Sigma^{\text{H}} \cap \Sigma = \emptyset$; a *transition relation* $\delta \subseteq S \times (\Sigma \cup \Sigma^{\text{H}}) \times S$. L is denoted by the tuple $(S, S^{\text{init}}, \delta, \Sigma, \Sigma^{\text{H}})$. We sometimes index a component by L, unless L is clear from the context. Note that the sets of states and actions may be infinite. Given a transition $e = (s, a, t) \in \delta$; s is the *source* of e, t is the *target* of e, and a is the *label* of e; if $a \in \Sigma^{\text{H}}$ then e is an *internal* transition. The set of actions *enabled* or *defined* in a state s, denoted by $En(s)$, is the set of all labels of transitions whose source is s:

$$En(s) = \{a \in \Sigma \cup \Sigma^{\text{H}} | (\exists t \in S)(s, a, t) \in \delta\}.$$

A nonempty sequence α of external actions is called a *trace of L in state* s_1 if there exist actions $a_1, \ldots, a_k \in \Sigma \cup \Sigma^{\text{H}}$ and states $s_1, \ldots, s_{k+1} \in S$ such that $(s_i, a_i, s_{i+1}) \in \delta$ for $1 \leq i \leq k$ and α is the projection of $a_1 \cdots a_k$ onto the set Σ. We write $Tr(s)$ to denote the set of all traces of L in state s; given $X \subseteq S$ we write $Tr(X)$ to denote $\bigcup_{s \in X} Tr(s)$, and we write $Tr(L)$ for $Tr(S^{\text{init}})$.

An LTS is *deterministic* if it has a single initial state, it has no internal transitions, and it has no transitions with the same source and label but distinct targets. If an LTS L is deterministic, it is convenient to view the transition relation as a partial function so that, given an action a that is enabled in a state s, $\delta_L(s, a)$ denotes the target of the transition in L whose source is s and label is a. For any LTS L there exists a deterministic LTS $Det(L)$ such that $Tr(L) = Tr(Det(L))$.

Example 1. The state machines in Figure 2 are deterministic LTSs. They model components of a multi-threaded program that adds and deletes elements from a shared bag R_1. For simplicity, the maximum capacity of the bag is restricted to a single element here but can easily be generalized to any number of elements. The bag is empty in the initial

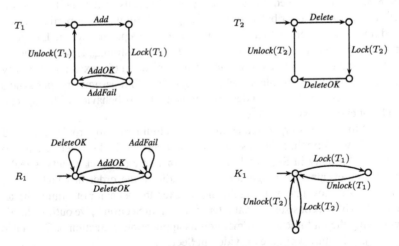

Fig. 2. Components of a system with two threads adding and deleting elements from a bag

state and full in the other state. When empty, an element can be added to the bag, that is denoted by the action *AddOK*. Intuitively this action represents a successful attempt (method invocation) to add an element to the bag. The other action *AddFail* represents a failing attempt to add an element to the bag. Deleting an element from the bag always succeeds, even if there is nothing to delete. K_1 models a lock that protects the bag; it can be acquired (locked) and released (unlocked) by the two threads T_1 and T_2. T_1 models a thread executing a function *Add*. After *Add* is called, the thread acquires the lock K_1. It then either successfully adds an element or fails to add an element to the bag. This nondeterminism is resolved by the state of the bag (whether it is full or not). Finally, the lock is released and the behavior is repeated. T_2 models a thread that deletes elements from the bag.

Parallel composition of LTSs formalizes the interaction of several systems. In a composition of two LTSs the two systems will synchronize on shared external actions, and asynchronously interleave all other actions. Let $L_1 = (S_1, S_1^{\text{init}}, \delta_1, \Sigma_1, \Sigma_1^{\text{H}})$ and $L_2 = (S_2, S_2^{\text{init}}, \delta_2, \Sigma_2, \Sigma_2^{\text{H}})$ be two LTSs such that $\Sigma_i^{\text{H}} \cap \Sigma_j = \emptyset$, The (*parallel*) composition of L_1 and L_2 is an LTS $L_1 \parallel L_2 = (S, S^{\text{init}}, \delta, \Sigma, \Sigma^{\text{H}})$ where

- $S^{\text{init}} = S_1^{\text{init}} \times S_2^{\text{init}}$,
- $\Sigma = \Sigma_1 \cup \Sigma_2$, $\Sigma^{\text{H}} = \Sigma_1^{\text{H}} \cup \Sigma_2^{\text{H}}$,

and S is the smallest set of states and δ the smallest transition relation such that

- $S^{\text{init}} \subseteq S \subseteq S_1 \times S_2$,
- $a \in \Sigma_1 \cap \Sigma_2, \langle s_1, s_2 \rangle \in S, (s_1, a, t_1) \in \delta_1, (s_2, a, t_2) \in \delta_2 \Rightarrow \langle t_1, t_2 \rangle \in S, (\langle s_1, s_2 \rangle, a, \langle t_1, t_2 \rangle) \in \delta$,
- $a \in \Sigma_1^{\text{H}} \cup (\Sigma_1 - \Sigma_2), \langle s, u \rangle \in S, (s, a, t) \in \delta_1 \Rightarrow \langle t, u \rangle \in S, (\langle s, u \rangle, a, \langle t, u \rangle) \in \delta$,
- $a \in \Sigma_2^{\text{H}} \cup (\Sigma_2 - \Sigma_1), \langle u, s \rangle \in S, (s, a, t) \in \delta_2 \Rightarrow \langle u, t \rangle \in S, (\langle u, s \rangle, a, \langle u, t \rangle) \in \delta$.

Let $L = (S, S^{\text{init}}, \delta, \Sigma, \Sigma^{\text{H}})$ be an LTS. Let $B \subseteq \Sigma$. The LTS obtained by *internalizing* or *hiding* all the actions in B is the LTS $Hide[B](L) = (S, S^{\text{init}}, \delta, \Sigma - B, \Sigma^{\text{H}} \cup B)$. It is often convenient to assume, without loss of generality, that there is a single internal action τ, i.e., $\Sigma_L^{\text{H}} = \{\tau\}$, since the distinction of internal actions is unimportant in the definition of traces. We use $DH[B](L)$ as a shorthand for $Det(Hide[B](L))$.

Example 2. Consider the LTSs in Figure 2. $DH[\Sigma_{K_1}](T_1 \parallel T_2 \parallel R_1 \parallel K_1)$ is shown in Figure 3, where $\Sigma_{K_1} = \{Lock_{K_1}(T_1), Unlock_{K_1}(T_1), Lock_{K_1}(T_2), Unlock_{K_1}(T_2)\}$. Usually lock events are considered to be internal, so they are hidden in the composition.

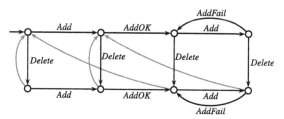

Fig. 3. The composition of the LTSs in Figure 2. Gray unlabeled arrows correspond to *DeleteOK*-transitions

Similar to [12], we use a *renaming* operator "$'$" for the purpose of reusing the external actions of an LTS. The renaming operator is a bijection on actions. We lift the operator to sets of actions: for an action set A, $A' = \{a'|a \in A\}$. Given an LTS L we write L' for the LTS where are all actions in L have been renamed.

3   System Modeling

We use LTSs to model multi-threaded programs. A thread is a sequential process modeled as an LTS. Two threads are *disjoint* if they do not share any actions. We consider a fixed collection *Threads* of n pairwise disjoint threads T_i for $1 \leq i \leq n$.

A *shared resource* is an LTS that models a state variable whose value is updated or read by threads. We consider a fixed collection *Resources* of m pairwise disjoint shared resources R_i, such that $\Sigma_{R_i} \subseteq \bigcup_{T \in Threads} \Sigma_T$, for $1 \leq i \leq m$.

Threads can communicate with each other through shared resources, but shared resources do not communicate with each other. For example, R_1 in Figure 2 is a shared resource.

A *lock* is a special type of shared resource that protects access to other shared resources. We model a lock K as a resource shared among the threads as follows.

$$S_K = (\{locked_K\} \times Threads) \cup \{unlocked_K\},$$
$$S_K^{init} = \{unlocked_K\},$$
$$\Sigma_K = \{Lock_K(T)|T \in Threads\} \cup \{Unlock_K(T)|T \in Threads\},$$
$$\delta_K = \{(unlocked_K, Lock_K(T), \langle locked_K, T\rangle)|T \in Threads\} \cup$$
$$\{(\langle locked_K, T\rangle, Unlock_K(T), unlocked_K)|T \in Threads\}.$$

We consider a fixed collection *Locks* of l pairwise disjoint locks K_i for $1 \leq i \leq l$. For example, K_1 in Figure 2 is a lock.

This notion of locks does not allow a lock being acquired more than once without being released first. In some programming languages, such as C#, a thread can acquire a lock more than once, but it has to release the lock for the same number of times before the lock can be acquired by other threads. The locks as defined above are adequate for the purposes of this paper.

In the following, we use thread to refer to any program thread T_i above and we use shared resource only to refer to a shared resource that is not a lock.

Program threads, shared resources, and locks constitute a *(multi-threaded) program* $P = (Threads, Resources, Locks)$. The *behavior* of P is described by the composition of the components denoted by $B(P)$. We hide *Lock* and *Unlock* actions in the composition, because they occur usually below the level of abstraction that is desired when viewing the composition, i.e. the lock events are not considered in the model.

$$B(P) \stackrel{\text{def}}{=} DH[\cup_{i=1}^l \Sigma_{K_i}](\|_{i=1}^n T_i \|_{i=1}^m R_i \|_{i=1}^l K_i).$$

Example 3. Consider the components in Figure 2 and let $P_1 = (\{T_1, T_2\}, \{R_1\}, \{K_1\})$. Figure 3 shows $Det(B(P_1))$. A practical concern when observing the behavior of such a system is to guarantee that the causal order of events is preserved. Since two threads are executing independently, it may happen for example that *AddFail* is observed after *DeleteOK*, resulting in an observed sequence *Add, AddOK, Add, Delete, DeleteOK, AddFail* that is not a trace of P_1, while in reality the trace *Add, AddOK, Add, Delete, AddFail, DeleteOK* happened.

The situation described in Example 3 can be formalized with the help of queues. Since threads are sequential processes, events from the same thread can be observed by a tester in the order they occur. Events from different threads could, however, have races. An event occurring earlier in one thread can be observed after an event occurring later in another thread. Recording of events can be formalized as buffering of events in thread-wise queues. Events are consumed in a random order from the queues by a tester. One can define queues similarly to those in [13], to model the effect of communication delay between the thread and the tester.

An *event queue* for a thread records events in the order produced by the thread and makes those events readable in FIFO order. Formally, given a thread $T \in Threads$, Q_T is the following LTS:

$$
\begin{aligned}
S_{Q_T}^{\mathrm{init}} &= \{\varepsilon\}, \\
S_{Q_T} &= (\Sigma_T)^*, \\
\Sigma_{Q_T} &= \Sigma_T \cup (\Sigma_T)', \\
\delta_{Q_T} &= \{(\alpha, a', \alpha a) | \alpha, \alpha a \in S_{Q_T}\} \cup \{(\alpha a, a, \alpha) | \alpha, \alpha a \in S_{Q_T}\}.
\end{aligned}
$$

Intuitively, a transition whose label is the renamed action a' corresponds to recording the event a in the queue, and a transition whose label is a corresponds to removing the recorded event a from the queue. Figure 4 illustrates an event queue of a thread with a single event a.

The queued behavior of a thread T can be described by composing T' with Q_T, hiding the shared actions, and making the result deterministic, i.e. the queued behavior is $DH[\Sigma_T'](T' \parallel Q_T)$. Unsurprisingly, $Tr(T) = Tr(DH[\Sigma_T'](T' \parallel Q_T))$ because events from the same thread are observed in the order they occur.

Let **T**, **R**, **K** and **Q** denote the parallel compositions of threads, resources, locks, and queues respectively. For the program P as above, the external behavior of P composed with queues gives rise to the *queued behavior* $Q(P)$ of P,

$$
Q(P) \stackrel{\mathrm{def}}{=} DH[\Sigma_\mathbf{T}'](B(P)' \parallel \mathbf{Q}) = DH[\Sigma_\mathbf{T}'](DH[\Sigma_\mathbf{K}](\mathbf{T} \parallel \mathbf{R} \parallel \mathbf{K})' \parallel \mathbf{Q}).
$$

The set of traces of $Q(P)$ corresponds to the set of traces that may be observed by a tester. The set $Tr(Q(P))$ is a superset of $Tr(B(P))$, so a tester might observe some traces not in the original behavior of the program.

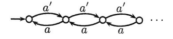

Fig. 4. An event queue for a thread with a single event a

Example 4. In Figure 3, *Add AddOK Add Delete AddFail DeleteOK* is a trace of $B(P_1)$ for the program $P_1 = (\{T_1, T_2\}, \{R_1\}, \{K_1\})$ in Figure 2. This trace, however, could correspond to the following trace in $Q(P_1)$: *Add AddOK Add Delete DeleteOK AddFail* which is not in $B(P_1)$, as pointed out in Example 3.

4 Multiplexer

As described above, in order to avoid possible discrepancies between the observed and the actual behavior of a multi-threaded program, we use a multiplexer to create a linearization of the observed events. To this end, we instrument threads and locks to keep track of lock events with lock-wise counts, called *usage counts*. The usage count of a lock indicates the number of times the lock has been used. When the multiplexer reads events that have been logged in the queues, it keeps track of the usage counts and does not read a lock entry from a queue unless that entry has the expected usage count.

A lock K with a usage count is unlocked when the usage count is an even number; it is locked otherwise. Initially the usage count is 0 and K is unlocked. We model a lock K with a usage count as the following LTS:

$$S_K = (\{unlocked_K\} \times \mathbb{N}^{even}) \cup (\{locked_K\} \times Threads \times \mathbb{N}^{odd}),$$
$$S_K^{init} = \{\langle unlocked_K, 0 \rangle\},$$
$$\Sigma_K = \{Lock_K(T, i) | T \in Threads, i \in \mathbb{N}^{even}\} \cup$$
$$\quad \{Unlock_K(T, i) | T \in Threads, i \in \mathbb{N}^{odd}\},$$
$$\delta_K = \{(\langle unlocked_K, i \rangle, Lock_K(T, i), \langle locked_K, T, i+1 \rangle) | T \in Threads, i \in \mathbb{N}^{even}\} \cup$$
$$\quad \{(\langle locked_K, T, i \rangle, Unlock_K(T, i), \langle unlocked_K, i+1 \rangle) | T \in Threads, i \in \mathbb{N}^{odd}\}.$$

In order to observe the usage counts in traces, the usage counts are made an explicit part of the lock transition labels.

Example 5. Figure 5 shows the two threads T_1 and T_2 and the lock K_1 from Figure 2 extended with usage counts.

Given P, **T**, **R**, **K** and **Q** as above, the queued behavior of the program with lock events visible is described by the LTS $S(P)$,

$$S(P) \stackrel{\text{def}}{=} DH[\Sigma_T']((\mathbf{T} \parallel \mathbf{R} \parallel \mathbf{K})' \parallel \mathbf{Q})$$

The multiplexer communicates with $S(P)$ by reading events from the queues. Lock events are used to create a linearization of all the other events from different queues that respects the causal order of the events. If the first event in an event queue is a lock event, then the multiplexer checks whether its usage count is the expected one. If yes, then it deletes this event from the queue and increases the expected usage count of the lock; otherwise, it leaves the queue intact. If the first event in an event queue is not a lock event, which means that the event can be executed without violating the ordering

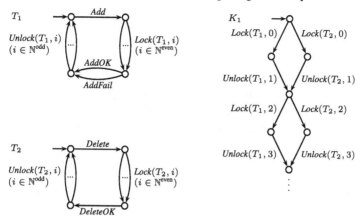

Fig. 5. Threads T_1 and T_2 and the lock K_1 from Figure 2 extended with usage counts

constraint, the multiplexer can simply remove the event from the queue and puts it in the output queue read by the tester.

Formally, the multiplexer M is an LTS obtained from the composition $\mathbf{K}$ of locks with usage counts by adding self-loops for all non-locking actions:

$$S_M^{\text{init}} = S_{\mathbf{K}}^{\text{init}},$$
$$S_M = S_{\mathbf{K}},$$
$$\Sigma_M = \Sigma_{\mathbf{T}},$$
$$\delta_M = \delta_{\mathbf{K}} \cup \{(s, a, s) | a \in \Sigma_M - \Sigma_{\mathbf{K}}, s \in S_M\},$$

The *multiplexed behavior* $M(P)$ of P is the composition of the queued behavior of P with the multiplexer where locking actions are hidden,

$$M(P) \overset{\text{def}}{=} DH[\Sigma_{\mathbf{K}}](S(P) \parallel M).$$

With the help of the multiplexer, we want to ensure that the multiplexed behavior $M(P)$ is the same as the behavior of P, i.e., $Tr(B(P)) = Tr(M(P))$. In general, this is only true if shared resources are properly protected by locks.

Example 6. Assume for a moment that the threads T_1 and T_2 in Figure 2 do not use locks. In Figure 6, we show the threads without lock events as threads T_3 and T_4, respectively. The behavior $B(P_2)$ of the program $P_2 = (\{T_3, T_4\}, \{R_1\}, \{K_1\})$ with R_1

Fig. 6. Threads T_1 and T_2 from Figure 2 after removal of lock events

as in Figure 2 and K_1 as in Figure 5, happens to be the same as the LTS in Figure 3. It is easy to see that $Tr(B(P_2)) \neq Tr(M(P_2))$ because the shared resource R_1 is not protected by a lock.

One can see that if an event a of one thread, say T_1, must precede an event b of another thread, say T_2, in $B(P)$, then there must be lock events between a and b that effectively enforce this order. Since a lock has to be released by a thread before it can be acquired by another, if there are lock events between a and b in that order, there must be an *Unlock* event from T_1 before a *Lock* event from T_2. It is intuitively clear that we only need to protect events of shared resources (e.g. thread-local events need no protection).

Let P be as above. We say that P is *lock-protected*, if every shared resource R is associated with a lock K_R and for every trace $\alpha a \beta \in Tr(P)$ and thread T, where $a \in \Sigma_T \cap \Sigma_R$, there is a *Lock* event $Lock_{K_R}(T, k)$ in α and a corresponding *Unlock* event $Unlock_{K_R}(T, k+1)$ in β for some k. In other words, P is lock-protected if there is a lock for each shared resource that assures exclusive access to that resource one thread at a time.

The following theorem shows that multiplexing does not affect the traces of lock-protected programs.

Theorem 1. *Given P as above. If P is lock-protected then $Tr(B(P)) = Tr(M(P))$.*

Proof (outline). We show first that $Tr(S(P) \parallel M) \subseteq Tr(T \parallel R \parallel K)$. Consider a trace α of $S(P) \parallel M$. From the construction of $S(P)$ it follows that all events of a given thread appear in the correct order in α as renamed events. The events from queues are merged arbitrarily in $S(P)$ so causal ordering constraints between events from different threads is not preserved. However, composition with M and the assumption of P being lock-protected excludes illegal interleavings of the queues so that α is again a possible trace of $Tr(T \parallel R \parallel K)$.

To see that $Tr(T \parallel R \parallel K) \subseteq Tr(S(P) \parallel M)$ consider a trace $u = b_1 b_2 \cdots \in Tr(T \parallel R \parallel K)$. There is the particular trace $b_1' b_1 b_2' b_2 \cdots \in Tr((T \parallel R \parallel K)' \parallel Q)$ corresponding to the special case when an event is removed from a queue immediately after it has been added to the queue, and thus $u \in Tr(S(P))$. Moreover, since the lock event ordering is not violated in u, $u \in Tr(S(P) \parallel M)$.

From $Tr(S(P) \parallel M) = Tr(T \parallel R \parallel K)$ follows that

$$Tr(B(P)) = Tr(Hide[\Sigma_K](T \parallel R \parallel K))$$
$$= Tr(Hide[\Sigma_K](S(P) \parallel M)) = Tr(M(P)). \qquad \square$$

5 Multiplexing Algorithm

In this section we describe the multiplexing algorithm that underlies a multiplexer. To make the description precise, we use the modeling language AsmL [2] as pseudo-code to describe the algorithm.

The multiplexer reads events from input queues. Each queue is associated with a particular thread. The multiplexer merges the events into a possible linearization and stores the merged sequence in a designated output queue.

```
type Queue
var inQueues as Set of Queue
var outQueue as Queue
```

The elements in the queues are lock events and other observable events, called update events. Each lock event is associated with a given lock and a usage count for that lock. (Each lock event is further classified as either acquiring or releasing of the lock, but this distinction is irrelevant for the purposes of this description.) The thread operating on the lock is implied by the input queue from which the multiplexer reads the lock event.

```
type Lock
structure Event
  case LockEvent
    lock as Lock
    count as Integer
  case UpdateEvent
```

We assume that one can perform the following operations on a queue: add a new event at the end of the queue by invoking Enqueue; remove the first event by invoking Dequeue; check if the queue is empty by invoking IsEmpty; and get the first event from the queue by invoking Head.

```
class Queue
  IsEmpty() as Boolean
  Enqueue(event as Event)
  Dequeue()
  Head() as Event
```

The multiplexer keeps a map from locks to expected usage counts. Initially, the map is empty, so the expected usage count of each lock is set to 0.

```
locks as Map of Lock to Integer = {->}
GetLockCount(lock as Lock) as Integer
  if lock notin locks then return 0
  else return locks(lock)
IncrementLockCount(lock as Lock)
  if lock notin locks then locks(lock) := 1
  else locks(lock) := locks(lock) + 1
```

The main part of the algorithm is described by the following while loop. A nonempty input queue of events is chosen randomly. If the first event is a lock event with a matching expected usage count then the event is removed from the queue and the expected usage count is incremented. If the event is an update event it is removed from the input queue and appended at the end of the output queue. From the point of view of external behavior, lock events are internal and are therefore not added to the output queue but are used solely for the purposes of ordering the update events.

```
while true
  choose queue in inQueues where not queue.IsEmpty()
```

```
let e = queue.Head()
if e is LockEvent then
   if e.count = GetLockCount(e.lock) then
      queue.Dequeue()
      IncrementLockCount(e)
   else
      skip
else
   queue.Dequeue()
   outQueue.Enqueue(e)
```

This description of the algorithm is simplified. The actual implementation of the multiplexer is itself multi-threaded, where the input queues may be updated while the multiplexer is running. Moreover, the number of input queues may grow or shrink dynamically as the number of threads changes.

Example 7. Figure 7 shows a possible run of the system in Figure 1. The event sequence of thread T_1 is $(a,\ Lock_K(T_1, 0),\ b,\ Unlock_K(T_1, 1),\ c)$, and the event sequence of thread T_2 is $(d,\ e,\ Lock_K(T_2, 2),\ f,\ Unlock_K(T_2, 3))$. The partial order of update events in the runs of the two threads depends on the total order of lock events associated with lock K. The solid arrow indicates that $Unlock_K(T_1, 1)$ happens before $Lock_K(T_2, 2)$. Consequently, event b must precede event f, as indicated with the dashed arrow. A possible event sequence produced by the multiplexer is $daebfc$. Notice that with the multiplexer, a tester always observes event b before event f since the order of update events is restrained by the order of lock events.

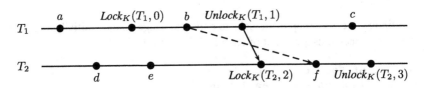

Fig. 7. Sample run of the threads in Figure 1

6   Application

The multiplexer is used together with the Spec Explorer tool for system-level conformance testing of multi-threaded and distributed systems. It is used by several Microsoft product groups that test highly concurrent subsystems of the forthcoming version of the Windows operating system. The Spec Explorer tool is briefly described in [8]. The tool is available from [1]. The threads or processes of the system under test produce thread-based event logs. These logs are serialized by the multiplexer into a single event trace. The trace is fed into a conformance checking engine that checks whether the observed trace is valid with respect to a given specification or model. The model is described by a model program written in AsmL [9] or Spec# [3]. The use of a model program as a behavioral specification is explained in [4, 17]. The formal conformance relation that is checked between the model and the system under test is a variation of alternating refinement of interface automata [6, 7]. An event trace is viewed as a particular run of a game between two players: a tester (or testing tool) and a system under test. In this setting, the role of the multiplexer is to produce a serial view of the moves of the system, viewed as a single player, as a response to a move of the tester.

7   Conclusion

In this paper we considered model-based testing of multi-threaded programs with a single, sequential tester. Such a tester requires a linearized view of all the events that occurred in a given test run. We proposed a method for reordering of events from multiple threads so that partial order constraints concerning locks are not violated.

Our method requires some instrumentation of the program so that the partial order of lock events is used to help to reorder other events. We do not assume the existence of a globally visible clock, and our approach does not create additional synchronization between threads. In this sense, our method tries to avoid major impact on the system performance. We validated our approach, by modeling multi-threaded programs in terms of LTS, and formulated a sufficient condition in terms of lock usage.

Based on the assumption of lock-protection, our method ensures the soundness of a tester using the multiplexer. If a correct implementation is lock-protected, which is usually the case, the multiplexer can correctly reconstruct the events from the implementation, and the latter does not fail a test case derived from the model. On the other hand, if an implementation is correct but not lock-protected, possibly due to performance considerations, then the multiplexer can still produce some traces not belonging to the system. In this case, the correct implementation might fail a test.

The multiplexer is used together with the Spec Explorer tool for system-level conformance testing of multi-threaded and distributed systems. It is used by several Microsoft product groups that test highly concurrent subsystems of the forthcoming version of the Windows operating system.

As to the future work, we would like to extend our method to other applications where events have partial order constraints. For example, in communicating systems, a send event precedes the corresponding receive event and a request precedes the corresponding acknowledgment.

Also, the lock-protection condition looks a little too stringent. It could be relaxed by requiring lock-protection only when two events of a shared resources executed by different threads are totally ordered.

Moreover, the multiplexer could be extended to detect potential deficiencies of multithreaded programs, such as anti-patterns related to synchronization abuse and deadlock [10].

References

1. Spec Explorer. URL:http://research.microsoft.com/specexplorer, released January 2005.
2. AsmL. URL: http://research.microsoft.com/fse/AsmL/.

3. M. Barnett, R. Leino, and W. Schulte. The Spec# programming system: An overview. In M. Huisman, editor, *Construction and Analysis of Safe, Secure, and Interoperable Smart Devices: International Workshop, CASSIS 2004*, volume 3362 of *LNCS*, pages 49–69. Springer, 2005.

4. A. Blass, Y. Gurevich, L. Nachmanson, and M. Veanes. Play to test. Technical Report MSR-TR-2005-04, Microsoft Research, January 2005. Extended version of a paper submitted to CAV'05.

5. L. Cacciari and O. Rafiq. Controllability and observability in distributed testing. *Inform. Software Technology*, 41:767–780, 1999.

6. L. de Alfaro. Game models for open systems. In N. Dershowitz, editor, *Verification: Theory and Practice: Essays Dedicated to Zohar Manna on the Occasion of His 64th Birthday*, volume 2772 of *LNCS*, pages 269 – 289. Springer, 2004.

7. L. de Alfaro and T. Henzinger. Interface automata. In *Proceedings of the 8th European Software Engineering Conference held jointly with 9th ACM SIGSOFT international symposium on Foundations of Software Engineering*, volume 26(5) of *ACM SIGSOFT Software Engineering Notes*, pages 109 – 120. ACM Press, 2001.

8. W. Grieskamp, N. Tillmann, and M. Veanes. Instrumenting scenarios in a model-driven development environment. *Information and Software Technology*, 46(15):1027–1036, December 2004.

9. Y. Gurevich, B. Rossman, and W. Schulte. Semantic essence of AsmL. In *Formal Methods for Components and Objects, Second International Symposium, FMCO 2003*, volume 3188 of *LNCS*, pages 240–259. Springer, 2004. Extended version to appear in special issue of *Theoretical Computer Science*, preliminary version available as Microsoft Research Technical Report MSR-TR-2004-27.

10. H. Hallal, E. Alikacem, P. Tunney, S. Boroday, and A. Petrenko. Antipattern-based detection of defficiencies in java multithreaded software. In *Proceedings of the Fourth International Conference on Quality Software (QSIC2004)*, Braunschweig, Germany, September 2004.

11. H. Hallal, S. Boroday, A. Ulrich, and A. Petrenko. An automata-based approach to property testing in event traces. In *Proceedings of the IFIP TC6/WG6.1 XV International Conference on Testing of Communicating Systems (TestCom 2003)*, volume 2644 of *LNCS*, pages 180–196. Springer, 2003.

12. J. Huo, R. Negulescu, and A. Petrenko. A study of robustness and delay-insensitivity of discrete action systems. Technical Report CRIM-03/04-02, Centre de Recherche Informatique de Montréal, Montreal, Quebec, Canada, 2003.

13. J. Huo and A. Petrenko. On testing partially specified IOTS through lossless queues. In *Proceedings of the 16th IFIP International Conference, TestCom 2004*, volume 2978 of *LNCS*, pages 76 – 94. Springer, 2004.

14. C. Jard. How to observe interoperability at the service level of protocols. In *7th IFIP WG6.1 International Workshop on Protocol Test Systems (IWPTS'94)*, Tokyo, Japan, November 1994.

15. L. Lamport. Time, clocks, and the orderings of events in a distributed system. *Communications of the ACM*, 21(7):558–565, 1978.

16. S. Tasiran and S. Qadeer. Runtime refinement checking of concurrent data structures. *Electronic Notes in Theoretical Computer Science*, 113:163–179, January 2005. Proceedings of the Fourth Workshop on Runtime Verification (RV 2004).

17. M. Veanes, C. Campbell, W. Schulte, and P. Kohli. On-the-fly testing of reactive systems. Technical Report MSR-TR-2005-05, Microsoft Research, January 2005.

Testing Communicating Systems: a Model, a Methodology, and a Tool[*]

Ismaïl Berrada, Richard Castanet, and Patrick Félix

LaBRI - CNRS - UMR 5800 Université Bordeaux 1,
33405 Talence cedex, France
{berrada, castanet, felix}@labri.fr

Abstract. This paper follows two main lines of research. The first line is related to the study of models for the description of systems. For this line, we introduce the model of *Communicating Systems* (CS), which defines a set of common resources, a set of entities, and a topology of communication. The second line focuses on testing methodologies adapted to protocol testing. For this line, we give a formal definition of a generic generation algorithm (GGA). We demonstrate that the CS model with a GGA supports various 1) test architectures, 2) test types: conformance, interoperability, embedded, component testing, and 3) test approaches: passive and active testing. The paper presents also the main characteristics of the TGSE tool (Test Generation, Simulation, and Emulation). TGSE is made-up of a test case generator, based on the CS model and implementing a GGA, a graphic simulator of the execution of a sequence generated by TGSE, and a real-time emulator of communicating specifications. In its current version, TGSE supports the passive and active testing of one or several components with data and temporal constraints.

1 Introduction

Protocol specifications are used to develop products and services. To ensure correctness of such products (implementations), testing, the process of checking that a system possesses a set of desired properties and/or behaviors, is one of the most used validation techniques.

Testing process is a hard work that is long, repetitive and which represents a potential source of errors. The use of formal specifications provides support for automating this process. Different models (FSM, EFSM, CEFSM, LTS, IOLTS, TIOA,...) and languages (SDL, Lotos, IF, UML,...) have been proposed to describe protocols and the desired behaviors about them in a formal way. Due to the nature of protocols/functions being tested, various test types are required. For example, in conformance testing, a single implementation is compared to relevant standards. In interoperability testing, two or more implementations are

---

[*] This research has been supported by the French RNTL project Avérroes and the Marie Curie RTN TAROT (MCRTN 505121).

F. Khendek and R. Dssouli (Eds.): TestCom 2005, LNCS 3502, pp. 111–128, 2005.

tested directly against each other, with the standard used primarily as a reference to adjudicate problems and incompatibilities, and secondarily as a guide to the functions to be tested. Embedded testing considers an implementation communicating through its environment. The ways to test communicating systems can be classified into two basic groups. The most natural way, namely the active testing approach [1, 2, 3, 4, 5, 6, 7, 8, 9, 10, 11, 12, 13, 14, 15, 16, 17], consists in carrying out the test derivation starting from specifications. Another possibility is the passive testing approach [21]. The absence of observations allows only the validation of traces, and thus this approach checks that a trace of an implementation is a valid execution of the specification.

From our point of view, this diversity of types, models and approaches points only to the specificity of requirements. Indeed, the different types of test are a consequence of the composition of the systems to be tested : conformance testing considers only one entity while interoperability and embedded testing consider several communicating components interacting according to a test architecture. The considered model is justified by needs of system description: systems have behaviors and can handle data and temporal constraints. With either the passive testing or the active testing, we are confronted with the same problem: the accessibility problem of states or transitions.

Thus, the aim of this paper is not to introduce a new test generation technique, but rather to show that it is possible to treat the different types (conformance, interoperability, embedded, component) and approaches (passive and active) of testing in a unified manner. Our main contributions are the following:

First, we introduce the model of communicating systems (CS). This model defines (i) a set of communicating entities (components), (ii) a set of common resources (variables and parameters) shared by these entities, and (iii) a topology of communication, inspired by [19, 20], which specifies the different possible synchronizations in a global state of the system. We have chosen to model entities by extended timed automata but other models may be used.

Second, we demonstrate that the CS model is a generic model for testing in the sense that (i) it offers mechanisms for modeling different types of communications and test architectures, and (ii) it allows the possibility of applying the same generic generation algorithm (GGA) with different test types and approaches. As we will see, these results have a consequence on the classical test activities in the sense that the specification modeling and the use of a test approach and a test architecture are not two separate steps.

Finally, by presenting the TGSE tool (Test Generation, Simulation and Emulation), we show that our framework is usable in practical tools. TGSE implements an on-the-fly GGA, and supports the passive and active testing (with test purpose) of one or several components with data and temporal constraints.

The paper is organized as follows. Section 2 introduces the CS model. The generic character of this model and its suitability for protocol testing are discussed in section 3. Section 4 gives some elements of the implementation of the test generator tool TGSE. Section 5 reports our experimental results on

CSMA/CD protocol. Finally, we conclude and draw some perspectives in section 6.

2   Model and Methodology

The behavior of a communication protocol can be described by means of formal models such as communicating systems (CS). In this paper, $\mathbb{R}$ will denote the set of reals, and $\mathbb{R}^+$ will denote the set of positive reals.

2.1   Preliminaries

Clocks and Constraints. A clock is a variable that allows to record the passage of time. It can be set to a certain value and inspected at any moment to see how much time has passed. In the Alur-Dill model [18], clocks increase at the same rate, they are ranged over $\mathbb{R}^+$, and the only assignments allowed are clock resets of the form $x := 0$. For a set C of clocks, a set P of parameters, and a set V of variables, the set of clock constraints $\Phi(C, P, V)$ is defined by the grammar:

$$\phi := \phi_1 \,|\phi_2|\, \phi_1 \wedge \phi_2, \quad \phi_1 := x \leq f(P, V), \quad \phi_2 := f(P, V) \leq x$$

where x is a clock of C, and $f(P, V)$ is a linear expression of P and V. For two sets L_1 and L_2, $L_1 \backslash L_2$ will denote the set $L_1 \backslash L_2 = \{a \,|\, a \in L_1 \wedge a \notin L_2\}$.

Definition 1 (ETIOA). *An extended timed input/output automaton (ETIOA) is a 10-tuple $M = (S, L, C, P, V, V_0, Pred, Ass, s_0, \rightarrow)$ where :*

- *S is a finite set of states.*
- *s_0 is the initial state.*
- *L is a finite alphabet of actions, $L = L_i \cup L_o \cup I$.*
- *C is a finite set of clocks.*
- *P is a finite set of parameters.*
- *V is a finite set of variables.*
- *V_0 is a finite set of the initial values for variables of V.*
- *$Pred = \Phi(C, P, V) \cup \tilde{P}[P, V]$, where $\tilde{P}[P, V]$ is a set of linear inequalities on V and P.*
- *$Ass = \{x := 0 \,|\, x \in C\} \cup \{v := f(P, V) \,|\, v \in V\}$ is a set of updates on clocks and variables.*
- *$\rightarrow \subseteq S \times L \times Pred \times Ass \times S$ is a set of transitions.*

The alphabet L is partitioned into three sets: L_i (resp. L_o) is the input (resp. output) alphabet, and I is the alphabet of internal actions. $t = (s, a, pred, ass, s') \in \rightarrow$ represents an edge from state s to state s' on symbol a. $pred \subseteq Pred$ is a set of constraints, and $ass \subseteq Ass$ is a set of updates.

Example 1. Fig. 1 illustrates an example of an ETIOA.

- $S = \{s_0, s_1, s_2, s_3\}$ and s_0 the initial state.
- $L = \{!a, ?b, !c, ?d\}$, $C = \{x, y\}$, $P = \{\beta, \lambda\}$, $V = \{v1\}$ and $V_0 = \{\beta\}$.
- The variable $v1$ has the initial value β.

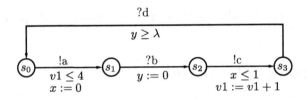

Fig. 1. ETIOA

- $Pred = \{y \geq \lambda, x \leq 1, v1 \leq 4\}$, $Ass = \{x := 0, y := 0, v1 := v1 + 1\}$.
- The transition t from s_2 to s_3 is: $t = (s_2, !c, \{x \leq 1\}, \{v1 := v1 + 1\}, s_3)$.

Remark 1. For an ETIOA $M = (S, L, C, P, V, V_0, Pred, Ass, s_0, \rightarrow)$:

- When $P = \emptyset$ and $V = \emptyset$, then we find the usual definition of a timed i/o automaton (TIOA). In this case, M will be simply noted $(S, L, C, s_0, \rightarrow)$.
- When $C = \emptyset$, $P = \emptyset$ and $V = \emptyset$, then we find the usual definition of an i/o automaton (IOA). In this case, M will be simply noted $M = (S, L, s_0, \rightarrow)$.

2.2   Topologies of Communication and Communicating Systems

A topology of communication **Top** of a set of processes is a synchronization model of the different processes. It describes the dynamic configurations of processes, and the possible synchronizations in a given configuration. The definition of **Top** is inspired by [19, 20]. It defines a set of global actions, a set of sets of actions, and a Transducer (this terminology is borrowed from [20]) modeled by an automaton.

Definition 2 (Topology). *The topology of communication Top of a set of n processes is a 3-tuple (G, I, Tr), with G a finite set of global actions, $I = \{I_i\}_{1 \leq i \leq n}$ a finite set of sets, and $Tr = (S_{tr}, L_{tr}, s_{0tr}, \rightarrow_{tr})$ an automaton such that the events of L_{tr} are vectors $\vec{v}$ of $n + 1$ elements, and $\forall \vec{v} \in L_{tr}$, $\vec{v} =< a_g, a_1, ..., a_n >$ with $a_g \in G$ and $\forall i \in [1, n]$, $a_i \in I_i \cup \{idle\}$.*

A vector $\vec{v} =< a_g, a_1, ..., a_n >$ of L_{tr} describes the action a_i that the process i, $i \in [1, n]$, has to perform. The synchronization of the actions $(a_i)_{i \in [1,n]}$ gives place to the global action a_g. When a vector $\vec{v} =< a_g, idle, ..., a_i, ..., idle >$ defines only one action, the process i executes lonely a_i, and changes its state. For a topology $Top = (G, I, Tr)$, when the number of states of Tr is equal to 1 then Top is called a *static* topology.

A topology offers the possibility of modeling communications between one, two or several processes: unicast, multicast, and broadcast. It can be used, in certain cases, as a kind of controller on actions allowed by processes in a given configuration of the global system. Note that, in order to describe inter-component communications, a process algebra can be more expressive than the topology, however, this latter offers suitable modeling mechanisms and algorithms usable in practical tools.

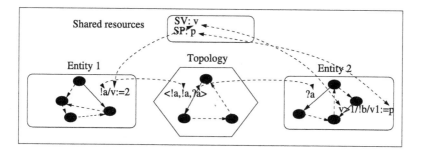

Fig. 2. CS model

Definition 3 (Communicating System). *A communicating system CS is a 5-tuple $(SP, SV, SV_0, (M_i)_{1 \le i \le n}, Top)$ where:*

- *SP is a set of shared parameters.*
- *SV is a set of shared variables.*
- *SV_0 is a set of the initial values for variables of SV.*
- *$Top = (G, \{I_i\}_{1 \le i \le n}, Tr)$ is a topology.*
- *$M_i = (S_i, L_i, C_i, P_i, V_i, V_{0i}, Pred_i, Ass_i, s_{0i}, \rightarrow_i)$ is an ETIOA such that $I_i \subseteq L_i$, $\forall i \in [1, n]$.*

Fig. 2 illustrates an example of a CS. Entities represent processes. They are modeled by ETIOAs. The topology of communication describes the different possible synchronizations between the entities. We assumed in the definition of entities that $\forall i \in [1, n]$, $I_i \subseteq L_i$. This enables the definition of partial topologies in which only allowed synchronizations are reported (in the next section, we will give some examples of such topologies). The common resources represent the shared data of the CS. We will restrict the shared data to variables and parameters. The parameters (resp. variables) can be read (resp. read and modified) by the CS entities [1]. The semantics of a CS is defined by an ETIOA. To simplify, we will assume that the names of parameters and variables of entities are different, and different from those of the CS.

Definition 4 (Semantics). *The semantics of a communicating system $S = (SP, SV, SV_0, (M_i)_{1 \le i \le n}, Top)$, with $M_i = (S_i, L_i, C_i, P_i, V_i, V_{0i}, Pred_i, Ass_i, s_{0i}, \rightarrow_i)$ and $Top = (G, I, (S_{tr}, L_{tr}, s_{0tr}, \rightarrow_{tr}))$, is defined by the ETIOA $\zeta(S) = (S, L, C, P, V, V_0, Pred, Ass, s_0, \rightarrow)$ such that :*

---

[1] Shared parameters and variables can appear in the definition of a transition of an entity.

- $S = \{s = (s_{tr}, s_1, ..., s_n) \mid s_{tr} \in S_{tr}, \forall i \in [1, n], s_i \in S_i\}$
- $s_0 = (s_{otr}, s_{01}, ..., s_{0n})$.
- $L = G, C = C_1 \cup ... \cup C_n, P = SP \cup P_1 \cup ... \cup P_n$.
- $V = VP \cup V_1 \cup ... \cup V_n, V_0 = VP_0 \cup V_{01} \cup ... \cup V_{0n}$.
- $Pred = Pred_1 \cup ... \cup Pred_n, Ass = Ass_1 \cup ... \cup Ass_n$.
- $\rightarrow = \{(s_{tr}, s_1, ..., s_n) \xrightarrow{a, pred, ass} (s'_{tr}, s'_1, ..., s'_n) \mid \exists \vec{v} = <a, a_1, ..., a_n> \in L_{tr}, s_{tr}$
  $\xrightarrow{\vec{v}}_{tr} s'_{tr}, \forall i \in [1, n], (((a_i = idle) \wedge (s_i = s'_i)) \parallel ((a_i \neq idle) \wedge (s_i \xrightarrow{a_i, pred_i, ass_i}_i$
  $s'_i))), pred = pred_1 \wedge ... \wedge pred_n, ass = ass_1 \wedge ... \wedge ass_n\}$.

The alphabet L of $\zeta(S)$ is the set G of global actions of Top. A state of $\zeta(S)$ consists of a state of Top and states of $(M_i)_{i \in [1,n]}$. A transition $(s_{tr}, s_1, ..., s_n) \xrightarrow{a, pred, ass}$ $(s'_{tr}, s'_1, ..., s'_n)$ of $\zeta(S)$ is conditioned by the existence of a transition of Top from s_{tr} to s'_{tr} on a vector having the global action a.

Thus, the semantics of a CS allows the possibility of the synchronization with other CSs, which gives a hierarchical definition for CSs. A possible extension of the CS model consists in the definition of extended topologies: the transducer modeled by an ETIOA (could be useful for modeling network latencies). Note that, the size (number of transitions) of the semantics automaton is linear in the size of entities times the size of the topology. In practice, however, this size is orders of magnitude less. For example, the size of a CS, such that its topology is a tree, is linear in the size of its topology.

2.3   Methodology of Generic Generation Algorithms

The majority of test generation algorithms are based on a depth-first search of a target state or transition in the accessibility graph. It is then possible to define generic generation algorithms for various test types. In this part, we show how to define such algorithms.

Definition 5. *A communicating system under test (CSUT) is a communicating system $S = (SP, SV, SV_0, (M_i)_{1 \le i \le n}, Top)$, such that there is at least one entity $M_i, i \in [1, n]$, defining one or several states labeled by $ACCEPT$.*

States labeled by $ACCEPT$ define the behaviors to be tested. Our definition of CSUT considers only states labeled by $ACCEPT$, but it is possible to define transitions labeled by $ACCEPT$. This last case is not treated in this paper, but the approach remains the same. Let us note by $\mathcal{CSUT}$, the set of all CSUTs.

Definition 6. *For a $S \in \mathcal{CSUT}$, a state $s = (s_{tr}, s_1, ..., s_n)$ of $\zeta(S)$ and $\rho = t_0...t_n$ a sequence of transitions in $\zeta(S)$ from the initial state:*

- *s is an accepting state of $\zeta(S)$ if there exists $i \in [1, n]$ such that s_i is a state labeled by $ACCEPT$.*
- *ρ is an accepting path of $\zeta(S)$, if*
  1. *ρ is an executable path.*
  2. *The target state of the last transition t_n is an accepting state of $\zeta(S)$.*

A state s of the ETIOA $\zeta(S)$, the semantics of S, is an accepting state of $\zeta(S)$, if one of the states that compose it, is a state labeled by $ACCEPT$. A path $\rho = t_0...t_n$ of $\zeta(S)$ from the initial state is an accepting path of $\zeta(S)$ if 1) the state s_n of the last transition $t_n = (s_{n-1}, a, pred, ass, s_n)$ is an accepting state of $\zeta(S)$ and 2) ρ is an executable (feasible) path, i.e, the different constraints on the transitions are all satisfied. The executability of a path is treated in [21, 22].

Definition 7. *A generic generation algorithm (GGA) for $CSUT$ is an algorithm that computes, for all $S \in CSUT$, all accepting paths of $\zeta(S)$.*

An algorithm gga is a GGA, if gga applied to $\zeta(S)$ returns a set $PATH(S)$ containing all accepting paths of $\zeta(S)$. Examples of GGA can be found in [21, 23, 22]. Note that the Hit-or-Jump algorithm [23] does not deal with the temporal aspect of systems and considers $ACCEPT$ transitions.

Finally, an algorithm gga does not depend on a CSUT. It can be applied to any ETIOA and it is exhaustive in the sense that all accepting paths are returned by gga. Its complexity depends on the size of entities and the size of the topology used. We have chosen the state coverage criterion for defining gga but the transition (or other) coverage criterion can also be chosen [22].

3   CS: A Generic Model for Testing

In this section we present the expressivity and the generic character of CSs for describing and testing protocols. Modeling specifications is presented in 3.1. Testing with different types and approaches is presented in 3.2.

In the remainder of this section, we will consider two specifications S_A and S_B, sharing the set of parameters SP, and the set of variables SV, such that SV_0 is a finite set of the initial values for variables of SV. We model S_A (resp. S_B) by the ETIOA $A = (S_A, L_A, C_A, P_A, V_A, V_0, Pred_A, Ass_A, s_0, \rightarrow_A)$ (resp. $B = (S_B, L_B, C_B, P_B, V_B, V_0', Pred_B, Ass_B, s_0', \rightarrow_B))$. L_{AB} (resp. L_{BA}) will denote the set of events of L_A (resp L_B) which synchronize with an event of L_B (resp. L_A). For example, if $L_A = \{?a_1, ?a_2, !a_3\}$ and $L_B = \{!a_2, ?a_3, !a_4\}$ then $L_{AB} = \{?a_2, !a_3\}$, $L_{BA} = \{!a_2, ?a_3\}$, and $?a_2$ (resp. $!a_3$) synchronizes with $!a_2$ (resp. $?a_3$). To simplify, we will assume that $\forall a \in L_{AB}$, there is a unique $b \in L_{BA}$ such that a synchronizes with b.

3.1   CS as a Specification Model

Observable events. Suppose that S is the specification made up of specifications S_A and S_B. A CS modeling of S is : $CS_1 = (SP, SV, SV_0, (A, B), TopS)$, with $TopS$ the automaton of Fig. 3 (a). $TopS$ is a static topology. Vector $< G, L_{AB}, L_{BA} >$ denotes the vectors $< g_{ab}, a, b >$ such that $a \in L_{AB}$ synchronizes with $b \in L_{BA}$, and their synchronization gives place to an observable action g_{ab}. An example of g_{ab} can be a (resp. b) if a (resp. b) is an emission (the visible action of an emission and a reception is an emission). In the same way, $< G_A, L_A \backslash L_{AB}, idle >$ denotes the vectors $< g_a, a, idle >$ such that

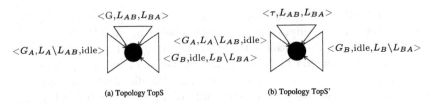

(a) Topology TopS   (b) Topology TopS'

Fig. 3. Different topologies

$a \in L_A \backslash L_{AB}$. In $< g_a, a, idle >$, the ETIOA A performs the action a giving place to the observable action g_a, and the ETIOA B remains in the same state ($idle$). The set G_A corresponds, in general, to the set $L_A \backslash L_{AB}$. Finally, $TopS$ allows the application of each vector (if it is possible) in a global state of S.

Non-observable events. Now, suppose that the synchronizations of L_{AB} events with L_{BA} events are non-observable (as it is the case of the black-box test architecture), then modeling S in CS is: $CS_2 = (SP, SV, SV_0, (A, B), TopS')$, with $TopS'$ the automaton of Fig. 3 (b). In $< \tau, a, b >$ of $< \tau, L_{AB}, L_{BA} >$, the synchronization of a with b gives place to an internal action τ. Generally, we can describe the synchronization on internal actions only for a part of the synchronization events as it is the case of a test architecture.

Thus, from a testing standpoint, the CS model is not only a formal model allowing the description of inter-component communications, but also a model that is able to incorporate the test architectures.

3.2   CS as a Test Generation Model

Two major approaches were used for protocol testing: *Active Testing* and *Passive Testing*. In active testing, the derivation is made from specifications. The derivation can consider only a part of the specification with the aim of limiting the state space explosion which occurs during the system composition and analysis. This approach is known as the test purpose technique. Active testing can deal with one or several communicating entities [1, 2, 3, 4, 5, 6, 7, 8, 9, 10, 11, 12, 13, 14, 15, 16, 17]. On the other hand, passive testing considers execution traces of an implementation, which can contain values of variables and clocks, and checks the validity of these traces with respect to the specification. In the works relating to passive testing [21], the authors consider only one untimed specification.

To simplify, let us call *one-component testing* the test of one specification (conformance testing) and *several-component testing* the test of several specifications (interoperability, embedded, component testing). In the rest of this section, we consider that gg^a is a GGA. This section shows that the test activities amount to a CS modeling, by deferring the different characteristics of a test to the topology of communication, and the application of the algorithm gg^a to validate a trace (passive testing) or to generate traces (active testing).

Passive testing. Suppose that I is an implementation of the specification S_A, and the trace modeled by the ETIOA of Fig. 4 (a) is a trace of I. This trace

(a) PTrace   (b) PTop

Fig. 4. Passive testing

reports that I has executed $a \in L_A$ (we recall that A is the ETIOA of S_A) at moment 3, followed by $b \in L_A$ at moment 5 such that the shared variable $v \in SV$ is equal to 4. Checking the validity of this trace consists in modeling a CS $CS_3 = (SP, SV, SV_0, (A, PTrace), PTop)$, with $PTrace$ the ETIOA of Fig. 4 (a) and $PTop$ the automaton of Fig. 4 (b).

The topology $Ptop$ is partial, i.e, it defines only the synchronizations on $PTrace$ events. $< a, a, a >$ (resp. $< b, b, b >$) considers that A and $PTrace$ synchronize on a (resp. b), and the visible action will be a (resp. b). We have labeled the state reached by the action b in $PTrace$ by $ACCEPT$ in order to make CS_3 a CSUT and to be able to apply gga. Consequently, gga allows to decide if $PTrace$ is a valid trace of A: if gga returns an empty set ($PATH(CS_3) = \emptyset$) then $PTrace$ is not a valid trace of A (we recall that gga is applied to the semantics of CS_3).

Remark 2. -Generally, the construction of $PTop$ depends strongly on $PTrace$. It should define only synchronizations on $PTrace$ events and in the same order.

-The trace $PTrace$ is considered as an entity of CS_3 without any distinction compared to the other entities. This allows to enlarge the form of the considered traces to any traces modeled by an ETIOA defining some accepting states.
-The example of the passive testing of the specification S_A is one-component testing, but the approach remains the same in the case of several-component testing. In this setting, the difficulty is to reorder various traces from the different components to construct only one trace. We think that the stamp mechanisms, and especially the stamp process presented in [24], could be used. This subject goes beyond the framework of this paper and needs more investigation.

Active testing. For a CSUT S, the paths $PATH(\zeta(S))$ generated by gga can be used to derive test cases that cover, for example, all S states. This amounts to define all S states as being accepting states (gga could be an adaptation of the TT/UIO/Wp methods for untimed systems). Thus, we consider here only the test purpose technique.

Definition 8. *A test purpose (TP) is an ETIOA $(S, L, C, P, V, V_0, Pred, Ass, s_0, \rightarrow)$ having two sets of states $ACCEPT$ and $REJECT$ characterizing the behaviors to be tested.*

A TP is a property that one would like to check on implementation behavior. $TP1$ of Fig. 5 (a) illustrates an example of a TP for the specification S_A. $TP1$ tests that an implementation I of S_A can execute a followed by b at an instant between $[2, Sig]$ according to the clock h ($Sig \in SP$ is a shared parameter of S_A). The label '*' denotes the alphabet L_A of A. We assume here that $a, b, c \in L_A$.

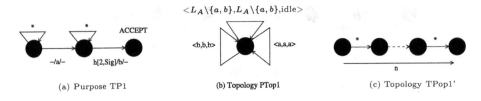

(a) Purpose TP1   (b) Topology PTop1   (c) Topology TPop1'

Fig. 5. Active testing: one-component testing (1)

One-component testing.
Suppose that $TP1$ is a TP for specification S_A. A modeling of this test in CS is: $CS_4 = (SP, SV, SV_0, (A, TP1), TPop1)$, with $TPop1$ the topology of Fig. 5 (b). The vectors $< L_A\backslash\{a, b\}, L_A\backslash\{a, b\}, idle >$ denote free evolutions of specification A on events other than a and b. CS_4 is a CSUT and thus gga will generate paths checking $TP1$.

Note that for the same TP, several CS modelings can be formulated, considering different topologies. In fact, the definition of the topology gives more expressivity to the behaviors awaited by a TP. A typical example of this expressivity is as follows: since paths generated by gga for CS_4 are of arbitrary lengths (the number of transitions), one can wish to generate only paths of lengths less than $n \in \mathbb{N}$. This wish cannot be expressed by a TP (there is no mechanism to count the event occurrences). Now, let us consider the CS $CS_5 = (SP, SV, SV_0, (A, TP1), TPop1')$, with $TPop1'$ the topology of Fig. 5 (c). The label '*' in $TPop1'$ denotes vectors $< a, a, a >$, $< b, b, b >$, and $< L_A\backslash\{a, b\}, L_A\backslash\{a, b\}, idle >$ (a transition '*' is then the set of transitions on these vectors). With $TPop1'$ the semantics of CS_5 is a tree of depth less than n and thus the lengths of paths generated by gga are less than n.

To close the part of one-component testing, let us take the TP $TP2$ of Fig. 6 (a). $TP2$ tests the same functionalities as $TP1$, but prohibits the appearance of c in the two first states of $TP2$. The label *'other'* in $TP2$ denotes the events $L_A\backslash\{c\}$. Note that the definition of $REJECT$ states is only a manner of prohibiting synchronizations on a set of events. This prohibition can be formulated in the topology instead of the test purpose. In this case, we can use $TP1$ instead of $TP2$. Indeed, the active testing of S_A with test purpose $TP2$ can be modeled

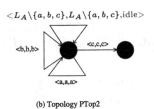

(b) Topology PTop2

Fig. 6. Active testing: one-component testing (2)

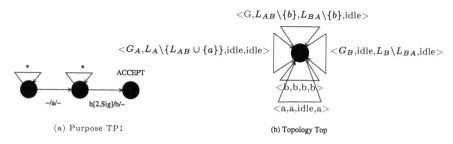

(a) Purpose TP1   (b) Topology Top

Fig. 7. Active testing: several-component testing

by the CS $CS_6 = (SP, SV, SV_0, (A, TP1), TPop2)$, with $TPop2$ the topology of Fig. 6 (b). In $TPop2$, when a synchronization on c occurs, the communicating system evolves/moves to a blocking/deadlock state and thus during the application of gga to CS_6, gga is forced to dequeue this synchronization. Finally, note that we have used $TP1$ in CS_6 to test $TP2$, and therefore a test purpose can contain only $ACCEPT$ states.

Several-component testing.
Suppose that S is the specification made up of specifications S_A and S_B, and $TP1$ (Fig. 7 (a)) is a TP for S. To simplify, we assume here that $a \in L_A$, $a \notin L_{AB}$ (a is not a synchronization event), and $b \in L_{AB} \cap L_{BA}$. A modeling of this test in CS is as follows: $CS_7 = (SP, SV, SV_0, (A, B, TP1), Top)$, with Top the topology of Fig. 7 (b). The vector $< b, b, b, b >$ considers that A, B and $TP1$ synchronize on b. The vector $< a, a, idle, a >$ considers that only A and $TP1$ synchronize on a. Again, the application of gga allows generating paths checking $TP1$.

To summarize this section, Fig. 8 presents the test activities (without the implementations). Three main steps are identified. Firstly, from (i) an informal specification(s), (ii) a test approach (passive or active testing), and (iii) a test architecture, a description S in the CS model is elaborated. Secondly, a GGA algorithm (with a coverage criterion) is applied to $\zeta(S)$ to generate a set of executable paths $PATH(\zeta(S))$. Finally, this set is interpreted according to the test

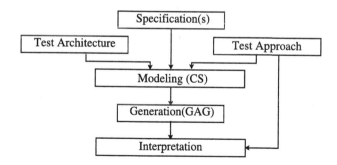

Fig. 8. Test activities

approach: for passive testing, if $PATH(\zeta(S)) = \emptyset$ then the implementation(s) is (are) incorrect. For active testing, test cases are generated from this set. In the opposite, the classical test activities involve the specification, the generation algorithm and the test architecture in three separate steps and thus looses the generic character of our framework.

Thus, there is no reason to make distinction between these types and approaches of protocol testing.

4   TGSE: A Generic Test Generation Tool

The automation of the test generation becomes a need faced with the growth of the complexity of the protocols being tested. This section describes the main characteristics of the implementation of the TGSE tool (Test Generation, Simulation and Emulation) based on the CS model. Due to space restrictions, we present only the test case generator. The interested readers are referred to [22].

TGSE Interfaces. The French RNRT project Calife and its successor Averroès are an academic and industrial projects gathering France Telecom R&D, CRIL Technology, LaBRI, LSV, Loria, LRI. The goal of this project is to define a generic platform (Open Source) able to interface verification and test generation tools. The Calife platform [25] comprises an editor and a simulator. The editor provides a pleasant and easy-to-handle graphical user interface of various types of automata (timed, hybrids, and extended automata). The simulator allows the graphical execution of automata.

The input of TGSE is the description of a CS following a simple syntax. Each ETIOA of a CS is defined in a separate file. A system file describes the access paths to each component, as well as the shared data and the topology of communication. The output of TGSE is an XML (eXtensible Markup Language) file according to a Calife DTD defining a test sequence.

TGSE can also be used in a graphical mode through Calife. In this case, the description of a specification is done through the Calife editor that allows the automatic generation of the synchronization vectors. Many synchronization modes are offered: rendez-vous, broadcast, identical labels and the Uppaal binary synchronization. The call to TGSE is done through the editor that generates the input files of TGSE. TGSE produces a test case to be simulated in Calife.

Generation Techniques. TGSE implements an on-the-fly algorithm gg^a. It is based on a depth-first traversal of the CS semantics. The traversal is parameterized by the maximum number allowed for a transition to appear in the generated sequence. The choice of a transition, a synchronization vector and the automaton that performs an action is parameterized (RANDOM or FIFO access). The algorithm gg^a computes an accepting path for a given CS. During the traversal, several computations are performed:

Step 1: Successor Computation. From the current state s of the semantics automaton, the synchronization vectors are evaluated in a parameterized way to compute a successor state s'. The API *SymbolicTrace*() is then called.

Step 2: Symbolic Trace. SymbolicTrace() calculates the symbolic trace of the new fired transitions and updates the predicates and the context (assignments and resets of the new transitions,see annex).

Step 3: Constraint Resolution. Once the symbolic trace is calculated, the API *feasible*() is called. In the case of a parameterized trace, *feasible*() calls *checkParams*(). This latter interacts with the linear programming tool *lp_solve* v4 for instancing parameters. In the opposite case, *checkClocks*() is carried out for computing the fastest/slowest timed executions [11, 22].

Step 4: Test Case Computation. If during the traversal an accepting state is met, the search ends by a call to the *writeTrace*() to decorate the path obtained by the different verdicts. The output is an XML file according to a Calife DTD.

The algorithm *gga* is explained in more detail in the annex and in [22]. Its complexity is linear in the size of the CS times the complexity for solving linear programming problems. Finally, if no accepting state is met, *gga* is automatically started for a new attempt (the launching is parametrized). Moreover, it is possible to generate a test case that has the minimal number of transitions for a given number of attempts. We point out that TGSE is based on a conformance relation (traces inclusion) taking into account data and clocks [22].

5   Case Study: CSMA/CD Protocol

The CSMA/CD Protocol (Fig. 9) is made up of a bus (medium of communication) and one or more senders (transmitting stations). We do not model here the receivers. When two or several senders transmit simultaneously data on the bus (!*begin*), a collision event (!*CD*) is sent by the bus to all senders. These

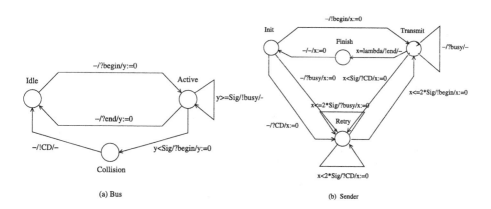

Fig. 9. CSMA/CD specifications

latter have to retransmit later. Thereafter, *Senders* (resp. *Bus*) will denote the ETIOA representing the specification of the sender (resp. bus) (Fig. 9).

The next table reports the experimental results of applying TGSE to CSMA/ CD with one bus, several senders and the TP: $1 \xrightarrow{-/!begin/-} 2 \xrightarrow{h=5/!CD/-} 3$. TP checks that a sender sends data (*!begin*), and the bus detects a collision at instant 5 (*!CD*). A test case generated by TGSE for this test appears bellow. In this case, Sender 1 transmits at 0, Sender 2 transmits at 0 and the Bus detects a collision at 5.

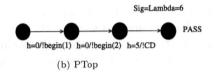

(b) PTop

The experience is run on a INTEL P4 DELL INSPIRON 5100 PC, with 256Mo of RAM running Mandrake 10.0. Each input of the table was launched 2000 times. Lock represents the number of times that a transition can appear in a path, Size TC the average size of a test case, Nb Sender the number of senders considered and CPU Time the average generation time. The reader can notice that the generation with Lock equal to 1 takes more time. In fact, with Lock equal to 1, *gga* moves to locked states and thus dequeues several times.

Lock	Nb Sender	TC Size	CPUs Time (s)
1	5	3	0.303
1	10	3	0.621
1	20	3	0.914
10^3	5	55	0.098
10^3	10	79	0.234
10^3	20	130	0.793

Although the CSMA/CD protocol is of a reduced size, the use of several senders increases its complexity. The obtained results are encouraging and improvements are at hand.

6   Conclusion

The aim of this paper is to show that different types (conformance, interoperability, embedded, component) and approaches (passive and active) of protocol testing can be treated in a unified manner. To achieve this aim, we have presented a testing framework based on the generic model of communicating systems (CS) and the methodology of generic generation algorithms (GGA). The CS model defines a set of communicating entities (components) modeled by extended timed input/output timed automata (ETIOAs), a set of common resources (variables and parameters) shared by these entities, and a topology of communication specifying the different synchronizations allowed in a system configuration. We showed that the test activities consist then in modeling a CS and applying an algorithm GGA. To our knowledge, this is the first framework that can fully handle various test types and approaches. Our framework was implemented in TGSE tool (Test Generation, Simulation and Emulation). The current version of TGSE can be used both for passive and active testing of one or several components but supports only deterministic ETIOAs and the definition of a test purpose.

Regarding future work, our intention is to study the impact of a coverage criterion on the definition of GGA, and to realize a realistic performance evaluations of TGSE on complex protocols. Finally, until very recently, research had been carried out with almost no interactions between the software and protocol testing communities. So, our framework might bring the two communities together, since object-oriented programming languages and component-based approaches (code testing) are now widely used in software development, and these lead to the need of state-based test techniques.

Acknowledgments

We would like to thank the members of the specific action AS 32 carried out by Ana Cavalli for their fruitful remarks. We would like also to thank the ENSEIRB students Dimitri Kandassamy, Jamel Semeh, David Dogoh and Carine Beduz for their participations in the realization of TGSE.

References

1. Jan Tretmans. Test Generation with Inputs, Outputs and Repetitive Quiescence, *Software - Concepts and Tools* 17(3): 103-120 (1996).
2. Laura BrandSSn and Ed Brinksma. A test generation framework for quiescent real-time systems. *FATES2004*, Linz, Austria September 21 2004.
3. S. Seol, M. Kim, S. Kang, J. Ryu. Fully automated interoperability test suite derivation for communication protocols, *Computer Networks* Volume 43, Pages 735 - 759, December 2003.
4. Rachel Cardell-Oliver. Conformance Testing of Real-Time Systems with Timed Automata Specifications, *Formal Aspects of Computing*, 12(5):350-371,2000.
5. Duncan Clarke and Insup Lee. Automatic Test Generation for the Analysis of a Real-Time System: Case Study. In *3rd IEEE RTSS*, 1997.
6. A. En-Nouaary, R. Dssouli, F. Khenedek, and A. Elqortobi. Timed test cases generation based on state characterization technique, *In 19th IEEE RTSS*, Madrid, Spain, 1998.
7. T. Higashino, A. Nakata, K. Taniguchi, and A. Cavalli. Generating Test Cases for a Timed I/O Automaton model, *TESTCOM99*, Budapest, Hungary, September 1999.
8. A. Koumsi, M. Akalay, R. Dssouli, A. En-Nouaary, L. Granger. An approach for testing real time protocols, *TESTCOM*, Ottawa, Canada, 2000.

9. Dino Mandrioli, Sandro Morasca, and Angelo Morzenti. Generating Test Cases for Real-Time Systems from Logic Specifications, *ACM Transactions on Computer Systems*, 13(4):365-398, 1995.
10. Jan Springintveld, Frits Vaandrager, Pedro R. D'Argenio. Testing Timed Automata. *Theoretical Computer Science*, 252(1-2):225-257, March 2001.
11. I. Berrada, R. Castanet, P. Félix. From the Feasibility Analysis to Real-Time Test Generation, *Studia Informatica Universalis* Volume 3 (2) pp.203-230 2004.
12. K. Larsen, M. Mikucionis, and B. Nielsenn. Real-time system testing on-the-fly. *In the 15th Nordic Workshop on Programming Theory (NWPT)*, 2003.
13. M. Krichen and S. Tripakis. Black-box conformance testing for real-time systems. *In SPIN 2004* (2004), Spring-Verlag Heidelberg, pp. 109-126.
14. Abdeslam En-Nouaary, Rachida Dssouli: A Guided Method for Testing Timed Input Output Automata. TestCom 2003: 211-225
15. Ahmed Khoumsi, Thierry JTron, HervT Marchand. Test Cases Generation for Nondeterministic Real-Time Systems. FATES 2003: 131-146
16. K. El-Fakih and N. Yevtushenko. Fault Propagation by Equation Solving. *Proceeding of FORTE*, Madrid, Spain. LNCS 3235, September 2004.
17. S. Boroday, A. Petrenko, R. Groz and Y.M. Quemener. Test Generation for CEFSM Combining Specification and Fault Coverage. *TESTCOM02*, Berlin, Germany, March 2002.
18. R. Alur and D. Dill. A theory of timed automata, *Theoretical Computer Science*, 126:183-235, 1994.
19. AndrT Arnold et M. Nivat. Comportements de processus. *In Colloque AFCET "Les mathTmatiques de l'Informatique"*, pages 35-68, 1982.
20. TomSSs Barros, RabTa Boulifa and Eric Madelaine. Parameterized Models for Distributed java Objects. *FORTE*, Madrid, Spain. LNCS 3235, September 2004.
21. Baptiste Alcalde, Ana Cavalli, Dongluo Chen, Davy Khuu, and David Lee. Network Protocol System Passive Testing for Fault Management: A Backward Checking Approach. *Proceeding of FORTE*, Madrid, Spain. LNCS 3235, September 2004.
22. Ismail Berrada, Richard Castanet and Patrick FTlix. Techinques de Test d'InteropTrabilitT. Fourniture Calife, 2005.
23. Ana Cavalli, David Lee, Christian Rinderknecht and Fatiha Zandi. Hit-or-Jump: An algorithm for embedded testing with applications to IN services. *FORTE/PSTV'99*, Beijing, China. October 1999.
24. Claude Jard, Thierry JTron, LTnanck Tanguy and CTsar Viho. Remote testing can be as powerful as local testing. *FORTE/PSTV'99*, Beijing, China. October 1999.
25. http://www.cril-technology.fr.

Annex

Description. The generation algorithm gg^a applied to a CS S performs a depth-first traversal of $\zeta(S)$. During the traversal, gg^a computes the symbolic trace and checks the feasibility of the new fired transitions. When an accepting state is met (the function $AcceptStates()$), a backtracking in the synchronization path is performed to decorate this latter with verdicts (function $writeTrace()$). Due to the space limit, we will present only the $gg^a()$ and $SymbolicTrace()$ functions.

Data Structure.
States: a n+1-tuple $(s_{tr}, s_1, ..., s_n)$.
Context: records the values of variables and last resets for clocks.

Transition: a n+1-table of pointers on the current transitions.
Element is a structure composed of a *States*, a *Context* and a *Transitions*.
Path: a stack of Elements. It managed by the operations "push", "top" and "pop".

Other functions.
SynchronizationOnEvents(): chooses a synchronization vector from the current state and returns a structures Element composed of the new transitions and states reached.
getSuccessors(): returns a successor state of the current state.
getInitStates: returns the initial state of $\zeta(S)$.

Function gga():
1.   **Begin**
2.   States:= getInitialStates(), Element := NULL, Path := $\emptyset$;
3.   **Do**
4.   Element := SynchronizationOnEvents(States);
5.   If (Element $\neq$ NULL) then
6.   push(Element,Path);
7.   SymbolicTrace(Path);
8.   If(!feasible(Path)) then
9.   pop(Element,Path);
10.   States := getSuccessors(Element);
11.   Else
12.   pop(Path); States := getSuccessors(top(Path)) ;
13.   If(AcceptStates(States))
14.   writeTrace(Path);
15.   **While**(Path $\neq \emptyset$);
16.   **End**

Symbolic Trace. Let us assume that $M = (S, L, C, P, V, V_0, Pred, Ass, s_0, T)$ is an ETIOA such that $C = \{c_1, ..., c_k\}$, $V = \{v_1, ..., v_m\}$, $V_0 = \{v_{01}, ..., v_{0m}\}$ and $\rho = t_1...t_n$ is a suite of transitions of M from the initial state. The symbolic trace of ρ is ρ such that $\forall\ t_i = (s_{i-1}, a, pred, ass, s_i)$ of ρ, and $\forall v \in V$, v is replaced in $pred$ by its last value before t_i (see [22]). **SymbolicTrace()** uses two vectors: $V1$ contains the current values of variables (may depend on P parameters). $V2$ is a vector of natural numbers. $V2[q]$ stocks the index of transition where the clock $x_q \in C$ was last reseted.

Function SymbolicTrace():
1.   **Input/output:** $\rho = t_1...t_n$, with $t_i = (s_{i-1}, a, pred_i, ass_i, s_i)$,
2.   **Temporary Data** Two vectors: $V1$ of size m and $V2$ of size k.
3.   **Begin**
                    /*Initialization */
4.   For $i := 1$ to m Do $V1[i] \leftarrow v_{0i}$;
5.   For $i := 1$ to k Do $V2[i] \leftarrow 0$;
                    /*Updating */
6.   For $i := 1$ to n Do
7. $pred_i \leftarrow updatePredicates(pred_i, V1, V2, i)$;
8. $updateContext(ass_i, V1, V2, i)$;
9.   **End**

The function **UpdatePredicates** replaces the variables with their current values from $V1$. For clocks, if c_p is last reseted in the t_j and i is the index of the current step then c_k is replaced by $h_i - h_j = h_i - h_{V2[p]}$ (line 4).

Function UpdatePredicates():
1. **Input:** A predicate *pred*, an index i, and two vectors $V1$ and $V2$.
2. **Output:** A predicate *predUpdated*.
3. **Begin**
4. $predUpdate \leftarrow pred[h_i - h_{V2[1]}, ..., h_i - h_{V2[k]}, V1[1], ..., V[m], P]$;
5. **End**

The function **UpadateContext** updates 1) the current values of variables in $V1$ from the new assignments (lines 4 and 5), and 2) the clock resets $V2$ by assigning the index of the current step (lines 6 et 7).

Function UpdateContext():
1. **Input:** An assignment *ass*, and an index i.
2. **Input/Output:** Two vectors $V1$ and $V2$.
3. **Begin**
4.   For $j := 1$ to m Do
5.   If $v_j := f(v_1, .., v_m, P) \in ass$ then $V1[j] := f(V[1], .., V[m], P)$;
6.   For $j := 1$ to m Do
7.   If $c_j := 0 \in ass$ then $V2[j] := i$;
8. **End**

Coping with Nondeterminism in Network Protocol Testing

R.E. Miller[1], D.-L. Chen[2], D. Lee[3], and R. Hao[4]

[1] Department of Computer Science, University of Maryland
[2] Department of Computer Science, Tsinghua University, China
[3] Department of Computer Science and Engineering, Ohio State University
[4] Bell Labs Research China, Lucent Technologies

Abstract. Given a nondeterministic protocol specification, we want to determine the deterministic implementation under test with a conformance of trace inclusion in the specification. We identify them using both active and passive testing. Four cases are studied with experiments on Internet protocols. In the first two cases, the implementation machine is a derived machine of the specification. In the third case, the implementation machine is a derived machine of the k-way expansion of the specification machine. The fourth case deals with the general case of nondeterministic machines.

1 Introduction

Network protocols are often partially specified, the unspecified inputs may be ignored, or cause an error message [1]. The choices depend on the design of an implementation. Often network protocols contain optional requirements, which are specified by "MAY" statements in many RFCs. These two cases can be regarded as options in network protocol specifications, providing certain flexibility to protocol implementations. Due to the options, a protocol cannot be modelled by a deterministic finite state machine (DFSM). The common approach is to use a non-deterministic finite state machine (NFSM) to model these protocols instead. This situation has complicated the protocol testing operations. There are several studies on testing NFSMs, both active testing [2], [3], [4], [5] and passive testing [6].

When a vendor implements a protocol, it may implement some of the options and discard the others, or implement all the options with configuration parameters and let the user make the decision. Hence, given a protocol, there may be different deterministic implementations that conform to the specification. Often we need to identify the deterministic implementation of the object system. For example, there are several TCP variants deployed on the Internet. [7] provided test scenarios to examine these deployments. In general, it is a machine identification problem, however, it is rather complex.

In this paper, we assume the specification machine A is an NFSM and the implementation machine B which conforms to A is a DFSM. We study the

F. Khendek and R. Dssouli (Eds.): TestCom 2005, LNCS 3502, pp. 129–145, 2005.

problem of identifying the DFSM implementation, given its NFSM specification. The specification machine is assumed to have n states, p inputs and q outputs. For such a machine, there are totally $(qn)^{pn}/n!$ candidate machines. The problem of identifying B is difficult, because the distinguishing sequences for a NFSM may not exist, when there is a distinguishing sequence, it can be of exponential length [8]. Due to the difficulty in the general case, some work [3], [5] focus on the special case of *Observable* NFSM (ONFSM).

Our approach is different from the exist works in several aspects. First we provide both passive testing and active testing algorithms for this machine identification problem. Passive testing/monitoring [6], [9] has been a important area in network analysis. Our passive testing algorithm can be used to identify new features of the protocols, like routing protocols, HTTP and TCP. Second we study the cases of both ONFSM and general NFSM. According to the NFSM is observable or not and the implementation is a subautomaton or not, there are four cases. We study the complexity of each case and provide algorithms when it is feasible. We propose the concept *derived machines* to study the relationship between implementation and specification in the first three cases. Third we study the nondeterminism in Internet protocols and propose algorithms to solve the identification problem. Third we use simulation to show the efficiencies of the algorithms.

In Section 2 we provide the basic concepts for NFSM. We propose the definition of *derived machines* when a DFSM is a subautomaton of an NFSM specification. Section 3, 4, 5 and 6 study the four cases, respectively. We discuss both active and passive testing approaches with experiments on Internet protocols. Conclusion is drawn on Section 7.

2   Preliminaries

The following definitions and properties about NFSMs are based on [8].

Definition 1. *A nondeterministic finite state machine (NFSM) M is a 4-tuple $M = (I, O, S, h)$ where I is a finite set of input symbols, O is a finite set of output symbols, S is a finite set of states, h is the transition function: $S \times I \to \mathcal{P}(S \times O)$, where $\mathcal{P}$ denotes the power set operator.*

Definition 2. *The transition function f is defined for $s, s' \in S, x \in I, y \in O$ as follows:*

$$f(s, x) \stackrel{\text{def}}{=} \{s' \mid \exists y \ [s', y] \in h(s, x)\}.$$

The conditional transition function h_y is defined for $s, s' \in S, x \in I, y \in O$ as follows:

$$h_y(s, x) \stackrel{\text{def}}{=} \{s' \mid [s', y] \in h(s, x)\}.$$

Definition 3. *A NFSM is observable if for all $s \in S, x \in I, y \in O$, we have $Card(h_y(s, x)) \leq 1$, where $Card(Z)$ denotes the cardinal number of the set Z.*

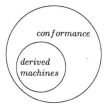

Fig. 1. Derived Machine and Conformance

In this paper, the specification is assumed to be reduced[8]. Our conformance relation is defined by *trace inclusion* [10]. Let s_A, s_B be the initial states of machine A, B respectively. The *trace* of machine M from its initial state s_M is denoted by $T(M, s_M)$.

Definition 4. *An implementation machine* (B, s_B) *conforms to a specification machine* (A, s_A) *if and only if* $T(B, s_B) \subseteq T(A, s_A)$.

We use *derived machine* when an implementation machine is a *subautomaton* of the specification machine. A derived machine is required to be connected and deterministic.

Definition 5. *Given a NFSM* $A = (I, O, S, h)$, *an implementation machine* $B = (I', O', S', h')$ *is called a* derived machine *of* A *if* B *is deterministic, connected, and a subautomaton of* A.

Since a derived machine B is a subautomaton of the specification machine A, its trace is included in the trace of A; hence it conforms to A. Note when B conforms to A, B is not required to be a derived machine of A, which is discussed in Section 5. There relationship is shown in Figure 1.

We now proceed to investigate four different cases of determining the implementations from active and passive testing.

3   Case 1: Derived Machine of Observable NFSM

Network protocol specifications may allow different responses according to an input. This kind of nondeterminism is *observable* and can be judged by the appearance of the output.

3.1   Active Testing Approach

Usually network protocol systems have *reset capability*, an input symbol, denoted by r, leading the machine back to its initial state, and it can be realized by a restart of the device. Obviously, taking an i/o pair as a symbol, ONFSM can be regarded as a deterministic finite automaton. To identify the implementation machine, we have to traverse the transitions with the same input from a state. The following procedure will construct the implementation machine.

begin
1. $B = (I, O, S = \{s_0\}, h = \{r\})$;   /* s_0: initial state, r: reset */
2. **while** ($\exists s_i \in S, a \in I$, $h(s_i, a)$ not specified in B)
3.   trap B in s_i;   /* usually with a sequence started by r */
4.   send input a to B, assume output b;
5.   find the unique transition $h(s_i, a) = (s_j, b)$ in the transition table of A;
6.   add $h(s_i, a) = (s_j, b)$ to h;
7.   **if** ($s_j \notin S$)   /* a new state explored in B */
8.   add s_j to S;
end

In step 5, there is a unique transition $h(s_i, a) = (s_j, b)$ in the transition table of A because A is observable and B conforms to A. If we use a breadth-first search (BFS) strategy to explore the transitions from the states, the ith explored state is reachable in i steps with prefix r. Assume the ith state has k_i undecided inputs, $k_i \leq p$. The complexity of the construction is $C \leq \sum_{i=1}^{n} i * k_i = O(p \sum_{i=1}^{n} i) = O(pn^2)$.

Theorem 1. *If A is an ONFSM and B is a derived machine of A, the construction procedure takes time $O(pn^2)$ to build the derived machine .*

3.2   Passive Testing Approach

The passive testing approach is divided into a *homing* phase and an *identification* phase, similar to [6]. The procedure traces the current states of the specification NFSM A using the observed I/O sequence from the implementation machine B. A *passive testing map* records the possible states and their related transitions during a passive testing.

Definition 6. *A passive testing map is a directed graph $G = (V, E)$. For an observed sequence $e_1, e_2, \ldots, e_k$, $V = L_0 \cup L_1 \cup \ldots \cup L_k$, where L_j records the possible states after event e_j, a node $v_{ij} = (s_i, j) \in L_j$ if s_i is a possible state after event e_j. $E = tr(0,1) \cup tr(1,2) \cup \ldots \cup tr(k-1,k)$, where $tr(j, j+1)$ records the possible transitions from L_j to L_{j+1}. If $(s_i, j) \in L_j$, and there is a transition $s_i \xrightarrow{e_j} s_v$ in the specification, then $(s_v, j+1) \in L_{j+1}$ and $\{(s_i, j) \xrightarrow{e_j} (s_v, j+1)\} \in tr(j, j+1)$.*

Figure 2 gives an example of passive testing map. We use the following notations in our passive testing algorithms:

L^-, L^+ - the level before and after level L in state tracing
$e_L = x_L / y_L$ - the input/output pair at level L
C - the current state set (C^- is the level before the current level)

If a state in the specification can trigger multiple transitions upon an input, it is a *branching state* for this input. A derived machine selects from the candidate transitions.

ON-LINE CHECKING - ALGORITHM I

input: ONFSM A and observed sequence

output: fault_detected or machine B

begin
1. $B := A$; /* B is derived from A by deleting transitions from the branching states */
2. $C := \{s_0, s_1, ..., s_{n-1}\}$; /* the initial possible state set */
3. **while** ($|C| > 1$ & $next(x/y)$) /* the homing phase */
4. $C := h_y(C, x)$; /* state tracing */
5.   record the transitions from C^- to C in $tr(C^-, C)$; /* for backtracking */
6. $L := C^-$; /* the current level C is a singleton */
7. **do** /* the backtracking phase */
8.   remove states from L with no outgoing transition in $tr(L, L^+)$;
9.   remove transitions leading to the removed states from $tr(L^-, L)$;
10.   **if** ($|L| \equiv 1$)
11.   remove transitions $\{(s, s', x_L/y')|s \in C, y' \neq y_L \}$ from B;
12. **while** ($|L| \equiv 1$); /* backtrack to decide the past before C */
13. **while** ($|C| \equiv 1$ & $next(x/y)$) /* the forward phase */
14.   **if** ($f(C, x) > 1$) /* branching state for x */
15.   remove transitions $\{(s, s', x/y')|s \in C, y' \neq y \}$ from B;
16.   **if** (B becomes deterministic) /* all the branchings are decided */
17.   **return** B;
18. $C := h_y(C, x)$; /* state tracing */
19. **if** ($|C| \equiv 0$) /* fault detected */
20.   **return** fault_detected;
21. **if** ($next(x/y) \equiv null$) /* passive testing ends */
22.   **return** B; /* B is not decided yet */
end

The algorithm is mainly composed of three phases, a homing phase (line 2-5), a backward tracking phase (line 6-12), and a forward tracking phase (line 13-18).

We use an example in Figure 2 to illustrate these phases. Assume the current state set is $\{s_1, s_2\}$ when a sequence a/x b/y c/z is observed. *Homing* is reached at the observation of b/y and the current state set is $\{s_6\}$. *Backtracking* removes $\{s_5, s_2\}$ from the levels. The transition $s_1 \xrightarrow{a/y} s_4$ is removed from B. The forward checking of c/z removes $s_6 \xrightarrow{c/y} s_9$ from B.

In Algorithm I, since back-tracking is triggered by homing, a node in the passive testing map can be back-tracked at most once. Hence the time complexity of this algorithm is $O(L)$, where L is the length of the test sequence. Because the passive testing map is recorded for backtracking, it has at most $n * L$ nodes.

Theorem 2. *If A is an ONFSM and B is a derived machine of A, Algorithm I is correct. Its time complexity is $O(L)$ and its space complexity is $O(n * L)$, where L is the length of the test sequence.*

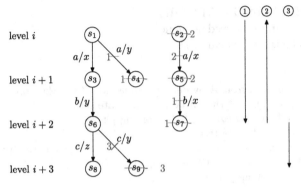

level i

level $i+1$

level $i+2$

level $i+3$

process 1 : homing phase
process 2 : backward tracking phase
process 3 : forward tracking phase
$-j$: this transition(state) is removed in process j from the passive testing map
$\times j$: this transition is removed in process j from the implementation machine

Fig. 2. The passive testing map

3.3   An Example from RIP

In the Routing Information Protocol (RIP) [11], "split horizon" is a scheme for avoiding problems caused by including routes in updates sent to the gateway from which they were learned. There are two types of split horizon. The "simple split horizon" scheme omits routes learned from one neighbor in updates sent to that neighbor. While "split horizon with poisoned reverse" includes such routes in updates, but sets their metrics to *infinity*. In Fig.3, the transition from $S1$ to $S2$ represents "simple split horizon" and the transition from $S1$ to $S3$ represents "split horizon with poisoned reverse". The two transitions are exclusive.

To identify the implementation machine, in active testing, the test sequence is $r.a.$ In passive testing, the derived machine can be decided at the observed output b_1 or b_2. We have tried both active testing and passive testing to identify the RIP implementation. Most vendors set "simple split horizon" as the default configuration; but Cisco (with IOS version 12) only supports "split horizon with poisoned reverse".

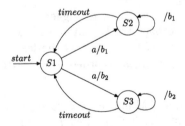

Fig. 3. Split horizon in RIP

4   Case 2: Derived Machine of NFSM

In this section we study the case when the specification A is a general NFSM (including non-observable transitions) and the implementation B is a derived machine of A. In active testing, two approaches, machine enumeration and machine construction, are proposed to solve the machine identification problem. In passive testing, *backtracking* is used to eliminate the unselected transitions.

4.1   Active Testing Approaches

In this case, it is *NP-hard* to determine the implementation machines:

Theorem 3. *Given NFSM A, B is a derived machine of A, the problem of deciding B is NP-hard.*

Deciding Hamiltonian Path can be reduced to deciding B out of A, thus the algorithm is NP-hard. The proof is given in [12] .   □

Two methods are proposed here to identify the derived machine under test. The first method is on-line machine enumeration. Candidate machines are enumerated on-line and then use cross verification to separate the candidate machines. The second method is on-line machine construction using distinguishing sequences. We want to reduce the number of candidate machines by eliminating the inconsistent transitions with distinguishing sequences. The first method is "generate then distinguish", while the second is "distinguish when generating". We will compare their efficiencies by simulation experiment.

4.1.1 On-line Machine Enumeration
Commonly the number of derived machines is quite large with nondeterministic transitions. On-line machine enumeration dose not generate all the derived machines. Instead it constructs machines on-the-fly. It removes inconsistent transitions according to the output of machine B.

On-line Machine Enumeration

queue Q contains machines to explore
begin
1. Insert A into Q;   /*initialization */
2. **while** $Q \not\equiv \phi$
3.   take a machine M from Q;
4.   **for** each unexplored state s in M;
5.   **for** each input i
6.   get the last y from machine B with input $prefix(s).i$;
7.   remove transitions $s \times i/y' \rightarrow s'$ $(y' \neq y)$ from M;
8.   **if** there is no transition with output y from $s \times i$
9.   **goto** 2;   /*for another candidate machine*/
10.   **if** there exists multiple transitions with output y from $s \times i$
11.   **for** each transition $t = s \times i/y \rightarrow s'$
12. M' clones M, M selects t and removes others transitions with $s \times i$;

```
13                    Insert M' to Q;
14.                      goto 3;   /*for another candidate machine*/
15.          mark state s as explored;
16.     print M;   /* M is a derived machine */
17. apply cross verification to identify the derived machine;
end
```

On-line enumeration generates a set of candidate deterministic machines. *Cross verification* [13] is applied to rule out the wrong ones(line 17).

If the specification has l nonobservable branching points of degree $r_1, r_2, ..., r_l$, there is at most $K = \prod_{i=1}^{l} r_i$ candidate machines generated from the enumeration. At each branching point, a sequence with length less than n is applied to machine B to get the corresponding output. It is known that the minimization of an DFSM is $O(pn \log n)$ [14], where p is the number of input symbols. The standardization takes time $O(pn)$ [15]. It takes $O(pn)$ to determine if two machines are isomorphic or not. If the two machines are not isomorphic, it takes $O(pn)$ to find a distinguishing sequence with length not greater than $2n - 1$ which can separate the two machines. The confirmation experiment takes time $O(pn^3)$ [13].

Theorem 4. *The on-line enumeration algorithm takes $O(Kpn \log n + pn^3)$ steps to identify the derived machine B, where K is the product of all the branching degrees in the specification machine.*

4.1.2 On-line Machine Construction

The second method constructs the machine using *pairwise distinguishing sequences*. The on-line enumeration method generates many candidate machines when the number of nonobservable transitions increases. If pairwise distinguishing sequences [16] exist, the end states of nonobservable transitions can be decided, reducing the number of candidate machines.

On-line Machine Construction

queue Q contains machines to explore
```
begin
1.  Insert A into Q;   /*initialization */
2.  while Q ≢ φ
3.     take a machine M from Q;
4.     while M is not decided
5.        explore the visited states in M;
6.        for each state with nonobservable transitions
7.           generate pairwise distinguishing sequences;
8.           if pairwise distinguishing sequence ds exists
9.              use ds to remove inconsistent transitions;
10.          if only one candidate state s left
11.             marked s as visited;
12.          else   /*the end states are not distinguishable now*/
13.             generate multiple copies according to the nonobervable transitions;
14.             add the copies to Q;
```

15.   **if** M is decided
16.   print M;
17. **if** there are multiple candidate machines
18.   apply cross verification to identify the derived machine;
end

This is an *adaptive strategy*. The construction procedure approximates the object derived machine by iterations. When more states are decided, the possibilities of pairwise distinguishing sequences increase and their lengths decrease.

For an NFSM, a distinguishing sequence of two state s_i and s_j may not exist. If it does, in the worst case, its length is up to $(2^n - 2)$[12]. But in practice they do exist and are not long.[1]

4.1.3 Experiments
Table 1 gives the experimental results of our simulations. In a simulation, a NFSM specification is generated according to four parameters: *number of states, input/output alphabet, branching rate*, where *branching rate* indicates the possi-

Table 1. Experiments

# of states	# of inputs	# of outputs	branching rate	average time(msec)	
				on-line enumeration	on-line construction
4	2	2	0.2	115	70
4	2	2	0.4	121	42
4	3	3	0.2	335	27
4	3	3	0.4	50	18
8	2	2	0.2	55	16
8	2	2	0.4	66	14
8	3	3	0.2	38	20
8	3	3	0.4	387	34
10	2	2	0.2	63	25
20	2	2	0.2	104	22

bility of having multiple transitions for an input. Then on-line enumeration and on-line construction are applied to the NFSM. Each simulation was done 4 times with the same parameters and calculates the average cost[2]. From Table 1 we can tell that in most cases, on-line construction takes less time to identify the object machine than on-line enumeration.

---

[1] Note that even pairwise distinguishing sequence does not exist, the algorithm still works by generating multiple copies and then using cross verification.
[2] The simulations are carried out on a Pentium 1.2GHz PC. Note that the absolute time is not important here. Different simulations should not be compared because the complexity of a NFSM is not merely decided by its parameters.

Table 2. Experiment Results on Active Testing

		1	2	3	4	5
# of requests for DS		19296	240	64	16	532
DS not exist		0	0	0	2	200
DS exist	len = 1	17376	162	32	12	266
	len = 2	1920	78	32	2	57
	len = 3	0	0	0	0	9

When multiple copies are generated in on-line enumeration, further splitting has to be done for each copy. Also a state distinguishing may have to be repeated on these copies. That is the reason that on-line enumeration takes more time.

For NFSMs with {8 states, 3 inputs, 3 output, branching rate=0.2}, we use on-line construction to identify the derived machines and study the distribution of distinguishing sequences, as shown in Table 2. In most cases, pairwise distinguishing sequences exist and their length is less than 3. This explains the advantage of the on-line construction method.

4.2   Passive Testing Approach

4.2.1 Algorithm

The passive testing procedure for identifying derived machines from NFSM with non-observable transitions is different from ALGORITHM I. The current state set may not converge even after it reaches a singleton state. To identify B, *backtracking* is used to rule out the unselected transitions from A.

ON-LINE CHECKING - ALGORITHM II

input: ONFSM A and observed sequence
output: fault_detected or machine B

begin
1. $B := A$; /* B is derived from A by deleting transitions from the branching states */
2. $C := \{s_0, s_1, ..., s_{n-1}\}$;   /* the initial possible state set */
3. **while** ($|C| > 0$ & $next(x/y)$)
4.   **if** ($|C| \equiv 1$)   /* singleton */
5.   remove the transitions $\{(s, s', x/y')|s \in C, y' \neq y \}$ from B;
6. $C := h_y(C, x)$;   /* state tracing */
7.   record the transitions from C^- to C in $tr(C^-, C)$;
8.   **if** ($\exists s \in C^-, h_y(s, x) \equiv 0$)   /* discrepancies from the current state set */
9. $L := C^-, level\_changed := true$;   /* the backtracking start level */
10.   **while** ($level\_changed$)   /* backtrack until the current level unchanged */
11.   **if** ($\exists s \in L$ with no outgoing transitions)
12.   **foreach** ($s \in L$ with no outgoing transitions)
13.   delete transitions leading to s in $tr(L^-, L)$;
14.   delete s from L;   /* s is not in the current path */
15. $L := L^-$;   /* set L to a upper level */
16.   **else**   /* the current level unchanged */
17. $level\_changed := false$;   /* backtracking ends */

18.   **while** $(L < C)$ /* go from the unchanged level to the end of the explored levels */
19.   **if** ($|L| \equiv 1$)   /* the current level is a singleton */
20.   remove $\{t | s \in L, t = (s, s', x_L/?), t \notin tr(L, L^+)\}$ from B; /*? means *don't care*/
21.   **if** (B becomes deterministic)   /* all the branchings are decided */
22.   **return** B;
23. $L := L^+$;   /* set L to the next level */
24. **if** ($|C| \equiv 0$)   /* fault detected */
25.   **return** fault_detected;
26. **if** ($next(x/y) \equiv null$)   /* passive testing ends */
27.   **return** B;   /* B is not decided yet */
end

Algorithm II is different from Algorithm I. Since the current state set is not monotonously decreased, the *backward checking* and *forward checking* are combined together. Whenever a discrepancy in outputs is observed in the current state set, backward checking is triggered to remove the invalid paths in the past. Then forward checking is used to select transitions from singletons.

We use an example specified in Figure 4 to illustrate the procedure. Assume the current level is $\{s_1\}$ and a sequence a/x b/y c/z is observed. Backward checking starts at the third level when s_5, s_7 cannot fire any transitions with c/z. Backtracking removes s_3, s_5 from the levels. Hence the upper levels become singletons. Then forward checking removes the following three transitions from B: $s_1 \xrightarrow{a/x} s_3$, $s_2 \xrightarrow{b/y} s_5$, $s_2 \xrightarrow{b/z} s_6$.

Backtracking stops when the level L stays unchanged in this tracking. We call a level L visited in backtracking if one or more states are removed in this backtracking. A level is at most visited n times in backtracking during the whole procedure, where n is the number of states in A. The forward checking is similar.

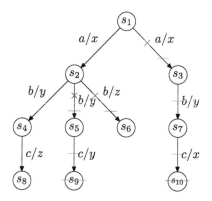

— : this transition(state) is removed from the passive testing map
× : this transition is removed from the implementation machine

Fig. 4. The passive test map

In Algorithm II, the state tracing levels are required to be stored for backtracking. Note that when a level becomes a singleton, backtracking will not overcome it and the level information before it can be discarded.

Theorem 5. *If A is a NFSM and B is a derived machine of A, Algorithm II is correct and takes time $O(n * L)$ and space $O(nl)$ for checking where L the test sequence length, and $l < L$ is the maximum length of a backtracking.*

4.2.2 Experiments

In a passive testing simulation, a NFSM and its derived machines are generated at first; then for each derived machine, multiple observed sequences are generated; after that the passive testing algorithm is applied to check if the derived machine can be identified. In Table 3 , the 4 columns in the left are parameters of the NFSMs; the length of a random generated sequence is $n * p$. A set of observed sequences are generated from the derived machine. If there exists 22 derived machines, 14 are identified by the current set of sequences, it is denoted as 14/22. The other 8 derived machines are not identified by the observed sequences. It is clear that the observed behavior increases the possibility of machine identification.

Table 3. The effect of multiple observed sequences

# of states	# of inputs	# of outputs	branching rate	length of a sequence	# of observed sequences			
					0.5*n	n	4n	8n
4	2	2	0.1	n*p	5/5	5/5	5/5	5/5
4	2	2	0.2	n*p	10/22	11/22	14/22	14/22
8	2	2	0.2	n*p	11/22	17/22	22/22	22/22

Also some observed sequences should be long enough to reach the all the states in the machine. Table 4 shows long observed sequences increase the possibility of machine identification by passive testing.

Table 4. The effect of lengths of observed sequences

# of states	# of inputs	# of outputs	branching rate	# of sequences	length of observed i/o sequence			
					0.5 n*p	n*p	2n*p	10n*p
4	2	2	0.1	n	5/5	5/5	5/5	5/5
4	2	2	0.2	n	4/22	11/22	13/22	14/22
8	2	2	0.2	n	6/22	14/22	22/22	22/22

4.3   TCP Congestion Control

Congestion control is required in TCP implementations. Several algorithms have been proposed and standardized [17] in the network community. In RFC2581

[17], *Slow Start* and *Congestion Avoidance* are mandatory , while *Fast Retransmit* and *Fast Recovery* (FR/FR) are recommended. Figure 5 shows the difference between them. The FR/FR algorithm has one more state, *FR/FR*, than the basic requirement. When duplicate ACKs (*dupAck*) are observed, the FR/FR algorithm counts its number and fires the transition to state *FR/FR* when there are 3 *dupAck*s. The transitions about *dupAck* are non-observable.

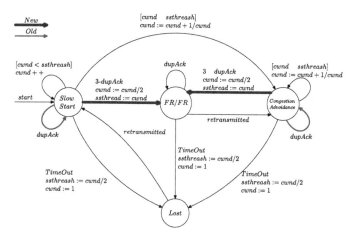

Fig. 5. TCP Congestion Control Algorithms

Different congestion control algorithms are deployed in the Internet. It is a job to study their deployment and their influence on TCP performance. In [7], the authors designed test scenarios to identify what algorithm is used in the remote web server. It is an active testing approach.

5   Case 3: Conformance Relation in Observable NFSM

The specification machine A is observable but the implementation machine B is not restricted to a derived machine of A. Fig.6 gives an example that B conforms to A but B is not equivalent to any derived machine of A.

We will prove that B is a derived machine of the *k-way expansion* of A, where k is the upper bound of the state number of B.

Definition 7. *Given a NFSM $A = (I, O, S, h)$, a k-way expansion of A is a machine $\overline{A} = (I, O, S', h')$ that*

$\forall s_i \in S, s_i^m \in S', 1 \leq m \leq k;$

$\forall [s_j, y] \in h(s_i, x), [s_j^m, y] \in h'(s_i^l, x), 1 \leq m \leq k, 1 \leq l \leq k$ □

We can see that $\overline{A}$ has k times the number of states in A and k^2 transitions for each transition in A. Our idea is that each state in B may be constructed by a set of states in $\overline{A}$. Intuitively each state in B may be constructed from a copy

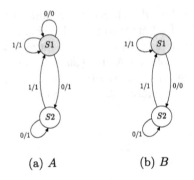

(a) A (b) B

Fig. 6. Machine A, B, $T(B, S1) \subseteq T(A, S1)$

of A, by selecting the features it needed. If each state in B can be simulated by one copy of A, then B may be constructed in the k-way expansion of A.

Theorem 6. *Suppose A is a minimal ONFSM specification and B is a minimal DFSM that conforms to A that has k states. Then B is equivalent to some derived machine of the k-way expansion of A.*

The proof is given in [12].   □

Fig.7(b) is a derived machine of the 2-way expansion of machine A in Fig.6. It is equivalent to machine B in Fig.6.

We show in [12] that B may not be a derived machine of $(k-1)$-way expansion of A. $k-way$ expansion is the upper bound and the bound is tight.

There are totally $k^{knp}/(k!)^n$ derived machines from the k-way expansion of A. See [12] for an explanation of the calculation.

For this case we only consider the active testing approach. Enumerating the derived machines can only be applied when k, n, p are very small numbers. We

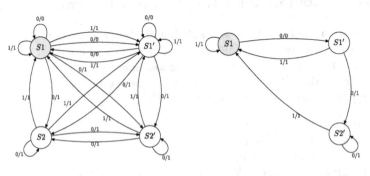

(a) 2-way expansion of A in 6(a)   (b) a derived machine of $\overline{A}$

Fig. 7. 2-way expansion and its derived machine

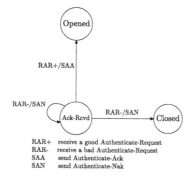

Fig. 8. PAP Authentication with retries

examine the topological structure of the graph of the machine, take into consideration of the strongly connected components(SCC) and the branching to them, and apply heuristics to reduce the candidate derived machines. We use the following PPP Authentication to illustrate.

The Password Authentication Protocol (PAP) is used as a PPP authentication protocol [18]. The dial-in system sends its PAP authentication information (*username, password*) in an Authenticate-Request to the server. The server sends an Authenticate-Ack to indicate the success of authentication. If authentication fails, the server sends an Authenticate-Nak. It should also attempt to terminate the link to frustrate a would-be system cracker, although a small number of attempts are often permitted. Most dial-up systems permit users to retry several times. We take state *Ack-Rcvd* and its neighbor states from the state machine. {*RAR+, RAR-* } are valid inputs for *Ack-Rcvd*. Another input *RAA* is for the PAP server and is ignored in *Ack-Rcvd*, since *Ack-Rcvd* is a state for the PAP client. The SCC containing *Ack-Rcvd* and its outgoing transitions are shown in Fig 8.

Assume that the retries number is not greater than 3, we can generate the derived machines from *3-way expansion* of state *Ack-Rcvd*. The derived machines can be easily classified into 4 equivalent classes [19]. Since *RAR+/SAA* is a distinguishing sequence for state *Ack-Rcvd* and *Closed*. We can use it to judge which derived machine is the implementation machine.

6   Case 4: General NFSM

The specification machine A is a general NFSM and the implementation machine B is not restricted - may not be a derived machine of A. It can be shown [19] that B can not be constructed from k-*way expansion* of A, no matter how large k is [12]. Obviously, we can disregard the specification A and apply a test to identify B [16] with an exponential cost. Can we take advantage of the information in the specification machine and identify the implementation machine more efficiently? As a pathological case, the given NDFS A may not contain any information, eg, upon each input/output, there is a transition from each state to all other states.

It remains to be investigated that how to explore the structure and available information of A to derive B efficiently or that how to characterize A such that B can be constructed in polynomial time.

7   Conclusion

We have studied the problem of identifying the deterministic implementation from nondeterministic specification using active or passive testing. From experiences in real network protocol system implementations, we introduce the concept of derived machines, developed efficient algorithms for determining the implementation machines, and analyzed the complexity of various cases with different assumptions on the specifications and implementations. The results are summarized in Table 5.

Table 5. Derived Machine and Conformance

Case	complexity	active testing	passive testing
derived machine of ONFSM	$O(pn^2)$	√	√
derived machine of NFSM	NP-hard	on-line exploration	back-tracking
conformance of ONFSM	k-way expansion	expand SCC	?
conformance of NFSM	exponential	?	

We only explored limited structures of the nondeterministic specifications, i.e., their observability and k-way expansions. In practice, the nondeterminism is more restricted, as seen from the case studies of PPP, RIP and TCP. It remains to be studied how to further explore and classify the nondeterministic structure so that the implementations can be determined more efficiently.

References

1. Yannakakis, M., Lee, D.: Testing finite state machines: Fault detection. J. Computer Science and Systems **50** (1995) 209–227
2. Luo, G., v. Bochmann, G., Petrenko, A.F.: Test selection based on communicating nondeterministic finite state machines using a generalized wp-method. IEEE Transactions on Software Engineering **20** (1994) 149–162
3. Petrenko, A., Yevtushenko, N., Bochmann, G.: Testing deterministic implementations from nondeterministic fsm specifications. In: Proc. of the 9th Intern Workshop on Protocol Test Systems. (1996)
4. Alur, R., Courcoubetis, C., Yannakakis, M.: Distinguishing tests for nondeterministic and probabilistic machines. In: Symposium on Theory of Computer Science, 1995, ACM. (1995) 363–372
5. Hierons, R.: Generating candidates when testing a deterministic implementation against a non-deterministic finite-state machine. The Computer Journal **46** (2003) 307–318

6. Lee, D., N.Netravali, A., Sabnani, K.K., Sugla, B., John, A.: Passive testing and applications to network management. In: Proceedings of IEEE International Conference on Network Protocols. (1997)
7. Padhye, J., Floyd, S.: On inferring TCP behavior. In: ACM SIGCOMM. (2001) 287–298
8. Starke, P.H.: Abstract Automata. American Elsevier Publishing Company, Inc (1972)
9. Lee, D., Chen, D., Hao, R., Miller, R.E., Wu, J., Yin, X.: A formal approach for passive testing of protocol data portions. In: International Conference on Network Protocols. (2002) 122–131
10. Milner, R.: Communication and Concurrency. Prentice Hall International (1989)
11. Malkin, G.: RIP version 2 - carrying additional information. RFC 1723 (1994)
12. Miller, R.E., Chen, D., Lee, D., Hao, R.: Coping with nondeterminism in network protocol testin, full version. (2005)
13. Lee, D., Sabnani, K.: Reverse-engineering of communication protocols. In: International Conference on Network Protocols. (1993) 208–216
14. Hopcroft, J.: An nlogn algorithm for minimizing states in a finite automaton. The Theory of Machines and Computations (1971) 189–196
15. Kohavi, Z.: Switching and Finite Automata Theory. second edition edn. McGraw-Hill, Inc., New York (1978)
16. Lee, D., Yannakakis, M.: Principles and methods of testing finite state machines - a survey. Proceedings of The IEEE **84** (1996) 1090–1123
17. Allman, M., Paxson, V., Stevens, W.: TCP Congestion Control. RFC 2581 (1999)
18. Carlson, J.D. In: PPP Design, Implementation, and Debugging. 2nd edition edn. Addison Wesley Professional (2000) 99
19. Lee, D., Miller, R.: Passive testing of network protocols specified by nondeterministic finite state machines, draft document. (1999)

Eliminating Redundant Tests in a Checking Sequence

Jessica Chen[1], Robert M. Hierons[2],
Hasan Ural[3], and Husnu Yenigun[4]

[1] School of Computer Science,
University of Windsor, Windsor,
Ontario, N9B 3P4, Canada
[2] Department of Information Systems and Computing,
Brunel University, Uxbridge,
Middlesex, UB8 3PH, UK
[3] School of Information Technology and Engineering,
University of Ottawa, Ottawa,
Ontario, K1N 6N5, Canada
[4] Faculty of Engineering and Natural Sciences,
Sabanci University, Tuzla 34956, Istanbul, Turkey

Abstract. Under certain well–defined conditions, determining the correctness of a system under test (SUT) is based on a checking sequence generated from a finite state machine (FSM) specification of the SUT. When there is a distinguishing sequence for the FSM, an efficient checking sequence may be produced from the elements of a set $E_{\alpha'}$ of α'-sequences that verify subsets of states and the elements of a set E_C of subsequences that test the individual transitions. An optimization algorithm may be used in order to produce a shortest checking sequence by connecting the elements of $E_{\alpha'}$ and E_C using transitions drawn from an acyclic set. Previous work did not consider whether some transition tests may be omitted from E_C. This paper investigates the problem of eliminating subsequences from E_C for those transitions that correspond to the last transitions traversed when a distinguishing sequence is applied in an α'–sequence to obtain a further reduction in the length of a checking sequence.

1 Introduction

Finite state machines (FSMs) can be used to model many types of systems including communication protocols [1] and control circuits [2]. A number of specification languages such as SDL, Estelle, X-machines and Statecharts are based on extensions of FSMs. FSM based test techniques can often be applied to systems specified using such languages [3, 4, 5, 6, 7, 8].

Given a formal model or specification of the required behaviour of the *system under test (SUT)* I it is normal to assume that I behaves like some unknown model that can be described using some particular formalism [9]. Given an FSM

F. Khendek and R. Dssouli (Eds.): TestCom 2005, LNCS 3502, pp. 146–158, 2005.

M, that models the required behaviour of SUT I, it is normal to assume that I behaves like some (unknown) FSM M_I with the same input and output alphabets as M. A common further assumption is that M_I has no more states than M.

Suppose M has n states. Let the set of deterministic FSMs with the same input and output alphabets as M and no more than n states be denoted $\Phi(M)$. A finite set of input sequences is a *checking experiment* for M if, between them, they distinguish M from every element of $\Phi(M)$ which is not equivalent to M. Given FSM M, there is some checking experiment [10]. A *checking sequence* is an input sequence that forms a checking experiment.

The problem of generating a checking sequence for an FSM M is simplified if M has a distinguishing sequence: an input sequence $\bar{D}$ with the property that the output sequence produced by M in response to $\bar{D}$ is different for the different states of M. There has been much interest in the generation of short checking sequences from an FSM M when a distinguishing sequence is known [11, 12, 13, 14]. Hierons and Ural [13] showed that an efficient checking sequence may be produced by combining the elements in some predefined set $E_{\alpha'}$ of α'–sequences that verify subsets of states and the elements of a set E_C of subsequences that test individual transitions using an acyclic set E'' of transitions from M. An optimization algorithm is then used in order to produce a shortest checking sequence by connecting the elements of $E_{\alpha'}$ and E_C using transitions drawn from E''. Their work did not consider whether some transition tests may be omitted from E_C.

In this paper, we show that the length of the checking sequences can be reduced even further, since not every element in E_C needs to be included in a checking sequence. Specifically, we eliminate subsequences from E_C for each transition that corresponds to the last transition traversed when a distinguishing sequence is applied in an α'–sequence to obtain further reductions in the length of a checking sequence. The reason we can eliminate the tests for such transitions is that, the existence of α'–sequences and the existence of the other transition tests in the checking sequence, already guarantee the correctness of the transitions for which the test segments are eliminated.

The shortest prefix of a distinguishing sequence $\bar{D}$ that distinguishes a state in M can actually be used as a special distinguishing sequence for that state [15]. Based on this observation, we use prefixes of distinguishing sequences as well, in order to further reduce the length of checking sequences.

The remaining of this paper is structured as follows. Section 2 introduces the basic concepts and notations used in this paper. Elements of an existing checking sequence construction method [13] which will be utilized in the proposed approach are also summarized here for completeness. Section 3 gives the details of the proposed approach to elimination of redundant transition tests in a checking sequence. A running example is used to illustrate the proposed approach and to compare the length of the resulting checking sequence to the one constructed by [13]. Conclusions are drawn in Section 4.

2   Preliminaries

2.1   Finite State Machines

A deterministic FSM M is defined by a tuple $(S, s_1, X, Y, \delta, \lambda)$ in which S is a finite set of *states*, $s_1 \in S$ is the *initial state*, X is the finite *input alphabet*, Y is the finite *output alphabet*, δ is the *next state function* and λ is the *output function*. The functions δ and λ can be extended to input sequences in a straightforward manner. The number of states of M is denoted n and the states of M are enumerated, giving $S = \{s_1, \ldots, s_n\}$. An FSM is *completely specified* if the functions λ and δ are total. If an FSM M is not completely specified, it is possible to make M completely specified by either adding an error state or, for each $s_i \in S, a \in X$ such that $(s_i, a) \notin dom\ \delta$, adding the transition $(s_i, s_i, a/null)$ where *null* represents no output being produced.

A transition τ is defined by a tuple $(s_i, s_j, x/y)$ in which s_i is the *starting state*, x is the input, $s_j = \delta(s_i, x)$ is the *ending state*, and $y = \lambda(s_i, x)$ is the output.

Two states s_i and s_j of M are *equivalent* if, for every input sequence $\bar{x}$, $\lambda(s_i, \bar{x}) = \lambda(s_j, \bar{x})$. If $\lambda(s_i, \bar{x}) \neq \lambda(s_j, \bar{x})$ then $\bar{x}$ *distinguishes* between s_i and s_j. An FSM M is *minimal* if no FSM with fewer states than M is equivalent to M. A sufficient condition for M to be minimal is that every state can be reached from the initial state of M and no two states of M are equivalent. Throughout this paper $M = (S, s_1, X, Y, \delta, \lambda)$ will denote a deterministic, minimal, and completely specified FSM that describes the required behaviour of the SUT I.

An FSM, that will be denoted M_0 throughout this paper, is described in Figure 1. Here, $S = \{s_1, s_2, s_3, s_4, s_5\}$, $X = \{a, b\}$ and $Y = \{0, 1\}$.

Two FSMs M_1 and M_2 are *equivalent* if and only if for every state of M_1 there is an equivalent state of M_2 and vice versa. An input sequence distinguishes between two FSMs if its application leads to different output sequences for these FSMs. An input sequence $\bar{x}$ is a *checking sequence* for M if and only if $\bar{x}$ distinguishes between M and all elements of $\Phi(M)$ that are not equivalent to M.

Given FSM M, a *distinguishing sequence* is an input sequence $\bar{D}$ whose output distinguishes all the states of M. More formally, for all $s_i, s_j \in S$ if $s_i \neq s_j$ then $\lambda(s_i, \bar{D}) \neq \lambda(s_j, \bar{D})$. Thus, for example, M_0 has distinguishing sequence aba.

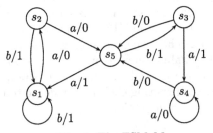

Fig. 1. The FSM M_0

We will use the notation $\bar{D}_i$ to denote the prefixes of distinguishing sequences that is sufficient to distinguish the states. Formally, given a distinguishing sequence $\bar{D}$ and a state s_i, $\bar{D}_i$ is the shortest prefix of $\bar{D}$ such that for any state s_j, if $s_i \neq s_j$ then $\lambda(s_i, \bar{D}_i) \neq \lambda(s_j, \bar{D}_i)$.

While not every minimal FSM has a distinguishing sequence and determining whether a minimal FSM has a distinguishing sequence is PSPACE-Complete [16], there has been interest in the problem of generating a checking sequence in the presence of a distinguishing sequence [12, 13, 17, 14]. This paper considers the problem of generating an efficient checking sequence from a deterministic, minimal, and completely specified FSM M with a known distinguishing sequence $\bar{D}$.

2.2   Directed Graphs

A *directed graph (digraph)* G is defined by a tuple (V, E) in which V is a set of vertices and E is a set of directed edges between the vertices. Each edge may have a label. An edge e from vertex v_i to vertex v_j with label l will be represented by (v_i, v_j, l). Edge e *leaves* v_i and *enters* v_j. For a vertex $v \in V$, $indegree_E(v)$ denotes the number of edges from E that enter v and $outdegree_E(v)$ denotes the number of edges from E that leave v.

Given an FSM, it is possible to produce a corresponding digraph in which each state is represented by a vertex and each transition is represented by an edge. Throughout this paper $G = (V, E)$ ($V = \{v_1, \ldots, v_n\}$) will be a digraph, that represents M, in which state s_i is represented by vertex v_i. A transition from state s_i to state s_j with input x and output y is represented by edge $e = (v_i, v_j, x/y)$ from E.

A sequence $\bar{P} = (n_1, n_2, x_1/y_1), \ldots, (n_{r-1}, n_r, x_{r-1}/y_{r-1})$ of pairwise adjacent edges from G forms a *walk* in which each *node* n_i represents a vertex from V and thus, ultimately, a state from S. Here $initial(\bar{P})$ denotes n_1, which is the *initial node* of $\bar{P}$, and $final(\bar{P})$ denotes n_r, which is the *final node* of $\bar{P}$. The sequence $\bar{T} = (x_1/y_1), \ldots, (x_{r-1}/y_{r-1})$ is the *label* of $\bar{P}$ and is denoted $label(\bar{P})$. In this case, $\bar{T}$ is said to *label* the walk $\bar{P}$. $\bar{T}$ is said to be a *transfer sequence* from n_1 to n_r. The walk $\bar{P}$ can be represented by the tuple $(n_1, n_r, \bar{T})$ or by the tuple $(n_1, n_r, \bar{x}/\bar{y})$ in which $\bar{x} = x_1, \ldots, x_{r-1}$ is the *input portion* of $\bar{T}$ and $\bar{y} = y_1, \ldots, y_{r-1}$ is the *output portion* of $\bar{T}$.

A *tour* is a walk whose initial and final nodes are the same. Given a tour $\bar{\Gamma} = e_1, \ldots, e_k$, $e_i = (n_i, n_{i+1}, l_i)$, $(1 \leq i \leq k)$ then $e_j, \ldots, e_k, e_1, \ldots, e_{j-1}$ is a walk formed by *starting* $\bar{\Gamma}$ with edge e_j, and hence by *ending* $\bar{\Gamma}$ with edge e_{j-1}. An *Euler Tour* is a tour that contains each edge exactly once. If the set of vertices represented by the nodes of walk $\bar{P}$ are distinct, $\bar{P}$ is said to be a *path*. A sequence of edges $e_1, \ldots, e_k$, $e_i = (n_i, n_{i+1}, l_i)$, $(1 \leq i \leq k)$ forms a *cycle* if $e_1, \ldots, e_{k-1}$ is a path and n_1 and n_{k+1} represent the same vertex. A set E' of edges from G is *acyclic* if no subset of E' forms a cycle.

A digraph is *strongly connected* if for any ordered pair of vertices (v_i, v_j) there is a walk from v_i to v_j. An FSM is *strongly connected* if the digraph that represents it is strongly connected. It will be assumed that any FSM considered in this paper is strongly connected.

2.3   Recognizing States and Verifying Edges

The algorithms of Ural et al. [14] and Hierons and Ural [13] use the notion of recognizing a node, corresponding to the state reached by a given input/output sequence, and verifying an edge of E. These notions, which are defined in terms of a given distinguishing sequence $\bar{D}$, are defined below. The key point is that, since the SUT I has no more states than M, if we observe the n possible responses of M to $\bar{D}$ when applied to I, then $\bar{D}$ must also be a distinguishing sequence for I. Once this has been demonstrated, we can use $\bar{D}$ to investigate the structure of I and thus to determine whether it is equivalent to M.

Consider a walk $\bar{P}$ and the nodes within it. Let $\bar{Q} = label(\bar{P})$.

Definition 1.   1. A node n_i of $\bar{P}$ is d–recognized in $\bar{Q}$ as state s of M if n_i is the initial node of a subpath of $\bar{P}$ whose label is input/output sequence $\bar{D}/\lambda(s, \bar{D})$.

  2. Suppose that $(n_q, n_i, \bar{T})$ and $(n_j, n_k, \bar{T})$ are subpaths of $\bar{P}$ and $\bar{D}/\lambda(s, \bar{D})$ is a prefix to $\bar{T}$ (and thus n_q and n_j are d–recognized in $\bar{Q}$ as state s of M). Suppose also that node n_k is d–recognized in $\bar{Q}$ as state s' of M. Then n_i is t–recognized in $\bar{Q}$ as s'.

  3. Suppose that $(n_q, n_i, \bar{T})$ and $(n_j, n_k, \bar{T})$ are subpaths of $\bar{P}$ such that n_q and n_j are either d–recognized or t–recognized in $\bar{Q}$ as state s of M and n_k is either d–recognized or t–recognized in $\bar{Q}$ as state s' of M. Then n_i is t–recognized in $\bar{Q}$ as s'.

  4. If node n_i of $\bar{P}$ is either d–recognized or t–recognized in $\bar{Q}$ as state s then n_i is recognized in $\bar{Q}$ as state s.

  5. Edge $e = (v_a, v_b, x/y)$ is verified in $\bar{Q}$ if there is a subpath $(n_i, n_{i+1}, x_i/y_i)$ of $\bar{P}$ such that n_i is recognized as s_a in $\bar{Q}$, n_{i+1} is recognized as s_b in $\bar{Q}$, $x_i = x$ and $y_i = y$.

The first rule says that a node is d–recognized as a state s if it is followed by the input/output sequence $\bar{D}/\lambda(s, \bar{D})$. This is essentially saying that $\bar{D}$ defines a one–to–one correspondence between the states of the SUT and the states of M: this must be the case if the n different responses to $\bar{D}$ are observed in the SUT. The second and third rules say that if an input/output sequence is observed from two different nodes n and n' that are both recognized (d–recognized or t–recognized) as the same state then their final nodes should correspond to the same state of M.

The fifth rule is related to a transition test that is defined as follows: The transition test for a transition $\tau = (s_i, s_j, x/y)$ is $x/y\bar{D}/\lambda(s_j, \bar{D})\bar{T}_j$ for some transfer sequence $\bar{T}_j$. The following result, that provides a sufficient condition for an input sequence to be a checking sequence, may now be stated.

Theorem 1.   (Theorem 1, [14]) Let $\bar{P}$ be a walk from G representing M that starts at v_1 and $\bar{Q} = label(\bar{P})$. If every edge $(v_i, v_j, x/y)$ of G is verified in $\bar{Q}$, then the input portion of $\bar{Q}$ is a checking sequence of M.

In this paper checking sequence generation is based on this result.

2.4   Defining α'-Sequences

Suppose that an input/output sequence $\bar{x}/\bar{y}$, that labels a walk from the initial state of M, contains the n subsequences of the form $\bar{D}_i/\lambda(s_i, \bar{D}_i)$ $(1 \le i \le n)$. If $\bar{x}/\bar{y}$ labels a walk from the initial state of the SUT then, since the SUT has at most n states, $\bar{D}$ must be a distinguishing sequence for the SUT. Further, the response to $\bar{D}$ defines a bijection between the states of M and the states of the SUT. This observation lies at the heart of algorithms for generating a checking sequence on the basis of a distinguishing sequence and motivates the use of α'-sequences. We now adapt α'-sequences [13], so that they use prefixes of $\bar{D}$, and then explain their role in the construction of a checking sequence.

The first step is to choose a set $V_1, \ldots, V_q$, $q \ge 1$, of non-empty subsets of V whose union is V. We then order the elements of each V_k, $1 \le k \le q$, to give $V_k = \{v_1^k, \ldots, v_{m_k}^k\}$. Each v_i^k represents a state $s_{f(i,k)}$ of M (defining a function f). For each v_i^k, we produce a sequence $\bar{D}_{f(i,k)}/\lambda(s_{f(i,k)}, \bar{D}_{f(i,k)})\bar{T}_i^k$ that is the result of applying $\bar{D}_{f(i,k)}$ in state $s_{f(i,k)}$ followed by a (possibly empty) transfer sequence $\bar{T}_i^k = (\bar{x}_i^k/\bar{y}_i^k)$ whose final state corresponds to v_{i+1}^k, $1 \le i \le m_k$, $(v_{m_k+1}^k$ can be any v_w^j, $1 \le j \le q, 1 \le w \le m_j)$. Each V_k thus defines a walk $\bar{P}_k$ whose starting state is $s_{f(1,k)}$ and whose label is the α'-sequence $\bar{\alpha}_k' = \bar{D}_{f(1,k)}/\lambda(s_{f(1,k)}, \bar{D}_{f(1,k)})\bar{T}_1^k \bar{D}_{f(2,k)}/\lambda(s_{f(2,k)}, \bar{D}_{f(2,k)})\bar{T}_2^k \ldots \bar{D}_{f(m_k,k)}/\lambda(s_{f(m_k,k)}, \bar{D}_{f(m_k,k)})\bar{T}_{m_k}^k \bar{D}_{f(w,j)}/\lambda(s_{f(w,j)}, \bar{D}_{f(w,j)})\bar{T}_w^j$ $(1 \le j \le q, 1 \le w \le m_j)$. The set $A = \{\bar{\alpha}_1', \ldots, \bar{\alpha}_q'\}$ is called an α'-set. Given $\bar{\alpha}_i' \in A$, $\bar{\alpha}_i'$ is called an α'-sequence from A. Where A is clear, its members are simply called α'-sequences.

The α'-sequences play the following roles in checking sequence generation.

1. They verify that $\bar{D}$ is a distinguishing sequence for the SUT since they contain the n different $\bar{D}_i/\lambda(s_i, \bar{D}_i)$.
2. For each $s_i \in S$ they d–recognize the final state of the walk from s_i with label $\bar{D}_i/\lambda(s_i, \bar{D}_i)\bar{T}_i^k$. This is achieved by the subsequence $\bar{D}_i/\lambda(s_i, \bar{D}_i)\bar{T}_i^k$ followed by the sequence $\bar{D}_j/\lambda(s_j, \bar{D}_j)$ for some $1 \le j \le n$. Thus, if the subsequence $\bar{D}_i/\lambda(s_i, \bar{D}_i)\bar{T}_i^k$ is seen elsewhere in the label of a walk, then the final node of this is t–recognized as the state s_j reached from s_i by a walk with label $\bar{D}_i/\lambda(s_i, \bar{D}_i)\bar{T}_i^k$.
3. An α'-sequence with starting state s_i starts with $\bar{D}_i/\lambda(s_i, \bar{D}_i)$ and thus its initial node is recognized.
4. If the label of a walk $\bar{P}$ contains every α'-sequence from α'-set A then the final node of each $\bar{P}_k$ is t–recognized.

2.5   Checking Sequence Construction: An Existing Approach

The proposed reduction of the length of a checking sequence is an enhancement of the checking sequence generation approach given in [13] where first a digraph $G' = (V', E')$ is obtained by augmenting the given digraph $G = (V, E)$, representing an FSM as follows:

Let the labels $\bar{\alpha}_1', \ldots, \bar{\alpha}_q'$ of walks $\bar{P}_1, \ldots, \bar{P}_q$ form an α'-set A. Then, from the elements of A, a set of transfer sequences, called T-set, is formed as a set of labels of subpaths $\bar{R}_1, \ldots, \bar{R}_p$ of walks $\bar{P}_1, \ldots, \bar{P}_q$, such that each element $\bar{T}_i$ of T-set is $label(\bar{R}_i)$ where $\{\bar{R}_i : i = 1, 2, \ldots, p\} = \{(v_j^k, \delta(v_j^k, \bar{D}_{f(j,k)}\bar{x}_j^k),$ $\bar{D}_{f(j,k)}/\lambda(v_j^k, \bar{D}_{f(j,k)})\bar{T}_j^k : 1 \le k \le q$ and $1 \le j \le m_k\}$. Thus, the starting state of $\bar{R}_i$ is recognized in some $\bar{\alpha}_k'$ because $\bar{D}_{f(j,k)}$ is applied to the starting state of $\bar{R}_i$ and the ending state of $\bar{R}_i$ is recognized in some $\bar{\alpha}_k'$ because the ending state of $\bar{R}_i$ is $\delta(v_j^k, \bar{D}_{f(j,k)}\bar{x}_j^k)$ to which $\bar{D}_{f(j+1,k)}$ is applied. The set of walks $\bar{P}_1, \ldots, \bar{P}_q$ and the set of subpaths $\bar{R}_1, \ldots, \bar{R}_p$ are included in G' as edges in $E_{\alpha'} \subset E'$ and in $E_T \subset E'$, respectively, in order to facilitate the recognition of vertices in the label $\bar{Q}$ of the solution $\bar{P}$. Moreover, a transition test for each edge of G is induced in G' as edges in $E_C \subset E'$ in order to verify every transition of M in $label(\bar{P}) = \bar{Q}$. Furthermore, a set of edges from E are included in G' as edges in $E'' \subset E'$ to increase the connectivity of the vertices in G'.

Formally, $G' = (V', E')$ is obtained from $G = (V, E)$ as follows:
$V' = V \cup U'$ where $U' = \{v_i' : \text{for every } v_i \in V\}$ and $E' = E_{\alpha'} \cup E_C \cup E_T \cup E''$,
$E_{\alpha'} = \{((\text{starting state of } \bar{P}_k), (\text{ending state of } \bar{P}_k)', \bar{\alpha}_k') : 1 \le k \le q\}$,
$E_C = \{(v_i', v_j, x/y) : (v_i, v_j, x/y) \in E\}$,
$E_T = \{((\text{starting state of } \bar{R}_i), (\text{ending state of } \bar{R}_i)', \bar{T}_i) : 1 \le i \le p\}$,
E'' is a subset of $\{(v_i', v_j', x/y) : (v_i, v_j, x/y) \in E\}$ such that $G'' = (U', E'')$ has no tour and G' is strongly connected.

Once G' is formed, a minimal symmetric augmentation G^* of the graph induced by the edges in $E_{\alpha'} \cup E_C$, that may be produced by adding edges from E', is found. If G^*, with its isolated vertices removed, is connected, G^* has an Euler tour. Otherwise, a heuristic is applied to make G^* connected and an Euler tour is formed. This Euler tour $\bar{\Gamma}$ of G^* contains all edges in $E_{\alpha'} \cup E_C$. Let τ be a transition with ending state s_1 which is represented by an edge $e = (v_i', v_1, x/y) \in E_C$ in $\bar{\Gamma}$. Let $\bar{P}$ be a walk of G' that is formed by ending $\bar{\Gamma}$ with edge e. Then, the input portion of $\bar{Q} = label(\bar{P})\bar{D}_1/\lambda(s_1, \bar{D}_1)$ is a checking sequence of M that starts at v_1, in accordance with Theorem 1.

3   Producing Checking Sequences

This section explains how, given an α'-set A, we can produce a checking sequence without considering some of the edges in E_C which represent test segments for a subset L of E. Thus, L is a set of edges which stand for transitions whose transition tests are redundant and can be eliminated. In this paper, we use prefixes of distinguishing sequences wherever it applies, and we use empty transfer sequences in the formation of α'-sequences. In the following, we first define L, and then explain the algorithm to generate the checking sequence.

3.1   Transition Test Exemption

Similar to showing an edge being verified as given in Definition 1, in order to show a sequence of edges being verified we first introduce the notion of a sequence of edges being traced.

Definition 2. *Let $\bar{\rho} = e_1 e_2 \ldots e_h$ be a sequence of edges in G, where $e_m = (v_{i_m}, v_{i_{m+1}}, x_m/y_m)$ for $1 \leq m \leq h$. $\bar{\rho}$ is traced in $\bar{Q} = label(\bar{P})$ of a walk $\bar{P}$ in G if there exists a subpath $(n_1, n_{h+1}, x_1' x_2' \ldots x_h'/y_1' y_2' \ldots y_h')$ in $\bar{P}$ such that n_1 is recognized as v_{i_1}, n_{h+1} is recognized as $v_{i_{h+1}}$, and $x_m/y_m = x_m'/y_m'$ for $1 \leq m \leq h$.*

Lemma 1. *Let $\bar{\rho} = e_1 e_2 \ldots e_h$ ($h \geq 1$) be a sequence of edges in G, where $e_m = (v_{i_m}, v_{i_{m+1}}, x_m/y_m)$ for $1 \leq m \leq h$, and $\bar{Q} = label(\bar{P})$ be the label of a walk $\bar{P}$ in G. Assume that $\bar{\rho}$ is traced in $\bar{Q}$. Further assume that $e_1, e_2, \ldots, e_{h-1}$ (all the edges in $\bar{\rho}$ except the last one) are all verified in $\bar{Q}$. Then, e_h is also verified in $\bar{Q}$.*

Proof. The proof is by induction on h. When $h = 1$ the lemma holds trivially, since $\bar{\rho}$ has only one edge, hence Definition 1 applies.

For the induction step, since e_1 is verified in $\bar{Q}$, there must exist a subpath $\bar{P}_1 = (n_j, n_k, x_1'/y_1')$ in $\bar{P}$ where n_j is recognized as v_{i_1}, n_k is recognized as v_{i_2}, and $x_1'/y_1' = x_1/y_1$. Since $\bar{\rho}$ is traced $\bar{Q}$, there must exist a subpath $\bar{P}_2 = (n_q, n_s, x_1'' x_2'' \ldots x_h''/y_1'' y_2'' \ldots y_h'')$ in $\bar{P}$ where n_q is recognized as v_{i_1}, n_s is recognized as $v_{i_{h+1}}$, and $x_m''/y_m'' = x_m/y_m$ for $1 \leq m \leq h$. Let us divide the path $\bar{P}_2$ into two as $\bar{P}_{21} = (n_q, n_i, x_1/y_1)$ and $\bar{P}_{22} = (n_i, n_s, x_2 x_3 \ldots x_h/y_2 y_3 \ldots y_h)$. According to Definition 1, the paths $\bar{P}_1$ and $\bar{P}_{21}$ recognize n_i as v_{i_2}. Then, the existence of $\bar{P}_{22}$ in $\bar{P}$ implies that $\bar{\rho}' = e_2 e_3 \ldots e_h$ is traced in $\bar{Q}$. This concludes the proof since the length of $\bar{\rho}'$ is $h - 1$, $\bar{\rho}'$ is traced in $\bar{Q}$ and e_m (for $2 \leq m < h$) is verified in $\bar{Q}$. □

Lemma 1 suggests that if there is a sequence of edges which is traced in the label $\bar{Q}$ of a path, then $\bar{Q}$ already includes what it takes to verify the last edge in the sequence, provided that all the other edges in the sequence are verified in $\bar{Q}$. In fact, inclusion of α'–sequences in the checking sequences guarantee that there are some sequences of edges which are traced.

For each $s_i \in S$, there exists an α'-sequence in the α'-set that can d-recognize the final state of the walk from s_i with label $\bar{D}_i/\lambda(s_i, \bar{D}_i)$, as the subsequence $\bar{D}_i/\lambda(s_i, \bar{D}_i)$ is followed by $\bar{D}_j$ for some $1 \leq j \leq n$. This is due to the fact that we use empty transfer sequences between the applications of $\bar{D}_i$ and $\bar{D}_j$ in α'–sequences. Formally, we have the following result.

Lemma 2. *Let A be an α'-set, and $\bar{Q} = label(\bar{P})$ be the label of a walk $\bar{P}$ in G. If $\bar{Q}$ includes all the α'–sequences in A, then for all $s_i \in S$, $\bar{\rho}_i = e_{j_1} e_{j_2} \ldots e_{j_{|D_i|}}$, where $label(\bar{\rho}_i) = D_i/\lambda(s_i, D_i)$, $\bar{\rho}_i$ is traced in $\bar{Q}$.*

Proof. Note that $\bar{\rho}_i$ corresponds to the application of $\bar{D}_i$ at state s_i. Consider the occurrence of $\bar{D}_i/\lambda(s_i, \bar{D}_i)$ in $\bar{Q}$ which is immediately followed by an occurrence of $\bar{D}_j/\lambda(s_j, \bar{D}_j)$, for some $1 \leq j \leq n$, which is guaranteed since all α'–sequences are included in $\bar{Q}$. $initial(\bar{\rho}_i)$ will be recognized as state s_i. Since there exists an application of some $\bar{D}_j$ after $\bar{D}_i$, $final(\bar{\rho}_i)$ will be recognized as state $s_j = \delta(s_i, \bar{D}_i)$. □

Lemma 3. *Let A be an α'-set, and $\bar{Q} = label(\bar{P})$ be the label of a walk $\bar{P}$ in G such that $\bar{Q}$ includes all the α'-sequences in A. Let $\bar{\rho}_i = e_{j_1} e_{j_2} \ldots e_{j_{|D_i|}}$, be a sequence of edges where $label(\bar{\rho}_i) = D_i/\lambda(s_i, D_i)$ for some state $s_i \in S$. If all the edges $e_{j_1} e_{j_2} \ldots e_{j_{|D_i|}-1}$ are verified in $\bar{Q}$, then $e_{j_{|D_i|}}$ is also verified in $\bar{Q}$.*

Proof. The result follows from Lemma 1 and Lemma 2.   □

Suppose Figure 2 shows a subgraph of G where $\bar{D}_1 = \bar{D}_2 = x_1 x_2 x_2$. Suppose also that $\bar{Q}$ contains α'-sequences with

- x_1/y_1 x_2/y_2 x_2/y_3 $\bar{D}_3/\lambda(s_3, \bar{D}_3)$ and
- x_1/y_4 x_2/y_3 x_2/y_2 $\bar{D}_4/\lambda(s_4, \bar{D}_4)$

as subsequences. Then using the above lemma, we know that

- if edges $(n_1, n_3, x_1/y_1)$, $(n_3, n_4, x_2/y_2)$ are verified in $\bar{Q}$, then $(n_4, n_3, x_2/y_3)$ is verified in $\bar{Q}$;
- if edges $(n_2, n_4, x_1/y_4)$, $(n_4, n_3, x_2/y_3)$ are verified in $\bar{Q}$, then $(n_3, n_4, x_2/y_2)$ is verified in $\bar{Q}$.

Of course, we cannot draw conclusion in this case that if edges $(n_1, n_3, x_1/y_1)$ and $(n_2, n_4, x_1/y_4)$ are verified in $\bar{Q}$, then $(n_3, n_4, x_2/y_2)$ and $(n_4, n_3, x_2/y_3)$ are verified in $\bar{Q}$.

The following procedure shows a possible way to calculate a set of edges that can be excluded from the transition tests.

Let $P_S = \{\bar{\rho}_i \mid \forall s_i \in S, \bar{\rho}_i$ is a sequence of edges such that $label(\bar{\rho}_i) = \bar{D}_i/\lambda(s_i, \bar{D}_i)\}$. For any $\bar{\rho} \in P_S$, the last edge of $\bar{\rho}$, denoted as $last(\bar{\rho})$, is verified in $\bar{Q}$ provided that all other edges in $\bar{\rho}$ are verified in $\bar{Q}$ as proposed by Lemma 3.

Let $L_0 = \{e \mid e = last(\bar{\rho}), \bar{\rho} \in P_S\}$. Obviously, we want to have as many edges in L_0 as possible to be excluded from being considered for transition test.

First note that, for an α'-sequence $\bar{\alpha}'_k$ with starting state s_i, if we do not test any of the incoming transitions of s_i, then $\bar{\alpha}'_k$ will not be included in the

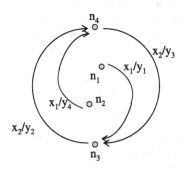

Fig. 2. An example to illustrate the edges that can be excluded from the transition tests

generated checking sequence, since each α'–sequence is used to test the end state of a transition. Similarly, since we want to generate a checking sequence that starts from s_1, the initial state of M, at least one incoming transition of s_1 must be tested, so that the tour generated passes over v_1. Therefore let L_1 be a maximal subset of L_0 such that, $indegree_{L_1}(v_i) < indegree_E(v_i)$ for each v_i corresponding to a state s_i which is s_1 or a starting state of an α'–sequence.

Further note that according to Lemma 1, the test for a transition can be exempted only if some other transitions are tested. Therefore, we need to make sure that there is no cyclic dependency between the transitions that are exempted from transition tests. The following algorithm can be used for this purpose: Construct a digraph $G_S = (V_S, E_S)$ where V_S contains one node for each $e \in L_1$. $(v_1, v_2) \in E_S$ if and only if $v_1 \neq v_2$, and for some $\bar{p} \in P_S$, v_2 corresponds to $e_2 = last(\bar{p})$, and v_1 corresponds to some e which appears in $\bar{p}$. Now, if G_S is cyclic, remove the minimal number of nodes from G_S so that it becomes acyclic. For each removed node, also remove its corresponding edge in L_1. This is an instance of Feedback Vertex Set problem [18], which is NP–complete. However certain heuristic approaches exist for this problem [19, 20].

The remaining edges in L_1 then represent transitions for which we do not need a transition test. We use L below to denote this set of edges. Since there can be at most n edges in L_0, there can be at most n transition tests that can be removed from the checking sequence.

3.2   Checking Sequence Construction

Now using L, we can improve on the algorithm in [13] for the checking sequence generation, by reducing the set of edges that must be included in the checking sequence. This is summarized below. Recall that we use prefixes of a distinguishing sequence and empty transfer sequences. The digraph $G' = (V', E')$ is obtained from $G = (V, E)$ as follows

- $V' = V \cup U'$ where $U' = \{v_i' : \text{for every } v_i \in V\}$, and $E' = E_{\alpha'} \cup E_C \cup E_T \cup E''$,
- $E_{\alpha'} = \{((\text{starting state of } \bar{P}_k), (\text{ending state of } \bar{P}_k)', \bar{\alpha}_k') : 1 \leq k \leq q\}$,
- $E_C = \{(v_i', v_j, x/y) : (v_i, v_j, x/y) \in E\}$,
- $E_T = \{(v_i, (\delta(v_i, \bar{D}_i))', \bar{D}_i/\lambda(v_i, \bar{D}_i))\colon \text{for every } v_i \in V \text{ s.t. there exists an edge in } E_C \text{ ending at } v_i\}$,
- E'' is a subset of $\{(v_i', v_j', x/y) : (v_i, v_j, x/y) \in E\}$ such that $G'' = (U', E'')$ has no tour and, excluding isolated nodes in G', G' is strongly connected.

E'' can be constructed similarly as discussed in [14]. However, we obtain an additional issue in the proposed algorithm; since we are using empty transfer sequences in the α'-sequences, such a set E'' might not exist. Where this is the case it is necessary to use non-empty transfer sequences, along the lines of [14,13]. It is straightforward both to extend the approach given in this paper to the case where non-empty transfer sequences are used and to show how a set of transfer sequences can be chosen in order to ensure the existence of E''.

Theorem 2. Let E_C' be defined as $E_C' = \{(v_i', v_j, x/y) : (v_i, v_j, x/y) \in E - L\}$. Let $\bar{\Gamma}$ be a tour of G' that contains all edges in $E_{\alpha'} \cup E_C'$ which is found in *the same manner as in [13]. Let τ be a transition with ending state s_1 which is represented by an edge $e = (v'_i, v_1, x/y) \in E'_C$ in $\bar{\Gamma}$. Let $\bar{P}$ be a walk of G' that is formed by ending $\bar{\Gamma}$ with edge e, and $\bar{Q} = label(\bar{P})\bar{D}_1/\lambda(s_1, \bar{D}_1)$. Then the input portion of $\bar{Q}$ is a checking sequence of M.*

Proof. All edges in $E - L$ are verified in $\bar{Q} = label(\bar{P})\bar{D}_1/\lambda(s_1, \bar{D}_1)$. According to Lemma 3 and the way L is constructed, if all edges in $E - L$ are verified in $\bar{Q}$, then all edges in L are verified in $\bar{Q}$. Thus, all edges of G are verified in $\bar{Q}$, and by Theorem 1, the input portion of $\bar{Q}$ is a checking sequence of M. □

3.3   Application

Let us consider FSM M_0 given in Figure 1. A distinguishing sequence for M_0 is $\bar{D} = aba$. The shortest prefixes of $\bar{D}$ that are sufficient to distinguish each state are: $\bar{D}_1 = aba$, $\bar{D}_2 = aba$, $\bar{D}_3 = ab$, $\bar{D}_4 = ab$, and $\bar{D}_5 = ab$. Using these $\bar{D}_i$'s, the α'-set for M_0 is $\{\bar{\alpha}'_1\}$, where $\bar{\alpha}'_1$, the label of $\bar{P}_1 = (v_3, v_1, \bar{\alpha}'_1)$, is

$$\bar{D}_3\bar{D}_5\bar{D}_1\bar{D}_2\bar{D}_4\bar{D}_5/\lambda(v_3, \bar{D}_3\bar{D}_5\bar{D}_1\bar{D}_2\bar{D}_4\bar{D}_5)$$

The set L_0 consists of the edges corresponding to the last transition of $\bar{D}_i$ when applied at s_i, $1 \le i \le 5$, hence $L_0 = \{(v_1, v_2, a/0), (v_3, v_4, a/1), (v_4, v_5, b/0), (v_1, v_1, b/1)\}$. The starting state of the only α'-sequence is s_3 and we have at least one incoming edge of v_3 (e.g. $(v_5, v_3, b/1)$) which is not included in L_0. Similarly, we have at least one incoming edge of v_1 (e.g. $(v_2, v_1, b/1)$) which is not in L_0. Therefore $L_1 = L_0$. The graph G_S for L_1 can shown to be acyclic, hence we also have $L = L_1$.

$E_T = \{\bar{T}_1, \bar{T}_2, \bar{T}_3, \bar{T}_4, \bar{T}_5\}$ where $\bar{T}_i = \bar{D}_i/\lambda(s_i, \bar{D}_i)$. The graph $G' = (V', E')$ is given in Figure 3.

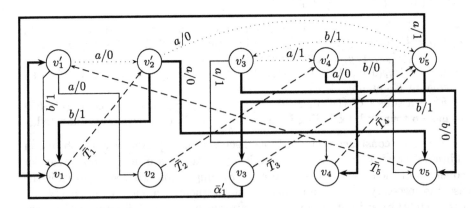

Fig. 3. $G' = (V', E')$ for M_0. The nodes in V and U' are at the bottom, and at the top respectively. The dashed lines are the edges in E_T, and the dotted lines are the edges in E''. The edges in $E_{\alpha'} \cup E_C$ are given in solid lines. The bold solid lines are the edges in $E_{\alpha'} \cup E'_C$, and the remaining solid lines are the edges in L

A tour $\bar{\varGamma}$ over G' that contains all the edges in $E_{\alpha'} \cup E'_C$ is

$$(v_1, v'_2, \bar{T}_1), (v'_2, v'_5, a/0), (v'_5, v'_3, b/1), (v'_3, v'_4, a/1), (v'_4, v_4, a/0), (v_4, v'_5, \bar{T}_4),$$
$$(v'_5, v'_3, b/1), (v'_3, v_5, b/0), (v_5, v'_1, \bar{T}_5), (v'_1, v'_2, a/0), (v'_2, v_1, b/1), (v_1, v'_2, \bar{T}_1),$$
$$(v'_2, v_5, a/0), (v_5, v'_1, \bar{T}_5), (v'_1, v'_2, a/0), (v'_2, v'_5, a/0), (v'_5, v_3, b/1), (v_3, v'_1, \bar{\alpha}'_1),$$
$$(v'_1, v'_2, a/0), (v'_2, v'_5, a/0), (v'_5, v_1, a/1)$$

Note that $\bar{\varGamma}$ already starts at v_1. Hence when we consider the the walk $\bar{P}$ corresponding to $\bar{\varGamma}$ given above, the input portion of $\bar{Q} = label(\bar{P})\bar{D}_1/\lambda(s_1, \bar{D}_1)$ forms a checking sequence of length 44, which is a shorter checking sequence than the one given in [13], which was reported as 64.

4   Conclusion

We have shown that, when α'–sequences are used in constructing a checking sequence, some transitions tests can be identified as redundant. Such tests are then eliminated by the optimization algorithm used to construct a shorter checking sequence, and hence a further reduction is obtained in the length of a resulting checking sequence.

The approach proposed in this paper starts with a given set of α'–sequences where empty transfer sequences are used after the application of each distinguishing sequence or its prefix at a state. We believe that selecting α'–sequences judiciously will result in further reductions in the length of a checking sequence. A recent study by Hierons and Ural [21] show how α'–sequences can be chosen so that their use minimizes the sum of the lengths of the subsequences to be combined in checking sequence generation. The related checking sequence generation algorithm then produces the set of connecting transitions *during* the optimization phase. Our proposed approach can also be incorporated to the method given in [21].

Acknowledgment

This work was supported in part by "Natural Sciences and Engineering Research Council of Canada under grant RGPIN 976", "Leverhulme Trust grant number F/00275/D, Testing State Based Systems", and "Engineering and Physical Sciences Research Council grant number GR/R43150, Formal Methods and Testing (FORTEST)".

References

1. Tanenbaum, A.S.: Computer Networks. 3rd edition edn. Prentice Hall International Editions, Prentice Hall (1996)
2. Pomeranz, I., Reddy, S.M.: Test generation for multiple state–table faults in finite-state machines. IEEE Transactions on Computers **46** (1997) 783–794

3. Hierons, R.M., Harman, M.: Testing conformance to a quasi–non–determinstic stream X–machine. Formal Aspects of Computing **12** (2000) 423–442

4. Holcombe, M., Ipate, F.: Correct Systems: Building a Business Process Solution. Springer–Verlag (1998)

5. Luo, G., Das, A., v. Bochmann, G.: Generating tests for control portion of SDL specifications. In: Proceedings of Protocol Test Systems VI, Elsevier (North-Holland) (1994) 51–66

6. Tan, Q.M., Petrenko, A., v. Bochmann, G.: Modeling basic lotos by fsms for conformance testing. In: IFIP Protocol Specification, Testing, and Verification XV. (1995) 137–152

7. Ural, H., Saleh, K., Williams, A.: Test generation based on control and data dependencies within system specifications in SDL. Computer Communications **23** (2000) 609–627

8. v. Bochmann, G., Petrenko, A., Bellal, O., Maguiraga, S.: Automating the process of test derivation from SDL specifications. In: SDL Forum'97, Paris, France (1997)

9. International Telecommunications Union Geneva, Switzerland: Recommendation Z.500 Framework on formal methods in conformance testing. (1997)

10. Moore, E.P.: Gedanken-experiments. In Shannon, C., McCarthy, J., eds.: Automata Studies. Princeton University Press (1956)

11. Gonenc, G.: A method for the design of fault detection experiments. IEEE Transactions on Computers **19** (1970) 551–558

12. Hennie, F.C.: Fault–detecting experiments for sequential circuits. In: Proceedings of Fifth Annual Symposium on Switching Circuit Theory and Logical Design, Princeton, New Jersey (1964) 95–110

13. Hierons, R.M., Ural, H.: Reduced length checking sequences. IEEE Transactions on Computers **51** (2002) 1111–1117

14. Ural, H., Wu, X., Zhang, F.: On minimizing the lengths of checking sequences. IEEE Transactions on Computers **46** (1997) 93–99

15. Lee, D., Yannakakis, M.: Principles and methods of testing finite–state machines – a survey. Proceedings of the IEEE **84** (1996) 1089–1123

16. Lee, D., Yannakakis, M.: Testing finite state machines: state identification and verification. IEEE Trans. Computers **43** (1994) 306–320

17. Kohavi, I., Kohavi, Z.: Variable-length distinguishing sequences and their application to the design of fault–detection experiments. IEEE Transactions on Computers (1968) 792–795

18. Garey, M.R., Johnson, D.S.: Computers and Intractability. W. H. Freeman and Company, New York (1979)

19. Bar-Yehuda, R., Geiger, D., Naor, J., Roth, R.: Approximation algorithms for the vertex feedback set problem with applications to constraint satisfaction and bayesian inference. In: Proceedings of Fifth ACM-SIAM Symposium on Discrete Algorithms. (1994) 344–354

20. Fujito, T.: A note on approximation of the vertex cover and feedback vertex set problems. Information Processing Letters **59** (1996) 59–63

21. Hierons, R.M., Ural, H.: Optimizing the length of checking sequences. (submitted)

On FSM-Based Fault Diagnosis

Zoltán Pap[1], Gyula Csopaki[1] and Sarolta Dibuz[2]

[1] Department of Telecommunications and Media Informatics,
Budapest University of Technology and Economics,[**]
Magyar tudósok körútja 2, H-1117, Budapest, Hungary
{pap, csopaki}@tmit.bme.hu,
[2] Ericsson, Armborstvägen 14., P.O.B. 1505,
125 25 Älvsjö, Stockholm
sarolta.dibuz@ericsson.com

Abstract. We study the problem of fault diagnosis, i.e., localization of difference(s) between an implementation and a specification in systems modelled by finite state machines. We show that even considering only a single fault in a finite state machine there are some situations when the exact diagnosis of the fault cannot be assured. We give an algorithm for fault diagnosis. If it is possible the procedure exactly locates a single fault, and in case exact localization is unfeasible it provides the set of all potential differences between the implementation and the specification.

Keywords: Finite state machine, fault diagnosis, fault localization, output fault, transfer fault

1 Introduction

Conformance testing provides the means to check whether a system behaves according to its specification. Given an implementation, which is a black box – i.e., we can only observe its input/output behavior – and the specification of the system, we test if the implementation conforms to the specification. In case the specification is given as a finite state machine we want to determine whether there are difference(s) between the behavior function of the specification and the implementation machines.

Fault diagnosis – in contrast – addresses the more complex problem of locating the difference(s) between the protocol specification and an implementation if they are found to be different. A solution to this problem has various applications [1]. One of the most important being the correction of a protocol implementation so that it conforms to its specification.

Much research has been done concerning fault diagnosis for different formalisms [2] [3], and using different restrictions on the cardinality of faults . All papers on fault diagnosis in FSMs are considering a fault model with two types of changes between the implementation and the specification: output faults and

---

[**] This research is supported by Inter-University Centre for Telecommunications and Informatics (ETIK).

F. Khendek and R. Dssouli (Eds.): TestCom 2005, LNCS 3502, pp. 159–174, 2005.
© IFIP 2005

transition faults. A number of papers are using the assumption, that the implementation contains only one – transition or output – fault. There are heuristic procedures presented for diagnosis of single faults in FSMs (finite state machines) [4], and in CFSMs (communicating finite state machines) [5] [6]. An exact fault localization procedure is reported by D. Lee and K. Sabnani capable of locating a single fault in a finite state machine [7]. Limiting the number of differences between the specification and the implementation to a single fault, all of these papers claim to guarantee the precise localization of the difference.

Other contributions consider the case of multiple faults. Procedures for diagnosing multiple faults in FSMs and CFSMs were also reported [8] [9]. These algorithms are not always able to locate the multiple faults of the implementation [9]. The multiple fault diagnosis method for FSMs only guarantees the correct diagnosis of certain configurations of faults in an implementation, which are characterized by a certain type of independence of the different faults [8].

In this paper we concentrate on the case of a single transition or output fault in an FSM. We show that reduced implementation machines with different single faults may have the same observable behavior, and consequently – contrary to the statements found in the literature ([4] [7]) – it is in general not possible to guarantee the precise localization of a single fault in a finite state machine.

We determine a set of sufficient conditions for the guaranteed exact localization of a single output or transfer fault. Based on the analytical results we give an algorithm, a modified version of Lee's procedure [7], for the fault diagnosis problem. If it is possible, the method exactly locates the difference between the implementation and the specification, and in case exact localization is unfeasible it provides the set of all potential single faults.

The rest of the paper is organized as follows. Section 2 provides the definitions of basic terms and notations used in the paper. In Section 3 we show that in some cases fault diagnosis fails to exactly locate a single fault in a finite state machine. In Section 4 we investigate the conditions for guaranteed the exact localization of a single fault in an FSM. In Section 5 we give an algorithm for fault diagnosis, and finally summarize our work in Section 6.

2 Preliminaries

A finite state machine can be used to model a software system. Many specification languages, such as SDL [10] and ESTELLE [11], are extensions of the FSM formalism. Specifications in such languages may be converted into FSMs from which tests can be generated [12]. Finite state systems produce outputs on their state transitions after receiving inputs. A finite state machine A is a 4-tuple (I, O, S, h) where

- I is the finite set of input symbols,
- O is the finite set of output symbols,
- S is the finite set of states,
- $h: D \to 2^{O \times S} \setminus \emptyset$ is a behavior function where $D \subseteq S \times I$ is the specification domain and $2^{O \times S}$ is the set of all subsets of the set $S \times O$.

In case the specification domain $D = S \times I$, the behavior function is defined for all state-input combinations and the FSM A is said to be completely specified (or completely defined) what we assume for the rest of the paper.

If for each pair $(s, i) \in D$ it holds that $|h(s, i)| = 1$ then FSM A is said to be deterministic. In case of a deterministic FSM instead of behavior function h we use two functions, the transition function $\delta\colon S \times I \to S$ and the output function $\lambda\colon S \times I \to O$.

For the rest of the paper, we will focus on completely specified and deterministic machines.

FSM A is said to be strongly connected, if for each pair of states (s_j, s_l), there exists an input sequence which takes A from s_j to s_l.

An FSM can be represented by a state transition diagram, a directed graph whose vertices correspond to the states of the machine and whose edges correspond to the state transitions. Each edge is labeled with the input and output associated with the transition. Supposing that the machine is currently in state s_3 and upon input c the machine moves to state s_2 and outputs 1. This transition can be written in a form $s_3 \xrightarrow{\;c/1\;} s_2$.

We extend the transition function δ and output function λ from input symbols to finite input sequences (strings) I^* as follows: For a state s_1, an input sequence $x = i_1, ..., i_k$ takes the machine successively to states $s_{j+1} = \delta(s_j, i_j), j = 1, ..., k$ with the final state $\delta(s_1, x) = s_{k+1}$, and produces an output sequence $\lambda(s_1, x) = o_1, ..., o_k$, where $o_j = \lambda(s_j, i_j), j = 1, ..., k$. The input/output sequence $i_1 o_1 i_2 o_2 ... i_k o_k$ is then called a trace of M. Note that since the FSMs in our model are deterministic all their traces are deterministic, because there are no transitions with different next states and/or outputs for the same state-input combination.

Finite state machines may contain redundant states. State minimization is a transformation into an equivalent state machine to remove redundant states.

Two states are equivalent written $s_j \cong s_l$ if and only if for every input sequence the machine will produce the same output sequence regardless of whether s_j or s_l is the starting state. In other words, for all input sequences $x \in I^*$, $\lambda(s_j, x) = \lambda(s_l, x)$. (Note that their succeeding states for a particular input sequence are also pairwise equivalent).

Two states s_j and s_l are distinguishable (inequivalent) if there exists a finite input sequence x which when applied to FSM M causes different output sequences starting in either state. In other words $\exists x \in I^*, \lambda(s_j, x) \neq \lambda(s_l, x)$. Such an input sequence is called a separating sequence of the two inequivalent states. If the shortest such sequence is of length k then (s_j, s_l) are k-distinguishable. A FSM M is reduced (minimized), if no two states are equivalent, that is, each pair of states (s_j, s_l) are distinguishable.

Machine equivalence is an equivalence relation on all FSMs with the same input and output sets.

Completely specified deterministic FSMs $M_1 = (I, O, S, \delta, \lambda)$ and $M_2 = (I, O, S', \delta', \lambda')$ are equivalent written $M_1 \cong M_2$ if their sets of traces coincide.

From an other point of view two machines M_1 and M_2 are equivalent if and only if for every state in M_1 there is at least one corresponding equivalent state in M_2, and vice versa.

A homomorphism from M_1 to M_2 is a mapping ϕ from S to S' such that for every state $s \in S$ and for every input symbol $i \in I$, it holds that $\delta'(\phi(s), i) = \phi(\delta(s, i))$ and $\lambda'(\phi(s), i) = \lambda(s, i)$ [13]. If ϕ is a bijection, then it is called an isomorphism. In this case M_1 and M_2 must have the same number of states, and they are identical except for a renaming of states. Two machines are called isomorphic if there is an isomorphism from one to the other. Two isomorphic FSMs are equivalent, but the converse is not true in general.

In each equivalence class there is a reduced machine with the minimal number of states. In an equivalence class, any two reduced machines have the same number of states, furthermore, there is a one-to-one correspondence between equivalent states, which gives an isomorphism between the two machines. That is, the reduced machine in an equivalence class is unique up to isomorphism.

Note that there is a number of equivalence relations of states of machines. They are, however, all the same for completely specified and deterministic machines, and they are only different in case of more general machines like nondeterministic machines.

We say that machine M has a reset capability if there is an initial state $s_0 \in S$ and an input symbol $r \in I$ that takes the machine from any state back to s_0. That is, $\delta(s_j, r) = s_0$ for all states $s_j \in S$. The reset is reliable if it is guaranteed to work properly in any implementation machine M', i.e., $\delta'(s'_j, r) = s'_0$ for all states $s'_j \in S'$, otherwise it is unreliable. Note that reset r is also an input symbol. Thus, if M has reset then M is considered to be strongly connected if all the other states can be reached from the initial state s_0.

According to the previous works on fault diagnosis, we are considering a fault model with two types of faults: the output and the transition fault. We say that a transition has an output fault if, for the corresponding state and received input, the implementation provides an output different from the one specified by the output function. We say that a transition has a transition fault if, for the corresponding state and received input, the implementation enters a different state than specified by the transition function. An implementation has a single output (transition) fault if one and only one of its transitions has an output (transition) fault.

3   Failure of Exact Fault Diagnosis in FSMs

We show that even in the most 'simple' case it is not always possible to solve the fault localization problem. That is, even when considering the strictest assumptions – a single fault in a finite state machine (investigated by Ghedamsi et al. [4] and Lee at al. [7]) – there are some situations where the exact localization of the fault cannot be assured.

For the rest of the paper we will consider a specification finite state machine $Spec = (I, O, S, \delta, \lambda)$. We denote the number of states, inputs, and outputs by

$n = |S|$, $p = |I|$, and $q = |O|$, respectively. We also consider implementation machines $Impl_a = (I, O, S', \delta', \lambda')$, $Impl_b = (I, O, S'', \delta'', \lambda'')$ and so on with the same input and output sets, and the same number of equally labeled states. We use the term "same states" written $s'_j = s''_j$ for states that are labeled alike in different machines. Of course, these states are not necessary equivalent written $s'_j \cong s''_j$.

Obviously, without any assumptions conformance testing and fault diagnosis are impossible problems; for any test sequence we can easily construct a machine M_2, which is not equivalent to M_1 but produces the same outputs as M_1 for the given test sequence. There is a number of natural assumptions that are usually made in the literature in order for the test to be at all possible [1]:

- The specification FSM $Spec$ is deterministic, completely specified, strongly connected and reduced.
- Implementation machines do not change during the experiment, and have the same input I and output O alphabet as $Spec$.

Furthermore we concentrate on systems with reliable reset capability, and we assume that there is only one difference – an output or a transition fault – between an implementation and the specification machine.

All previous works on the diagnosis of a single fault in a FSM ([4] [7]) used the same assumptions, and they claim to provide methods to precisely locate the single fault.

We show that – contrary to the statements found in the literature – it is in general not possible to guarantee the precise localization of a single fault in a finite state machine, not even considering the assumptions above: Take specification machine $Spec$ and two implementation machines: $Impl_a$ differing from $Spec$ by a single fault $Fault_a$, and $Impl_b$ differing from the specification by a single fault $Fault_b$. $Fault_a$ and $Fault_b$ are different faults. Evidently, neither $Impl_a$ nor $Impl_b$ can be equivalent to $Spec$, since $Spec$ is deterministic, completely specified, strongly connected and reduced. Interestingly, however, $Impl_a$ and $Impl_b$ might be equivalent to each other even though the faults they contain differ. In this case it is impossible to decide between the faults, i.e., it is impossible to exactly locate the fault. The next simple example demonstrates the situation.

Example 1. Take specification machine $Spec$ shown on Figure 1. The set of input symbols is $I = \{a, r\}$, where r is the reset input, the set of output symbols is $O = \{1, 2\}$ and the set of states is $S = \{s_0, s_1, s_2\}$ where s_0 is the initial state. Specification machine $Spec$ is deterministic, completely specified, strongly connected and reduced. Note that the (reliable) reset transitions are omitted on the figure for the sake of perspicuity. Let us consider two implementation machines $Impl_a$ on Figure 2(a) and $Impl_b$ on Figure 2(b) with the same input and output alphabet as $Spec$.

The difference between $Impl_a$ and $Spec$ is a a single transition fault at state s_0, $Fault_a : \delta'(s'_0, a) = s'_0$ instead of s'_1. In case of $Impl_b$ the difference is a single output fault at s_2, $Fault_b : \lambda''(s''_2, a) = 1$ instead of 2.

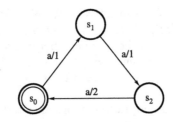

Fig. 1. Specification machine *Spec*

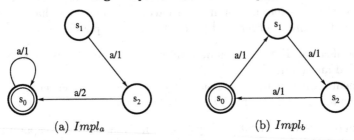

(a) *Impl_a*   (b) *Impl_b*

Fig. 2. Faulty implementation machines: (a) *Impl_a* contains a single transition fault at state s_0, (b) *Impl_b* contains an output fault at s_2

The two implementation machines are equivalent, as they both produce the same trace for every input string. Thus, it is impossible to distinguish between them and therefore between the two faults. Or, to formulate more precisely, is it is impossible to distinguish among any faulty implementation machines belonging to the same equivalence class, and therefore among the faults that they contain.

4   Conditions for Guaranteed Fault Diagnosis

We determine a set of sufficient conditions for the guaranteed exact localization of a single output or transfer fault. That is, we analyze when two (or more) implementation machines, each differing from the specification by a single dissimilar fault, cannot be equivalent. Note that we still consider the assumptions made in the previous section, therefore the specification FSM *Spec* is deterministic, completely specified, strongly connected and reduced with reliable reset.

First we show that it is always possible to distinguish two different output faults if the specification machine has reliable reset capability.

Lemma 1. *Suppose that the specification machine under consideration is deterministic, completely specified, strongly connected and reduced with reliable reset capability. Two implementation machines, each differing from the specification by a single and dissimilar output fault, cannot be equivalent, thus any two output faults can be distinguished.*

Proof. Let us consider two implementation machines *Impl_a* and *Impl_b*, both differing from the specification *Spec* by a single dissimilar output fault. We reset the machines and start to explore the state-space of the two implementations and the specification in parallel. Clearly, until we reach a faulty transition in one of the machines, for any input string x, the traversed states – and the output sequences – are the same in the two implementations and the specification: $\delta'(s'_0, x) = \delta''(s''_0, x) = \delta(s_0, x)$, and $\lambda'(s'_0, x) = \lambda''(s''_0, x) = \lambda(s_0, x)$. When we traverse a faulty transition in one of the implementations (let's say $Impl_a$) with an input string y, we find an inconsistency between $Impl_a$ and $Spec$: $\lambda'(s'_0, y) \neq \lambda(s_0, y)$. However, since $Fault_a \neq Fault_b$ the output of $Impl_b$ at the given transition also cannot be equivalent to the output of $Impl_a$. Therefore, $\lambda'(s'_0, y) \neq \lambda''(s''_0, y)$, i.e., $Impl_a$ and $Impl_b$ are inequivalent, and input sequence y can distinguish them.

Note that the statement made in Lemma 1 only holds if the specification machine has reliable reset capability. We demonstrate a counter-example of Lemma 1 in case the specification machine does not have reliable reset capability.

Example 2. Take specification machine $Spec$ shown on Figure 3.

The set of input symbols is $I = \{a\}$, the set of output symbols is $O = \{1, 2\}$ the set of states is $S = \{s_1, s_2, s_3, s_4\}$.

Specification machine $Spec$ is deterministic, completely specified, strongly connected and reduced. Take two implementation machines $Impl_a$ on Figure 4(a) and $Impl_b$ on Figure 4(b) with the same input and output alphabet as $Spec$.

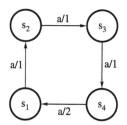

Fig. 3. Specification machine $Spec$ without reliable reset capability

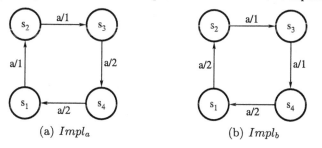

(a) $Impl_a$ (b) $Impl_b$

Fig. 4. Faulty implementation machines: (a) $Impl_a$ contains a single output fault at state s_3, (b) $Impl_b$ contains an output fault at s_1

The difference between $Impl_a$ and $Spec$ is a a single output fault at state s_3, $Fault_a : \lambda'(s_3', a) = 2$ instead of 1. In case of $Impl_b$ the difference is a single output fault at s_1, $Fault_b : \lambda''(s_1'', a) = 2$ instead of 1. The two implementation machines are clearly equivalent.

Next we show that it is always possible to distinguish a single output and a single transition fault if the *faulty machines* are reduced.

Lemma 2. *Suppose that the specification machine under consideration is deterministic, completely specified, strongly connected and reduced with reliable reset capability. Two implementation machines, one differing from the specification by a single output fault, the other by a single transition fault cannot be equivalent if the implementation machines are reduced.*

Proof. Let us consider two implementations $Impl_a$ and $Impl_b$. One of the implementations (let's say $Impl_a$) contains a transition, the other ($Impl_b$) an output fault. The two implementation machines are reduced therefore they must be isomorphic to be equivalent. That is, there has to be a one-to-one mapping ϕ from S' to S'' such that for every state s' in S' and for every input symbol i in I, $\delta''(\phi(s'), i) = \phi(\delta'(s', i))$ and $\lambda''(\phi(s'), i) = \lambda'(s', i)$ should hold.

Let's say the output fault in $Impl_b$ is at s_x''. Since the output of one of its transitions has changed s_x'' has to map to an other state (say s_y') of $Impl_a$ where $\lambda''(s_x'', i) = \lambda'(s_y', i)$, $\forall i \in I$. However, this mapping cannot be one-to-one, as there is no output fault in $Impl_a$, and therefore $Impl_a$ has one less states with the same output characteristic as s_x''. Thus, there is clearly no one-to-one mapping ϕ fulfilling $\lambda''(\phi(s'), i) = \lambda'(s', i)$, $\forall s' \in S'$, $\forall i \in I$.

Finally we show that it is always possible to distinguish two different single transition faults if the *faulty machines* are reduced.

Lemma 3. *Suppose that the specification machine under consideration is deterministic, completely specified, strongly connected and reduced with reliable reset capability. Two implementation machines, each differing from the specification by a single and dissimilar transition fault, cannot be equivalent if the implementation machines are reduced.*

Proof. Let us assume the following situation:

$Fault_a$ in $Impl_a$: $(s_c \xrightarrow{i_l/o_f} s_d) \Rightarrow (s_c' \xrightarrow{i_l/o_f} s_e')$

$Fault_b$ in $Impl_b$: $(s_u \xrightarrow{i_m/o_g} s_v) \Rightarrow (s_u'' \xrightarrow{i_m/o_g} s_w'')$

First, take the special case when the two faults are applied to the same transition in the two implementations, i.e., $c = u$ and $l = m$. In this case the outputs are also the same ($f = g$) but the next states are not ($e \neq w$) because $Fault_a$ and $Fault_b$ are dissimilar. In this case there is only one difference between $Impl_a$ and $Impl_b$, and therefore, if the implementation machines are reduced ($s_e' \not\cong s_w'$) we can certainly find an input sequence distinguishing them for example using Chow's method [14]: Let y be a separating sequence distinguishing states s_e' and s_w'. We apply an input sequence (say x) corresponding to the path of the tree from the initial state to s'_c, input i_l and then apply y. This input sequence $x \cdot i_l \cdot y$ certainly distinguishes $Impl_a$ and $Impl_b$, thus the implementation machines cannot be equivalent.

Now take the general case when the two faults are applied to different transitions. Let's reset the machines and start to explore the state-space of the two implementations and the specification in parallel. Until we reach a faulty transition in one of the machines for any input string the traversed states – and the output sequences – are the same in the two implementations and the specification. Let's say we first encounter $Fault_a$ in $Impl_a$ with an input string x, i.e., with x we reach the state s'_c in $Impl_a$, s''_c in $Impl_b$ and s_c in $Spec$. If we input i_l after x, $Impl_a$ will transit to s'_e, $Spec$ to s_d and $Impl_b$ to s''_d. Let Y be the set of all separating sequences distinguishing states s_e and s_d. Any input sequence $x \cdot i_l \cdot y_j$ where $y_j \in Y$ will clearly distinguish $Impl_a$ and $Spec$. Any of these input sequences will also distinguish $Impl_a$ and $Impl_b$, except if all $y_j \in Y$ starting from s''_d in $Impl_b$ traverse $Fault_b$ making $\lambda(s'_0, x \cdot i_l \cdot y_j)$ and $\lambda(s''_0, x \cdot i_l \cdot y_j)$ consistent for all $y_j \in Y$. For that, also in $Spec$ all separating sequences distinguishing states s_e and s_d starting from s_d traverse transition (s_u, i_m); and if $\delta(s_u, i_m) = s_v$ then s_e and s_d are separable, if $\delta(s_u, i_m) = s_w$ then they are not separable. From that it follows that s''_e and s''_d in $Impl_b$ are not separable. Thus, the implementation machines cannot be minimal.

Theorem 1. *Suppose that the specification machine under consideration is deterministic, completely specified, strongly connected and reduced with reliable reset capability. Two implementation machines, each differing from the specification by a single and dissimilar fault, cannot be equivalent if the implementation machines are reduced.*

Proof. The proof follows from Lemmas 1, 2 and 3.

The theorem shows that if there is only one difference between an implementation and a specification and the implementation is minimal then it is unique, no other fault can induce the same change in behavior. Thus it is possible to identify the given fault.

5   Exact Algorithm for Fault Diagnosis

We give an algorithm – a modification of Lee's method [7] – for the localization of single transfer or output faults in finite state machines. We incorporate the analytical results of Section 4. to quickly verify if the first fault candidate the algorithm identifies is certainly the only possible one. If it is we conclude that the difference between the implementation and the specification can be exactly located, otherwise the algorithm moves on and provides the set of all potential single faults.

Let us consider a specification finite state machine $Spec$ and an implementation $Impl$ to be diagnosed. The algorithm is made up of two steps:

Step 1 Conformance testing is used to determine if there is difference between the specification and the diagnosed implementation.

Step 2 Localization of the fault.

5.1   Step 1: Detection of the Fault

For Step 1 of the algorithm a checking sequence needs to be constructed.

Definition 1. *Let M be a finite state machine with n states and initial state s_0. A checking sequence for M is an input sequence x that distinguishes M from all other machines with n states. That is, any machine with at most n states not equivalent to M produces a different output than M on input x starting from the initial state.*

There are a number of conformance testing methods developed for finite state machines constructing checking sequences. These include the transition tour [15], the Unique Input Output (UIO) method [16], the Distinguishing Sequence method [17], the "W-method" [14] and the Wp method [18]. In our algorithm we create the checking sequence using the W-method proposed by Chow for machines with reliable reset. It consists of no more than pn^2 test sequences of length less than $2n$ interposed with reset. We apply the checking sequence to the specification and to the diagnosed implementation. If we do not find an inconsistency of the observed outputs then we conclude that the implementation machine is equivalent to the specification, thus there is either no fault in the implementation or there are more than one, and end of the algorithm. If we find a difference we move on to Step 2.

5.2   Step 2: Localization of the Fault

During conformance testing an inconsistency was found between the specification and the diagnosed implementation. Thus, there is at least one of the pn^2 test sequences (say x) detecting the fault, i.e. $\lambda(s_0, x) \neq \lambda'(s_0', x)$. Let us assume that the earliest inconsistency between $\lambda(s_0, x)$ and $\lambda'(s_0', x)$ is at the kth output symbol where $1 \leq k \leq 2n$. Let's say that the first k elements (inputs) of x carry the specification machine from s_0 to $s_1, s_2, ..., s_k$, where these $k+1$ states may or may not be different.

We assume *Impl* has only a single output or transition fault. In case the diagnosed implementation machine contains an output fault, x has to traverse the fault at the kth transition. If *Impl* contains a transition fault, then x has to traverse the fault during the first $k-1$ transitions.

Note that if there are more than one test sequences detecting the fault, we may use either of them for the localization of the fault (for practical reasons we should choose the shortest sequence). If multiple test cases detect the fault, we might also check if the set of possibly faulty transitions can be narrowed: For each test sequence detecting the fault we determine the transitions it traverses in the specification machine prior to the first inconsistency. Trivially, in Step 2, we only have to consider the intersection of these traversed transitions.

In the algorithm we consider two cases. First we presume that the fault in *Impl* is an output fault and verify if it's a potential candidate. If the verification succeeds, then we try to confirm whether it is the only potential candidate. If it is the only one, then we located the fault and end of algorithm. Otherwise we move on and presume that the fault could be a transition fault, and similarly analyze each possibilities. If at the end we don't find any potential candidates we conclude that there are more than one fault in *Impl*.

Output Fault. We assume that the fault in *Impl* is an output fault, i.e., $\lambda(s_{k-1}, x_k) \neq \lambda'(s'_{k-1}, x_k)$ where x_k is the kth input of x. For the verification we modify *Spec* according to the supposed fault: we change the output symbol at state s_{k-1} upon input x_k to the faulty output symbol $\lambda'(s'_{k-1}, x_k)$. We denote the modified specification C_1. We conduct a checking experiment (conformance testing) on *Impl* with respect to C_1.

C_1, however, is not necessarily minimal. To use Chow's method for checking sequence generation, we first have to minimize machine C_1 and get $C_{1\ reduced}$. Let m be the number of states of reduced machine $C_{1\ reduced}$. If $m < n$, that is, if the reduced conjectured machine has less states than the specification, then according to Chow we have to use a Z set instead of a W set for test sequence generation. A Z set can be created by extending the W set the following way [14]:

$$Z:\ W\ U\ I \cdot W\ U\ \ldots U\ I^{n-m} \cdot W$$

Where "U" is the union operator, "$\cdot$" is the string concatenation operator and I is the input alphabet. The checking sequence is then created by the concatenation of the sets of sequences P and Z.

If we find that *Impl* conforms to C_1, we conclude that C_1 is a potential candidate. Then we try to confirm if it is the only possible candidate. For that we simply have to check if the reduced machine $C_{1\ reduced}$ has equivalent number of states to the specification. If it has, we conclude that C_1 is certainly the only potential candidate, and therefore we exactly located the fault in *Impl*, end of algorithm.

If *Impl* conforms to C_1, but the reduced machine has less states than the specification, we conclude that C_1 is a potential candidate, store it in the set of potential candidate machines PC, and proceed to the following step.

If *Impl* does not conform to C_1 we proceed to the following step.

Transition Fault. A transition fault can occur in one of the first $k-1$ transitions, i.e., $\delta(s_j, x_{j+1}) \neq \delta'(s'_j, x_{j+1})$ where $j = 0, ..., (k-2)$. We assume, that the fault occurs in the jth transition and verify each assumption in turn. On input x_{j+1} at state s_j the implementation machine is supposed to transit to s_{j+1}. But instead *Impl* transits to s_r, where s_r can be any of the $n-1$ states except the right state s_{j+1}. We verify each possibilities in turn.

In each turn we modify *Spec* according to the supposed fault: we create candidate machine C_{l+1} where l is the cardinality of the set PC, by changing the next-state symbol of the given transition to the supposed wrong state s_r.

We minimize the candidate machine and conduct a checking experiment on $Impl$ with respect to $C_{l+1\ reduced}$.

If we find that $Impl$ conforms to $C_{l+1\ reduced}$, we conclude that C_{l+1} is a potential candidate. If PC is not empty ($l \geq 1$), we store C_{l+1} in PC, conclude that the exact localization of the fault is not possible and move on to the next turn.

If $l = 0$ then we try to confirm if it is the only possible candidate. We simply check if the reduced machine $C_{l+1\ reduced}$ has equivalent number of states to the specification. If it has, we conclude that C_{l+1} is certainly the only candidate, and therefore we exactly located the fault in $Impl$, end of algorithm.

If $l = 0$ and $Impl$ conforms to C_{l+1}, but the reduced machine has less states than the specification, we conclude that C_{l+1} is a potential candidate, store it in set PC, and proceed to the next turn.

If $Impl$ does not conform to C_{l+1} we move on to the next turn.

For each assumed transition there are $n - 1$ possible next states. Thus, there are no more than $2n^2$ turns. At the end of the last turn there are three possibilities:

- If $l = 0$, we conclude that there are more than one faults in $Impl$, end of algorithm.
- If $l = 1$, there is only one potential candidate, therefore we exactly located the fault in $Impl$, end of algorithm.
- If $l > 1$, we conclude that the exact localization of the fault is not possible, and PC is the set of all potential candidates i.e., we determined the set of all potential single faults, end of algorithm.

Example 3. We use an example to demonstrate the algorithm given above. Take the specification machine *Spec* shown on Figure 5(a) The set of input symbols is $I = \{a, b, r\}$, where r is the reset input, the set of output symbols is $O = \{1, 2\}$ and the set of states is $S = \{s_0, s_1, s_2, s_3\}$ where s_0 is the initial state. Reset transitions are again omitted on the figure. Implementation machine on Figure 5(b) contains a single transition fault at state s_2. This transition fault is to be located using the algorithm.

For the detection of the fault (step 1 of the algorithm) we need to construct a checking sequence. Since our emphasis is not on checking experiments, we omit the details. A P-set of *Spec* can be constructed based on a testing tree.

$$P : \ \{r, ra, raa, rab, rb, rba, rbb, rbaa, rbab\}$$

The characterizing set (W-set) of *Spec* is:

$$W : \ \{ab, b\}$$

By concatenating P and the characterizing set we get a basic test set of the checking sequence, interposed with reset. Obviously, if a prefix of a sequence can detect a fault then the whole sequence also can. Thus, we can remove all the

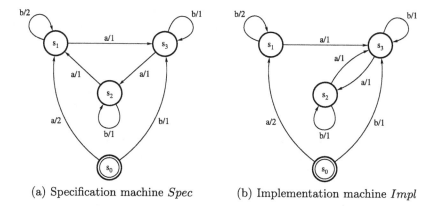

(a) Specification machine *Spec*   (b) Implementation machine *Impl*

Fig. 5. Faulty implementation machine *Impl* contains a single transition fault at state s_2

sequences that are prefix of other sequences. As a result we get the following test set:

$$\{raaab, raab, rabab, rabb, rbaaab, rbaab^*, rbabab^*, rbabb, rbbab, rbbb\}$$

We execute the test set on *Impl*. The test sequences marked with * detect the fault. We use the shortest sequence – *rbaab* – for the rest of the algorithm. Note that we can not narrow the set of possibly faulty transitions, because in *Spec* sequence *rbabab* traverses all transitions that *rbaab* does.

If applied to *Spec rbaab* produces the output sequence 1112, and if applied to *Impl* we get 1111. That is, the fourth outputs are different ($k = 4$). First we presume that the fault in *Impl* is an output fault (occurring at the fourth

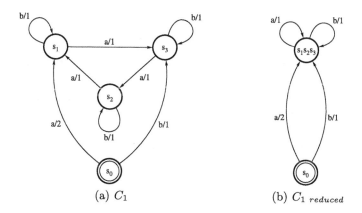

(a) C_1 (b) C_1 *reduced*

Fig. 6. Conjectured machine C_1 with an output fault at state s_1 (a), and C_1 after minimization (b)

transition). Since the sequence *rbaab* carries *Spec* from s_0 to s_3, s_2, s_1, s_1, we change the output at state s_1 input b from 2 to 1. We get the machine C_1 on Figure 6(a) reduce C_1 and get the machine C_1 *reduced* on Figure 6(b) We conduct a checking experiment (conformance testing) on *Impl* with respect to C_1 *reduced*. We find that the two machines are not equivalent (for example *rab* finds the difference), therefore, we move on and presume that the fault is a transition fault occurring in one of the first three $(k - 1)$ transitions.

We first conjecture that the first transition goes to a different state than specified. We have three possibilities: at state s_0, on input b the machine goes to s_0, s_1 or s_2 instead of s_3. We build the according conjectured machines and verify them in turn. Omitting the details, we find that none of the machines conform to *Impl* (*rba*, *rbb* and *rbab* rule out the possibilities respectively).

We move on and conjecture that the fault is at the second transition: at state s_1, on input a the machine goes to s_0, s_1 or s_3 instead of s_2. After building the machines and conducting the checking experiments we rule out the first two possibilities with sequences *rbaa* and *rbab* respectively. We also find that the third conjectured machine (C_1 on Figure 7(a)) conforms to *Impl*. Since the set of potential candidate machines *PC* is empty, we try to confirm if it is the only possible candidate. We find that after minimization C_1 has less states than the specification. Thus, we conclude that C_1 is a potential candidate, store it in set *PC*, and proceed to the next turn. We conjecture that the fault is at the third transition: at state s_2, on input a the machine goes to s_0, s_2 or s_3 instead of s_1. The sequence *rbaaa* rules out the first possibility, but the other two conjectured machines – C_2 (Figure 7(b)), and C_3 (Figure 5(b)) – conform to *Impl*. Since *PC* is not empty, we know that the exact localization of the fault is not possible and store both machines in *PC*. As $k = 4$, transition fault may only occur at the first three transitions, therefore, we have reached the end of the algorithm.

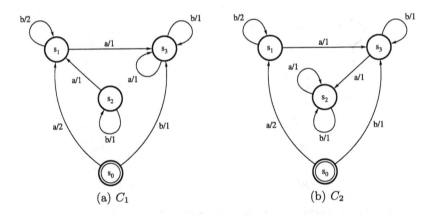

(a) C_1 (b) C_2

Fig. 7. Conjectured machines C_1 and C_2

As a result we conclude that the exact localization of the fault is not possible. PC is the set of possible faulty machines C_1, C_2 and C_3 including all potential single faults.

6 Conclusion

We study the problem of fault diagnosis. The scope of fault diagnosis is beyond the scope of the fault detection (or conformance testing) problem. While the latter is concerned with determining if there are difference(s) between the behavior of the specification and the implementation machines, the former also tries to identify and locate the difference(s).

We concentrate on the diagnosis of a single transition or output fault in an FSM. Clearly, the problem cannot be exactly solved if there are two or more equivalent implementation machines, each differing from the specification machine by a single dissimilar fault. We show that implementation machines with different single faults may have the same observable behavior and thus in general it is not possible to guarantee the exact localization of a single fault in a finite state machine.

We analyze under what circumstances the exact localization of a single output or transfer fault can be guaranteed. That is, we determine a set of sufficient conditions when two (or more) implementation machines, each differing from the specification by a single dissimilar fault, cannot be equivalent. We incorporate the analytical results into an algorithm for the fault diagnosis problem. In case it is possible, the algorithm exactly locates the difference between the implementation and the specification, and when the exact localization is not possible, it provides the set of all potential single faults.

References

1. Lee, D., Yiannakakis, M.: Principles and methods of testing finite state machines – a survey. Proc. IEEE **43** (1996) 1090–1123
2. El-Fakih, K., Prokopenko, S., Yevtushenko, N., Bochmann, G.V.: Fault diagnosis in extended finite state machines. Testing of Communicating Systems - Proceedings of 15th IFIP International Conference, TestCom 2003 (2003)
3. Ghedamsi, A., Dssouli, R., Bochmann, G.V.: Diagnostic tests for single transition faults in non-deterministic finite state machines. Proceedings of the IFIP TC6/WG6.1 Fifth International Workshop on Protocol Test Systems V (1992)
4. Ghedamsi, A., v. Bochmann, G.: Test result analysis and diagnostics for finite state machines. Proc. 12th Int. Conf. on Distributed Systems (1992)
5. Ghedamsi, A., Bochmann, G., Dssouli, R.: Diagnosis for single transition faults in communicating finite state machines. IEEE International Conference on Distributed Computing Systems (ICDCS'93), Pittsburgh, USA (1993)
6. Ghedamsi, A., Dssouli, R., Bochmann, G.: Diagnosing distributed systems modeled by communicating finite state machines. Revue Reseaux et Informatique Repartie **3** (1993) 343–363
7. Lee, D., Sabnani, K.: Reverse-engineering of communication protocols. Proc. of the IEEE International Conference on Network Protocols, California (1993) 208–216

8. Ghedamsi, A., Bochmann, G., Dssouli, R.: Multiple fault diagnostics for finite state machines. IEEE INFOCOM'93 (1993)
9. El-Fakih, K., Yevtushenko, N., von Bochmann, G.: Diagnosing multiple faults in communicating finite state machines. Formal Techniques for Networked and Distributed Systems, FORTE 2001, IFIP TC6/WG6.1 - 21st International Conference on Formal Techniques for Networked and Distributed Systems (2001) 85–100
10. ITU-T: Recommendation z.100: Specification and description language (2000)
11. TC97/SC21, I.: Estelle – a formal description technique based on an extended state transition model. international standard 9074 (1988)
12. Luo, G., Das, A., Bochmann, G.V.: Generating tests for control portion of sdl specifications. Proceedings of the IFIP TC6/WG6.1 Sixth International Workshop on Protocol Test systems VI (1993)
13. Moore, E.F.: Gedanken-experiments on sequential machines. In: Automata Studies. Princeton University Press, Princeton, N.J. (1956) 129–153
14. Chow, T.: Testing software design modelled by finite-state machines. IEEE Trans. Software Eng. 4 (1978)
15. Naito, S., Tsunoyama, M.: Fault detection for sequential machines by transition tours. Proc. of FTCS (Fault Tolerant Computing Systems (1981) 238–243
16. Sabnani, K., Dahbura, A.: A protocol testing procedure. Computer Networks and ISDN Systems 15 (1988) 285–297
17. Gonenc, G.: A method for the design of fault detection experiments. IEEE Trans. Computer C-19 (1970) 551–558
18. Fujiwara, S., Bochmann, G.V., Khendec, F., Amalou, M., Ghedamsi, A.: Test selection based on finite state model. IEEE Trans. Softrw. Eng. 17 (1991) 591–603

State Identification Problems
for Timed Automata*

Moez Krichen and Stavros Tripakis

Verimag Centre Equation,
2, avenue de Vignate, 38610 Gières, France
{krichen, tripakis}@imag.fr

Abstract. A well-established theory exists for testing finite state machines. One fundamental class of problems handled by this theory is state identification: we are given a machine with known state space and transition relation, but unknown initial state, and we are asked to find tests which identify the initial or final state of the machine. In this paper, we study state identification in the context of timed automata which contrary to, say, Mealy or Moore machines, is a suitable model for real-time systems. We are interested in digital-clock tests which have a finite clock precision and are thus implementable. We develop a general technique, based on time-abstracting bisimulation, which reduces the problem to the case of non-deterministic finite-state Mealy machines. We illustrate our technique on a toy example.

1 Introduction

Testing is a fundamental step in any development process. It consists in applying a set of experiments to a system, with multiple aims, from obtaining some piece of unknown information to checking correctness or measuring performance. These different aims give rise to different classes of testing problems, for instance, conformance testing or performance testing.

A particularly interesting class of testing problems, pioneered in the seminal 1956 paper of Moore [9], is *state identification*. We are given a *machine* with known state-transition diagram but unknown initial state. We are asked to perform an experiment in order to, either find the unknown initial state (*distinguishing* experiments), or verify that the machine is indeed in an assumed-to-be state (*state-verification* experiments), or identify the final state, reached at the end of the experiment (*homing* experiments), or lead the machine to a given state (*synchronizing* experiments), etc.

An extensive theory is available on state identification problems for finite-state machine models such as Mealy or Moore machines (see [8] for an excellent survey). These models are well-suited for some applications (e.g., synchronous

---

* Work partially supported by CNRS STIC project "CORTOS" and by IST Network of Excellence "ARTIST2".

F. Khendek and R. Dssouli (Eds.): TestCom 2005, LNCS 3502, pp. 175–191, 2005.

circuits) but not for others. In particular, the assumption that inputs and outputs are synchronous makes these models unsuitable when modeling real-time systems, where outputs are produced with variable delays governed by complex timing constraints.

In this paper, we study state identification (in particular, distinguishing and homing) problems in the context of *timed automata* [2]. The latter have been recognized as a useful model for real-time systems. Although some work has been done for this model on problems of conformance testing (e.g., see references in [7]) we are not aware of any previous work on problems of state identification in a real-time setting.

Since timed automata (TA) are based on a *dense-time* semantics, the first choice to make when dealing with testing on such a model is to define the observation capabilities of the tester, in particular in what concerns time. Two types of testers can thus be defined: *analog-clock* testers which can observe real-time precisely; *digital-clock* testers which can only observe the "ticks" of a digital clock (i.e., a counter). Caring about the implementability of our approach, we consider digital-clock testers in this paper. Indeed, analog-clock testers rely on an infinite-precision clock thus are difficult, if not impossible, to implement.

Assuming digital-clock testers has an additional benefit. It opens up the possibility for reducing the problem from the timed to the untimed case. However, carrying out this idea is less obvious than one may think. We summarize the main steps of the procedure in the sequel. The details are given in the main body of the paper.

The first thing to do is to compute the product $A\|\mathsf{Tick}$ of the TA under test A with Tick, which is a TA modeling the digital clock of the tester. Tick emits the special output tick and does not synchronize with A except in time. Since the tester does not have access to any other timing information except the number of ticks, it becomes an "untimed controller" of the product TA, call it $A\|\mathsf{Tick}$.

Thus, in principle, it seems possible at this point to reduce the problem to a problem of "untimed" testing by working on some kind of *time-abstracting* graph of $A\|\mathsf{Tick}$. One choice is the *region graph* [2] but this is obviously to be avoided if we want our method to be tractable. An alternative is to use the *forward reachability graph* used in TA model-checking tools such as Kronos [4]. Unfortunately, this graph does not have the necessary properties for testing purposes. In particular, it is not *pre-stable*, that is, if $S_1 \xrightarrow{a} S_2$ is a transition in the abstract graph then there might be (concrete) states in the abstract state S_1 which have no a-transition in some state in S_2. To see why this is problematic, suppose a is an input: if the tester issues a in the abstract state S_1 then the abstract system will move to S_2; however, the concrete system is not guaranteed to do so. Our choice is, then, to use the *time-abstracting bisimulation* (TAB) quotient graph [11]. This graph has the same properties as the region graph (in particular, pre-stability) and is typically much smaller than the latter. Thus, it presents a good compromise between property preservation and size.

Once we have generated the TAB quotient graph of $A\|\mathsf{Tick}$, call it G, we have a finite-state model which can be treated algorithmically. However, G is not a

Mealy machine: it is a labeled transition system (LTS) the transitions of which are labeled with input or output actions, ticks, or τ labels. The latter correspond to either *unobservable* actions of A or time-elapsing transitions abstracted by the bisimulation. Notice that we make no assumption on A (or Tick), in particular, it can be non-deterministic and partially observable. The reason is that we have to confront non-determinism anyway, even if A is deterministic: two distinct output sequences may appear the same to the tester because of its digital clock.

The last step consists in transforming G into a non-deterministic Mealy machine M, on which state-identification problems can be solved using existing techniques [1]. This is an original, to our knowledge, transformation technique which is general enough to be used for any finite LTS provided it satisfies some properties on boundedness of number of outputs (see below). Thus, the technique can be useful in an "untimed" context to reduce testing problems from asynchronous LTS models to synchronous Mealy machines.

In a nutshell, the transformation is as follows. For every pair of nodes v_1, v_2 of G, we compute the language L_{v_1,v_2} of *vertebrae* linking v_1 and v_2. A vertebra is a finite word ending with a tick symbol and containing a single tick. L_{v_1,v_2} is a regular language. We then compute L_{v_1,v_2}^O, the *projection* of L_{v_1,v_2} into *output vertebrae*, that is, vertebrae containing only outputs and tick. Using the hypothesis that A is *bounded output* (i.e., can only emit a bounded number of outputs in a bounded amount of time) we can show that L_{v_1,v_2}^O is a finite language. For each $\sigma \in L_{v_1,v_2}^O$, we compute $L_{v_1,v_2,\sigma}^I$, the projected language of input vertebrae corresponding to σ. Finally, for each such σ, we construct a transition in M of the form $v_1 \xrightarrow{L/\sigma} v_2$, where L is an appropriate regular language derived from $L_{v_1,v_2,\sigma}^I$.

Intuitively, an input vertebra like $a \cdot b \cdot$ tick corresponds to a basic command of the tester which is to issue input a followed by b and then wait until the next tick before it proceeds. An output vertebra like $c \cdot$ tick corresponds to what the tester observes after executing the input vertebra. Notice that the lengths of the two need not be the same, although both end with a unique tick, since, according to the interpretation above, tick can be seen both as an input and output. $v_1 \xrightarrow{L/\sigma} v_2$ can be seen as a *symbolic* transition: L is the input symbol and σ is the output symbol. To exercise this transition, a tester chooses some input vertebra in L and then may observe the output vertebra σ. Notice that M is non-deterministic, thus, the same input can also result to another output σ'. The correctness of the method lies on the fact that input and output vertebrae end with their unique tick symbols. Thus, there is no danger that concatenating vertebrae may result in ambiguity for the tester. In particular, if σ_1, σ_2 are two vertebrae such that $\sigma_1 \neq \sigma_2$ then for any vertebrae σ_1', σ_2', $\sigma_1 \cdot \sigma_1' \neq \sigma_2 \cdot \sigma_2'$.

The rest of this paper is organized as follows. In Section 2 we recall our model of timed automata with input, output and unobservable actions. In Section 3 we define the various state-identification problems. In Section 4 we recall the time-abstracting quotient graph and identify its properties of interest for our purposes. In Section 5 we show how to transform this graph to a non-deterministic Mealy machine and reduce the problems from the timed to the untimed case. Section 6 summarizes the paper and gives some directions for future work.

2   The Model

The basic model is timed automata with inputs and outputs (TAIO) as defined in [7]. These are timed automata with *deadlines* to capture urgency [10, 3] and edges labeled by an *input action* in a finite set $\mathsf{Act}_{in} = \{a, b, \cdots\}$, an *output action* in a finite set $\mathsf{Act}_{out} = \{v, w, \cdots\}$ or an *unobservable action* $\tau \notin \mathsf{Act}_{in} \cup \mathsf{Act}_{out}$.

Let R be the set of non-negative reals. Given a finite set of *actions* Act, the set $(\mathsf{Act} \cup \mathsf{R})^*$ of all finite *real-time sequences* over Act will be denoted $\mathsf{RT}(\mathsf{Act})$. The *length* of a sequence ρ is denoted $|\rho|$. $\epsilon \in \mathsf{RT}(\mathsf{Act})$ is the empty sequence. Given $\mathsf{Act}' \subseteq \mathsf{Act}$ and $\rho \in \mathsf{RT}(\mathsf{Act})$, $P_{\mathsf{Act}'}(\rho)$ denotes the *projection* of ρ to Act', obtained by "erasing" from ρ all actions not in Act' and all delays. For example, if $\mathsf{Act} = \{a, b\}$, $\mathsf{Act}' = \{a\}$ and $\rho = a\,1\,b\,2\,a\,3$, then $P_{\mathsf{Act}'}(\rho) = a\,a$. $P_{\mathsf{Act}' \cup \mathsf{R}}(\rho)$ denotes the projection of ρ to $\mathsf{Act}' \cup \mathsf{R}$, obtained by "erasing" from ρ all actions not in Act' (but not delays). For example, $P_{\mathsf{Act}' \cup \mathsf{R}}(\rho) = a\,3\,a\,3$. The time spent in a sequence ρ, denoted $\mathsf{time}(\rho)$ is the sum of all delays in ρ, for example, $\mathsf{time}(\epsilon) = 0$ and $\mathsf{time}(a\,1\,b\,0.5) = 1.5$.

A *timed automaton over* Act is a tuple (Q, X, Act, E) where Q is a finite set of *locations*; X is a finite set of *clocks*; E is a finite set of *edges*. Each edge is a tuple (q, q', ψ, r, d, a), where $q, q' \in Q$ are the source and destination locations; ψ is the *guard*, a conjunction of constraints of the form $x\#c$, where $x \in X$, c is an integer constant and $\# \in \{<, \leq, =, \geq, >\}$; $r \subseteq X$ is the set of clocks to be *reset*; $d \in \{\mathsf{lazy}, \mathsf{delayable}, \mathsf{eager}\}$ is the *deadline*; and $a \in \mathsf{Act}$ is the action. Intuitively, a lazy deadline imposes no urgency on the transition; delayable means the transition, once enabled, must be taken before it becomes disabled; eager means the transition must be taken as soon as it becomes enabled. We will not allow eager edges with guards of the form $x > c$.

A TA A defines an infinite labeled transition system (LTS) the states of which are pairs $s = (q, v) \in Q \times \mathsf{R}^X$, where $q \in Q$ is a location and $v : X \to \mathsf{R}$ is a clock *valuation*. Given state $s = (q, v)$ and clock x, we write $x(s)$ to denote the value of x at s, i.e., $v(x)$. **0** is the valuation assigning 0 to every clock of A. S_A is the set of all states. There are two types of transitions, discrete and timed. Discrete transitions are of the form $s = (q, v) \xrightarrow{a} s' = (q', v')$, where $a \in \mathsf{Act}$ and there is an edge $e = (q, q', \psi, r, d, a)$, such that v satisfies ψ and v' is obtained by resetting to zero all clocks in r and leaving the others unchanged. We say that e is enabled at s and write $s \models e$ (or $s \models \psi$). Timed transitions are of the form $(q, v) \xrightarrow{t} (q, v + t)$, where $t \in \mathsf{R}, t > 0$ and there is no edge (q, q'', ψ, r, d, a), such that: either $d = \mathsf{delayable}$ and there exist $0 \leq t_1 < t_2 \leq t$ such that $v + t_1 \models \psi$ and $v + t_2 \not\models \psi$; or $d = \mathsf{eager}$ and there exists $0 \leq t_1 < t$ such that $v + t_1 \models \psi$. We use notation such as $s \xrightarrow{a}$, $s \not\xrightarrow{a}$, ..., to denote that there exists s' such that $s \xrightarrow{a} s'$, there is no such s', and so on. This notation naturally extends to timed sequences. For example, $s \xrightarrow{a1b} s'$ if there exist s_1, s_2 such that $s \xrightarrow{a} s_1 \xrightarrow{1} s_2 \xrightarrow{b} s'$.

A *timed automaton with inputs and outputs* (TAIO) is a timed automaton over $\mathsf{Act}_\tau = \mathsf{Act} \cup \{\tau\}$. A TAIO is called *observable* if none of its edges is labeled by τ. A TAIO A is called *input-complete* if it can accept any input at any state: $\forall s \in S_A . \forall a \in \mathsf{Act}_{in} . s \xrightarrow{a}$. It is called *deterministic* if $\forall s, s', s'' \in S_A . \forall a \in \mathsf{Act}_\tau . s \xrightarrow{a} s' \wedge s \xrightarrow{a} s'' \Rightarrow s' = s''$. It is called *non-blocking* if

$$\forall s \in S_A . \forall t \in \mathbb{R} . \exists \rho \in \mathsf{RT}(\mathsf{Act}_{out} \cup \{\tau\}) . \mathsf{time}(\rho) = t \wedge s \xrightarrow{\rho} . \tag{1}$$

The non-blocking property states that at any state, A can let time pass forever, even if it does not receive any input. This is a sanity property which ensures that a TAIO does not "force" its environment to provide an input by blocking time.

A is called *output-bounded* if there is a bound on the number of outputs A can produce in a bounded amount of time (say, one time unit). Formally:

$$\exists n . \forall s \in S_A . \forall \rho \in \mathsf{RT}(\mathsf{Act}_\tau) . (s \xrightarrow{\rho} \wedge \mathsf{time}(\rho) = 1) \Rightarrow |P_{\mathsf{Act}_{out}}(\rho)| \leq n. \tag{2}$$

An example of a TAIO is shown in Figure 1. This TAIO has three locations (q_1, q_2 and q_3), one input (click), two outputs (simple and double) and one clock (x). It models a mouse which produces a double-click when the button is pressed twice (or more) in one time unit, a simple-click otherwise. We will use this automaton as a running example in the rest of the paper. We annotate actions with ? and ! to denote inputs and outputs, respectively. Unless otherwise noted, deadlines are lazy.

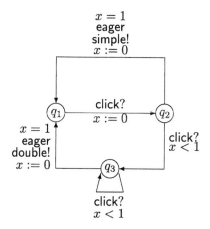

Fig. 1. An example of a TAIO: the simple- and double-click mouse

3   State-Identification Problems on Timed Automata

We consider a TAIO A which is non-blocking and output-bounded (but possibly non-deterministic, partially-observable or non input-complete) and the current state of which is unknown. We wish to perform an input/output experiment from which we can deduce either the initial state (the state A was occupying at the beginning of the experiment – the *distinguishing* problem) or the final state (the state A is occupying at the end of the experiment – the *homing* problem).

An input/output experiment consists in applying inputs on A and observing the generated outputs. The experiment may be *preset* or *adaptive* [5].[1] In a preset experiment the input sequence the tester applies is totally known in advance (before the experiment starts). In an adaptive experiment the tester is allowed to decide which inputs to apply depending on the outputs observed so far. Clearly, adaptive experiments are more general. While a preset experiment can simply be modeled as an input sequence, an adaptive experiment needs to be modeled as a decision tree (e.g., see Figure 3).[2]

In our case, the tester is "timed": it observes not only the outputs of the machine under test but also the time when these outputs occur. In practice, it is not possible to observe time in an infinitely-precise way, due to the fact that the tester has access only to a digital clock (i.e., a discrete counter updated by some physical process). In this paper, we make the assumption that the clock of the tester can be modeled by a timed automaton called Tick. Examples of Tick automata are given in Figure 2. Tick is a TAIO with a single action tick $\notin \mathsf{Act_{in}} \cup \mathsf{Act_{out}} \cup \{\tau\}$ and no inputs. Tick must be non-blocking and ensure that tick always eventually occurs. Our method works for any such Tick model.

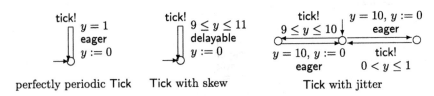

perfectly periodic Tick   Tick with skew   Tick with jitter

Fig. 2. Possible tester clock models

The initial uncertainty of the tester is modeled by a set of states $S_0 \subseteq S_A$. In other words, we assume that A is initially in some state in S_0. Notice that

---

[1] Adaptive experiments are called *branching* experiments in [9].

[2] In the literature a distinction is made between *simple* and *multiple* experiments [9, 5]. A multiple experiment can be executed multiple times and the assumption is that the machine is always at the same state at the beginning of each execution: this essentially means there is a special "reset" button which brings the machine back to the same (unknown) initial state at the beginning of each experiment. We only consider simple experiments in this paper, since they assume less power on the tester side.

S_0 may equal S_A, which means we have no knowledge of the initial state. We are also given m pairwise disjoint subsets of S_A, $C_1, ..., C_m$. In the case of the distinguishing problem, $C_1, ..., C_m$ form a *partition* of S_0 (thus, $S_0 = \bigcup_i C_i$). This partition models our requirements from the tester: we want the tester to tell us, at the end of the experiment, in which of the m subsets A was at the beginning of the experiment. In the case of the homing problem, $C_1, ..., C_m$ form a partition of S_A (thus, $S_A = \bigcup_i C_i$). Here, we want the tester to tell us in which of the m subsets A is at the end of the experiment. For example, we might associate one set C_i with each location q_i of A, meaning we want to know the final location.

A *vertebra* is an element of $\mathsf{Vert} = (\mathsf{Act_{in}} \cup \mathsf{Act_{out}})^* \cdot \{\mathsf{tick}\}$. An *input-vertebra* (respectively, *output-vertebra*) is an element of $\mathsf{Vert_{in}} = (\mathsf{Act_{in}})^* \cdot \{\mathsf{tick}\}$ (respectively, $\mathsf{Vert_{out}} = (\mathsf{Act_{out}})^* \cdot \{\mathsf{tick}\}$). At each vertebra corresponds a unique input-vertebra and a unique output-vertebra which can be obtained by projection. For instance, $a? \cdot v! \cdot b? \cdot v! \cdot w! \cdot \mathsf{tick}$ is a vertebra with corresponding input-vertebra $a? \cdot b? \cdot \mathsf{tick}$ and output-vertebra $v! \cdot v! \cdot w! \cdot \mathsf{tick}$.

A *digital preset experiment* (PX for short) is a finite sequence $\pi \in (\mathsf{Vert_{in}})^*$, for example

$$\pi = a \cdot \mathsf{tick} \cdot b \cdot c \cdot \mathsf{tick}.$$

This experiment is to be interpreted as follows:

> Issue input a; wait until the next clock tick occurs; issue input b, then input c; wait until the next clock tick occurs; collect the observed output.

This interpretation assumes that the tester has enough time to issue the entire sequence of input actions appearing between two successive ticks before the next tick is received. However, this is not a restrictive assumption: as we make no assumption on input-completeness on A, assumptions on A's environment can be *modeled directly* within A. In particular, timing constraints on the tester, such as how much time it takes to issue an input can be modeled this way. As we shall see later, the tester is not allowed to issue an input which may not be accepted by A, thus, must obey the modeled timing restrictions.

A *digital adaptive experiment* (AX for short) is defined as a finite decision tree like the ones shown in Figure 3. Each internal node of the tree is labeled with an input-vertebra. Each edge is labeled with an output-vertebra: the labels of two edges emanating from the same internal node must be distinct. Each leaf is labeled with an element from $\{C_1, ..., C_m\}$. The AX to the left of the figure is to be interpreted as follows:

> Issue input a, issue input b, wait until the next tick and collect the observed output sequence. If the latter equals $v \cdot w \cdot \mathsf{tick}$ then stop the experiment and declare that the result of the experiment is C_2. Otherwise (i.e., $v \cdot \mathsf{tick}$ is observed), issue input a twice, wait until the next tick and collect the observed output sequence. If the latter equals $v \cdot \mathsf{tick}$ then the

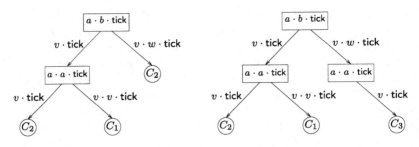

Fig. 3. Two digital experiments: adaptive (left) and preset (right)

result of the experiment is C_2. Otherwise (i.e., $v \cdot v \cdot \text{tick}$ is observed) the result is C_1.[3]

Notice that we allow decisions to be taken in an AX only after ticks. Indeed, this is the only choice that makes sense implementation-wise, because this is the point where the inputs and outputs of the tester *synchronize*. Suppose we allowed the AX to make a decision after every input it issues. This would give a tree where an internal node could be labeled, say, by $a \in \text{Act}_{in}$. How would such an experiment be interpreted? It is not legal to interpret it as: "Issue input a and observe the output. If the latter is b then ... else ...". This is because the output cannot always be observed immediately after an input is given, but only after some time. Indeed, for some inputs, there might be no output at all until the next tick. Thus, it is natural to interpret the above experiment as: "Issue input a and wait for the next output. If the latter is ...". But waiting for the next output is equivalent to waiting for the next tick and then observing the output, since the tester does not know how much it has to wait. This is precisely the same as labeling the internal node by $a \cdot \text{tick}$, which brings us to our case where nodes are labeled with input-vertebrae.

Another thing to point out on AX is the fact that the branches from an internal node do not cover all possible outputs. Indeed, they cannot, since the AX needs to be finite and the number of output-vertebrae is infinite. However, as we shall see, for an output-bounded TAIO, the above number turns out to be finite. We shall use this hypothesis in the following sections. In terms of execution of an AX, if the tester observes an output sequence which is not in the set of possible outputs in the current node of the decision tree, then the tester declares the system under test or the tester's clock as *non-conforming* to their respective models.

Notice that a PX is a special type of an AX, where the inputs given do not depend on the outputs observed during the experiment. Thus, an AX T is a PX if all leaves of T are at the same depth and all internal nodes of T which are at the same depth are labeled with the same input-vertebra. For example, the AX to the right of Figure 3 is preset.

---

[3] Depending on whether we are dealing with the distinguishing problem or the homing problem, the result of the experiment is interpreted differently, see below.

Before giving the definitions of distinguishing and homing sequences, we need to make the link between the possible observable input- and output-vertebrae and the real-time traces of the model. For that, we consider $A^{\text{tick}} = A\|\text{Tick}$ the product of A and Tick. A *timed-vertebra* is an element of $\text{Vert}_{\text{RT}} = \text{RT}(\text{Act}) \cdot \{\text{tick}\}$, for example, $\rho = a \cdot 0.4 \cdot v \cdot \tau \cdot 0.6 \cdot \text{tick}$. Let $\text{Act}_{\text{in}}^{\text{tick}} = \text{Act}_{\text{in}} \cup \{\text{tick}\}$ and $\text{Act}_{\text{out}}^{\text{tick}} = \text{Act}_{\text{out}} \cup \{\text{tick}\}$. To each $\rho \in (\text{Vert}_{\text{RT}})^*$ correspond the unique sequences $\pi = P_{\text{Act}_{\text{in}}^{\text{tick}}}(\rho) \in (\text{Vert}_{\text{in}})^*$ and $\sigma = P_{\text{Act}_{\text{out}}^{\text{tick}}}(\rho) \in (\text{Vert}_{\text{out}})^*$. For example, ρ given above matches $\pi = a \cdot \text{tick}$ and $\sigma = v \cdot \text{tick}$. Intuitively, if ρ matches π and σ then ρ is a possible behavior of A^{tick} for which the latter can produce σ when "fed" with π.

For some set of states $S \subseteq S_A$ and an input-vertebra sequence $\pi \in (\text{Vert}_{\text{in}})^*$ we say that π is *accepted* by S if $\forall s \in S \cdot \exists \rho \in (\text{Vert}_{\text{RT}})^* \cdot s \xrightarrow{\rho} \wedge \pi = P_{\text{Act}_{\text{in}}^{\text{tick}}}(\rho)$. The set of output-vertebra sequences that can be observed starting from some state in S, due to the execution of π is $outputs(S, \pi) = \{\sigma \in (\text{Vert}_{\text{out}})^* \mid \exists s \in S \cdot \exists \rho \in \text{Vert}_{\text{RT}} \cdot s \xrightarrow{\rho} \wedge \pi = P_{\text{Act}_{\text{in}}^{\text{tick}}}(\rho) \wedge \sigma = P_{\text{Act}_{\text{out}}^{\text{tick}}}(\rho)\}$. Moreover for some output-vertebra sequence $\sigma \in (\text{Vert}_{\text{out}})^*$, we introduce the two following sets of states $init(S, \pi, \sigma) = \{s \in S \mid \exists \rho \in \text{Vert}_{\text{RT}} \cdot s \xrightarrow{\rho} \wedge \pi = P_{\text{Act}_{\text{in}}^{\text{tick}}}(\rho) \wedge \sigma = P_{\text{Act}_{\text{out}}^{\text{tick}}}(\rho)\}$ and $succ(S, \pi, \sigma) = \{s' \in S_A \mid \exists s \in S \cdot \exists \rho \in \text{Vert}_{\text{RT}} \cdot s \xrightarrow{\rho} s' \wedge \pi = P_{\text{Act}_{\text{in}}^{\text{tick}}}(\rho) \wedge \sigma = P_{\text{Act}_{\text{out}}^{\text{tick}}}(\rho)\}$. Intuitively, $init(S, \pi, \sigma)$ corresponds to the subset of states of S from which it is possible to observe σ after applying π and $succ(S, \pi, \sigma)$ the subset of states of S_A to which it is possible to move after applying π and observing σ.

Definition 1 (Valid experiments). *Let T be an AX, A a TAIO and $S_0 \subseteq S_A$. T is said to be valid w.r.t. A and S_0 if for each node u of T it is possible to assign a set of states $S_u \subseteq S_A$ such that the following hold:*

- *for r, the root of T, we have $S_r = S_0$;*
- *for each internal node u of T, if π is the input-vertebra label of u, then:*
  - *π is accepted by S_u;*
  - *for each $\sigma \in outputs(S_u, \pi)$, there exists an outgoing edge from u labeled with σ; furthermore, u has as many outgoing edges as the number of elements of $outputs(S_u, \pi)$;*
  - *if $u \xrightarrow{\sigma} u'$ is an edge of T then $S_{u'} = succ(S_u, \pi, \sigma)$.* $\square$

Validity guarantees that, at each step of its execution, the input provided by the experiment is accepted by the current state of the machine, no matter what this state is. Validity also ensures that any output the machine may produce is taken into account in the experiment.

Let T be an AX. For each leaf u of T, π_u denotes the unique sequence of input-vertebrae obtained by concatenating the labels of the internal nodes on the path from the root of T to u. Similarly, σ_u denotes the unique sequence of output-vertebrae obtained by concatenating the labels of the edges on this path. Finally, C_u denotes the label of u (i.e., $C_u \in \{C_1, ..., C_m\}$).

Definition 2 (Distinguishing and homing experiments). *An experiment T is* distinguishing *(respectively,* homing*) for A w.r.t. Tick, S_0 and $\{C_1, ..., C_m\}$*

iff T is valid w.r.t. A and S_0 and for any leaf u of T we have: $succ(S_0, \pi_u, \sigma_u) \subseteq C_u$ *(respectively, $init(S_0, \pi_u, \sigma_u) \subseteq C_u$).*   □

We use abbreviations DAX, DPX, HAX and HPX for distinguishing or homing, adaptive or preset experiments.

The objective of this paper is to develop algorithms which, given A, Tick, S_0 and $\{C_1, ..., C_m\}$, check whether there exists a DPX, HPX, DAX, or HAX and if so construct one. It can be easily shown that for any type of experiment, a solution does not always exist. This is no surprise, since A is generally partially observable and non-deterministic. But also because the tester only has limited observation capabilities regarding time (i.e., a digital-clock). Notice that even in the case of finite Mealy machines, non-determinism implies that solutions do not always exist for any of these experiments [1]. On the other hand, in the case of deterministic Mealy machines, a homing (preset) experiment always exists, whereas distinguishing experiments may or may not exist [9, 8]. Also note that there are cases where an adaptive experiment exists whereas no preset experiment exists.

4   The Time-Abstracting Bisimulation Quotient Graph

The first step toward solving the state-identification problems defined in the previous section is to generate the *quotient graph* G of the product A^{tick} with respect to the *time-abstracting bisimulation* (TAB). Due to space limitations, we will not define what a TAB is, nor show how to construct G. These topics are presented in detail in [11]. Here, we only recall the basic properties of G which are relevant for the purposes of this paper. Readers not familiar with TABs may think of G as the *region graph* of A^{tick}. Indeed, the latter is in fact a TAB quotient graph, but not the coarsest possible in general.

G is a finite graph. The edges of G are labeled either with some $a \in \text{Act}_{\text{in}} \cup \text{Act}_{\text{out}} \cup \{\text{tick}, \tau\}$ (corresponding to the discrete transitions of A^{tick}), or with ϵ (corresponding to the passage of time). For our purposes, both τ and ϵ transitions model events which are unobservable to the tester. Thus, we rename all ϵ transitions into τ transitions. From now on, we assume that G has been transformed in that way. That is, the set of labels of G is $\Sigma = \text{Act}_{\text{in}} \cup \text{Act}_{\text{out}} \cup \{\text{tick}, \tau\}$.

Every node v of G corresponds to a set of states of A^{tick} and consequently to a set of states of A, S_v. We assume that G *respects* all sets $S_0, C_1, ..., C_m$. This means that either $S_v \subseteq S_0$ or $S_v \cap S_0 = \emptyset$ and similarly for every C_i. Constructing G in order to respect such subsets of the state space is not a problem (see [11] for details).

Finite paths of G define sequences of symbols which are in Σ^*. In particular, a *discrete-vertebra* is an element of $\text{Vert}_{\text{disc}} = (\Sigma \backslash \{\text{tick}\})^* \cdot \{\text{tick}\}$. As in the TAIO case, we make the link between these discrete-vertebrae and the corresponding observable input- and output-vertebrae. For $\rho \in (\text{Vert}_{\text{disc}})^*$, $\pi \in (\text{Vert}_{\text{in}})^*$ and $\sigma \in (\text{Vert}_{\text{out}})^*$, we say that ρ matches π (resp. σ) if the projection of ρ to $\text{Act}_{\text{in}}^{\text{tick}}$ (resp. $\text{Act}_{\text{out}}^{\text{tick}}$) equals π (resp. σ).

The sanity properties of A and Tick induce similar properties on G. G is *non-blocking* in the sense that for any node v of G there exists a node v' of G and a sequence $\rho \in$ Vert$_{\text{disc}}$ such that $v \xrightarrow{\rho} v'$ is a possible path in G and ρ matches the input-vertebrae tick (i.e., if no input is given, time will elapse). An equally important property is that G is also *output-bounded* in the sense that the output-vertebrae that G can produce are of bounded length. In other words, there exists n such that for any discrete-vertebra ρ of G, the length of the output-vertebra corresponding to ρ is at most n.

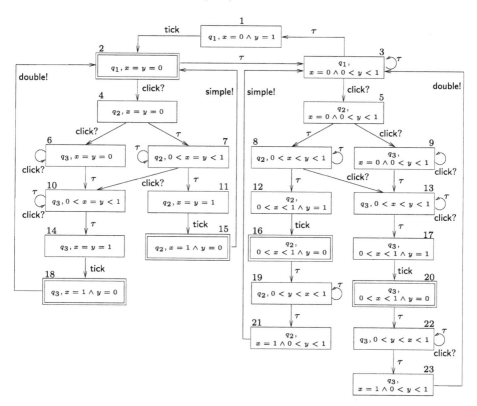

Fig. 4. A time-abstracting bisimulation quotient graph

The graph G shown in Figure 4 is the TAB quotient graph of the product of the TAIO of Figure 1 and the left-most Tick automaton of Figure 2. [4] The nodes of G are numbered from 1 to 23. G is made up of three subblocks:

- The cycle made by nodes $1, 2$ and 3 models the behavior of the system when no stimuli are received from the external environment (i.e., only time elapses).

---

[4] Notice that since the automaton of Figure 1 is not input-complete, click? actions are not allowed at every node of the quotient graph.

- The subgraph of G induced by nodes $2, 4, 6, 7, 10, 11, 14, 15$ and 18 models the behavior of the system when a first click and the tick actions happen simultaneously.
- The second subgraph of G induced by the rest of the nodes models the behavior of the system when the first click and the tick actions happen at different times.

G is not a Mealy machine, thus, existing methods for solving state identification problems [8] do not apply. Indeed, in Mealy machines inputs and outputs are *synchronous* whereas in G they are inherently *asynchronous*: an input may result in some output later in time, or even not at all; an output may be emitted without any explicit input but simply with the passage of time; a single input may produce more than one outputs or more than one inputs may be necessary to produce an output; and so on. This motivates the next section, which proposes a transformation of G to a Mealy machine M capturing all necessary information in order to solve the problems of the previous section. Notice that M is a non-deterministic machine, that is, a given input may result in more that one outputs and/or lead to more that one states. This is to be expected, as mentioned above. Still, input and output symbols in M are synchronous, which allows us to use existing methods on non-deterministic such machines [1].

5   Transformation to a Non-deterministic Mealy Machine and Reduction

As explained in Section 4 the main objective of the transformation is to remove the asynchronism between inputs and outputs in G. To do this, we observe that the basic external stimuli in G are input-vertebrae. Thus, it should suffice to consider the way in which G behaves w.r.t. elements in Vert_{in}. For this we need to identify the response of G w.r.t. any possible input-vertebra which is "accepted" by the current considered node. An input-vertebra π is accepted by node v if there exists a discrete-vertebra ρ such that $v \xrightarrow{\rho}$ and ρ matches π.

Consequently, a first idea is to transform G into a Mealy machine M with the same set of nodes as G and label the edges of M with pairs $(\pi, \sigma) \in \mathsf{Vert}_{in} \times \mathsf{Vert}_{out}$. Formalizing this, we get that for any two nodes v, v' of G and any pair $(\pi, \sigma) \in \mathsf{Vert}_{in} \times \mathsf{Vert}_{out}$, we add an edge $v \xrightarrow{\pi/\sigma} v'$ in M iff there exists $\rho \in \mathsf{Vert}_{disc}$ such that

$$v \xrightarrow{\rho} v' \text{ is a path of } G \text{ and } \rho \text{ matches both } \pi \text{ and } \sigma.$$

For instance, the Mealy machine deduced from the graph shown in Figure 4 has an edge from node 2 to node 18 labeled with click $\cdot$ click $\cdot$ tick/tick and another edge from 2 to 15 labeled with click $\cdot$ tick/tick.

The problem with the above definition is that some nodes of M may have an infinite number of outgoing edges, since the number of paths $v \xrightarrow{\rho} v'$ is a-priori unbounded. For instance, in the preceding example, we need to draw an edge from node 2 to node 18 for each input-vertebrae which is in click · click · click* · tick. Observe, however, that any of these input-vertebrae produces the same output-vertebra, namely, tick. Thus, we can remedy the above problem by grouping all input-vertebrae together and representing them *symbolically* in a single transition. More precisely, we will only add a single edge $2 \xrightarrow{L/\text{tick}} 18$, where L is the regular language click · click · click* · tick.

The method we propose consists of the following steps:

Step 1 We identify the nodes of G with an incoming edge labeled with tick. These nodes are called tick-*nodes*. The latter are these nodes which can be reached by an input-vertebra. In Figure 4, the tick-nodes are drawn with double rectangles.

Step 2 For every node v and every tick-node v_{tick} of G, we compute the language $L_{v,v_{\text{tick}}}$ containing all $\rho \in \text{Vert}_{\text{disc}}$ such that $v \xrightarrow{\rho} v_{\text{tick}}$. $L_{v,v_{\text{tick}}}$ is a regular language since it is induced by a subgraph of G.

Step 3 For each v and v_{tick}, we compute $L^O_{v,v_{\text{tick}}} = \{P_{\text{Act}^{\text{tick}}_{\text{out}}}(\rho) \mid \rho \in L_{v,v_{\text{tick}}}\}$, the projection of $L_{v,v_{\text{tick}}}$ to the set of outputs and tick actions. $L^O_{v,v_{\text{tick}}}$ is a set of output-vertebrae. Since G is output-bounded, $L^O_{v,v_{\text{tick}}}$ is a finite set.

Step 4 For each $\sigma \in L^O_{v,v_{\text{tick}}}$, we compute $L^I_{v,v_{\text{tick}},\sigma} = \{\pi \mid \exists \rho \in L_{v,v_{\text{tick}}} \text{ such that } \rho \text{ matches both } \pi \text{ and } \sigma\}$, the set of input-vertebrae the execution of which may generate σ. $L^I_{v,v_{\text{tick}},\sigma}$ can be defined equivalently as

$$L^I_{v,v_{\text{tick}},\sigma} = P_{\text{Act}^{\text{tick}}_{\text{in}}}(P^{-1}(\sigma) \cap L_{v,v_{\text{tick}}})$$

where $P^{-1}(\cdot)$ denotes the *inverse projection* function. Since all the operations in the right-hand side of the above formula preserve regular languages, $L^I_{v,v_{\text{tick}},\sigma}$ is a regular language.

After computing $L^I_{v,v_{\text{tick}},\sigma}$, we add in M a new edge from v to v_{tick} labeled with $L^I_{v,v_{\text{tick}},\sigma}/\sigma$.

At this point, we have obtained a finite, non-deterministic Mealy machine which has the same nodes as G and the edges of which are labeled with pairs (L,σ) where L is a regular language of input-vertebrae (called the *language-symbol* of the edge) and σ is an output-vertebra. Unfortunately, we are still not done. The problem is that language-symbols must be disjoint across the entire set of edges of M. Only if this holds we have the right to consider two different (and disjoint) language-symbols L_1 and L_2 as different input symbols in M.[5] The example shown in Figure 5 illustrates the problem. If we consider L_1 and L_2 as different input symbols then we do not find a homing preset experiment for this machine: L_1 is not a HPX because L_1 is not accepted at state 2; similarly for L_2. However, a HPX exists, namely, $a \cdot a \cdot$ tick. In order to be able to detect this, we need to "split" L_1 into L'_1 and L'_2 and to update the edges as shown in the figure.

---

[5] Notice that for the output symbols of M there is no such issue: two output symbols σ_1 and σ_2 are the same iff the output-vertebrae σ_1 and σ_2 are identical.

In the general case, this transformation is done as follows:

Step 5 We collect the language-symbols that appear on the edges of the machine M so far constructed. Let $L_1, ..., L_N$ be the list of these language-symbols. Then we compute $L'_1, ..., L'_{N'}$, the coarsest partition of $L_1 \cup L_2 \cup ... \cup L_N$ which respects each L_i. Thus, L'_k are pairwise disjoint and each L_i is "split" into a number of L'_k, namely:

$$L_i = L'_{j_1} \cup \cdots \cup L'_{j_i}.$$

Then, we replace each edge $v \xrightarrow{L_i/\sigma} v'$ by the edges $v \xrightarrow{L'_{j_1}/\sigma} v', ..., v \xrightarrow{L'_{j_i}/\sigma} v'$.

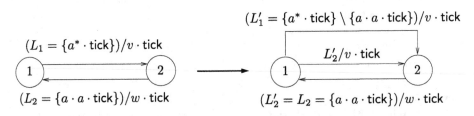

Fig. 5. A time-abstracting bisimulation quotient graph

Step 5 completes the transformation. Figure 6 shows the result of the transformation technique applied up to Step 4 to our running example (Step 5 is omitted because it results in a graph too complex to be readable). In the figure, the tick-nodes are drawn with double circles. The rest of the nodes are drawn with rectangles. In order not to overload the figure, we group together some nodes which are equivalent in the sense that no input sequence can distinguish them (nodes 19 and 21 for example). We also duplicate the nodes 15 and 18. The list of (non-disjoint) input language-symbols for this machine are: $A = \text{tick}$, $B = \text{click} \cdot \text{tick}$, $C = \text{click} \cdot \text{click}^* \cdot \text{tick}$, $D = \text{click} \cdot \text{click} \cdot \text{click}^* \cdot \text{tick}$, $E = \text{click}^* \cdot \text{tick}$. The corresponding disjoint input language-symbols are: $A' = \text{tick} \ (= A)$, $B' = \text{click} \cdot \text{tick} \ (= B)$, $C' = \text{click} \cdot \text{click} \cdot \text{click}^* \cdot \text{tick} \ (= D)$. The output symbols are: $X = \text{tick}$, $Y = \text{simple} \cdot \text{tick}$, $Z = \text{double} \cdot \text{tick}$.

Once we have transformed G into M we can reduce the problem of finding a digital-clock experiment for A to the problem of finding the corresponding (untimed) experiment for M. We omit the definitions of untimed preset/adaptive homing/distinguishing experiments for non-deterministic Mealy machines, as they can be found in [1].[6] The following proposition gives the main result of this work.

---

[6] There are slight differences in the framework considered in the above paper, namely, the machines considered there are input-complete and homing experiments are not studied. However, extending the definitions and algorithms to cover these cases is straightforward.

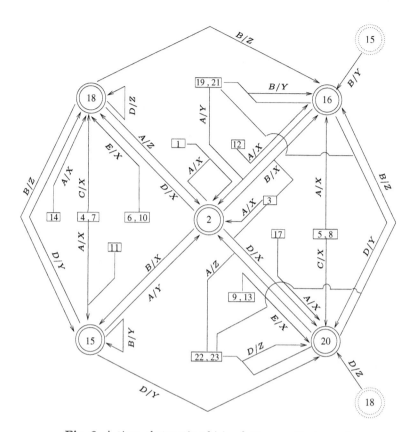

Fig. 6. A time-abstracting bisimulation quotient graph

Proposition 1. *A has a DPX (resp., HPX, DAX, HAX) iff M has a DPX (resp., HPX, DAX, HAX).*

Checking whether M has a given type of experiment can be done using the algorithms of [1]. These algorithms permit not only to check existence but also to construct an experiment in case it exists. The algorithms are based on the synthesis of *strategies* in *games with incomplete information*. The game is played between the tester who provides the inputs and the system under test who provides the outputs. The strategy of the system corresponds to resolving its non-determinism. The strategy of the tester corresponds to choosing the inputs. The tester has incomplete information because it only observes the output, not the current state of the game. Finding preset experiments corresponds to finding a *blindfold* strategy for the tester, that is, a strategy which is totally defined in advance. Finding preset and adaptive experiments is shown in the above paper to be PSPACE-complete and EXPTIME-complete problems, respectively.

It remains to show how to construct an experiment for A given an experiment for M. We explain this in the case of preset homing experiments. The idea carries to other types of experiments as well. A HPX for M is a finite sequence of language-symbols $L_1 \cdot L_2 \cdot \ldots \cdot L_m$, where each L_i is a regular language of input-vertebrae. For each i we choose arbitrarily an input-vertebra $\pi_i \in L_i$ (e.g., we may choose a π_i of minimal length). We claim that $\pi = \pi_1 \cdots \pi_m$ is a HPX for A. This is based on the following. First, the fact that different language-symbols in M are disjoint. Thus, when issuing a certain input-vertebra π_i, there is no ambiguity as to which language-symbol in M this π_i corresponds to. In our example above, it will be the language-symbol L_i. Second, the fact that all output-vertebrae end with a tick symbol. This ensures that when concatenating output-vertebrae to form the final output sequence given to the tester, the latter will have no ambiguity in interpreting the result. In particular, if σ_1, σ_2 are two vertebrae such that $\sigma_1 \neq \sigma_2$ then for any vertebrae σ_1', σ_2', $\sigma_1 \cdot \sigma_1' \neq \sigma_2 \cdot \sigma_2'$. Thus, if the output sequences are different at the level of M they will also differ at the level of A.

6   Summary and Future Work

We presented a method for solving state-identification problems for timed automata by generating their time-abstracting bisimulation quotient graph and then transforming the latter into a non-deterministic Mealy machine on which the same problems can be solved. Although we only studied distinguishing and homing experiments in this paper, the method should adapt easily to state-verification and synchronizing experiments as well. In the short term, we plan to identify upper and lower complexity bounds on the problems studied in this paper and experiment with a prototype implementation. One direction for future work is to consider analog-clock experiments. Apart from their theoretical interest, such experiments could also be useful in limiting state-explosion, in particular in cases where the constants involved in the Tick automaton are significantly smaller than those in the automaton under test. Still, a solid theory for implementation of analog-clock devices is lacking, thus should also be topic of future research. Another direction would be to remove, if possible, the bounded-output hypothesis used in this paper. Since most realistic systems meet this hypothesis, removing it is probably only of theoretical interest. However, it gives rise to an interesting question, namely, studying testing problems in the context of generalized Mealy machines or *sequential transducers*. Finally, another interesting direction is to consider related problems such as machine identification and learning. Some work in this direction has recently been reported in [6].

References

1. R. Alur, C. Courcoubetis, and M. Yannakakis. Distinguishing tests for nondeterministic and probabilistic machines. In *27th ACM Symposium on Theory of Computing (STOC'95)*, pages 363–372, 1995.
2. R. Alur and D. Dill. A theory of timed automata. *Theoretical Computer Science*, 126:183–235, 1994.

3. S. Bornot, J. Sifakis, and S. Tripakis. Modeling urgency in timed systems. In *Compositionality*, volume 1536 of *LNCS*. Springer, 1998.

4. C. Daws, A. Olivero, S. Tripakis, and S. Yovine. The tool Kronos. In *Hybrid Systems III, Verification and Control*, volume 1066 of *LNCS*, pages 208–219. Springer-Verlag, 1996.

5. A. Gill. State-identification experiments in finite automata. *Information and Control*, 4:132–154, 1961.

6. O. Grinchtein, B. Jonsson, and M. Leucker. Learning of event-recording automata. In *Joint conference on Formal Modelling and Analysis of Timed Systems and Formal Techniques in Real-Time and Fault Tolerant System (FORMATS-FTRTFT'04)*, volume 3253 of *LNCS*. Springer, 2004.

7. M. Krichen and S. Tripakis. Black-box conformance testing for real-time systems. In *11th International SPIN Workshop on Model Checking of Software (SPIN'04)*, volume 2989 of *LNCS*. Springer, 2004.

8. D. Lee and M. Yannakakis. Principles and methods of testing finite state machines - A survey. *Proceedings of the IEEE*, 84:1090–1126, 1996.

9. E.F. Moore. Gedanken-experiments on sequential machines. In *Automata Studies*, number 34. Princeton University Press, 1956.

10. J. Sifakis and S. Yovine. Compositional specification of timed systems. In *13th Annual Symposium on Theoretical Aspects of Computer Science, STACS'96*, volume 1046 of *LNCS*. Spinger-Verlag, 1996.

11. S. Tripakis and S. Yovine. Analysis of timed systems using time-abstracting bisimulations. *Formal Methods in System Design*, 18(1):25–68, January 2001.

Timing Fault Models for Systems with Multiple Timers

M. Ümit Uyar[1], Yu Wang[1], Samrat S. Batth[1], Adriana Wise[2], and M.A. Fecko[3]

[1] The City College of the City University of New York, New York, USA
[2] Department of Computer Science, Graduate Center, CUNY, New York, USA
[3] Applied Research Area, Telcordia Technologies Inc., New Jersey, USA

Abstract. Multiple timing faults, although detectable individually, can hide each other's faulty behavior making the faulty system indistinguishable from a non-faulty one. A set of graph augmentations are introduced for single timing faults. The fault detection capability of the augmentations is analyzed in the presence of multiple timing faults and shown that multiple occurrences of a class of timing faults can be detected.

Keywords: Conformance Testing; Timer Constraints; Multiple Faults; Fault Modeling; Timed Automata

1 Introduction

This paper analyzes the fault detection capability of the timed FSM model introduced in Ref. [7] in the presence of multiple timing faults. It is shown here that multiple timing faults, although detectable individually, can hide each other's faulty behavior thereby making the faulty system indistinguishable from a non-faulty one. A set of graph augmentations are introduced for single timing faults. It is shown that the augmentations for single faults can also detect the presence of multiple faults occurring simultaneously.

Fault coverage has been studied mostly with respect to transfer/output faults for FSMs [1, 9, 11, 15]. Petrenko et al. [9] investigate fundamental underlying concepts of fault coverage analysis, whose primary focus is protocol conformance testing. The detection of such faults, which is not part of the timing-fault analysis, depends on the adopted conformance relation, the underlying fault models, and the state verification method [4, 8, 10, 13]. If a timing fault results in a transfer/output fault, we assume that it is detected with high probability under the widely accepted assumption that the faults do not increase the number of states in an implementation under test (IUT).

The related work on testing systems with timing dependencies focuses on testing Timed Automata (TA) [2], with a theoretical framework in Ref. [12] achieving a provably complete test coverage at the expense of a prohibitively large number of test cases. Dssouli et al. [5, 6] introduce a method based on the state characterization technique using a timed extension of the Wp-method [8].

F. Khendek and R. Dssouli (Eds.): TestCom 2005, LNCS 3502, pp. 192–208, 2005.

The technique formulates fault models for timed systems by considering time specific one-clock and multi-clock timing faults in addition to FSM-like transfer/output faults. The aim of a complete test coverage is relaxed—by choosing a proper granularity, a "good" fault coverage is achieved with reasonably long test sequences. Dssouli et al. are the first to present a classification of timing faults [6], and formally prove that their technique detects all single faults of a given type [5]. None of the above techniques are shown to have the ability to detect multiple simultaneous timing faults. A major contribution of this paper is a formal analysis of such a fault detection capability for the testing methodology introduced in Ref. [7].

Section 2 of this paper gives the basic definitions. The simplified version of the timed FSM model of [7] is given in Section 3. Single and multiple timing faults are discussed in Sections 4 and 5, respectively.

2   Definitions

A communicating protocol can be modeled as a Finite State Machine (FSM) represented by a directed graph $G(V, E)$. Vertex set V and edge set E represent the states and transitions triggered by events of a system, respectively. For time-related FSM, FSM can be extended to consider of a set of timers $\mathcal{T}$ that may be arbitrarily started or stopped.

Timed FSM is a tuple $M = (V, A, O, \mathcal{T}, E, v_0)$ where V is a finite set of states, $v_0 \in V$ is the initial state, A is a finite set of inputs, O is a finite set of outputs, $\mathcal{T}$ is a finite set of timers, and $E \subseteq V \times (A \times \mathcal{T} \times O) \times V$ is a set of transitions $V \times A \times \mathcal{T} \longrightarrow O \times V$.

In the presence of timers, an FSM becomes an Extended Finite State Machine (EFSM). Timer-related variables will appear in addition to the variables from the tuple above, in the form of conditions $\langle \mathbf{t}_j \rangle$ on the timer variables and of actions $\{\mathbf{t}_j\}$ on variable values. A tuple $e_i = (v_p, v_q, a_i, o_i, \langle \mathbf{t}_j \rangle, \{\mathbf{t}_j\})$ is a transition $e_i \in E$, where v_p is a current state, v_q is a next state, a_i is the input defined in current state v_p or in current transition $v_p \xrightarrow{e_i} v_q$, o_i is the output from current transition $v_p \xrightarrow{e_i} v_q$, $\mathbf{t}_j$ is a vector of timer variables, $\langle \mathbf{t}_j \rangle$ are the conditions on time-related variables, and $\{\mathbf{t}_j\}$ are the actions which update time-related variables.

A timer $T_j \in \mathcal{T}$ can be defined with a timer vector $\mathbf{t}_j = (T_j, D_j, f_j, L_p)$ where $T_j \in \{0, 1\}$ is a timer running status variable denoted by a boolean variable, $D_j \in R^{o+}$ is a time-characteristic variable that indicates the length of timer T_j, $f_j \in R^{\infty}$ is a time-keeping variable that indicates the time elapsed since timer T_j started, and $L_p \in \{0, 1\}$ is a flow enforcing variable that forces the test sequence to traverse the augmented graph according to model specific rules. Timer $T_j \in \mathcal{T}$ is expired iff $\langle (T_j == 1) \wedge (f_j \geqslant D_j) \rangle$ and is running iff $\langle (T_j == 1) \wedge (f_j < D_j) \rangle$.

$T_j == 1$ (depicted as T_j henceforth) denotes a timer is running and $T_j == 0$ (depicted as $\neg T_j$ henceforth) denotes a timer is not running (i.e., stopped, expired or not started yet). D_j is the length for T_j and $\forall f_j \in \mathbf{Z}^{\infty}$ is the time elapsed since its start. When T_j has just started, $f_j := 0$, and $f_j := -\infty$ if T_j is not running. Over an edge e_i the value of f_j is increased by the cost c_i of e_i as

$f_j := f_j + c_i$. Once f_j becomes $(f_j \geqslant D_j)$, T_j is said to be expired or timed-out. The difference of $(D_j - f_j)$ represents the remaining time until T_j's expiry. L_p is a flow enforcing variable where $L_p = 0$ implies that no transition can leave the current state v_p and $L_p = 1$ means that all transitions are allowed to leave v_p.

For $h_k = (v_k, v_{k+1}, a_k, o_k, \langle t_j \rangle, \{t_j\})$ $(\forall h_k \in E, \forall v_k \in V, \forall k \in \mathbf{Z}^+)$, a finite transition sequence is represented as $\rho = h_1, \cdots h_k, h_{k+1}, \cdots h_n$ in the graph G associated with M. For any $\forall k \in [1, n-1]$, h_k was progressed before h_{k+1}.

Assume that there are K running timers: $\{T_1, T_2, \cdots T_j, \cdots T_K\} \subset \mathcal{T}$. Then edge cost $c_i \in R^{\circ +}$ is the amount of time required to completely traverse the current edge e_i. Timeout transition $e_i = (v_p, v_q, a_i, o_i, \langle t_j \rangle, \{t_j\})$ is triggered by T_j expiry and it becomes feasible if at least one of the running timers T_j expires, $\forall T_k \neq T_j$, which can be described as follows:

$$\langle t_j \rangle : \langle T_j \wedge (f_j \geqslant D_j) \wedge T_k \wedge (f_k < D_k) \wedge (D_j - f_j < D_k - f_k) \rangle$$
$$\{t_j\} : \{T_j := 0; \quad f_j := -\infty; \quad T_k := T_k; \quad f_k := f_k + c_i\} \quad k \in \{1, 2, \cdots K, \forall k \neq j\}$$

A transition in which timer T_j, $\forall j \in [1, K]$, does not expire is defined as a non-timeout transition. A timer can be started in an action as follows:

$$\langle t_j \rangle : \langle \neg T_j \wedge T_k \wedge (f_k < D_k) \rangle$$
$$\{t_j\} : \{T_j := 1; \quad f_j := 0; \quad T_k := T_k; \quad f_k := f_k + c_i\} \quad k \in \{1, 2, \cdots K\}, \forall k \neq j.$$

A timer can be stopped as follows:

$$\langle t_j \rangle : \langle T_j \wedge (f_j < D_j) \wedge T_k \wedge (f_k < D_k) \rangle$$
$$\{t_j\} : \{T_j := 0; \quad f_j := -\infty; \quad T_k := T_k; \quad f_k := f_k + c_i\} \quad k \in \{1, 2, \cdots K\}, \forall k \neq j.$$

3   Modeling Timed FSM

To simplify the test generation from timed FSM models (which are essentially EFSMs due to the timing variables as described in Section 2), we introduce a graph augmentation for conversion of G to G' as follows:

Step (i): All the self loops in G are represented as ordinary (i.e., state-to-state) edges in G';

Step (ii): For every state v_p in G, an additional state called v'_p is introduced in G', which becomes the ending state for all of self-loops defined in v_p;

Step (iii): For self-loops of v_p in G, the return from v'_p to v_p is ensured by the introduction of an additional edge called return edge e_p^{ret} in G':

$$e_{p,k} = (v_p, v'_p) \text{ (self-loop converted as state-to-state edge)}$$
$$e_p^{ret} = (v'_p, v_p) \text{ (return edge from replica state } v'_p)$$

Step (iv): A new *observer state* is appended to v_p in G', namely v''_p. This state can be reached from and to v_p via additional edges $e_{p,obs}, e_{p,wait}$ and $e_{p,obs}^{ret}$, respectively:

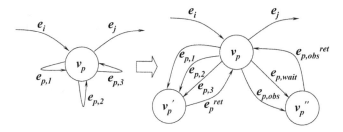

Fig. 1. Self-loops and traversal enforcement rules for v_p in G into v_p, v'_p and v''_p in G'

$$e_{p,obs} = (v_p, v''_p) \text{ (observer edge)}$$
$$e_{p,wait} = (v_p, v''_p) \text{ (wait edge)}$$
$$e^{ret}_{p,obs} = (v''_p, v_p) \text{ (return edge from observer state)}$$

In this model, the new states in G' are introduced to convert the self-loop transitions as state-to-state transitions. The role of the observer state is to "consume" pending timeouts and enable outgoing edges by setting L_p to 1. Figure 1 shows, for state v_p, an example conversion of self-loops to state-to-state transitions and the introduction of observer states/edges by our model. Augmented graph G' will contain two types of transitions, as defined below:

Type 1 *Timeout transition e^j_i defined as the transition triggered by the expiry of timer T_j. (Note that in the original graph G, e^j_i corresponds to either a state-to-state edge or a self-loop).*

Type 2 *Non-timeout transition e_i, which may start/stop a timer, may be a regular, non-timeout, state-to-state transition or may have been converted from a non-timeout self-loop transition.*

3.1   Edge Conditions and Actions for New Model

The original edge conditions and the actions of G are modified by appending timer-related conditions and actions, as described below.

Edge conditions that need to be satisfied before an edge can be traversed are formulated using the three variable types described in Section (2): *timer status variables* (T_j—on or off), *time-keeping variables* (D_j—timer length, f_j—time elapsed) and *flow-enforcing variables* (L_p—edge traversal control). Below are the edge conditions used by our model:

A *Type 1* (timeout) transition is feasible if all of the following conditions are true during the traversal:

- at least one of the running timers expires (for any two running timers, T_j and T_k, either T_j or T_k expires, and thus enables the timeout edge): $((T_j \wedge \neg T_k) \vee (\neg T_j \wedge T_k))$ $\forall T_j \neq T_k$

- the timer that expired was the timer with the least remaining time (i.e., if some T_k was also running, and if T_j's remaining time was less, then it was T_j that expired): $T_j \wedge \left(\neg T_k \vee \left(T_k \wedge (D_j - f_j < D_k - f_k) \right) \right)$ $\forall T_j \neq T_k$
- the flow-enforcing variable is set as follows:

$$L_p == \begin{cases} 0, \text{ if the edge was a timeout self loop edge in } G \\ 1, \text{ if the edge was a timeout state-to-state edge in } G \end{cases}$$

These three components of a *Type 1* edge condition can be, therefore, combined and formalized as:

- for a converted edge in G' (i.e., a self-loop edge in G): $\langle T_j \wedge (f_j \geqslant D_j) \wedge T_k \wedge (f_k < D_k) \wedge (D_j - f_j < D_k - f_k) \wedge (L_p == 0) \rangle$
- for an original edge in G' (i.e., a state-to-state edge in G): $\langle T_j \wedge (f_j \geqslant D_j) \wedge T_k \wedge (f_k < D_k) \wedge (D_j - f_j < D_k - f_k) \wedge (L_p == 1) \rangle$

The above equations imply that before a timeout transition, T_j should be still running, remaining time should be the least among all other running timers and the flow-enforcing variable is appropriately set for either a converted or an original edge in G'. Any nondeterminism due to multiple timeouts can be detected during test-sequence generation, e.g., if tm_j and tm_k are to expire simultaneously, then $(D_j - f_j = D_k - f_k)$ and their conditions cannot be satisfied.

Similarly, during the traversal, a *Type 2* (non-timeout) transition becomes feasible if both of the following conditions are true:

- either there is no running timer started in a previous transition (there may be a timer started on the current transition): $\langle \neg T_j \rangle$; or, if there is, it did not expire over a previous transition (time variable f_j of running timer T_j is less than timer's length D_j): $\langle T_j \wedge (f_j < D_j) \rangle$
- the flow-enforcing variable is set as:

$$L_p == \begin{cases} 0, \text{ if the edge was a non-timeout self-loop in } G \\ 1, \text{ if the edge was a non-timeout state-to-state edge in } G \end{cases}$$

Therefore, the time conditions for *Type 2* edges can be formalized as follows:

- for a converted edge in G' (i.e., a self-loop edge in G): $\langle (\neg T_j \vee (f_j < D_j)) \wedge (L_p == 0) \rangle$
- for an original edge in G' (i.e., a state-to-state edge in G): $\langle (\neg T_j \vee (f_j < D_j)) \wedge (L_p == 1) \rangle$

The time condition for the wait edge $e_{p,wait}$ and observer edge $e_{p,obs}$, from the original state v_p to the observer state v_p'' is formulated as: $\langle L_p == 0 \rangle$.

The return edges (i.e., e_p^{ret} and $e_{p,obs}^{ret}$) added by the graph augmentation to G' are no-cost edges with time condition as true: $\langle 1 \rangle$.

Action list can be executed by an edge whose traversal was determined by its time condition being satisfied. Such an edge may proceed and update all variables that changed during the current transition accordingly:

- If a timer expires, the timeout edge will reset the status variable T_j to 0 and the time-keeping variable to $-\infty$: $\{T_j := 0; \quad f_j := -\infty\}$
- If a timer started on a previous transition is still running, the current edge e_i will update its value with its cost c_i (which may bring $f_j \geqslant D_j$, and thus timeout T_j and trigger a timeout transition): $\{f_j := f_j + c_i\}$
- If a timer is started on the current transition, the current action list will initialize the timer state T_j to 1 and the time-keeping variable f_j to 0: $\{T_j := 1; \quad f_j := 0\}$
- The flow-enforcing variable L_p is also set by every edge according to its type:

$$L_p := \begin{cases} 1, \text{ set by observer edge to allow traversal of state-to-state edges} \\ 0, \text{ set by either } \textit{Type 1} \text{ or } \textit{Type 2} \text{ edges} \end{cases}$$

Each edge type will perform a subset of the above listed actions, according to its specifics, as follows:

- *Type 1* (timeout) edge: $\{T_j := 0; \quad f_j := -\infty; \quad T_k := T_k; \quad f_k := f_k + c_i; \quad L_p := 0\}$
- *Type 2* (non-timeout) edge: $\{f_k := f_k + c_i; \quad L_p := 0\}$ if the edge starts no timers; $\{T_j := 1; \quad f_j := 0; \quad T_k := T_k; \quad f_k := f_k + c_i; \quad L_p := 0\}$ if the edge starts timer T_j
- *Wait* (artificial) edge: $\{f_j := f_j + 1\}$ or $\{f_j := f_j + (D_j - f_j)\}$ where $D_j - f_j$ is the remaining time of timer T_j to timeout
- *Observer* (artificial) edge: $\{L_p := 1\}$
- *Return* (artificial) edge: $\{\ \}$ (i.e., there is no actions for this edge)

Since both edge types, namely *Type 1* and *Type 2*, disable outgoing transitions by setting $L_p := 0$ the only edges whose actions will enable these transitions are the artificially-created observer edges.

4 Modeling Timing Faults

In general, timing faults in an IUT can be classified into: (*i*) 1-clock interval faults, (*ii*) n-clock interval faults (introduced by Dssouli et al. [5, 6]), and (*iii*) incorrect settings of timer lengths. The goal is to detect such faults during testing through special-purpose timers and graph augmentations that force a test sequence to take a different path for a faulty IUT than for the conformant one.

In our model during the testing of transition $e_i = (v_p, v_q, a_i, o_i, \langle t_j \rangle, \{t_j\})$, after input a_i is applied, the expected output o_i should be generated no later than θ time units, $\theta \in \mathbf{R}^+$. If there is no output observed in θ time units (represented as $\neg o_i$) or output o_i is observed after θ time units, a fault occurs. The θ time units is part of a test harness rather than the IUT.

4.1 1-Clock Interval Faults

1-Clock Interval Faults are related to timing conflicts due to one clock/timer regardless of other concurrent clocks/timers. Unacceptable input timing (i.e., an input may be 'rushed' or 'delayed') results either in an unacceptable output value for a transition or unexpected output timing (i.e., an output may be 'rushed' or 'delayed'). 1-clock interval faults occur either when at least one input interval boundary is violated in the IUT or no interval boundary is modified but no output is observed.

Timing Requirement: Transition $e_i = (v_p, v_q, a_i, o_i, \langle t_j \rangle, \{t_j\})$ can correctly trigger only if applied input a_i is within the required time interval $[\alpha, \beta]$ measured from the traversal of h_k—an edge prior to e_i in a test sequence.

Based on this requirement, two faults, namely *Timing Faults I* and *II*, can be defined as follows:

Timing Fault I: Input a_i is applied either too early ($\delta' < \alpha$) or too late ($\delta' > \beta$), but output o_i may still be observed and state v_q be verified in no later than θ time units from the instance input a_i is applied.

Timing Fault II: Input a_i is applied within the required time interval $[\alpha, \beta]$, but either the output is not observed (i.e., $\neg o_i$) or state v_q cannot be verified in less than $\delta + \theta$ time units. The detection of Fault II has not been included in the analysis presented in this paper since it has been handled by transfer fault detection models reported in literature [9].

Graph Augmentation to Detect Timing Fault I: The modeling of 1-clock timing requirement for an edge $e_i = (v_p, v_q, a_i, o_i, \langle t_j \rangle, \{t_j\})$, is accomplished by using two *special purpose timers* and creating the so-called *observer states/edges*. The special purpose timers are called T_α and T_β with lengths $D_\alpha = \alpha$ and $D_\beta = \beta$ time units, respectively, where $\alpha < \beta$. Note that timers T_α and T_β are not the part of the IUT, but maintained by the test harness run by the tester.

The edge e_i triggers only after input a_i is applied within time interval $[\alpha, \beta]$ (i.e., after timer T_α but before timer T_β expires), and in its action stops timer T_β. Therefore, in our augmentation, the modified timing conditions for h_k (which starts T_α and T_β timers) and e_i are as follows:

$$h_k : \langle \neg T_\alpha \wedge \neg T_\beta \rangle \qquad \{T_\alpha := 1; \ f_\alpha := 0; \ T_\beta := 1;$$
$$f_\beta := 0\}$$

$$e_i : \langle \neg T_\alpha \wedge T_\beta \wedge (f_\beta \in [\alpha, \beta]) \wedge (L_p == 1) \rangle \quad \{T_\beta := 0; \ f_\beta := -\infty; \ L_p := 0\}$$

Additionally, v_p (starting state of e_i) is replaced by two new states, $v_{p,1}$ and $v_{p,2}$, connected by a new edge $e_{p,1,2}$ from $v_{p,1}$ to $v_{p,2}$; the original incoming and outgoing edges of v_p are connected to $v_{p,1}$ and $v_{p,2}$, respectively. The time condition for $e_{p,1,2}$ is the expiry of T_α with the cost of zero:

$$e_{p,1,2} : \langle T_\alpha \wedge (f_\alpha \geqslant \alpha) \wedge T_\beta \wedge (L_p == 1) \rangle \quad \{T_\alpha := 0; \ f_\alpha := -\infty; \ L_p := 0\}$$

Two new observer states, namely $v'_{p,1}$ and $v'_{p,2}$, with their associated observer edges, $e_{p,1,obs}$ and $e_{p,2,obs}$, are appended to $v_{p,1}$ and $v_{p,2}$, respectively. The new wait edges $e_{p,1,wait}$ from $v_{p,1}$ to $v'_{p,1}$ (with cost $c_{p,1,wait} = 1$ time unit) and $e_{p,2,wait}$ from $v_{p,2}$ to $v'_{p,2}$ (with cost $c_{p,2,wait} = 1$ time unit), and their return edges, namely $e^{ret}_{p,1}$ and $e^{ret}_{p,2}$ (both with zero cost), are created:

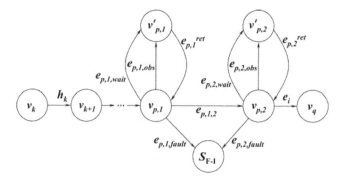

Fig. 2. Augmenting state v_p for Timing Fault I detection

$$e_{p,1,wait} : \langle T_\alpha \wedge (f_\alpha < \alpha) \wedge T_\beta \wedge (f_\beta < \alpha) \wedge (L_p == 0) \rangle \quad \{f_\alpha := f_\alpha + c_{p,1,wait};$$
$$f_\beta := f_\beta + c_{p,1,wait}\}$$
$$e_{p,1,obs} : \langle T_\alpha \wedge (f_\alpha \geqslant \alpha) \wedge T_\beta \wedge (L_p == 0) \rangle \quad \{L_p := 1\}$$
$$e_{p,2,wait} : \langle \neg T_\alpha \wedge T_\beta \wedge (f_\beta < \beta) \wedge (L_p == 0) \rangle \quad \{f_\beta := f_\beta + c_{p,2,wait}\}$$
$$e_{p,2,obs} : \langle \neg T_\alpha \wedge T_\beta \wedge (f_\beta \in [\alpha, \beta]) \wedge (L_p == 0) \rangle \quad \{L_p := 1\}$$

Finally, two new *fault edges*, named $e_{p,1,fault}$ and $e_{p,2,fault}$, from $v_{p,1}$ and $v_{p,2}$ to a new *fault state* called S_{F-I}, respectively, are introduced. The edge conditions and actions of $e_{p,1,fault}$ and $e_{p,2,fault}$ are formulated such that if the input is applied before T_α's expiry (i.e., the lower boundary of $[\alpha, \beta]$) and after T_β's expiry (i.e., the upper boundary of $[\alpha, \beta]$), respectively, the sequence is forced to move into state S_{F-I}. In other words, when input a_i is applied, if the following timing conditions are true, the IUT will be assumed to be in state S_{F-I}, where the test will be declared as failed:

$$e_{p,1,fault} : \langle T_\alpha \wedge (f_\alpha < \alpha) \wedge T_\beta \wedge (f_\beta < \alpha) \wedge (L_p == 0) \rangle \quad \{T_\alpha := 0; \quad f_\alpha := -\infty;$$
$$T_\beta := 0; \quad f_\beta := -\infty\}$$
$$e_{p,2,fault} : \langle \neg T_\alpha \wedge T_\beta \wedge (f_\beta > \beta) \wedge (L_p == 0) \rangle \quad \{T_\beta := 0; \quad f_\beta := -\infty\}$$

Therefore, e_i triggers only when a_i is applied after T_α's and before T_β's expiry. But if the input interval condition is not satisfied, G' forces the traversal of either $e_{p,1,fault}$, or $e_{p,2,fault}$, making the tester declare the IUT in the fault state of S_{F-I} (Figure 2).

4.2   n-Clock Interval Fault

Timing conflicts due to n-clock interval faults are concerned with n clocks/timers running concurrently. In a faulty IUT, this fault may result in an altered traversal sequence which can go unnoticed during testing. n-clock interval fault occurs when at least one edge is traversed out of the required testing sequence.

Timing Requirement: Edge $e_i = (v_p, v_q, a_i, o_i, \langle t_j \rangle, \{t_j\})$, can be only traversed after a sequence of transitions $\rho = h_1, h_k, h_{k+1} \cdots h_n$, such that h_k was executed before h_{k+1} ($\forall k \in [2, n] \subset \mathbf{Z}^+$).

Timing Fault III: The required order of edges is not respected and the relation between them does not hold true (i.e., for at least one edge $\exists k \in [2, n]$, h_{k+1} was executed before h_k). As a result, for a test sequence, the final state $v_q' \neq v_q$ is verified and the final output $o_i' \neq o_i$ is observed.

The graph augmentation for this case has been skipped due to space constraints, but an extensive study can be found in Refs. [3, 14].

4.3   Incorrect Timer Setting Faults

Timing conflicts which arise due to faulty timer length settings in an IUT are called incorrect timer setting faults where the timer length is incorrectly set either too short or too long (i.e., the timer expires too early or too late).

Timing Requirement: In a test sequence, edge h_k starts timer T_j and is traversed before e_i. Timeout transition $e_i = (v_p, v_q, a_i, o_i, \langle t_j \rangle, \{t_j\})$ triggers exactly in D_j time units, where D_j is the timer length.

Timing Fault IV: Timeout transition e_i triggers in D_j' time units and output o_i is observed and state v_q is verified in shorter than the expected time (i.e., $D_j' < D_j$).

Timing Fault V: Timeout transition e_i triggers in D_j' time units and output o_i is observed and state v_q is verified in longer than the expected time (i.e., $D_j' > D_j$).

Graph Augmentation to Detect Timing Fault IV: Let us consider timer T_j with length D_j defined by the specification to be started by the actions of edge h_k and to be expired at edge e_i (reachable from h_k). To detect if the length for T_j is set to D_j' which is shorter than D_j, we introduce a special purpose timer T_s where D_s is the correct timer length as defined by the specification. Timer T_s will be started by edge h_k, which also starts T_j. Therefore, after the augmentation, the time-related conditions and actions for h_k are modeled as:

$$h_k : \langle 1 \rangle \qquad \{T_j := 1; \quad f_j := 0; \quad T_s := 1; \quad f_s := 0\}$$

An observer state v_p' is appended to state v_p via a new *observer edge* $e_{p,obs}$, *wait edge* $e_{p,wait}$ and *return edge* e_p^{ret} (with cost $c_{p,wait} := 1$ time unit and $c_p^{ret} := 0$, respectively).

$$e_{p,obs} : \langle T_s \wedge (f_s \geqslant D_s) \wedge (T_j \text{ timeout}) \wedge (L_p == 0) \rangle \qquad \{L_p := 1\}$$
$$e_{p,wait} : \langle T_s \wedge (f_s < D_s) \wedge (\neg T_j \text{ timeout}) \wedge (L_p == 0) \rangle \qquad \{f_s := f_s + 1\}$$

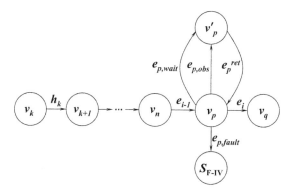

Fig. 3. Graph augmentation of state v_p for detecting Timing Fault IV (a similar augmentation is also applicable to Timing Fault V)

Finally, a new *fault state* S_{F-IV} is created which is connected to v_p via $e_{p,fault}$. The edge condition of $e_{p,fault}$ is modified such that if timer T_j expires earlier than expected, the sequence is forced to move to state S_{F-IV} where the tester declares the verdict of the test as failure:

$$e_{p,fault} : \langle T_s \wedge (f_s < D_s) \wedge (T_j \text{ timeout}) \wedge (L_p == 0) \rangle \quad \{T_s := 0; \ f_s := -\infty\}$$

The edge condition of e_i is also modified such that it traverses only when $f_s \geqslant D_s$ and T_j expires as shown in Figure 3:

$$e_i : \langle T_s \wedge (f_s \geqslant D_s) \wedge (T_j \text{ timeout}) \wedge (L_p == 1) \rangle \quad \{T_s := 0; \ f_s := -\infty;$$
$$L_p := 0\}$$

Graph Augmentation to Detect Timing Fault V: Graph augmentation for Fault V is similar to that of Fault IV (Figure 3), except that the edge conditions are formulated differently:

$$h_k : \langle 1 \rangle \qquad\qquad\qquad\qquad\qquad\qquad \{T_j := 1; \ f_j := 0;$$
$$T_s := 1; \ f_s := 0\}$$
$$e_{p,obs} : \langle T_s \wedge (f_s \geqslant D_s) \wedge (T_j \text{ timeout}) \wedge (L_p == 0) \rangle \quad \{L_p := 1\}$$
$$e_{p,wait} : \langle T_s \wedge (\neg T_j \text{ timeout}) \wedge (L_p == 0) \rangle \quad \{f_s := f_s + 1\}$$
$$e_{p,fault} : \langle T_s \wedge (f_s \geqslant D_s) \wedge (\neg T_j \text{ timeout}) \wedge (L_p == 0) \rangle \quad \{T_s := 0; \ f_s := -\infty\}$$
$$e_i : \langle T_s \wedge (f_s \geqslant D_s) \wedge (T_j \text{ timeout}) \wedge (L_p == 1) \rangle \quad \{T_s := 0; \ f_s := -\infty;$$
$$L_p := 0\}$$

5   Multiple Faults

It is possible that, for a given test sequence, a single timing fault, occurring simultaneously with a fault of different type, can exhibit a behavior indistin-

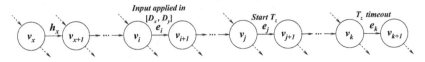

Fig. 4. Generalization of timer specification where Faults I and V hide each other

guishable from an IUT without any faults. We prove in this section that the graph augmentations introduced for single timing faults in Section 4 are capable of detecting such multiple faults. Due to space constraints, only the pairwise combinations of Timing Faults I, IV and V are presented in detail. The other combinations with Timing Fault III are available in [3, 14].

5.1   Multiple Faults of I and V

It is possible that a single Fault I and a single Fault V can hide each other such that the observable behavior of a faulty system is not distinguishable from a non-faulty system.

Lemma 1: Graph augmentation for Fault I (Section 4.1) and Fault V (Section 4.3) can detect simultaneous presence of a single Fault I and a single Fault V in an IUT, irrespective of the order they occur in an edge sequence.

Proof: It is possible to construct an edge sequence such that an input applied too early violating a timing interval requirement of a specification (i.e., Fault I) followed by a timer expiring too late (i.e., Fault V) can generate an output as if the IUT is non-faulty. For the general case, consider a test sequence containing $\cdots, h_x, \cdots, e_i, \cdots, e_j, \cdots, e_k, \cdots$ (Figure 4) where:

- Edge e_i has a timing interval requirement that input a_i be applied within the interval of $[\alpha, \beta]$ (i.e. $\delta \in [\alpha, \beta]$, where δ is the instant at which input is applied, measured from edge h_x).
- Edge e_j from state v_j to state v_{j+1} starts timer T_z with length D_z. e_j : $\langle \neg T_z \rangle \{T_z := 1; \quad f_z = 0\}$
- T_z timeout triggers edge e_k which generates an observable output o_k in $\delta + c_i + c_{(i+1 \longrightarrow j+1)} + D_z + c_k$ time units from h_x, where $c_{(i+1 \longrightarrow j+1)}$ is the total cost of all edges used in the sequence between states v_{i+1} and v_{j+1}.

If input a_i is applied too early (i.e., Fault I where $\delta' < \alpha$) and, at the same time, D_z is incorrectly implemented as too long (i.e., Fault V where $D'_z > D_z$) such that $\delta - \delta' \equiv D'_z - D_z$, the time at which the output o_k is generated remains the same for both the faulty and non-faulty IUTs. The output o_k is generated in $\delta + c_i + c_{(i+1 \longrightarrow j+1)} + D_z + c_k$ time units for non-faulty IUT and in $\delta' + c_i + c_{(i+1 \longrightarrow j+1)} + D'_z + c_k$ time units for faulty IUT after h_x. Since $\delta - \delta' \equiv D'_z - D_z$, Faults I and V can hide each other.

To detect the simultaneous existence of a single Fault I and a single Fault V, the original graph (Figure 4) is augmented (Figure 5) to include new wait and fault states with their associated edges (as in Sections 4.1 and 4.3, respectively).

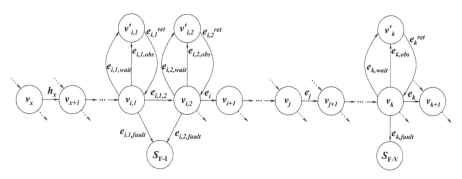

Fig. 5. Graph augmentation for a single occurrence of Faults I and V

For the above generalized sequence, our graph augmentation introduces special timers T_x and T_y in the test harness with lengths D_x and D_y, respectively, to test the requirement of applying input a_i in the interval $[\alpha, \beta]$, where $\alpha = D_x$ and $\beta = D_y$. Augmentation in Section 4.1 state that both special timers to be started at edge h_x:

$$h_x : \langle \neg T_x \wedge \neg T_y \rangle \qquad \{T_x := 1; \; f_x := 0; \; T_y := 1; \; f_y := 0\}$$

Edge e_i triggers after applying input a_i within time interval $\delta \in [D_x, D_y]$ and stops T_y in its actions:

$$e_i : \langle \neg T_x \wedge T_y \wedge (f_y \in [D_x, D_y]) \wedge (L_p == 1) \rangle \quad \{T_y := 0; \; f_y := -\infty; \; L_p := 0\}$$

Similarly, a special purpose timer T_s at the test harness with length D_s is introduced to define the correct timer length for T_z. Therefore, edge e_j starts both T_z and T_s:

$$e_j : \langle \neg T_z \wedge \neg T_s \rangle \qquad \{T_z := 1; \; f_z := 0; \; T_s := 1; \; f_s := 0\}$$

For Fault I augmentation, v_i (starting state of e_i) is replaced by two new states, $v_{i,1}$ and $v_{i,2}$, connected via $e_{i,1,2}$. S_{F-I} and its incoming edges ($e_{i,1,fault}$ and $e_{i,2,fault}$) are created for states $v_{i,1}$ and $v_{i,2}$, respectively. Then, an observer state $v'_{i,1}$ with its associated edges $e_{i,1,wait}$, $e_{i,1,obs}$ and $e_{i,1}^{ret}$ to the $v_{i,1}$ are introduced. Similarly, $v'_{i,2}$, $e_{i,2,wait}$, $e_{i,2,obs}$ and $e_{i,2}^{ret}$ are created for T_β (Section 4.1). For Fault V, state v'_k with edges $e_{k,wait}$, $e_{k,obs}$ and e_k^{ret} are attached to v_k whose outgoing edge is the T_j timeout edge e_k. also state S_{F-V} and edge $e_{k,fault}$ are added to the graph:

$$e_{k,obs} : \langle T_s \wedge (f_s \geqslant D_s) \wedge (T_z \text{ timeout}) \wedge (L_p == 0) \rangle \qquad \{L_p := 1\}$$

$$e_{k,wait} : \langle T_s \wedge (\neg T_z \text{ timeout}) \wedge (L_p == 0) \rangle \qquad \{f_s := f_s + 1\}$$

$$e_{k,fault} : \langle T_s \wedge (f_s \geqslant D_s) \wedge (\neg T_z \text{ timeout}) \wedge (L_p == 0) \rangle \quad \{T_z := 0; \; f_z := -\infty;$$
$$T_s := 0; \; f_s := -\infty\}$$

$$e_k : \langle T_s \wedge (f_s \geqslant D_s) \wedge (T_z \text{ timeout}) \wedge (L_p == 1) \rangle \quad \{T_z := 0; \; f_z := -\infty;$$
$$T_s := 0; \; f_s := -\infty;$$
$$L_p := 0\}$$

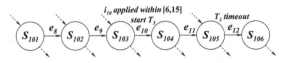

Fig. 6. Timed FSM: T_3 is started by applying i_{10} within time interval $[6, 15]$

After augmentation for both Faults I and V, a correct edge traversal sequence for a non-faulty IUT can be given as: $\cdots$, h_x, $\cdots$, $e_{i,1,wait}$, $e_{i,1}^{ret}$, $e_{i,1,obs}$, $e_{i,1}^{ret}$, $e_{i,2}$, $e_{i,2,wait}$, $e_{i,2}^{ret}$, $e_{i,2,obs}$, $e_{i,2}^{ret}$, e_i, $\cdots$, e_j, $\cdots$, $e_{k,wait}$, e_k^{ret}, $e_{k,obs}$, e_k^{ret}, e_k, $\cdots$. A faulty IUT with Faults I and V, where Fault I is traversed before Fault V, will not follow this traversal, but, instead, will end up at state S_{F-I}. Similarly, it can be shown that a sequence where a single Fault V is traversed before a single Fault I will end up at state S_{F-V}. Therefore, a single Fault I and a single Fault V, irrespective of the order of their occurrences, can be detected by our augmentations as indicated in Sections 4.1 and 4.3.   □

An example test sequence of containing $\cdots$, e_8, e_9, e_{10}, e_{11}, e_{12}, $\cdots$ is given for the FSM of Figure 6. Suppose the FSM specification defines that, for e_{10}, the input i_{10} should be applied within time interval of $[6, 15]$ seconds (measured from e_8) and that e_{10} starts T_3 with length $D_3 = 4$ seconds. Edge e_{12} is a timeout transition for T_3, and for edges e_9, e_{10}, e_{11}, and e_{12} the costs are $c_9 = 4$, $c_{10} = 1$, $c_{11} = 4$, and $c_{12} = 2$ seconds, respectively. In a correct implementation, i_{10} is applied 6 seconds after e_8 and timer T_3 expires in 4 seconds (i.e. $D_3 = c_{11} = 4$ seconds). Hence, the output o_{12} generated by e_{12} is observed in 13 seconds after e_8 traversal (i.e., $\delta + c_{10} + D_3 + c_{12} = 6 + 1 + 4 + 2$ seconds). Now suppose input i_{10} is applied too early at 5 seconds after e_8, and T_3 is incorrectly implemented too long as $D_3' = 5$ seconds. In this scenario, output o_{12} is also observed in 13 seconds (i.e., $\delta' + c_{10} + D_3' + c_{12} = 5 + 1 + 5 + 2$ seconds). Therefore, without the augmentations, this single occurrences of Faults I and V cannot be detected. However, in the augmented graph G', the sequence will detect single Fault I by forcing the traversal to state S_{F-I} as proven by Lemma 1.

Corollary 1: The multiple occurrences of Faults I and V, irrespective of their occurrence order, are detectable after the graph is augmented for single Faults I and V as in Sections 4.1 and 4.3.

5.2   Multiple Faults of I and IV

Lemma 2: Graph augmentation for Fault I (Section 4.1) and Fault IV (Section 4.3) can detect simultaneous presence of a single Fault I and a single Fault IV, irrespective of the order they occur in an edge sequence (proof analogous to that for Lemma 1).

Corollary 2: Multiple occurrences of Faults I and V, irrespective of their occurrence order, are detectable after the graph is augmented for single Faults I and IV as in Sections 4.1 and 4.3.

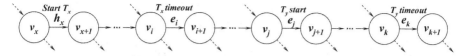

Fig. 7. Generalization of timer specification where Faults IV and V hide each other

5.3   Multiple Faults of IV and V

Lemma 3: Graph augmentations for Fault IV and Fault V (Section 4.3) can detect simultaneous presence of a single Fault IV and a single Fault V, irrespective of the order they occurren an edge sequence.

Proof: Let us first prove that timing faults can hide each other such that the observable behavior for an IUT with Faults IV and V, and a non-faulty IUT are identical. Consider an edge sequence over which two timers, namely T_x and T_y, are started and expired. For the general case, such a sequence can be defined as $\cdots, h_x, \cdots, e_i, \cdots, e_j, \cdots, e_k, \cdots$ (Figure 7) where:

- Edge h_x from state v_x to v_{x+1} starts timer T_x with length D_x. $h_x : \langle 1 \rangle \{T_x := 1; f_x := 0\}$
- Expiry of T_x triggers edge e_i, for which no observable output is generated. $e_i : \langle T_x \wedge (f_x \geqslant D_x) \rangle \{T_x := 0; \quad f_x := -\infty\}$
- Reachable from e_i, an edge e_j, from state v_j to v_{j+1}, starts timer T_y with length D_y. $e_j : \langle \neg T_x \rangle \{T_y := 1; \quad f_y := 0\}$
- Expiry of T_y triggers edge e_k such that output o_k is observed in $(D_x + c_{(i \longrightarrow j+1)} + D_y + c_k)$ time units after h_x is traversed, where $c_{(i \longrightarrow j+1)}$ is the cost of all the edges between states v_i and v_{j+1}. $e_k : \langle T_y \wedge (f_y \geqslant D_y) \rangle \{T_y := 0; \quad f_y := -\infty\}$
- The inputs for the edges between e_i and e_k do not have input interval requirements (i.e., input timing requirements pertaining to Fault I, which would have been detected by Corollary 2).

Let us suppose now that T_x is implemented too short (i.e., Fault IV with $D'_x < D_x$) and T_y is implemented too long (i.e., Fault V with $D'_y > D_y$) such

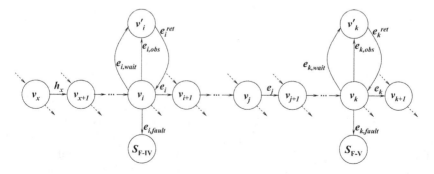

Fig. 8. Graph augmentation for a single occurrence of Faults IV and V

that $D_x - D'_x \equiv D'_y - D_y$. For a non-faulty IUT, the output o_k will be generated in $(D_x + c_{(i \longrightarrow j+1)} + D_y + c_k)$ time units after the traversal of h_x. For an IUT with Faults IV and V, it will take $(D'_x + c_{(i \longrightarrow j+1)} + D'_y + c_k)$ time units to generate the output o_k. Therefore, since $D_x - D'_x \equiv D'_y - D_y$, it is possible that Timing Faults IV and V can hide each other.

Applying the graph augmentation methods described in Section 4.3, the generalized case of Figure 7 can be modified to include the new wait and fault states with their associated edges. As shown in Figure 8, our graph augmentation introduces special purpose timers T_{sx} and T_{sy} with lengths D_{sx} and D_{sy}, respectively, to define the correct timer lengths for timer T_x and T_y, where $D_{sx} \equiv D_x$ and $D_{sy} \equiv D_y$ time units. In the augmented graph, h_x starts both T_x and T_{sx}, and e_j starts both T_y and T_{sy}:

$$h_x : \langle \neg T_x \wedge \neg T_{sx} \rangle \qquad \{ T_x := 1; \quad f_x := 0; \quad T_{sx} := 1; \quad f_{sx} := 0 \}$$

$$e_j : \langle \neg T_y \wedge \neg T_{sy} \rangle \qquad \{ T_y := 1; \quad f_y := 0; \quad T_{sy} := 1; \quad f_{sy} := 0 \}$$

For Fault IV augmentation, a wait state v'_i with its associated edges $e_{i,wait}$, $e_{i,obs}$ and e_i^{ret} are attached to v_i whose outgoing edge is the timeout edge e_i. A new state S_{F-IV} and its edge $e_{i,fault}$ is added to state v_i:

$$e_{i,obs} : \langle T_{sx} \wedge (f_{sx} \geqslant D_{sx}) \wedge (T_x \text{ timeout }) \wedge (L_p == 0) \rangle \quad \{ L_p := 1 \}$$

$$e_{i,wait} : \langle T_{sx} \wedge (f_{sx} < D_{sx}) \wedge (\neg T_x \text{ timeout}) \wedge (L_p == 0) \rangle \quad \{ f_{sx} := f_{sx} + 1 \}$$

$$e_{i,fault} : \langle T_{sx} \wedge (f_{sx} < D_{sx}) \wedge (T_x \text{ timeout }) \wedge (L_p == 0) \rangle \quad \{ T_{sx} := 0;$$
$$f_{sx} := -\infty \}$$

$$e_i : \langle T_{sx} \wedge (f_{sx} \geqslant D_{sx}) \wedge (T_x \text{ timeout }) \wedge (L_p == 1) \rangle \quad \{ T_{sx} := 0;$$
$$f_{sx} := -\infty; L_p := 0 \}$$

Similarly, for Fault V augmentation, an observer state v'_k with its associated edges $e_{k,wait}$, $e_{k,obs}$ and e_k^{ret} are attached to v_k whose outgoing edge is the timeout edge e_k. A new state S_{F-V} and its associated edge $e_{k,fault}$ is added to state v_k:

$$e_{k,obs} : \langle T_{sy} \wedge (f_{sy} \geqslant D_{sy}) \wedge (T_y \text{ timeout }) \wedge (L_p == 0) \rangle \quad \{ L_p := 1 \}$$

$$e_{k,wait} : \langle T_{sy} \wedge (\neg T_y \text{ timeout}) \wedge (L_p == 0) \rangle \quad \{ f_{sy} := f_{sy} + 1 \}$$

$$e_{k,fault} : \langle T_{sy} \wedge (f_{sy} \geqslant D_{sy}) \wedge (\neg T_y \text{ timeout }) \wedge (L_p == 0) \rangle \quad \{ T_{sy} := 0;$$
$$f_{sy} := -\infty \}$$

$$e_k : \langle T_{sy} \wedge (f_{sy} \geqslant D_{sy}) \wedge (T_y \text{ timeout }) \wedge (L_p == 1) \rangle \quad \{ T_{sy} := 0;$$
$$f_{sy} := -\infty; L_p := 0 \}$$

After these augmentations, a test sequence for a non-faulty IUT is $h_x, \cdots,$ $e_{i,wait}, e_i^{ret}, e_{i,obs}, e_i^{ret}, e_i, \cdots, e_j, \cdots, e_{k,wait}, e_k^{ret}, e_{k,obs}, e_k^{ret}, e_k$. For a faulty IUT where Fault IV is reached before Fault V, the test sequence will end up in state S_{F-IV} (i.e., the edge $e_{i,fault}$ will be traversed instead of e_i), and hence will detect Fault IV.

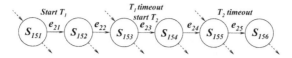

Fig. 9. Timed FSM: T_1 is started by T_1 expiry

Similarly, it can be shown that a test sequence can be constructed such that, if a single Fault V is traversed before a single Fault IV, the test sequence will be forced to state S_{F-V}. Therefore, a single Fault IV and a single Fault V, irrespective of the order of their occurrence, can be detected by augmentations given in Section 4.3.   □

Let us illustrate the simultaneous occurrence of Faults IV and V with an example. In Figure 9, the FSM specification defines that edges e_{21} and e_{23} start timers T_1 (expires in e_{23} with $D_1 = 5$ seconds) and T_2 (expires in $e25$ with $D_2 = 4$ seconds), respectively. The costs for the edges e_{22}, e_{23}, e_{24} and e_{25} are given as $c_{22} = 5$, $c_{23} = 2$, $c_{24} = 4$ and $c_{25} = 3$ seconds, respectively.

The test sequence for a non-faulty IUT can be constructed as e_{21}, e_{22}, e_{23}, e_{24}, e_{25} such that timer T_1 expires in 5 seconds and T_2 in 4 seconds. Therefore, using this test sequence, a non-faulty IUT will generate o_{25} by e_{25} 14 seconds after e_{21} traversal (i.e., $D_1 + c_{23} + D_2 + c_{25} = 5 + 2 + 4 + 3$ seconds). Now suppose T_1 is incorrectly implemented as $D_1' = 4$ seconds and T_2 as $D_2' = 5$ seconds. This faulty IUT would also generate o_{25} in 14 seconds after e_{21} is traversed (i.e., $D_1' + c_{23} + D_2' + c_{25} = 4 + 2 + 5 + 3$ seconds). This example illustrates that, without our augmentations, simultaneous occurrence of single Faults IV and V may be indistinguishable from the non-faulty IUT for certain test cases. However, after graph augmentations, the sequence will detect single occurrences of Fault IV and V by forcing the faulty IUT into state S_{F-IV}.

Corollary 3: The multiple occurrences of Faults IV and V, irrespective of their occurrence order, are detectable after the graph is augmented for single Faults IV and V as in Section 4.3.

6   Concluding Remarks

A number of individually detectable timing faults can hide each other's faulty behavior, making the faulty system indistinguishable from a non-faulty one. A set of augmentations for the timed FSM model introduced in Ref. [7] is presented for single timing faults. The augmentations for the single faults are shown to be capable of detecting multiple occurrences of pairwise combinations of these timing faults. Fault detection capabilities of existing timed automata models and the model studied in this paper will be compared as an extension of this work.

References

[1] J. ALILOVIC-CURGUS AND S.T. VUONG. A metric-based theory of test selection and coverage. In *Proc. IFIP Protocol Specif. Test. Verif. (PSTV)*, Liege, Belgium, 1993.

[2] R. ALUR AND D.L. DILL. A theory of timed automata. *[Elsevier] Theoret. Comput. Sci.* **126**, pp. 183–235, 1994.

[3] S.S. BATTH. *Fault Models for Timed EFSMs*. MS thesis, The City College of CUNY, New York, NY, 2004.

[4] W.Y.L. CHAN AND S.T. VUONG. The UIOv—method for protocol test sequence generation. In *Proc. IFIP Int'l Wksp Protocol Test Syst. (IWPTS)*, Berlin, Germany, 1989.

[5] A. EN-NOUAARY, R. DSSOULI, AND F. KHENDEK. Timed Wp-method: Testing real-time systems. *IEEE Trans. Softw. Eng.* **28**(11), pp. 1023–1038, 2002.

[6] A. EN-NOUAARY, R. DSSOULI, F. KHENDEK, AND A. ELQORTOBI. Timed test cases generation based on state characterisation technique. In *Proc. IEEE Real-Time Syst. Symp. (RTSS)*, pp. 220–229, Madrid, Spain, 1998.

[7] M.A. FECKO, M.U. UYAR, A.Y. DUALE, AND P.D. AMER. A technique to generate feasible tests for communications systems with multiple timers. *IEEE/ACM Trans. Netw.* **11**(5), pp. 796–809, 2003.

[8] G. LUO, G.V. BOCHMANN, AND A.F. PETRENKO. Test selection based on communicating nondeterministic finite state machines using a generalized Wp-method. *IEEE Trans. Softw. Eng.* **20**(2), pp. 149–162, 1994.

[9] A.F. PETRENKO, G.V. BOCHMANN, AND M.Y. YAO. On fault coverage of tests for finite state specifications. *[Elsevier] Comput. Netw. ISDN Syst.* **29**(1), pp. 81–106, 1996.

[10] A. REZAKI AND H. URAL. Construction of checking sequences based on characterization sets. *[Elsevier] Comput. Commun.* **18**(12), pp. 911–920, 1995.

[11] D.P. SIDHU AND T.K. LEUNG. Fault coverage of protocol test methods. In *Proc. IEEE INFOCOM*, pp. 80–85, New Orleans, LA, 1988.

[12] J. SPRINGINTVELD, F. VAANDRAGER, AND P.R. D'ARGENIO. Testing timed automata. *[Elsevier] Theoret. Comput. Sci.* **254**(1-2), pp. 225–257, 2001.

[13] H. URAL AND K. ZHU. Optimal length test sequence generation using distinguishing sequences. *IEEE/ACM Trans. Netw.* **1**(3), pp. 358–371, 1993.

[14] Y. WANG. *Timing Faults in EFSM Models with Multiple Concurrent Timers*. PhD thesis, Graduate Center of CUNY, New York, NY. (in progress).

[15] J. ZHU AND S.T. CHANSON. Toward evaluating fault coverage of protocol test sequences. In *Proc. IFIP Protocol Specif. Test. Verif. (PSTV)*, pp. 137–151, Vancouver, Canada, 1994.

An Expressive and Implementable Formal Framework for Testing Real-Time Systems[*]

Moez Krichen and Stavros Tripakis

Verimag Centre Equation,
2, avenue de Vignate, 38610 Gières, France
{krichen, tripakis}@imag.fr

Abstract. We propose a new framework for black-box conformance testing of real-time systems, based on the model of timed automata. The framework is expressive: it can fully handle partially-observable, non-deterministic timed automata. It also allows the user to define, through appropriate modeling, assumptions on the environment of the system under test (SUT) as well as on the interface between the tester and the SUT. The framework is implementable: tests can be implemented as finite-state machines accessing a finite-precision digital clock. We propose, for this framework, a set of test-generation algorithms with respect to different coverage criteria. We have implemented these algorithms in a prototype tool called TTG. Experimental results obtained by applying TTG on the Bounded Retransmission Protocol show that only a few tests suffice to cover thousands of reachable symbolic states in the specification.

1 Introduction

Our work targets black-box conformance testing for real-time systems. By "black box" we mean that the tester has no knowledge nor access in the internals of the system under test (SUT), thus, can only rely on its observable input/output behavior. We follow a formal, *model-based* testing approach, in the sense that we assume a formal specification is available and conformance is also defined in a formal way.

Real-time systems operate in an environment with strict timing constraints. Examples of such systems are many: embedded systems (e.g., automotive, avionic and robotic controllers, mobile phones), communication protocols, multimedia systems, and so on. When testing real-time systems, one must pay attention to two important facts. First, it is not sufficient to check whether the system under test (SUT) produces the correct outputs; it must also be checked that the timing of the outputs is correct. Second, the timing of the inputs determines which outputs will be produced as well as the timing of these outputs.

---

[*] Work partially supported by CNRS STIC project "CORTOS" and by IST Network of Excellence "ARTIST2".

F. Khendek and R. Dssouli (Eds.): TestCom 2005, LNCS 3502, pp. 209–225, 2005.

Many formal testing frameworks use models such as (extended) Mealy machines (e.g., see [11, 14, 16]) or labeled transition systems (e.g., see [18, 8, 13]). These models are not well-suited for real-time systems. In Mealy machines, inputs and outputs are synchronous, which is a reasonable assumption when modeling synchronous hardware, but not when outputs are produced with variable delays, governed by complex timing constraints. In labeled transition systems (LTSs) inputs and outputs are asynchronous. However, there is no explicit modeling of time. In some cases [18], the notion of *quiescence* is used: timeouts are modeled by special δ actions which can be interpreted as "no output will be observed". This is problematic, because timeouts need to be instantiated with concrete values upon testing (e.g., "if nothing happens for 10 seconds, output FAIL"). However, there is no systematic way to derive the timeout values (indeed, durations are not expressed in the specification). Thus, one must rely on empirical, ad-hoc methods.

We advocate an *explicit* specification of timing assumptions and requirements for testing real-time systems. For this, we need a specification model which explicitly talks about time. We opt for the model of *timed automata* (TA) [1]. TA have been established during the past decade as a suitable model for real-time systems. With respect to existing testing methods based on TA (see [12] and references therein) our framework presents two major contributions.

First, the framework is *expressive*: it can handle the full class of *partially-observable, non-deterministic* TA. In existing works, only subclasses of the TA model are considered. For example, [17, 9] consider TA with "isolated" and "urgent" outputs, which means that for each input sequence there is a unique output emitted at a precise point in time. A simple specification such as *"when input a is received, output b must be emitted within at most 10 time units"* cannot be expressed in this model. Other works use event-recording automata [15] or TA with restricted clock resets [10] or guards [5].

Second, our framework is *implementable*: the tests we generate can be executed by an automatic tester which uses a *digital clock* of finite precision. In most existing works the tester is implicitly assumed to have access to an infinite-precision clock, allowing, for instance, to distinguish between an event observed at time 1 or at time $1 + \epsilon$, for ϵ arbitrarily close to 0. An exception is the work [5] where a *digitization* of the TA semantics is used to model the tester clock. Our approach is more general in the sense that the digital-clock model is not "hard-wired" in the test generation algorithm. Rather, it is provided explicitly by the user as a Tick automaton (see Section 2). Tick automata can model not only fixed-step digitization but also skewed or diverging clocks, or any other sampling and interfacing mechanism the tester might use to observe and control the SUT.

In this paper we describe our framework from a methodological point of view (Section 2). We give special emphasis on modeling expressiveness and show through examples that the framework is rich enough to capture assumptions on the environment of the SUT, event-based or variable-based interfaces between the SUT and the tester, delays introduced by such interfaces, digital-clock sampling, and so on. Such *explicit* modeling is important for two reasons. First, it provides the user of the framework with full control on the assumptions made on the testing infrastructure and how these affect the generated tests. Second, it avoids the need for special algorithms (e.g., digitization [5]) in order to treat the above features: the latter simply become part of an extended specification model. Indeed, our test generation method uses standard *symbolic reachability* techniques available in most TA model-checking tools. Also note that symbolic reachability techniques scale much better than testing techniques based on the *region graph* [7, 17].

The framework is accompanied by a prototype tool called TTG (Timed Test Generator), built on top of the IF tool-suite [3]. To control the explosion of the potential number of tests, we have implemented in TTG a set of test selection techniques, among which a set of test generation algorithms with respect to various coverage criteria, such as state, location, action or selected-variable coverage. To illustrate the practical interest of our approach, we have used TTG to generate tests for the well-known Bounded Retransmission Protocol (BRP). The results are described in Section 3 and show that a few tests suffice to cover thousands of reachable symbolic states.

2   The Testing Framework

In this section we present the essential features of our testing framework. For more details, the reader is referred to [12]. We also illustrate some methodological aspects of our framework, especially modeling issues regarding environment assumptions and interface conditions between the tester and the SUT.

The Model: Timed Automata with Inputs, Outputs and Unobservable Actions. To model the specification, we use timed automata (TA) [1]. As the TA model is well-known, we only give a brief overview here. We also present a "pure" TA model without discrete variables and omit discussion on how to compose TA. In practice, these features are essential for ease and clarity of modeling: they are indeed part of our tool, see Section 3.

Let R be the set of non-negative reals. Given a set of *actions* Σ, the set $(\Sigma \cup R)^*$ of all finite *real-time sequences* over Σ will be denoted $RT(\Sigma)$. $\epsilon \in RT(\Sigma)$ is the empty sequence. Given $\Sigma' \subseteq \Sigma$ and $\rho \in RT(\Sigma)$, $\Pi_{\Sigma'}(\rho)$ denotes the *projection* of ρ to Σ', obtained by "erasing" from ρ all actions not in Σ'. For example, if $\Sigma = \{a, b\}$, $\Sigma' = \{a\}$ and $\rho = a\,1\,b\,2\,a\,3$, then $\Pi_{\Sigma'}(\rho) = a\,3\,a\,3$. The time spent in a sequence ρ, denoted $time(\rho)$ is the sum of all delays in ρ, for example, $time(\epsilon) = 0$ and $time(a\,1\,b\,0.5) = 1.5$.

A *timed automaton* over Σ is a tuple (Q, q_0, X, Σ, E) where Q is a set of *locations*; $q_0 \in Q$ is the initial location; X is a set of *clocks*; E is a set of *edges*. Each edge is a tuple (q, q', ψ, r, d, a), where $q, q' \in Q$ are the source and destination locations; ψ is the *guard*, a conjunction of constraints of the form $x \# c$, where $x \in X$, c is an integer constant and $\# \in \{<, \leq, =, \geq, >\}$; $r \subseteq X$ is the set of clocks to be *reset*; $d \in \{\text{lazy}, \text{delayable}, \text{eager}\}$ is the *deadline* (lazy deadlines impose no urgency, **delayable** means that once enabled the transition must be taken before it becomes disabled and **eager** means the transition must be taken as soon as it becomes enabled); and $a \in \Sigma$ is the action. We will not allow **eager** edges with guards of the form $x > c$.

A TA A defines a labeled transition system (LTS). Its states are pairs $s = (q, v)$, where $q \in Q$ and $v : X \to$ R is a clock *valuation*. **0** is the valuation assigning 0 to every clock of A. S_A is the set of all states and $s_0^A = (q_0, \mathbf{0})$ is the initial state. There are two types of transitions. Discrete transitions of the form $(q, v) \xrightarrow{a} (q', v')$, where $a \in \Sigma$ and there is an edge (q, q', ψ, r, d, a), such that v satisfies ψ and v' is obtained by resetting to zero all clocks in r and leaving the others unchanged. Timed transitions of the form $(q, v) \xrightarrow{t} (q, v + t)$, where $t \in$ R, $t > 0$ and there is no edge (q, q'', ψ, r, d, a), such that: either $d = $ **delayable** and there exist $0 \le t_1 < t_2 \le t$ such that $v + t_1 \models \psi$ and $v + t_2 \not\models \psi$; or $d = $ **eager** and $v \models \psi$. We use notation such as $s \xrightarrow{a}$, $s \not\xrightarrow{a}$, ..., to denote that there exists s' such that $s \xrightarrow{a} s'$, there is no such s', and so on. This notation naturally extends to timed sequences. For example, $s \xrightarrow{a1b} s'$ if there exist s_1, s_2 such that $s \xrightarrow{a} s_1 \xrightarrow{1} s_2 \xrightarrow{b} s'$. A state $s \in S_A$ is *reachable* if there exists $\rho \in$ RT(Σ) such that $s_0^A \xrightarrow{\rho} s$. The set of reachable states of A is denoted Reach(A).

In the rest of the paper, we assume given a set of actions Σ, partitioned in two disjoint sets: a set of *input actions* Σ_{in} and a set of *output actions* Σ_{out}. We also assume there is an *unobservable action* $\tau \notin \Sigma$. Let $\Sigma_\tau = \Sigma \cup \{\tau\}$.

A *timed automaton with inputs and outputs* (TAIO) is a timed automaton over Σ_τ. A TAIO is called *observable* if none of its edges is labeled by τ. A TAIO A is called *input-complete* if it can accept any input at any state: $\forall s \in$ Reach$(A) . \forall a \in \Sigma_{\text{in}} . s \xrightarrow{a}$. It is called *deterministic* if $\forall s, s', s'' \in$ Reach$(A) . \forall a \in \Sigma_\tau . s \xrightarrow{a} s' \wedge s \xrightarrow{a} s'' \Rightarrow s' = s''$. It is called *non-blocking* if $\forall s \in$ Reach$(A) . \forall t \in$ R $. \exists \rho \in$ RT$(\Sigma_{\text{out}} \cup \{\tau\}) .$ time$(\rho) = t \wedge s \xrightarrow{\rho}$. The non-blocking property states that at any state, A can let time pass forever, even if it does not receive any input. This is a sanity property which ensures that a TAIO does not "force" its environment to provide an input by blocking time. The set of *observable timed traces* of A is defined to be Traces$(A) = \{\Pi_\Sigma(\rho) \mid \rho \in$ RT$(\Sigma_\tau) \wedge s_0^A \xrightarrow{\rho}\}$.

Specifications, Implementations and Conformance. We assume that the specification of the system to be tested is given as a non-blocking TAIO A_S. We assume that the SUT, also called *implementation*, can be modeled as a non-blocking, input-complete TAIO A_I. Notice that we do not assume that A_I is known, simply that it exists. The assumption of A_S and A_I being non-blocking is natural, since in reality time cannot be blocked. The assumption of A_I being input-complete is also reasonable, since a system usually accepts all inputs at any time, possibly ignoring them or issuing an error message when the input is not valid. Notice that we do not assume, as is often done, that the specification A_S is input-complete. This is because A_S needs to be able to model assumptions on the environment, i.e., restrictions on the inputs, as we show below.

We also do not assume that A_S is deterministic. In fact, A_S may contain un-observable actions. Partially-observable or non-deterministic models often arise in practice. For instance, when specifications are built of many components (Figure 1), internal communication among these components is not observable to the tester (in fact it may simply be an artifact of modeling). This is indeed true in the case of the communication protocol we treat in Section 3. Non-determinism may also result when abstractions are applied to the model in order to reduce its size.

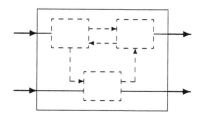

Fig. 1. A specification with internal (unobservable) actions

The *timed input-output conformance relation*, denoted tioco, requires that after any observable sequence specified in A_S, every possible observable output of A_I (including delays) is also a possible output of A_S. tioco is inspired from its "untimed" counterpart, ioco [18]. The key idea is that time delays, along with output actions, are considered to be observable events. More precisely, define A after σ as the set of all states of A that can be reached by some timed sequence ρ whose projection to observable actions is σ and let out(S) be the set of all observable events (output actions or delays) that can occur when the automaton is at some state in S. Formally, A after $\sigma = \{s \in S_A \mid \exists \rho \in \mathsf{RT}(\Sigma_\tau) . s_0^A \xrightarrow{\rho} s \wedge \Pi_\Sigma(\rho) = \sigma\}$, out($S$) $= \bigcup_{s \in S}$ out(s), out(s) $= \{a \in \Sigma_{\mathsf{out}} \mid s \xrightarrow{a}\} \cup$ elapse(s) and elapse(s) $= \{t > 0 \mid \exists \rho \in \mathsf{RT}(\{\tau\}) . \mathsf{time}(\rho) = t \wedge s \xrightarrow{\rho}\}$. Then, A_I conforms to A_S, denoted A_I tioco A_S, if

$$\forall \sigma \in \mathsf{Traces}(A_S) . \mathsf{out}(A_I \text{ after } \sigma) \subseteq \mathsf{out}(A_S \text{ after } \sigma). \tag{1}$$

Figure 2 shows an example of a specification Spec_1, which could be expressed in English as follows: "after the first a received, the system must output b no earlier than 2 and no later than 8 time units".[1] Thus, this specification requires that the output b is not emitted neither too early nor too late. Implementations Impl_1 and Impl_2 conform to Spec_1. Impl_1 produces b exactly 5 time units after reception of a. Impl_2 produces b sometime in the interval $[4, 5]$. Implementations Impl_3 and Impl_4 do not conform to Spec_1. Impl_3 may produce a b after 1 time unit, which is too early. Impl_4 fails to produce a b at all. Formally, letting $\sigma = a\,1$, we have out($\sigma(\mathsf{Impl}_3)$) $= (0, 4] \cup \{b\}$ and out($\sigma(\mathsf{Impl}_4)$) $= (0, \infty)$, whereas out($\sigma(\mathsf{Spec}_1)$) $= (0, 7]$. The last example shows that "doing nothing" is not an option for the SUT, since doing nothing is equivalent to letting time pass, resulting in a tester timeout when the deadline for producing an output is reached. This example also illustrates how our framework handles timeouts in a seamless way, without the need of modeling artifacts such as quiescence [18].

---

[1] Unless otherwise mentioned, deadlines of output edges are delayable and deadlines of input edges are lazy. In order not to overload the figures, we do not always draw input-complete automata. We assume that implementations ignore the missing inputs (this can be modeled by adding self-loop edges covering these inputs).

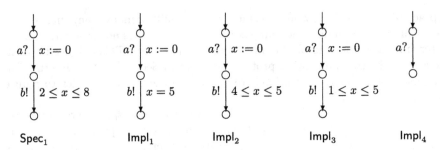

Fig. 2. Examples of specification and implementations

Modeling Assumptions on the Environment. Often, the SUT is supposed to operate correctly only in a particular environment, not in any environment. This brings up the issue of how to incorporate *assumptions* on the environment when building a model of specification. Figure 3 shows how this can be done. The specification can be modeled compositionally, in two parts: one part modeling the environment (assumptions) and another part the nominal behavior of the SUT in this environment (requirements). In this case, the interactions between the two components are not unobservable, but are exported as inputs and outputs of the global specification. A simple example of such a situation is shown in Figure 3. The specification expresses schedulability of an aperiodic task in a typical real-time operating system: "assuming the minimal inter-arrival time of task A is 20 time units, the task must be executed within 10 time units". Notice that environment assumptions generally make the specification non-input-complete. In the above example, the second **arrive** input cannot be accepted until at least 20 time units have elapsed since the first **arrive**.

Modeling Input/Output Variables. The TA model we have presented uses the notion of input/output *actions*, implying an event-based interface between the tester and the SUT. In practice, many systems communicate with the external world using input/output *variables*. We now show how to model such situations in our framework.

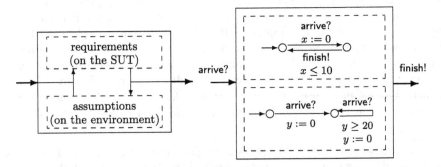

Fig. 3. Specification including assumptions on the environment: generic scheme (left) and example of a task scheduler (right)

There are basically two possibilities to specify real-time requirements related to variables. One is to refer to variable *updates* and the other to refer to value *durations*. The first can be modeled in our framework using an action for each update. The second can be modeled using a "begin" action for the point in time where a variable changes its value to the value that is of interest and an "end" action for the moment where the variable changes to a different value. For example, assume x is an input variable and y an output variable. Consider the requirement "y will be updated at most 10 time units after x is updated". Notice that x is updated by the environment (or the tester) while y is updated by the SUT. Thus, update$_x$ can be introduced as an input action and update$_y$ as an output action. The specification can be modeled as a TA similar to the one for Spec$_1$ of Figure 2, with a replaced by update$_x$ and b replaced by update$_y$.

This simplistic way of modeling supposes that updates are immediately perceived (by the SUT or by the tester) when they occur. This is obviously not always true. For instance, a sampling controller typically reads its inputs only periodically (but may write the outputs as soon as they are ready). In this case, it could be that the specification only requires that the output be produced at most 10 time units after the input is sampled by the controller, not after it is updated by the environment. This situation can also be modeled in our framework by explicitly adding automata modeling the sampling (either at the SUT side, or at the tester side, or both). In fact, we will add such an automaton, called the Tick automaton in order to generate digital-clock tests (see below). The Tick automaton models in some sense sampling at the tester side. A similar automaton can be used to model sampling at the SUT side, with the difference that the tick event would in this case be an input event. More elaborate interfaces (e.g., event handlers with buffering, and so on) can also be modeled, as long as they can be expressed as (extended) timed automata.

Modeling Interfacing Delays. As a last example of modeling methodology, we show how to model interfacing delays between the tester and the SUT. This can again be done by composing the specification with "delay automata", as shown in Figure 4. A simple input delay automaton is shown to the right of the figure. Input action a is the original action whereas a_t is the output command of the tester. This automaton models the assumption that the tester output may experience a delay of at most 2 time units until it is perceived by the SUT. Notice that this automaton does not allow a new input to be produced while the previous one is still in "transit". For this, a more complicated automaton is necessary, which buffers input events. The point is that, as mentioned above, such elaborate interfaces can all be modeled explicitly. Thus, the user has full control on how the assumptions made on the tester equipment affect the generated tests.

Digital-Clock Test Generation. The conformance relation tioco is "ideal" in the sense that it captures non-conformance of a SUT at an infinite-precision time-measuring level. For instance, if the guard $1 \leq x \leq 5$ of SUT Impl$_3$ of Figure 2 was replaced by $1.9 \leq x \leq 5$ then Impl$_3$ would still be non-conforming.

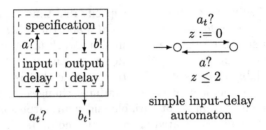

simple input-delay
automaton

Fig. 4. Specification composed with interface-delay automata

In fact, the same would be true if the guard was replaced by $2-\epsilon \le x \le 5$, for any $\epsilon > 0$. It is reasonable to define tioco in such an "ideal" way, since we do not want conformance to depend on implementation details such as tester equipment. On the other hand, the tester's time-observation capabilities are limited in practice: testers only dispose of a finite-precision digital clock (a counter) and cannot distinguish among observations which elude their clock precision. Our framework takes this limitation into account. First, we allow the user to explicitly model the assumptions on the tester's digital clock. Second, we generate tests with respect to this model.

Note that generating digital-clock tests does *not* mean that we discretize time: the specification still has a continuous-time semantics. It is the tester which "samples" this semantics with a digital clock. Also note that the tests we generate are both *sound* and *precise* with respect to tioco. Intuitively, soundness means that if the tester announces "fail" then the SUT is indeed non-conforming w.r.t. tioco. The test is precise in the sense that the tester announces "fail" *as soon as possible*: as soon as the observations the tester disposes of permit to conclude that the SUT is non-conforming, the tester will announce "fail". It may, however, be the case that the observations do not permit such a conclusion to be made: this situation occurs, for instance, when a faulty behavior gives the same digital-clock observation as a non-faulty behavior.

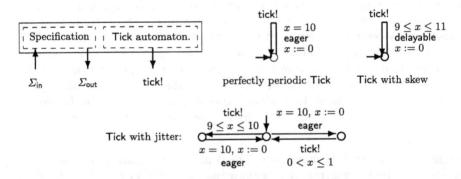

Fig. 5. Extending the specification with a tester clock model and possible such models

The tester's digital clock is modeled as a Tick automaton, which is a special TAIO with a single output action tick. Three possible Tick automata are shown in Figure 5. The first models a perfectly periodic clock with period equal to 10 time units: in this case, the n-th tick occurs precisely at time $10n$. The second automaton models a clock with "skew": in this case, the n-th tick may occur anywhere in the interval $[9n, 11n]$. The third automaton models a clock with "jitter": in this case, the n-th tick may occur anywhere in the interval $[10n - 1, 10n + 1]$. Notice that this automaton contains unobservable transitions (the ones with deadline eager).

Once a Tick automaton is chosen, it is composed with the specification automaton A_S as shown in Figure 5. This yields a new TAIO, denoted A_S^{Tick}, which has as inputs the inputs of A_S and as outputs the outputs of A_S plus the new output tick. Notice that A_S and Tick do not synchronize on any discrete transitions, they only synchronize in time (time elapses at the same rate for both).

Test generation is done based on the extended specification, A_S^{Tick}.[2] A test is represented as a finite tree like the one shown in Figure 6 and is generated using an algorithm similar to the one presented in [18]. Nodes of the tree are either input nodes (where the tester issues an input to the SUT) or output nodes (where the tester awaits for an output from the SUT or for the next tick of its own clock). Leaves are marked "pass" or "fail" indicating conformance or not. Each node of the tree corresponds to a set of states of A_S^{Tick}. Such sets are generally *dense* due to the continuous state-space of

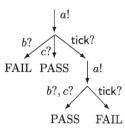

Fig. 6. A digital-clock test represented as a finite tree

the clocks. The sets are represented *symbolically* using simple constraints on clocks. For instance, the constraint $1 \leq x \leq 2 \wedge x = y$ represents the fact that clock x has some value within $[1, 2]$ and clock y is equal to x. The constraints are implemented using a matrix data structure called DBM (*difference bound matrix*) [2, 6]. Computing successor nodes is also done symbolically, using a *bounded-time reachability analysis* for timed automata, as shown in [19, 12].

Test Selection with Respect to Coverage Criteria. At each point during test generation, the generation algorithm has a number of choices to make: stop the test or continue, wait for an output or issue an input, which of the possible inputs, etc. There are different ways to resolve these choices. For instance: *interactively* (the user guides the test generation), *randomly* (the algorithm takes decisions at random), *exhaustively* (generate all possible tests, up to a given

---

[2] The extended specification may also include other automata to model environment assumptions, interface delays, etc., as shown previously.

depth provided by the user), or guided by some *coverage criterion*. Our tool implements all these choices.[3] We briefly elaborate on the last one.

At the moment, we consider simple coverage criteria such as *state*, *location* or *edge* coverage, aiming to cover, respectively, all reachable states, locations or edges of the specification. The state and location criteria are based on the fact that each node of a digital test tree corresponds to a set of states (thus also a set of locations) of the specification. Therefore, each such node "covers" the corresponding set. The edge criterion is similarly based on the fact that each edge of the test tree corresponds to a set of transitions (thus also a set of edges) of the specification.

We also consider simple variations of the above criteria. For instance, *input/output action* coverage seeks to cover reachable input/output actions of the specification. In a context of extended TA such as those used by our tool, we can also define *partial* state coverage, with respect to a subset of the variables making up the state space. It should be noted that some of these criteria subsume others. For instance, achieving state coverage implies location coverage, partial state coverage and action coverage.

We now briefly describe the test-generation algorithm w.r.t. a coverage criterion. The algorithm starts by choosing at random a point p in the space to be covered (e.g., a location for location coverage, a symbolic state for state coverage, etc.). Then a reachability algorithm is run on the product A_S^{Tick} in order to find a discrete path reaching the point p to be covered. Note that, since we consider coverage only for reachable states (or locations, or actions, etc.) the point is reachable, thus, a path exists. Also note that this path is labeled only with observable (input or output) actions. Once the path is found, it is extended into a test tree: this is done by completing all nodes in the path whose outgoing edge is labeled with an output action or tick, by the remaining outputs. This is the first generated test which covers not only p but other points as well (e.g., all locations encountered in the test tree). The algorithm proceeds by choosing a new uncovered point and repeating the above process, until all points are covered. This algorithm has been implemented in our tool TTG, described below.

3   Tool and Case Study

The TTG Tool. We have built a prototype test-generation tool, called TTG (Timed Test Generator), on top of the IF environment [3]. The IF modeling language allows to specify systems consisting of many processes communicating through message passing or shared variables and includes features such as hierarchy, priorities, dynamic creation and complex data types. The IF tool-suite includes a simulator, a model checker and a connection to the untimed test generator TGV [8]. TTG is implemented independently from TGV. TTG is written

---

[3] Another way to select tests is using a *test purpose*. This approach is taken, for instance, in the TGV tool [8].

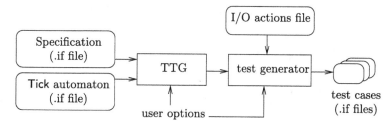

Fig. 7. The TTG tool

in C++ and uses the basic libraries of IF for parsing and symbolic reachability of timed automata with deadlines.

TTG takes as inputs the specification and Tick automata, written in IF language, as well as a set of user options specifying the test-generation mode. There are four modes: *interactive* (user-guided); *random*; *exhaustive* up to a user-defined depth; or *coverage* with respect to a criterion among *state*, *location*, *action* or *partial state*. TTG generates an executable which will perform the test generation when run. The executable takes additional options (e.g., depth) and generates one or more tests, depending on the chosen mode. The tests are output in IF language.

Case Study: The Bounded Retransmission Protocol. The Bounded Retransmission Protocol (BRP) is a protocol for transmitting files over an unreliable (lossy) medium. The architecture of the protocol is shown in Figure 8. The protocol is implemented by the Transmitter and the Receiver. The users of the protocol are the Sending and Receiving clients. The medium is modeled by the Forward and Backward channels. Upon receiving a file from the Sending client (action put), the Transmitter fragments the file into packets and sends each packet to the Receiver (action send), awaiting an acknowledgment for each packet sent (action ack). If a timeout occurs without receiving an acknowledgment, the Transmitter resends the packet, up to a maximum number of retrials. At the end, if the file is transmitted successfully the Transmitter does not output anything to the Sending client. Otherwise, the Transmitter responds either with

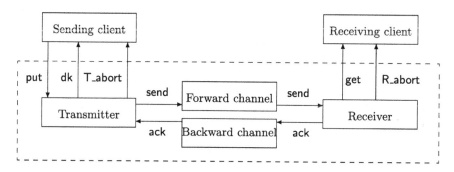

Fig. 8. The BRP specification and interfaces

"abort" (action T_abort) if the packet that failed was a "middle" one, or with "don't know" (action dk) if the packet was the first or last one (in this case the file may or may not be received at the other end). In case of success, the Receiving client receives the file (action get). In case the Receiver does not hear from the Transmitter for some time, it outputs R_abort to the Receiving client.

Here, we use the BRP model developed in [4]. The model has been initially developed in SDL, then automatically translated in IF. The model is shown in Figure 9.[4] States in red (labeled "decision_....") are *transient* states, meaning that time does not elapse and the automaton moves through these states without being interrupted by other concurrent automata. The Transmitter has two clocks, "t_repeat" and "t_abort", and the Receiver one clock, "r_abort".[5] The keyword "when" preceeds a clock guard and "provided" precedes a guard on discrete variables. Keyword "task" is for assignments. The model is parameterized by five parameters: p, the number of packets in a file; max_retry, the maximum number of retries in sending a packet (after timeout); dt_repeat, the timeout delay; dt_abort, the time the Transmitter waits before outputting T_abort; dr_abort, the time the Receiver waits before outputting R_abort. The values used in our case study are:

$$p = 2, \quad \text{max\_retry} = 4, \quad \text{dt\_repeat} = 2, \quad \text{dt\_abort} = 15, \quad \text{dr\_abort} = 13.$$

For testing, we view the four components enclosed in dashed square in Figure 8 as the BRP specification. The Sending and Receiving clients play the role of the environment, but they are not explicitly modeled, i.e., no assumptions are made on the environment. The interface of the SUT with its environment is captured by actions put (input) and get, dk, T_abort, R_abort (outputs).

Using TTG, we generate tests for the perfectly periodic Tick automaton with clock period equal to 1, with respect to various coverage criteria. The results are shown in Table 1. The criteria used are: (reachable) configurations, locations, actions, and the values of the five discrete variables of the model, namely, m, b, c, i, j. A configuration corresponds to an entire symbolic state and includes a vector of locations and values of variables for each automaton, plus a DBM representing symbolically the set of clock states. Thus, this criterion is the same as state coverage discussed in Section 2.

Column "size" shows the number of elements to be covered. Thus, there are 14687 reachable configurations in total[6], there are 4 global locations (we do not count transient locations) and 6 actions (the 5 input/output actions plus tick). Variables b and c are booleans (they encode the *alternating bit* for the

---

[4] The automata have been drawn automatically using the if2eps tool by Marius Bozga. The model of BRP that we use in this paper can be found in the IF web page: http://www-verimag.imag.fr/ async/IF/ http://www-verimag.imag.fr/~async/ IF/ under "examples".

[5] The clocks are reset to a negative value and count upwards. This is not an essential difference with the TA model presented earlier.

[6] The forward and backward channels are modeled by lossy FIFO buffers. These buffers remain bounded because reception of messages are eager.

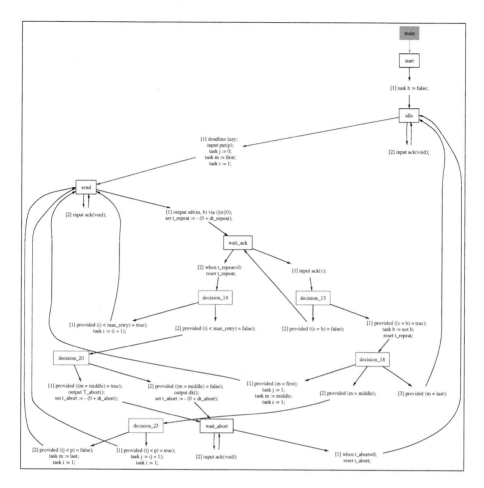

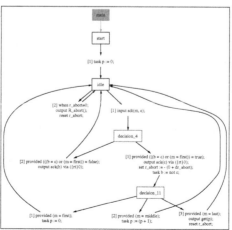

Fig. 9. Transmitter (up) and Receiver (down)

Table 1. Test generation results for the BRP case study

criterion used	size	time (sec)	# of tests	depth	coverage of other criteria							
					config.	locations	actions	m	b	c	i	j
config.	14687	400	24	6 - 53	100%							
locations	4	37	1	12	21%	100%	100%	100%	100%	100%	25%	100%
actions	7	76	1	43	36%	100%	100%	100%	100%	100%	25%	100%
m	3	17	1	2	1%	75%	50%	100%	100%	100%	25%	100%
b	2	16	1	2	1%	75%	50%	100%	100%	100%	25%	100%
c	2	17	1	2	1%	75%	50%	100%	100%	100%	25%	100%
i	4	35	1	9	20%	75%	50%	100%	100%	100%	100%	100%
j	3	16	1	2	1%	75%	50%	100%	100%	100%	25%	100%

Transmitter and Receiver, respectively). Variable m takes three possible values (beginning, middle or end of file). Variable i takes four possible values, from 1 to max_retry. Variable j takes three possible values, from 0 to p. Column "time" shows the time in seconds taken by TTG to generate a test suite with respect to the corresponding coverage criterion. Column "# of tests" shows the number of tests in the suite. Notice that the configuration criterion requires 24 tests whereas all other criteria can be covered with just one test. Column "depth" shows the depth of the generated tests (i.e., the length of the longest path from the root to a leaf). For the configuration criterion, the depth varies between 6 and 53. The rest of the columns show the percentage of coverage of the other criteria by the test suite generated for the given criterion. For example, the test covering the four global locations also covers 3105 configurations, which amounts to approximately 21% of the total number of configurations.

Perhaps the most interesting finding from the above experiments is that a relatively small number of tests suffices to cover all reachable configurations of the specification (in fact, we cover the states of the product automaton A_S^{Tick}). It is worth comparing this number to the number of tests generated with the "exhaustive up to given depth" option. As shown in Table 2, the size of exhaustive test suite grows too large even for relatively small depths. The table also shows the percentage of the above criteria covered by the exhaustive test suite. It can

Table 2. Exhaustive test suites for the BRP case study

depth	time (sec)	# of tests	coverage of other criteria							
			config.	locations	actions	m	b	c	i	j
1	17	2	0.2%	75%	33%	100%	100%	100%	25%	100%
2	17	3	2%	75%	50%	100%	100%	100%	50%	100%
3	22	5	5%	75%	50%	100%	100%	100%	50%	100%
4	39	11	8%	75%	50%	100%	100%	100%	75%	100%
5	168	41	14%	75%	50%	100%	100%	100%	75%	100%
6	1677	371	18%	75%	50%	100%	100%	100%	100%	100%

be seen that even though the number of tests is large, only a small percentage of coverage is achieved: for instance, 18% configuration coverage for 371 tests at depth 6.

Sometimes not only the number of tests but also their size is important. By looking at our test generation algorithm, where a test is obtained by completing a path, we can say that the size of a test is essentially its depth. As one can see from Table 1 the largest test depth is 53. This can be explained as follows. In our implementation we use the following heuristic to choose which configuration to cover next: we pick a configuration which is "far" from the initial one, that is, at a large depth. The expectation is to cover as many configurations as possible with every new test. Thus, this heuristic tends to favor the generation of fewer but "longer" tests. Obviously, a different approach is to favor "shorter" (but perhaps

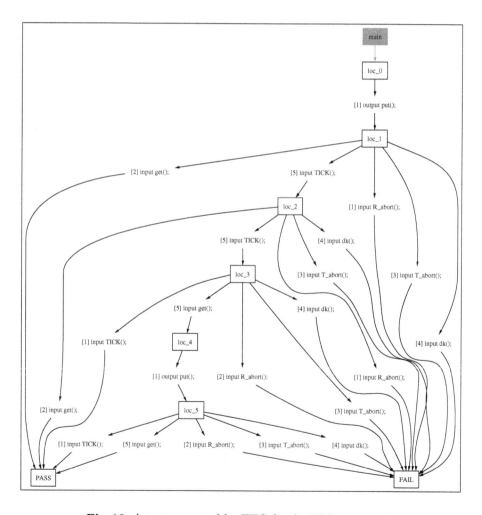

Fig. 10. A test generated by TTG for the BRP case study

more) tests. This can be done by changing the heuristic to pick configurations which are "close" to the initial one.

A test generated by TTG for the configuration coverage option is shown in Figure 10.

4   Summary and Future Work

We have proposed a testing framework for real-time systems based on partially-observable, non-deterministic timed-automata specifications and on digital-clock tests. To our knowledge, this is the first framework that can fully handle such specifications and such tests. We showed that, through appropriate modeling, assumptions on the environment and the interface between the tester and SUT can be captured in the framework in a seamless way, without need for extra notions or algorithms. We also reported on a recent implementation of a test generation algorithm with respect to coverage criteria and experimental results obtained for the Bounded Retransmission Protocol. These results show that a few tests suffice to cover thousands of reachable symbolic states of the specification. We are currently studying alternative notions of coverage and methods to generate *minimal* test suites (without redundant tests). We are also examining how to adapt other testing problems than conformance, for instance, fault detection or state identification [14], to the timed setting.

References

1. R. Alur and D. Dill. A theory of timed automata. *Theoretical Computer Science*, 126:183–235, 1994.
2. B. Berthomieu and M. Menasche. An enumerative approach for analyzing time Petri nets. *IFIP Congress Series*, 9:41–46, 1983.
3. M. Bozga, J.C. Fernandez, L. Ghirvu, S. Graf, J.P. Krimm, and L. Mounier. IF: a validation environment for timed asynchronous systems. In *Proc. CAV'00*, volume 1855 of *LNCS*. Springer, 2000.
4. M. Bozga, S. Graf, A. Kerbrat, L. Mounier, I. Ober, and D. Vincent. SDL for Real-Time: What is Missing? In *Proceedings of SAM'00: 2nd Workshop on SDL and MSC (Grenoble, France)*, pages 108–122. IMAG, June 2000.
5. R. Cardell-Oliver. Conformance tests for real-time systems with timed automata specifications. *Formal Aspects of Computing*, 12(5):350–371, 2000.
6. D.L. Dill. Timing assumptions and verification of finite-state concurrent systems. In J. Sifakis, editor, *Automatic Verification Methods for Finite State Systems*, volume 407 of *LNCS*, pages 197–212. Springer–Verlag, 1989.
7. A. En-Nouaary, R. Dssouli, F. Khendek, and A. Elqortobi. Timed test cases generation based on state characterization technique. In *RTSS'98*. IEEE, 1998.
8. J.C. Fernandez, C. Jard, T. Jéron, and G. Viho. Using on-the-fly verification techniques for the generation of test suites. In *CAV'96*, volume 1102 of *LNCS*. Springer, 1996.
9. A. Hessel, K. Larsen, B. Nielsen, P. Pettersson, and A. Skou. Time-optimal real-time test case generation using UPPAAL. In *FATES'03*, 2003.

10. A. Khoumsi, T. Jéron, and H. Marchand. Test cases generation for nondeterministic real-time systems. In *FATES'03*, 2003.
11. Z. Kohavi. *Switching and finite automata theory, 2nd ed.* McGraw-Hill, 1978.
12. M. Krichen and S. Tripakis. Black-box conformance testing for real-time systems. In *11th International SPIN Workshop on Model Checking of Software (SPIN'04)*, volume 2989 of *LNCS*. Springer, 2004.
13. V. Kuliamin, A. Petrenko, N. Pakoulin, A. Kossatchev, and I. Bourdonov. Integration of functional and timed testing of real-time and concurrent systems. In *Ershov Memorial Conference*, volume 2890 of *LNCS*. Springer, 2003.
14. D. Lee and M. Yannakakis. Principles and methods of testing finite state machines - A survey. *Proceedings of the IEEE*, 84:1090–1126, 1996.
15. B. Nielsen and A. Skou. Automated test generation from timed automata. In *TACAS'01*. LNCS 2031, Springer, 2001.
16. A. Petrenko, S. Boroday, and R. Groz. Confirming configurations in EFSM testing. *IEEE Trans. Software Eng.*, 30(1), 2004.
17. J. Springintveld, F. Vaandrager, and P. D'Argenio. Testing timed automata. *Theoretical Computer Science*, 254, 2001.
18. J. Tretmans. Testing concurrent systems: A formal approach. In J.C.M Baeten and S. Mauw, editors, *CONCUR'99 – 10th Int. Conference on Concurrency Theory*, volume 1664 of *LNCS*, pages 46–65. Springer-Verlag, 1999.
19. S. Tripakis. Fault diagnosis for timed automata. In *Formal Techniques in Real Time and Fault Tolerant Systems (FTRTFT'02)*, volume 2469 of *LNCS*. Springer, 2002.

Firewall Conformance Testing*

Diana Senn, David Basin, and Germano Caronni

ETH Zürich, 8092 Zürich, Switzerland
{dsenn, basin}@inf.ethz.ch, gec@acm.org

Abstract. Firewalls are widely used to protect networks from unautho-
rised access. To ensure that they implement an organisation's security
policy correctly, they need to be tested. We present an approach that
addresses this problem. Namely, we show how an organisation's network
security policy can be formally specified in a high-level way, and how
this specification can be used to automatically generate test cases to test
a deployed system. In contrast to other firewall testing methodologies,
such as penetration testing, our approach tests conformance to a specified policy. Our test cases are organisation-specific — i.e. they depend on
the security requirements and on the network topology of an organisation — and can uncover errors both in the firewall products themselves
and in their configuration.

1   Introduction

Firewalls are a common and widely deployed technology to control access to
networked systems. Although they are sometimes viewed as an "appliance" that
can be used out of the box, considerable work is required in practice to configure them so that they implement an organisation's network security policy. To
ensure that this is done properly and that the employed firewalls then behave
as expected, the entire setup must be tested. This is particularly important in
high-security environments like banking or in military settings.

In this paper we present an approach to specification-based firewall testing,
where an organisation's network security policy comprises the specification. This
can also be called firewall conformance testing, as it tests if the firewalls conform
to the network security policy. Our motivation to follow this path comes from
the fact that there is a wide range of security needs and network topologies, and
a firewall testing procedure should be tailored to both of these. Note that such
testing says nothing about the appropriateness of the security policy itself. For
this, a separate analysis of the security policy is needed.

Our approach is based on the following ideas: First, we propose a formal
language for specifying network security policies. Second, we show how to automatically generate test cases from formal policies. A *test case* consists of test

---

* This work was partially supported by armasuisse. It represents the views of the
authors.

F. Khendek and R. Dssouli (Eds.): TestCom 2005, LNCS 3502, pp. 226–241, 2005.

input, also called *test data*, and the expected test output. Our test cases consist of a series of network packets (test data) and a statement per packet whether we expect this packet to reach its destination or not. We are testing firewalls and use the term *firewall implementation* to denote everything that is delivered by the firewall manufacturer, and the term *firewall configuration* (or *firewall rule set*) to denote its configuration by the customer. By executing the generated test cases directly on the real network (as opposed to simulation), we can find errors both in the firewall configuration and in the firewall implementation. These tests can be done just before deploying a network, or after configuration updates. Note that we do not explicitly search for all possible bugs in the firewall implementation as is sometimes done in penetration testing. Rather, our method succeeds in finding all policy related errors.

The contributions of this paper are a language for the formal specification of network security policies, the novel combination of different methods for generating abstract test cases, and an algorithm for generating concrete test cases from policies. As firewalls can be very complex, we have made some simplifying assumptions in this paper: We assume that all firewalls are stateful packet filters[1], and we do not test for problems with timing or sequence numbers. Future work will aim at eliminating these simplifications and at carrying out large-scale case studies.

This paper is organised as follows: We give a comparison with related work in Section 2. Then we present our formal policy specification language in Section 3, and the process of test case generation in Section 4. The entire process is then illustrated on an example in Section 5. We conclude and report on future work in Section 6.

2   Related Work

Most preexisting work on firewall testing covers different aspects of testing by hand [Hae97, Sch96]. Constructing these tests relies on human experts who mainly focus on detecting known vulnerabilities, for example forwarding external packets that claim to come from an internal source. Most of this testing falls under the heading of *penetration testing*.

Over the last few years, a new approach to firewall testing was taken by [BMNW99, JW01], which can be called *specification-based firewall testing*. The general idea comes from specification-based software testing: The specification is used to generate test cases, against which the system implementation is tested. In the case of specification-based firewall testing, the system is the firewall and

---

[1] A *packet filter* can filter traffic only at OSI Layer 4 (TCP and UDP), whereas an *application level firewall* can interpret and filter higher-level protocols. A *stateful packet filter* can forward (changed or unchanged), drop, or reject a packet based on its source IP address, the packet's source port, its destination IP address, its destination port, its TCP flags, and the state of the connection the packet belongs to.

the specification is a security policy. The difference to penetration testing is substantial: Whereas penetration testing tends to always use the same test cases, in specification-based testing they depend on the policy and are designed explicitly to test conformance with the policy.

These specification-based approaches share some similarities with ours. Wool et al. [BMNW99, BMNW03, MWZ00, Woo01], for example, gather the configurations of the network and the firewalls, and then simulate the network under test, i.e. they start with the firewall rules instead of with the policy. In their simulation, tests can then be executed easily and without doing harm. There are a number of tools (Firmato [BMNW99, BMNW03], Fang [MWZ00], LFA [Woo01]) implementing this approach. The disadvantages of this approach are twofold: First it relies on the correctness of the firewall implementations and second it needs to interpret the different firewall rule languages (of the different vendors). Thus it tests a model, which will never model reality perfectly. We treat firewalls as black boxes and therefore can test firewalls without having to formalise and provide a semantics for their rule language. Additionally, by carrying out tests on the real network, we can find errors in not only the firewall configuration, but also in the firewall implementation. The advantage of testing a model, as Wool et al. do, is that there is no interaction with a running system and that the tests themselves can do no harm.

An approach similar to specification-based firewall testing is to generate the firewall rules from a formal policy [Gut97, BCG+01]. What firewall rule generation has in common with specification-based firewall testing is that both need a formal specification. Guttman [Gut97], for example, takes an approach similar to formalising policies as we do, but includes all the low-level details. He then models the network as a bipartite graph and computes the individual rules for each firewall from the global policy by completing a graph traversal of this model. His aim is different from ours: he generates the firewall rules from the policy, whereas we assume that there are firewall rules whose correctness we would like to check. What our work has in common is that we also need a formal policy. However, his policies are specified in a way that they easily become too detailed and therefore are subject to policy errors. In contrast, in our approach, we separate the low-level details from the policy, thereby making policies easier to understand and policy writing less error-prone.

3   A Formal Network Security Policy

A network security policy formalises what kind of traffic is allowed between different zones. A *zone* is a part of a network that is separated from the rest of the network by means of one or more firewalls. In what follows, we will use the term *policy* to denote any part of a security policy, be it formal or informal, and the term *formal policy* for our formalisation of the *network security policy*. Note that in our work, we shall assume that users do not play a role in policies.

Figure 1 illustrates a network with three zones: the public Internet, the demilitarised zone (DMZ), and the private Intranet of a company. In this example,

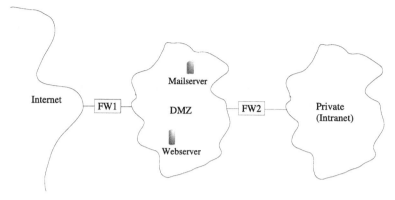

Fig. 1. A sample graphical network layout

our network also has two servers, a Mailserver and a Webserver, standing in the DMZ. A policy for this network defines what traffic is allowed to flow between these different zones. This can be direction dependent (for example, there may be different restrictions on what connections are allowed to be initiated from the private zone to the Internet than the other way) and thus we need two rules per pair of zones. We assume that all clients in a zone are equivalent, in that differences in their IP addresses have no effect on the firewalls' behaviours[2]. In contrast, we do distinguish between servers, as we would like to be able to state different policies for different servers. Thus, in the example given, instead of stating policies for traffic flowing to and from the DMZ, we state individual policies for the two servers. Policies for traffic within zones need not be specified, since compliance with these policies cannot be enforced by firewalls.

```
@ Connections to Private
DMZ → Private:              ACCEPT securetraffic
Internet → Private:         DENY *

@ Connections to the DMZ
* → Webserver:              ACCEPT webtraffic
* → Mailserver:             ACCEPT mailtraffic

@ Connections to the Internet
Private → Internet:         ACCEPT *
DMZ → Internet:             DENY *
```

Fig. 2. A sample formal policy

Figure 2 gives an example of a formal policy for the given network, where lines starting with @ are comments, and where * means everything. The second

---

[2] This represents our *uniformity hypothesis*.

line, for example, states that only secure traffic is allowed from the DMZ zone to the private zone. But which connections are secure? This can change quickly (for example, when a new ssh weakness is found) and is therefore stated separately from the policy in what we call *keyword definitions*. The idea is that our policy is expressed at a high-level; this way it is both manageable and understandable by managers as well as security specialists. Because of this, we also use names for network zones. The low-level details (IP-addresses, etc.), which may be subject to frequent change, are stored separately in what we call a *textual network layout*. The graphical version presented in Figure 1 does not contain these low-level details.

securetraffic = ssh, scp, https, imaps
webtraffic   = http, https
mailtraffic   = smtp, imap, imaps

Fig. 3. Keyword definitions

An example of keyword definitions is given in Figure 3. Here the security engineer has decided that SSH, SCP, HTTPS, and IMAPS are secure protocols. These protocols are application level protocols. At the TCP level — where stateful packet filters work — they are represented by their TCP port number.

DMZ: 129.132.178.192/27
Private (Intranet): 192.168.1.0/24
Internet: !DMZ, !Private
* * *

@ Name of the Firewall	Interface	Comment
FW1	eth0 (0.0.0.1)	
FW1	eth1 (129.132.178.193)	
FW2	eth0 (129.132.178.194)	Packet filter
FW2	eth1 (192.168.1.1)	Packet filter

* * *

@ Name (fac.)	IP	Service
Mailserver	129.132.178.200	smtp
Mailserver	129.132.178.200	imap
Webserver	129.132.178.197	http

Fig. 4. A sample textual network layout

An example of a textual network layout, providing the low-level details of the network shown in Figure 1, is given in Figure 4. The first part gives the IP-address-ranges for the zones in CIDR notation [FLYV93]. For example, 129.132.178.192/27 means that the first 27 bits are used to represent the network and the remaining 5 bits are used to identify hosts, which results in the 30 hosts starting at 129.132.178.193 and ending at 129.132.178.222 (note that 129.132.178.192 represents the network address, and 129.132.178.223 represents the broadcast address). The ! operator represents set complement with respect to the universe of all possible IP addresses (from 0.0.0.0 to 255.255.255.255) and thus the third line means that the Internet consists of everything other than the DMZ and the Private zone. The second part provides the IP addresses of the firewall-interfaces along with some comments. The last part lists the IP addresses of the servers together with the service they provide. The stars separate the different parts and @ again represents comments.

The grammars for formal policies, keyword definitions, and textual network layout can be found in the Appendix.

4   Test Case Generation

In this Section, we first present our method for test case generation in detail, before giving a concrete example in Section 5. Our test case generation consists of two parts. First we generate *test tuples* from the formal policy. Afterwards we generate *abstract test cases*. The idea of the abstract test cases is to test the correct stateful handling of a protocol by a firewall. For example, a stateful packet filter may be tested to determine whether it correctly handles TCP traffic. To generate the *concrete test cases*, we instantiate the abstract test cases with the test tuples.

4.1   Abstract Test Cases

We must generate a set of abstract test cases for every protocol we want to test. Once we have these test cases, we can use them for every test concerning this protocol. The generation consists of two steps: We first construct a Mealy automaton describing the protocol for which we want to generate abstract test cases. Then we generate test cases for this Mealy automaton using the well known UIO-sequences method [SD88]. We will now explain the generation in detail.

Mealy Automata

Definition 1. *A Mealy automaton is a six-tuple $M = (Q, \Sigma, \Gamma, \delta, \lambda, q_1)$, where $Q = \{q_1, q_2, ..., q_{|Q|}\}$ is a finite set of states, $\Sigma = \{\sigma_1, \sigma_2, ..., \sigma_{|\Sigma|}\}$ is a finite input alphabet, $\Gamma = \{\gamma_1, \gamma_2, ..., \gamma_{|\Gamma|}\}$ is a finite output alphabet, $\delta : Q \times \Sigma \to Q$ is the transition function, $\lambda : Q \times \Sigma \to \Gamma$ is the output function, and $q_1 \in Q$ is the initial state.*

In our models, the input of a transition represents the packet (we only model the parts of it essential for determining the firewall's action) reaching the firewall, and the output represents the corresponding packet leaving the firewall. A typical input has the form $x : A \to B$, where x represents packet information being sent from source A to destination B. The output packet can either be the same as the input packet, different from the input packet (i.e. changed by the firewall), or non-existent (dropped by the firewall). Thus $\Sigma = \Gamma \cup \{-\}$, where the "$-$" symbol represents no output.

Test Cases for Mealy Automata

The general idea behind testing a specification given as a Mealy automaton M_{spec} is to ensure that every transition of M_{spec} is correctly implemented, where the implementation is also assumed to be a Mealy automaton M_{imp}. This is achieved by testing every transition in M_{spec}, say from state s_i to state s_j, according to the following steps:

1) Bring the implementation automaton M_{imp} into the initial state s_1.
2) Transfer M_{imp} into the state s_i.
3) Test the transition (apply its input and see if the output is correct).
4) Verify that M_{imp} is now in the state s_j.

Step one is easy if there is a reliable reset: Just apply the reset input to go back to the initial state. The TCP protocol, which we present in the next Section, has such a reliable reset.

Steps two and three can be solved by building a *test tree* T according to the following rules and afterwards traversing all the paths [Cho78]:

Level 1: Label the root of T with the initial state of M_{spec}.

Level (k+1): Examine the nodes in the k-th level from left to right. A node in the k-th level is terminated if its label is the same as a nonterminal at some level j, $j \leq k$. Otherwise, let M_{spec_i} denote its label. If on input x, machine M_{spec} goes from state M_{spec_i} to state M_{spec_j}, then we attach a branch and a successor node to the node labelled M_{spec_i} in T. The branch and the successor node are labelled with x and M_{spec_j}, respectively.

Step 4 can be achieved by using either the *W-method* [Cho78], *UIO sequences* [SD88], or *distinguishing sequences* [Gil61, Gil62]. All these methods achieve the same fault coverage. We have chosen the UIO sequences because they generate the shortest test cases of the three methods. In brief, a UIO sequence is an input/output sequence x for a state s that distinguishes s from all other states, i.e. $\lambda(s_i, x) \neq \lambda(s, x)$, for all $s_i \neq s$.

We can now fit the pieces together to generate our abstract test cases: We take every possible path in the test tree, prepend it with the reset input, and append the UIO sequence of the end state (of the path). Thus we get a set of abstract test cases, where every abstract test case consists of a series of I/O tuples (describing input and expected output). Every abstract test case starts with the reset input to bring the machine back into its initial state, followed by a series of I/O tuples to bring the machine into some state s_i and one I/O tuple to test the transition from state s_i to state s_j (extracted from the test tree), and finally a series of I/O tuples (the UIO sequences) to verify that state s_j was reached.

4.2   Test Tuples

A test tuple is a four-tuple *(sIP, dIP, proto, exp)*, where *sIP* and *dIP* represent IP addresses, *proto* is the name of a protocol, and *exp* ∈ {*ACCEPT, DROP*} represents an expectation. A test tuple describes whether a connection from the source *sIP* to the destination *dIP* using protocol *proto* is allowed by the formal policy. If the policy allows a connection, we expect the firewalls to let this data through, and therefore *exp* in this case would be *ACCEPT*. If a connection is not allowed (or explicitly forbidden) by the policy, *exp* will be *DROP*. This means that the test tuples are policy-specific and thus must be generated for every policy. Note that the statefulness of a connection is not modelled by these test tuples, but rather by the abstract test cases.

We generate test tuples in two steps. First we combine the formal policy with the low-level details contained in the keyword definitions and the textual network layout. This means that we transform every rule

source → destination: action keyword

from the formal policy into n low-level rules, where n is the number of protocols named in the keyword definitions. In these low-level rules, the names of source and destination are replaced with the corresponding IP ranges.

These low-level rules can be represented graphically using one two-dimensional graph per protocol, where the x-axis represents the source IP addresses and the y-axis represents the destination IP addresses. For each low-level rule

sIPr dIPr protocol action

the cross-product $sIPr \times dIPr$ defines a rectangular region in the graph. We colour this region according to the given action (grey for ACCEPT, black for DROP). An example of this is given in Section 5, Figure 7.

In a second step, we choose our test tuples from these low-level rules. This is necessary because it is generally infeasible to test every possible combination of IP addresses. However, as we assume uniformity within zones, it is sufficient to choose for each low-level rule an arbitrary IP from the source IP range and an arbitrary IP from the destination IP range. As boundary points are a source of errors in practice, we also select addresses to test these. That is, we choose the lowest IP address, an arbitrary (intermediate) IP address, and the highest IP address per range. This results in nine (three times three) test tuples per low-level rule.

Until now, we just considered what the policy explicitly states. But we should also test implicit statements, i.e. what is not explicitly allowed is forbidden. This is best explained on the graphical representation (see Figure 7 for an example). In the graph, we coloured all the areas where we have an explicit policy statement (either in grey or black). This means that for all the uncoloured areas there exists no explicit policy statement. Note that a part of the uncoloured area is not testable since, as we stated earlier, policies for traffic within zones cannot be enforced by firewalls. But the rest of the uncoloured areas can be partitioned into rectangles and then test tuples can be chosen, analogous to the procedure given above, where the expectation is set to DROP.

The resulting test tuples are then used to instantiate the abstract test cases. How this is done is explained in the next Subsection.

4.3   Concrete Test Cases

In the last two Subsections, we have explained the generation of test tuples and abstract test cases. Recall that abstract test cases test the correct stateful handling of a protocol, and they contain variables for source and destination addresses (A and B respectively). Recall further that test tuples are of the form *(sIP, dIP, proto, exp)*, formalising whether a connection from the IP address *sIP* to the IP address *dIP* using protocol *proto* is allowed or not. We now explain how to instantiate the abstract test cases with the test tuples and thereby generate concrete test cases that test if the policy is correctly implemented in a stateful manner. Given a test tuple *(sIP, dIP, proto, exp)* and abstract test cases a_i for the protocol *proto*, the instantiation proceeds as follows:

- replace every occurrence of A in every a_i with *sIP*,
- replace every occurrence of B in every a_i with *dIP*, and
- if *exp* == *DENY* then replace the expected output in every a_i with "–".

The resulting test data represents network packets. These packets can then be built and injected into the actual network and the results can be compared to the expectations of the given test cases.

In this paper, we only consider the testing of stateful packet filters. This means that we only need abstract test cases for TCP and UDP, but not for every possible (application-level) protocol. Thus, instead of instantiating the abstract test cases generated for *proto* with test tuples of the form *(sIP, dIP, proto, exp)*, we instantiate the abstract test cases for TCP with these tuples. To model *proto* at the TCP-level, we use the TCP port-number *pnum* of *proto* as the destination port. Thus, B in the abstract test cases is replaced with *dIP:pnum* (instead of *dIP*) in this case, to produce the concrete test cases.

As described above, our abstract test cases are generated from Mealy automata using the UIO sequences method. The resulting unoptimised test sequences have length $O(mn^2)$ per automaton, where m denotes the number of transitions and n denotes the number of states of the automaton (Theorem 3 of [SD88]). As test sequences can be optimised, i.e. subsequences completely contained in others can be eliminated, the above complexity bound represents the worst case.

The work needed for generating test tuples is the following: If we have a policy containing r rules, and at most p protocols per keyword, we get $O(rp)$ test tuples. The generation of the abstract test cases needs only be done once per protocol, i.e. this is a one-time cost. The generation of the test tuples and the instantiation of concrete test cases based on them has to be done once per policy. As we use each test tuple to instantiate at most $O(mn^2)$ abstract test cases, in the worst case we generate $O(rpmn^2)$ concrete test cases.

When testing Mealy automata, we can distinguish between two types of errors: *operation errors*, which are errors in the output function, and *transfer errors*, which are errors in the next state function. If the implementation automaton has the same number of states as the specification automaton, then we can detect all errors of both kinds, and our abstract test cases are reliable and valid in the sense described by [GG75]. If there are extra states in the implementation, the UIO sequences method we use may however miss errors.

If our uniformity hypothesis holds, i.e. the firewall reacts in the same way to all clients within a zone, then our test tuples represent all possible connections (between every possible source and destination). Hence instantiating the abstract test cases with these test tuples, the resulting concrete test cases are reliable and valid.

5   An Example

Abstract Test Cases for TCP.

A graphical Mealy automaton for the TCP protocol is given in Figure 5. The automaton is not a full specification: sequence numbers and acknowledgement numbers have been omitted. Also the input alphabet does not contain all possible combinations of flags. But the central parts of the protocol are specified. The respective input and output of each transition are written next to the transition and are separated by a slash. The input fin: A → B, for example, stands for a TCP packet sent from A to B, where exactly the fin flag is set. A and B stand for two hosts and are instantiated with concrete IP addresses later.

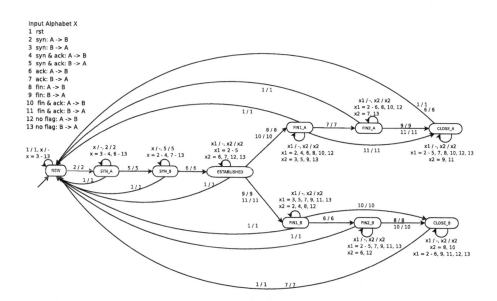

Fig. 5. Automaton for TCP

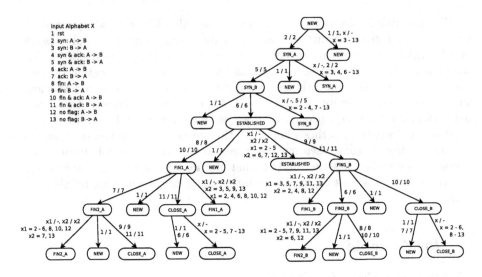

Fig. 6. Test Tree for TCP

From the Mealy automaton for TCP, we construct a test tree using the method given in Section 4.1. The test tree for TCP is given in Figure 6: NEW is the start state of the Mealy automaton and represents level 1 of the test tree. From the state NEW there are two transitions, one back to NEW and one to the state SYN_A. Thus the states NEW and SYN_A represent level 1 of the test tree. As we already had state NEW in the test tree, the test tree is continued only for state SYN_A.

Proposition 1. *The UIO sequences for TCP are:*

NEW:	*(5/-)(2/2)*
SYN_A:	*(6/-)(5/5)*
SYN_B:	*(7/-)(6/6)(9/9)(10/10)*
ESTABLISHED:	*(8/8)(11/11)*
FIN1_A:	*(7/7)(9/9)(6/6)(2/2)*
FIN2_A:	*(9/9)(6/6)(2/2)*
CLOSE_A:	*(6/6)(2/2)*
FIN1_B:	*(6/6)(8/8)(7/7)(2/2)*
FIN2_B:	*(8/8)(7/7)(2/2)*
CLOSE_B:	*(7/7)(2/2)*

As an example, consider the UIO sequence of the state NEW. On input **syn: A → B**, only the states NEW and SYN_A will respond with output **syn: A → B**; all the other states will have no output. As the state SYN_A, in contrast to state NEW, will also respond to **syn & ack: B → A**, we identify the state NEW if we send the packets **syn: A → B** and **syn & ack: B → A** and only see the second packet behind the firewall.

We will now construct two test cases according to the four step procedure given in Section 4.1. Our first test case should test the transition from state NEW to itself.

1) Bring the machine into its initial state: (1 / 1).
2) Transfer the machine into state NEW: no action is needed here.
3) Test the transition: (8 / -) is one possibility.
4) Verify that the machine is now in state NEW: (5 / -)(2 / 2) is the UIO sequence of state NEW.

Thus the resulting test case is (1 / 1)(8 / -)(5 / -)(2 / 2).

Our second test case should test the transition from state SYN_B to state ESTABLISHED.

1) Bring the machine into its initial state: (1 / 1).
2) Transfer the machine into state SYN_B: (2 / 2)(5 / 5).
3) Test the transition: (6 / 6).
4) Verify that the machine is now in state ESTABLISHED: (8 / 8)(11 / 11) is the UIO sequence of state ESTABLISHED.

Thus the resulting test case is (1 / 1)(2 / 2)(5 / 5)(6 / 6)(8 / 8)(11 / 11). Analogous to the two examples given, test cases for all the other transitions need to be constructed.

An Example of Test Tuples
We will illustrate the generation of test tuples on the example of the formal policy given in Figure 2. Apart from the policy, we need the keyword definitions given in Figure 3 and some knowledge (i.e. IP addresses) of the network under test (given in Figure 1). Let us assume that we have the information about the network under test given in Figure 4.

As an example, we generate test tuples for the HTTPS protocol. HTTPS is contained in the keywords *securetraffic* and *webtraffic*. Therefore we have to build and colour a graph for all rules of the formal policy except the fourth one. The result can be seen in Figure 7. In this graph, test tuples are marked by a circle, and untestable areas are marked with a question mark. One example of such a test tuple is (129.132.178.192, 192.168.0.255, https, DENY).

An Example of a Concrete Test Case
In this example, we have only generated abstract test cases for TCP. Thus we instantiate these abstract test cases with the above test tuples, to generate concrete test cases. For this, we represent every application level protocol with its TCP port number (e.g. 443 for HTTPS).

As an example, we present the instantiation of one abstract test case with two test tuples.

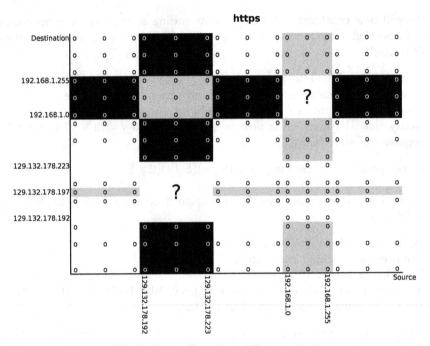

Fig. 7. Policy for https with test points

Example 1. Test Case Instantiation
an abstract test case for TCP: (1 / 1)(8 / -)(5 / -)(2 / 2).
test tuple 1: (129.132.178.192, 192.168.0.255, HTTPS, DENY)
test tuple 2: (129.132.178.192, 192.168.1.0, HTTPS, ACCEPT)

Using the first test tuple we get the concrete test case:
(rst: 129.132.178.192 → 192.168.0.255:443 / −)
(fin: 129.132.178.192 → 192.168.0.255:443 / −)
(syn & ack: 192.168.0.255:443 → 129.132.178.192 / −)
(syn: 129.132.178.192 → 192.168.0.255:443 / −)

Using the second test tuple we get:
(rst: 129.132.178.192 → 192.168.1.0:443 / rst 129.132.178.192 → 192.168.1.0:443)
(fin: 129.132.178.192 → 192.168.1.0:443 / −)
(syn & ack: 192.168.1.0:443 → 129.132.178.192 / −)
(syn: 129.132.178.192 → 192.168.1.0:443 / syn: 129.132.178.192 → 192.168.1.0:443)

Let us explain these two test cases. Recall that a test case (this holds for
the abstract and the concrete test cases) is composed of a series of input and
expected output packets. Each of the above test cases contains four such I/O
pairs. Thus for the first concrete test case we try to initiate a https-connection
from 129.132.178.192 to 192.168.0.255, where we expect the firewall to drop all

these packets. That is we test that a https-connection from 129.132.178.192 to 192.168.0.255 is not allowed.

The second concrete test case belongs to a series of test cases that test if a https-connection can be initiated from 129.132.178.192 to 192.168.1.0 and if this is done correctly, i.e. they test whether the firewall handles the TCP connection correctly. This specific test case tests the start of such a connection (as explained in the last Subsection). The first packet resets the connection and should be accepted by the firewall. The second packet attempts to close the connection, but as the connection no longer exists (it was reset before), this packet should not be allowed, and therefore should be dropped by the firewall. The third packet is not the start of a new connection and thus should be dropped as well, and finally the fourth packet initiates a new connection and should be let through.

With the second concrete test case we can find different kinds of errors: 1) A bug in the firewall implementation if the `fin` or the `syn & ack` packet is let through (i.e. the stateful connection handling is incorrect), and 2) a bug in the firewall configuration if the `syn` packet is blocked.

6   Conclusion

We have presented a new approach to test the conformance of firewalls to a given security policy. Our contributions are the following: a language for the formal specification of network security policies, the novel combination of different methods for generating abstract test cases, and an algorithm for generating concrete test cases from the policy. Overall, our method is designed to find errors both in the firewall implementation and the firewall specification.

In this paper our focus has been on the theoretical basis of our approach. We are currently implementing a prototype testing tool based on this work. We plan to use this tool to conduct case studies, to see how effective our method is in finding errors as well as to determine its robustness. An interesting scenario will be to stress test the firewalls, i.e. to run many different test cases at the same time.

To reduce the complexity of the problem, we have simplified matters by assuming that our firewalls are stateful packet filters and by not testing for problems with timing or sequence numbers. As a next step, we plan to eliminate these simplifications. In particular, we shall adapt our approach to application-level firewalls. As some application-level protocols are difficult to handle by a firewall, e.g. SIP [RSC+02] needs dynamic port opening, this problem is quite challenging. With respect to timing properties, at the moment we can only test the correct ordering of test packets over time. It would be interesting to test, for example, what happens when there is a long pause between test packets belonging to the same test case.

References

[BCG+01]   J. Burns, A. Cheng, P. Gurung, S. Rajagopalan, P. Rao, D. Rosenbluth, A.V. Surendran, and D.M. Martin. Automatic management of network security policy. In *Proceedings of DISCEX II*, 2001.

[BMNW99]   Yair Bartal, Alain J. Mayer, Kobbi Nissim, and Avishai Wool. Firmato: A novel firewall management toolkit. In *IEEE Symposium on Security and Privacy*, pages 17–31, 1999.

[BMNW03]   Yair Bartal, Alain J. Mayer, Kobbi Nissim, and Avishai Wool. Firmato: A novel firewall management toolkit. Technical report, Dept. Electrical Engineering Systems, Tel Aviv University, Ramat Aviv 69978 Israel, February 2003.

[Cho78]   Tsun S. Chow. Testing software design modeled by finite-state machines. In *IEEE Transactions on Software Engineering, Vol. SE-4, No 3*, pages 178–187, May 1978.

[FLYV93]   V. Fuller, T. Li, J. Yu, and K. Varadhan. RFC 1519: Classless interdomain routing (CIDR): an address assignment and aggregation strategy. http://www.ietf.org/rfc/rfc1519.txt, September 1993.

[GG75]   John B. Goodenough and Susan L. Gerhart. Toward a theory of test data selection. In *IEEE Transactions on Software Engineering (TSE), Volume 1, Number 2*, pages 156–173, June 1975.

[Gil61]   A. Gill. State-identification experiments in finite automata. In *Information and Control, vol. 4*, pages 132 – 154, 1961.

[Gil62]   A. Gill. *Introduction to the Theory of Finite-state Machines*. McGraw-Hill, 1962.

[Gut97]   J. D. Guttman. Filtering postures: Local enforcement for global policies. In *1997 IEEE Symposium on Security and Privacy*, pages 120–129, Oakland, CA, 1997. IEEE Computer Society Press.

[Hae97]   Reto E. Haeni. Firewall penetration testing. Technical report, The George Washington University Cyberspace Policy Institute, 2033 K St, Suite 340N, Washington, DC, 20006, US, January 1997.

[JW01]   Jan Jürjens and Guido Wimmel. Specification-based testing of firewalls. In Andrei Ershov, editor, *4th International Conference Perspectives of System Informatics (PSI'01)*, LNCS. Springer, 2001.

[MWZ00]   Alain Mayer, Avishai Wool, and Elisha Ziskind. Fang: A firewall analysis engine. In *Proceedings of the 2000 IEEE Symposium on Security and Privacy (S&P 2000)*, pages 177–187, May 2000.

[RSC+02]   J. Rosenberg, H. Schulzrinne, G. Camarillo, A. Johnston, J. Peterson, R. Sparks, M. Handley, and E. Schooler. RFC 3261 SIP: Session initiation protocol. http://www.ietf.org/rfc/rfc3261.txt, June 2002.

[Sch96]   E. Schultz. How to perform effective firewall testing. In *Computer Security Journal, vol. 12, no. 1*, pages 47–54, 1996.

[SD88]   Krishan Sabnani and Anton Dahbura. A protocol test generation procedure. In *Computer Networks and ISDN Systems 15*, pages 285–297, 1988.

[Woo01]   A. Wool. Architecting the lumeta firewall analyzer. In *Proceedings of the 10th USENIX Security Symposium*, pages 85–97, August 2001.

A   Grammars

A.1   General

IP	= DDD'.'DDD'.'DDD'.'DDD .
D	= [digit] .
PROTO	= letter {letter | '-' | '+' | digit | '.' | '_'} | NUM .
NUM	= {digit} .
NAME	= letter {letter | digit} .
ACTION	= 'accept' | 'deny' .
PRE	= 'pre' .
POST	= 'post' .
COMMENT	= '@' TEXT '\n'
TEXT	= {letter | digit ...}

A.2   Formal Network Policy

POLICY	= {RULE | COMMENT}
RULE	= SOURCE '→' DEST : ACTION KEYWORDS
SOURCE	= NETWORK
DEST	= NETWORK
NETWORK	= NAME
KEYWORDS	= ('*' | NAME) {',' KEYWORDS}

A.3   Keyword Definitions

KEYWORD-DEFINITIONS	= {DEFINITION | COMMENT}
DEFINITION	= NAME '=' PROTO {',' PROTO}

A.4   Network Layout

NETLAYOUT	= NETWORKS '***' FIREWALLS '***' SERVERS
NETWORKS	= {NET | COMMENT}
NET	= NAME':' RANGE {',' RANGE}
RANGE	= IP'/'DD | '!'NAME
FIREWALLS	= {FIREWALL | COMMENT}
FIREWALL	= FW IF TEXT
FW	= NAME
IF	= ['eth0' | 'eth1' ...] '('IP')'
SERVERS	= {SERVER | COMMENT}
SERVER	= NAME IP PROTO

Test Generation for Interaction Detection in Feature-Rich Communication Systems

Caixia Chi and Ruibing Hao

Bell Labs Research China, Lucent Technologies,
Beijing, China, 100080
chic@lucent.com, rhao@research.bell-labs.com

Abstract. This paper proposes a technique to generate test sequences to check the conformance of an implementation of a feature-rich communication system to its specification, as well as to detect the interactions between the features of the system. A concept called *color span* is introduced to measure the extent of the interactions between different features. A modified *Chinese postman tour* algorithm is proposed to produce an approximate minimum-cost and minimum *color span* tour of the transition graph of a finite-state machine. Test generation using the proposed algorithm for the SIP-based Internet telephony end system and for the Link Management Protocol are reported.

1 Introduction

With the convergence of 3G wireless and mobile Internet, more and more feature-rich communication systems are designed and deployed. An example is the popular MSN messenger client which provides voice call, instant messaging and video communication services. A feature-rich communication system is a system that can offer many value-added services to its users, in which different services may interfere with each other, and result in a problem known as feature interaction [1]. For example, Internet telephony end systems can offer basic call functions, as well as some value-added services including automatic call answering, call forwarding, call waiting, call redirection, etc. When a user wants to apply a feature to automatically accept an incoming call in addition to an existing call forwarding feature, the interaction between automatic call answering and call forwarding occurs. Feature interactions also occur in very low level communication protocol systems. In [2], we have identified some feature interactions in the protocols for core optical networks. Interactions between features of a communication system are usually caused by different reasons such as resource sharing or requirement violation, and can be identified through various ways including protocol verification, simulation, or testing. In this paper, we focus our discussion on how to identify feature interactions in a real system by means of testing.

As stated in [3], a communication protocol system can be specified as a deterministic finite-state machine (FSM), conformance test can be to present a

F. Khendek and R. Dssouli (Eds.): TestCom 2005, LNCS 3502, pp. 242–257, 2005.

method to test whether there is a discrepancy between the specification and the implementation of an FSM. Typically, the implementation of a system is tested for conformance by applying a sequence of inputs from an external tester, and then verifying that the corresponding sequence of outputs is what is expected[3]. Lots of work has been done on generating test sequences for FSM's [4][5][6][7], and all these work focus on finding a tour of the transition graph of the FSM that meets certain coverage criteria, such as a transition tour [7], or a postman tour [3].

With the richness of features in modern communication systems, it is important to make sure that a feature that works correctly in a stand alone mode also works as expected in an integrated multi-feature system. Thus to guarantee the reliability and usability of whole system, identifying the interactions between features becomes more important. Generating conformance test cases that at the same time can detect feature interactions in a feature-rich communication system can be an efficient way to achieve this goal. Unfortunately we have not seen any previous work on this aspect.

This paper describes a technique for generating optimal test sequences for an implementation of a feature-rich communication system with an emphasis on detecting the system's malfunctions resulted by interactions between different features. The mechanism proposed in this paper tries to interleave the operations of different features as much as possible such that interactions between different features can be tested. A concept called *color span* is introduced in this paper to specify the interleaving extent of multiple features, then an optimization technique is used to find test sequences with minimum *color span* such that transitions from different features interleave with each other as much as possible in order to test interactions between different features.

In section II, some preliminary knowledge on graph theory and finite automata theory is introduced. Section III describes the algorithm to generate test sequence minimal in time and with the minimum *color span*, section IV extends the algorithm to generate test sequence with minimum *color span* only. In Section V, the algorithm is applied to generate test sequence for the SIP-based Internet telephony end systems. In Section VI, we report the conformance test sequence generated for the Link Management Protocol [15]. The paper concludes in section VII.

2   Preliminaries

2.1   Graphs

Let $G = (V, E)$ be a labelled directed graph with vertex set V, edge set E, where $V = \{v_1, \cdots, v_n\}$ and $m = |E|$. G may contain loops and parallel edges, which are distinguished from one another by different labels. An edge e from vertex v_i to v_j is represented by a triple (v_i, L_e, v_j), where L_e is a label such that each edge in E has an unique representation.

A *walk* in G is a finite, non-null sequence of consecutive edges: $W = (v_{i_1}, L_1, v_{i_2})(v_{i_2}, L_2, v_{i_3}) \cdots (v_{i_{r-1}}, L_{r-1}, v_{i_r})$. Note that in a walk, a particular edge may appear more than once. Vertex v_{i_1} is called the *origin* of W, and v_{i_r} the *tail* of W. A *tour* is a walk that starts and ends at the same vertex[8]. An *Eulerian tour* of G is a tour which contains every edge of E exactly once.

Graph G is *strongly connected* if for any pair of distinct vertices v_i and v_j, there exists a walk W in G with v_i as the origin and v_j as the tail[9].

The in-degree and out-degree of a vertex v_i in G are denoted by $d_G^-(v_i)$ and $d_G^+(v_i)$, respectively. The index G is omitted if G is obvious in the context. A directed graph is *balanced* if for every vertex v_i, $d^+(v_i) = d^-(v_i)$. For each $v_i \in V$, set $\sigma_i = d^-(v_i) - d^+(v_i)$. Let $S = \{v_i \in V | \sigma_i > 0\}$, $T = \{v_i \in V | \sigma_i < 0\}$, $\sigma = \sum_{v_i \in S} \sigma_i$.

A *postman tour* of G is a tour which contains every edge of E at least once. The *Chinese postman problem* is to find an optimal (minimum-cost) *postman tour* of a directed, strongly connected graph G; such a tour is called a *Chinese postman tour*.

2.2   Finite-State Machines

A given finite-state machine (FSM) M can be taken as a directed graph $G = (V, E)$, where $V = \{v_1, \cdots, v_n\}$ represents the specified states of the FSM and a directed edge represents a transition from one state to another in the FSM [3]. In this paper, it is assumed that G is strongly connected.

The following symbols are introduced in [3] and we include them here for the convenience of the reader. There is an edge in E from v_i to v_j with label a_k/o_l if and only if the FSM M, in state s_i upon receiving input a_k produces output o_l, and moves into state s_j. When there are multiple transitions from state s_i to s_j, there are multiple parallel edges from vertex v_i to v_j in the corresponding graph G. Therefore, an edge in G is fully specified by a triple (v_i, L, v_j), where $L \equiv a_k/o_l, L^{(i)} \equiv a_k$, and $L^{(o)} \equiv o_l$. It is assumed here that M is a deterministic FSM, that is, for a vertex $v_i \in V$ which has two outgoing edges $(v_i, L_1, v_j) \in E$, and $(v_i, L_2, v_k) \in E$, $L_1^{(i)} \neq L_2^{(i)}$, although it is permissible that $L_1^{(o)} = L_2^{(o)}$. In this case, a walk W in G which corresponds to a sequence of state transitions is specified by its origin(the initial state) and a sequence of input operations.

For a state machine that describes the behaviors of a feature-rich communication system, different features will often trigger different transitions of the state machine. For the ease of better presentation, we assign each system feature with a distinguished color, then G can be transformed into a colored graph, in which the color associated with each edge is the same as the color of the feature that realizes the corresponding transition in M.

Let $G = (V, E, C)$ be a colored graph with vertex set V, edge set E and color set C, where $V = \{v_1, \cdots, v_n\}$ and $n = |V|, m = |E|$, $C = \{c_1, \cdots, c_k\}$. Each edge $e \in E$ is assigned a color $c_e \in C$.

3   Problem Statement

3.1   Mathematical Model

In an implementation, features of a complex communication system are often implemented in different processes or invoked according to different rules, thus concurrent operation of these features are inevitable. Interleaving the operations of different features and invoking features in different orders may result in some intricate interaction problems. Previous research efforts have been mostly focused on the general conformance testing problem, whose purpose is to establish the confidence that a given implementation is in compliance with every function/feature description of a specification. It emphasizes on checking the compliance of individual feature of a system. However, many field observations have shown that even if an implementation passes the tests for all individual features, it still might fail to perform a function when there are other features running in the system concurrently. There is little work on systematically generating test sequences to test the interactions between the features.

In this work, we study the test sequence generation problem with a stress on testing the interactions between different features. We propose an algorithm to generate test sequences with requests from different features interleaving with each other as much as possible. A parameter to measure the interleaving extent of features in a test sequence is defined at first, then the test sequence generation problem is stated as an optimization problem which strives to maximize the interleaving extent of features, and finally an algorithm is proposed to solve the problem.

For a given walk W of a colored graph G, the associated *color sequence* of W is denoted as $CS(W) = c_{i_1}, c_{i_2}, \cdots, c_{i_{r-1}}$, where c_{i_j} is the color assigned to edge $e_j = (v_{i_j}, L_j, v_{i_{j+1}})$ in G.

For an edge e_j in W, its *color span* in W, $s_W(e_j)$, is defined as the length of the longest same color sub-walk in W starting with e_j. For example, if $W = (v_1, l_1, v_2)(v_2, l_2, v_3)(v_3, l_3, v_4)(v_4, l_4, v_5)$ and the color sequence of W is $CS(W) = c1, c1, c1, c2$, according to this definition, the *color span* of edge $e_1 = (v_1, l_1, v_2)$ in W is 3 and the *color span* of edge $e_3 = (v_3, l_3, v_4)$ in W is 1. Based on the *color span* definition of edges in a walk, we can also give the *color span* definition for a walk. The *color span* of a walk W is defined as the maximum of all the edge *colorspans* in the walk, $s(W) = max\{s_W(e_i), e_i \in W\}$. If all edges in a walk are of the same color, the *colorspan* of the walk is the length of the walk. The longest same color sub-walks in a walk W are also called the *critical sections* of W.

For example, given a walk $W = e_1, e_2, e_3, e_4, e_5, e_6, e_7$, and its color sequence $CS(W) = c_1, c_1, c_1, c_1, c_2, c_2, c_3$, the *color span* of W is 4 and the *critical section* of W is e_1, e_2, e_3, e_4. If all edges in W are of the same color, e.g., $CS(W) = c_1, c_1, c_1, c_1, c_1, c_1, c_1$, then $s(W) = 7$.

As we have described earlier, for a state machine M, transitions resulted from different features are assigned with different colors. Given a test sequence consisting of the edges in M, the *color span* of the test sequence reflects the interleaving extent of features. The larger the *color span*, the less the interleaving. Thus different from the traditional test sequence generation problem, which tries to find a *Chinese postman tour*, we need to find a *postman tour* which has the minimum *color span*. In summary, the problems we need to solve are as follows:

Problem 1: Given a colored digraph $G = (V, E, C)$, find a *postman tour* T such that $|T|$ and $s(T)$ are both minimized, where $|T|$ is the number of edges in T and $s(T)$ is the *color span* of T.

Problem 2: Given a colored digraph $G = (V, E, C)$, find a *postman tour* T such that $s(T)$ is minimized.

The first problem is to find a *Chinese postman tour* such that $s(T)$ is minimized, while the second problem only has one optimization object that is to minimize $s(T)$. For the optimal solution T to problem 1 and the optimal solution T' to problem 2, it is easy to prove that $s(T') \le s(T)$, $|T| \le |T'|$.

3.2   Algorithm for Problem 1

If a colored digraph G is an Eulerian graph, Problem 1 is reduced to find an *Euler tour* T in G such that its *color span* $s(T)$ is minimized. If G is not an Eulerian graph, from [11] we know that G must have un-balanced vertex, and the number of such un-balanced vertex is even. For any *postman tour* of G, some edges are traversed more than once. Suppose that a *postman tour* T passes edge $e_{ij} = (v_i, v_j)$ for k_{ij} times, we add $k_{ij} - 1$ new edges between v_i and v_j and associate each new edge with the same color as e_{ij}, these new edges are called the augmented edges of e_{ij}. The resulted augmented graph is denoted as $\tilde{G}$, then $\tilde{G}$ is an Eulerian Graph, and T is an *Euler tour* of $\tilde{G}$, apparently, $s(T)$ is determined by the color of the newly added edges and the way to form the tour.

To solve Problem 1, we need augment graph G to guarantee the existence of an *Euler tour* and then from the augmented graph find such a tour with the minimum *color span*. The solution can be summarized as the following steps:

Step 1. Get $E_1 \subset E$ in G with the condition that when G is augmented with only edges in E_1, the new graph $\tilde{G}$ has an *Euler tour*.
Step 2. On the condition that step 1 is satisfied, choose E_1' that has the minimum number of edges.
Step 3. For $\tilde{G}$, augmented from G using only edges in E_1', find an *Euler tour* T, such that $s(T)$ is minimized.

When an edge set satisfies condition in step 1, it is referred to as a feasible augment edge set of G. When an edge set satisfies condition in both step 1 and step 2, it is referred to as the optimal augment edge set of G. If a tour satisfies condition in step 3, it is called the optimal tour.

In [11], the author gives an algorithm to find the optimal augment edge set for G in polynomial time, so we only need to find an optimal tour on the augmented

Eulerian graph $\tilde{G}$. In the following we will show that to find such an optimal tour on $\tilde{G}$ is a NP-Complete problem.

Theorem 1. *For a given balanced graph $G = (V, E, C)$, and an integer $k \leq |E|$, deciding if there is a tour T in G that traverses each edge once and has a color span $s(T) \leq k$ is a NP-Complete problem.*

Proof. For a given colored digraph $G = (V, E, C)$, a dual graph $\hat{G} = (U, A, \hat{C})$ can be constructed according to the following steps:

Step 1: $U = E$, that is, each edge in G corresponds to a node in $\hat{G}$. Let $u_i \in U$ corresponds to $e_i \in E$.

Step 2: For $e_i = (v_r, v_s), e_j = (v_p, v_q) \in E$, if $v_s = v_p$, that is, e_i and e_j are adjacent via node v_s in G, then $(u_i, u_j) \in A$, in $\hat{G}$.

Step 3: $\hat{C}$ has an initial value of NULL. For any $(u_i, u_j) \in A$, if $c(e_i) = c(e_j)$ in G, that is, e_i and e_j have the same color in G, then $\hat{c}(u_i, u_j) = 1$, $\hat{C} = \hat{C} \cup \{1\}$; otherwise, $\hat{C}(u_i, u_j) = n, n \in N^+$ and $n \notin \hat{C}$, $\hat{C} = \hat{C} \cup \{n\}$.

By above construction, if two adjacent edges in G have different colors, their corresponding nodes are connected in $\hat{G}$ by an edge with a color different from all the other colors assigned to edges in A.

Fig. 1 (1) (2) give a graph G and its dual graph $\hat{G}$. The label on edges of Fig.1(1) is (l, c), where l is the the edge index and the c is the color assigned to the edge. The label edges of Fig.1(2) is the color assigned to the edge. Each edge index in Fig.1(1) corresponds to a vertex in Fig.1(2).

Finding a tour T in G that traverses each edge exactly once and has $s(T) \leq k$ is equivalent to finding a simple path p in $\hat{G}$ that passes each node in $\hat{G}$ exactly once and has $s(p) \leq k - 1$. As a special case of this problem, if all edges in G have the same color, the problem is equivalent to finding a travelling salesman

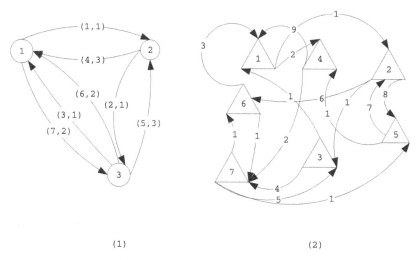

(1)   (2)

Fig. 1. A Prime Graph G (1) and its Dual Graph $\hat{G}$ (2)

path in $\hat{G}$, which is known to be a NP-C problem. So the original problem is also NP-Complete.

In the following we give a heuristic algorithm to find an *Euler tour* in G with an approximately minimum *color span* in time complexity $O(m)$, where m is the number of edges of G.

Algorithm 1: Find an *Euler tour* with an approximately minimal *color span* on a balanced digraph.

Input: $G = (V, E, C)$ /* a balanced colored digraph */
Output: An *Euler tour* with an approximately minimal *color span*.

begin
1. $i := 0$.
2. Get an arbitrary vertex $v_1 \in V$, call subroutine $getCircuit(v_1, G)$ to get a circuit T_i with v_1 as the beginning and ending vertex.
3. $G := G - T_i$, if $G = NULL$, stop and return T_i as the optimal tour.
4. Otherwise, arbitrarily select a vertex v in T_i such that $d_G^+(v) \geq 1$
5.   Call subroutine $getCircuit(v, G)$ to find a circuit C starting from and ending at v; Replace v in T_i with C to get T_{i+1};
6. $i := i + 1$; Go to step 3.
end

Procedure $getCircuit(v, G)$
Output: A circuit in G that begins with and ends at v with an approximately minimal *color span*.

begin
1. Let $\bar{E} := \{e_1, e_2, \cdots, e_k\}$ be the set of all edges in G.
2. Arbitrarily select an edge $e = (v, v') \in \bar{E}$, $T := e$;
3. $\bar{E} := \bar{E} \backslash e$, $v_1 := v$, $v_2 := v'$;
4. If $v_2 = v$, return T;
5. If $\exists e' = (v_2, v'') \in \bar{E}$ such that the color of e' is different from (v_1, v_2)
6. $T := T \cdot e'$; /* append edge e' to T */
7. otherwise arbitrarily select an edge $e' = (v_2, v'')$ from $\bar{E}$
8. $T := T \cdot e'$;
9. $e := e'$, Goto step 3;
end

Combining the algorithm to find an optimal augment edge set for G given in [11] and algorithm 1, we give a heuristic solution to Problem 1 in Algorithm 2.

Algorithm 2: A Heuristic Solution to Problem 1
Input: $G = (V, E, C)$ /* a strongly connected colored digraph */
Output: A shortest Postman Tour with an approximately minimal *color span*.

begin

1. For each $v_i \in V$, set $\sigma_i := d^-(v_i) - d^+(v_i)$.
2. If $\sigma_i = 0, i = 1 \ldots n$, then set $\tilde{G} := G$ goto step 7; Otherwise,
3. Let $S = \{v_i \in V | \sigma_i > 0\}$, $T = \{v_j \in V | \sigma_j < 0\}$. For $\forall v_i \in S, \forall v_j \in T$, find the shortest path from v_i to v_j;
4. Construct a complete bi-partite graph $H = (X, Y, E_H, W)$, with $X = \{x_{i,p} | v_i \in S, p = 1, 2, \cdots, \sigma_i\}$, $Y = \{y_{j,q} | v_j \in T, q = 1, 2, \cdots, |\sigma_j|\}$, $E_H = \{x_{i,p} y_{j,q} | x_{i,p} \in X, y_{j,q} \in Y\}$. Associates each edge $x_{i,p} y_{j,q}$ in H, $p = 1, 2, \cdots, \sigma_i$, $q = 1, 2, \cdots, |\sigma_j|$, a weight $w(v_i, v_j) \in W$, where $w(v_i, v_j)$ is the length of the shortest path between v_i and v_j in G.
5. Find the perfect match $M = \{e_1, e_2, \cdots, e_k\}$ in H, such that
$$w(M) = \sum_{e \in M} w(e) \text{ is minimized.}$$
6. For each edge $x_{i,p} y_{j,q} \in M$, suppose the shortest path between v_i and v_j in G is $P_{i,j}$, add every edge in $P_{i,j}$ to G. Set the newly augmented balanced graph as $\tilde{G}$.
7. Call Algorithm 1 to find the *Euler tour* T in $\tilde{G}$ such that $s(T)$ is minimized .
8. Return T.

end

3.3   A Heuristic Solution to Problem 2

The *color span*, $s(T)$, of an *Euler tour* T depends largely on the color of the feasible edges added to graph G and also the algorithm to find the *Euler tour*. Intuitively, a tour with less $s(T)$ can be found when the colors of the feasible edges become more. Based on such an intuition, we modify the process to find the feasible edges for G in a way such that the path formed by the feasible edges has a minimum *color span*.

Definition 1. *Given a graph $G = (V, E, C)$, the minimum color span path C_{ij} for node pair (v_i, v_j) is the one with the minimum color span value among all the paths from node v_i to v_j.*

Following we present an algorithm to find the minimum *color span* path from a given node s to every other node in a graph. The complexity of the algorithm is $O(n^2 m)$, where m, n is the number of edges and vertices of G.

Algorithm 3: Find the Minimum *color span* Paths.
Input: $G = (V, E, C), v$ /* a strongly connected colored digraph and a source node*/
Output: Minimum *color span* path from node v to every other node in G.
Notations: $l(v_i)$ - the current minimum *color span* value for all the paths from v to v_i;
$p(v_i)$ - the current minimum *color span* path from v to v_i;
$a(v_i)$ - the immediate ancestor for v_i on the current minimum *color span* path from v to v_i;
F - visited node set; M - unvisited node set.

begin

1. $l(v) := 0$, $p(v) := v$, $F := \{v\}$, $M := V\backslash\{v\}$;
2. For any $v_j \in V$ and $v_j \neq v$ /* initialization */
     $p(v_j) := NULL$;
     if $(v, v_j) \in E, l(v_j) := 1, a(v_j) := v$;
     otherwise $l(v_j) := \infty, a(v_j) := NULL$;
3. Select a node v_i in M such that $l(v_i) = \min\limits_{v_j \in M} l(v_j)$.

     If $l(v_i) = \infty$, stop, no path between v_i and all the nodes in M;
     Otherwise, $p(v_i) := p(a(v_i)) \cdot v_i$;
4. Set $F := F \cup \{v_i\}$, $M := M\backslash\{v_i\}$. If $M = \emptyset$, stop, the minimum *color span*
     paths from v to all the other nodes have been found; otherwise,
5. For all $v_j \in M$, if $(v_i, v_j) \in E$ and $l(v_j) > s(p(v_i) \cdot (v_i, v_j))$
     /* $s()$ is defined in Section 3.1. */
         set $l(v_j) := s(p(v_i) \cdot (v_i, v_j))$, $a(v_j) := v_i$;
6. Go to step 3.

end

In algorithm 2, when we augment the graph to find the shortest *postman tour*, we only search for a perfect matching in which the sum of weights of these augmented edges is minimized, and have not considered the *color span* of each augmented path. However, in problem 2, we only care about the *color span* of the final generated tour and the length of the tour is no longer an issue. An intuitive heuristic approach to problem 2 is to use path with smaller *color span* when augmenting. This is very similar to what is called the *minimax matching* problem [16].

Definition 2. *Given a bi-partite graph $H = (X, Y, E_H, W)$, M is a matching of H, let $\tilde{w}(M) = max\{w_{x_i,y_j} | (x_i, y_j) \in M\}$. If H has a maximum matching M^*, such that for all maximum matchings of H, $\tilde{w}(M^*) = min\{\tilde{w}(M)\}$, then M^* is called the minimax matching of H.*

The algorithm proposed in [10] can be modified to get the *minimax matching* of a bi-partite graph in time complexity $O(m^2)$, as shown in Algorithm 4.

Algorithm 4: Find the *Minimax Matching*.
Input: $H = (X, Y, E_H, W)$ /* Directed bi-partite graph H with assigned weight on each edge */
Output: Matching M of H such that $\max\limits_{e \in M}\{w(e)\}$ is minimized.

begin

1. For any edge in H, assign a new weight $w'(e) = W - w(e)$,
     where W is a real number larger than any $w(e), e \in E_H$;
2. Call *maximin matching* algorithm [10] to get the *maximin matching* M
     of H based on the new weight;
3. M is the *minimax matching* of the original graph H.

end

If we use the value of *color span* for each edge as the weight for each edge in the bi-partite graph H, then Algorithm 4 can be used to find a matching whose edge's maximum *color span* is the minimal among all the matchings. By combining algorithm 1, 3 and 4, we now give a heuristic algorithm for problem 2 with complexity $O(m^2 + n^2m)$, where m is the number of vertices and n is the number of edges of G.

Algorithm 5: A Heuristic Solution to Problem 2
Input: $G = (V, E, C)$ /* a strongly connected colored digraph */
Output: A *Postman Tour* with an approximately minimal *color span*.

begin

1. For each $v_i \in V$, set $\sigma_i := d^-(v_i) - d^+(v_i)$.

2. If $\sigma_i = 0, i = 1 \ldots n$, then set $\tilde{G} := G$ goto step 7; Otherwise,

3. Let $S = \{v_i \in V | \sigma_i > 0\}$, $T = \{v_j \in V | \sigma_j < 0\}$. $\forall v_i \in S, \forall v_j \in T$, find the minimum *color span* path from v_i to v_j using Algorithm 3;

4. Construct a complete bi-partite graph $H = (X, Y, E_H, W)$,with
   $X = \{x_{i,p} | v_i \in S, p = 1, 2, \cdots, \sigma_i\}$, $Y = \{y_{j,q} | v_j \in T, q = 1, 2, \cdots, |\sigma_j|\}$,
   $E_H = \{x_{i,p} y_{j,q} | x_{i,p} \in X, y_{j,q} \in Y\}$.
   Associates each edge $x_{i,p} y_{j,q}$ in H, $p = 1, 2, \cdots, \sigma_i$, $q = 1, 2, \cdots, |\sigma_j|$,
   a weight $w(v_i, v_j)$, where $w(v_i, v_j)$ is the *color span* of the
   minimum *color span* path from v_i to v_j in G.

5. Find the *minimax match* $M = \{e_1, e_2, \cdots, e_k\}$ in H using Algorithm 4.

6. For each edge $x_{i,p} y_{j,q} \in M$, suppose the minimum *color span* path between v_i and v_j in G is $C_{i,j}$, add every edge in $C_{i,j}$ to G.
   Set the newly augmented balanced graph as $\tilde{G}$.

7. Call Algorithm 1 to find the *Euler tour* T in $\tilde{G}$ such that $s(T)$ is minimized .

8. Return T.

end

4   Test Generation for Internet Telephony End System

SIP-based Internet telephony systems have become popular with the introduction of 3GPP. Service creation, as well as feature interactions, has been well studied for the Internet telephony systems [1][12][13][14]. However we haven't seen any test generation work that considers the interaction detection problem for SIP-based Internet telephony systems. In the following, we use an FSM to model an Internet telephony end system and apply the algorithms we discussed above to generate test sequences for the Internet telephony end system.

4.1   Model of the Internet Telephony End System

An Internet telephony end system can support many services and as a case study, we suppose the end system only supports the services discussed in [1],

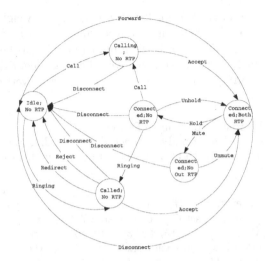

Features: Basic Call Feature; Hold; Mute; Forward; Redirect; Reject.

Fig. 2. Internet Telephony End System FSM

which include basic call functions such as call, accept, and disconnect, and also other features such as call reject, call redirect, call transfer, call hold, and mute.

Fig. 2 gives the FSM of an Internet telephony end system. Since the end system is the only entity where signaling and media flows are guaranteed to converge, the state of the end system should include both control signalling state and media state. In the FSM, each state of the end system is denoted as (*Control State*; *Audio State*), the combination of the signaling state and the audio media state. Basic call functions include the following actions: *call*, *ring*, *accept* and *disconnect*. The actions of the call hold feature include: *hold* and *unhold*; the actions of mute feature include: *mute* and *unmute*.

Fig. 3 gives the augmented graph of Fig. 2 after applying algorithm 2. There is a label $c : a$ on each transition, c is the color assigned to the transition, and a is the action that results in this transition. For this example FSM, since every shortest path used by algorithm 2 in finding the *perfect match* is also the minimum *color span* path, the same augmented graph can be generated when applying algorithm 5.

Using algorithm 1, we generate the following *Euler tour T* for Fig. 3:
$Call \rightarrow Accept \rightarrow Hold \rightarrow Disconnect \rightarrow Call \rightarrow Accept \rightarrow Hold \rightarrow Call \rightarrow Disconnect \rightarrow Call \rightarrow Accept \rightarrow Hold \rightarrow Ring \rightarrow Reject \rightarrow Call \rightarrow Accept \rightarrow Hold \rightarrow Unhold \rightarrow Mute \rightarrow Disconnect \rightarrow Ring \rightarrow Redirect \rightarrow Ring \rightarrow Accept \rightarrow Mute \rightarrow Unmute \rightarrow Forward \rightarrow Ring \rightarrow Accept \rightarrow Disconnect$

The corresponding color sequence for this test sequence is:
$CS(T) = 11211121111216112231151134111$, and its *color span* is $s(T) = 4$.

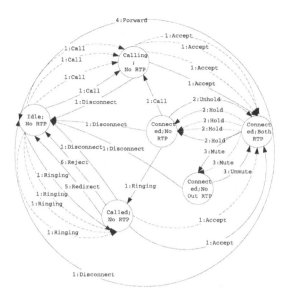

Color Assignment: 1: Basic Call Feature; 2: Hold; 3: Mute; 4: Forward; 5: Redirect; 6:Reject

Fig. 3. Augmented Graph for Internet Telephony End System FSM

5   Test Generation for LMP

5.1   Introduction to LMP

Generalized Multiprotocol Label Switching (GMPLS) is being standardized by Internet Engineering Task Force (IETF) to serve as an integral protocol for the next generation of data networks. Link Management Protocol (LMP)[15] is one of the control plane components of GMPLS, and it provides the fundamental functions to support GMPLS routing and signaling protocols.

The features of LMP include: control channel management, link property correlation, link connectivity verification, and fault management. Control Channel Management allows two nodes in optical network to establish and maintain control channels between adjacent nodes. Link Property Correlation allows two nodes in optical network to automatically exchange their TE link properties, verify the TE link configuration. Link Connectivity Verification provides functions such that two nodes in optical network can discover their data plane neighbor, exchange their interface ID, and verify their physical connectivity. Fault Management makes nodes in optical network suppress downstream alarms, localize faults for protection and restoration.

LMP features are specified using the Control Channel FSM, the Data Link FSM and the TE Link FSM in the LMP draft [15]. In most cases, Control Channel Management controls the state transition of a control channel, Link Property Correlation controls the state of a TE link, while behaviors of Link Connectivity Verification and Fault Management can change the state transition of a data link.

On the other hand, these features are not independent, they interact with each other via the operation on the shared state machine. For example, Link Property Correlation can change a data link's state when it finds the data link property is not correlated in both sides, Control Channel Management can change a TE link's state when there is no active control channels for the TE link.

Some feature interaction problems of LMP have been identified in [2]. In the following, we study the feature interaction testing problem of LMP.We use the active data link FSM of LMP as an example, applying algorithm 2 to generate a test sequence to guarantee that each transition is traversed at least once and the operations of different features are interleaved with each other as much as possible such that their interactions can be checked.

5.2   Data Link Model of LMP

Fig. 4 shows the active LMP data link FSM. The label on each transition is $c : i/o$, where c is the color assigned to the transition, i is the input event for the transition and o is the output event of the transition. Explanation of the transitions are given in the following table, in which ! represents the event of sending out a message and ? represents the event of receiving a message.

Inputs:
1 :   evCCUp: Control channel has gone up.
2 :   evCCDown: LMP neighbor connectivity is lost.
3 :   ?msgBeginVerifyAck: Receive BeginVerifyAck message.
4 :   ?msgBeginVerifyOK: Receive correct BeginVerify message.
5:      ?msgTstSuccess: Receive TestStatusSuccess message.

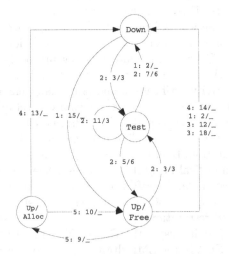

Color Assignment: 1: CCM; 2: LCV; 3: LPC; 4: FM; 5: LDP.

Fig. 4. Active LMP Data Link FSM

6 : ?msgTestOK: Receive compatible Test message.

7 : ?msgTstStatusFailure: Receive TestStatusFailure message.

8 : evPsvTestFail: VerifyDeadInterval has expired.

9 : evLnkAlloc: Allocate the data link.

10: evLnkDealloc: Deallocate the data link.

11: evTestRet: A retransmission timer expires.

12: ?msgLinkSumErr: Receive error LinkSummary.

13: evLocalizeFail: FM localizes a Failure.

14: evDlDown: The data link is down.

15: inBandConfigOK: Link is ready for path establishment.

16: evTstFail: Verification fails.

17: ?msgEndVerify: Receive EndVerify message.

18: ?msgLinkSumNack: Receive LinkSummaryNack message.

Output:

1 :   !msgBeginVerify: Send out BeginVerify message.

2 :   !msgBeginVerifyAck: Send out BeginVerifyAck message.

3 :   !msgTest: Send out Test message.

4 :   !msgTestSuccess: Send out TestSuccess message.

5 :   !msgTestFailure: Send out TestFailure message.

6 :   !msgTstStatusAck: Send out TstStatusAck message.

7:         !msgEndVerify: Send out EndVerify message.

8:         !msgEndVerifyAck: Send out EndVerifyAck message.

9:         !msgBeginVerifyNack: Send out EndVerifyNack message.

10:        !msgLinkSumNack: Send out LinkSumNack message.

5.3   Optimal Test Sequence for LMP

Fig. 5 shows the balanced augmentation of the active LMP data link FSM. Since the shortest paths adopted to augment Fig. 4 is also the minimum *color span* paths, the same augmented graph will be generated no matter which of algorithm 2 and algorithm 5 is used. In Fig. 5 the dashed links are the links augmented to Fig. 4. There is a label (l, c) on each link, l is a label assigned to the link and c is the color of the link.

Using algorithm 1, we get an *Euler tour* T_1 for Fig. 5:
$T_1 = 1, 3, 2, 4, 12, 9, 11, 13, 10, 8, 17, 14, 18, 15, 20, 16, 7, 5, 6, 19$. Its corresponding color sequence is $CS(T_1) = 21221541553131412221$, and its *color span* is $s(T_1) = 3$. The following gives the test sequence corresponding to tour T_1.
?msgBeginVerifyAck/!msgTest → evCCDown/_ → ?msgBeginVerifyAck/ !msgTest → ?msgTstStatusFailure/ !msgTstStatusAck → inBandConfigOK/_ → evLnkAlloc/_ → evLocalizeFail/_ → inBandConfigOK/_ → evLnkAlloc/_ → evLnkDealloc/_ → ?msgLinkSumErr/ !msgLinkSumNack → inBandConfigOK/_ → ?msgLinkSumNack/_ → inBandConfigOK/_ → evDlDown/_ → inBandConfigOK/_ → ?msgBeginVerifyAck/!msgTest → evTestRet/!msgTest → ?msgTstSuccess/!msgTstStatusAck → evCCDown/_

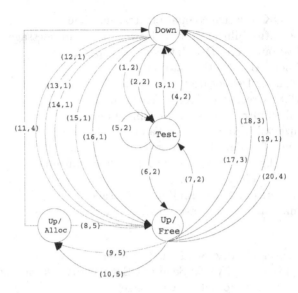

Color Assignment: 1: CCM; 2: LCV; 3: LPC; 4: FM; 5: LDP.

Fig. 5. Symmetric Augmentation of the Active LMP Data Link FSM

6   Conclusion

In this paper, a technique is proposed to generate optimal conformance test sequences for the purpose of feature interaction detection for a complex feature-rich communication system. A feature-rich communication system may offer many features and these features can be implemented in multiple processes and as a result their operations can interleave with each other. Whether or not the implemented system can work correctly when such an interleaving occurs needs to be verified. We define a parameter *color span* to measure the extent of the interactions between different features, propose an algorithm to find test sequences with minimum length and minimum color span such that all the transitions of the FSM are traversed at least once and the features of the system are interleaved with each other as much as possible.

With the protocol being modelled as a finite-state machine, the same approach can be used for many other purposes such as inter-operability testing and fault detection. Some state verification techniques such as UIO sequences can also be combined to make the algorithm more powerful and practical.

Acknowledgement

We are indebted to the colleagues in Bell Labs Research China for the valuable comments and stimulating discussions.

References

1. Xiaotao Wu, Henning Schulzrinne, "Feature Interactions in Internet Telephony End Systems", Technical Report, Department of Computer Science, Columbia University, January 2004.
2. Caixia Chi, Dong Wang, Ruibing Hao, "A Framework on Feature Interactions in Optical Network Protocols", Feature Interaction Workshop'2003, June 2003.
3. Alfred V.Aho, Anton T.Dahbura, David Lee, and M.Ümit Uyar, "An Optimization Technique for Protocol Conformance Test Generation Based on UIO Sequences and Rural Chinese Postman Tours", IEEE Tran. on Communications, Vol.39,NO.11, Nov.1991, 1604-1615.
4. David Lee, Mihalis Yannakakis, "Principles and Methods of Testing Finite State Machines - A Survey", Proceedings of the IEEE, Vol.84,No.8,August 1996.
5. T.S.Chow,"Testing software design modeled by finite-state machines ",IEEE Trans. Software Eng. Vol.SE-4,No.3,pp.178-187,1978.
6. K.K.Sabnani and A.T.Dahbura,"A protocol test generation procedure", Computer Networks and ISDN Syst.Vol.15,No.4,pp285-297,1988.
7. S.Naito and M.Tsunoyama,"Fault detection for sequential machines by transitions tours", in Proc.IEEE Fault Tolerant Comput. Symp.,IEEE Computer Soc.Press,pp.238-243,1981.
8. T. H. Cormen, C. E. Leiserson and R. L. Rivest, Introduction to Algorithms. The MIT Press, 1997.
9. J.A.Bondy and U.S.R.Murty, Graph Theory With Applications. New York: Elsevier North Holland,1976.
10. Gross O. The bottleneck assignment problem: an algorithm. In: Procedings, and Symposium on Mathematical Programming(Wolfe Ped), Rand Publication, 1960,87-88.
11. A.Gibbons, Algorithmic Graph Theory. Cambridge, MA:Cambridge University Press,1985.
12. John de Keijzer, Douglas Tait, and Rob Goedman, "JAIN: a new approach to services in communication networks". IEEE Communications Magazine, 38(1), January 2000.
13. Jonathan Lennox and Henning Schulzrinne, "Feature interaction in Internet telephony", In Feature Interaction in Telecommunications and Software Systems VI, Glasgow, United Kingdom, May 2000.
14. J. Rosenberg, J. Lennox, and Henning Schulzrinne. "Programming Internet telephony services". IEEE Network, 13(3):42C49, May/June 1999.
15. Jonathan P. Lang, "Link Management Protocol (LMP)", Internet draft, draft-ietf-ccamp-lmp-10.txt, October 2003, work in progress.
16. K. Imai, S. Sumino and H. Imai," Minimax Geometric Fitting of Two Corresponding Sets of Points and Dynamic Furthest Voronoi Diagrams", IEICE Transactions on Information and Systems, Vol.E81-D, No.11 (November 1998), pp.1162-1171.

Fault Detection of Hierarchical Networks with Probabilistic Testing Algorithms

Keqin Li[1] and David Lee[2]

[1] Bell Labs Research, Lucent Technologies
[2] Department of Computer Science and Engineering,
The Ohio State University

Abstract. As communications networks are expanding to larger areas the control and maintenance of routing information are becoming a formidable task. To cope with its size and complexity and to make the network reliable and scalable hierarchical network has been proposed with new features to support the information infrastructure. However, the network hierarchy adds more complications to the network design and implementations and that hampers the network reliability and quality of services. Conformance testing is known to be a powerful tool for network fault detection yet most of the works in the published literature are on networks without hierarchy. We present probabilistic algorithms for testing hierarchical networks along with the added features. Based on a formal model of the networks, we provide a formal analysis that shows that our probabilistic algorithms guarantee a high fault coverage with a feasible number of tests. To further reduce the number of tests we identify test equivalence classes and that enables us to significantly reduce the number of tests yet without losing the fault coverage. Experimental results on Internet OSPF protocol are reported.

1 Introduction

Networks are indispensable for our daily communications, including PSTN (Public Switched Telephone Network), ATM, wireless, and Internet. With the expanding networks and new and sophisticated services, which are demanded by the user applications, the networks become more complex, and their reliability and scalability pose a challenge yet are essential for the QoS (Quality of Services). For the reliability of a large network, a key function is to ensure correct routing of information, and, consequently, routing protocols play a critical role. In this work we investigate conformance testing of routing protocols that checks whether an implementation of a routing protocol conforms to its specification.

As networks grow in size, the control and maintenance of routing information become difficult if not impossible. In order to improve the scalability of routing systems, hierarchy is introduced into networks [10] where large networks are partitioned into several subdomains. The routing information within a subdomain is first aggregated and then shared with other subdomains; the detailed internal network structure of a subdomain is hidden from each other while networking

F. Khendek and R. Dssouli (Eds.): TestCom 2005, LNCS 3502, pp. 258–274, 2005.

devices in different subdomains are still reachable from each other. Hierarchy in PSTN [18], PNNI [2] in ATM network, and OSPF [15] [16] in Internet are typical hierarchical mechanisms in networks.

The telephone networks worldwide are classical hierarchical routing networks [18]. Telephone-switching offices or exchanges are classified according to their level in a hierarchy. Routing in PSTN is performed as follows. When a call is coming, the switch checks its routing database to match the prefix of the destination phone number. If there is a match, the call is routed to the next switch. Otherwise, the call is routed to the higher-level switch/exchange. When the call arrives at the destination switch, the suffix of the number is checked for ringing the callee phone.

The PNNI (Private Network-Network Interface) [2] protocol provides mechanisms to support scalable, QoS-based ATM routing and switch-to-switch Switched Virtual Connection (SVC) interoperability. To create a PNNI network hierarchy, ATM switches at the lowest hierarchical level can be organized into multiple peer groups, each of which elects a Peer Group Leader (PGL) and its parent node becomes active. The purpose of the active parent node, or Logical Group Node (LGN), is to represent the entire peer group to other LGNs. Within each peer group, all nodes exchange complete topology database information among them. However, the LGN reduces the amount of information shared with other peer groups by sending only a limited amount of aggregated information to its neighbor LGNs, which in turn flood that information down to all nodes within their child peer group.

In order to improve scalability, a two level hierarchy is proposed in OSPF [15] [16], which is a widely used routing protocol in the Internet. An Autonomous System (AS) is divided into areas. Each area has been assigned an area ID and contains a group of routers, called Internal Routers. In order to avoid routing loops, these areas are organized in a hub-and-spoke structure. Area 0 is the backbone area and all the other areas attach to area 0 by one or more Area Border Routers (ABR). Routers in area 0 is at level 1 and all the other routers at level 2; it is a two-level hierarchy.

Routers in one area operate as if there is no hierarchy imposed. The routers originate and exchange LSAs (Link State Advertisement) which contains the topology update information so that each router has an identical Link State Database (LSDB), which represents the topology of the area for routing table computation. In each routing table entry, destination, cost to the destination and nexthop are specified. Note that the destinations of routing table entries are all in this area. Since an ABR belongs to multiple areas, logically there is one routing table entry for each area to which an ABR belongs.

In order to make the destinations in one area at level 2, e.g., area 1, reachable for routers and hosts outside the area, Summary-LSAs are originated and advertised outside the area by ABRs. The main fields of Summary-LSA are destination and metric to the destination. For each entry of area 1's routing table, a Summary-LSA is originated, in which the destination field is the destination of the routing table entry, and the metric field is the cost. This procedure is referred to as summarization.

In order to reduce the control traffic, a procedure referred to as aggregation is used. In an ABR of an area at level 2, e.g., area 1, several address ranges can be configured, and each address range can cover several entries in a routing table. For each address range, the ABR originates one Summary-LSA, instead of several Summary-LSAs from these routing table entries.

Upon receiving a Summary-LSA originating by an ABR, the router performs inter-area route calculation. One inter-area routing table entry is generated for each Summary-LSA received. In the routing table entry, the destination is the one described in the Summary-LSA, the cost is the sum of cost to the ABR and the metric specified in the Summary-LSA, and the nexthop is the same as the nexthop to the ABR.

In summary, when an AS is divided into areas and ABRs are designated, the following additional operations are performed by routers in the AS:

- Summary-LSA origination, performed by ABRs; and
- Inter-area route calculation, performed by every router.

To establish hierarchy in networks, new features are added into routing systems of networking devices. For example, when a hierarchy is structured in OSPF, router needs to originate a new type of Link State Advertisement (LSA) and perform different routing table calculations. These new features and operations are essential for the reliability of hierarchical networks. On the other hand, the implementations of the hierarchical OSPF are rather complex, and practical experiences show [15] that the hierarchy of OSPF is also a source of implementation faults and that often leads to the degradation of Internet performances. Consequently, their conformance testing is essential for the correct implementations of the OSPF routing protocol.

Currently, most testing tools conduct a test of routers in an isolated environment and check the conformance of router's behaviors in accordance with RFCs. Available commercial tools include Agilent RouterTester [1], Spirent AX/4000 and SmartBits TeraRouting Tester [19] and IXIA IxANVL [9]. A main function of these tools is to generate a set of tests corresponding to each of the requirements in the design/RFC for "typical" network configurations/topologies. Most of these tools also test on the hierarchical features of OSPF, yet in an ad hoc way and on a static network environment.

We study conformance testing of hierarchy features of routing protocols of networking devices. We propose probabilistic testing algorithms on routers connected to the networks and in a dynamic environment. Furthermore, we study test equivalence class of network configurations to selectively test representative configurations; we can significantly cut down the configurations to test yet without sacrificing the fault coverage. We provide a formal analysis of the fault coverage of our probabilistic algorithms and show that a high fault coverage can be guaranteed yet with a reasonable testing cost.

Given its importance in the current Internet, the testing of hierarchy of OSPF is our focus of investigation, and we take it as a case study of our general theory.

The rest of the paper is organized as follows. In Section 2, we describe a formal model of hierarchical networks and the basics of conformance testing with OSPF as a case study. We then discuss in Section 3 equivalence classes of network topologies and present our probabilistic algorithms for testing the hierarchy features with a fault coverage analysis. Experimental results on Cisco and Zebra OSPF implementations are reported in Section 4.

2   Conformance Testing and Modeling

In recent years, there are a lot of activities in the area of protocol conformance testing. We only mention a few related publications here. For instance, [17] highlights works in the area of algorithmic test generation from formal specifications with fault model-driven test derivation, [4], [5] and [6] describe methods for testing real time systems with fault coverage analysis, and [3] and [12] contain a survey.

As an important and complex routing protocol, testing of OSPF has been studied [8] [21], however, the approaches are on OSPF protocols without hierarchy. In this case, a bipartite graph $G_b = < R, W, E_b >$ is used to model the network in which RUT (Router Under Test) locates. As in Figure 1, Router Nodes in the set R represent routers in the network, and Network Nodes in the set W are used to model networks or LANs (Local Area Network). Edges in set E_b connect Router Nodes and Network Nodes, i.e., a router is in a LAN. A router can be in more than one LAN and a LAN can contain more than one router. For the completeness of tested network configurations and topologies, the number of Network Nodes $m = |W|$ has to satisfy $m = \lfloor \frac{n}{2} \rfloor \lceil \frac{n}{2} \rceil$ where $n = |R|$ is the number of Router Nodes [8].

In order to test hierarchical OSPF, a two-level bipartite graph can be used to model the network in which RUT locates. It can be considered as an extension of the basic model in Figure 1.

At the first level, a bipartite graph $G_0 = < R_0, W_0, ABR, E_0 >$ is used to model the backbone area 0 as in Figure 2 where

- $R_0 = \{r_x^{(0)} | x = 1, 2, \cdots, n_0\}$ is the set of $n_0 = |R_0|$ Internal Router Nodes in area 0.

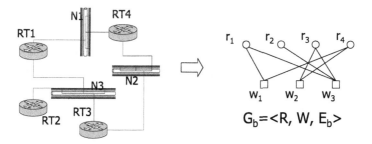

Fig. 1. Basic Model

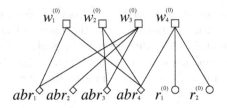

Fig. 2. The First Level Bipartite Graph

- $W_0 = \{w_x^{(0)}|x = 1, 2, \cdots, m_0\}$ is the set of $m_0 = |W_0|$ Network Nodes in area 0.
- $ABR = \{abr_x|x = 1, 2, \cdots, k\}$ is the set of $k = |ABR|$ ABR Nodes in area 0.
- E_0 is the set of edges connecting router and network nodes.

For instance, internal router nodes $r_1^{(0)}$ and $r_2^{(0)}$ are connected together with ABR router node abr_4 by network (LAN) node $w_4^{(0)}$; and ABR nodes abr_3 and abr_4 are connected by network node $w_2^{(0)}$.

A second level bipartite graph $G_i =< R_i, W_i, ABR_i, E_i >$ is used to model a non-backbone area $i(i \neq 0)$. In Figure 3, area 1, which connects to abr_1 in Figure 2, is expanded as an example.

- $R_i = \{r_x^{(i)}|x = 1, 2, \cdots, n_i\}$ is the set of $n_i = |R_i|$ Internal Routers in area i.
- $W_i = \{w_x^{(i)}|x = 1, 2, \cdots, m_i\}$ is the set of $m_i = |W_i|$ Network Nodes in area i.
- ABR_i is the set of $b_i = |ABR_i|$ ABR Nodes in area i. In OSPF, all ABRs must attach to the backbone area, thus, $ABR_i \subseteq ABR$.
- E_i is the set of edges connecting router nodes and network nodes in area i.

When all the ABR Nodes are expanded the whole two-level bipartite graph is in Figure 4. Note that more than one ABR router can be in a same area. Suppose that there are l non-backbone areas. Then, there are n_0 internal non-

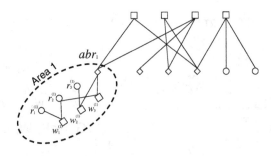

Fig. 3. A Second Level Bipartite Graph

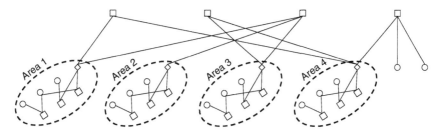

Fig. 4. The Two-Level Bipartite Graph Model

ABR router nodes in the backbone area 0, $\sum_{i=1}^{l} n_i$ internal non-ABR router nodes in the l non-backbone areas at the second level, and $\sum_{i=1}^{l} b_l = k$ ABR routers.

For clarity, we make the following assumptions.

No Range Assumption. *An ABR only advertises metrics to Internal Router Nodes in the areas to which it attaches, i.e., no address range is configured at ABR.*

Link Cost Assumption. *All the link costs from Router Node to Network Node are 1, and all the link costs from Network Node to Router Node are 0.*

Single Entry Assumption. *There is only one ABR per non-backbone area.* Note that the above assumptions are only for clarity and that they can be relaxed or modified with due changes in our algorithms.

With these assumptions, the whole hierarchical network contains k ABR Nodes, the number of non-backbone areas is also k, i.e., $l = k, b_i = 1(1 \leq i \leq k)$, the total number of routers is $\sum_{i=0}^{k} n_i + k$, and the total number of networks is $\sum_{i=0}^{k} m_i$.

Based on the formal model, we now present our probabilistic testing algorithms.

3   Probabilistic Testing Algorithms

In order to test the behaviors of the RUT in dynamic environment in a structured manner, we need to generate all the possible network topologies, and, taking each network topology as a test case, we check the RUT. However, it is formidable to generate and test all the possible topologies. We need to reduce

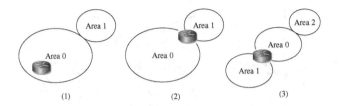

Fig. 5. Positions of RUT

the number of test cases without losing the fault coverage. We achieve this by the following two approaches: identifying test equivalence classes and randomization.

A randomized algorithm is an algorithm that uses random numbers to influence the choices it makes in the course of its computation. Once viewed as a tool in computational number theory, it has by now found widespread applications, fueled by the two major benefits of randomization: simplicity and speed. Randomized algorithms have been used for conformance testing. For instance, [11] applies a random walk for fault detection. For many applications, a randomized algorithm is the fastest algorithm available, or the simplest, or both [7]. [13] and [14] provide a comprehensive introduction survey of paradigms underlying randomized algorithms.

We are focused on testing the hierarchy of OSPF. Since Summary-LSA origination and inter-area route calculation are two new functions/features from the hierarchy of OSPF, we conduct tests on their implementations and analyze the fault coverage. According to the different positions and hence functions of RUT in an AS, different testing algorithms are needed, as enumerated in Figure 5:

1. RUT is an internal router. In this case, RUT receives Summary-LSA and performs inter-area route calculation. When RUT is an internal router in a non-backbone (level 2) area, it receives Summary-LSAs originated by one ABR. And when it is in the backbone (level 1) area, it receives Summary-LSAs originated by multiple ABRs. Thus, the testing algorithm for internal router in the backbone (level 1) area can test internal router in non-backbone (level 2) area. In the following, we only consider the case in which RUT is an internal router in the backbone (level 1) area.
2. RUT is an ABR and there is only one non-backbone (level 2) area. In this case, RUT originates Summary-LSA, but no inter-area route calculation is performed.
3. RUT is an ABR and there are two or more non-backbone (level 2) area. In this case, RUT performs Summary-LSA origination and also inter-area route calculation.

According to the three different cases, we design and analyze the corresponding probabilistic testing algorithms.

3.1   Internal Router in Backbone Area 0

In this subsection, we consider the case when RUT is an Internal Router in the backbone area 0. In this case, RUT receives Summary-LSA and performs inter-area route calculation. We first identify equivalent Summary-LSAs advertised by ABRs; we only need to test on one Summary-LSA among each equivalence class and that significantly reduces the number of tests. We then present a probabilistic testing algorithms to test the inter-area route calculation by RUT with a fault coverage analysis. Recall that in this case the following functions of an ABR have to be tested. An RUT in area 0 receives Summary-LSAs originated by ABRs, and calculates/updates inter-area routes accordingly. Therefore, the inter-area route calculation is to be checked. We only need to consider ABRs, which are reachable from RUT.

Since an ABR summarizes the topology of a non-backbone area by Summary-LSAs, the topologies of this non-backbone area are invisible to RUT. The inter-area route calculation is conducted by the combination of the known topology of area 0 and Summary-LSAs originated by ABRs.

Under the *No Range Assumption*, ABR_i advertises metrics to the internal routers $r_1^{(i)}, r_2^{(i)}, \cdots, r_{n_i}^{(i)}$ in area i where $(1 \leq i \leq k)$. These Summary-LSAs can be taken as a Distance Vector $v^{(i)} = (v_1^{(i)}, v_2^{(i)}, \cdots, v_{n_i}^{(i)})$, advertised into area 0. For a reachable Internal Router Node $r_j^{(i)} (1 \leq j \leq n_i)$, $v_j^{(i)}$ is the length of the shortest path from ABR_i to this Router Node. Under the *Link Cost Assumption*, it is obvious that $v_j^{(i)} \geq 1 (1 \leq i \leq k, 1 \leq j \leq n_i)$.

In order to generate all the possible topologies in area i, the number of LANs in this area is at least $m_i = \lfloor \frac{n_i+1}{2} \rfloor \lceil \frac{n_i+1}{2} \rceil$. It is obvious that $m_i \geq n_i (n_i \geq 1)$. Obviously, the longest path from ABR_i to an Internal Router is n_i. As a convention, if $r_j^{(i)}$ is not reachable from ABR_i, we set $v_j^{(i)} = \infty$.

Proposition 1. *If an internal router node $r_j^{(i)}$ is reachable from ABR_i, then $1 \leq v_j^{(i)} \leq n_i (1 \leq i \leq k, 1 \leq j \leq n_i)$. Otherwise, $v_j^{(i)} = \infty$.*

Consider the distance vector advertised by ABR_i from area i, i.e., $v^{(i)} = (v_1^{(i)}, v_2^{(i)}, \cdots, v_{n_i}^{(i)})$. We construct $u^{(i)} = (u_1^{(i)}, u_2^{(i)}, \cdots, u_{n_i}^{(i)})$ where

$$u_j^{(i)} = \begin{cases} 1, & \text{if } v_j^{(i)} < \infty \\ \infty, & \text{if } v_j^{(i)} = \infty \end{cases} \quad 1 \leq j \leq n_i.$$

Then we construct $\overline{u^{(i)}}$, which is obtained by permuting components of $u^{(i)}$.

Since we only consider ABR_i's, which are reachable from RUT, its cost (path length) is finite x. Therefore, the n_i internal nodes in area i correspond to n_i entries in the routing table of RUT, and their costs are $x + u_j^{(i)}, j = 1, \cdots, n_i$, respectively. It is natural to assume that the correctness of the routing table computation of RUT is not affected by the permutation of the internal nodes in an area i, which correspond to the identical n_i entries in the routing table; we claim that they are equivalent.

In summary, for each area i, we have a set of $n_i + 1$ Characteristic Distance Vectors, each of which represents an equivalence class of distance vectors:

$$\left\{ \underbrace{(\infty, \infty, \cdots, \infty)}_{n_i}, \underbrace{(1, \infty, \cdots, \infty)}_{n_i}, \underbrace{(1, 1, \cdots, \infty)}_{n_i}, \cdots, \underbrace{(1, 1, \cdots, 1)}_{n_i} \right\}. \text{ For each } ABR_i,$$

we only need to test these $n_i + 1$ vectors. However, there are still $\prod_{i=1}^{k} n_i$ possible combinations of Characteristic Distance Vectors to test, and it is impossible to test on each of them in real OSPF networks. We apply probabilistic algorithms [8] with the following constants, parameters and variables:

1. k (input parameter): number of non-backbone areas;
2. $n_0, n_1, n_2, \cdots, n_k$ (input parameters): number of internal routers in area 0, 1, 2, $\cdots$, k respectively;
3. $0 \le p_1, p_2, p_3, p_4 \le 1$ (input parameters): probability of edge insertion, node insertion, edge deletion, and node deletion, respectively in area 0; $p_1 + p_2 + p_3 + p_4 = 1$.
4. $G_0 = <R_0, W_0, ABR, E_0>$ (variable): topology graph of area 0 with internal router nodes R_0, network nodes W_0, set of ABR nodes ABR, and edges E_0;
5. $v^{(1)}, v^{(2)}, \cdots, v^{(k)}$ (variable): distance vectors advertised by ABR_1, ABR_2, $\cdots$, ABR_k, respectively, into area 0;
6. $v_0 \in R_0$ (constant): router under test.

Algorithm 1
Input: $k, n_0, n_1, n_2, \cdots, n_k, 0 \le p_1, p_2, p_3, p_4 \le 1$
Output: implementation fault in hierarchy of OSPF or conformance

```
1.  repeat
2.       Construct initial network topology graph G_0 with
         R_0 = {v_0}, W_0 = ABR = E_0 = φ;
3.       while (G_0 is not a complete graph)
4.            UPDATE(G_0);
5.            if ROUTE(G_0) = FALSE;
6.                 return "faulty";
7.       end-while
8.  end-repeat
9.  return "conforms"
```

The algorithm is probabilistic in nature. Line 2 constructs an initial network topology graph G_0 of area 0 with only one router node: v_0 (RUT). The while-loop from Line 3 to Line 7 continues until a complete bipartite graph is obtained. Subroutine UPDATE(G_0) in Line 4 gets a new network topology of area 0. Subroutine ROUTE(G_0) in Line 5 generates distance vectors advertised by ABRs, and checks LSDB and routing table of RUT. If any faults are detected, the process is aborted and "faulty" is reported in Line 6. Otherwise, after sufficient repetition of the repeat-loop from Line 1 to Line 8, "conforms" is declared in Line 9 with a good confidence in the topologies and router behaviors that have been tested.

Subroutine UPDATE(G_0)

In Algorithm 1, while-loop is repeated until network topology graph of area 0 becomes a complete bipartite graph. Each repetition of the loop runs the subroutine UPDATE(G_0) in Line 4, which updates G_0 incrementally.

Subroutine UPDATE(G_0)

Parameters: $n_0, m_0, 0 \le p_1, p_2, p_3, p_4 \le 1$
Variables: $G_0 = < R_0, W_0, ABR, E_0 >$

```
1.   switch(p)
2.       case 'p₁': if( |E₀| < (|R₀| + |ABR|) * |W₀| )
3.           /* graph is not complete */
4.           insert an edge u.a.r. in E₀;
5.       case 'p₂': if( |R₀| + |ABR| + |W₀| < n₀ + m₀ )
6.           /* nodes below upper bounds */
7.           insert a node u.a.r. in R₀ ∪ ABR ∪ W₀;
8.           Add all related physical links to E₀.
9.       case 'p₃': if( |E₀| > 0 )
10.          /* edge set is not empty */
11.          delete an edge u.a.r. from E₀;
12.      case 'p₄': if( |R₀| + |ABR| + |W₀| > 1 )
13.          /* node set is not empty */
14.          delete a node u.a.r. from R₀ ∪ ABR ∪ W₀;
15.          Remove all related physical links from E₀;
16.  return
```

For a network topology, one of the four operations on edge or node insertion or deletion is performed with probability $0 \le p_1, p_2, p_3, p_4 \le 1$. We can partition the unit interval into four subintervals $I_1 = [a_0, a_1), I_2 = [a_1, a_2), I_3 = [a_2, a_3), I_4 = [a_3, a_4]$ with $|I_1| = p_1, |I_2| = p_2, |I_3| = p_3, |I_4| = p_4$. We then sample uniformly at random (u.a.r.) in the unit interval and obtain $0 \le p \le 1$. We then "switch" on the value of p in Line 1. Specifically, depending on $p \in I_i, i = 1, 2, 3, 4$, one of the cases is executed at Line 2, 5, 9, or 12. This subroutine is similar to the corresponding one described in [8] and we omit the details.

Subroutine ROUTE(G_0)

In Algorithm 1, once G_0 is updated, the subroutine ROUTE(G_0) is called. This subroutine has the following functions:

1. Generating distance vectors advertised by ABRs into area 0;
2. Calculating routing update information, i.e., Link State Update packets (LSU packets), and sending to RUT;
3. Obtaining LSDB and routing table from RUT, and checking correctness.

Function 2 and 3 are similar to the corresponding ones described in [8]. The subroutine ROUTE(G_0) is described in the following where Line 4 is for Function 2 and 3.

Subroutine ROUTE(G_0)

    1.   **for** $i \leftarrow 1$ **until** k **do**
    2.   generate 1 possible value of $v^{(i)}$ u.a.r.;
    3.   **for** each possible combination $< v^{(1)}, v^{(2)}, \cdots, v^{(k)} >$ **do**
    4.   <Function 2 and 3>

In this subroutine, the one vector of area i is generated uniformly at random. Thus, the calculation and correctness checking operations are performed only once for each topology in area 0.

Combining Distance Vector
Recall that we only take into account ABRs which are reachable from RUT and there are k of them. For $ABR_i, i = 1, \cdots, k$, there are n_i distinct Characteristic Distance Vectors, which we have to test on, and there are a total of $\prod_{i=1}^{k} n_i$. It can be shown that each of them is to be tested by Algorithm 1 with a non-zero probability.

Fault Coverage
The inter-area route calculation/update is performed upon receiving each Summary-LSAs, and a reasonable fault model is that a calculation, which is based on a specific Summary-LSA, is performed incorrectly. This is often referred to as a single-fault model. A single fault involves an ABR Node ABR_x that is reachable from RUT and an internal router $r_y^{(x)}$ of area x. When ABR_x advertises a Summary-LSA destined for $r_y^{(x)}$ to area 0, RUT calculates inter-area route to $r_y^{(x)}$ incorrectly.

We present the following result on fault coverage. Due to space limit we omit the proof.

Proposition 2. *There exists a polynomial $P(k, n_0, n_1, \cdots, n_k)$ such that for any $0 < \varepsilon \leq 1$, with no more than $P(k, n_0, n_1, \cdots, n_k) \ln \frac{1}{\varepsilon}$ repetitions of the repeat-loop in Algorithm 1, any single-fault is to be detected with a probability at least $1 - \varepsilon$.*

It shows that with a polynomial number of tests Algorithm 1 detects any single fault with a high probability.

3.2   Area Border Router: Only One Non-backbone Area

In this subsection, we consider the case when RUT is an ABR and there is only one non-backbone level 2 area, i.e., area 1. In this case, RUT originates Summary-LSA, but no inter-area route calculation is needed since there is only one level 2 area. We present a probabilistic testing algorithm to test the Summary-LSA origination feature with a fault coverage analysis. Recall that in this case the following functions of an ABR have to be tested:

- Area 0 Summary-LSA origination. RUT originates Summary-LSA from area 1 into the backbone area. This function is only determined by the topology of area 1, more specifically, by the routing table of area 1.
- Area 1 Summary-LSA origination. RUT originates Summary-LSA from area 0 into the non-backbone area 1. This function is only determined by the topology of area 0, more specifically, by the routing table of area 0.

Testing Algorithm

We present a probabilistic testing algorithm with the following:

1. n_0, n_1(input parameters): number of internal routers in area 0 and area 1;
2. $0 \leq p_1, p_2, p_3, p_4 \leq 1$(input parameters): probability of edge insertion, node insertion, edge deletion, and node deletion, respectively in area 0; $p_1 + p_2 + p_3 + p_4 = 1$.
3. v_0 (constant): router under test.
4. $G_0 = < R_0, W_0, \{v_0\}, E_0 >$ (variable): topology graph of area 0 with internal router nodes R_0, network nodes W_0, an ABR node v_0, and edges E_0;
5. $G_1 = < R_1, W_1, \{v_0\}, E_1 >$ (variable): topology graph of area 1 with internal router nodes R_1, network nodes W_1, an ABR node v_0, and edges E_1.

Algorithm 2

input: $n_0, n_1, 0 \leq p_1, p_2, p_3, p_4 \leq 1$
output: implementation fault in hierarchy of OSPF or conformance

1. **repeat**
2.   construct initial network topology graph G_0 with $R_0 = W_0 = E_0 = \phi$;
3.   **while**(G_0 is not a complete graph)
4.   UPDATE(G_0);
5.   GENERATE(G_1);
6.   **if** ROUTE(G_0, G_1) = FALSE;
7.   **return** "faulty";
8.   **end-while**
9. **end-repeat**
10. **return** "conforms"

The algorithm is probabilistic in nature. Line 2 constructs an initial network topology graph G_0 of area 0 with only one ABR node: v_0 (RUT). The while-loop from Line 3 to Line 8 continues until a complete bipartite graph is obtained. Subroutine UPDATE(G_0) in Line 4 gets a new network topology of area 0. It is the similar to the one in Algorithm 1. Subroutine GENERATE(G_1) in Line 5 generates a new network topology of area 1. Subroutine ROUTE(G_0, G_1) in Line 6 checks LSDB and routing table of RUT. If any faults are detected, the process is aborted and "faulty" is reported in Line 7. Otherwise, after sufficient repetition of the repeat-loop from Line 1 to Line 9, "conforms" is declared in Line 10 with a good confidence in the topologies and router behaviors that have been tested.

Subroutine GENERATE(G_1)

In Algorithm 2, while-loop is repeated until network topology graph of area 0 becomes a complete bipartite graph. In each repetition of the loop, subroutine UPDATE(G_0) is called to updates G_0 incrementally. After that, subroutine GENERATE(G_1) is called to generate a new topology graph G_1:

Subroutine GENERATE(G_1)

1. Construct initial graph $G_1 = < R_1, W_1, \{v_0\}, E_1 >$ with
   $R_1 = \{r_x^{(1)}|x = 1, 2, \cdots, n_1\}, W_1 = \{w_x^{(1)}|x = 1, 2, \cdots, m_1\}, E_1 = \phi$;
2. Choose l from $[n_1 + 1..(n_1 + 1)m_1]$ u.a.r.;
3. Insert l edges u.a.r. into E_1.

In Line 1, an initial G_1 is constructed with all the nodes yet without any edges. In Line 2, the number of edges to be inserted into G_1 is determined randomly. In Line 3, these edges are inserted into G_1 randomly to obtain G_1.

Subroutine ROUTE(G_0 , G_1)

In Algorithm 2, after G_0 is updated and G_1 is generated, subroutine ROUTE(G_0, G_1) is called to check the correctness of RUT. It is similar to that in [8] and we omit the details. Note that LSU packets are calculated and sent to RUT for both areas, and LSDBs of the two areas are obtained, respectively. Routing table of RUT is also computed based on the LSDBs. If any of them is incorrect, "faulty" is returned.

Fault Coverage

The Summary-LSA origination is performed based on routing table entries one by one, a reasonable fault model is to assume that the origination based on a specific routing table entry is performed incorrectly. Since the Summary-LSA originations of the two areas are performed at the same time, and there may be interactions of them in an implementation, we need to consider the routing table entries in both areas. Again this is a single-fault model; a single fault about Summary-LSA origination involves an internal router $r_x^{(0)}$ of area 0 and an internal router $r_y^{(1)}$ of area 1. When both of them are reachable from RUT, RUT originates one or two Summary-LSAs incorrectly.

Similar to the fault coverage analysis of Algorithm 1, we have the following:

Proposition 3. *There exists a polynomial $P(n_0, n_1)$ such that for any $0 < \varepsilon \le 1$, with no more than $P(n_0, n_1) \ln \frac{1}{\varepsilon}$ repetitions of the repeat-loop in Algorithm 2, any single-fault is to be detected with a probability at least $1 - \varepsilon$.*

It shows that with a polynomial number of tests Algorithm 2 detects any single fault with a high probability.

3.3   Area Border Router: More than One Non-backbone Area

In this subsection, we consider the case when RUT is an ABR and there is more than one non-backbone (level 2) area, i.e., $k \geq 2$. Specifically, suppose that RUT is ABR_1 which connects the backbone area and the non-backbone (level 2) area 1. In this case, both Summary-LSA origination and inter-area route calculation are performed, since there are two or more level 2 areas. Obviously, it is a combination of the previous two cases, and we can apply both Algorithm 1 and 2 to test the two functions as follows. Initially network topology graph G_0 of area 0 is constructed with only one router node: v_0 (RUT). Then G_0 is updated until it becomes a complete bipartite graph. With each G_0, network topology G_1 of non-backbone area 1 is generated using Algorithm 2, and characteristic distance vectors $v^{(i)}, i = 2, \cdots, k$ of the other non-backbone areas are originated using Algorithm 1. We check the valid performance of RUT using Algorithm 2. On the other hand, the corresponding LSDB and routing table of RUT are also tested using Algorithm 1. Upon detecting any faults, the process is aborted and "faulty" is reported. Otherwise, after sufficient repetition, "conform" is declared. Obviously, the fault coverage of both Algorithm 1 and 2 apply, and faults in this case can be detected with a high probability in polynomial number of repetitions.

In summary:

Theorem 1. *For testing the hierarchy features of an IP router OSPF protocol with the probabilistic algorithms, any single fault can be detected with a high probability and in a number of tests that is polynomial in the size of the network.*

4   Experiments

We implemented both probabilistic algorithms in a software tool to test IP routers. For this experiment we use a software tool, Socrates. It was developed at Bell Labs [8], and can simulate IP network topologies. We further enhance the software to simulate hierarchical IP network topologies for our testing. When an RUT is connected to simulator it perceives itself is connected to a real network of IP routers and interacts as if it is a router connected with Internet, performing due operations: it exchanges messages, including LSAs, with other routers and computes routing tables with each network topology update.

In order to test the inter-area route calculation, Algorithm 1 is implemented and integrated with the simulator with the following configuration in Figure 6.

In this configuration, RUT is $r_1^{(0)}$, and $w_1^{(0)}$ and $w_2^{(0)}$ are physical networks connecting RUT and the software tool. The other routers and networks in area 0 are simulated by the software tool. For this experiment, we set $k = 1$, i.e., there is only one ABR with one non-backbone area. The distance vectors advertised by ABR_1 into area 0 are generated by the software tool.

In order to test the summary-LSA origination function, Algorithm 2 is applied, and the experiment configuration is in Figure 7.

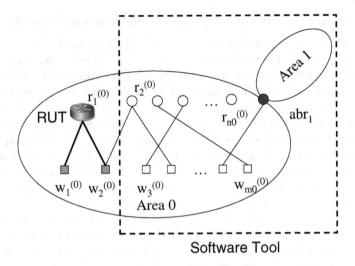

Fig. 6. Experiment Configuration 1

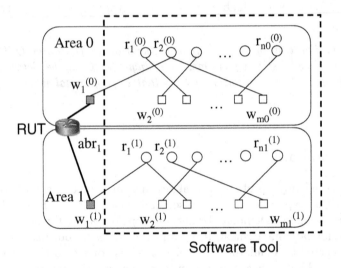

Fig. 7. Experiment Configuration 2

In this configuration, RUT is abr_1, and $w_1^{(0)}$ and $w_1^{(1)}$ are physical networks connecting RUT and the software tool. The other routers and networks in area 0 and 1 are simulated.

We tested OSPF implementations of Cisco router and Zebra [20]. We used several combinations of n_0 and n_1 in the experiments and most of the tests went well without reporting any faults.

In order to verify the fault detection capability, we intentionally introduced some errors into the implementation of Zebra. For example, one of the added errors was that during Summary-LSA origination when both $r_{n0}^{(0)}$ and $r_{n1}^{(1)}$ were reachable from RUT and that the modified implementation of RUT originated summary-LSAs with wrong value in the metric field. We applied our algorithms against the faulty implementation, and all the faults were detected. Specifically, for $n_0 = n_1 = 4$, after a large number of runs of the testing algorithm, the average time to detect the fault was 10.25 minutes. For $n_0 = n_1 = 6$, the average time was 22 minutes. When $n_0 = n_1 = 8$, the average time was 33.5 minutes. Note that our algorithms detected the faults in the first run of the repeat-loop before the network topology became a complete graph.

5   Conclusion

We study testing of hierarchical networks with Internet OSPF routing protocol as a case study. Due to the size and complexity of all the possible network topologies it is impossible to test on each network configuration. We discuss network topology equivalence and reduce the testing to the characteristic topology representation for each equivalence class. We then provide probabilistic algorithms for testing the hierarchy features and show that a high fault coverage can be achieved with a polynomial number of tests. The basic ideas and mechanisms can be applied to the testing of the hierarchy features of PSTN, ATM PNNI and other hierarchical networks.

We have analyzed the fault coverage with a single fault model. Apparently, multiple faults are easier to detect since they result in more violations of the network protocol specifications. However, a rigorous analysis is yet to be obtained. One of the difficulties is that different faults might "cover up" each other, and how to model their interactions and show rigorously the fault coverage remains to be investigated.

Acknowledgement

We are indebted to Caixia Chi for part of the analysis of the fault coverage and to Ruibing Hao and Dawei Wang for their help with the experiments.

References

1. Agilent Technologies: URL=http://advanced.comms.agilent.com/routertester/
2. ATM Forum: Private Network-Network Interface Specification Version 1.1 (PNNI 1.1). 2002
3. Gregor v. Bochmann, Alexandre Petrenko: Protocol Testing: Review of Methods and Relevance for Software Testing. International Symposium on Software Testing and Analysis, August 1994, Seattle, Washington, USA
4. Abdeslam En-Nouaary, Ferhat Khendek, Rachida Dssouli: Fault Coverage in Testing Real-Time Systems. Proceedings of the Sixth International Conference on Real-Time Computing Systems and Applications, 1999

5. Ahmed Khoumsi, Mehdi Akalay, Rachida Dssouli, Abdeslam En-Nouaary, Louis Granger: An Approach for Testing Real Time Protocol Entities. Proceedings of the IFIP TC6/WG6.1 13th International Conference on Testing Communicating Systems: Tools and Techniques, 2000

6. Abdeslam En-Nouaary, Rachida Dssouli, Ferhat Khendek: Timed Wp-Method: Testing Real-Time Systems. IEEE Transactions on Software Engineering, Volume 28, Issue 11, November 2002

7. Rajiv Gupta, Scott A. Smolka, Shaji Bhaskar: On Randomization in Sequential and Distributed Algorithms. ACM Computing Surveys, Vol. 26, No. 1, 1994

8. Ruibing Hao, David Lee, Rakesh Sinha, Dario Vlah: Testing IP Routing Protocols - From Probabilistic Algorithms to Software Tool. FORTE/PSTV 2000

9. Ixia: URL= http://www.ixiacom.com/products/conformance_applications/

10. Leonard Kleinrock, Farouk Kamoun: Hierarchical Routing for Large networks Performance Evaluation and Optimization. Computer Networks, Vol. 1, No. 3, (1977) 155-174

11. David Lee, K. K. Sabnani, D. M. Kristol and Sanjoy Paul: Conformance Testing of Protocols Specified as Communicating Finite State Machines - a Guided Random Walk Based Approach. IEEE Trans. on Communications, Vol. 44, No. 5, (1996) 631-640

12. David Lee, Mihalis Yannakakis: Principles and Methods of Testing Finite State Machines - a Survey. Proceedings of the IEEE, vol. 84, pp. 1090–1123, Aug 1996

13. Rajeev Motwani, Prabhakar Rafhavan: Randomized Algorithms. Cambridge University Press, New York, 1995

14. Rajeev Motwani, Prabhakar Raghavan: Randomized Algorithms. ACM Computing Surveys, Vol. 28, No. 1, 1996

15. John Moy: OSPF - Anatomy of an Internet Routing Protocol. Addison-Wesley, 1997

16. John Moy: OSPF Version 2. Internet RFC 2328

17. Alexandre Petrenko: Fault Model-Driven Test Derivation from Finite State Models: Annotated Bibliography. In the Proceedings of Modelling and Verification of Parallel Processes (MOVEP'2k). Nantes, France, June 19-23, 2000

18. Misha Schwartz: Telecommunication Networks: Protocol, Modeling and Analysis. Addison-Wesley, 1987

19. Spirent Communications: URL=http://www.spirentcom.com/

20. Zebra: URL=http://www.zebra.org/

21. Yixin Zhao, Xia Yin, Bo Han, Jianping Wu: OnLine Test System Applied in Routing Protocol Test. International Symposium on Modeling, Analysis and Simulation of Computer and Telecommunication Systems (MASCOTS), 2001

Detecting Trapdoors in Smart Cards Using Timing and Power Analysis *

Jung Youp Lee[1], Seok Won Jung[2], and Jongin Lim[1]

[1] Graduate School of Information Security,
Korea University, Anam Dong, Sungbuk Gu, Seoul, Korea
[2] Department of Information Security,
Mokpo National University, ChonNam, Korea

Abstract. For economic reasons, in spite of security problems, the commands of re-initializing the card and writing patch code are widely used in smart cards. The current software tester has difficulty in detecting these trapdoor commands by reason that trapdoors are not published and programmed sophisticatedly. Up to now the effective way to detect them is to completely reveal and analyze the entire code of the COS with applications such as the ITSEC. It is, however, very time-consuming and expensive processes. We propose a new approach of detecting trapdoors in smart cards using timing and power analysis. By experiments, this paper shows that this approach is a more practical method than the current methods.

Keywords: Smart Card, Trapdoor, Timing Analysis, Power Analysis

1 Background

The smart card has a high level of security, since it could safely store secret keys and execute cryptographic algorithms. In addition, smart cards are so small and easy to handle that they are replacing magnetic-stripe cards as bank cards and credit cards in electronic payment systems.

Since enormous amounts of money flow in a widely-distributed system, the service provider of an electronic payment system must have a high degree of confidence in the IC chip manufacturer, the producer of the Chip Operating System (COS) with applications, and the smart card issuer. The service provider must be able to be certain that the software in the COS performs the required financial transactions without any errors and that the software is free of security leaks, not to mention trapdoors deliberately introduced into the software.

Evaluating and testing smart cards could provide the service provider with confidence. Evaluations are generally applied to the description documents or

---

* This research was supported by the MIC(Ministry of Information and Communication), Korea, under the ITRC(Information Technology Research Center) support program supervised by the IITA(Institute of Information Technology Assessment).

F. Khendek and R. Dssouli (Eds.): TestCom 2005, LNCS 3502, pp. 275–288, 2005.

the program code with static procedures. In contrast to static methods, tests are applied to the real smart card in operation with dynamic procedures.

The Trusted Computer System Evaluation Criteria (TCSEC) [1], the Information Technique System Evaluation Criteria (ITSEC) [2], and the Common Criteria (CC) [3] are representative evaluation methods. The TCSEC were created in order to establish a catalog of criteria for evaluating the trustworthiness of software products by the American Department of Defense (DoD) in 1985. The ITSEC published in 1990 were European criteria based on TCSEC. The CC were made in order to provide a uniform standard for evaluating the correctness of a software in 1996. The CC have also been published as international standard ISO 15408. The basic procedure for evaluating a system is to rate the mechanisms that it uses to maintain security with regard to the pre-defined basic threats. For example, the ITSEC have six quality levels from E1 to E6. If the software satisfies minimum requirements such as informal descriptions of functions, it has the lowest level E1. For the highest level E6, a complete evaluation is required. For instance, full source code and object code testing are necessary for level E6.

As well as the software, the hardware could be evaluated by various criteria. The VISA corporation requires the Chip Hardware Architecture Review for their smart cards [4]. This is an evaluation of the basic chip, without a COS or an application. This evaluation identifies features that the COS and applications must enable properly in order to achieve the security desired.

To test the software of a smart card, the service provider or its agency examines the input and output data with regard to their relationship to each other, as defined in the specifications. If the examiner knows the internal data structures and processes of the COS with applications, the number of possible input values could be reduced. Besides the functional tests of the COS with applications, the VISA corporation performs risk testing [4]. This testing verifies that the security features provided by the IC chip are appropriately implemented by the COS, and evaluates the protection that a card provides against various documented and well-known attacks.

The hardware of a smart card is tested by the IC chip manufacturer and by the card body manufacturer. The card body is verified by mechanical, chemical, and thermal test regulations of the ISO/IEC 10373. In every fabrication processes of a smart card, the ATR test and the EEPROM test are performed to check whether the IC chip has been damaged by being packaged into the module or by being heated during the embedding process.

In the real smart card fields, the commands of re-initializing the card and writing patch code are widely used. For economic reasons, the re-initializing command is intentionally inserted into the COS to reuse incorrectly issued cards which should be cut into pieces using a pair of scissors. This command clears the EEPROM of a smart card. Nowadays the patch command is almost always used at initial stage that a new COS with applications is introduced. This command is used to correct the errors of the COS or to adapt the minor changes of the specifications. This command writes patch code into the EEPROM. In many cases, these commands are not published. Such unpublished commands could be trapdoors. The malicious developer of the COS could easily introduce trapdoors in the form of patch code that reads all of the EEPROM memory including the key information. This is a serious risk, especially to the electronic payment system that uses only the symmetric key. The exposure of the key means a crash of the system.

By means of the software test of a smart card, the service provider could have the confidence that the smart card of its system complies with the specifications and that it operates without errors or security weakness including trapdoors. However, it is sometimes incorrectly assumed that these tests can discover all Trojan horses in the software. Although the unsophisticated trapdoors could be detected, an experienced programmer can easily create trapdoors that are not detected by current tests. Up to now the effective way to detect them is to completely reveal and analyze the entire code of the COS with applications. However, it is very time-consuming and expensive processes. The ITSEC level E4 which is the lowest level of the source code testing can cost around 300,000 euro. In order to be certified of the level E6, it takes several years and costs several million euros [5].

We propose a new approach of detecting trapdoors in smart cards using timing analysis and power analysis. The basic idea is as follows: if a terminal transmits the commands which are not in the specifications into a smart card, their response time and power consumption are same. However, the trapdoor command which is also not in the specifications has the different response time and the different power consumption as compared with the other commands. This idea provides a fast and inexpensive method for detecting trapdoors compared to known test methods.

The following section classifies the types of trapdoors in smart cards. Section 3 illustrates the current test methods to detect trapdoors. Section 4 introduces the timing analysis and the power analysis. Section 5 presents the methods to detect the defined trapdoors using timing and power analysis, and shows the practice.

2 Types of Trapdoors in Smart Cards

The smart card has a interface so-called Application Protocol Data Unit (APDU) that consists of a command APDU and a response APDU to communicate with the terminal [6]. This tells us that a trapdoor in a smart card also has a APDU format and that it could be detected by the analysis of the APDU format.

A command APDU, which is sent by the terminal to the card, consists of a mandatory header and an optional body in Figure 1. The header is composed

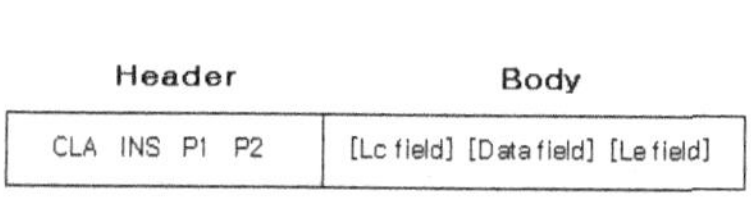

Header	Body
CLA INS P1 P2	[Lc field] [Data field] [Le field]

Fig. 1. Structure of a command APDU

of four elements: the class byte (CLA), the instruction byte (INS), and two parameter bytes (P1 and P2). The body is composed of the length of input data (Lc field), the input data (data field), and the expected length of output data (Le field).

A response APDU, which is sent by the card in reply to a command APDU, consists of an optional body and a mandatory trailer in Figure 2. The body is the output data and the trailer is a status word.

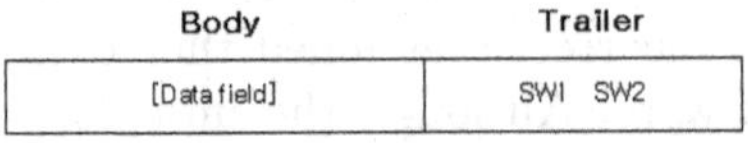

Body	Trailer
[Data field]	SW1 SW2

Fig. 2. Structure of a response APDU

Trapdoors could be inserted in a command APDU that is in the published documents such as the specifications or a manual. This command operates the defined function as well as the hidden function and it returns the response with the hidden information. Trapdoors could be a new command APDU that is not in the published documents. Also, a series of commands could be a trapdoor. If the commands of this trapdoor executes in order, the last command performs a hidden function. Otherwise, it performs a normal function. We classify these trapdoors into three types: steganographic commands, trapdoor commands, and trapdoor sequences. In the following subsections, we will define the types of trapdoors in detail.

2.1   Steganographic Commands

Definition 1. *A steganographic command is a command defined in the published documents and implemented in the smart card, which has one or more hidden functions than defined in the published documents.*

Almost all smart card operating systems contain the GET CHALLENGE command for generating and issuing random numbers [7]. This command could be modified to a steganographic command. If a smart card generates a 16-byte random number, The first 8-byte number of the random number is actually generated by the pseudo-random number generator. The remaining 8-byte number would then consist of an 8-byte value taken from the EEPROM and XORed with the first 8-byte random number. An external program could then be used to read out the entire memory contents, including all of the keys. Incidentally, this is a good example of a steganographic trapdoor.

2.2   Trapdoor Commands

Definition 2. *A trapdoor command is a command that is not defined in the published documents and is implemented in the smart card.*

To make a trapdoor in smart cards, the developer of the COS and applications usually defines a new command rather than modifies an existing command. The reason is that he could handle the trapdoor as a normal command.

A command APDU consists of CLA, INS, P1-P2, Lc, Data, and Le. Therefore a trapdoor command could use one or more elements of a command APDU as the trapdoor awareness data. According to that data, trapdoor commands could be defined by CLA trapdoor commands, INS trapdoor commands, P1-P2 trapdoor commands, and so on.

If an experienced programmer inserts a trapdoor command into the COS, he would use one or more commands before the trapdoor command to block easy detecting. The successful authentication command, for example, may be requested before the patch command is applied. Also he would intentionally use the error status word for the successful trapdoor command to pretend that the smart card does not support that command.

2.3   Trapdoor Sequences

Definition 3. *A trapdoor sequence is a sequence of commands defined in the published documents and implemented in the smart card, of which the last command operates as a trapdoor if the commands are executed in predefined order.*

Suppose a trapdoor sequence is a sequence of the GET RESPONSE command, the PUT DATA command, and the GET CHALLENGE command. The GET CHALLENGE command, which returns a random number in normal state, could respond to the key information if the above sequence of commands are sent into a smart card according to the defined order.

Trapdoor sequences are usually defined to avoid the collision with the possible command sequences of transactions in the specifications.

3   Current Test Methods to Detect Trapdoors

A functional test is commonly used to discover trapdoors in a real smart card in operation. Figure 3 illustrates the method used to determine the unpublished commands. A CLA in the APDU is sent into the smart card, being changed from '00' to 'FF'. As soon as a return code other than 'invalid class' is received, the first valid class byte has been determined. Then all possible INSs are sent with the determined CLA. The unsupported INS returns the status word 'unknown instruction', and the supported INS does return the other status word. In a similar manner, the possible parameters of a command could be determined. If suitable software is available in the terminal, this method can be used determine which commands are supported by a smart card in a few minutes.

The reason that this simple search algorithm for CLA, INS, and P1-P2 is possible is that practically most of command interpreters in smart card operating systems evaluate received commands by starting with the CLA byte and working through the following bytes.

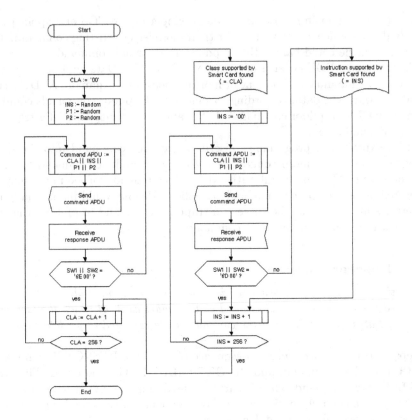

Fig. 3. Basic procedure for determining the commands set of a smart card

However, an experienced programmer can easily create trapdoors that are not detected by this test as mentioned in Subsection 2.2. If he uses the error status word 'unknown instruction' for the successful trapdoor command, there is no way to detect them by this test. What is worse, this test could not practically detect a steganographic command or a trapdoor sequence.

4   Timing Analysis and Power Analysis

In the previous section, we show that the current test methods are not sufficient to detect trapdoors in smart cards. It is well known fact that a timing analysis and a power analysis are powerful methods to attack the smart card. This paper explains how these methods could be applied to detect trapdoors effectively in the next section. We introduce the concept of a timing analysis and a power analysis in the following subsections.

We suggest that the side channel attacks which are focus to on the cryptographic algorithms in the smart card could be used for detecting trapdoors. It would be powerful methods as much for the cryptographic algorithms.

4.1   Timing Analysis

This subsection briefly describes the timing analysis of [10]. A timing attack can be mounted if the execution time of the cipher depends on the value of the key. For example, consider the square-and-multiply algorithm for modular exponentiation, which is the basis of many public-key cryptosystems. If no special precautions are taken, the total execution time of the cipher will vary depending on the key. Hence, it is possible to deduce the key by comparing the cipher execution times for different keys.

4.2   Power Analysis

This subsection briefly describes the power analysis of [11] and how it can be used to attack encryption algorithms. Simple Power Analysis (SPA) involves directly interpreting the power consumption measurement of a device like a smart card. SPA can yield information about a device's operation as well as key material. For example, when an attacker can find out which branch of a jump instruction is taken in the DES operation, it becomes possible to use such information to draw conclusions about the secret key because a conditional branch is commonly used to compute the DES key scheduling.

Differential Power Analysis (DPA) is a statistical approach, where many traces are collected, and are examined for correlations. A partial guess of a key could determine whether the value of a particular bit in the outputs is 0 or 1. The value divides the traces into two sets. Then, the averages of the traces for the two sets are compared. If the guess is incorrect, there will be no correlation between the two sets. However if the guess is correct, the first set will have a different bias than the second one. When the averages of the two sets are subtracted, there will be a spike in the difference. In such manner, the entire key can be derived.

5   Detecting Trapdoors in a Smart Card

Most smart cards support the protocol T=0, half-duplex transmission of asynchronous characters [6]. In the protocol T=0, the COS has to parse the received INS in order to distinguish the commands that are incoming data transfers to the smart card and the commands that are outgoing data transfers to the terminal. Therefore, the COS commonly has the command processing steps as the following Algorithm 1.

Algorithm 1. APDU command processing steps

Step 1. Receive a command APDU header.
Step 2. Parse the command according to INS.
Step 3. Receive a command APDU body if it is the incoming data transfer command.
Step 4. Process the secure messaging.

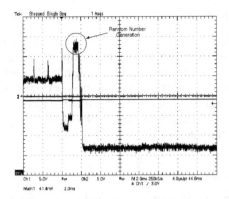

Fig. 4. Power consumption of a general GET CHALLENGE command

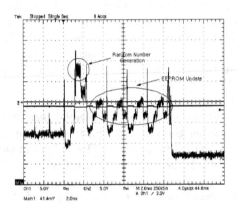

Fig. 5. Power consumption of a trapdoor GET CHALLENGE command

Step 5. Check the input command according to the specifications.
Step 6. Performs the command.
Step 7. Send a response APDU.

If the smart card supports only block transmission protocols such as T=1, type A, type B [6, 8, 9], the steps may differ from the above. For example, Step 3 could be merged to step 1. Step 2 and 4 could be swapped. Since most of smart cards supporting block transmission protocols are implemented T=0 also, without loss of generality, we assume that the smart cards have T=0 protocol.

For experiments, the sample COS is developed on the Samsung OPENice i500 smart card development tools. The power consumption graph is the difference of the voltages over 50 ohms between Vcc of the smart card and Vcc of the terminal measured by the Tektronix TDS 5052 Digital Phosphor Oscilloscope.

Detecting Steganographic Commands

This trapdoor executes an ordinary function and a trapdoor function at the same time. It should be implemented in Step 6 of Algorithm 1, and it has additional operations compared with an original command.

Let us use an example where a trapdoor GET CHALLENGE command generates a random number and operates XOR with one byte of the EEPROM memory. After that, it updates the EEPROM area for the next address to read.

Most smart card ICs have a hardware random number generator, so the power consumption graph of the GET CHALLENGE command is generally simple like Figure 4. On the other hand, because the trapdoor GET CHALLNGE command has additional operations, the power consumption graph differs compared with the general implementation of the GET CHALLENGE command if the same IC is used. Figure 5 tells us that it has additional operations that are not known, so we suspect this as a trapdoor.

Detecting Trapdoor Commands

This trapdoor has one or more new CLA, INS, P1-P2, Lc, Data, or Le. We illustrate a INS trapdoor command first, which is the representative trapdoor. In Step 2, the INS of an input command APDU is compared within the switch clause or the if-else clause. If it is matched, the COS calls the function and

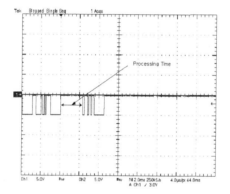

Fig. 6. Processing time of commands that are not in a command parser

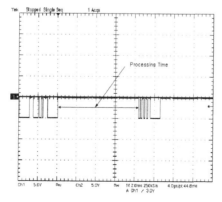

Fig. 7. Processing time of an INS trapdoor command

returns an ordinary status word. Otherwise, the COS returns the status word '6D00' (unknown instruction).

The INS trapdoor command can be implemented in Step 2 of Algorithm 1. Although this trapdoor returns the status word '6D00' as Example 1, we could easily guess that this command of which the processing time is different from those of other commands would be a trapdoor. In a similar manner like Figure 3, INSs from '00' to 'FF' are sent into the smart card. Figure 6 shows that the processing time of INSs that are not in the command parser and Figure 7 shows an INS trapdoor command.

Because the INS value is between 0 and 255, the full search time of INS trapdoor commands is only about 8 seconds assuming that the processing time of one command is 30ms as [5].

Example 1. Pseudo-code for command parser and trapdoor function

```
command_parser ()
{
    switch (apdu.ins)
    {
        case TRAPDOOR:
            trapdoor();
        break;
        case READ_BINARY:
            read_binary();
        break;
        case WRITE_BINARY:
            if (apdu.lc > 0)
                receive_arr(apdu.body, apdu.lc);
            write_binary();
        break;
        // *** Abbr. ***//
        case GET_CHALLENGE:
            get_challenge(&tApdu);
        break;
        // *** Abbr. ***//
        default:
            send_sw(0x6D00);
        return;
    }
}

trapdoor()
{
    format_file_system();
    send_sw(0x6D00);
}
```

Although an experienced programmer can enforce a delay that the command parser matches the processing time with a trapdoor command. Since instructions are different, the power consumption of a trapdoor command would be different from those of other commands. Figure 8 shows the power consumption of commands which return the status word '6D00' with a enforced delay, and Figure 9 shows the power consumption of a trapdoor.

In Step 5 of Algorithm 1, P1 and P2 are checked whether they comply with the specifications or not, respectively. Generally P1 is checked first and P2 second. For example, that the P1-P2 trapdoor command operates as a trapdoor only when P1 = 0x37 and P2 = 0xBF. Matching P1 causes a small difference of the processing time because matching P1 enables P2 to be compared. To search the matching P1, the same method for detecting the INS trapdoor command is applied. After the full search of P1, P2 could be searched by the same way.

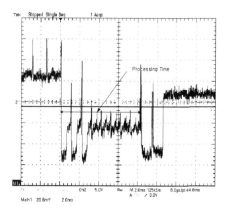

Fig. 8. Power consumption of commands which return the status word '6D00' with a enforced delay

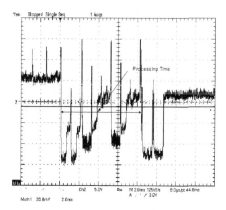

Fig. 9. Power consumption of a trapdoor command

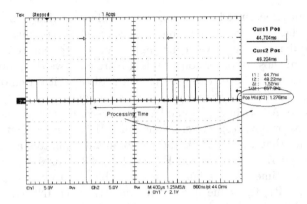

Fig. 10. Processing time of a P1-P2 trapdoor command when P1 != 0x37

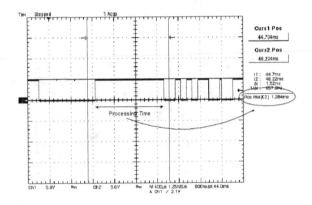

Fig. 11. Processing time of a P1-P2 trapdoor command when P1 = 0x37

Figures 10 and 11 show the processing time of the P1-P2 trapdoor command with matching P1 or not.

Detecting other trapdoor commands are the extension of detecting INS trapdoor commands or P1-P2 trapdoor commands.

Detecting Trapdoor Sequences

To implement a trapdoor sequence, the commands in a sequence have to save the current state for the next command to execute. Suppose that a trapdoor sequence is a sequence of the GET RESPONSE command, the PUT DATA command, and the GET CHALLENGE command. The variable CUR_STATE in RAM of a smart card is for the current state. If the GET RESPONSE command is executed, the CUR_STATE will be set the GET RESPONSE state as defined by S1. If the PUT DATA command is executed and the CUR_STATE is S1, the CUR_STATE will be set the PUT DATA state as defined by S2. If the GET CHALLENGE command is executed and the CUR_STATE is S2, a trapdoor

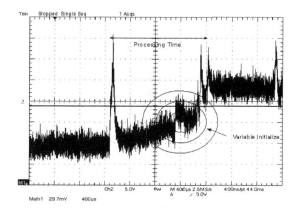

Fig. 12. Power consumption of the PUT DATA command if the previous command is not the GET RESPONSE command

will be executed and the CUR_STATE will be initialized to S0. Any other cases make the CUR_STATE to S0.

With respect to the PUT DATA command, the CUR_STATE will be set the next state if the previous command is the GET RESPONSE command, or it will be initialized. This means that the power consumption difference exists. Figure 12 and 13 show the difference of the power consumption.

The number of commands in most electronic payment systems is 30, more or less. The number of states is about 10 in one command. In other words, one command may return one of about 10 status words. To find one chain, a minimum of two command executions is needed. The full search time of a trapdoor sequence is estimated only about 90 minutes assuming that the processing time of one command is 30ms.

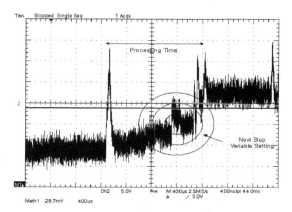

Fig. 13. Power consumption of the PUT DATA command if the previous command is the GET RESPONSE command

6   Conclusion

In the real field, even though the COS developers often insert trapdoors for economic reasons, the current analyzing methods for source code of the COS or the functional test software for smart cards could not detect trapdoors efficiently.

In this paper, trapdoors are classified into steganographic commands, trapdoor commands, and trapdoor sequences, based on the idea that the number of the smart card trapdoors are finite apart from general software because they should follow the APDU format. They are implemented with various ways in the special area of source code according to the basic COS structure.

Side channel attacks which are used to expose secret values of the crypto algorithms in the smart card could be applied to detect trapdoors in the smart card. The timing analysis is useful to detect trapdoor commands which are representative trapdoors in the real smart cards. The power analysis could be used to detect steganographic commands and trapdoor sequences which are more difficult to detect than trapdoor commands. We explain that this idea is very useful to detect trapdoors compared with the current methods.

Furthermore, they also provide the practical and inexpensive methods in the real smart card world. We want this paper to be the start of detecting trapdoors for real smart cards using a timing analysis and a power analysis.

References

1. Trusted Computer Systems Evaluation Criteria, US DoD 5200.28-STD, Dec. 1985.
2. Information Technology Security Evaluation Criteria, Version 1.2, Office for Official Publications of the European Communities, June 1991.
3. Common Criteria for Information Technology Security Criteria, Version 2.1, Aug. 1999.
4. VISA Corporation, Chip Card: Testing and Approval Requirements Version 7.0, Industry Services, Dec. 2002.
5. W. Rankl and W. Effing, "Smart Card Handbook," Third Edition, John Wiley & Sons, Ltd, 2003, pp.244, pp.544-546, pp.579, pp.589.
6. ISO/IEC 7816-3:1997, Identification cards - Integrated circuit(s) cards with contacts - Part 3: Electronic signals and transmission protocols.
7. ISO/IEC 7816-4:1995, Identification cards - Integrated circuit(s) cards with contacts - Part 4: Interindustry commands for interchange.
8. ISO/IEC 14443-3:2001, Identification cards. Contactless integrated circuit(s) cards. Proximity cards. Part 3: Initialization and anticollision.
9. ISO/IEC 14443-4:2001, Identification cards. Contactless integrated circuit(s) cards. Proximity cards. Part 4: Transmission protocol.
10. P. Kocher, "Timing Attacks on Implementation of Diffie-Hellman, RSA, DSS, and Other Systems," CRYPTO 1996, LNCS 1109, Springer-Verlag, 1996, pp.104-113.
11. P. Kocher, J. Jaffe, and B. Jun, "Differential Power Analysis," CRYPTO 1999, LNCS 1666, Springer-Verlag, 1999, pp.388-397.

From U2TP Models to Executable Tests with TTCN-3
- An Approach to Model Driven Testing -

Justyna Zander[1], Zhen Ru Dai[1], Ina Schieferdecker[1,2], and George Din[1]

[1] Fraunhofer Fokus, TIP,
Kaiserin-Augusta-Allee 31,
10589 Berlin, Germany
{j.zander,dai,schieferdecker,din}@fokus.fraunhofer.de
[2] Technical University Berlin, Faculty IV,
Straße des 17. Juni 135,
10623 Berlin,
Berlin, Germany

Abstract. The approach towards system engineering according to Model-Driven Architectures (MDA) with code generation derived from model implies also an increased need for research on automation of the test generation process. This paper presents an approach to derive executable tests from UML 2.0 Testing Profile diagrams automatically. In particular, an approach to derive executable tests within the Testing and Test Control Notation (TTCN-3) is discussed. The transformation rules between the source U2TP meta-model to the target TTCN-3 meta-model are given.

Keywords: UML 2.0 Testing Profile, UML, Testing, TTCN-3, QVT, Model transformation, MOF, MDA.

1 Introduction

Recently, the attention around automatic derivation of executable code from abstract models has been raised in the context of MDA (Model Driven Architecture [1]). We believe that that this concept can also be used also in testing area. Therefore, it is proposed to enhance MDA with a separate development line for testing artefacts [12]. We believe that derivation of executable tests from their models is possible to some extent. Due to complete test designs we gain the advantage of reduced work on pure tests programming. Several efforts have been undertaken to establish an approach to automate - or at least to provide significant support for an automated - test generation. Algorithms have been defined to derive tests from formal system specification given in various notations. But today, none of the approaches is widely used in the industrial practice for large applications [17]. As UML and MDA have gained much momentum in industry, we focus on using these concepts to show that retrieving executable test instances from system model can be supported via test skeleton generation combined with manual completion of the tests.

MDA prescribes certain model artefacts to be used along system development, how those models may be prepared and their relationship [1]. It is an approach to system development that separates the specification of functionality from the specification of

F. Khendek and R. Dssouli (Eds.): TestCom 2005, LNCS 3502, pp. 289–303, 2005.

the implementation of that functionality on a specific technology platform [3]. Main MDA artefacts are platform independent system models (PIMs), platform specific system models (PSMs) and system code [1][14]. There is a clear distinction between PIM, PSM and system code although it depends on the context, the development process and the details of the system and target platform, where the border between PIM, PSM and system code is to be placed. Within these three abstraction levels, transformation techniques are used to translate model parts of one abstraction level into model parts on another abstraction level. These transformations can also be used to specify the relations and invariants between the models on different abstraction levels, which are the base to check the consistency between models and to validate models against each other. These MDA abstraction levels can also be applied to test modelling [15] as according to the philosophy of MDA, the same modelling mechanism can be re-used for multiple targets [16]. Similarly, test models can be specified platform independently and platform specific before generating executable test codes [8].

As shown in Fig. 1, platform independent system design models (PIM) can be transformed into platform specific system design models (PSM). While PIMs focus on describing the pure functioning of a system independently from potential platforms that may be used to realize and execute the system, the relating PSMs contain a lot of information on the underlying platform. In another transformation step, system code may be derived from the PSM. Certainly, the completeness of the code depends on the completeness of the system design model [8].

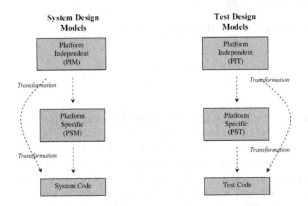

Fig. 1. System and Test Development

According to model driven testing[1] approach, a platform independent test design model (PIT) can be transformed either directly to test code or to a platform specific test design model (PST) [10]. Finally, the test design model can be transformed into executable test code from either PST or PIT.

This paper presents transformations between UML 2.0 Testing Profile (U2TP [4]) specifications used to represent PITs and Testing and Test Control Notation (TTCN-3 [5]). The transformations are specified as transformation rules between the U2TP

---

[1] We define model driven testing as testing based-MDA.

meta-model [4] and the TTCN-3 meta-model [10]. Afterwards, the generated output is completed and compiled to executable test code in Java [18].

U2TP and TTCN-3 meta-models are both defined as Meta Object Facility (MOF) models [1]. Transformation rules provided in this paper define relation between source and target meta-classes of these meta-models, while the transformations are performed on model (instance) level, i.e. deriving parts of TTCN-3 modules from parts of U2TP specifications. This procedure is shown in Fig. 2.

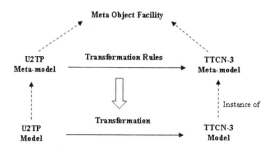

Fig. 2. Transformation of U2TP to TTCN-3

The goal is to get executable tests from U2TP models automatically, however, in general the generation will only be semi-automatic as U2TP specifications can be very abstract so that further details are needed to make the tests executable. Examples include the addition of concrete data, timing or default behaviours.

The environment, which is used to demonstrate the feasibility of our approach is Eclipse with its UML2.0 plug-in [19]. U2TP is realized as an extension of the UML 2.0 plug-in via its Java API. The transformation rules are also realized in Java. The transformations generate objects within a TTCN-3 meta-model instance, which enables the compilation and execution of the tests designed previously in U2TP.

The paper is divided into six sections. After the introduction, Section 2 is devoted to the U2TP and TTCN-3 meta-models which are used as source and target for the transformations. Additionally, we discuss Eclipse and its UML 2.0 plug-in as a tool which is used to implement and demonstrate our approach. In Section 3, the transformation theory in the context of model driven testing is discussed. Section 4 provides the methodology of retrieving the executable test code, which is possible by applying presented transformation rules and appropriate compilation. The transformation rules could be formalized in Query/View/Transformation (QVT) rules defined by CBOP/IBM/DSTC [3]. However due to lack of vendors providing appropriate tools and because of the limitations of the UML 2.0 profiling support in Eclipse, we had to realize the transformation rules directly in Java. Thus, we define our own mapping language and rules based on meta-model classes. In Section 5, an example of U2TP diagram is presented and the transformation rules for this example are described. Furthermore, the same example analysis, but resulting from application of the transformer implementation is continued. In Section 6, the results are discussed and conclusions are taken. Finally, future work challenges are outlined.

2 Related Work

Research as well as industrial work related to generation of executable tests from UML models according to MDA concepts is being continuously developed. LEIRIOS Test Generator™ tool (LTG) [23] implements the Smart Testing concept. It supports Model Based Testing - an approach in which one defines the behaviour of a system in terms of actions that change the state of the system (state machine). UML 2.0 models are used for automatic generation of test sequences. LEIRIOS core technologies implement smart heuristics to compute the test cases.

Objecteering Software [24] on the other side provides the opportunity of working with pragmatic design and coding tools, which combine UML modelling, code production, debugging and Java application testing in a single environment. Objecteering/UML tool is integrated into the Eclipse 2.0 platform. This integration allows the Java developer to take advantage of a strongly model-oriented tool, which, when integrated with a dedicated Java environment, associates the support of UML modelling with the support of Java development. Objecteering/UML tool bases however on UML 1.4 meta-model.

Finally, Telelogic TAU Generation2 [25] represents generation of advanced software development and testing tools, supporting the latest industry-standards for visual systems and software development (UML 2.0 Testing Profile) and systems and integration testing (TTCN-3). Telelogic team provides an approach that automates testing activities covering test specification, development of testing software and execution of test campaigns. U2TP is selected as modelling language for test case specification. The models are then transformed to TTCN-3 language, which is used for describing executable test cases.

Our approach is to use similar methodology as LEIRIOS deriving executable tests from UML 2.0 models, however we extend the models with U2TP concepts and integrate our tool with Eclipse platform as Objecteering team does. We develop also transformation rules from U2TP to TTCN-3 as offered by Telelogic, but we define the rules on the meta-model level using methods available in Eclipse to implement our approach.

3 Theoretical Background

The transformation between U2TP and TTCN-3 is obtained by use of the Eclipse framework for meta-modelling, repository generation and read/write access to model data in repositories. We store model information in Eclipse meta-modelling framework (EMF [21]) based repositories. The transformation rules are defined between source and target meta-models (see Fig. 3) and applied to concrete meta-model instances, i.e. source and target models in U2TP and TTCN-3 respectively. We design and develop test specifications in U2TP and perform the transformations on model level so as to get TTCN-3 test model instances.

In the following section we describe the main concepts of U2TP and TTCN-3, as well as introduce Eclipse being the tool used for the transformation.

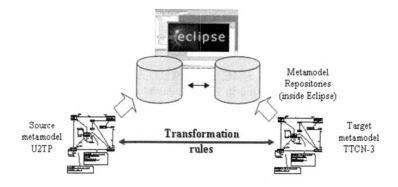

Fig. 3. Transformation Architecture

3.1 The UML 2.0 Testing Profile

The UML 2.0 Testing Profile (U2TP) defines a language for designing, visualizing, specifying, analyzing, constructing and documenting the artefacts of test systems. It is a test modelling language that can be used with all major object and component technologies and be applied to test systems in various application domains. U2TP can be used stand alone for the handling of test artefacts or in an integrated manner with UML for a handling of system and test artefacts together [4]. The UML 2.0 Testing Profile extends UML 2.0 with test specific concepts like test components, verdicts, defaults, etc. These concepts are grouped into concepts for test architecture, test data, test behaviour and time. Being a profile, the U2TP seamlessly integrates into UML. It is based on the UML 2.0 meta-model [2] and reuses UML 2.0 syntax. The U2TP concepts are structured into:

– Test architecture concepts defining concepts related to test structure and test configuration, i.e. the elements and their relationships involved in a test,
– Test behaviours concepts defining concepts related to the dynamic aspects of test procedures and addressing observations and activities during a test,
– Test data concepts defining concepts for test data used in test procedures, i.e. the structures and meaning of values to be processed in a test, and
– Time concepts defining concepts for a time quantified definition of test procedures, i.e. the time constraints and time observation for test execution [9].

A detailed structure of U2TP concepts is given in Table 1.

Table 1. Overview of the Testing Profile concepts [8]

Architecture concepts	Behaviour concepts	Data concepts	Time Concepts
SUT	Test objective	Wildcards	Timer
Test components	Test case	Data pools	Time zone
Test context	Defaults	Data partitions	
Test configuration	Verdicts	Data selectors	
Arbiter	Test control	Coding rules	
Scheduler			

In [4], the meta-model of U2TP is also introduced and explained. It is the source meta-model for the transformation and hence a basis for defining the mapping rules as well as to develop source test models being transformed. It is the input for our transformation work.

Although Eclipse provides EMF, the UML2 plug-in of Eclipse [19] and the profiling mechanism of this plug-in for extensions of UML require that the U2TP meta-model is written in Java from scratch. The UML2 plug-in is based on the UML 2.0 meta-model [2] but provides a specific realization of this in the context of EMF. It allows us to develop a U2TP plug-in for Eclipse and to integrate it with the TTCN-3 plug-in for Eclipse [18].

3.2 TTCN-3 and Its Meta-model

The Testing and Test Control Notation version 3 (TTCN-3 [5]) has been developed at the European Telecommunication Standardization Institute (ETSI) and has been also standardized at the International Telecommunication Union (ITU-T). TTCN-3 is a test specification and implementation language to define test procedures for black-box testing of distributed systems. It enables tests execution, if appropriate tools and system under test (SUT) are available. In [10] a meta-model for TTCN-3 is provided, which represents the concept space of TTCN-3 and enables the use of TTCN-3 in the context of meta-modelling, repositories and model transformations.

The main objectives for the development of the TTCN-3 meta-model were:
- The separation of concerns by separating the TTCN-3 concept space and semantics (represented in the TTCN-3 meta-model) from TTCN-3 syntactic aspects (defined in the core language and the presentation formats).
- The ability to define the semantics on concept space level without being affected by syntactic considerations e.g. in case of syntax changes.
- To ease the exchange of TTCN-3 specifications of any presentation format and not of textual TTCN-3 specifications only.
- To ease the definition of external language mappings to TTCN-3 as such definitions can reuse parts of the conceptual mapping from other languages.
- To integrate TTCN-3 tools into MDA based processes and infrastructures[1].

The TTCN-3 test meta-model defines the TTCN-3 concept space with additional support for the different presentation formats. It does not directly reflect the structure of a TTCN-3 modules but rather the semantics structure of the TTCN-3 language definition. It is defined as a single package with concept structures for types and expressions, modules and scopes, declarations, and statements and operations.

The TTCN-3 meta-model is the target used in our transformation and another base for the definition of the mapping rules. Each meta-class of the target meta-model is named applying the same convention: the logical name for the TTCN-3 concept represented by the meta-class being prefixed with "TT" to make the meta-classes easily identifiable as meta-classes from TTCN-3. The meta-model for TTCN-3 language is technically defined in UML by using the Rational Rose tool [22]. The EMF [21] generator provided by Eclipse was used to generate the TTCN-3 repository by the creation of a corresponding set of Java implementation classes from this Rose model.

3.3 Eclipse

The Eclipse Project [19] is an open source software development project dedicated to providing a robust, full-featured, commercial-quality, industry platform for the development of highly integrated tools. It is composed of three subprojects: the Eclipse Platform, the Java Development Tools (JDT), and the Plug-in Development Environment (PDE). The success of the Eclipse Platform depends on how well it enables a wide range of tool builders to build advanced integrated tools. The Eclipse Platform provides building blocks and a foundation for constructing and running integrated software-development tools [20].

We use PDE to create the U2TP plug-in for Eclipse based on the UML2 Project [19]. Additionally, the Eclipse Modelling Framework (EMF) [21] being a modelling framework and code generation facility enables us to build partly the tools based on the structured meta-models. EMF is a Java framework and code generation facility for building tools and other applications based on meta-models defined in EMF. The EMF Ecore defines the meta-model for all the models handled by the EMF.

4 Transformation Approach

We define transformation from U2TP models to TTCN-3 models. Since TTCN-3 provides a direct generation of executable tests we provide by this translation also a direct way towards test code. Based on concrete U2TP specifications the user is enabled to generate TTCN-3 code, to complete the TTCN-3 definitions if needed afterwards and to execute his/her tests finally. The idea is to provide transformation rules which enable to map the concepts on meta-model level. However, the transformation itself is performed on the model level.

The UML 2.0 Testing Profile is targeted at UML 2.0 providing selected extensions to the features of TTCN-3 as well as restricting/omitting other TTCN-3 features. In general, a mapping from TTCN-3 to U2TP is possible but not the other way around. For the U2TP to TTCN-3 mapping, restrictions on U2TP level are necessary that restrict the U2TP definitions to executable models. In the following, we assume U2TP models which can be mapped to TTCN-3. The principal approach towards the mapping to TTCN-3 consists of two major steps. U2TP stereotypes and associations are selected and assigned to TTCN-3 concepts. Afterwards, procedures to collect required information for the generated TTCN-3 modules are defined [5].

In Fig. 4, the specific application of U2TP to TTCN-3 transformation is considered in the general framework of MDA-based testing [11], where platform-independent tests (PIT) relate to platform-independent system models (PIM) and platform-specific tests (PST) relate to platform-specific system models (PSM). We provide in this paper mapping from a more abstract test design in U2TP down to a detailed technical level in TTCN-3.

Afterwards, the generated test code is completed in TTCN-3 and changed into executable test code. The translation from PITs to PSTs for specific target system platforms is not considered in this work. Also, we do not explicitly model the target test platform (and hence the specifics of the test code dealing with technical test platform characteristics) but rely here on the capabilities of TTCN-3 to generate and adapt executable tests by use of the TTCN-3 runtime interfaces (TRI [6]) and the TTCN-3 control interfaces (TCI [7]).

The way of getting the test code from TTCN-3 repository is performed by using a TTCN-3 compiler (e.g. TTthree [18]). After provision of a test adaptor, the tests originally being designed in U2TP can be performed.

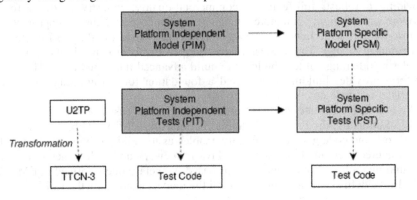

Fig. 4. Transformation of PIT/PST in U2TP to Test Code in TTCN-3

Mapping rules (provided in the next section) define the connection between appropriate nodes of source and target meta-models. These nodes are stereotypes (and extensions of UML 2.0 meta-classes), primitive types or interfaces in case of U2TP and meta-classes in case of TTCN-3 meta-model.

4.1 Mapping Rules Between U2TP and TTCN-3 on Meta-model Level

Mapping is a mechanism for transforming the elements of a model conforming to a particular meta-model into elements of another model that conforms to another meta-model [12]. Mapping is specified using some languages. The description may be in natural language, an algorithm in an action language, or in a model mapping language. A desirable quality of a mapping language is portability. This enables use of a mapping with different tools [13].

The mapping language used in this paper is developed by us. A transformation rule represents the basic unit of mapping between an arrangement of source elements and an arrangement of target elements [13]. Transformation rules are used in our case to express mappings from concepts of the U2TP meta-model to concepts of the TTCN-3 meta-model. For example, we map each U2TP TestComponent stereotype to the TTComponentType meta-class of TTCN-3. Such a procedure is needed for each element of the source meta-model. Thus, we map each stereotype, interface, primitive type, as well as properties, operations and parameters to appropriate meta-classes and associations of the target meta-model. We used the comparison provided in [4], Chapter 6.6.2 as the base for developing the transformation rules and concretized and completed these rules (Table 2), which defines the semantic relation between U2TP elements and TTCN-3 meta-model elements. Mapping rules provided at this part present selected, the most important, however relatively simple issues. The meta-classes of source meta-model have a correspondence in target meta-model. Hence, concrete mapping rules between elements of U2TP and TTCN-3 meta-models are provided.

Table 2. Relation between U2TP and TTCN-3 meta-model elements (excerpt)

U2TP Element	TTCN-3 Meta-model Element
SUT	*system association of TTTestcase* *TTVariable*
TestComponent	*TTComponentType*
TestCase	*TTTestcase*
TestContext	*TTModule* *TTComponentType for the MTC type*
TestConfiguration	*TTFunction* *TTPortLinkKind* *TTCreateTC* *TTStartTC*
TestObjective	*TTComment*
Arbiter	*TTComponentType* *TTExternalFunction or TTFunction*
Verdict	*TTVerdict*
ValidationAction	*TTExternalFunction or TTFunction*
Default	*TTDefaultType* *TTAltstep*
DefaultApplication	*TTDefaultKind*
Stimuli	*TTOutputKind*
Observation	*TTInputKind*
Coordination	*TTOutputKind* *TTInputKind*
LogAction	*TTLog*
InteractionOperator(alt,determAlt)	*TTAlternative*
InteractionOperator(loop)	*TTLoopKind*
DataSelector	*TTExternalFunction or TTFunction*
DataPartition	*TTExternalFunction or TTFunction,* *TTTemplate*
CodingRule	*TTWithKind*
LiteralAny	*matching/expression*
Timer	*TTTimer,* *TTTimerType*
StartTimerAction	*TTTimerStatementKind*
StopTimerAction	*TTTimerStatementKind*
ReadTimerAction, TimerRunningAction	*TTTimerOp*
TimeOutAction, TimeOut, TimeOutMessage,	*TTTimeOut*
Duration	*TTFloatType*
Port	*TTPort , TTPortKind, TTPortType*
Parameters	*TTModuleParameter*

All the mapping rules presented above are connected mostly with single concepts. However, there are such elements like time zone or scheduler that cannot be transformed one by one. The time zone concept cannot be directly expressed in TTCN-3 so that it has been not yet considered in the mapping. Furthermore, it is assumed that the scheduler is implicitly present in the TTCN-3 semantics and therefore realized by every TTCN-3 run time environment, so that there is no need to transform it.

Further investigations in the context of U2TP diagrams are done. The attention is focused especially on Class Diagram, Sequence and Interaction Diagrams. Prototypical implementation of the transformations serves as reliable proof of described concepts. Here, appropriate algorithms to order mapping of various elements are investigated. Different approaches for each type of UML 2.0 diagrams are elaborated.

5 An Example

Hence we would like to introduce an example of diagram mapping so as to show how the mentioned U2TP meta-model concepts can be mapped to TTCN-3 meta-model concepts. In the example, we show how the particular elements of U2TP given in Fig. 5 are mapped to TTCN-3 meta-classes on the base of a Sequence Diagram.

The **sequence diagram** in Fig. 5 specifies the behaviour for *InvalidPIN()* Test Case. The test objective of this test case is: Verify that if a valid card is inserted, and an invalid pin-code is entered, the log with the content *"PIN incorrect"* is stored.

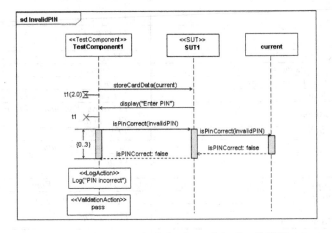

Fig. 5. Sequence Diagram – the behaviour of the *InvalidPIN* test case

The interaction specifies the expected sequence of messages (Stimuli – e.g. *storeCardData(current)*, Observation – e.g. *display("Enter PIN")*) between *Test Component1* and *SUT1*, when used as a test behaviour. During a Test Case, *Log("PIN incorrect")* is used to store log event information. Validation Action sets the verdict to pass. Validation Actions use an arbiter to calculate and maintain a verdict for a Test Case. Test Cases always return verdicts. This is normally done implicitly through the arbiter and doesn't have to be shown in the test case behaviour. In the example, an arbitrated verdict is returned implicitly.

The diagram also illustrates the use of a Timer – *t1* and a duration constraint (*{0..3}*). The Timer is used to specify how long the Test Component1 will wait for the Observation. Thus the Timer – *t1* is started after sending a Stimulus by *Test Component1* to *SUT1*. Once the message (Observation) has been received by the *Test Component1*, the Timer is stopped.

Mapping rules given below are extended in such a way that the whole path of the inheritance of TTCN-3 meta-classes is given. In this way better overview on the meta-models structure is presented. Additional restrictions, like associations are provided to enable the recognition of some important relations in the TTCN-3 meta-model.

Let us consider `TestComponent` stereotype, which is used for the creation of test components and their connection to the SUT and to other test components. It specifies *TestComponent1* in Fig. 6. `TestComponent` is mapped to `TTComponentType`. `TTComponentType` has a `TTScope` which is an abstract meta-class in the TTCN-3 meta-model. It is also a `TTComplexType`, which inherits from `TTType`. `TTType` inherits from `TTDeclaration` and this respectively is associated with `TTModule` which inherits from `TTScope` (see Fig. 6).

```
U2tp::TestComponent →
TTCN3::TTScope::TTComponentType
TTCN3::TTScope::TTModule@TTDeclaration::TTType
::TTComplexType::TTComponentType
```

Fig. 6. Test Component mapping

Symbols used in the creation of mapping rules are given in Table 3:

Table 3. Symbols and their Meaning used in Mapping Language

Symbols	Meaning
meta-class1::meta-class2	inheritance of meta-class2 from meta-class1
meta-class1@meta-class2	meta-class1 is composed of meta-class2
meta-class$enumeration	enumeration is included in the meta-class as an attribute type
enumerationExample(value)	represents the value of given enumeration

Applying the transformation rules to all the concepts presented in Fig. 5, we get the following results. `Stimulus` is the element of U2TP meta-model responsible for sending messages, calling operations, and replying to operation invocations. An element corresponding to `Stimulus` on model level is i.e. *storeCardData(current)* in Fig. 5. Stimulus is mapped to `TTOutputKind(OutputKind_call)` in our example. `TTOutputKind` is included in `TTOutput` meta-class as an attribute type. `TTOutput` meta-class inherits from `TTOtherStatements`, while this inherits from `TTFunctionElement`. `TTFunctionElement` is associated with `TTModule`, which inherits from `TTScope`.

```
U2tp::Stimulus →
TTCN3::TTScope::TTModule@TTFunctionElement::TTOtherStatements
::TTOutput$TTOutputKind(OutputKind_call)
```

Fig. 7. Stimulus mapping

Observation means according to U2TP specification - receiving messages (receive), operation invocations (getcall), and operation replies (getreply). An element corresponding to Observation in the example is e.g. *display("Enter PIN")* in Fig. 5. Here, observation is mapped into TTInputKind (InputKind_getreply).

TTInputKind is included in TTInput meta-class as an attribute type. TTInput meta-class inherits from TTOtherStatements, while this inherits from TTFunctionElement. TTFunctionElement is associated with TTModule, which inherits from TTScope.

```
U2tp::Observation →
  TTCN3::TTScope::TTModule@TTFunctionElement::TTOtherStatements::TTI
nInput$ TTInputKind(InputKind_getreply)
```

Fig. 8. Observation mapping

For the time-quantified control of the communication between two components, a Timer is used. The U2TP stereotypes StartTimerAction and StopTimerAction are responsible for *t1(2.0)* starting and *t1* stopping (see Fig. 5). They are mapped to TTTimerStatementKind(start, stop) respectively. TTTimerStatementKind is included in TTTimerStatement meta-class as an attribute type. TTTimerStatement meta-class inherits from TTControlStatements, while this inherits from TTFunctionElement. TTFunctionElement is associated with TTModule, which inherits from TTScope.

```
U2tp::StartTimerAction →
U2tp::StopTimerAction →
TTCN3::TTScope::TTModule@TTFunctionElement::TTControlStatements
::TTTimerStatement$TTTimerStatementKind(stop, stop)
```

Fig. 9. StartTimerAction, StopTimerAction mapping

LogAction is a stereotype of U2TP. *Log("PIN incorrect")* shows its use in the example (see Fig. 5). TTCN-3 provides a log operation for logging test information in the test trace. The LogAction is mapped to the TTLog meta-class of the TTCN-3 meta-model. TTLog meta-class inherits from TTControlStatements, while this inherits from TTFunctionElement. TTFunctionElement is associated with TTModule, which inherits from TTScope.

```
U2tp::LogAction →
TTCN3::TTScope::TTModule@TTFunctionElement
::TTControlStatements::TTLog
```

Fig. 10. LogAction mapping

Validation. Action is another stereotype of U2TP. It is an external function resulting in a value of the specific verdict type. It is mapped to `TTExternalFunction` inheriting directly from `TTScope` in TTCN-3 meta-model (see Fig. 11).

```
U2tp::ValidationAction →
TTCN3::TTScope::TTExternalFunction
```

Fig. 11. ValidationAction mapping

The TTCN-3 code created after applying the transformation according to the rules defined above is presented in Fig. 12.

```
function invalidPIN_TestComponent1() //parameters not specified yet
runs on                              // not specified yet
    {
        TestComponent1Port.call(storeCardData:{current}, nowait);
        t1.start;

        TestComponent1Port.getreply(display_:{"EnterPIN"});
        t1.stop;

        TestComponent1Port.call(isPinCorrect:{invalidPIN}, 3.0) {
            [] TestComponent1Port.getreply(isPinCorrect:{?} value false){}
        }
        log("PIN incorrect");
        setverdict(pass);
    }
```

Fig. 12. TTCN-3 code retrieved from the U2TP Diagram

The U2TP test configuration or types definition deserve special attention as they are examples of more complex transformations. Furthermore, for fully specified test cases, all elements of a diagram should be transformed so as to get the whole TTCN-3 code.

In the following, we provide a concrete example of mapping using the whole test specification. Implementation of all the rules mentioned before is the proof of their correctness. We obtained a transformer being able to provide tests in TTCN-3.

Not all the diagrams specified in U2TP are necessary condition to get the full TTCN-3 code. State machine for message flow on one test component presents the same point of view as sequence diagram of the same test behaviour in the context of TTCN-3. Thus, not all available diagrams are used so as to obtain the complete code.

The results of the transformer work for diagram from Fig. 5 are given in Fig. 13.

Behavioural function's name results from test configuration, while body of it is defined alternatively either by sequence diagram or state machine for a test component.

```
function invalidPIN_TestComponent1(inout integer invalidPIN)
runs on TestComponent1_CType
    {
        activate(TestComponent1_classifierdefault());
        TestComponent1Port.call(storeCardData:{current}, nowait);
        t1.start;
        TestComponent1Port.getreply(display_:{"EnterPIN"});
        t1.stop;
        TestComponent1Port.call(isPinCorrect:{invalidPIN}, 3.0);
        alt {
            [] TestComponent1Port.getreply(isPinCorrect:{?} value false
            }
        };
        log("PIN incorrect");
        setverdict(pass);
    }
```

Fig. 13. Transformer Output - TTCN-3 code retrieved from the U2TP Diagram

6 Outlook and Future Work

This paper is devoted to transformation from U2TP test specifications to TTCN-3 code. Transformation rules are defined on meta-model level. Elements of a source U2TP repository (defined by a meta-class of the source U2TP meta-model) are mapped to elements in the target TTCN-3 repository (defined by meta-classes in the target TTCN-3 meta-model). The transformations follow the principles of MDA-based testing, which differentiates between platform-independent tests (PIT), platform-specific tests (PSTs), test code and the relations to the corresponding model artefacts for the system. In particular, a transformation on PIT level is discussed. Selected examples of diagram interactions are provided and the transformation according to the previously defined rules is presented.

The definition of the transformation rules is almost completed. However, special cases of diagrams set are to be considered. This applies especially to test designs specifying Sequence Diagrams, Activity Diagrams or Interaction Overview Diagrams for the same test behaviours at the same time. Additional algorithms should be developed to let the transformation recognise the same behaviour so as not to repeat the same specification in the final TTCN-3 code. Also huge effort must be undertaken so as to map all possible concepts of U2TP, especially such like timezone or scheduler. We have created Eclipse U2TP Plug-in based on the UML2 Project. Furthermore, we developed a tool enabling the transformation and aim to provide the full transformation with graphical front end in future work.

The transformation results provide skeletons of TTCN-3 code only, which means that additional effort must be taken by the user so as to produce complete test definitions. We believe that a fully automated, complete test generation into TTCN-3 will not be feasible in general as test specifications on detailed concrete level contain additional definitions, which are not available in abstract test models. Still, the details of this deserve further investigation. Last but not least, a further aim will be to consider also the generation of PSTs from PITs and/or from platform-specific system models (PSMs). Which of these two ways of transformations towards PSTs should be taken is not clear yet. Research on this will allow us to investigate the relation between platform specifics on system model and test model side.

References

[1] OMG: Model-Driven Architecture (MDA) http://www.omg.org/docs/omg/03-06-01.pdf, http://www.omg.org/docs/formal/02-04-03.pdf

[2] OMG: UML 2.0 Superstructure Final Adopted Specification, www.omg.org/cgi-bin/doc?ptc/2003-08-02

[3] OMG: MOF Query/Views/Transformations, 2nd Revised Submission, ad/04-01-06, 2004.

[4] OMG: UML 2.0 Testing Profile. Final Adopted Specification, ptc/04-04-02, 2004

[5] ETSI ES 201 873-1 V2.2.1: The Testing and Test Control Notation version 3; Part 1: TTCN-3 Core Language, 2003.

[6] ETSI ES 201 873-5 V2.2.1: The Testing and Test Control Notation version 3; Part 5: TTCN-3 Runtime Interfaces, 2003.

[7] ETSI ES 201 873-6 V2.2.1: The Testing and Test Control Notation version 3; Part 6: TTCN-3 Control Interfaces, 2003.

[8] Z. R. Dai: Model-Driven Testing with UML 2.0, Second European Workshop on Model Driven Architecture (MDA) with an emphasis on Methodologies and Transformations (EWMDA'04), Canterbury, England, September 2004.

[9] Z. R. Dai, I. Schieferdecker: Time Concepts for UML 2.0 Based Testing. Workshop on the usage of the UML profile for Scheduling, Performance and Time (SIVOES 2004), hold in conjunction with the 10TH IEEE Real-Time and Embedded Technology and Applications Symposium (RTAS 2004), Toronto, Canada, May 2004

[10] D. Thomas: MDA Revenge of the Modellers or UML Utopia ? IEEESoftware, May/June 2004

[11] I. Schieferdecker, G. Din: A meta-model for TTCN-3. 1st International Workshop on Integration of Testing Methodologies, ITM 2004, Toledo, Spain, Oct. 2004.

[12] M. Born, I. Schieferdecker, O. Kath and C. Hirai: Combining System Development and System Test in a Model-centric Approach, RISE 2004, Luxembourg.

[13] G. Caplat, J.L. Sourouille: Considerations about Model Mapping, Workshop in Software Model Engineering Oct. 2003, San Francisco, USA, http://www.metamodel.com/wisme-2003/18.pdf

[14] A. Kleppe, J. Warmer, W. Bast: MDA Explained: The Model Driven, Architecture–Practice and Promise. Addison-Wesley Pub Co, 2003.

[15] Gross, H.: Testing and the UML – a perfect fit. Fraunhofer IESE, Technical Report 110.03E, 2003.

[16] J. Siegel, OMG Staff Strategy Group: Developing in omg's model-driven architecture., 2001.

[17] I. Schieferdecker, Z. R. Dai, J. Grabowski, A. Rennoch: The UML 2.0 Testing Profile and its Relation to TTCN-3, IFIP 15th Intern. Conf. on Testing Communicating Systems - TestCom 2003, Cannes, France, May 2003.Eclipse UML2 Project, http://www.eclipse.org/uml2/

[18] Testing Technologies: TTworkbench - TTCN-3 IDE in Eclipse, www.testingtech.de

[19] Eclipse UML2: http://www.eclipse.org/uml2/

[20] Eclipse Platform: http://www.eclipse.org/platform/

[21] Eclipse Modelling Framework: http://www.eclipse.org/emf/

[22] Rational Rose Tool, http://www-306.ibm.com/software/awdtools/developer/datamodeler/

[23] LEIRIOS Test Generator™ tool, http://www.leirios.com/products.php

[24] Objecteering/UML tool, http://www.objecteering.com/news_events_news_oct2002_eclipse.php

[25] P. Leblanc, White Paper, Implementation of the UML Testing Profile and Production of Executable Test Cases, Telelogic France, 2003

Using TTCN-3 for Testing Platform Independent Models

Gabor Batori and Domonkos Asztalos

Software Engineering Group, Ericsson Hungary Ltd.,
P.O.B.107, H-1300 Budapest, Hungary
{Gabor.Batori, Domonkos.Asztalos}@ericsson.com

Abstract. In the field of telecommunication UML and Model Driven Architecture (MDA) have an increasing acceptance. MDA brings up new questions about the testing of the application developed by this technology. In MDA, Platform Independent Model (PIM) is the source of the system, and all maintenance and enhancement is performed at the platform independent level. However, MDA supporting tools provide only limited means for describing model level test procedures so a framework for model testing is indispensable. This paper investigates how to assist the model level test development with TTCN-3. We found that with the help of model translators we can facilitate and partly automate the test development process.

1 Introduction

The Model Driven Architecture (MDA) [1] of the Object Management Group has become the dominating trend in software engineering. MDA recommends starting the design of an application with a Platform-Independent Model (PIM) representing the business functionality and behavior, undistorted by technology details in the form of a UML model. In the next phase, Platform-Specific Models (PSM) containing software architecture dependent information are generated from the PIM by applying mappings in an MDA tool, preferably by automatic model transformations. Finally, in the code generation phase MDA tools automatically generate all or most of the implementation code for the deployment technology. Model transformation methodologies have been under extensive research recently. These transformation techniques provide higher quality compared to manually written programs but they require that the PIM contains the smallest possible number of faults. Unfortunately, it does not matter what technology we use and how much time we put into design and how careful we are when programming; mistakes are inevitable. Automation does not alone guarantee neither the proper choice of underlying architecture nor the elimination of conceptual flaws from the analysis model because defects injected in the requirements analysis are also deployed automatically into the implementation.

Due to the increased complexity of IT systems and increased customer requirements for quality of service (QoS) and reliability, mathematical-based test generation techniques often fail, because of the difficulty to select test cases from a (theoretical) unbounded number of tests. However, there is a strong need for effective testing of complex applications, because it is a well known fact that the development and implementation of tests is very time consuming and labor intensive. MDA based software develop-

F. Khendek and R. Dssouli (Eds.): TestCom 2005, LNCS 3502, pp. 304–317, 2005.
© IFIP 2005

ment offers an effective way to analyze computer systems with early-phase simulation and the tests created at the early-phase analysis can be reused on the implementation level.

We use TTCN-3 [2] as a test description language for platform independent model tests. One essential benefit of TTCN-3 is that the specification of tests is possible in a platform independent way. Our goal is to develop a framework for testing Platform Independent Model with TTCN-3, and analyze the possibility of reusing the analysis level tests on the implementation level.

This paper is organized as follows. In Section 2, we examine existing researches related to testing UML models. We will present a brief review of Model Driven Architecture focusing on the testing concepts in Section 3 and address our testing approach. Section 4 concludes the TTCN-3 language architecture and its relation to MDA. In Section 5 we present the structure of a model testing framework and the generation of this framework with a model transformer. In Section 6, we summarize the current status of the tester and our future plans.

2   Related Work

Lots of approaches have been taken to use the early-phase model as a basis of test development. Classic problems of model-based testing are [3]:

1. the generation of test cases from model according to a given coverage criterion,
2. the generation of a test oracle to determine the expected result of a test,
3. the execution of tests in test environments, possibly also generated from models.

Model-based testing is used to define tests which verify that a specific implementation accurately capture its requirements. Algorithms [4, 5, 6] have been defined to derive tests from formal system specification given in UML notation and their usage has been demonstrated with sample applications. But today none of the approaches are widely used in the industrial practice for large applications. One reason may be the difficulty to define selection criterions that result test cases with high coverage in respect to the requirements of the application. Furthermore, if MDA and code generation techniques are used, the test generation can apply with a purpose different of the classical approach. The difficulty that restricts the usage of problem (1) is: the code and test generation algorithms have the same source, the *PIM*. In this case only the correctness of the translation method could be verified.

UML technology focuses primarily on the definition of system structure and behavior and provides only limited means for describing complex test procedures [7]. CASE tools provide only minimal support for developing tests. They only assist to create unit tests, therefore:

– We can execute only a small number of tests.
– We have to execute and estimate them manually.
– The scope of a test is only an object or a small cluster of objects.

A special UML profile based on the UML 2.0 specification was initiated for test description using UML [8]. This profile aims at bridging the gap between designers and testers by providing a means for using UML for system modeling and test development. This allows a re-use of UML design documents for testing and makes test development possible in an early system development phase. But UML is not the appropriate language to address executable tests, because it is hard to define complex structures of test data and the graphical notation is sometimes inconvenient especially in case of a complex test description. The authors of paper [9] showed a methodology of how to use the UML 2.0 Testing Profile on an existing UML design model. The usability of the method was demonstrated by developing a test model for a Bluetooth roaming model.

The paper [10] describes a MOF (Meta-Object Facility) based meta-model of TTCN-3 and the realization of the meta-model in Eclipse. Moreover, it shows how to integrate TTCN-3 tools via this meta-model.

3   Testing Concepts in MDA

MDA envisages systems being designed independently of the eventual technologies, and a PIM can then be transformed into specific platforms. This section provides an overview of the model driven architecture focusing on the testing aspect.

3.1   Software Development with Executable UML

The OMG Model Driven Architecture addresses the complete life cycle of designing, deploying, integrating and managing applications using open standards. The MDA aims at providing a framework for the creation of applications in such a context where even the interface between the target application and the underlying execution platform is changing. MDA is a new way of writing specifications and developing applications, based on a platform-independent model (PIM) and using transformations to create platform-specific models (PSMs) and source code. The idea is that in a platform independent model the developer concentrates on a description of *what* the system has to do without going into details of *how* that will be achieved. The platform specific model, by contrast, describes how the system will realize the behavior implied by the analysis model [11]. MDA uses the Unified Modeling Language (UML) as notation. The UML 1.4 standard had relatively little to say about the detailed behavior that might be specified for the action associated with transitions and states or the methods implementing operation. In UML 1.5 and UML 2.0 specification, a UML Action Semantics [12] has been introduced. With the Action Semantics (AS) we can create executable models [13] with a detailed dynamic behavior description. This model can be executed in an appropriate simulator. The benefits of this approach go well beyond simply reducing or eliminating the coding stage. It also ensures platform independence, avoids obsolescence (programming languages may change, the model does not) and allows full verification of the models by executing them in a test and debug environment.

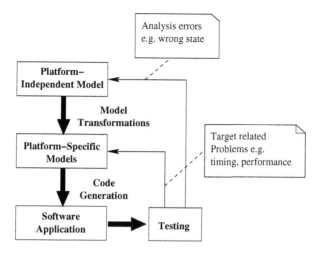

Fig. 1. The MDA architecture

3.2   Testing in MDA

The designated architecture of MDA is summarized in Fig. 1. Firstly, analysts create the analysis model[1] based on the system requirements. Then automatic transformations are used to create platform specific models (PSMs) and source code. The last phase is the testing of the implementation. In this method the testing phase only starts after the code generation has finished. There are two main problems in this method: (1) The creation of a new model transformer for a new platform is very time consuming, hence the code generation and the testing phase can be delayed, although there is an executable and testable model. (2) The model transformation can lead to the mixing up of platform independent and platform specific information in the implementation. This makes it difficult to eliminate the errors from the PIM.

In our approach (Fig. 2), we split the testing into two phases. In the first phase, the simulated platform independent model is verified. In this early stage only the functional correctness of the model could be tested. Since the analysis model is the source of the system and the following model transformations, it requires rigorous testing. The errors found during this phase are related to the analysis model, therefore we call them analysis errors.

In the second phase, the testing of the implementation is started. Based on the early-phase tests the testers can build performance, inter-operability etc. test cases. The functional tests can be also repeated in order to verify that the model transformations do not make any unexpected changes. To minimize the work invested to the testing of the application we should reuse the early-phase tests. In order for testing to reach its full potential, it is essential to use the same testing framework throughout the entire MDA software development process. We use a dashed arrow between the implementation testing and the platform independent model in Fig. 2 because the early-phase

---

[1] Analysis model and Platform Independent Model (PIM) are used as synonyms in this paper.

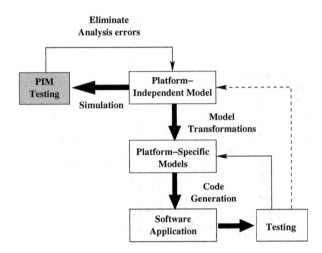

Fig. 2. Extended test model in MDA

testing ensures that the implementation does not contain analysis errors, hence during the implementation testing only platform related errors can be found. We present some exceptions in the end of Section 5.2

In the following section we demonstrate that the TTCN-3 language is a feasible candidate for this purpose. We present a short overview of the standardized language for test description, focusing on how to depict tests on analysis as well as on implementation level.

4   TTCN-3 and Its Relation to MDA

TTCN-3 (Testing and Test Control Notation 3) is the new industry-standard test specification language that was developed and standardized by the European Telecommunication Standards Institute (ETSI). TTCN-3 can be applied for all kinds of black-box testing for reactive and distributed systems and makes it possible to be used not only in conformance testing of telecommunication protocols but as well for testing Internet, mobile, data base access etc. protocols and also for inter-operability, robustness etc. testing. Use of TTCN-3 to support test development has been investigated to encourage the parallel development of a test suite together with a standard system analysis. TTCN-3 language consists of three main units:

Test Behavior. Test behavior is a specification of what to test with which input, result, and under which conditions. The TTCN-3 language defines several constructs for describing the functionality of a test system. TTCN-3 allows an easy and efficient description of complex test behavior in terms of sequences, alternatives, loops and parallel stimuli and responses.

Test Configuration. This part is responsible for the communication between the System Under Test (SUT) and the test system. However, the real physical connection is outside the scope of TTCN-3. Instead, a well defined (but abstract) test system interface shall be associated with each test case. A complex test configuration may contain several test components which could communicate with each other and the system under test.

Test Data Definition. One of the key elements of TTCN-3 is the ability to send and receive complex messages over the communication ports defined by the test configuration. TTCN-3 supports a number of predefined basic data types and structured types constructed from the basic data types. The TTCN-3 has a special language element, the template, that provides sophisticated means for describing test data. Templates are used either to transmit a set of distinct values or to test whether a set of received values match the template specification.

The general testing process with TTCN-3 includes the following main steps: the developed abstract test suite is compiled and extended with an adaptor (one special implementation of an abstract TTCN-3 test port) that provides the connection between the tested system and the executable test suite. Then, the executable test suite is executed against the system under test. Finally, the results are evaluated. The TTCN-3 is an abstract language, hence one can describe the test behavior independently of the underlying communication architecture and data presentation. The structure of a TTCN-3 tester is summarized in Fig. 3. Note that the basic conception of the model driven architecture is almost the same (see in Section 3.2), but the TTCN-3 focusing on the testing domain.

There are two ways to alter the behavior of a test suite. One solution is to change the communication interface and the data encoding/decoding rules. In the field of wireless communication there are many protocols that are able to transmit data in several different ways depending on how reliable the connection is or how important the message is etc. A good example is the WAP (Wireless Application Protocol) protocol, which can work on various bearers i.e. SMS, GPRS, Circuit Switched Data etc. This functionality is especially important in the 3G or 4G mobile technologies where many high level applications have to work on different transaction protocols.

The second solution is to change the test data definitions. TTCN-3 provides a simple form of inheritance that enables us to modify an existing template without changing the

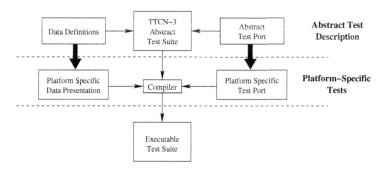

Fig. 3. The Architecture of the TTCN-3 language

original definition. This makes the adaptation of templates to different testing situations possible and avoids the duplication of similar test data.

In accordance with the discussion above this approach allows to use TTCN-3 during all part of the model-driven software development. The functionality and the specification details are separated, therefore the early-phase functional tests can be reused on implementation level.

5   Testing Framework for Platform Independent Models with TTCN-3

In this section, we show how to use the TTCN-3 language in model driven software development.

5.1   Simulating Executable UML Models

Model execution enables developers to focus on the appropriate behavior of the problem to be solved, independently of platform dependent problems at an early development phase. Executable models allow the early verification with simulation, since they completely describe the dynamic behavior of the system. In order to simulate a model we need a special environment that is capable to interpret executable models. This environment is referred to as a *UML Virtual Machine*. As input, the Virtual Machine requires an executable UML model (class diagram, state-chart, action specification) and executes the model according to the initial state and the receiving inputs. Having this Virtual Machine we are able to define test interfaces.

According to [17], PIMs suffer from testability problems in the area of *observability*, the ability to detect errors in control flows, and *controllability*, the capability to cause the software to execute an appropriate path. An OMG Request For Proposal (RFP) has been initiated on a standardized interface of testing and debugging executable UML models [16]. In Fig. 4, the structure of the interface is concluded.

The goal of the Test Instrument Interface is to standardize the hooks into model execution to allow test setup, stimulus, and data collection. Model simulators have some support for model connection, they provide the ability to define breakpoints in the executable model, to log the actions during the execution. But they do not allow to use

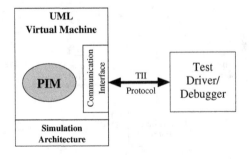

Fig. 4. Test Instrumentation Interface

external testers for the testing of the model. In our approach, we transform UML models to be able to communicate with an external tester, so that the original simulation framework can be used. The interface definitions between the test system and the UML model are addressed on UML level and the physical communication interfaces are derived from these definitions. The extension of executable models with communication ability is provided through model transformations.

5.2   Towards the Mapping of UML Models into TTCN-3

To create executable tests three partly coherent tasks have to be carried out:

- Define the data uses in the test cases
- Define the behavior of the test cases
- Define the test framework (test configuration)

In this paper we concentrate on the solution of the first and the third problem with the help of a model translators. A test framework covers the concepts for specifying test components, the interfaces of and connections between the test components to the System Under Test. Telecommunication protocols and softwares are distributed applications, therefore our testing framework was designed to allow the definition of complex distributed test scenarios on model level. We defined a model transformer which is capable to extend an executable UML model in order to test in a distributed test configuration.

Most tedious activities during test development are to accurately define the interfaces between the system under test (SUT) and the test system, and specify the test data sending and receiving on these interfaces. Therefore, another model transformer was defined to create the data definition and the testing framework in TTCN-3 core language. The test cases can be written manually based on the derived definition.

MDA offers the potential to automatically transform a PIM, perhaps after annotating it with some platform information, to different PSMs. Modeler will *tag* their PIM component with information to control the translation. This approach allows us to store test specific information in the analysis model independently of the design aspects.

To create a model transformer in UML we have to create the meta-model of the target language, in our case the meta-model of the TTCN-3 language. Fig. 5 depicts the communication and data representation part of our meta-model.

The elements of the meta-model are populated (instantiate the elements of the meta-model) depending on the platform-independent model. According to our experience the communication interfaces on the implementation level are represented by operations of classes on the model level. Hence, we specify a *tagging* structure in order to mark the operations that are relevant for testing. *Tags* may denote the direction of the communication channel created from the *tagged* operation or the name of the test port which the given operation belongs to. The data presentation of UML differs from the one of TTCN-3, therefore we had to define mapping rules between them. Because of the lack of space only the main mapping rules are summarized in Table 1.

The simple UML data types have unambiguous representation in TTCN-3. The only exception is the text type because in TTCN-3 five different basic string types can be defined. We selected the charstring type to represent the UML text type in TTCN-3.

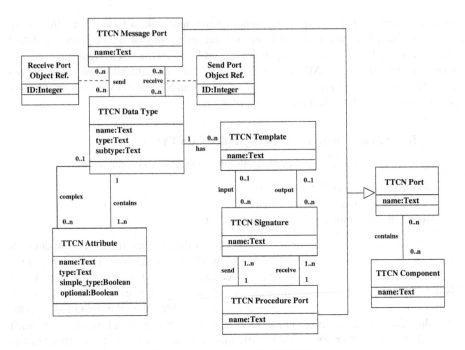

Fig. 5. Meta-model of the TTCN-3

Table 1. Data presentation mapping rules

UML	TTCN
Simple types (Boolean, Double,Integer)	Simple TTCN-3 types
Text	charstring
Data set	record of
Operation parameters	record
Polymorphic operations (with small changes)	optional parameters
Polymorphic operations	union types

We map the input and output parameters of the operations into record types. TTCN-3 ports are also generated which allows to send and receive these record types. We can define sending templates for these records to test the operation with various input parameters. In addition, we can define receiving templates to automatically verify the results of the operation using the TTCN-3 matching mechanism.

The last two rows of Table 1 show an example how the structure of the platform independent model influence the TTCN-3 data presentation. If analysts create generalization relations with many sub-classes and with polymorphic operations then the structure of the derived TTCN-3 data types have to reflect this inheritance tree. An operation of the parent-class can be the representation of a communication port and the sub-classes inherit this operation but in some sub-classes the operation is overridden. In this case some parameters of the operation may become *optional* parameters in TTCN-3 if only small changes (one or two parameters appear or disappear in the operation definition) occurred during the redefinition of the operation. If the changes in the parameters of the operation are considerable then it is more profitable to create a new *record* for this parameter structure. In order to refer that the new *record* is derived from a parent-class we compose a *union* type which contains the different definitions of the records corresponding to the operation.

To achieve testability, we also use the *tagged* elements of the model as weaving points where we should insert new instructions to extend the UML model. The extended model is capable of communicating with a tester in the simulator. The extension is based on the definition of the tagged operation.

With MDA we can develop a translator model [14] which is capable to collect information from high level, platform independent models and generate the TTCN-3 test interfaces and data definitions. Accordingly, the technical problems related to the communication between the test system and the UML Virtual Machine can be hidden from the testers as well as the analysts. Fig. 6 depicts the structure of the PIM tester. A distributed client-server based environment is responsible for the communication between the two parts of the model tester. This communication interface is also generated from the analysis model. The interface has two part. The first part is running in the UML Virtual Machine. This part is capable to access the model. The second part is the implementation of TTCN-3 test ports. This implementation contains the mappings between the UML and TTCN-3 data types.

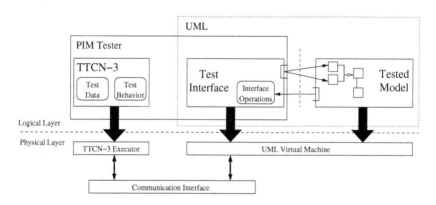

Fig. 6. Structure of the PIM tester

The different parts of the platform independent model testing are summarized in Fig. 7. The test development is started with the transformation of the PIM. The TTCN-3 translator creates the communication interfaces and the data definitions. Based on this definitions the test data and the test behavior can be defined. The model translator creates the extended PIM, which is executed in a simulator. The TTCN-3 test cases are executed on the simulated extended platform independent model.

The model-based testing usually not enough to eliminate all faults from the software because of the following reasons:

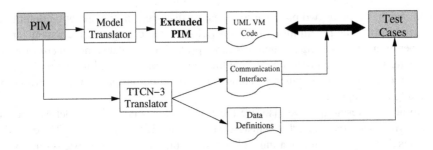

Fig. 7. Mapping to TTCN-3

- The model may contain special object structures.
- Usage of native codes in the model.
- Usage of third party libraries, existing components.

There are special object structures [15] whose functions depend on the architecture, hence the functions of these objects have to be tested on implementation level as well. Some MDA tools allow to insert INLINE (platform specific, native language) codes into the body of the platform independent action code that can be tested only after the mapping to the platform specific implementation occurs. Furthermore, one can use third party libraries or existing components that were created without model driven technology. In this case, the integration with these components have to be tested, but it is only possible on implementation level. In spite of these limitations of the platform independent testing, according to our experience approximately 50-60% of the errors can be found and eliminated in analysis phase.

5.3   Testing Through a MDA Software Development

We experimented on our testing framework during the development of a network management software. The test environment is depicted in Fig. 8. The test architecture consists of three different elements.

Managed Network. A managed network may contain a few or several hundreds of managed nodes (MN). The managed nodes provide support to ATM switching and IP forwarding system. An arbitrary mix of different traffic types – data, voice, and video type of traffic – can be handled with preserved quality of service and with efficient use of bandwidth for each traffic type.

Network Management Server. This application is required by telecommunication operators for providing reliable operations of the communication network. The tasks involved include monitoring, troubleshooting, and control operations in a wide range of network management areas.

Web clients. The operators of the network are able to access the management software through web-based clients. In case of error the operators can reconfigure the network topology manually.

The main component, the management server, is modeled in UML and the other components (client, managed nodes) are emulated by TTCN-3 components. This heterogeneous infrastructure can be tested with TTCN-3 parallel components. Our goal hereby is to test the functionality of the server with different network structures or with erroneous network topologies. In case of a complex real network it is difficult to configure the network to generate incorrect answers. With TTCN-3 and simulation we can easily establish these situations and can verify that our application (the simulated PIM model) works as we expect.

A typical problem in model driven development is that the development of the platform-independent model finishes before the development of the transformation rules for the specific platform would be completed. In this case we can test the PIM in a simulator but the test environment act as a real network.

5.4   Empirical Experiences

We used a sample TTCN-3 test module to investigate what kind of modifications were needed to rerun the early-phase tests on the implementation. At first, we defined manually 20 test cases to verify the main functionality of the network management application. The test module contained 25 type definitions and 30 template specifications for the data types. Two types of TTCN-3 test port were used during the testing: a HTTP-based test port for the client and a SNMP port for the communication to the managed nodes. For simulation testing purposes the test ports, the test components and the data type definitions were automatically generated from the PIM model. The test port implementations for the Ericsson's TTCN-3 test executor were also generated from the PIM model. Three parallel test components were used during the testing, one for the

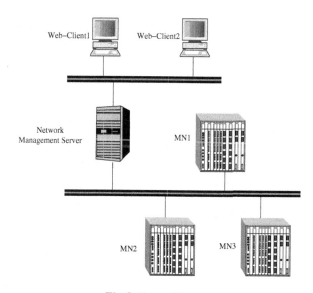

Fig. 8. Test architecture

emulation of the web-client and two for the emulation of the managed network. The test suite was executed against the simulated model and 5 errors were found in the PIM.

Secondly, we executed this test suite on the implementation. The implementation was generated from the platform independent model with a model transformer developed in Ericsson Hungary. Naturally, we had to change the implementation of the test ports. We also needed one new data type and 2 new templates. With these modifications every test case could be executed on the implementation. One additional error was found in the implementation which was caused by an integration problem between an existing and a newly developed component.

6   Conclusion and Future Work

In this article we propose an approach for model level testing of applications designed with model-driven technology. We can adapt this test design process into the standard model-driven software development process. By using this approach, we are able to analyze Platform Independent Models with tests written in a standardized test description language. These early-phase tests primarily focus on the functional correctness of the software. Moreover, by extending the platform independent tests, other types of tests (e.g. inter-operability, performance) can be derived. Accordingly, the implementation level test development time can be reduced.

Regarding further investigation, it would be interesting to study the possibility of using this testing concept throughout the entire model-driven software development process and work out a general *Model-Driven Test Development* method.

References

1. R. Soley: Model Driven Architecture: An Introduction. http://www.omg.org/mda.
2. ETSI ES 201 873-1: The Testing and Test Control Notation version 3; Part 1: TTCN-3 Core Language. V2.2.1 (2003-02), 2003; also an ITU-T standard Z.140.
3. R.Heckel, M.Lohmann: Towards Model-Driven Testing, Electronic Notes in Theoretical Computer Science Vol.82 (6), 2003.
4. J. Hartman, C. Imoberdorf, M. Meisinger: UML-Based Integration Testing, ISSTA 2000.
5. J. Offut, A. Abdurazik: Generating Tests from UML Specification, UML99 Fort Collins (CO), October 1999.
6. L. C. Briand , Y. Labiche: A UML-Based Approach to System Testing, Journal of Software and Systems Modeling (SoSyM) Vol. 1 No.1 2002 pp. 10-42.
7. I. Schieferdecker, Z. R. Dai, J. Grabowski, A. Rennoch: The UML 2.0 Testing Profile and its relation to TTCN-3, Testing of Communicating Systems – 15th IFIP International Conference, TestCom2003, Sophia Antipolis (F), May 2003. Lecture Notes in Computer Science (LNCS) 2644, Springer, May 2003.
8. UML Testing Profile (Final Submission), April 2004 http://www.fokus.gmd.de/u2tp/.
9. Z. R. Dai, J. Grabowski, H. Neukirchen, H. Pals: From Design to Test with UML – Applied to a Roaming Algorithm for Bluetooth Devices. Testing of Communicating Systems – 16th IFIP International Conference, TestCom2004, Oxford, United Kingdom, March 2004. Lecture Notes in Computer Science (LNCS) 2978, Springer, March 2004.

10. I. Schieferdecker, G. Din: A Meta-model for TTCN-3, Applying Formal Methods: Testing, Performance, and M/E-Commerce: FORTE 2004 Workshops, Toledo, Spain. Lecture Notes in Computer Science (LNCS) 3236, Springer, October 2004.
11. S. Shlaer, S. J. Mellor: Recursive Design of an Application-Independent Architecture, IEEE Software, pp. 61-72, January/February 1997.
12. I. Wilkie, A. King, M. Clarke, C Raistrick: UML ASL Reference Guide, Kennedy Carter, 2001.
13. Supporting Model Driven Architecture with eXecutable UML Kennedy Carter 2002.
14. I. Wilkie, A. King, M. Clarke, C Raistrick: The Intelligent OOA Strategy for Configurable Code Generation, Kennedy Carter, 1997.
15. S. Shlaer, N. Lang: Shlaer-Mellor Method: The OOA96 Report. http://www.projtech.com.
16. Model-level Testing/Debug RFP (Final Submission) April 2004 http://www.omg.org.
17. G. Eakman: Verification of Platform Independent Models, Workshop on Model Driven Architecture in the Specification, Implementation and Validation of Object-oriented Embedded Systems (SIVOES-MDA), San Francisco, October 2003.

Some Lessons from an Experiment Using TTCN-3 for the RIPng Testing

Annie Floch[1], Frédéric Roudaut[1], Ariel Sabiguero[1,2], and César Viho[1]

[1] IRISA, Campus de Beaulieu, 35042 Rennes Cedex, France
{afloch, froudaut, asabigue, viho}@irisa.fr,
http://www.irisa.fr/armor
[2] Instituto de Computación, Facultad de Ingeniería,
Universidad de la República, J. Herrera y Reissig 565,
Montevideo, Uruguay
asabigue@fing.edu.uy
http://www.fing.edu.uy/inco

Abstract. This paper presents an experiment in using TTCN-3 for developing conformance test suite for the RIPng protocol. Main issues that any new TTCN-3 user may deal with are highlighted. Some methodological constraints imposed by TTCN-3 development process are exposed. Provided solutions are presented together with main features that have to be included in TTCN-3 based tools to ease test development.

Keywords: Conformance testing, TTCN-3, RIPng, IPv6.

1   Introduction

The European community, through the European Telecommunications Standards Institute (ETSI), promotes the use of the TTCN-3 language for testing purposes [1, 2]. Several leading communication protocols and standards followed the ETSI IEC/OSI 9646 recommendations for testing, both on methodology and tools. TTCN-3 has been designed to provide a well suited environment for any kind of testing activity [3, 4, 5, 6], from abstract test suites specification to executable test suites [7, 8]. As it is a new language, there is not enough maturity regarding its usage and environments that are supposed to ease TTCN-3 usage.

In the Internet community in general, TTCN-3 is not widely adopted. Moreover, it is even unfavorably criticized. This is mainly due to the confusion with it's predecessor TTCN-2, which was considered too formal and inadequate for Internet related protocol testing. TTCN-2 was considered a rigid language and difficult to generate tests for new protocols. This 'bad reputation' applies for testing the new protocols developed for the new version of the Internet protocol, called IPv6. Indeed, most of the existing test suites are developed using IPv6 dedicated languages and tools. The most famous one is the v6eval toolbox (http://www.tahi.org/) developed by the Japanese TAHI project. In this context, it is difficult to convince people to use TTCN-3 without showing real executable test suites for at least a simple IPv6 related protocol.

F. Khendek and R. Dssouli (Eds.): TestCom 2005, LNCS 3502, pp. 318–332, 2005.

The objective of the present work is to gain experience using the general purpose TTCN-3 language and tools while addressing an IPv6 specific test conformance problem. The protocol selected for testing was RIPng protocol [9], presented later in section 2.1. The RIPng routing protocol has the advantage of being relatively simple (at least compared to other IPv6 related routing protocols), while an important and widely deployed protocol in small to medium organizations. This work also aims at proving to the Internet community that TTCN-3 is ready to be used for testing, covering all steps from abstract test suites (ATS) specification to executable test suites (ETS). It was also important identifying main issues when testing with TTCN-3 and providing solutions that may help simplifying future test generation.

The methodology behind this work was restricted in scope as the goal was to to be able to obtain ETS to be executed against real implementations during the IPv6 interoperability event[1] organized by the ETSI/PlugTests Service in October 2004. Thus, we followed a straightforward approach due to time constraints: some decisions were based on *time-to-executable-test* parameters. On the other hand, one may notice that this kind of requirements also corresponds to the real Internet community context of having ETS as soon as the need of testing is identified.

Amongst all available TTCN-3 tools, the choice was made in favor of a free of charge toolkit for academic research purpose. Indeed, due to the youngness of TTCN-3 and our small knowledge in using this new language, it was important to use a tool which allows libraries source code modifications if needed.

As a result of this work, a RIPng conformance ATS/ETS based on TTCN-3 is now available. These tests have been ran against real implementations during the last IPv6 ETSI-PlugTests interoperability event. Test results were considered interesting by participants.

Doing this work and following the approach indicated above, we face main issues that any new TTCN-3 user may deal with. As other results, these main issues have been highlighted. Solutions that we provided are explained. Some ideas that may help in easing test development using TTCN-3 are proposed.

The paper is structured as follow. At first, Section 2 explains the context of the work. A short description of the RIPng protocol is given followed by main components that have to be developed when using TTCN-3 for testing. Section 3 outlines different steps to obtain TTCN-3 based test suites for the RIPng protocol. Problems encountered during the test development phase and provided solutions are also presented. Section 4 presents some results gathered and lessons learned from this first experiment in using TTCN-3 for RIPng testing. Some ideas that may help in easing other similar effort are presented. The conclusion of this paper is summarized in Section 5, and future work is suggested.

---

[1] An interoperability event is a session of about one week where real implementations are tested against several test suites provided by test generation companies and laboratories.

2   The Context of the Experiment

We have been involved for years developing IPv6 conformance tests suites. The tool used is v6eval, developed by TAHI project (http://www.tahi.org/). In such line of research, we are working now to produce test suites for several IPv6 routing protocols.

One important reason behind the present work for us is to find provider-independent tools and languages for defining test suites. TTCN-3 is presented as a modern standardized abstract language, test oriented and provider independent. Tool providers implement their solutions according to the standards, but independently. It is widely accepted that multi-provider scenarios lead to more complete and general languages and tools than single provider ones.

Our primary motivation was to experiment with the ability of TTCN-3 for our testing purposes with real and concrete IPv6 protocol. On the other hand, we wanted to show to the IPv6 community that TTCN-3 can be used for this purpose. One way to prove that is to have executable test suites built with TTCN-3 language and tools, which can be used during interoperability sessions.

2.1   A Short Overview of RIPng

RIPng[9] is the logical step of the well known IPv4 family of RIP protocols into IPv6 world. RIPng stands for *Routing Information Protocol - Next Generation*. RIP belongs to the class of algorithms known as "distance vector algorithms". Distance-vector algorithms are based on the exchange of only a small amount of information. Each network node that participates in the routing protocol must be a router as IPv6 protocol provides other mechanisms for router discovery, and it is assumed to keep information about all destinations within the system.

Limitations of RIP include network diameter restrictions, counting to infinity to resolve loop situations and the lack of metrics based on dynamic. Some of the limitations are not *per se* limitations, but they are a consequence of the design of the protocol. RIP is not intended to be used as Internet's single routing protocol, but as an Autonomous System (AS) internal protocol. RIPng is an UDP-based protocol and listens on the port 521. It is a message oriented protocol (1-request; 2-response), based on distributed intelligence, without any distinguished node. The figure 1 shows a typical RIPng deployment scenario, where 6 interconnected routers exchange routing information as request-response messages.

IPv6 protocol defines and implements four different types of communication destinations, which are: anycast, unicast, multicast and broadcast. This enhancements at network/transport layers provides better support for protocols using their services. RIPng uses both unicast and multicast mechanisms for inter router communication, according to the kind of message exchanged. The multicast address ff02::9 is reserved as the all-rip-routers group, which is used except in some non-multicast channels, where explicit network addresses have to be used.

Authentication mechanisms have better grounds on IPv6 protocol stack and thus, are removed from RIPng protocol itself.

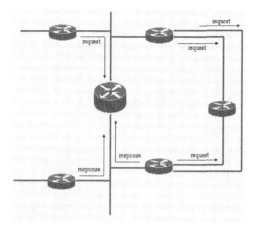

Fig. 1. Autonomous System RIPng messaging

2.2   A Short Description of TTCN3 Main Components

TTCN-3 is a pretty new language (current TTCN-3 Core Language[10] was published on 02-2003) with only a first generation of compliers and tools supporting it. TTCN-3 was designed to be able to incorporate testing capabilities not present on other programming languages, and was also cleared from OSI peculiarities (that previous versions suffered). TTCN-3 is now flexible enough to be applied to any kind of reactive system tests.

The structure of a TTCN-3 test system general structure is shown in the figure 2. As usual, this test system is supposed to be executed against a system

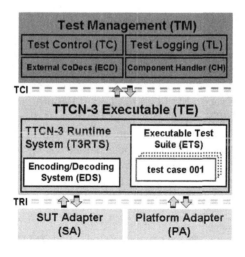

Fig. 2. TTCN-3 Test System Architecture

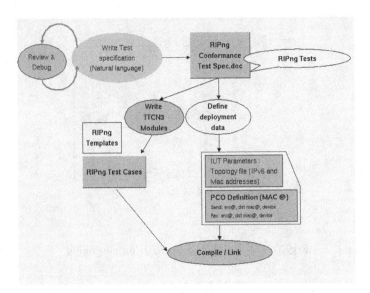

Fig. 3. TTCN-3 based initial approach of test specification

under test (SUT). Each block in the figure represents an entity implementing a particular aspect required by a test system. The test system user interacts with the Test Management (TM) and uses the general test execution management functionality. The TM entity is responsible for the global test management. The TTCN-3 Executable (TE) implements the functionality defined as TTCN-3 modules, which can be structured into sub-modules and import definitions from other modules. Modules have a definition part (defines test components, communication ports, data types, constants, test data templates, etc.) and a control part (which is responsible for calling test cases and controlling their execution). Other test layout dependent parameters are defined at the SUT Adapter (SA) and the Platform Adapter (PA). A TTCN-3 test system has two main internal interfaces, the TTCN-3 Control Interface (TCI) and the TTCN-3 Runtime Interface (TRI). TCI interface specifies the interface between Test Management (TM) and TTCN-3 Executable (TE) entities. TRI interface specifies the interfaces between TE, SUT Adapter (SA) and Platform Adapter (PA) entities.

Figure 3 shows the modules and main methodological tasks that have to be developed to produce test suites. The blocks named `RIPng Test Cases` and `RIPng Templates` corresponds to the tasks required to define the TTCN-3 Executable block on figure 2. The blocks named `SUT Parameters` and `PCO Definition` corresponds to parameters required by the SA to interface with the SUT.

3   TTCN3 Based Test Generation for RIPng

We have a broad experience on the IPv6 field, while this is our first practical approach to TTCN-3. Nevertheless, both our experience and the methodology used in the IPv6 community matches the principles suggested in [11]. The hands-on experience with TTCN-3 presented in this paper tries to answer whether the language and methodology are ready for addressing to the strong needs of the IPv6 test community. It is worth mentioning that the Internet community is a very pragmatic environment, who do not care about the way the tools are designed, but focus on the way they can quickly answer to their needs. Our goal was to develop tests for RIPng in a short time with existing new tools. This work documents field experience with TTCN-3, but does not intend to promote a methodology.

It is known that a black-box approach to conformance testing will only allow us to exchange signals with the System Under Test (SUT): in this case, signals are RIPng messages. Changes in the routing tables of the SUT could be observed only through the way routing is performed by the SUT and RIPng messages sent. Most routers implement the *Simple Network Management Protocol* (SNMP) [12], which allows inspection of network entities (like interfaces, routing tables, etc ...) specified by the network administrator. It might have been possible to consider SNMP inspection of the routing tables of the SUT(gray-testing), but as SNMP is not required for IPv6 compliance, the idea was dropped. Designed test cases consisted of exchanging routing information with the SUT and later sending IP probes to selected destinations so as to determine the way routing information is not only learned and shared by the SUT, but also, applied on its own routing decisions.

To be able to specify TTCN-3 test cases we had to obtain a tool and define the needed modules according to our test purposes. It was also required to provide the SA with proper definitions so that the mapping between TTCN-3 components communication ports and test system interface ports is done. After this, the ETS is generated.

3.1   Approach for TTCN-3 Test Specification

Routing Table Entries (RTE) are the key elements exchanged within RIPng messages. Each router is supposed to have some sort of routing table with at least the following information: the IPv6 prefix of the destination, a metric, the IPv6 address of the next router along the path to that destination, a flag and various timers associated with the route. This suggests that basic routing operations to test shall be related to RTE maintenance like: RTE creation, RTE update, RTE deletion, RTE request.

Maybe the simplest test topology would consist of two routers and the SUT, each connected to a different physical interface of the SUT. From the test purposes settled we were able to build a more complex network layout, shown on figure 4. The small box in the center represents the role that the SUT plays in the topology, while the rest of it, marked as **Tester** represents what has to be developed to perform the tests. For specific test purposes we selected -projected-the relevant routers that allow inspection of the desired property and specified the particular ATS only considering it. This methodology simplifies test design because we have a single well known network, and it allows us to concentrate

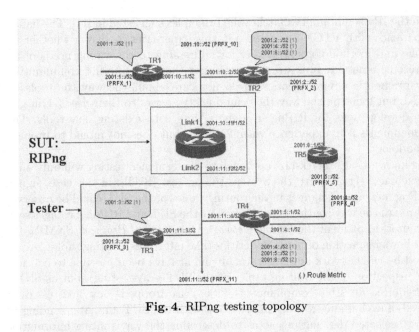

Fig. 4. RIPng testing topology

on details of each test purpose by projection of relevant smaller parts of the network.

It was required right from the first test definitions to be able to emulate more than one router to explore even simple protocol behavior and properties. This fact makes us define and handle several Points of Control and Observation PCO. The distribution of PCO over single or multiple test execution threads or processes promotes the discussion between parallel *vs.* single party testing, or in other words, a Master Test Component (MTC) with Parallel Test Components (PTC) *vs.* single MTC. Protocol complexity was not an issue at this point, as the protocol itself is simple: both solutions are adequate for test requirements. From our previous experiences and the lack of time for enough testing of the TTCN-3 parallel possibilities and API, we decided for a solution with a single MTC that handles all required PCO. The decision of using a single node to emulate the whole network topology allows us to avoid all parallel synchronization problems. We believe that naive deployment of PTC corresponding to each emulated router would have produced test suites with different characteristics. Complexity of test setup would have increased considerably as separate process on different machines had to be configured, etc.

Another important decision was the tool selection, which was done considering all the existing tools known to us (testing_tech, Telelogic, Danet, OpenTTCN, etc.). At the time of the selection all available tools were equally eligible as they all implemented TTCN-3 required components. Also, none of them provided already built IPv6 libraries that might have helped with the building blocks for RIPng tests. The decision was based on our experience testing with C++ tools and licensing conditions that allowed us not only to use the tool for academic purposes, but also to have access to the source code when needed. Other aspects considered were Integrated Development Environments (IDE) and tools provided that help with simple and repetitive tasks. From all those testing tools available the choice was made for Danet's testing tool (`http://www.danet.de`).

3.2   PCOs Management

Points of Control and Observation (PCO) play a very important role on what can be observed out of a system. Proper selection of PCO placement would allow better and detailed protocol inspection. As RIPng is a UDP based protocol the first test design tried to place PCO at UDP level, as shown in the figure 5.

It was not possible to code a single tester using TTCN-3 that was able to emulate several routers. The tester is implemented using underlying operating system protocol stack services, thus it is not possible to simulate traffic to and from different routers: it would be necessary to define different IPv6 addresses and Ethernet MAC addresses. TTCN-3 does not allow dynamic definition of MAC/IPv6 addresses associated to ports. Another observation is that we do not only need UDP services: ICMP echoes are sent through the SUT so as to check the routing decisions at a certain moment.

The figure 6 shows all the parts -grayed- of the protocol stack that had to be addressed with the test. The main difficulty was that when more than one router had to be emulated using a single MTC, IPv6 native stack on the host had to be disabled and all the steps of the communication had to be emulated from TTCN-3 modules. It would have been also the same situation with several PTC running on the same machine. Several issues arose during the development phase.

Fig. 5. RIPng testing architecture, UDP level PCO

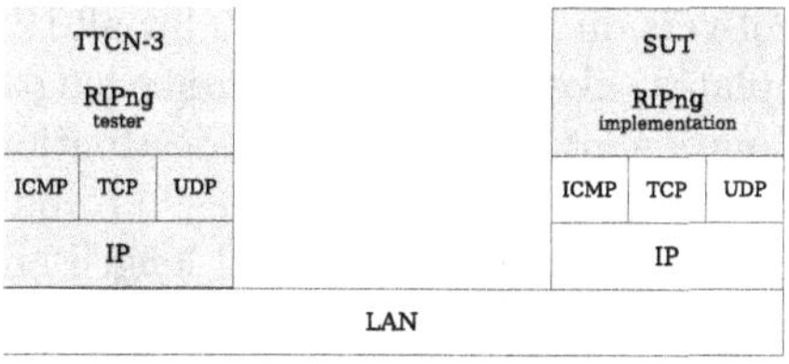

Fig. 6. RIPng testing architecture, link layer/IP level PCO

Both the TTCN-3 tool and language were not designed to handle this situation of multiple host emulation using a single Network Interface Card (NIC). Due to time constraints we worked out the problems by changing some aspects of the tool implementation by recoding parts of TTCN-3 primitives. We changed TRI basic primitives so as to handle link layer PCO, which were not implemented in Danet's tool. With the modifications introduced we were able to emulate as many hosts -form data link layer up- as required from a single real host.

This kind of handling increased the complexity of the ATS as not only RIPng protocol communications had to be implemented. Required UDP assembly and disassembly of packets also was needed, including checksum and packet length calculation. IPv6 layer assembly and disassembly of packets was also mandatory. In the end also data link layer parameter handling had to be introduced to transmit packets with the corresponding MAC address of the router emulated. Moreover, reception of the packets and their corresponding processing had to be handled.

Other link maintenance aspects of IPv6 Neighbor Discovery[13] (ND) algorithm had to be addressed. IPv6 relies several host autoconfiguration tasks to the ND. Thus, for correct node emulation, ND signaling is necessary.

TTCN-3 template definition was not versatile enough to allow efficient matching of incoming data. The solution found was to create as many PCO as couples of communicating addresses required. Due to the way IPv6 handles addresses, each emulated node was associated to several addresses (unicast, broadcast and multicast). To fulfill this multiple addressing scenario, several PCO were introduced. The complexity generated by this fact was significant, both at ATS coding and at tool modification level. ATS legibility was also an important issue as classification of messages received becomes complicated.

3.3   Coding/Decoding, Libraries, etc.

As stated before, the communication between RIPng nodes is message-oriented. Message definition has a low level of abstraction and coding/decoding is done dependent on the position of bits within the frame. Figure 7 presents RIPng packet as defined in the RFC 2080[9] with its corresponding IPv6 header prepended, without any IPv6 options.

Several codification issues needed to be resolved in order to define a TTCN-3 module that abstracts the RIPng packet. First of all, some fields are hard-coded always, like the protocol version, which is 0b0110 for all IPv6 tests. Other fields are parameters of templates, like prefixes and prefix length values. Some fields are parameters of the component, like source and destination addresses (different from one tested router to other). Finally, others need to be calculated each time a packet is about to be transmitted, like payload length and checksum values.

We found that there is no easy mechanism, like the ones defined on the RFC 2373[14], for IPv6 address text representation. When defining parameters for a component, its IPv6 address 2001:2::1 had to be coded. In our environment, XML files are used (see figure 8).

```
 0                   1                   2                   3
 0 1 2 3 4 5 6 7 8 9 0 1 2 3 4 5 6 7 8 9 0 1 2 3 4 5 6 7 8 9 0 1
+-+-+-+-+-+-+-+-+-+-+-+-+-+-+-+-+-+-+-+-+-+-+-+-+-+-+-+-+-+-+-+-+
|Version| Traffic Class |            Flow Label                 |
+-+-+-+-+-+-+-+-+-+-+-+-+-+-+-+-+-+-+-+-+-+-+-+-+-+-+-+-+-+-+-+-+
|        Payload Length         |  Next Header  |  Hop Limit    |
+-+-+-+-+-+-+-+-+-+-+-+-+-+-+-+-+-+-+-+-+-+-+-+-+-+-+-+-+-+-+-+-+
|                                                               |
~                     Source Address                            ~
|                                                               |
+-+-+-+-+-+-+-+-+-+-+-+-+-+-+-+-+-+-+-+-+-+-+-+-+-+-+-+-+-+-+-+-+
|                                                               |
~                   Destination Address                         ~
|                                                               |
+-+-+-+-+-+-+-+-+-+-+-+-+-+-+-+-+-+-+-+-+-+-+-+-+-+-+-+-+-+-+-+-+
|          Source  Port         |        Destination Port       |
+-+-+-+-+-+-+-+-+-+-+-+-+-+-+-+-+-+-+-+-+-+-+-+-+-+-+-+-+-+-+-+-+
|             Length            |            Checksum            |
+-+-+-+-+-+-+-+-+-+-+-+-+-+-+-+-+-+-+-+-+-+-+-+-+-+-+-+-+-+-+-+-+
|   command   |   version   |           must be zero            |
+-+-+-+-+-+-+-+-+-+-+-+-+-+-+-+-+-+-+-+-+-+-+-+-+-+-+-+-+-+-+-+-+
|                                                               |
~                   Route Table Entry 1                         ~
|                                                               |
+-+-+-+-+-+-+-+-+-+-+-+-+-+-+-+-+-+-+-+-+-+-+-+-+-+-+-+-+-+-+-+-+
|                                                               |
~                   Route Table Entry 2                         ~
|                                                               |
+-+-+-+-+-+-+-+-+-+-+-+-+-+-+-+-+-+-+-+-+-+-+-+-+-+-+-+-+-+-+-+-+
```

Fig. 7. RIPng packet format

```
<RUT_LINK2_GLOBAL_ADDRESS1  moduleId="IPv6RouterInterface\">
    <OctetStringValue valueKind="4\">
        20010002000000000000000000000001
    </OctetStringValue>
</RUT_LINK2_GLOBAL_ADDRESS1>
```

Fig. 8. Markup defining an IPv6 address

To ease TTCN-3 based IPv6 test generation, a test environment shall provide standardized methods for network address handling and representation.

TTCN-3 data type definitions were coded to provide abstract description of IPv6 packets. Templates are built based on data type definitions. Figure 9 shows an example of a template defined.

It can be noted that assigning values to non byte-oriented fields could not be done in a standard way as it could be done in C++ or Java. Fields like Protocol Version could be properly type-defined as Bit4, but it was not possible to assign a "6" value, like it was possible to do with many others like Traffic Class or Destination Port. The solution found was to invoke an encoding function that encoded the "6" in binary using four digits (Version := int2bit (6, 4)). Even though this is not particularly a problem, the solution does not seem natural.

Another relevant limitation found was that we were not able to specify a template with "any number of RTE". The template shown in the figure 9 is defined for a RIPng packet with exactly two RTE. Pattern matching rules embedded in TTCN-3 might allow definition of repetitive parts of structures that might help decreasing the number of data types and templates defined.

Upon message reception, the message classification presented several difficulties, both for handling interleaved reception of RIPng packets and ND ones. This

```
template IPv6PacketType RIPngRequestTable_tp
  (IPv6AddressType source, IPv6AddressType est,
   IPv6AddressType P1, UInt8 PF1, IPv6AddressType P2, UInt8 PF2) :=
{
Ipv6Header := { Version := int2bit (6, 4),
                TrafficClass := 0,
                FlowLabel := int2bit (0, 20),
                PayloadLength := 0, // CALCULATED BEFORE SENDING
                NextHeader := NextHeaderUDP,
                HopLimit := 255,
                SourceAddress := source, // TEMPLATE PARAMETER
                DestinationAddress := dest // TEMPLATE PARAMETER
              }
Data := { UDPHeader := {
                SourcePort := 777, // NEVERMIND
                DestinationPort := 521, // SERVICE PORT
                Length := 0, // CALCULATED BEFORE SENDING
                Checksum := 0, // CALCULATED BEFORE SENDING
                Payload := { Command := 1, // RIPng Request
                             Version := 1,
                             MustBeZero := 0,
                             RTE := { // First RTE
                                      IPv6Prefix := P1,
                                      RouteTag := 0,
                                      PrefixLen := PF1,
                                      Metric := 0
                                    },{ // Second RTE
                                      IPv6Prefix := P2,
                                      RouteTag := 0,
                                      PrefixLen := PF2,
                                      Metric := 0
                                    }
                           }
                       }
            }
}
```

Fig. 9. TTCN-3 template for a RIPng packet

fact conspired against legibility of the test. It is desirable to have some aggregation of "similar" packets. In this way, logical separation of message reception and handling would lead to more structured ATS.

Also some kind of inspection of unknown packets shall be provided. Reception message queues are processed sequentially. Upon arrival of a non-matching packet, the reception queue stalls. A "wildcard" default packet matching rule was introduced, but TTCN-3 does not provide methods for inspecting the unknown packet. Reception of unmatched packets was logged and the analysis had to be done with external tools like ethereal (http://www.ethereal.com/), something that was important during test debugging and log analysis.

3.4   Test Execution

From the methodological point of view we intended to perform stepwise refinements of our ATS until we produce the definitive one. Spiral patterns or incremental iterations could not be performed the way that they should. The amount of modules and things to be generated delayed the first ETS test production. The delay introduced until we had the first executable version of the test made that several different pieces of testing code had to be debugged at once and also, feedback for refining the test suites was delayed.

The lack or building blocks stopped us from concentrating only on RIPng templates and test cases. Representation of network topology, like routing tables, were needed. The lack of IPv6 extensions or libraries also forced us to model from simple things, like IPv6 packets, to complex behavior like ND algorithms.

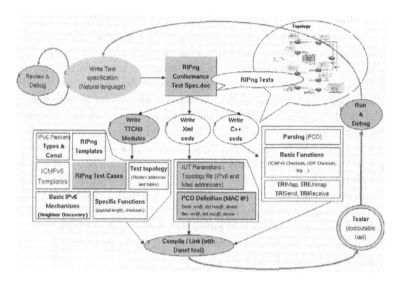

Fig. 10. Test development cycle

We are aware that this was our first TTCN-3 implementation, but all the facts suggests that the *test development cycle* was too big and only few iterations could be performed. The figure 10 shows the effective RIPng test development cycle and the main tasks needed for closing it. It is worth comparing our initial test development plan (see figure 3) with the actual work done. Our experience suggests that network layer support from the tool is needed to reduce the gap and, consequently, development overhead.

The tests performed in our laboratory were done against both a `GNU/Linux` system running `Zebra/RIPngd` and `FreeBSD` system running `routed6`. From the test development point of view, Danet's tool gave the required support for analyzing and debugging purposes. From the test execution point of view we found that log information was hard to analyze. One possible reason is that our changes at PCO were not propagated by the tool to the log files, thus, Link Layer information was stripped from the packets and did not reach log files.

Five test cases were developed in time. Generated tests were successfully run during PlugTests, October 2004 with interesting results. But still, we found it not easy to use TTCN-3 tools compared to what we can do with `v6eval`.

4   Main Issues

The objective of the present work was to gain experience using TTCN-3 language and tools while addressing an IPv6 test conformance problem. As stated before, one important reason behind the experience was to find provider-independent tools and languages for defining test suites.

We found that there are no standard extensions to handle IPv6 level data. Moreover, there is no easy mechanism for standard IPv6 address representation. For modeling network layer protocols, tester network stack has to be disabled. At that moment all IPv6 implementation details, including packet assembly/disassembly, ND becomes part of our test and had to be emulated. It is desirable that an IPv6 oriented test tool provide as many tools as possible to the expert to help him concentrate on the test purpose. Even though we partially succeeded, our test suites rely on PCO behavior not defined in TTCN-3 standard language, thus running them over an of-the-shelf TTCN tool might be impossible. All our results indicate that it is not possible to provide standard TTCN-3 test suites for IPv6 protocols based on our test architecture built on multiple host emulation from a single test node. Experimental results suggest that the minor changes performed to the tools would benefit TTCN-3 usage (maybe an IPv6 specialized version of the tools). Field experience supports that the ability of emulating a complex network from a single host is beneficial from the point of view of test execution and is worth considering it as a requirement for the TTCN-3 language.

Ongoing work complementing the RIPng test suite requires usage of other IPv6 features not implemented in the tool. RIPng relies on the IP Authentication Header and IP Encapsulated Security Payload to ensure integrity, authentication and confidentiality of routing exchanges. IPv6 stacks must include IPSec support, used by RIPng, and we have to manually code IPSec from scratch in TTCN-3 for testing SUT security capabilities.

It seems that TTCN-3 template definition was not versatile enough to allow efficient matching of incoming data. It might be interesting to have hierarchical incoming data matching or at least being able to group similar matching rules. This has a direct impact on ATS legibility as the number of entries in matching statements grow considerably. We foresee that the problems of expressiveness would remain also if we use several PTC instead of a single MTC, but the impact on ATS legibility is so far unpredictable. The experience of such implementation would help understanding other TTCN-3 aspects, while contrasting single tester vs parallel testers on the same matter.

We found no way to define recursive or iterative data templates. Repetitive structures (like routing tables) are sets of individual RTE. The definition of individual templates for packets with one, two, three, etc. RTE again made the code difficult to maintain, unnecessarily large and hard to read.

As a consequence of previous limitations, we were unable to find a pleasant methodology for test creation. It is difficult to abstract parts of the components and protocols for re-using in future implementations. It takes more time than expected to produce runnable ETS. This fact makes that feedback from real execution returns late in test development cycle and the risk of delay due to redesign need is high.

5   Conclusion

The work presented in this paper shows that it was possible to develop abstract test suites for RIPng protocol using TTCN-3 language. Indeed, we were able to fulfill all steps from abstract test suite definition to executable test suite derivation and execution.

We have presented the most important lessons we found when applying the young TTCN-3 language to produce test suites for RIPng protocol. We were able to meet the schedule and the resulting test suite was successfully presented at 50th ETSI PlugTests event. This fact shows that it was possible to develop test suites using TTCN-3, but under special circumstances like having access to the tool source code and changing its implementation.

The use of TTCN-3 is still in its early phases. Success of the language is tightly related to the availability of tools and their capacity to cope in time with the requirements of different fields of application. A careful analysis of enhancement requests has to be combined with pushing industrial requirements.

There are also pending issues regarding language constructs and style that would lead to readable ATS. It seems that a strong community working and proposing solutions to those problems is the most feasible way to find the answer.

The time constraint imposed affected somehow the way things were done. Several important decisions were taken without enough study and experimentation. Ongoing work addresses more detailed study of identified problems. In this new stage we are putting special emphasis on all TTCN-3 modular capabilities. Our goal is to achieve a modular specification architecture that allows easier test specification.

Among further aspects of the protocol testing have to be addressed are security and fragmentation aspects.

Acknowledgements. The authors would like to thank Wolfgang Sachse and Danet technical team for their support during the work.

References

1. Jens Grabowski and Dieter Hogrefe. Towards the third edition of ttcn. In Gyula Csopaki, Sarolta Dibuz, and Katalin Tarnay, editors, *(TestCom 1999) Testing of Communicating Systems, Methods and Applications, ISBN 0-7923-8581-0*, pages 19–30. Kluwer Academic Publishers, 1999.
2. Jens Grabowski, Anthony Wiles, Colin Willcock, and Dieter Hogrefe. On the design of the new testing language ttcn-3. In Hasan Ural, Robert L. Probert, and Gregor v. Bochmann, editors, *(TestCom 2000) Testing of Communicating Systems, Tools and Techniques, ISBN 0-7923-7921-7*, pages 161–176. Kluwer Academic Publishers, 2000.
3. Andreas Ulrich, Hartmut Köoning, and Thomas Walter. Architectures for testing distributed systems. In Gyula Csopaki, Sarolta Dibuz, and Katalin Tarnay, editors, *(TestCom 1999) Testing of Communicating Systems, Methods and Applications, ISBN 0-7923-8581-0*, pages 93–108. Kluwer Academic Publishers, 1999.
4. Ina Schieferdecker and Theofanis Vassiliou-Gioles. Realizing distributed TTCN-3 test systems with TCI. In Dieter Hogrefe and Anthony Wiles, editors, *(TestCom 2003) Testing of Communicating Systems In 15th IFIP Testing of Communicating Systems, Tools and Techniques, ISBN 3-540-40123-7*, pages 95–109. Springer, 2003.

5. Stephan Schulz and Theofanis Vassiliou-Gioles. Implementation of ttcn-3 test systems using the tri. In Ina Schieferdecker, Hartmut Köning, and Adam Wolisz, editors, *(TestCom 2002) Testing of Communicating Systems, Application to Internet Technologies and Services, ISBN 0-7923-7695-1*, pages 425–442. Kluwer Academic Publishers, 2002.
6. Theofanis Vassiliou-Gioles, Ina Schieferdecker, Marc Born, Mario Winkler, and Mang Li. Configuration and execution support for distributed tests. In Gyula Csopaki, Sarolta Dibuz, and Katalin Tarnay, editors, *(TestCom 1999) Testing of Communicating Systems, Methods and Applications, ISBN 0-7923-8581-0*, pages 61–67. Kluwer Academic Publishers, 1999.
7. Roland Gecse and Sarolta Dibuz. An intuitive ttcn-3 data presentation format. In Dieter Hogrefe and Anthony Wiles, editors, *(TestCom 2003) Testing of Communicating Systems In 15th IFIP Testing of Communicating Systems, Tools and Techniques, ISBN 3-540-40123-7*, pages 63–78. Springer, 2003.
8. Törö. Decision on tester configuration for multiparty testing. In Gyula Csopaki, Sarolta Dibuz, and Katalin Tarnay, editors, *(TestCom 1999) Testing of Communicating Systems, Methods and Applications, ISBN 0-7923-8581-0*, pages 109–128. Kluwer Academic Publishers, 1999.
9. G. Malkin and R. Minnear. RFC 2080: RIPng for IPv6. http://www.rfc-editor.org/rfc/rfc2080.txt, 1997.
10. ETSI. Es 201 873-1 ttcn-3 core language, version: 2.2.1. http://www.etsi.org/ptcc/TTCN-3%20Downloads/es_20187301v020201p.zip, 2003.
11. Jianping Wu, Whongjie Li, and Xia Yin. Towards Modeling and Testing of IP Routing Protocols. In Dieter Hogrefe and Anthony Wiles, editors, *Testing of Communicating Systems In 15th IFIP Testing of Communicating Systems, ISBN 3-540-40123-7*, pages 49–62. Springer, 2003.
12. D. Harrington, R. Presuhn, and B. Wijnen. RFC 3411: An Architecture for Describing Simple Network Management Protocol (SNMP) Management Frameworks. http://www.rfc-editor.org/rfc/rfc3411.txt, 2002.
13. T. Narten, E. Nordmark, and W. Simpson. RFC 2461: Neighbor Discovery for IP Version 6 (IPv6). http://www.rfc-editor.org/rfc/rfc2461.txt, 1998.
14. R. Hinden and S. Deering. RFC 2373: IP Version 6 Addressing Architecture. http://www.rfc-editor.org/rfc/rfc2373.txt, 1998.

A Model-Based Approach for Robustness Testing

Jean-Claude Fernandez, Laurent Mounier, and Cyril Pachon

Verimag,- Centre Equation,
- 2 avenue de Vignate, - F38610 Gieres, France
{Jean-Claude.Fernandez, Laurent.Mounier, Cyril.Pachon}@imag.fr
http://www-verimag.imag.fr/

Abstract. Robustness testing is a part of the validation process which consists in testing the behavior of a system implementation under exceptional execution conditions in order to check if it still fulfills some robustness requirements. We propose a theoretical framework for model-based robustness testing together with an implementation within the IF validation environment. Robustness test cases are generated from both a (partial) operational specification and an abstract fault model. This generation technique is inspired from the ones used in (classical) conformance testing - already implemented in several tools. This framework is illustrated on a small example.

1 Introduction

Among the numerous techniques available to validate a software system, the purpose of testing is essentially to *find defects* on a *system implementation*. When theoretically founded, testing provides an efficient and rigorous way for error detection. For example, formal methods for *conformance testing* have been largely investigated in the telecomunication area, and the so-called "model based" approach was implemented in several tools (e.g., [4, 15, 9, 7, 1]) and taken into account by the standardization bodies (e.g., ISO standard 9646).

Robustness Testing. Informally, robustness can be defined as the ability of a software to keep an "acceptable" behavior, expressed in terms of *robustness requirements*, in spite of *exceptional* or *unforeseen* execution conditions (such as the unavailability of system resources, communication failures, invalid or stressful inputs, etc.). Such a feature is particularly important for software critical applications those execution environment cannot be fully foreseen at development time. Robustness requirements can then range from very general considerations ("there is no run-time error", "there is no system deadlock"), to more specific properties ("after entering a degraded mode, the system always goes back to a nominal one", "some system resources remains always available", etc.).

Even if this kind of testing has been less studied than in the hardware community, several approaches have been proposed to automate software robustness

F. Khendek and R. Dssouli (Eds.): TestCom 2005, LNCS 3502, pp. 333–348, 2005.

testing. Most of them are based on *fault-injection*, i.e., they consist in feeding the system under test with (sequences of) invalid inputs, chosen within a *fault-model*, and supposed to exhibit robustness failures. However, they differ in the way these inputs are chosen and we review below some of them we consider as the most representatives:

- A first approach consists in generating random inputs obtained by considering only the input domain definition. This technique is particularly adequate to test very large softwares (such an operating system), for which neither a specification nor even the source code is available. Several tools implement this technique. In FUZZ [14], inputs are randomly generated and a failure is detected if the system hangs or dumps a `core` file. In BALLISTA [2], test cases consist of combinations of both valid and invalid inputs focusing on particular parts of the system (e.g., the most frequently used systems calls of an operating system). The verdict distinguishes between several failure criteria (crash, restart, abort, silent, etc.). More recently, the RIDDLE tool [8] uses an input grammar to generate combinations of correct, incorrect and boundary inputs with a better coverage of the system functionalities. It also delivers more precise failure criteria than its predecessors.

- When the source code of the system is available, the generation of relevant inputs to test its robustness can be improved. For instance it becomes possible to use some kinds of static analysis techniques to choose the better inputs able to cover all parameter combinations (w.r.t. an equivalence relation) of public method calls. This idea is exploited for instance in the `JCrasher` testing tool [6], those purpose is to detect undeclared runtime exceptions in Java programs. However this tool only targets a particular kind of faults (unforeseen combinations of parameters in method calls), and issue a rather coarse verdict.

- Finally, some techniques may also rely on some abstract specification of the system behavior to select the test inputs. It is the case for instance in the so-called FOTG approach [11] (Fault Oriented Test Generation): starting from a fault introduced in a protocol specification (like a message loss, or a node crash), it consists in looking (forward) for an error state (a state in which a protocol fails to meet its requirement), and then to search (backward) for a test sequence leading from the initial state to this error state. Even if this approach seems well adapted to fault-tolerant protocols it only deals with single faults (one at a time), and uses a rather simple specification formalism (Finite State Machines). A similar technique has been also proposed in the PROTOS project [3]: it consists in mutating a high-level and abstract description (expressed by a context-free grammar) of the system behavior (the set of correct interactions) to introduce abnormal inputs. Test cases are then generated by performing simulations on this abstract description.

A Model-Based Approach for Robustness Testing. The objective of this paper is to extend the model-based approach used in conformance testing to the robustness testing framework. However, this extension is not straightforward and it raises the following problems:

- First, robustness is defined with respect to a *fault model* that may vary from an application to another. This element usually depends on the application architecture (e.g., unreliability of some communication links, lack of confidence in some external components, input channel feed by an untrusted user, etc.) and needs to be expressed at a rather abstract level. Note that some of these faults may be controllable by an external tester, whereas some others may not.

- Moreover, specifying the system behavior for *any* exceptional and/or invalid execution conditions expressed by a fault model is (by definition) hard to achieve. Therefore the specification should no longer be considered as "exhaustive" in this context (it may not always reflect the expected behavior of the implementation). In addition, in a real size system, the specification of some components may also be over-approximated (for instance when this specification is partially known, or too complex).

- As a consequence, test verdicts should no longer be based on a conformance relation between the implementation and this (approximated) specification, but directly with respect to the initial robustness requirements.

The solution we propose is based on the following elements: The initial *system specification* is expressed in a formalism those operational semantics can be defined in terms of Input-Outputs labelled transition systems and which explicits the system architecture (communication links attributes, component interface and internal structure). The *fault model* is expressed by *syntactic mutations* performed on this specification. The *robustness requirements* are expressed by a linear temporal logic formula describing the expected behavior of the system implementation in terms of tester interactions. Of course, checking whether a given implementation satisfies or not such a formula should remain decidable during a test (i.e., within a finite amount of time).

Paper Outline. The paper is organized as follows: first (in section 2) we introduce the models we used, and then (in section 3) we define formally our model-based approach for robustness testing. Section 4 presents an implementation of this technique within the IF environment, and section 5 illustrates its use on an example. We terminate by perspectives and future extensions.

2   Models

In this section, we introduce the models and notations used throughout the paper. The basic models we consider are Input-Output Labelled Transition Systems (IOLTS), namely Labelled Transition Systems in which input and output actions are distinguished (due to of the asymmetrical nature of the testing activity).

2.1   Input-Outputs Labelled Transition Systems

We consider a finite alphabet of actions A, partitioned into two sets: *input actions* A_I and *output actions* A_O. A (finite) IOLTS is a quadruplet $M = (Q^M, A^M, T^M, q_{init}^M)$ where Q^M is the finite set of states, q_{init}^M is the initial state, $A^M \subseteq A$ is a finite alphabet of actions, and $T^M \subseteq Q^M \times A^M \cup \{\tau\} \times Q^M$ is the transition relation.

Internal actions are denoted by the special label $\tau \notin A$. We denote by $\mathbb{N}$ the set of non negative integers. For each set X, $\mathbf{card}(X)$ is the number of element of X. For each set X, X^* (resp. $X^\omega = [X \to \mathbb{N}]$) denotes the set of finite (resp. infinite) sequences on X. Let $\sigma \in X^*$; σ_i or $\sigma(i)$ denotes the ith element of σ. We adopt the following notations and conventions: Let $\sigma \in A^*$, $\alpha \in A \cup \{\tau\}$, $p, q \in Q^{\mathrm{M}}$. We write $p \xrightarrow{\alpha}_{\mathrm{M}} q$ iff $(p, \alpha, q) \in T^{\mathrm{M}}$ and $p \xrightarrow{\sigma}_{\mathrm{M}} q$ iff $\exists\, p_0, \cdots, p_n \in Q^{\mathrm{M}}$ such that $p_0 = p$, $p_i \xrightarrow{\sigma(i+1)}_{\mathrm{M}} p_{i+1}$ for $i < n$, $p_n = q$. In this case, σ is called a *trace* or *execution sequence*, and $p_0 \cdots p_n$ a *run* over σ. An infinite run of M over an infinite execution sequence σ is an infinite sequence ρ of Q^{M} such that

1. $\rho(0) = q_{\mathrm{init}}^{\mathrm{M}}$ and 2. $\rho(i) \xrightarrow{\sigma(i)}_{\mathrm{M}} \rho(i+1))$. $\mathbf{inf}(\rho)$ denotes the set of symbols from Q^{M} occurring infinitely often in ρ: $\mathbf{inf}(\rho) = \{q \mid \forall n.\ \exists i.\ i \geq n \wedge \rho(i) = q\}$. Let V a subset of the alphabet A. We define a *projection operator* $\downarrow_V : A^* \to V^*$ in the following manner: $\epsilon \downarrow_V = \epsilon$, $(a.\sigma) \downarrow_V = \sigma \downarrow_V$ if $a \notin V$, and $(a.\sigma) \downarrow_V = a.(\sigma \downarrow_V)$ if $a \in V$. This operator can be extended to a language L (and we note $L \downarrow V$) by applying it to each sequence of L. The language recognized by M is $\mathcal{L}(M) = \{\sigma \mid \exists \rho$ such that ρ is a run of M over $\sigma\}$. The IOLTS M is *complete* with respect to a set of actions $X \subseteq A$ if and only if for each state q^{M} of Q^{M} and for each action x of X, there is at least one outgoing transition of T^{M} from q^{M} labelled by $x \in X$: $\forall p^{\mathrm{M}} \in Q^{\mathrm{M}} \cdot \forall x \in X \cdot \exists q^{\mathrm{M}} \in Q^{\mathrm{M}}$ such that $p^{\mathrm{M}} \xrightarrow{x}_{\mathrm{M}} q^{\mathrm{M}}$. The IOLTS M is said *deterministic* if and only:

$$\forall p^{\mathrm{M}} \in Q^{\mathrm{M}} \cdot \forall a \in A^{\mathrm{M}} \cdot p^{\mathrm{M}} \xrightarrow{a}_{\mathrm{M}} q^{\mathrm{M}} \wedge p^{\mathrm{M}} \xrightarrow{a}_{\mathrm{M}} q'^{\mathrm{M}} \Rightarrow q^{\mathrm{M}} = q'^{\mathrm{M}}.$$ A state p is said *quiescent* [16] in M either if it has no outgoing transition (deadlock), or if it belongs to a cycle of internal transitions (live-lock). Quiescence can be expressed at the IOLTS level by introducing an extra transition to each quiescent state labelled by a special output symbol δ. Formally, we associate to LTS M its so-called "suspension automaton" $\delta(M) = (Q^{\mathrm{M}}, A^{\mathrm{M}} \cup \{\delta\}, T^{\delta(M)}, q_0^{\mathrm{M}})$ where $T^{\delta(M)} = T^{\mathrm{M}} \cup \{(p, \delta, p) \mid p \in Q^{\mathrm{M}} \wedge p$ is quiescent$\}$.

2.2 Specification

We consider specifications, expressed in the IF language [1], consisting of components (called *processes*), running in parallel and interacting either through shared variables or asynchronous signals. Processes describe sequential behaviors including data transformations, communications and process creations/destructions. Furthermore, the behavior of a process may be subject to timing constraints. The behavior of a *process* is described as a (timed) automaton, extended with data. A process has a local memory consisting of variables, control states and a FIFO queue of pending messages (received and not yet consumed). A process can move from one control state to another by executing some *transition*. Notice that several transitions may be enabled at the same time, in which case the choice is made non-deterministically. Transitions can be either *triggered* by signals in the input queue or be *spontaneous*. Transitions can also be *guarded* by predicates on variables. A transition is enabled in a state if its trigger signal is present and its guard evaluates to true.

---

[1] http://www-verimag.imag.fr/ async/IF/index.shtml.en

Transition *bodies* are *sequential programs* consisting of elementary actions (variable assignments, message sending, process creation/destruction, etc) and structured using elementary control-flow statements (like if-then-else, while-do, etc). In addition, transition bodies can use external functions/procedures, written in an external programming language (C/C++). *Signals* are typed and can have data parameters. Signals can be addressed directly to a process (using its *pid*) and/or to a signal route which will deliver it to one or more processes. The destination process stores received signals in a FIFO buffer. *Signal routes* represent specialized communication media transporting signals between processes. The behavior of a signal route is defined by its connection policy (peer to peer, unicast or multi cast), and finally its reliability ("reliable" or "lossy"). We use below a simplified abstract syntax and we give its corresponding (informal) semantics in terms of IOLTS.

Definition 1 (specification syntax).
A specification SP is a tuple (S, C, P) where S is the set of signals, $C = C^{int} \cup C^{ext}$ is the set of queues (internal and external ones) and P is the set of processes. The external queues describe the interface between the specified system and its environment. A process $p \in P$ is a tuple (X_p, Q_p, T_p, q_p^0) where X_p is a set of local typed variables, Q_p is a set of states, Σ_p is a set of guarded commands which can be performed by p, and $T_p \subseteq Q_p \times \Sigma_p \times Q_p$ is a set of transitions. A guarded command has the form $[\ b\ ]\alpha$ where α can be either an assignment $x := e$, an input $c?s(x)$, or an output $c!s(e)$. Above, b and e are expressions, $x \in X_p$ is a variable, $c \in C$ is a queue and $s \in S$ is a signal. The set of types τ_i is partially ordered by the sub-typing relation $\leq_{s.t.}$.

We give the semantics of specifications in terms of labeled transition systems. For each type τ_i, we consider its domain D_i and we denote by D the disjoint union of all these domains. We define variable contexts as being total mappings $\rho : \bigcup_{p \in P} X_p \to D$ which associate to each variable x a value v from its domain. We extend these mappings to expressions in the usual way. We define internal queue contexts as being also total mappings $\delta : C^{int} \to (S \times D)^*$ which associates to each internal queue c a sequence $(s_1, v_1), ..., (s_k, v_k)$ of messages, that is pairs (s, v) noted also by $s(v)$, where s is a signal and v is the carried parameter value.

Definition 2 (specification semantics).
The semantics of a specification SP is given by a labeled transition system $S = (Q^s, A^s, T^s, q_{init}^s)$. States of this system are configurations of the form (ρ, δ, π), where ρ is a variable context, δ is a queue context and $\pi = \langle q_1, ... q_n \rangle \in \times_{p \in P} Q_p$ is a global control state. Transitions are either internal (and labeled with τ), when derived from assignments or internal communication, or visible when derived from external communication. There is a transition from a configuration (ρ, δ, π) to (ρ', δ', π') iff there is a transition $q_p \xrightarrow{[b]\alpha} q_p'$ in the specification such that the guard b is evaluated to true in the environment ρ. The set of actions is partitioned into A_I^s and A_O^s where
$A_I^s = \{c?s(v) \in A^s, c \in C^{ext}, v \in D\}$ and $A_O^s = \{c!s(v) \in A^s, c \in C^{ext}, v \in D\}$

2.3   Mutation

The abstract fault model we consider consists in a mutation function defined on the specification syntax. Formally, let (S, C, P) be a specification. A *fault model* is a function that transforms (S, C, P) into (S', C', P'). We give hereafter a (non exhaustive) set of possible transformations. Note that each transformation corresponds to a *fault* that can be produced by an external tester.

- Domain extension for a variable. For a process i, if an input signal has a parameter of type t_i, then we can extend t_i in t_i' where $t_i \leq t_i'$.
- Unreliable channel In a process i, each transition corresponding to an output on a channel c $(p_i \overset{[b]\ c!s(e)}{\longrightarrow} q_i)$ is "duplicated" into an internal transition $(p_i \overset{\tau}{\longrightarrow} q_i)$. At the IF level, this transformation simply consists in replacing a reliable channel by a lossy one.
- Input failure In a process i, if a state has only input entries, then we add a new transition from this state, labelled by τ and leading to a sink state.

3   Robustness Testing Framework

In this section we propose a formal framework to test the "robustness" of a software implementation with respect to a set of robustness requirements.

3.1   Robustness Requirements and Satisfiability Relation

A robustness requirement aims at ensuring that the software will preserve an "acceptable behavior" under non nominal execution conditions. This notion of "acceptable behavior" may not only correspond to safety properties (telling that something bad never happens), but also to liveness properties (telling that something good will eventually happen). Liveness properties are characterized by *infinite* execution sequences. From the test point of view, only the existence of a finite execution sequence can be checked on a given IUT (since the test execution time has to remain bounded). This restricts in practice the test activity to the validation of safety properties. Nevertheless, an interesting sub-class of safety properties are the so-called *parameterized liveness*. Such properties allow for instance to a express that the IUT will exhibit a particular behavior within a given amount of time, or before a given number of iterations has been reached. From a practical point of view, it is very useful to express such properties as liveness (i.e., in terms of infinite execution sequences), and then to bound their execution only at test time, depending on the concrete test conditions.

Robustness Requirements. In the approach we propose, a robustness requirement φ is directly modelled by an *observer automaton* $O_{\neg\varphi}$ recognizing all (infinite) executions sequences satisfying $\neg\varphi$. Several acceptance conditions (Büchi, Muller, Streett, Rabin, etc) have been proposed to extend finite-state IOLTS to recognize infinite sequences. For algorithmic considerations, it is more efficient to consider a *deterministic* observer. Since any ω-regular languages can be recognized by a deterministic Rabin automaton [2], we choose this kind of acceptance condition to model our robustness requirements. First we recall the definition of a Rabin automaton.

Definition 3. *A Rabin automaton is a pair $(B, \mathcal{T})$ where $B = (Q^B, A, T^B, q_{init}^B)$ is an IOLTS and $\mathcal{T} = \{(L_1, U_1), \cdots, (L_n, U_n)\}$ is a set of couple of subsets of Q^B. The language accepted by $(B, \mathcal{T})$ is $\mathcal{L}(B, \mathcal{T}) = \{\sigma \in A^\omega \mid \exists i.$
$\exists$ an infinite run ρ of B over σ such that $\mathbf{inf}(\rho) \cap L_i \neq \emptyset$ and $\mathbf{Inf}(\rho) \cap U_i = \emptyset\}$.*

Clearly, deciding if an execution sequence σ belongs or not to $\mathcal{L}(B, \mathcal{T})$ cannot be performed during a finite test execution. Therefore, this definition needs to be refined in order to approximate $\mathcal{L}(B, \mathcal{T})$ as a set of *finite* execution sequences. The solution we propose is to associate parameters (c_l, c_u) to each pair (L, U) of $\mathcal{T}$ in order to "bound" the acceptance condition. This notion of "parameterized" Rabin automaton is formalized in the following definition.

Definition 4. *Let $(B, \mathcal{T})$ be a Rabin automaton, $\mathcal{C} = \{(c_{l_1}, c_{u_1}), \cdots, (c_{l_n}, c_{u_n})\}$ a set of integer pairs. We define $\mathbf{inf}_a(\rho, n) = \{q \mid \mathtt{card}(\{i \mid \rho(i) = q\}) \geq n\}$.*
The language accepted by the parameterized Rabin automaton $(B, \mathcal{T}, \mathcal{C})$ is then: $\mathcal{L}(B, \mathcal{T}, \mathcal{C}) = \{\sigma \in A^* \mid \exists i.$
$\exists$ a run ρ of B over σ such that $\mathbf{inf}_a(\rho, c_{l_i}) \cap L_i \neq \emptyset$ and $\mathbf{Inf}_a(\rho, c_{u_i}) \cap U_i = \emptyset\}$.

Implementation. The Implementation Under Test (IUT) is assumed to be a "black box" those behavior is known by the environment only through a restricted interface (a set of inputs and outputs). From a theoretical point of view, this behavior can be considered as an IOLTS IUT$=(Q^{IUT}, A^{IUT}, T^{IUT}, q_{init}^{IUT})$, where $A^{IUT} = A_I^{IUT} \cup A_O^{IUT}$ is the IUT interface. We assume in addition that this IUT is complete with respect to A_I (it never refuses an unexpected input).

Satisfiability Relation. We are now able to formalize the notion of robustness of an implementation with respect to a robustness requirement φ.

Definition 5. *Let $\mathcal{I}$ be an IOLTS, φ a formula interpreted over execution sequences of $\mathcal{I}$. An observer $\mathcal{O}_{\neg\varphi} = (\mathcal{O}, \mathcal{T}^\mathcal{O}, \mathcal{C}^\mathcal{O})$ for φ is a parameterized Rabin automaton such that IOLTS $\mathcal{O}$ is deterministic, complete and $\mathcal{L}(\mathcal{O}_{\neg\varphi})$ is the set of execution sequences verifying $\neg\varphi$. We say that $\mathcal{I}$ satisfies φ iff $\mathcal{L}(\mathcal{I}) \cap \mathcal{L}(\mathcal{O}_{\neg\varphi}) = \emptyset$.*

3.2 Test Architecture and Test Cases

Test Architecture. At the abstract level we consider, a test architecture is simply a pair $(\mathcal{A}_c, \mathcal{A}_u)$ of actions sets, each of them being a subset of $\mathcal{A}$: the set of *controllable* actions $\mathcal{A}_c$, initiated by the tester, and the set of *observable* actions $\mathcal{A}_u$, observed by the tester. A test architecture will be said *compliant* with an observer $\mathcal{O}$ those action set is $A^\mathcal{O} = A_O^\mathcal{O} \cup A_I^\mathcal{O}$ iff it satisfies the following constraints : $A_I^\mathcal{O} \subseteq \mathcal{A}_c$ and $A_O^\mathcal{O} \subseteq \mathcal{A}_u$. In other words the tester is able to control (resp. observe) all inputs (resp. outputs) appearing in the observer.

---

[2] Which is not the case for deterministic Büchi automata.

Test Cases. Intuitively, a test case $\mathcal{TC}$ for a robustness requirement φ is a set of execution sequences, controllable, compatible with a given test architecture and accepted by an observer $O_{\neg\varphi}$. This notion can be formalized as parameterized Rabin automaton.

Definition 6. *For a given observer $\mathcal{O}$ those action set is $A^{\mathcal{O}}$, a test architecture (A_c, A_u) compliant with $\mathcal{O}$, a test case $\mathcal{TC}$ is a parameterized Rabin automaton $(TC, \mathcal{T}^{TC}, \mathcal{C}^{TC})$ with $TC = (Q^{TC}, A^{TC}, T^{TC}, q_{init}^{TC})$ satisfying the following requirements:*

1. $A^{TC} = A_I^{TC} \cup A_O^{TC}$ *with* $A_O^{TC} \subseteq A_c$ *and* $A_I^{TC} \subseteq A_u$.
2. *TC is deterministic wrt A^{TC}, controllable (for each state of Q^{TC} there is at most one outgoing transition labelled by an action of A_c), and input-complete (for each state of Q^{TC}, for each element a of A_u, there exists exactly one outgoing transition labelled by a).*
3. $\mathcal{L}(TC) \downarrow A^{\mathcal{O}} \subseteq \mathcal{L}(\mathcal{O})$

3.3   Test Cases Execution and Verdicts

A test case $\mathcal{TC}$ for a robustness requirement φ is supposed to be executed against an IUT by a tester. This IUT is then declared *non robust* (for φ) if such a test execution exhibits an execution sequence of the IUT that belongs to $\mathcal{L}(\mathcal{TC})$ (in other words if $\mathcal{L}(TC) \cap \mathcal{L}(IUT) \neq \emptyset$). In this case the tester should issue a **Fail** verdict, and it should issue a **Pass** verdict otherwise.

Test Execution. More formally, Let $IUT = (Q^{IUT}, A^{IUT}, T^{IUT}, q_{init}^{IUT})$ an implementation, $(TC, \mathcal{T}^{TC}, \mathcal{C}^{TC})$ a test case with $TC = (Q^{TC}, A^{TC}, T^{TC}, q_{init}^{TC})$, and (A_c, A_u) a test architecture. The test execution of TC on IUT can be expressed as a parallel composition between IUT and TC with synchronizations on action sets A_c and A_u. This test execution can be described by an IOLTS $\mathcal{E} = (Q^{\varepsilon}, A^{\varepsilon}, T^{\varepsilon}, q_{init}^{\varepsilon})$, where $A^{\varepsilon} = A^{TC}$, and sets Q^{ε} and T^{TC} are defined as follows:

- Q^{ε} is a set of *configurations*. A *configuration* is a triplet $(p^{TC}, p^{IUT}, \lambda)$ where $p^{TC} \in Q^{TC}, p^{IUT} \in Q^{IUT}$ and λ is a partial function from Q^{TC} to $\mathbb{N}$, which counts the number of times an execution sequence visits a state.

- T^{ε} is the set of transitions $(p^{TC}, p^{IUT}, \lambda) \xrightarrow{a}_{\varepsilon} (q^{TC}, q^{IUT}, \lambda')$ such that

  - $p^{TC} \xrightarrow{a}_{TC} q^{TC}$, $p^{IUT} \xrightarrow{a}_{IUT} q^{IUT}$ and

  - $\lambda'(q^{TC}) = \begin{cases} \lambda(q^{TC}) & \text{if } q^{TC} \notin \bigcup\limits_{i \in \{1, \cdots k\}} (L_i^{TC} \cup U_i^{TC}) \\ \lambda(q^{TC}) + 1 & \text{if } q^{TC} \in \bigcup\limits_{i \in \{1, \cdots k\}} (L_i^{TC} \cup U_i^{TC}) \end{cases}$

The initial configuration q_{init}^{TC} is $(q_{init}^{TC}, q_{init}^{IUT}, \lambda_{init})$, where for all q, $\lambda_{init}(q) = 0$.

T^{ε} describes the interactions between the IUT and the test case. Each counter associated with a state of $L_i^{\mathrm{TC}} \cup U_i^{\mathrm{TC}}$ is incremented when an execution sequence visits this state.

Verdicts. Test execution is supposed to deliver some *verdicts* to indicate whether the IUT was found robust or not. These verdicts can be formalized as a function **Verdict** on execution sequences of $\mathcal{E}$ to the set {**Pass, Fail**}. More precisely:

- **Verdict**$(\sigma) = $ **Fail** if there exists a run ρ of $\mathcal{E}$ over σ, $i \in \{1, 2, \ldots, k\}$ and $l \in \mathbb{N}$ such that:
  1. $\rho(l) = (p_l^{\mathrm{TC}}, p_l^{\mathrm{IUT}}, \lambda_l)$, $p_l^{\mathrm{TC}} \in L_i^{\mathrm{TC}}$ and $\lambda_l(p_l^{\mathrm{TC}}) \geq c_{l_i}$, and
  2. $\forall m \in [0 \cdots l].\rho(m) = (q_m^{\mathrm{TC}}, q_m^{\mathrm{IUT}}, \lambda_m) \wedge q_m^{\mathrm{TC}} \in U_i^{\mathrm{TC}} \implies \lambda_m(q_m^{\mathrm{TC}}) \leq c_{u_i}$.
- **Verdict**$(\sigma) = $ **Pass** otherwise.

In practice the test case execution can be performed as follows:

- At each step of the execution the controllability condition may give a choice between a controllable and an observable action. In this situation the tester can first wait for the observable action to occur (using a local timer), and then choose to execute the controllable one.
- Formal parameters $\mathcal{C}^{\mathrm{TC}}$ are instantiated according to the actual test environment. A **Fail** verdict is issued as soon as an incorrect execution sequence is reached (according to definition above), and a **Pass** verdict is issued either if the current execution sequence visits "too many often" a state of U_i^{TC} ($\lambda_m(q_m^{\mathrm{TC}}) > c_{u_i}$), or if a global timer, started at the beginning of test execution, expires. This last case occurs when an execution sequence enters a loop without any state belonging to L_i^{TC} or U_i^{TC}.

3.4   Test Graph

Intuitively, the purpose of a test graph TG is to gather a set of execution sequences, computed from a (mutated) specification S and an observer $\mathcal{O}$, defined over a test architecture TA, and belonging to $\mathcal{L}(\mathcal{O})$. The test graph is defined below by computing an asymmetric product $\otimes$ between S and $\mathcal{O}$.

Definition 7. *Let* $TA = (A_c, A_u)$ *a test architecture,* S_0 *a specification and* $S=(Q^s, A^s, T^s, q_{init}^s)$ *its deterministic suspension automaton with* $A^s \subseteq A_c \cup A_u$. *Let* $(\mathcal{O}, T^{\mathcal{O}}, \mathcal{C}^{\mathcal{O}})$ *be an observer with* $\mathcal{O}=(Q^{\mathcal{O}}, A^{\mathcal{O}}, T^{\mathcal{O}}, q_{init}^{\mathcal{O}})$ *and*
$T^{\mathcal{O}} = \langle (L_1^{\mathcal{O}}, U_1^{\mathcal{O}}), (L_2^{\mathcal{O}}, U_2^{\mathcal{O}}), \ldots, (L_k^{\mathcal{O}}, U_k^{\mathcal{O}}) \rangle$ *such that* TA *is compliant with* $\mathcal{O}$. *We define the Parameterized Rabin automaton* $(TG, T^{TG}, \mathcal{C}^{TG})$ *where*
$TG=(Q^{TG}, A^{TG}, T^{TG}, q_{init}^{TG})$, *such that* $Q^{TG} \subseteq Q^S \times Q^{\mathcal{O}}$, $A^{TG} \subseteq A^S$, $q_0^{TG} = (q_0^S, q_0^{\mathcal{O}})$, *and* Q^{TG}, T^{TG} *are obtained as follows:*

$$(p_S, p_{\mathcal{O}}) \xrightarrow{a}_{T^{\otimes}} (q_S, q_{\mathcal{O}}) \text{ iff } p_S \xrightarrow{a}_{T^S} q_S \text{ and } p_{\mathcal{O}} \xrightarrow{a}_{T^{\mathcal{O}}} q_{\mathcal{O}}$$

The pair table T^{TG} *is equal to* $\langle (L_1^{TG}, U_1^{TG}), (L_2^{TG}, U_2^{TG}), \ldots, (L_k^{TG}, U_k^{TG}) \rangle$ *where* L_i^{TG} *and* L_i^{TG} *are defined as follows:*
$$L_i^{TG} = \{(p_S, p_{\mathcal{O}}) \in Q^{TG} \mid q_{\mathcal{O}} \in L_i^{\mathcal{O}}\} \qquad U_i^{TG} = \{(p_S, p_{\mathcal{O}}) \in Q^{TG} \mid q_{\mathcal{O}} \in U_i^{\mathcal{O}}\}$$

3.5   Test Cases Selection

The purpose of the test case selection is to generate a particular test case TC from the test graph TG. Roughly speaking, it consists in "extracting" a subgraph of TG controllable with respect to the test architecture, and containing a least a sequence of $\mathcal{L}(TG)$ (and hence of $\mathcal{L}(\mathcal{O})$).

Clearly, to belong to $\mathcal{L}(TG)$, an execution sequence of TG has to reach a cycle containing a state belonging to some distinguished set L_i^{TG} (for some i) of the pair table associated to TG. Conversely, any sequence of TG not leading to a strongly connected component of TG containing a state of L_i^{TG} cannot belong to $\mathcal{L}(TG)$. Therefore, we first define on TG the predicate L2L (for "leads to L"), to denote the set of states leading to such a strongly connected component:

$$\text{L2L}\,(q) \equiv \exists(q_1, q_2, \omega_1, \omega_2, \omega_3).\ (q \overset{\omega_1}{\Longrightarrow}_{TTG} q_1 \overset{\omega_2}{\Longrightarrow}_{TTG} q_2 \overset{\omega_3}{\Longrightarrow}_{TTG} q_1 \text{ and } \exists i.\, q_2 \in L_i^{\mathrm{TG}})$$

We can now define a sub-graph of TG, controllable, and containing at least a sequence of $\mathcal{L}(\mathcal{O})$. This subset contains all non controllable transitions of T^{TG} (labelled by an element of A_u), and at most one (randomly chosen) controllable transition of T^{TG} leading to a state of L2L when several such transitions exist from a given state of TG. More formally, we introduce a selection function:

select $(T^{TG}) = \{(p, a, q) \in T^{TG} \mid$

$\qquad a \in A_u \text{ or } a = \text{one-of}(\{a_i \in A_c \mid p \overset{a_i}{\longrightarrow}_{TTG} q_i \text{ and L2L}\,(q_i)\})\}$

Finally, this subset of T^{TG} remains to be extended with all non controllable actions of A_u not explicitly appearing in T^{TG}, to ensure the input completness of the test case. The definition of a test case TC is then the following:

Definition 8. *let* $(TG, T^{TG}, \mathcal{C}^{TG})$ *with* $TG=(Q^{TG}, A^{TG}, T^{TG}, q_{init}^{TG})$ *a test graph and* $TA = (A_c, A_u)$ *a test architecture. A test case* $(TC, T^{TC}, \mathcal{C}^{TC})$ *is a Parameterized Rabin automaton with* $TC=(Q^{TC}, A^{TC}, T^{TC}, q_{init}^{TC})$ *such that* $q_0^{TC} = q_0^{TG}$, $A^{TC} = A^{TG} \cup A_u$, Q^{TC} *is the subset of* Q^{TG} *reachable by* T^{TG} *from* q_0^{TC} *and* T^{TC} *is defined as follows:*

$$T^{TC} = \text{select}(T^{TG}) \cup \{(p, a, p) \mid a \in A_u \text{ and } \not\exists q.\, (p, a, q) \in T^{TG}\}$$

4   Implementation

We present in this section a complete tool chain which automates the generation and execution of robustness test cases for Java programs. This tool chain is built upon the IF validation environment [5], and it integrates some components developed within the AGEDIS project. First we give the overall architecture of this tool chain, and we briefly explain how the main operations described in the previous sections have been implemented. Then we illustrate its use on a running example.

4.1   Platform Architecture

The overall architecture of the tool chain is depicted in figure 1. It is built upon several existing tools: model exploration is performed using the IF simulator

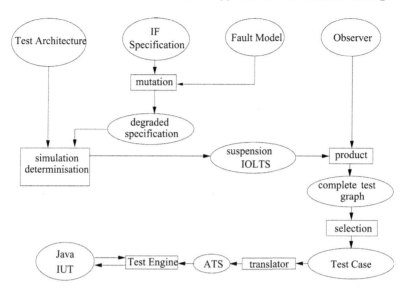

Fig. 1. Platform for the robustness testing

integrated into the IF environment, test generation uses some of the algorithmic techniques borrowed from the TGV tool [12], and test execution relies on the SPIDER [10] test engine developed in the AGEDIS project. This platform is dedicated to particular specification and target languages (IF and JAVA), but a similar architecture could be used with other specification formalisms or programming languages. The platform inputs are detailed below.

Implementation Under Test. the IUT is a (distributed) multi-threaded Java program, only accessed through a set of public methods (black box IUTs). The corresponding formal model is an IOLTS where input (*resp.* output) actions correspond to method calls (*resp.* return values).

Test Architecture. Formally, the test architecture is a pair $(\mathcal{A}_c, \mathcal{A}_u)$ of actions sets (section 3.2). In this particular platform the controllable actions $(\mathcal{A}_c)$ are the set of methods that can be called by an external tester and the observable actions $\mathcal{A}_u$ are the values returned to the tester when these method calls terminate.

Specification. In our context, the specification (partially) describes the expected behavior of the IUT under some nominal execution conditions. It is written using the IF formalism (see section 2.2 for a short description). In practice this IF specification can be automatically produced from high-level specification languages (like SDL or UML).

Fault Model. The fault model lists the potential failures and/or incorrect inputs supposed to occur within the actual execution environment. It is directly expressed by a set of syntactic mutations to be performed on the specification.

Observer. The observer is a parameterized Rabin automaton.

4.2   Implementation Issues

We now briefly sketch the main operators used in this platform to implement the test generation and test execution technique proposed in this paper. These operators are depicted by square boxes on figure 1.

Mutation. The mutation operation is a purely syntactic operation performed on the abstract syntax tree of the IF specification.

Simulation and Determinisation. This operator produces a deterministic suspension IOLTS from the mutated IF specification. It consists in three steps that are combined *on-the-fly*: 1. generation of an IOLTS from the mutated IF specification, 2. computation of the suspension IOLTS ; this step introduces the δ actions, and 3. determinisation and minimization with respect to the bisimulation equivalence.

Product. This operator computes the test graph from the deterministic suspension IOLTS associated to the mutated specification (S_{Sd}) and the observer (S_{obs}), as defined in section 3.4. It is implemented as a joint traversal of these two IOLTSs.

Test Selection. The test selection operation consists in extracting a test case TC from the complete test graph TG. TC is a parameterized Rabin automaton, controllable, and such that $\mathcal{L}(TC) \subseteq \mathcal{L}(TG)$. Practically this operation is performed in two successive steps (section 3.5):

Computation of State Predicate L2L: This computation is based on an algorithm due to R.E. Tarjan to compute in linear time the strongly connected components (SCCs) of TG. When necessary, an SCC can be refined into sub-SCCs to obtain the elementary cycles containing a distinguished state of the test graph.

Computation of Function Select*:* Once the state predicate L2L has been computed on TG, it remains to extract a sub-graph of TG containing only controllable execution sequences leading to a state satisfying L2L.

Test Case Translator and Test Execution Engine. Test execution is performed using the SPIDER test engine [10] developed in the AGEDIS project. This tool allows the automatic execution of test cases on multi-threaded (distributed) JAVA programs. Test cases are described in an XML-based format defined within Agedis. Extra test execution directives (supplied by the user) can also be used to map this abstract test case onto the actual implementation interface.

5   Example

We illustrate our approach on a small example describing a simple ticket machine. The system architecture is presented on figure 2. It consists of two components: a *coin tray*, able to store coins received from a user, and a machine *controller*, managing the interactions with this user. These components communicate each other by message exchanges via two channels C and A. The external user communicates with both components via the channel U.

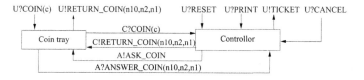

Fig. 2. Ticket machine architecture

Under nominal conditions, the expected behavior of the system is the following: the user puts some coins in the *coin tray* (U?COIN(c)), where possible coins values c belong to the set {1,2,10}. The *controller* receives these coins from the *coin tray*, ones by ones, (C?COIN(c)), and increases the user credit. The user can then ask for a ticket (U?PRINT). If his credit is sufficient, a ticket is delivered by the *controller* (U!TICKET), otherwise the machine simply waits for more coins. When a ticket is delivered the machine also needs to return some change to the user. This change is computed according to the coins available in the *coin tray*. To do that, the *controller* asks the *coin tray* about its current contain (A!ASK). The *coin tray* then returns its answer (A!ANSWER(n10, n2, n1)), where n10, n2 and n1 denote the number of coins available in each category. From this information the *controller* can then compute the change (function CompChange()) and ask the *coin tray* to return it to the user (C!RETURN_COIN(...)). Finally, instead of asking for a ticket the user may also choose to cancel the transaction (U?CANCEL) and the machine should then returns to him all the coins he put (C!RETURN_COIN(...)). This specification is formalized on Figure 3 (left, without considering the dashed transitions).

5.1   Robustness Test Cases Generation

We focus here on the *controller* component and we consider a test architecture where inputs received on channels U and C are controllable, outputs sent on channel C are observable, and communications on channel A are internal. The robustness property we want to ensure is the following: "If the *controller* receives at least one coin (C?COIN(c)), then it *must* output a C!RETURN_COIN action". Figure 3 (right) gives a parameterized Rabin automaton expressing the negation of this property. In this particular example, we assume that in the real execu-

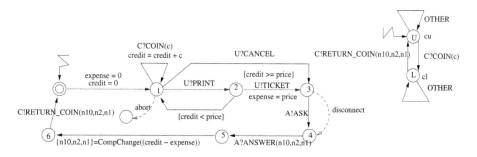

Fig. 3. Controller specification and robustness property

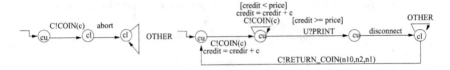

Fig. 4. Possible test cases

tion environment two "faults" may happen: the user may silently stop at any time all interaction with the machine, and communication failures may happen on channel A. Here the mutation operation introduces two new controllable actions (Figure 3, dashed lines): abort, starting from state 1 and leading to a sink state, and disconnect starting from state 3 and leading to state 4. The test generation technique described in the previous section produces the two (parameterized) test cases depicted in figure 4 to invalidate the robustness property. The first one involves a user abortion and the second one a communication failure.

5.2   Implementation and Test Execution

Two Java implementations of the *controller* have been written. The first one simply reproduces its expected behavior under nominal conditions. Running the above test cases on such an implementation (after instantiation of parameters c_l and c_u) leads to a **Fail** verdict: for both tests there exists a controllable execution sequence for which the limit value of the c_l parameter is reached. The second one (Figure 5) uses a timer T to detect user quiescence and communication failures. In such situations it calls a special function (CompDefChange()) to compute defaults coin values to return back to the user. This implementation is now considered as *robust*: the verdict obtained is **Pass**.

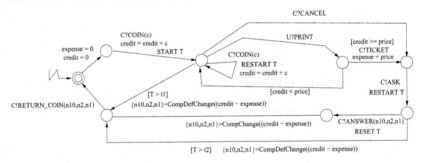

Fig. 5. A "robust" implementation of the controller

6   Conclusion

The current work extends a model based approach used in conformance testing to the validation of robustness properties. Starting from a (possibly incomplete) system specification it consists in producing a "mutated" specification by applying syntactic transformations described by an abstract fault model. This new specification is model-checked against the robustness requirements to produce diagnostic sequences. These diagnostic sequences are then turned into abstract test cases to be executed on the implementation. Robustness requirements are bounded liveness properties expressed by parameterized automata on infinite words. The corresponding test sequences are instantiated at test time to keep the test execution finite. This technique has been implemented inside a complete tool chain (integrating the test generation and test execution phases) and experimented on small Java programs.

Compared to existing robustness testing techniques (based on fault injection), the main advantage of this approach is to much better target the test cases with respect to expected robustness requirements. In particular "faults" are injected by the tester only when necessary, and the verdicts produced are sound (a **Fail** verdict always indicate a violation of a robustness requirement). However, this approach is effective only if there exists some (basic) formal specification of the software under test, describing at least some expected execution scenarios under nominal conditions (like UML use cases, or sequence diagrams).

A first perspective is to improve our implementation to validate this approach on larger case studies. A particular point that would require more investigations is the (static) refinement of the fault model according to a given specification and robustness property. This would allow to consider more accurate mutations and would contribute to limit the state explosion inherent to this kind of approach. Another perspective is to extend this framework to deal with *timed* models [13]. Thus, it would be possible to consider other kinds of faults (stress testing) or properties (response time). The IF specification language already includes a timed model which makes this extension relevant.

Acknowledgement. We thank the anonymous reviewers for their many helpful comments. This work was partly initiated in a joint work on *robustness testing* inside a French action supported by the CNRS and gathering members of IRISA, LAAS, LABRI, LRI and VERIMAG laboratories (http://www.laas.fr/TSF/AS23/).

References

1. *The Agedis Project.* http://www.agedis.de.
2. *The Ballista Project.* http://www.ece.cmu.edu/ koopman/ballista/.
3. *The Protos Project.* http://www.ee.oulu.fi/research/ouspg/protos/.
4. A. Belinfante, J. Feenstra, R. de Vries, J. Tretmans, N. Goga, L. Feijs, S. Mauw, and L. Heerink. Formal Test Automation : a Simple Experiment. In *12th International Workshop on Testing of Communicating Systems*, G. Csopaki et S. Dibuz et K. Tarnay, 1999. Kluwer Academic Publishers.
5. M. Bozga, S. Graf, and L. Mounier. If-2.0: A validation environment for component-based real-time systems. In K. L. Ed Brinksma, editor, *Proceedings of CAV'02 (Copenhagen, Denmark)*, volume 2404 of *LNCS*, pages 343–348. Springer-Verlag, July 2002.
6. C. Csallner and Y. Smaragdakis. JCrasher: an automatic robustness tester for Java. *Software - Practice and Experiece*, 1(7), 2000.

7. J.-. Fernandez, C. Jard, T. Jéron, and C. Viho. Using on-the-fly verification techniques for the generation of test suites. In *CAV'96*. LNCS 1102 Springer Verlag, 1996.
8. A. Ghosh, V. Shah, and M. Schmid. An approach for analyzing the Robustness of Windows NT Software. In *Proceedings of the 21st National Information Systems Security Conference*, pages 383–391, Crystal City, VA, 1998.
9. R. Groz, T. Jeron, and A. Kerbrat. Automated test generation from SDL specifications. In R. Dssouli, G. von Bochmann, and Y. Lahav, editors, *SDL'99 The Next Millenium, 9th SDL Forum, Montreal, Quebec*, pages 135–152, Elsevier, Juin 1999.
10. A. Hartman, A. Kirshin, and K. Nagin. A test execution environment running abstract tests for distributed software. In *Proceedings of Software Engineering and Applications, SEA 2002*, Cambridge, MA, USA, November 2002.
11. A. Helmy, D. Estrin, and S. K. S. Gupta. Fault-oriented test generation for multicast routing protocol design. In *Proceedings of the FIP TC6 WG6.1 Joint International Conference on Formal Description Techniques for Distributed Systems and Communication Protocols (FORTE XI) and Protocol Specification, Testing and Verification (PSTV XVIII)*, pages 93–109. Kluwer, B.V., 1998.
12. C. Jard and T. Jron. Tgv: theory, principles and algorithms. In *The Sixth World Conference on Integrated Design & Process Technology (IDPT'02)*, Pasadena, California, USA, June 2002.
13. M. Krichen and S. Tripakis. Black-box conformance testing for real-time systems. In *SPIN'04 Workshop on Model Checking Software*, 2004.
14. B. Miller, D. Koscki, C. Lee, V. Maganty, R. Murphy, A. Natarajan, and J. Steidl. Fuzz revisited: A re-examination of the reliabilty of UNIX utilities and services. Technical report, University of Wisconsin, Computer Science Dept., 1995.
15. M. Schmitt, B. Koch, J. Grabowski, and D. Hogrefe. Autolink - A Tool for Automatic and Semi-Automatic Test Generation from SDL Specifications. Technical Report A-98-05, Medical University of Lübeck, 1998.
16. J. Tretmans. Test Generation with Inputs, Outputs, and Quiescence. In T. Margaria and B. Steffen, editors, *Second Int. Workshop on Tools and Algorithms for the Construction and Analysis of Systems (TACAS'96)*, volume 1055 of *Lecture Notes in Computer Science*, pages 127–146. Springer-Verlag, 1996.

Content-Level Conformance Testing: An Information Mapping Case Study

Boonserm Kulvatunyou, Nenad Ivezic, and Albert T. Jones

National Institute of Standards and Technology, 100 Bureau Drive,
Gaithersburg, MD 20899, USA
{serm, nivezic, jonesa}@nist.gov

Abstract. Content-level conformance testing is a key to achieving interoperable
data exchange among applications deployed across collaborating, yet independent enterprises. In this paper, we identify four types of content-level conformance tests to support interoperable data exchange: document-verification tests,
information-mapping tests, transaction-behavior tests, and scenario-based tests.
We describe in substantial detail our experience with information-mapping tests
within an industrial B2B integration effort. We review different approaches to
information-mapping conformance verification including logical consistency
checking, human-computer interaction, and event-based checking. We adopt the
human-computer interaction approach and describe a test-case generation
methodology. The methodology details modeling, test requirements specification, abstract test-case definition, and, ultimately, executable test-case generation. Lastly, we provide experimental results of applying our methodology in
the context of an automotive industry development of data exchange standard
for interoperable inventory visibility applications.

1 Introduction

The research study described in this paper is a result of a large business-to-business
(B2B) integration initiative called Inventory Visibility and Interoperability (IV&I).
The initiative is a collaboration that includes the Automotive Industry Action Group
(AIAG) [1], its member companies, and the Manufacturing B2B Interoperability
Testbed at the National Institute of Standards and Technology (NIST) [2]. A key
objective of this initiative is to enable different tools supporting vendor-managed
inventory (VMI or Inventory Visibility (IV)) to interoperate using an internet-based
B2B integration infrastructure. In this paper, we explain the role of content-level
conformance testing in achieving this objective, detail the testing methodology, and
provide results from applying the methodology to one type of content-level conformance test: the information-mapping tests. In Section 2, we present the
interoperability problem addressed in the IV&I project. Section 3 summarizes the
content-level conformance tests needed to support interoperability. Section 4 provides
an overview of the information-mapping test, alternatives to the information-mapping
conformance verification, and the rationale for our selected approach. Section 5
describes the test-case generation methodology for the information-mapping test.

F. Khendek and R. Dssouli (Eds.): TestCom 2005, LNCS 3502, pp. 349–364, 2005.
© IFIP 2005

Section 6 illustrates experimental results from interaction with participating IV tool vendors. Finally, Section 7 concludes the paper by summarizing key research results.

2   Inventory Visibility and Interoperability Problem

Currently, the automotive customer companies typically require their suppliers to monitor customer inventory and replenish parts using IV tools that use proprietary formats to exchange data. Consequently, each supplier needs multiple IV tools to communicate with multiple customers. Fig. 1 shows the current status of the IV tool usage that involves costly data exchange using proprietary formats.

Fig. 2 shows the target usage scenario where IV tools interoperate in a federated architecture. In this case, each supplier needs only one tool since the IV tools exchange inventory data using a standard message called SyncQuantityOnHand (SQOH). SQOH is a Business Object Document (BOD) based on a standards specification from the Open Application Group Integration Specification (OAGIS) [3]. These OAGIS specifications use the eXtensible Markup Language (XML) format [4].

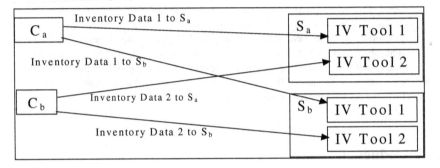

Fig. 1. In the current status of the IV tools usage, customer C_a sends inventory data in a proprietary format (Data 1) to IV Tool 1, while C_b uses another format (Data 2) with IV Tool 2. Both C_a and C_b trade with suppliers S_a and S_b that, consequently, need to employ both IV tools

Before interoperability can be achieved among IV tools, it is important to assure that each IV tool consistently uses the data in the SQOH BOD specification. This is the purpose for developing the content-level conformance testing methods. It should be noted that these conformance tests are not necessary in the Fig. 1 scenario, since the IV tools only operate using their own proprietary representations.

3   Types of Content-Level Conformance Testing

Content-level conformance testing is a function testing (also called functional testing) [17] focusing on the application-level interoperability in the B2B stack [14]. We classify the conformance tests at the content level into one of the following four types that are equally important and complementary: (1) document-verification tests, (2) information-mapping test, (3) transaction-behavior test, and (4) scenario-based test.

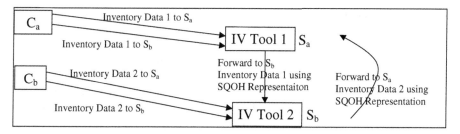

Fig. 2. The figure illustrates the target scenario for the IV tools usage. Customer C_a may still send inventory data in its proprietary format (Data 1) to IV Tool 1, while C_b may still use another proprietary format (Data 2) with IV Tool 2. However, both IV Tool 1 and IV Tool 2 are capable of exchanging the data using the SQOH BOD standard message. Therefore, suppliers S_a and S_b. may use only a single IV tool

3.1   Document-Verification Test

The document-verification test spells out structural, syntactic, and semantic rules that must hold for a message instance containing data exchanged between applications. A document-verification test includes a generation and a consumption test components. In the generation case, the tests verify whether the application under test can generate minimally valid message instances. In the consumption case, the tests verify whether the application under test appropriately consumes minimally valid message instances. In both cases, valid means structurally, syntactically, and semantically correct. This test is a pre-requisite for the three remaining tests.

3.2   Information-Mapping Test

The information-mapping test validates that the intended usage of exchanged data within the application under test in fact conforms to the agreed upon shared semantics, which is declared in the relevant content standard specification. For example, the SQOH specification includes data definitions for Customer Id, Inventory Id, and Storage Location Id. It is important that the applications exchanging the inventory data 'interpret' the data the same way. This means that they must support the use of the data in a manner consistent with the content standard specification. On one hand, an application may interpret 'Customer' as a manufacturing plant, 'Inventory' as the quantity on hand at a specific building that has associated delivery docks within a manufacturer's plant, and 'Storage Location' as the quantity on hand at specific bins or an area within the site. Another application, however, may interpret the 'Customer' as an OEM who has multiple manufacturing plants, 'Inventory' as quantity on hand at a specific plant (which has one or more buildings), and 'Storage Location' as a building within a plant. Such inconsistent interpretation of the business data by two applications could cause the execution of inappropriate business actions.

3.3   Transaction-Behavior Test

The transaction-behavior test focuses on transactional response of the application under test. In the transaction-behavior test, responses based on transactional success, partial success, and failure conditions are verified. These conditions are referred to as business rules, which must be agreed upon as part of the content standard specification. For example, there is a requirement for a protocol that specifies whether passing inventory information about an item, which is unknown to one IV system, should be treated as a success or a failure by another IV system. In Fig. 2, if IV Tool 1 considers the above circumstance a failure condition, while IV Tool 2 accepts partial successes, Tool 1 might end up resending duplicate data. In addition to testing the behavior based upon those business rules, we must test for the proper response, and the proper set of follow-up behaviors to other typical error conditions such as boundary conditions of the field's domain [16, 18]. Transactional behavior at the content level may potentially interact and be confused with the transport protocol level behavior. The boundary between the two levels needs to be well established before interoperability can be achieved.

3.4   Scenario-Based Test

While the previous types of tests typically involve only one business document at a time (not counting the transactional response document), the scenario-based test typically involves multiple business requests and responses. The scenario-based test seeks to verify the business logic of an application that must be common across data exchange steps and participating partners. It focuses on testing a high-level control flow of business actions and consequences. Transaction flow analysis [16] and cause-and-effect graphing [13] on an agreed upon business process could help generate test cases. For example, in some instantiations of the IV Min/Max business scenario, a business response to a shipment notice is expected within a certain time period when the inventory data shows that the available quantity is below a specified minimum level. In others, a receipt notice and purchase order transactions that are handled by multiple, segregated applications are required. As these examples show, scenario-based testing can be very involved, difficult to perform, and hard to verify [5].

4   Information-Mapping Test

Information-mapping tests have been developed for other data exchange standards such as the ISO 10303, informally known as, Standard for Exchange of Product Data (STEP) [6]. Building on the STEP testing methodology, we propose the addition of two steps to verify the information-mapping conformance: the Input Test and the Output Test [7]. The Input Test verifies that the application can read and correctly interpret the standard representation. The Output Test verifies that the application can translate correctly from its internal representation to the standard representation.

4.1   Overview of the Test Procedure

Fig. 3 illustrates the general procedure for the two testing steps. The outputs from both the Output Test and Input Test go through a verification process to determine conformance by checking syntactic and semantic integrity against the inputs.

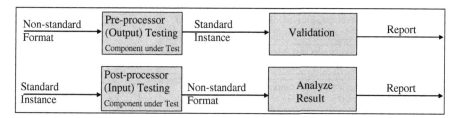

Fig. 3. General procedure for information-mapping test consists of the Output Test and Input Test. The Output Test requires the test data in a proprietary, non-standard format. The output from the Output Test is translated to the target standard representation, the standard instance. The input to the Input Test is the test data in the target standard representation, the standard instance, and the translated output is a non-standard format, a proprietary representation

4.2 Information-Mapping Test Challenges

Challenges associated with the information-mapping test include effective approaches for (1) creating the non-standard format as an input to the Output Test, (2) analyzing the non-standard format output from the Input Test, and (3) validating the standard instance from the Output Test.

Applications under test typically can read the target standard representation and at least one proprietary representation. Since the capability to read different formats varies among components under test, a straightforward way to handle this issue would be to create and maintain test data in multiple representations. However, this is a costly commitment. Similarly, analyzing different non-standard outputs from the Input Test becomes an unmanageable task. The level of difficulty in validating the output from the component under test is related directly to the target standard representation: the more flexible the standard is, the more complicated the validation. On the other hand, the more formally expressed the standard semantics are, the easier the validation.

To deal with the first and second challenges, we investigated a 'reflexive' testing approach (shown in Fig. 4) for both the Input and Output Tests. This approach would resolve issues stemming from proprietary representations because we would have to deal with the target standard representation only. However, it turns out that this approach only verifies the integrity of data passing between the input and output interfaces but not the data 'interpretation' within the application. The approach is easily compromised as it leaves the critical mapping mismatch undetectable (see Fig. 5).

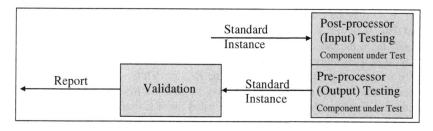

Fig. 4. An initial 'reflexive' testing approach was insufficient to detect mapping mismatch

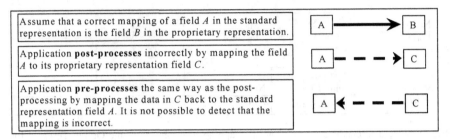

Fig. 5. The reflexive testing approach cannot detect incorrect mapping from field *A* to field *C* (i.e., coincidentally correct mapping error)

Our refined approach followed the argument that if either the Input Test or Output Test is verified to conform to the specification, then the other can rely on the reflexive testing approach. Fig.6 illustrates the proof for this argument when the Input Test is first verified to conform. It can be shown that the same conclusion holds when the Output Test is performed first. If this approach holds, then the challenge #1 is eliminated: we need to create test data only in the target standard representation. This is a major improvement from the STEP testing approach where test data are engineering graphics on the pieces of paper. In the Output Test, an engineer would draw the graphic using the tool under test and then push out the graphic data in the target standard representation.

In the next three subsections, we describe the three potential approaches to address the second and third challenges: to verify conformance of the Input and Output Tests.

4.2.1 Logical Consistency Approach

The logical consistency approach based on formal ontologies may be used to verify the results of both Output and Input Tests. However, an ontology of the standard terminology is needed for the Output Test and another ontology for each application vendor's proprietary terminology is needed for the Input Test. In practice, however, such ontologies are rarely available. Logical consistency alone may only confirm validity of a document but not correctness of the mapping. Additionally, verifying the correctness a document requires necessary and sufficient conditions for targeted terms. However, sufficient conditions often cannot be expressed nor validated from the data perspective alone but may need to be expressed in terms of business events.

Consider the term *ReceivedDate,* a data field in the SQOH BOD. Customers typically update this field whenever they receive a shipment of ordered goods from a supplier. Logical relationships between the *ReceivedDate* and other fields in the SQOH BOD may be established such that *ReceivedDate* must be before the BOD's current date. A better definition of the field would relate this field to be on or after the *ShippedDate* in the latest shipment BOD from the supplier. This requires information from another transaction. For some test cases, this information may be available; in others it may not. The two axioms about the *ReceivedDate* still represent only necessary conditions. A sufficient condition may be that the *ReceivedDate* correspond to the Date and Time at which the item is recorded into the inventory. If the item has to be inspected before it is considered received, then this sufficient condition involves

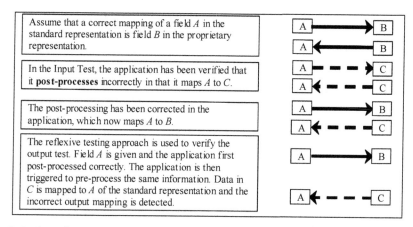

Fig. 6. In the refined testing approach, we rely on showing that Input Test is verified before using the reflexive testing approach

the execution of an event and requires knowledge about the inspection time. If the event is not broadcast and recorded somewhere, then there is no reference data to validate the condition. On the other hand, a research is being conduct in our team to combine the logical consistency approach with the model-based instance equivalence measurement as a test verification method [19]. The research have demonstrated that the logical consistency coupled with the instance equivalence measure performs well when sufficient conditions can be bound or assumed and have suggested a context where the assumption may hold.

4.2.2 Human-Computer Interaction Approach

In this approach, the user or the application developer manually encodes the data from its proprietary representation into the target standard representation for the Input Test. Therefore, the output from the Input Test will already be in the target standard representation. In such cases, the conformance verification can rely on one representation that is the target standard representation for both the Input and Output tests. Here we circumvent the second challenge. Fig. 7 illustrates this approach associated with the Input Test, while the Output Test is based on the refined reflexive testing approach as illustrated earlier in Fig. 6.

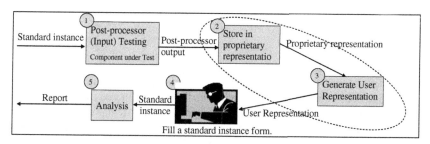

Fig. 7. Human-computer interaction-based conformance verification approach

The procedure for the Input Test would be as follows. (1) The application post-processes a test instance given in the target standard representation. (2) The application stores the data in its proprietary representation. (3) Another procedure in the application then renders the data for user consumption. (4) The user fills a new standard instance form. (5) The test verifies the syntax and semantic integrity against the original standard instance given in step 1. It should be noted that procedures in step 2 and 3 are treated as a black box, which means that we assume that the two steps, particularly the rendering of data onto the screen, are done correctly. In effect, we are testing the mapping implementation in step 1 and conceptual mapping in step 4. If a mapping mismatch is found in step 5, the vendor has to determine if the problem lies in the post-processor (step 1) or the conceptual mapping (step 4).

We note that this approach is not foolproof from the standpoint of coincidental correctness. Some incorrect mappings may still get through undetected if the vendor behavior in step 4 coincides with the symmetric mapping as described in Fig. 5. However, the chances of coincidental correctness decrease as there are two more mappings in between, from the proprietary representation to the UI representation and from the UI representation to the output. The test will have higher fidelity if a user who has no knowledge of the pre- and post-processing interfaces conducts the test.

4.2.3 Event-Based Approach

The event-based approach relies on one or more sequences of messages to trigger some events in the component under test whenever data changes. If the component under test triggers the events as expected, then it may conform to the specification. The event-based approach has a severe limitation in that there are few event-triggering fields in a typical exchange messages such as BODs. The test is harder to generate and automate the execution because multiple messages may be needed before the event is triggered and some events may be actual physical events.

5   Information-Mapping Test Case Generation Method

In this section, we describe the procedure to generate test cases for the information-mapping conformance test. As described in [8], the heart of this procedure is the business-case. The business case definition is described in Section 5.1. Then, a sample mapping table is described in Section 5.2. Finally, the detail test case generation is described in Section 5.3.

5.1 Business Case Definition

Business Case Definitions specify requisite constraints among the message elements and attributes in terms of usage occurrence and tool-support indicators.

The 'usage occurrence' for a BOD indicates the minimum and maximum allowable occurrences for each element/attribute in the context of particular data exchange (e.g., the IV&I project). These occurrence constraints are different from those expressed in the BOD schema because they reflect additional requirements. The occurrences of each element/attribute are specified conditionally on their parent elements. For example, within a SQOH document schema, the *ItemStatus* (parent) element may have a usage occurrence of 0, while the *ItemStatus/Code* (child) element may have a usage occurrence of 1. The meaning is that the *ItemStatus/Code* element must occur if the *ItemStatus* element occurs; otherwise, the *ItemStatus/Code* element must not occur. The following notation applies:

- **0** means an optional element/attribute that may occur 0 or 1 time.
- **C** means a conditional optional element/attribute may occur 0 or 1 time, based on conditions involving elements/attributes beyond the occurrences of their ancestors.
- **1** means a required element/attribute that must occur once and only once.
- **0+** means an optional element/attribute that may occur zero or more times.
- **C+** is similar to **C** where an element/attribute may occur multiple times.
- **1+** means a required element/attribute that must occur at least one time.

The 'tool support' indicates optionality of elements/attributes from a functional-requirements perspective and drives the definition of the business cases for testing purposes. If the field's usage occurrence is required (1 or 1+), that field always requires tool support (S). If the field's usage occurrence is optional or conditionally optional (0, 0+, C, C+), the tool support indicates whether the tool must be able to process the field, if it occurs in a message. The following notation applies:

- **S** means mandatory tool support for the field, i.e., the tool must be able to store, process, and/or interpret the field.
- **NS** means optional tool support for the field, i.e., the sending tool may not expect the receiving tool to interpret, process, and/or store the field.

The S and NS tool support indicators are also interpreted conditionally on the parent of the element/attribute in the same way as the usage occurrence. All the fields with mandatory tool support constitute one or more Base Business Cases dependent upon the optional and conditional usage occurrences.

5.2 Mapping Tables

Mapping Tables specify mappings between each XML-based message element/attribute and an intended vendor tool interface. Table 1 shows a mapping table example with usage occurrence and tool support specifications. Each row of the 'Element' column is an XPATH language representation of the document structure [9]. The row with the bold type font represents an aggregate (complex type) element, which has children elements/attributes. The 'Vendor Support' column shows a vendor support of each document schema element/attribute. The difference between the Tool Support and the Vendor Support suggests an additional implementation requirement for the vendor to satisfy the user's functional requirements. For example, the vendor support of the *From* and *To* components of the *EffectivePeriod* but not of the *Duration* component is a potential problem since the 'Tool Support' column indicates all three elements must be supported by the tool.

Table 1. An example mapping table with usage occurrence and tool support definitions

Element	Description	Usage Occurrence	Tool Support	Vendor Support
Item/CustomerItemId	Customer part number	1	S	Yes
Item/CustomerItemId/Id	Customer part number	1	S	Yes
Item/CustomerItemId/Revision	Part revision number	0	S	Yes
Item/EffectivePeriod	The period part will be in production	C	S	Yes
Item/EffectivePeriod/From	Start date of part production	C	S	Yes
Item/EffectivePeriod/To	Planned end date of production	C	S	Yes
Item/EffectivePeriod/Duration	Planned duration of production	C	S	No
Item/EndEffectiveQuantity	Planned part cumulative quantity	C	NS	No
Item/AvailableQuantity	Quantity available for production	1	S	Yes
Item/MinimumQuantity	The minimum inventory the customer wishes to have on-hand.	1	S	Yes
Item/MaximumQuantity	The maximum inventory the customer wishes to have on-hand.	1	S	Yes

5.3   Test Cases Generation Procedure

As mentioned previously, mandatory tool support specification defines one or more Business Cases with different combinations of optional and conditional elements/attributes. The specification of business cases defines testing requirements for the IV&I conformance tests.

Prior to test requirements generation, we must specify possible IV&I profiles (i.e., valid combinations of Tool Support and Conditional fields and type of data will be used such as language, standard identification code, and standard code lists). The IV&I profiles determine which individual business case makes sense to support from the business requirements standpoint. Once the profiles are determined, test requirements are created to indicate data elements/attributes that must appear in test cases.

Table 2 includes some examples of business cases and associated test requirements (TR). The numbers in the test requirement columns are 'Occurrence in Test'. The possible values are 1, 1+, or 0, which indicate whether the field will be instantiated in the test data once and only once, once or more, or not at all. Business case 1 represents a baseline functional requirement as indicated in the Tool Support and the Usage Occurrence columns. In the example, the base case has the first 3 and the last 3 elements' occurrences in test equal to 1, because they all have the Usage Occurrence equal 1 and the Tool Support equals S with an exception of the *Revision* field. The Revision field can have the Occurrence in Test equal 1 in the base case, because there is no condition on its occurrence. This helps reduce the number of tests.

The *EffectivePeriod* and its child elements as well as the *EndEffectiveQuantity* have additional logic associated to deal with the plan production period or quantity; hence, they constitute the second business case. Two test requirements are necessary for the business case, because the conditions in the Usage Occurrence column indicate

Table 2. Example business cases and test requirements

Element	Usage Occurrence	Tool Support	Bus. Case 1 (Base case)	Bus. Case 2	
			TR1-1	TR2-1	TR2-2
Item/CustomerItemId	1	S	1	1	1
Item/CustomerItemId/Id	1	S	1	1	1
Item/CustomerItemId/Revision	0	S	1	0	0
Item/EffectivePeriod	C	S	0	1	1
Item/EffectivePeriod/From	C	S	0	1	1
Item/EffectivePeriod/To	C	S	0	1	0
Item/EffectivePeriod/Duration	C	S	0	0	1
Item/EndEffectiveQuantity	C	NS	0	0	0
Item/AvailableQuantity	1	S	1	1	1
Item/MinimumQuantity	1	S	1	1	1
Item/MaximumQuantity	1	S	1	1	1

that the *To* and the *Duration* elements cannot be used at the same time. We note that the mutually exclusive condition between the *EffectivePeriod* and the *EndEffectiveQuantity* fields could constitute the third test requirement in the second business case. However, the *EndEffectiveQuantity* is excluded because the user indicates that the tool does not need to support the field.

In summary, the business case concept is a logical grouping of information elements to make the tests more manageable and understandable. In Table 2, for example, the TR 2-1 could be combined with the TR 1-1 for the information-mapping test because there is no conditional conflict. This could result in a smaller number of tests.

These test requirements (together with IV&I profiles) guide test data selection, which matches sample application data with test requirements to form test data. Then, the test data are assembled in the form of abstract (i.e., independent of a specific format) test cases that match test requirements. The semantic validation rules ensure valid abstract test cases.

Before generating the executable test cases, conformance level statements are created to aggregate abstract test cases that match some conformance testing strategy. Such a strategy identifies possible aggregation of IV&I profiles and the corresponding business cases.

6   Experimental Results

Using the approach described above, we have developed test cases and executed them against two IV applications. Initially, the vendors perform the document-verification testing which is a self-test using a Reflector Tool [20]. Fig. 8 summarizes the testing approach used for the mapping test. We validated the generated BOD instances (1) using an XML parser against the schema using XML Spy 2004 [10], (2) with additional structural and semantic rules encoded in Schematron [11] using the XT 20020426a XSLT transformation engine [12], and (3) with a Schematron diff tool using the same XT implementation. The Schematron diff tool has been developed in this project to assist the conformance verification process. The tool takes test data, such as a BOD instance, as input and generates Schematron rules that compare the BOD output from the Input or Output Test with the test data. Due to its limited capability, the tool cannot completely automate the conformance verification. For example, the current tool would raise a flag if the test data were specified in a different order from the ones in the BOD output from the test.

The rest of this section summarizes the experiment and highlights some results from the test with the IV applications using the test cases from the base business case of the SQOH BOD partially illustrated in Table 2.

6.1 Results from the Input Test

At the initiation of the test, we identified a number of mapping mismatches among the fields *Sender, Receiver, CustomerPartyId, SupplierPartyId, Inventory/SiteId*, and *StorageLocation/Id*. We discovered these mismatches right away because they were used for authentication and authorization. The BOD development experts define the *Sender* as the OEM, the *CustomerPartyId* as the OEM plants, the *Inventory/SiteId* as a pointer to an inventory facility inside the customer plant, and the *StorageLocation/Id* as a location within an inventory facility. This means that an OEM can update "on hand data" at the level of plant, building within a plant, and location within a building. On the other hand, the IV tool under test interpreted the *Sender* to be the same as the *CustomerPartyId*, which points to the OEM (the *Sender* serves only as routing information), *Inventory/SiteId* as pointing to the OEM's plant, while *StorageLocation/Id* is an identifier for arbitrary locations within the plant. These mismatches were later resolved with the team of business process experts to match interpretations suggested by the IV tool vendors. In addition, the XML parser validation and the Schematron rules validation indicated that a required field, *Inventory/LastModification DateTime*, was missing.

The Schematron diff also raised flags, which indicated either a mapping mismatch or a representation mismatch in a number of fields. Table 3 lists these fields and provides a list of input and output values for the tool under test. Table 4 lists the concerns raised in each case and their resolutions, if there were any.

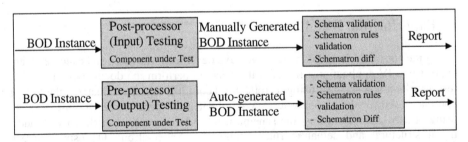

Fig. 8. Summary of the approach for BOD mapping test

Table 3. A list of fields in the SQOH with potential mapping problems as indicated by the information-mapping test

Field	Description	Test value	Return value
CreationDateTime	BOD timestamp	An arbitrary date time - 2003-11-10T11:30:47-08:00	Current date time - 2004-01-28T14:36:02-08:00
BODId	BOD unique Id in one year	An arbitrary string - 200311101130QOH442	An arbitrary string - 637a732d6c7415ee671:f a5e9fe859:-8000
LastShipment Info/ShipToParty	Location code of item's last shipment destination	DUNS number of customer plant – 832022258	DUNS number of supplier plant – 732022158
LastShipment Info/ShipFromParty	Location code of item's last shipment origin	DUNS number of supplier plant – 732022158	DUNS number of customer (OEM) – 132022257
LastShipment Info/ReceivedDateTi me	Date and Time of last shipment received by Customer.	An arbitrary date time before the current date - 2004-03-02T09:30:00-05:00	The date portion of the test value without time information - 2004-03-02T00:00:00-08:00
Inventory/ LastModification- DateTime	The last time the Inventory was changed via a (Shipment) BOD coming into the sending system or an event happened within the sending system (e.g., part consumption).	An arbitrary date time before the current date - 2004-02-28T12:00:00-05:00	Current date time - 2004-04-28T15:46:11-08:00.
Uom (unit of measure)	Quantity unit of measure	Each	An abbreviated form – ea

6.2 Results from the Output Test

In the Output Test, similar flags were raised with *CreationDateTime*, *BODId*, *ReceivedDateTime*, and *LastModificationDateTime*. The additional observations led to potential problems: (1) only one line item was returned when two were submitted; (2) the *LastShipmentInfo/ShipFromParty* and *LastShipmentInfo/ShipToParty* were missing; and (3) the field *Inventory/InTransitQuantity* contained value zero although it was not specified in the input. In the first case, we discovered that the test application did not allow inventory information (for a given item and inventory site) to be associated with more than one supplier. In the second case, it seems that a similar problem occurred in the Input Test, which could explain the observed mapping problem: If a field *A* was mapped (incorrectly) to *B* and vice versa in the first place and if this mapping were fixed (after running the input test) so that now *A* correctly maps to *C*, then the reverse output test may not have had a value in the field B to generate any output, as observed. This demonstrates the improvement of the refined reflexive testing approach as described earlier in Fig. 6.

In the third case, the *InTransitQuantity* means the inventory quantity being transported to, but not yet received by, the customer at the time of issuing the SQOH message. The difference between the data not being specified and the data using a default, not-agreed-upon value can result in a different interpretation. When the data is not specified, it means that the field is not used between the customer and the supplier. However, the supplier may use that particular field with another customer. Showing or generating a field with a default value (e.g., zero) when it is not actually in use could result in an incorrect decision made by the supplier (e.g., supplier repeating the part shipment assuming that it has not shipped the part yet). To avoid these problems, we recommended to the tool vendors that a null field should not be generated or displayed to the user. The tool vendors have agreed that this is an issue which requires attention.

Table 4. Comments and resolution to fields with potential mapping problems

Field	Comment and resolution
CreationDateTime	The integration scenario involves federation of business data exchanged among tools used by customers and suppliers. It might be necessary for the traceability purpose that the BOD CreationDateTime remains the same from customer to suppliers. However, the tool under test generates a new timestamp for every new BOD. A group of IV business process experts indicated that this is not an issue because the scenario involves continuous updates and traceability is not needed.
BODId	The BODId holds similar potential issue and resolution to the Creation-DateTime.
LastShipment Info/ShipToParty LastShipment Info/ShipFromParty	The mismatches of these two fields appear to result from incorrect mapping. The use of customer (OEM) identifier instead of the plant identifier is an incorrect mapping. Consequently, the engineer discovered that the incorrect placements of the customer identifier into the ShipFromParty field and of the supplier identifier into the ShipToParty field are mapping errors.
LastShipment Info/ReceivedDateT ime	The tool stores and/or retrieves only date portion of the input. This is discovered to be the tool implementation problem.
Inventory/ LastModification-DateTime	At the first pass, the tool did not generate this field. In the second pass, the tool interprets and generates this field as the current date time. Both passes indicate that the information mapping is incorrect.
Uom (unit of measurement)	This error indicates the representation mismatch in the unit of measure. Typically, this field should be based on a standard. However, the business experts have indicated that in this scenario, the IV tool should generate the Uom with the same representation as it receives from the customer.

7   Conclusion

Four types of content-level conformance tests have been identified and described. All of them can affect interoperability positively at the application level. Of the four, we discussed in detail various approaches to information-mapping conformance only. Although the logical consistency approach has attractive capabilities, it could be expensive and it has implementation limitations. The human-computer interaction approach is less expensive, but it does not guarantee absolute conformance. It helps reduce the test data generation effort to only include the target standard representation. Currently, we are studying how an ontological approach could address the deficiency in the Schematron diff tool when measuring the equivalence between the test input and the corresponding test output.

We also described information-mapping test-case generation in detail. The current approach relies on filling out a business case and test requirements spreadsheet manually. In the future, portions of this process will be automated as certain assumptions for XML schema design are enforced. In the present approach, we introduced the conditionally optional concept as distinct from the purely optional field. The result is a reduction in the number of tests as the optional fields need not be permutated. In addition, if the conditions are formally expressed, they can be used to automatically enumerate the test requirements. It should be noted that the proposed test cases and testing technique are based only on positive cases. We envision that the data validation testing techniques [15] might be useful for information-mapping test using negative test cases. The approach would rely on the implication that if the application correctly identifies an error, then it is likely that it has correctly mapped/interpreted the fields. However, there are subtle issues that require further studies and experimentation. An apparent issue is that the applicability of the test may be application specific. That is, some error conditions are not discovered by the application but by a middleware component such as a generic schema-based data parser. Another issue is that the content standards are created for flexible usage, with only a small number of usage conditions specified. In addition, these usage conditions could be application specific. In such situations, the only useful conditions could be the common business rules used in the transaction-behavior test and the scenario-based test.

Finally, we discussed experimental results of a mapping-conformance test using the human-computer interaction approach to verify the conformance of IV tool implementations with IV&I SQOH BOD specification. We witnessed a strong need for repeated cycles of testing whenever the vendors updated their tools in response to new conformance requirements or bug fixes. The feedbacks received from the IV tool vendors indicate significant benefits from the conformance testing runs, which identified a number of problems and inconsistencies. Currently, we are planning to run experiments to analyze benefits of performing the content-level conformance tests as a prerequisite for interoperability testing and system deployment.

Disclaimer

Certain commercial software products are identified in this paper. These products were used only for demonstration purposes. This use does not imply approval or endorsement by NIST, nor does it imply that these products are necessarily the best available for the purpose.

References

1. Automotive Industry Action Group Web Site, accessed December 2004. Available online via <http://www.aiag.org>
2. The Manufacturing Business-to-Business Interoperability Testbed Web Site, accessed December 2004. Available online via <http://www.mel.nist.gov/msid/b2btestbed/>
3. The Open Application Group: Open Application Group Integration Specification version 8.0 (2002). Available online via <http://www.openapplications.org/downloads>
4. World Wide Web Consortium: Extensible Markup Language (XML) 1.0 (Third Edition) W3C Recommendation (February 2004).
5. Morris, K.C., Flater, D. (September 1999): Standards-based Software Testing in a Net-Centric World. Proceedings of Ninth International Workshop on Software Technology and Engineering Practice, Computer Society, Pittsburgh, PA 115-122

6. Kemmerer, S.J. (July 1999). STEP the Grand Experience, National Institute of Standards and Technology Special Publication 939.
7. Morris, K.C., Mitchell, M.J., Barnard, A. (May 1993): Validating STEP Application Models at the National PDES Testbed.
8. Ivezic, N., Kulvatunyou, B.S., Jones, A.T., Frechette, S., Cho, H., and Jeong, B. (October 2004): An Interoperability Testing Study: Automotive Inventory Visibility and Interoperability. Fourteenth E-Challenge Conference, Vienna, Austria, 551-558.
9. World Wide Web Consortium: XML PATH Language Version 1.0 (November 1999). Available online via <http://www.w3.org/TR/xpath>
10. Altova GmbH: XML Spy 2004 Professional Edition
11. Jelliffe, R.: The Schematron Assertion Language 1.5. Academia Sinica Computing Center (2000). Available online via
12. Lindsey, B.: XT version 20020426a, Extensible Stylesheet Transformation Implementation in Java (2002). Available online via <http://www.blnz.com/xt/index.html>
13. Elmendorf, W.R. (1973): Cause-Effect Graph in Functonal Testing, TR-00.2487. IBM Systems Development Division, Poughkeepsie, NY.
14. Kulvatunyou, B.S., Ivezic, N., Martin, M.J., Jones, A.T (october 2003): A Business-to-Business Interoperability Testbed: An Overview. The 5th International Conference on ELECTRONIC COMMERCE (ICEC), Pittsburgh, PA.
15. Beizer, B. (1983): Software Testing Techniques. Van Nostrand Reinhold electrical/computer science and engineering series, NY.
16. Beizer, B. (1990): Software Testing Techniques, 2nd Ed. Van Nostrand Reinhold, NY.
17. Beizer, B. (1995): Black-Box TestingJohm Wiley & Sons, NY.
18. Myers, G.J. (1979): The Art of Software Testing. Wiley Series in Business Data Processing.
19. Anicic, N., Ivezic, N., and Jones, A (Feburary 2005): An Architecture for Semantic Enterprise Application Integration Standards. First International Conference on Interoperability of Enterprise Software and Applications, Geneva, Switzerland.
20. Accordare Web Site, accessed April 2004. Available at <http://www.accordare.com>

Quiescence Management Improves Interoperability Testing

Alexandra Desmoulin and César Viho

IRISA/Université de Rennes 1,
Campus de Beaulieu,
35042 Rennes Cedex,
France
{adesmoul, viho}@irisa.fr

Abstract. At any level of computer networks, interoperability testing generally deals with several components that communicate while trying to provide a designated service. When a component remains silent, the assigned testing verdict is generally Fail, assuming that its behavior is non-conformant. Sometimes, this silence may be anticipated given the component's specifications. In these cases, the fail verdict is not unsatisfactory. In this paper, we show that "quiescence management" improves interoperability testing. Based on formal definitions of interoperability testing, we introduce new definitions that take into account the possible quiescence of components under test. Through several examples and scenarios, we show that these new definitions detect non-interoperability cases with higher precision. Moreover, these new definitions more clearly distinguish specification-driven quiescences from others, leading to unbiased interoperability tests with accurate verdicts.

1   Introduction

Different methods have been developed to test network components. Among these methods, we will focus on conformance and interoperability testing. Conformance testing evaluates the ability of a component to behave as described in its specification, generally a standard. Interoperability testing deals with the ability of two or more components to interact in an operational environment. This notion can be intuitively defined by the capacity of two or more components to behave as described in their specification during their interaction, to communicate correctly together, and to provide the foreseen service.

Conformance testing is precisely characterized : testing architectures and conformance relations [1, 2, 3, 4] were defined. This allows automatic test generation and execution. This is not the case for interoperability testing although some definitions exist in [5, 6, 7]. Two main reasons explain the current situation : interoperability is more often regarded as being a practical requirement than conformance is. Yet conformance testing is also considered as being prerequisite to the achievement of interoperability.

F. Khendek and R. Dssouli (Eds.): TestCom 2005, LNCS 3502, pp. 364–378, 2005.

Conformance and interoperability concern the same objects (implementations, specifications, etc). For this reason, the different attempts to define the notion of interoperability use the concepts and theory defined for conformance testing. In [5], interoperability testing architectures and *interoperability relations* were defined. An interoperability relation defines the conditions that two implementations must satisfy to be considered interoperable. These interoperability definitions do not manage possible quiescence of implementations and this leads to incorrect verdicts during testing. For a black-box testing point of view, an implementation is quiescent when no observable event occurs. Quiescence may be foreseen in the specification. In this case, quiescence of an implementation should not be considered as a wrong behaviour. Based on the interoperability relations defined in [5], new interoperability relations with quiescence management have been defined. We show that these new relations can help in solving this problem.

This paper is structured as follows. First the model and notations used for the interoperability definitions are presented in Section 2. In Section 3, we summarize the interoperability definitions of [5]. Some testing results obtained with these definitions are presented in Section 4. The new interoperability relations with quiescence management are defined in Section 5. Then, the new testing results with these relations are presented in Section 6 showing the contribution of quiescence management in interoperability testing. Finally, conclusion and future work are to be found in Section 7.

2   Model and Notations

The model used to provide formal interoperability definitions, and which we consequently use, is the model of the IOLTS (Input-Output Labeled Transition System) [4]. We use it to model specifications. As usual in the black-box testing context, we also need to model implementations, even if their behaviors are supposedly unknown. They will also be represented by an IOLTS.

2.1   IOLTS Model

Definition 1. *An IOLTS is a tuple $M = (Q^M, \Sigma^M, \Delta^M, q_0^M)$ where*

- Q^M *is the set of states of the system and $q_0^M \in Q^M$ is the initial state.*
- Σ^M *denotes the set of observable (input and/or output) events on the interaction points (with the environment) of the system. We note $p?a$ for an input event and $p!a$ for an output event with p as an interaction point on which the event is executed and a as the message.*
- $\Delta^M \subseteq Q^M \times (\Sigma^M \cup \tau) \times Q^M$ *is the transition relation, where $\tau \notin A^M$ denotes an internal event. We note $q \xrightarrow{\alpha}_M q'$ for $(q, \alpha, q') \in \Delta^M$.*

Let us consider an IOLTS M, and let $\alpha \in \Sigma^M$ with $\alpha = p.\{?,!\}.m$, $\mu_i \in \Sigma^M \cup \tau$, $\sigma \in (\Sigma^M)^*$, $q, q', q_i \in Q^M$:

- $q \stackrel{\mu_1 \cdots \mu_n}{\longrightarrow}_M q' =_\Delta \exists\, q_0 = q, q_1 \ldots, q_n = q', \forall i \in [1, n], q_{i-1} \stackrel{\mu_i}{\longrightarrow}_M q_i$.
- $q \stackrel{\epsilon}{\Rightarrow}_M q' =_\Delta q = q'$ or $q \stackrel{\tau \ldots \tau}{\longrightarrow}_M q'$.
- $q \stackrel{\alpha}{\Rightarrow}_M q' =_\Delta \exists\, q_1, q_2, q \stackrel{\epsilon}{\Rightarrow}_M q_1 \stackrel{\alpha}{\rightarrow}_M q_2 \stackrel{\epsilon}{\Rightarrow}_M q'$.
- $q \stackrel{\sigma}{\Rightarrow}_M q' =_\Delta q \stackrel{\mu_1 \cdots \mu_n}{\Longrightarrow}_M q' =_\Delta \exists\, q_0 = q, q_1 \ldots, q_n = q', \forall i \in [1, n], q_{i-1} \stackrel{\mu_i}{\Rightarrow}_M$ $q_i, \sigma = \mu_1 \cdots \mu_n$.
- $out(q) =_\Delta \{\alpha \in \Sigma_O^M \mid \exists\, q'$ and $q \stackrel{\alpha}{\rightarrow}_M q'\}$ is the set of outputs from q.
- q after $\sigma =_\Delta \{q' \in Q^M \mid q \stackrel{\sigma}{\Rightarrow}_M q'\}$ is the set of states which can be reached from q by the sequence of actions σ. By extension, all the states reached from the initial state of the IOLTS M is (q_0^M after σ) and will be noted by (M after σ). In the same manner, $Out(M, \sigma) =_\Delta out(M$ after $\sigma)$.
- $Traces(q) =_\Delta \{\sigma \in (\Sigma^M)^* \mid q$ after $\sigma \neq \emptyset\}$ is the set of possible observable traces from q. And, $Traces(M) =_\Delta Traces(q_0^M)$.

- $\bar\mu =$ p!a if $\mu =$ p?a and $\bar\mu =$ p?a if $\mu =$ p!a. For internal events, $\bar\tau = \tau$.

2.2   Some Definitions

In interoperability testing, we usually need to observe some specific events among all possible traces of an IUT. These traces, reduced to the expected messages, can be obtained by a projection of those traces on a set. This latter being used to select the expected events.

Definition 2. *Let us consider an IOLTS M, a trace $\sigma \in (\Sigma^M)^*$, $\alpha \in \Sigma^M$, and a set X. The projection of σ on X is noted by σ/X and is defined by :*
$\epsilon/X = \epsilon, (\alpha.\sigma)/X = \sigma/X$ *if* $\alpha \notin X$, *and* $(\alpha.\sigma)/X = \alpha.(\sigma/X)$ *if* $\alpha \in X$.

Definition 3 (Projection of an IOLTS on a set). *Let us consider an IOLTS* $M = (Q, \Sigma, \Delta, q_0)$, *a set* X. *The projection of* M *on the set of events* X *is noted by* M/X *and is defined by :*

- $M_X = (Q, \Sigma_X, \Delta(X), q_0)$
  $\forall (q_1, a, q_1') \in \Delta$, $a \in X$, $(q_1, a, q_1') \in \Delta(X)$, $a \in \Sigma_X$
  $\forall (q_1, a, q_1') \in \Delta$, $a \notin X$, $(q_1, \tau, q_1') \in \Delta(X)$, $a \notin \Sigma_X$
- $M/X = (M/X, \Sigma_{M/X}, \Delta_{M/X}, q_0^X)$ *is the IOLTS* M_X *obtained after determinization :*
  - $Q_{M/X} = 2^Q$
  - $\Sigma_{M/X} = \Sigma \setminus \{a \in \Sigma \mid a \notin \Sigma_X\}$.
  - $q_0^X = q_0$ *after* ϵ
  - $\Delta_{M/X}$ *is obtained as :* $(p, a, p') \in \Delta_{M/X}$ *if* $p = p'$ *after* a, *with* p, p' $\in 2^Q$ *and* $a \in \Sigma_{M/X}$.

Interoperability testing concerns the interaction of two or more implementations. In order to provide a formal definition of interoperability, we need to model interaction. This is done in the definition 4. In this definition, Σ_U and Σ_L are the set of events on the different interaction points as described in the testing architecture (figure 1 of section 3.1).

Definition 4 (Synchronous interaction $\|_S$). *The synchronous interaction of two IOLTS M_1 and M_2 is noted $M_1\|_S M_2 = (Q^{M_1} \times Q^{M_2}, \Sigma^{M_1\|_S M_2}, \Delta^{M_1\|_S M_2}, (q_0^{M_1}, q_0^{M_2}))$ with $\Sigma^{M_1\|_S M_2} \subseteq \Sigma^{M_1} \cup \Sigma^{M_2}$, and the transition relation $\Delta^{M_1\|_S M_2}$ is obtained as follows : $\forall (q_1, q_2) \in Q^{M_1} \times Q^{M_2}$,*

$$\frac{(q_1, a, q_1') \in \Delta^{M_1}, a \in \Sigma_U^{M_1} \cup \{\tau\}}{((q_1, q_2), a, (q_1', q_2)) \in \Delta^{M_1\|_S M_2}}, \frac{(q_2, a, q_2') \in \Delta^{M_2}, a \in \Sigma_U^{M_2} \cup \{\tau\}}{((q_1, q_2), a, (q_1, q_2')) \in \Delta^{M_1\|_S M_2}} \quad (1)$$

$$\frac{(q_1, a, q_1') \in \Delta^{M_1}, (q_2, \bar{a}, q_2') \in \Delta^{M_2}, a \in \Sigma_L^{M_1}, \bar{a} \in \Sigma_L^{M_2}}{((q_1, q_2), a, (q_1', q_2')) \in \Delta^{M_1\|_S M_2}} \quad (2)$$

3 Summary of Quiescence-Less Interoperability Relations

Interoperability testing can be defined as a set of procedures used to verify if two or more implementations interact correctly. This test is not precisely characterized as conformance testing and is often considered as a pragmatic and a practical requirement. But different attempts to define interoperability exist [5, 8, 9, 7, 10, 6]. For the quiescence management, we used interoperability definitions of [5] called *interoperability relations*. These relations are based upon **ioconf** conformance relation and do not manage quiescence. These relations consider the testing architecture presented in section 3.1 and are presented in Section 3.2.

3.1 Test Architectures

In order to provide a formal definition of interoperability testing, we have taken into consideration the general testing architecture of figure 1. Different architectures may be obtained from this architecture as described in [11, 8, 7, 12].

This testing architecture is composed of two interacting IUTs. Each of these two IUTs has two kind of interfaces : UI_i and LI_i which are the Upper Interfaces and the Lower Interfaces through which the implementation communicates with its upper and lower layers. Testers are linked to these interfaces : UT_i (Upper Tester) and LT_i (Lower Tester). Depending on the accessibility of the interfaces, these testers can or can not exist. Thus, we obtained different testing architectures. The *unilateral*, *bilateral* and *global* interoperability testing architectures respectively correspond to the architecture with testers which observe/control interfaces of a unique implementation, both implementations separately or both implementations together. We can also distinguish architectures according to the accessibility of upper or lower interfaces. In this paper, we only consider the case of the accessibility of both interfaces : this architecture is called *total*.

With this architecture, the set Σ^M of observable events of the definition 1 can be decomposed as follows : $\Sigma^M = \Sigma_U^M \cup \Sigma_L^M$, where Σ_U^M (resp. Σ_L^M) is the set of messages exchanged on the upper (resp. lower) interface. Σ^M can be

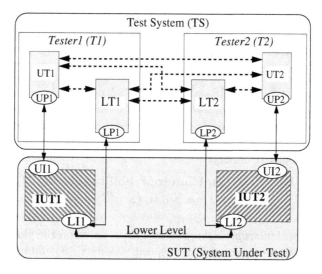

Fig. 1. General architecture of interoperability testing

also decomposed in order to distinguish input messages from output messages. $\Sigma^{\mathrm{M}} = \Sigma_I^{\mathrm{M}} \cup \Sigma_O^{\mathrm{M}}$, where Σ_I^{M} (resp. Σ_O^{M}) is the finite set of input (resp. output) messages.

3.2 Interoperability Relations

In [5], different *interoperability relations* have been defined. These relations formally specify conditions to be satisfied by two implementations in order to be considered interoperable. These interoperability relations are based upon a conformance relation : the **ioconf** conformance relation defined in [4] as follows

Definition 5 (Conformance Relation ioconf).
$$I \ \mathbf{ioconf} \ S =_{\Delta} \forall \sigma \in Traces(S), \ Out(I, \sigma) \subseteq Out(S, \sigma)$$.

Remark: In the conformance testing theory, the implementations are input-completed : in each state, an implementation is supposed to be able to receive any input message on any (upper or lower) interface. In the context of interoperability testing, testers can only control the upper interfaces, but not the lower interfaces which are only observable. Thus, the input-completion of the implementations concerns only events on the upper interfaces in this context.

The interaction considered is asynchronous : $M_i \| M_j = M_i \|_{\mathrm{s}} \mathcal{E} \|_{\mathrm{s}} M_j$ where $\mathcal{E}$ represents the asynchronous environment between the two IOLTS.

Definitions of the Interoperability Relations Without Quiescence Management. Different interoperability relations were defined depending of the considered testing architecture and thus, of the access on the different interfaces. The *unilateral total interoperability relation* $\mathcal{R}_1$ consider the case where we have only access to one IUT. This relation is based on the fact that, during the interaction between I_1 and I_2, the least we can expect from the implementation I_1 is to behave as expected according to its specification S_1.

Definition 6 (Unilateral Total Interoperability Relation $\mathcal{R}_1$).
$$\mathcal{R}_1(I_1, I_2) =_\Delta \forall \sigma_1 \in Traces(S_1), \forall \sigma \in Traces(S_1 \| S_2), \sigma/\Sigma^{S_1} = \sigma_1 \Rightarrow$$
$$Out((I_1 \| I_2)/\Sigma^{I_1}, \sigma) \subseteq Out(S_1, \sigma_1).$$

The relation $\mathcal{R}_1$ can be applied independently to I_2 (based on the specification S_2). The *bilateral lower interoperability relation* corresponds to the relation $\mathcal{R}_1$ applied for both I_1 and I_2.

Definition 7 (Bilateral Total Interoperability relation $\mathcal{R}_2$).
$$\mathcal{R}_2(I_1, I_2) =_\Delta \mathcal{R}_1(I_1, I_2) \wedge \mathcal{R}_1(I_2, I_1).$$

The *global total interoperability relation* $\mathcal{R}_3$ is based on the global behavior of the interactions between respectively : specifications $S_1 \| S_2$ and implementations $I_1 \| I_2$.

Definition 8 (Global Total Interoperability relation $\mathcal{R}_3$).
$$\mathcal{R}_3(I_1, I_2) =_\Delta \forall \sigma \in Traces(S_1 \| S_2), \ Out(I_1 \| I_2, \sigma) \subseteq Out(S_1 \| S_2, \sigma).$$

Remark: In [5], the formal interoperability relation definitions do not correspond to their literal definitions. Indeed, different relations have been defined corresponding to the different possible testing architectures. Thus, the interoperability relations must consider only events observable with the corresponding architecture during testing. But the interoperability relations were written in such a way that the traces also include non-observable events. For this reason, the formal definition of the interoperability relations were rewritten. The interoperability relations presented above are the corrected relations.

The properties of the interoperability relations proved in [5] are still true because the proofs were based on the literal definitions of the relations. Some of these properties are :

- $\mathcal{R}_3 \cong_\mathcal{R} \mathcal{R}_2$: this equivalence suggests that we may avoid the construction of the interaction of the specification.
- I_1 **ioconf** $S_1 \Rightarrow \mathcal{R}_1(I_1, I_2)$, and I_1 **ioconf** $S_1 \wedge I_2$ **ioconf** $S_2 \Rightarrow \mathcal{R}_2(I_1, I_2) = \mathcal{R}_3(I_1, I_2)$: two implementations conformant to their specification in the sense of **ioconf** are considered interoperable with these interoperability relations.

4   Interoperability Testing Without Quiescence Management: Some Examples

On the example of the figure 2, let us consider these four interactions : I_1 with I_4, I_2 with I_4, I_3 with I_4, and I_1 with I_5. The results with the interoperability relations on these interactions are :

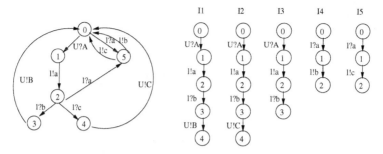

Fig. 2. Specification S and implementations I_1, I_2, I_3, I_4 and I_5

- For I_1 and I_4, we have : $\mathcal{R}_1(I_1, I_4)$, $\mathcal{R}_1(I_4, I_1)$, $\mathcal{R}_2(I_1, I_4)$ and $\mathcal{R}_3(I_1, I_4)$.
- For I_2 and I_4, we have : $\neg\mathcal{R}_1(I_2, I_4)$, $\mathcal{R}_1(I_4, I_2)$, $\neg\mathcal{R}_2(I_2, I_4)$ and $\neg\mathcal{R}_3(I_2, I_4)$.
- For I_3 and I_4, we have : $\mathcal{R}_1(I_3, I_4)$, $\mathcal{R}_1(I_4, I_3)$, $\mathcal{R}_2(I_3, I_4)$ and $\mathcal{R}_3(I_3, I_4)$.
- For I_1 and I_5, we have : $\mathcal{R}_1(I_1, I_5)$, $\mathcal{R}_1(I_5, I_1)$, $\mathcal{R}_2(I_1, I_5)$ and $\mathcal{R}_3(I_1, I_5)$.

This last result is unsatisfactory given I_5 sends a message that is unexpected in I_1. With an intuitive definition of interoperability, I_1 and I_5 should be considered non-interoperable.

Given the test architecture considered, the interoperability scenario (for each interaction) begins with the tester T_1 sending A to the upper interface of I_1 (or I_2). Then, the testers can not control the scenarios but only observe the message sent and received on the lower interfaces (communication between the two IUT). Testers can also receive messages sent by the IUT on its upper interface.

Notation: for the scenario description, the events in the traces are noted:

• For the exchange between a tester and an implementation $U_x\{!,?\}m$ where x is the number of the concerned IUT, $\{?,!\}$ the kind of the message from the point of view of the IUT, and m the message.

• For the exchange between the two implementations in interaction, the sending and the reception are modeled as explained in the definition 1 (cf. Section 2.1) with the number of the IUT concerned.

Thus the scenarios of interaction are :

1. For I_1 and I_4, we have : $U_1?A.l_1!a.l_4?a.l_4!b.l_1?b.U_1!B$.
2. For I_2 and I_4, we have : $U_2?A.l_2!a.l_4?a.l_4!b.l_2?b.U_2!C$.
3. For I_3 and I_4, we have : $U_3?A.l_3!a.l_4?a.l_4!b.l_3?b$.
4. For I_1 and I_5, we have : $U_1?A.l_1!a.l_5?a.l_5!c$ (with no reception of c by I_1).

For the second scenario (interaction of I_2 and I_4), the verdict of the test (when testing $\mathcal{R}_1(I_2, I_4)$ or $\mathcal{R}_3(I_2, I_4)$) is FAIL because of the output $U_2!C$ which is not allowed in the specification S_2 after the trace $U_2?A.l_2!a.l_4?a.l_4!b.l_2?b$ (only $U_2!B$ is allowed after this trace).

For the other scenarios above (1, 3 and 4), the verdicts are also FAIL whereas the corresponding interoperability relations are verified. The reason is the absence of quiescence management in the interoperability relations used as a basis for the tests. Indeed, in practice, quiescence is observed with timers : after each event a timer is started and a situation of quiescence is observed if a timeout occurs (the timer is restarted after each other event). All the scenarios presented terminate : after the last event takes place, the implementation does not return to the initial state. Thus, after the last event of the scenario, a timer is started. As there is no other event that can occur, a timeout is observed. The verdict is FAIL because this timeout (and quiescence corresponding) is considered as a not-allowed output of the implementations in interaction. But this quiescence can be foreseen in the specifications. In this case, the verdict must not be FAIL. For this reason, it is necessary to manage quiescence in interoperability relations.

5   Quiescence Management

To manage quiescence, we need to model this kind of event. The definition 1 of the IOLTS does not model quiescence. This is done in Section 5.1. Then, the operations on the IOLTS used in the interoperability relations are rewritten with quiescence management in Sections 5.2 and 5.3. Finally, the interoperability relations with quiescence management are defined section 5.4.

5.1   Quiescence and Suspensive IOLTS

Three main situations lead to quiescence of a system :

- A deadlock corresponds to a state after which no event is possible : $q \in deadlock(M) =_\Delta \Gamma(q) = \emptyset$.
- An outputlock corresponds to a state after which only transitions labeled with input exist and none of these inputs are observed. This is noted : $q \in outputlock(M) =_\Delta \Gamma(q) \subseteq \Sigma_I^{\mathrm{M}}$.
- A livelock corresponds to a loop of internal events : $q \in livelock(M) =_\Delta \exists \tau_1, \cdots, \tau_n, q \xrightarrow{\tau_1, \cdots, \tau_n} q$.

Thus, $q \in quiescent(M) =_\Delta q \in deadlock(M) \vee q \in outputlock(M) \vee q \in livelock(M)$. A quiescence state $q \in quiescent(M)$ is modeled by $q \xrightarrow{\delta}_{\mathrm{M}} q$ where δ is treated as an observable output event. The obtained IOLTS is called suspensive IOLTS [13, 2] and is noted $\Delta(M)$.

To study quiescence management in the interoperability relations, we consider the conformance relation **ioco** [13].

Definition 9 (Conformance Relation ioco). *I* ioco $S =_\Delta \forall \sigma \in STraces(S)$ $(= Traces(\Delta(S)))$,
$Out(\Delta(I), \sigma) \subseteq Out(\Delta(S), \sigma)$

Quiescence management in some operations used in the interoperability relations of [5] needs to be studied. These operations are the projection of an IOLTS on a set and the interaction between implementations.

5.2   Projection with Quiescence

To calculate the projection of an IOLTS M on a set X, the problem is to preserve information on all quiescent states. The steps to calculate this projection are :

1. Calculation of $\Delta(M)$
2. Substitution of events of $\bar{X}$ by internal events
3. Calculation of livelocks : these livelocks can be due to the precedent step.
4. Determinization

The steps 2 and 4 are the two steps of the calculation of the definition 3. The steps 1 and 3 are necessary to preserve all information on quiescence.

5.3   Interaction with Quiescence

The method chosen to calculate the interaction of two IOLTS with quiescence management is a method with calculation of the suspensive IOLTS followed by the calculation of the interaction. The steps to calculate the interaction with quiescence on M_1 and M_2 are :

1. Calculation of $\Delta(M_1)$ and $\Delta(M_2)$.
2. Then the following rules are applied :
   - Rules (1) and (2) of the definition 4 of the Section 2.2 i.e. propagation of events on the upper interface (rule (1)) and mapping of events on the lower interfaces (rule (2)).
   - propagation of quiescence modeled in the two IOLTS : a quiescent state is noted $(q_1, q_2) \xrightarrow{\delta(1)}_\text{M} (q_1', q_2')$ if $(q_1 \xrightarrow{\delta}_\text{M} q_1') \in \Delta(M_1)$, $(q_1, q_2) \xrightarrow{\delta(2)}_\text{M} (q_1', q_2')$ if $(q_2 \xrightarrow{\delta}_\text{M} q_2') \in \Delta(M_2)$, and we have $(q_1, q_2) \xrightarrow{\delta}_\text{M} (q_1', q_2')$ if $((q_1, q_2) \xrightarrow{\delta(1)}_\text{M} (q_1', q_2')) \wedge ((q_1, q_2) \xrightarrow{\delta(2)}_\text{M} (q_1', q_2'))$.
   - an other rule is necessary to model all quiescent states. This rule is applied on some particular states. The transitions starting from such states are labeled with output **and** input on the lower interface. Thus, no quiescence is modeled on the state. But if only the input events can be mapped with output events, quiescence must be modeled in the corresponding state of the interaction.
3. Calculation of all the deadlocks not already modeled.

Remark: Another method to calculate this interaction is the calculation of the interaction with the rules of the definition 4 followed by the calculation of quiescence on the interaction. But we observe that some situations of quiescence modeled, which are necessary for quiescence management in interoperability testing, are not modeled with this method. These situations correspond to the case where two kinds of events are possible : inputs on the upper interface of one of the implementations (I_i) and outputs on the upper interface of the other implementation (I_j). In this case, quiescence of I_i can be allowed but not quiescence of I_j. The corresponding $\delta(i)$ is only modeled with the chosen method of interaction calculation.

Notation: In the traces of a scenario, the events of the lower interface were noted $l_a!m.l_b?m$ and the considered interaction was asynchronous. In the following study on interoperability testing with quiescence management of the Section 6, the considered interaction is synchronous. Thus, to model the mapping of the outputs and inputs on the lower interface, we note $l_a!m(l_b?m)$ or $l_a?m(l_b!m)$ for a point of view from I_a and $l_b!m(l_a?m)$ or $l_b?m(l_a!m)$ for a point of view from I_b.

5.4   Interoperability Relations with Quiescence Management

With these operations (projection and interaction with quiescence), new interoperability relations can be defined. The different between these new relations noted $\mathcal{R}_x^\delta$ and the relations of section 3.2 is the quiescence management : for example, $\mathcal{R}_1^\delta$ can be deduced from $\mathcal{R}_1$ by using the projection and interaction of sections 5.2 and 5.3.

Definition 10 (Unilateral total interoperability relation).
$$\mathcal{R}_1^\delta(I_1, I_2) =_\Delta \forall \sigma_1 \in Traces(\Delta(S_1)), \forall \sigma \in Traces(S_1\|_\delta S_2),\, \sigma/\Sigma^{S_1} = \sigma_1 \Rightarrow$$
$$Out((I_1\|_\delta I_2)/\Sigma^{S_1}, \sigma) \subseteq Out(\Delta(S_1), \sigma_1).$$

The other interoperability relations with quiescence management can be written in the same way from the interoperability relations of section 3.2.

6   Interoperability Testing with Quiescence Management

The different scenarios of interaction presented in Section 4 are studied with quiescence management in this section.

6.1   Interaction Between I_1 and I_4

This example of interaction corresponds to the figure 3. Allowed quiescence is modeled on the specification : the concerned states are the states 0 and 2 with

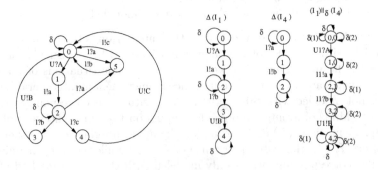

Fig. 3. Interaction between I_1 and I_4

outputlocks. Quiescence is also modeled on the IUT and on the interaction of I_1 and I_4. We can notice that this interaction ends with a deadlock. The results for the interoperability relations with quiescence management on the interaction of I_1 and I_4 are : $\mathcal{R}_1^\delta(I_1, I_4)$, $\mathcal{R}_1^\delta(I_4, I_1)$, $\mathcal{R}_2^\delta(I_1, I_4)$ and $\mathcal{R}_3^\delta(I_1, I_4)$. All outputs are allowed in the specification, but also all quiescent states. Thus, with the interoperability relations with quiescence management, this result of interoperability is preserved in this case.

The scenario of the interaction of I_1 and I_4 for a unilateral total interoperability relation is : $U1?A.l1!a.l1?b.U1!B$. Then this scenario terminates with a timeout (due to the deadlock at the end of the interaction). But this deadlock is allowed in the specification S_1 : the state 4 of I_1 corresponds to the state 0 of the specification where an outputlock is modeled.

The scenario of the interaction of I_1 and I_4 for a global total interoperability relation is : $U1?A.l1!a(l4?b).l1?b(l4!b).U1!B$ followed by a timeout. As the quiescence of the state 0 of S_1 is propagated to the interaction of the two specifications, the deadlock at the end of the scenario is also allowed for this architecture and the scenario based on the corresponding interoperability relation.

Conclusion: As quiescence at the end of the scenario is allowed in the specifications, the verdict of the test is PASS. Thus with quiescence management, the verdict corresponds to the result of the interoperability relations : all the interoperability relations are verified for this interaction, and the verdicts of the test based on these relations are PASS.

6.2   Interaction Between I_2 and I_4

The results with the interoperability relations with quiescence management on the interaction of I_2 and I_4 are : $\neg\mathcal{R}_1^\delta(I_2, I_4)$, $\mathcal{R}_1^\delta(I_4, I_2)$, $\neg\mathcal{R}_2^\delta(I_2, I_4)$ and $\neg\mathcal{R}_3^\delta(I_2, I_4)$. The result of non-interoperability is due to the output C on the upper interface of I_2 which is not allowed in S_2 after the executed trace.

The scenario of the interaction of I_2 and I_4 is : $U2?A.l2!a(l4?b).l2?b(l4!b).U2!C$. The verdict of this scenario is FAIL because of the output $U1!C$ which is not allowed in S_1. For the unilateral total architecture in the point of view of I_4, the timeout is allowed in the specification S_4 and the verdict is PASS : $\mathcal{R}_1^\delta(I_4, I_2)$.

Conclusion: Quiescence management does not change this verdict of non-interoperability due to a non-authorized output (for the unilateral total architecture in the point of view of I_2 and the global total architecture). In this scenario, the verdicts also correspond to the result of the corresponding interoperability relations.

6.3   Interaction Between I_3 and I_4

For this interaction (cf. figure 4), we have I_3 **ioconf** S but $\neg I_3$ **ioco** S : the deadlock at the end of I_3 is not allowed in the corresponding state (state 3) of S. The results with the interoperability relations with quiescence management on the interaction of I_3 and I_4 are : $\neg\mathcal{R}_1^\delta(I_3, I_4)$, $\mathcal{R}_1^\delta(I_4, I_3)$, $\neg\mathcal{R}_2^\delta(I_3, I_4)$ and $\neg\mathcal{R}_3^\delta(I_3, I_4)$.

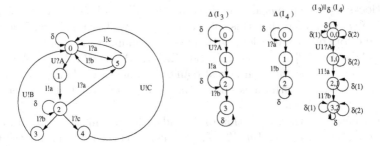

Fig. 4. Interaction between I_3 and I_4

The scenario of the interaction of I_3 and I_4 is : $U3?A.l3!a(l4?b).l3?b(l4!b)$. The timeout at the end of this scenario does not correspond to a quiescent state of the specification S_3 (but an outputlock exists in the specification of I_4 for the state corresponding to the state 4 of this implementation).

Conclusion: For this scenario, the verdict depends of the tested relation. For a global total interoperability relation or a unilateral total interoperability relation in the point of view of I_3, the verdict is FAIL. This verdict is due to the timeout at the end of the scenario. Indeed, no quiescence is foreseen in this state in the specification S_3 because in this state, I_3 must send the output B on its upper interface. For a unilateral total interoperability relation in the point of view of I_4, the verdict is PASS. Quiescence is allowed in S_4 after the trace $l_4?a.l_4!b$. All these verdicts correspond to the results of the considered interoperability relations for the tests.

6.4   Interaction Between I_1 and I_5

This interaction (cf. figure 5) corresponds to a case for which the results with the interoperability relations of [5] were not satisfying. All interoperability relations were verified but the message sent by I_5 does not correspond to the

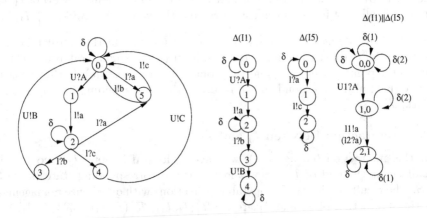

Fig. 5. Interaction between I_1 and I_5

message expected by I_1. The results with the interoperability relations with quiescence management on the interaction of I_1 and I_5 are : $\mathcal{R}_1^\delta(I_1, I_5)$, $\neg\mathcal{R}_1^\delta(I_5, I_1)$, $\neg\mathcal{R}_2^\delta(I_1, I_5)$ and $\neg\mathcal{R}_3^\delta(I_1, I_5)$. These results correspond more to the practical definition and intuitive notion of interoperability.

The scenario of the interaction of I_1 and I_5 is : $U1?A.l1!a(l5?a)$. The message $l5!c$ is not sent by I_5 because in the synchronous context an implementation can not send a message if it is not waited by the implementation in interaction. Thus, the scenario ends after the exchange of the message a between I_1 and I_5 with a deadlock.

Conclusion: For this scenario, the verdict also depends of the tested relation. For a global total interoperability relation or a unilateral total interoperability relation in the point of view of I_5, the verdict is FAIL. This verdict is due to the timeout at the end of the scenario. No quiescence is allowed at the corresponding state of the specification S_5 after the input a : an output must occur. This verdict correspond to the results of the considered interoperability relations : these results are more satisfying because these two implementations are not considered interoperable. For a unilateral total interoperability relation in the point of view of I_1, the verdict is PASS. Quiescence is allowed in S_1 after the trace $U_1?A.l_1!a$. Thus, the non-interoperability is not detected in the point of view of I_1.

6.5 Synthesis and Main Results

After the study of these interactions, the following properties of interoperability relations with quiescence management can be highlighted:

- With quiescence management, the verdicts of testing scenarios correspond to the results of the considered interoperability relations. This was not the case without quiescence management. Indeed, all timeouts gave a FAIL verdict, but these timeouts can be allowed in the specification and do not correspond to an error in the implementations.
- With quiescence management, we can have two conformant implementations that are not considered interoperable. The interaction of I_1 and I_5 can be taken as example for this property.
- The results for the interoperability relations (and the verdicts of the tests) correspond more to the practical definition and intuitive notion of interoperability. Two implementations considered non-interoperable with the interoperability relations without quiescence management remain non-interoperable with the new interoperability relations. But two other cases of non-interoperable exist with the interoperability relations with quiescence management. The first case corresponds to the non-conformance of one of the implementations due to quiescence not allowed : an example is the interaction of I_3 and I_4 where $\neg I_3$ **ioco** I_4. The second case corresponds to the interaction of an implementation who wants to send a message which is not expected by the implementation in interaction : example of I_1 and I_5. These two cases are no longer considered interoperable with the new in-

teroperability relations and the verdicts of the corresponding tests are FAIL.

This study considered a synchronous interaction between implementations. A point that remains to be studied is the difference between synchronous and asynchronous interaction. This study has already started but is not advanced enough to give formal results. Nevertheless, we give here some observations that seem interesting.

With an asynchronous interaction, the three first scenarios studied above (interaction of I_1 with I_4, I_2 with I_4 and I_3 with I_4) have the same results. But the last scenario (interaction of I_1 with I_5) is different if we consider an asynchronous interaction. Indeed, the message $l5!c$ can be sent by I_5 and is not received by I_1. But the timeout received after this event is foreseen in the specifications, the interoperability relations are verified and the verdict of the test is PASS even though the message c can not be received by I_1.

This latter situation proves that a more formal study is needed to examine the influence of an asynchronous environment on quiescence management in interoperability testing.

7   Conclusion

The goal of the study was to investigate the quiescence management in interoperability testing. Based on a previous work that gives formal definitions of interoperability, we provide new definitions that take into account predictable quiescences of components. Several examples and scenarios show that using these new definitions leads to more accurate verdicts in interoperability testing. The obtained results are more consistent with the intuitive notion of interoperability and practical usage. In light of this information, we can assume that quiescence management improves interoperability testing.

Our study considered a context of two implementations communicating via a synchronous environment. Future work will investigate interoperability criteria with quiescence management in an asynchronous context. We will also study the generalization of these interoperability criteria to a context with more than two implementations.

References

[1] ISO. Information Technology - Open Systems Interconnection Conformance Testing Methodology and Framework - Parts 1-7. *International Standard ISO/IEC 9646/1-7*, 1992.

[2] Thierry Jéron. Le test de conformité : état de l'art. Rapport pour l'AEE (Architecture Electronique Embarquée), 2001.

[3] E. Brinksma, R. Alderden, J. Langerak, R. Van de Lagemaat, and J. Tretmans. A Formal Approach to Conformance Testing. In J. De Meer, L. Mackert, and W. Effelsberg, editors, *Second International Workshop on Protocol Test Systems*, pages 349–363, North Holland, 1990.

[4] L. Verhaard, J. Tretmans, P. Kars, and E. Brinksma. On asynchronous testing. In G.V. Bochman, R. Dssouli, and A. Das, editors, *Fifth inteernational workshop on protocol test systems*, pages 55–66, North-Holland, 1993. IFIP Transactions.

[5] Sébastien Barbin, Lénaïck Tanguy, and César Viho. Towards a formal framework for interoperability testing. In M. Kim, B. Chin, S. Kang, and D. Lee, editors, *21st IFIP WG 6.1 International Conference on Formal Techniques for Networked and Distributed Systems*, pages 53–68, Cheju Island, Korea, Août 2001.

[6] R. Castanet and O. Kone. Test generation for interworking systems. *Computer Communications*, 23:642–652, 2000.

[7] J.P. Baconnet, C. Betteridge, G. Bonnes, F. Van den Berghe, and T. Hopkinson. Scoping further EWOS activity for interoperability testing. Technical Report EGCT/96/130 R1, EWOS, September 1996.

[8] R. Castanet and O. Koné. Deriving coordinated testers for interoperability. In O. Rafiq, editor, *Protocol Test Systems*, volume VI C-19, pages 331–345, Pau-France, 1994. IFIP, Elsevier Science B.V.

[9] T. Walter and B. Plattner. Conformance and interoperability a critical assessment. Technical Report 9, Computer engineering and networks laboratory (TIK), Swiss federal institute of technology Zurich, 1994.

[10] Machiel van der Bijl, Arend Rensink, and Jan Tretmans. Component based testing with **ioco**. In A. Petrenko and A. Ulrich, editors, *FATES 2003 — Formal Apporaches to Testing of Software*, volume 2931 of *Lecture Notes in Computer Science*, pages 86–100. Springer-Verlag, 2004.

[11] O. Rafiq and R. Castanet. From conformance testing to interoperability testing. In *Protocol Test Systems*, volume III, pages 371–385, North-Holland, 1991. IFIP, Elsevier sciences publishers B. V.

[12] T. Walter, I. Schieferdecker, and J. Grabowski. Test architectures for distributed systems : state of the art and beyond. In Petrenko and Yevtushenko, editors, *Testing of Communicating Systems*, volume 11, pages 149–174. IFIP, Kap, September 1998.

[13] J. Tretmans. Testing concurrent systems: A formal approach. In J.C.M Baeten and S. Mauw, editors, *CONCUR'99 – 10th Int. Conference on Concurrency Theory*, volume 1664 of *Lecture Notes in Computer Science*, pages 46–65. Springer-Verlag, 1999.

Author Index

Lecture Notes in Computer Science

For information about Vols. 1–3397

please contact your bookseller or Springer